Background Readings
for Instructors Using

THE
BEDFORD
HANDBOOK

Fifth Edition

Glenn Blalock

Stephen F. Austin State University

BEDFORD BOOKS ♨ BOSTON

Acknowledgments

Gloria Anzaldúa, "How to Tame a Wild Tongue," from *Borderlands/La Frontera: The New Mestiza* © 1987 by Gloria Anzaldúa. Reprinted by permission of Aunt Lute Books (415) 558–8116.

David Bartholomae, "Inventing the University." From *When a Writer Can't Write: Studies in Writer's Block and Other Composing Problems*, edited by Mike Rose. Reprinted by permission of The Guilford Press. "The Study of Error," *College Composition and Communication*, October 1980. Copyright © 1980 by the National Council of Teachers of English. Reprinted with permission.

Richard Beach, "Demonstrating Techniques for Assessing Writing in the Writing Conference," *College Composition and Communication*, February 1986. Copyright © 1986 by the National Council of Teachers of English. Reprinted with permission.

Stephen A. Bernhardt, "The Shape of Text to Come: The Texture of Print on Screens," *College Composition and Communication*, May 1993. Copyright © 1993 by the National Council of Teachers of English. Reprinted with permission.

Wendy Bishop, "Helping Peer Writing Groups Succeed," *Teaching English in the Two-Year College*, May 1988. Copyright © 1988 by the National Council of Teachers of English. Reprinted with permission.

Patricia Bizzell and Bruce Herzberg, "Research as a Social Act," *The Clearing House* 60 (March 1987): 303–306. Reprinted with permission of the Helen Dwight Reid Educational Foundation. Published by Heldref Publications, 1319 Eighteenth Street, NW, Washington, DC 20036–1801. Copyright © 1987. "Writing across the Curriculum: A Bibliographic Essay." This essay first appeared in *The Territory of Language: Linguistics, Stylistics, and the Teaching of Composition* (Carbondale: Southern Illinois University Press, 1986) and is reprinted with the permission of the authors and the copyright holder, Donald A. McQuade.

Acknowledgments and copyrights are continued at the back of the book on pages 518–520, which constitute an extension of the copyright page.

PREFACE

In her preface, Diana Hacker writes that she intends *The Bedford Handbook* to be useful to a wide range of students. Similarly, I intend *Background Readings for Instructors Using the Bedford Handbook* to be useful to a wide range of instructors with diverse backgrounds and different levels of experience. With this book, I invite new and experienced instructors to reflect carefully and critically on how and why they do what they do as writing teachers. Further, I want the readings in this book to suggest helpful, practical solutions to common problems and concerns and to provide useful and accessible references for further reading and study. I like to think that these readings will engage instructors in an ongoing professional conversation about teaching writing.

I selected the readings in this collection from among the extensive annotated bibliographical references that I provided for the *Instructor's Annotated Edition of The Bedford Handbook*. I selected these readings based on their potential to complement, supplement, or enhance the teaching done in courses using *The Bedford Handbook* and for their potential to stimulate further reading, research, and professional conversation. These selections are representative of the rich body of research that constitutes contemporary composition studies and that informs Diana Hacker's textbook.

The organization of *Background Readings* follows that of *The Bedford Handbook*, with at least one reading selection for each of the eleven parts of the handbook. The topics addressed in this collection are relevant to all writing courses. No matter how instructors might choose to use the handbook, they will find readings in this collection that will help them think about their course, their assignments and activities, and their various interactions with students.

In addition to selecting the readings for this collection I have written introductions for each part that explore connections between the readings and the topics addressed in that part of the handbook. For each of the readings, my introductory headnotes provide biographical information about the author, situate the reading in its original context, and offer a brief overview of the reading.

The third edition of *Background Readings* has several new features:

- Over one-third of the readings are new to this edition and represent the important ongoing work being done in composition studies.
- To match the handbook's new expanded coverage of critical thinking, I have included readings to help teachers focus more effectively on helping students develop critical literacy.
- A new appendix on computers and composition recognizes the way technology is changing definitions of literacy and writing instruction.

Acknowledgments

Working on this third edition has reaffirmed my appreciation for the collaborative nature of composing, and I want to acknowledge the individuals who have contributed to this book. Without Diana Hacker's *Bedford*

Handbook, this collection would have no reason to be. Her insightful comments on my revision plans have ensured that this new edition of *Background Readings* will be a popular and worthy accompaniment to the handbook.

Several reviewers commented on the second edition with thoughtful and detailed comments. Their responses invited me to reconsider many of the readings I selected and to recognize the book's strengths and weaknesses. Though I was unable to incorporate all of the reviewers' valuable suggestions, I know that this edition has benefited from their responses. I wish to thank Wendy Day, College of Redwoods; Mark Fulk, John Brown University; Phillip J. Hanse, Jamestown College; Woodrow L. Holbein, The Citadel; Sally Joranko, John Carroll University; Margaret J. Marshall, University of Pittsburgh; Timothy McLaughlin, Bunker Hill Community College; and Bernadette Wilkowski, Seton Hall University.

I assembled the first and second editions of this book while I was at the University of North Carolina at Chapel Hill, where Erika Lindemann created the environment that encouraged and valued this kind of work. She continues to inspire my work as a professional. At Stephen F. Austin State University, I am fortunate to be part of an active community of compositionists and dedicated, innovative teachers. I want to thank Sheryl Mylan, Ed Nagelhout, Jacky O'Connor, and Linda Feldmeier White for the support they provided while I was engaged with this project. In addition to these individuals, I extend my thanks to the larger community of teachers and scholars who constitute the field of composition studies. As I attempted to survey the scholarly work that represents our profession, I was humbled by its quality and intellectual vitality. Without this important ongoing work, books such as *Background Readings* could not exist.

Working with Bedford Books continues to be a wonderful and energizing experience for me. First, I want to thank Joan Feinberg, who initially conceived of this project. With each revision, I have tried to repay that trust with my work on the current edition. I would also like to thank Ara Salibian, who oversaw the production of the book with care and patience, and Joyce Churchill for her skillful copyediting.

I have worked on the third edition of *Background Readings* most closely with the developmental editor, Joanne Diaz. She deserves my highest praise and my sincere gratitude. I have been especially grateful for the ways she has handled what have often seemed to be unreasonable deadlines and demands, the ways she has absorbed pressure from many different directions, and the ways she has skillfully and thoughtfully managed the complex revision process and the complicated exchanges of documents and ideas. Perhaps most important, Joanne has been willing to listen, to read, and to respond to my ideas honestly and graciously. All writers deserve that kind of reader. Thanks, Joanne.

Glenn Blalock
Stephen F. Austin State University

CONTENTS

THE WRITING PROCESS

The first part of *The Bedford Handbook* introduces students to the writing process and guides them through it. The articles included in the first part of *Background Readings* complement that coverage by recognizing that writing is fundamentally a social activity, and that composing is a complex process. Our understanding of the writing situation and the writing process governs the ways we introduce students to the concepts of planning, drafting, revising, and editing. It influences our approaches to responding to and assessing student writing.

In addition to the traditional focuses of our composition courses, more and more of our students will benefit from attention to writing in business or professional settings. Part One of *The Bedford Handbook* includes a concise discussion of writing for business and professional purposes. This discussion helps writers understand that effective communication entails more than clear writing. Students and teachers must also attend fully to document design, to the visual rhetoric of the page and to the visual impact it will have.

The articles in Part One raise a number of important questions that instructors must consider as they develop their course plans and class activities:

- How can instructors most effectively characterize the writing situation? And how can they help students assess the complex variables that constitute any given writing situation?
- How can writers think of audience? What alternatives can students consider as they attempt to analyze their audience?
- What assumptions do instructors make when they teach the writing process in a certain way?
- How can instructors help students develop more effective strategies for exploring and developing a topic? How can instructors help students consider alternative plans for their writing?
- How does revision differ from writer to writer? How can instructors help students provide and receive more effective responses to their classmates' and their own writing-in-progress?
- What are alternatives to teaching students about paragraphs? How can teachers resist the teaching of rigid patterns and prescriptive rules about development and coherence?
- What should instructors consider as they respond to student writing? How can instructors help students become more effective self-evaluators?
- What can teachers of first-year composition courses do to prepare students for the kinds of writing they will have to do in business and professional situations?
- How can teachers help students attend to document design? How is our understanding of "text" and "document design" changing as more texts we read and compose are "screen-based" and not printed on paper?

THE WRITING SITUATION

COMMUNITY

Joseph Harris

[From *A Teaching Subject: Composition Since 1966.* Joseph Harris. Upper Saddle River, NJ: Prentice-Hall, 1997. 97–116.]

Joseph Harris is an associate professor of English at the University of Pittsburgh. In addition to serving as the chair of the composition program, Harris teaches undergraduate courses in composition, literature, and popular culture, and graduate courses in literacy and pedagogy. Harris is the current editor of *CCC: College Composition and Communication,* and he has published numerous articles about teaching composition. His 1989 article in *CCC,* "The Idea of Community in the Study of Writing," won the Richard Braddock Award in 1990. He has authored two books: *Media Journal: Reading and Writing About Popular Culture* (Allyn & Bacon, 1995) and *A Teaching Subject: Composition Since 1966* (Prentice-Hall, 1997).

Since the early 1980s, compositionists have been using the concept of "community" to explain the larger contexts in which writers and readers participate and interact. In this closing chapter from *A Teaching Subject,* Harris extends his 1989 CCC article. He suggests that discussions of "community" are couched in "romantic, organic, and pastoral terms," so that members of a discourse community are often characterized as sharing similar "values and concerns." Focusing on this homogenous and largely positive rendering of community glosses over the many differences among members of a "community." Harris suggests that in addition to (or perhaps instead of) talking about "community," we introduce the concept of "public," which "refers not to a group of people (like community) but to a kind of space and process, a point of contact that needs both to be created and continuously maintained." Harris helps teachers and students to recognize the complexity of any writing situation, which can complicate notions of "audience" and "purpose."

If you stand, today, in Between Towns Road, you can see either way: west to the spires and towers of the cathedral and colleges; east to the yards and sheds of the motor works. You see different worlds, but there is no frontier between them; there is only the movement and traffic of a single city.

– Raymond Williams, *Second Generation* (9)

In *The Country and the City,* Raymond Williams writes of how, after a boyhood in a Welsh village, he came to the city, to Cambridge, only then to hear "from townsmen, academics, an influential version of what country life, country literature, really meant: a prepared and persuasive cultural history" (6). This odd double movement, this irony, in which one only begins to understand the place one has come from through the act of leaving it, proved to be one of the shaping forces of Williams' career — so that, some 35 years after having first gone down to Cambridge, he was still to ask himself: "Where do I stand . . . in another country or in this valuing city" (6)?

A similar irony, I think, describes my own relations to the university. I was raised in a working-class home in Philadelphia, but it was only when I went away to college that I heard the term *working-class* used or began to think of myself as part of it. Of course by then I no longer was quite part of it, or at least no longer wholly or simply part of it, but I had also been at college long enough to realize that my relations to it were similarly ambiguous — that here too was a community whose values and interests I could in part share but to some degree would always feel separate from.

This sense of difference, of overlap, of tense plurality, of being at once part of several communities and yet never wholly a member of one, has accompanied nearly all the work and study I have done at the university. So when, in the past few years, a number of teachers and theorists of writing began to talk about the idea of *community* as somehow central to our work, I was drawn to what was said. Since my aim here is to argue for a more critical look at a term that, as Williams has pointed out, "never seems to be used unfavourably" (*Keywords* 66), I want to begin by stating my admiration for the theorists — in particular, David Bartholomae and Patricia Bizzell — whose work I will discuss. They have helped us, I think, to ask some needed questions about writing and how we might go about teaching it.

Perhaps the most important work of these theorists has centered on the demystifying of the concept of *intention*. That is, rather than viewing the intentions of a writer as private and ineffable, wholly individual, they have helped us to see that it is only through being part of some ongoing discourse that we can, as individual writers, have things like points to make and purposes to achieve. As Bartholomae argues: "It is the discourse with its projects and agendas that determines what writers can and will do" ("Inventing" 139). We write not as isolated individuals but as members of communities whose beliefs, concerns, and practices both instigate and constrain, at least in part, the sorts of things we can say. Our aims and intentions in writing are thus not merely personal, idiosyncratic, but reflective of the communities to which we belong.

But while this concern with the power of social forces in writing is much needed in a field that has long focused narrowly on the composing processes of individual writers, some problems in how we have imagined those forces are now becoming clear. First, recent theories have tended to invoke the idea of community in ways at once sweeping and vague: positing discursive utopias that direct and determine the writings of their members, yet failing to state the operating rules or boundaries of these communities. One result of this has been a view of "normal discourse" in the university that is oddly lacking in conflict or change. Recent social views of writing have also often presented university discourse as almost wholly foreign to many of our students, raising questions not only about their chances of ever learning to use such an alien tongue, but of why they should want to do so in the first place. And, finally, such views have tended to polarize our talk about writing: One seems asked to defend either the power of the discourse community or the imagination of the individual writer.

In trying to work towards a more useful sense of *community*, I will take both my method and theme from Raymond Williams in his *Keywords: A Vocabulary of Culture and Society*. Williams' approach in this vocabulary reverses that of the dictionary-writer. For rather than trying to define and fix the meanings of the words he discusses, to clear up the many ambiguities involved with them, Williams instead attempts to sketch "a history and complexity of meanings" (15), to show how and why the meanings of certain words — *art, criticism, culture, history, literature* and the like — are still being contested. Certainly *community*, at once so vague and suggestive, is such a word too, and I will begin, then, with what Williams has to say about it:

> Community can be the warmly persuasive word to describe an existing set of relationships, or the warmly persuasive word to describe an alternative set of relationships. What is most important, perhaps, is that unlike all other terms of social organization (*state, nation, society,* etc.) it seems never to be used unfavourably, and never to be given any positive opposing or distinguishing term. (76)

There seem to me two warnings here. The first is that, since it has no "positive opposing" term, *community* can soon become an empty and sentimental word. And it is easy enough to point to such uses in the study of writing, particularly in the many recent calls to transform the classroom into "a community of interested readers," to recast academic disciplines as "communities of knowledgeable peers," or to translate standards of correctness into "the expectations of the academic community." In such cases, *community* tends to mean little more than a nicer, friendlier, fuzzier version of what came before.

But I think Williams is also hinting at the extraordinary rhetorical power one can gain through speaking of community. It is a concept both seductive and powerful, one that offers us a view of shared purpose and effort and that also makes a claim on us that is hard to resist. For like the pronoun *we, community* can be used in such a way that it invokes what it seems merely to describe. The writer says to his reader: "We are part of a certain community; they are not" — and, if the reader accepts, the statement is true. And, usually, the gambit of community, once offered, is almost impossible to decline — since what is invoked is a community of those in power, of those who know the accepted ways of writing and interpreting texts. Look, for instance, at how David Bartholomae begins his remarkable essay on "Inventing the University":

> Every time a student sits down to write for us, he has to invent the university for the occasion — invent the university, that is, or a branch of it, like history or anthropology or economics or English. The student has to learn *to speak our language, to speak as we do,* to try on the peculiar ways of knowing, selecting, evaluating, reporting, concluding, and arguing that define *the discourse of our community.* (134, my emphases)

Note here how the view of discourse at the university shifts subtly from the dynamic to the fixed — from something that a writer must continually reinvent to something that has already been invented, a language that "we" have access to but that many of our students do not. The university becomes "our community," its various and competing discourses become "our language," and the possibility of a kind of discursive free-for-all is quickly rephrased in more familiar terms of us and them, insiders and outsiders.

This tension runs throughout Bartholomae's essay. On one hand, the university is pictured as the site of many discourses, and successful writers are seen as those who are able to work both within and against them, who can find a place for themselves on the margins or borders of a number of discourses. On the other, the university is also seen as a cluster of separate communities, disciplines, in which writers must locate themselves through taking on "the commonplaces, set phrases, rituals and gestures, habits of mind, tricks of persuasion, obligatory conclusions and necessary connections that determine 'what might be said'"(146). Learning to write, then, gets defined both as the forming of an aggressive and critical stance towards a number of discourses, and as a more simple entry into the discourse of a single community.

Community thus becomes for Bartholomae a kind of stabilizing term, used to give a sense of shared purpose and effort to our dealings with the various discourses that make up the university. The question, though, of just who this "we" is that speaks "our language" is never resolved. And so while Bartholomae often refers to the "various branches" of the university, he ends up claiming to speak only of "university discourse in its most generalized form" (147). Similarly, most of the "communities" to which other current theorists refer exist at a vague remove from actual experience: The University, The Profession, The Discipline, The Academic Discourse Community. They are all quite literally utopias — nowheres, meta-communities — tied to no particular time or place, and thus oddly free of many of the tensions, discontinuities, and conflicts in the sorts of talk and writing that go on everyday in the classrooms and departments of an actual university. For all the scrutiny it has drawn, the idea of community thus still remains little more than a notion — hypothetical and suggestive, powerful yet ill-defined.[1]

Part of this vagueness stems from the ways that the notion of "discourse community" has come into the study of writing — drawing on one hand from the literary-philosophical idea of "interpretive community," and on the other from the sociolinguistic concept of "speech community," but without fully taking into account the differences between the two. "Interpretive community," as used by Stanley Fish and others, is a term in a theoretical debate; it refers not so much to specific physical groupings of people as to a kind of loose dispersed network of individuals who share certain habits of mind. "Speech community," however, is usually meant to describe an actual group of speakers living in a particular place and time. Thus while "interpretive community" can usually be taken to describe something like a world-view, discipline, or profession, "speech community" is generally used to refer more specifically to groupings like neighborhoods, settlements, or classrooms.[2]

What "discourse community" means is far less clear. In the work of some theorists, the sense of community as an active lived experience seems to drop out almost altogether, to be replaced by a shadowy network of citations and references. Linda Brodkey, for instance, argues that:

> To the extent that the academic community is a community, it is a literate community, manifested not so much at conferences as in bibliographies and libraries, a community whose members know one another better as writers than speakers. (12)

And James Porter takes this notion a step further, identifying "discourse community" with the *intertextuality* of Foucault — an argument that parallels in interesting ways E. D. Hirsch's claim, in *Cultural Literacy*, that a literate community can be defined through the clusters of allusions and references that its members share. In such views, *community* becomes little more than a metaphor, a shorthand label for a hermetic weave of texts and citations.

Most theorists who use the term, however, seem to want to keep something of the tangible and specific reference of "speech community" — to suggest, that is, that there really are "academic discourse communities" out there somewhere, real groupings of writers and readers, that we can help "initiate" our students into. But since these communities are not of speakers, but of writers and readers who are dispersed in time and space, and who rarely, if ever, meet one another in person, they invariably take on something of the ghostly and pervasive quality of "interpretive communities" as well.

There have been some recent attempts to solve this problem. John Swales, for instance, has defined "discourse community" so that the common space shared by its members is replaced by a discursive "forum," and their one-to-one interaction is reduced to a system "providing information and feedback." A forum is not a community, though, and so Swales also stipulates that there must be some common "goal" towards which the group is working (212–13). A similar stress on a shared or collaborative project runs through most other attempts to define "discourse community."[3] Thus while *community* loses its rooting in a particular place, it gains a new sense of direction and movement. Abstracted as they are from almost all other kinds of social and material relations, only an affinity of beliefs and purposes, consensus, is left to hold such communities together. The sort of group invoked is a free and voluntary gathering of individuals with shared goals and interests — of persons who have not so much been forced together as have chosen to associate with one another. So while the members of an "academic discourse community" may not meet each other very often, they are presumed to think much like one another (and thus also much *unlike* many of the people they deal with everyday: students, neighbors, coworkers in other disciplines, and so on). In the place of physical nearness we are given like-mindedness. We fall back, that is, on precisely the sort of "warmly persuasive" and sentimental view of community that Williams warns against.

One result of this has been, in recent work on the teaching of writing, the pitting of a "common" discourse against a more specialized or "privileged" one. For instance, Bartholomae argues that:

> The movement towards a more specialized discourse begins . . . both when a student can define a position of privilege, a position that sets him against a "common" discourse, and when he or she can work self-consciously, critically, against not only the "common" code but his or her own. ("Inventing" 156)

The troubles of many student writers, Bartholomae suggests, begin with their inability to imagine such a position of privilege, to define their views against some "common" way of talking about their subject. Instead, they simply repeat in their writing "what everybody knows" or what their professor has told them in her lectures. The result, of course, is that they are penalized for "having nothing really to say."

The task of the student is thus imagined as one of crossing the border from one community of discourse to another, of taking on a new sort of language. Again, the power of this metaphor seems to me undeniable. First, it offers us a way of talking about why many of our students fail to think and write as we would like them to *without* having to suggest that they are somehow slow or inept because they do not. Instead, one can argue that the problem is less one of intelligence than socialization, that such students are simply unused to the peculiar demands of academic discourse. Second, such a view reminds us (as Patricia Bizzell has often argued) that one's role as a teacher is not merely to inform but to persuade, that we ask our students to acquire not only certain skills and data, but to try on new forms of thinking and talking about the world as well. The problem is, once having posited two separate communities with strikingly different ways of making sense of the world, it then becomes difficult to explain how or why one moves from one group to the other. If to enter the academic community a student must "learn to speak our language," become accustomed and reconciled to our ways of doing things with words, then how exactly is she to do this?

Bizzell seems to picture the task as one of assimilation, of conversion almost. One sets aside one's former ways to become a member of the new community. As she writes:

> Mastery of academic discourse must begin with socialization to the community's ways, in the same way that one enters any cultural group. One must first "go native." ("Foundationalism" 53)

And one result of this socialization, Bizzell argues, may "mean being completely alienated from some other, socially disenfranchised discourses" (43). The convert must be born again.

While Bartholomae uses the language of paradox to describe what must be accomplished:

> To speak with authority [our students] have to speak not only in another's voice but through another's code; and they not only have to do this, they have to speak in the voice and through the codes of those of us with power and wisdom; and they not only have to do this, they have to do it before they know what they are doing, before they have a project to participate in, and before, at least in the terms of our disciplines, they have anything to say. ("Inventing" 156)

And so here, too, the learning of a new discourse seems to rest, at least in part, on a kind of mystical leap of mind. Somehow the student must "invent the university," appropriate a way of speaking and writing belonging to others.

The emphasis of Bartholomae's pedagogy, though, seems to differ in slight but important ways from his theory. In *Facts, Artifacts, and Counterfacts,* a text for a course in basic writing, Bartholomae and Anthony Petrosky describe a class that begins by having students write on what they already think and feel about a certain subject (for example, adolescence or work), and then tries to get them to redefine that thinking through a seminar-like process of reading and dialogue. The course thus appears to build on the overlap between the students' "common" discourses and the "academic" ones of their teachers, as they are asked to work "within and against" both their own languages and those of the texts they are reading (8). The move, then, is not simply from one discourse to another but towards a "hesitant and tenuous relationship" to both (41).

Such a pedagogy helps remind us that the borders of most discourses are hazily marked and often traveled, and that the communities they define are thus often indistinct and overlapping. As Williams again has suggested, one does not step cleanly and wholly from one community to another, but is caught instead in an always changing mix of dominant, residual, and emerging discourses (*Marxism* 121–27). Rather than framing our work in terms of helping students move from one community of discourse into another, then, it might prove more useful (and accurate) to view our task as adding to or complicating their uses of language.

I am not proposing such addition as a neutral or value-free pedagogy. I would instead expect and hope for a kind of useful dissonance as students are confronted with ways of talking about the world with which they are not yet wholly familiar. What I am arguing against, though, is the notion that our students should necessarily be working towards the mastery of some particular, well-defined sort of discourse. It seems to me that they might better be encouraged towards a kind of polyphony — an awareness of and pleasure in the various competing discourses that make up their own.

To illustrate what such an awareness might involve, let me turn briefly to some student writings. The first comes from a paper on *Hunger of Memory,* in which Richard Rodriguez describes how, as a Spanish-speaking child growing up in California, he was confronted in school by the need to master the "public language" of his English-speaking teachers and class-mates. In her response, Sylvia, a young black woman from Philadelphia, explains that her situation is perhaps more complex, since she is aware of having at least two "private languages": A Southern-inflected speech which she uses with her parents and older relatives, and the "street talk" which she shares with her friends and neighbors. Sylvia concludes her essay as follows:

> My third and last language is one that Rodriguez referred to as "public language." Like Rodriguez, I too am having trouble excepting and using "public language." Specifically, I am referring to Standard English which is defined in some English texts as:
>
> "The speaking and writing of cultivated people . . . the variety of spoken and written language which enjoys cultural prestige, and which is the medium of education, journalism, and literature. Competence in its use is necessary for advancement in many occupations."
>
> Presently, I should say that "public language" is *becoming* my language as I am not yet comfortable in speaking it and even less comfortable in writing it. According to my mother anyone who speaks in "proper English" is "putting on airs."
>
> In conclusion, I understand the relevance and importance of learning to use "public language," but, like Rodriguez, I am also afraid of losing my "private identity" — that part of me that my parents, my relatives, and my friends know and understand. However, on the other hand, within me, there is an intense desire to grow and become a part of the "public world" — a world that exists outside of the secure and private world of my parents, relatives, and friends. If I want to belong, I must learn the "public language" too.

The second passage is written by Ron, a white factory worker in central Pennsylvania, and a part-time student. It closes an end-of-the-term reflection on his work in the writing course he was taking.

> As I look back over my writings for this course I see a growing accep-tance of the freedom to write as I please, which is allowing me to almost enjoy writing (I can't believe it). So I tried this approach in another class I am taking. In that class we need to write summations of articles each week. The first paper that I handed in, where I used more feeling in my writing, came back with a (√-) and the comment, "Stick to the material." My view is, if they open the pen I will run as far as I can, but I won't break out because I have this bad habit, it's called eating.

What I admire in both passages is the writer's unwillingness to reduce his or her options to a simple either/or choice. Sylvia freely admits her desire to learn the language of the public world. Her "I understand . . . but" suggests, however, that she is not willing to loosen completely her ties to family and neighborhood in order to do so. And Ron is willing to run with the more free style of writing he has discovered, "if they open the pen." Both seem aware, that is, of being implicated in not one but a number of discourses, a number of communities, whose beliefs and prac-tices conflict as well as align. And it is the tension between those discourses — none repudiated or chosen wholly — that gives their texts such interest.

There has been much debate in recent years over whether we need, above all, to respect our students' "right to their own language," or to teach them the ways and forms of "academic discourse." Both sides of this argument, in the end, rest their cases on the same suspect generalization: That we and our students belong to different and fairly distinct communities of discourse, that we have "our" "academic" discourse and they have "their own" "common" (?!) ones. The choice is one between opposing fictions. The "languages" that our students bring to us cannot but have been shaped, at least in part, by their experiences in school, and thus must, in some ways, already be "academic." Similarly, our teaching will and should always be affected by a host of beliefs and values that we hold regardless of our roles as academics. What we see in the classroom, then, are not two coherent and competing discourses but many overlapping and conflicting ones. Our students are no more wholly "outside" the discourse of the university than we are wholly "within" it. We are all at once both insiders and outsiders. The fear (or hope) of either camp that our students will be "converted" from "their" language to "ours" is both overstated and misleading. The task facing our students, as Min-zhan Lu has argued, is not to leave one community in order to enter another, but to *reposition* themselves in relation to several continuous and conflicting discourses. Similarly, our goals as teachers need not be to initiate our students into the values and practices of some new community, but to offer them the chance to reflect critically on those discourses — of home, school, work, the media and the like — to which they already belong.

"Alongside each utterance . . . off-stage voices can be heard," writes Barthes (21). We do not write simply as individuals, but we do not write simply as members of a community either. The point is, to borrow a turn of argument from Stanley Fish, that one does not *first* decide to act as a member of one community rather than some other, and *then* attempt to conform to its (rather than some other's) set of beliefs and practices. Rather, one is always *simultaneously* a part of several discourses, several communities, is always already committed to a number of conflicting beliefs and practices.[4] As Mary Louise Pratt has pointed out: "People and groups are constituted not by single unified belief systems, but by competing self-contradicting ones" ("Interpretive Strategies," 228). One does not necessarily stop being a feminist, for instance, in order to write literary criticism (although one discourse may try to repress or usurp the other). And, as the example of Williams shows, one does not necessarily give up the loyalties of a working-class youth in order to become a university student (although some strain will no doubt be felt).

In *The Country and the City*, Williams notes an "escalator effect" in which each new generation of English writers points to a lost age of harmony and organic community that thrived just before their own, only of course to have the era in which they were living similarly romanticized by the writers who come after them (9–12). Rather than doing much the same, romanticizing academic discourse as occurring in a kind of single cohesive community, I would urge that we instead think of it as taking place in something more like a city. That is, instead of presenting academic discourse as coherent and well-defined, we might be better off viewing it as polyglot, as a sort of space in which competing beliefs and practices intersect with and confront one another. One does not need consensus to have community. Matters of accident, necessity, and convenience hold groups together as well. Social theories of reading and writing have helped to deconstruct the myth of the autonomous essential self. There seems little reason now to grant a similar sort of organic unity to the idea of community.

The metaphor of the city would also allow us to view a certain amount of change and struggle within a community not as threats to its coherence but as normal activity. The members of many classrooms and academic departments, not to mention disciplines, often seem to share few enough beliefs or practices with one another. Yet these communities exert a very real influence on the discourses of their members. We need to find a way to talk about their workings without first assuming a consensus that may not be there. As Bizzell has recently come to argue:

> Healthy discourse communities, like healthy human beings, are also masses of contradictions. . . . We should accustom ourselves to dealing with contradictions, instead of seeking a theory that appears to abrogate them. ("What" 235)

I would urge an even more specific and material view of community: One that, like a city, allows for both consensus and conflict, and that holds room for ourselves, our disciplinary colleagues, our university coworkers, *and* our students. In short, I think we need to look more closely at the discourses of communities that are more than communities of discourse alone. While I don't mean to discount the effects of belonging to a discipline, I think that we dangerously abstract and idealize the workings of "academic discourse" by taking the kinds of rarefied talk and writing that go on at conferences and in journals as the norm, and viewing much of the other sorts of talk and writing that occur at the university as deviations from or approximations of that standard. It may prove more useful to center our study, instead, on the everyday struggles and mishaps of the talk in our classrooms and departments, with their mixings of sometimes conflicting and sometimes conjoining beliefs and purposes.

Indeed I would suggest that we reserve our uses of *community* to describe the workings of such specific and local groups. We have other words — *discourse, language, voice, ideology, hegemony* — to chart the perhaps less immediate (though still powerful) effects of broader social forces on our talk and writing. None of them is, surely, without its own echoes of meaning, both suggestive and troublesome. But none, I believe, carries with it the sense of like-mindedness and warmth that make community at once such an appealing and limiting concept. As teachers and theorists of writing, we need a vocabulary that will allow us to talk about certain forces as social rather than communal, as involving power but not always consent. Such talk could give us a fuller picture of the lived experience of teaching, learning and writing in a university today.

"I don't want no Jesuses in my promised land," is how Lester Bangs put it (259). The line comes near the end of a piece he wrote on the Clash, and to appreciate what he meant by it, you have to know that Bangs loved the Clash, admired not only their skill and energy as musicians, but also their lack of pretense, the wit and nerve of their lyrics, and, most of all, the open and democratic stance they took toward their fans. In their songs the Clash often railed against the culture and politics of Maggie Thatcher's Britain, but they had little interest in becoming the spokesmen for a cause or the leaders of a movement. But neither did they pose as celebrities or keep a distance from their fans. Instead, at least early in their career, they simply let themselves be part of the crowd, talking and drinking and hanging out with the people who came to listen to their music. Bangs saw in them what rock culture might look like if it wasn't divided into leaders and followers, stars and groupies, backstage insiders and outside nobodies. No Jesus, maybe not even a promised land, but a moment to be part of.

Like Bangs I don't want no Jesuses in my promised land either. Most talk about utopias scares me. What I value instead is a kind of openness, a lack of plan, a chance both to be among others and to choose my own way. It is a kind of life I associate with the city, with the sort of community in which people are brought together more by accident or need than by shared values. A city brings together people who do not so much choose to live together as they are simply thrown together, and who must then make the best they can of their common lot. The core values of this loose form of community, it seems to me, are a tolerance of diversity and a respect for privacy. For instance, I know very few of the people who live on my city block by name, and have at best only a vague idea of what they do for a living, much less of what their politics or beliefs or values are. And yet it is a great block to live on: People take care of their houses, shovel the snow from their walks, keep an eye out for the neighborhood kids, report prowlers, bring lost dogs back to their homes, buy church candy and Girl Scout cookies, and the like. We keep watch but we do not intrude, forming something like what Richard Sennett, also in writing about city life, has called a "community of strangers" (*Fall* 4).

Although of course such an absence of shared values has more often been viewed as a loss. There is a long tradition of lament among intellectuals about the disappearance of real community, a nostalgia for the closeness of the town or village or parish that, it is argued, has since given way to the anonymous crowds of the city. Such a yearning for community also marks many utopian dreams of reform. I know of very few utopias in film or literature that are set in large industrial cities, although many dystopias are. (Think of *Blade Runner, Robocop, Escape from New York*.) There are no Jesuses in the big city, or actually, there's often a new one on each corner, and their clamor and conflict doesn't much make for a vision of ideal community. But there is also a freedom to be had in the chaos and anonymity of city life. That has always been its allure. In the essay which begins this chapter, I argued that we have tended to talk about "discourse communities" in far too romantic, organic, and pastoral terms, that we have in effect pictured such communities more as small closely knit villages — where everyone pretty much shares the same set of values and concerns — than as large and heteroglot cities, where everyone doesn't. I want to push that contrast a little further here, to suggest how a more urban and less utopian view of social life might help us rethink the kinds of work that can go on in our classrooms.

In doing so, I want to bring a term back into our conversation that was once a key one in rhetoric but seems somehow recently to have fallen out of use or favor. Back in 1989, I cited Williams's famous remark that, alone among the words used to describe social groups, community seems "never to be used unfavourably, and never to be given any positive opposing or distinguishing term" (76). Since then no one has come up to me in order to say, why yes there is such a positive opposing term — but in continuing to read and think about the issue, I am growing more convinced that one does exist. The word is *public,* a term that does not even appear in Williams's *Keywords,* but that has been central to the work of many American intellectuals, among them John Dewey, Walter Lippmann, Hannah Arendt, C. Wright Mills, Richard Sennett, and, most recently, Kenneth Cmiel.[5] The peculiar importance of the term to these thinkers has to do with how they have tried to use it in theorizing a *large-scale* form of democracy, as a key (if troubled) means of bridging the interests of local communities and individuals with those of a state or nation. What I find most interesting and useful about this notion of a *public* is that it refers not to a group of people (like community) but to a kind of space and process, a point of contact that needs both to be created and continuously maintained.

Richard Sennett draws on a similar distinction in *The Fall of Public Man.* For Sennett, a public space is one where the members of various communities can meet to negotiate their differences. It is a site of conflict rather than consensus, of bartering rather than sharing. The classic example would be a thriving square or market in a cosmopolitan city. It makes little sense to talk of New York, for instance, as a community; it is too sprawling, diverse, heterogeneous. But there is some sense to speaking of it as a kind of public space where the representatives of various boroughs or neighborhoods, the advocates of competing interests or constituencies, can come to argue out their needs and differences. I don't mean here to argue for some idealized version of a public sphere, some free market of viewpoints and ideas. Not all communities or interests are allowed anything near a fair or equal hearing in most public debates, and some are not allowed access to them at all. I am instead thinking of a public space as a place where differences are made visible, and thus where the threat of conflict or even violence is always present. This means that we need to resist moves to romanticize conflict in order to argue for something more like *civility*, a willingness to live with difference. As Jane Jacobs puts it in her classic study of urban life, *The Death and Life of Great American Cities,* "The tolerance, the room for great differences among neighbors . . . are possible and normal only when streets of great cities have built-in equipment allowing strangers to dwell in peace together on civilized but essentially dignified and reserved terms."[6]

Thinking in terms of public rather than communal life can give us a way of describing the sort of talk that takes place *across* borders and constituencies. It suggests that we speak as public intellectuals when we talk with strangers rather than with the members of our own communities and disciplines (or of our own interdisciplinary cliques). And so what I do want to argue for here is a view of the classroom as a public space rather than as a kind of entry point into some imagined community of academic discourse. Most English classrooms are, I think, set up to move from conflict to consensus, from a diverse and competing set of readings (and maybe misreadings) to a single interpretation that teacher and students forge together as a group. The routine goes something like this: The teacher begins by asking for a reading of a certain line or passage from the text at hand and a student volunteers one. The teacher then points to a difficulty or problem with this reading (or asks another student to do so), and thus prompts an alternative reading of the passage. This second interpretation is also critiqued and then replaced by yet a third reading, and so on, until at some point the class arrives at a (more or less) common understanding of the passage. This problem-solving process is then repeated until the class builds a kind of consensual reading of the text as a whole. (A drawback of this approach is that when students are later asked to write on the text, they often feel there is nothing left for them to say about it.)

Imagine instead a class that worked not to resolve such differences in reading but to highlight them, that tried to show what might be involved in arguing for the various ways of understanding a text — as well as what might be at stake in the conflicts between them. Such a class would not try to get students to agree on what a certain text means but to see how and why various readers might disagree about what it means. And it would then ask each of them to take a stand, to commit herself to a position on the text and the issues around it. The aim of discussion in such a class would be for most people to leave thinking that just about everybody else has got it wrong, or at best only half right, and that they're going to write a paper over the weekend which shows why.

But I don't think that is likely to occur when the only alternative readings students come across are ones posed by their teacher. Many students are only too well used to coming to class only to find out, in effect, that they've blown it once again, that the poem or story they've just read doesn't mean what they thought it did — or what's probably worse, that the poem or story they couldn't figure out at all last night seems perfectly clear to their teacher. So even when we insist we are only posing an "other" way of looking at the text, many students are likely to take it (and with good reason) as the "right" way of reading it. But something else can happen when they begin to realize that other members of the class disagree with them about what a text means or how good it is. These are real people, after all. To find out that they disagree with you is both less threatening and more troubling than having your reading challenged as a matter of routine by your teacher.

This can become very clear when you have a group of students watch TV together in a classroom, for it turns what is usually a private experience into a public one. The freshman who chortles appreciatively at a sitcom line about dumb but sexy blondes, only to realize that the young woman he's been trying to impress for the last few weeks is now sitting in stony silence right next to him, suddenly has some explaining to do. And so does she, if others in the class see her response as being less correct than humorless. Similarly, the student who jokes that Roseanne Arnold is disgusting may soon find himself dealing with several others who think that actually she's pretty funny, much as the one who thinks *My So-Called Life* is moving and realistic will need to answer to those classmates who could care less about a group of whining suburban kids. What happens in such situations is that students start to hold each other to account for their readings. They begin to argue not with their teacher but among themselves about the meaning and value of what they've seen.

Let me try to give you a more detailed sense of what it might mean to set up a classroom as such a public space or zone of contact. In a previous interchapter I wrote of a beginning undergraduate class that I teach called Writing About Movies. Again, the goal of this course is not so much to introduce students to the academic study of the cinema as it is to get them thinking and writing about the ways they already have of looking at movies and TV. As a way of beginning to surface these kinds of viewing strategies, one of the first things I usually ask students to do is to locate a point where their understanding of a film breaks down, to write about a scene or image in a movie that they have trouble making sense of — that confuses or disturbs them, or that they have trouble fitting in with the rest of the film, or that just makes them angry somehow. I then ask them to recreate the scene as well as they can in their writing and to define the problem it poses for them as viewers.

One term we looked at Spike Lee's *Do The Right Thing.* Lee's movie is set in the Bed-Stuy neighborhood of Brooklyn and offers a picaresque series of glimpses into life on a city block on the hottest day of summer. Lee himself plays Mookie, a young black man who delivers pizzas for Sal (Danny Aiello), a likable Italian patriarch who owns and runs the neighborhood pizzeria, and who along with his two sons, both of whom work in his shop, are almost the only white characters we see. (City cops, a lost motorist, and a brownstoning yuppie are the only others.) Early on in the movie we see what seems a routine blowup between Sal and one of his customers, Buggin' Out, another young black man who fancies himself something of a political activist and tries to organize a neighborhood boycott of the pizzeria until Sal replaces some of the pictures of Italians — Rocky Marciano, Frank Sinatra, Al Pacino — on his "Wall of Fame" with photos of African Americans. The only support Buggin' Out is able to raise, though, comes from (even by the standards of this neighborhood) two fringe characters: Radio Raheem, a mean-looking hulk of a man with no visible occupation other than walking up and down the street blaring the rap music of Public Enemy from his giant boom box, and Smiley, a stuttering hawker of photographs of Malcolm X and Martin Luther King (which we see no one but Mookie buy). While tempers flare at a number of other points during the day, none of these exchanges come to much, and the overall mood of the film is comic and quick. So when near the end of the movie Sal decides to reopen his doors to give a few teenagers a late-night slice, it seems as if the boycott and whatever threat it might have posed to the routine peace of the block are over, that the neighborhood has managed to get through the hottest day of the year without serious incident. This isn't the case, though, as Buggin' Out, Raheem, and Smiley also take this occasion to renew their threat to close Sal down, and Sal and Raheem find themselves in a fight that erupts quickly and ends tragically. Harsh words lead to a wrestling match that sends the two men crashing into the street. Raheem pins Sal to the sidewalk and seems on the verge of strangling him when a white policeman pulls him away and, as a crowd watches in horror, chokes Raheem to death with his nightstick. Panicked, the police throw Raheem's lifeless body into a squad car and escape, leaving the enraged crowd to loot and burn Sal's pizzeria in revenge.[7]

About a third of the class that spring chose to write on this scene, and it's easy to see why, since it seems so unclear as to who if anyone "does the right thing" in it. So I decided to start our talk about the movie by looking at three of their responses to it. I began by noting that all three pieces had virtually the same concluding paragraph: a plea for greater openness and understanding among all people of all races — be they white, black, yellow, whatever. My sense was that these paragraphs had less to do with the ending of Lee's film than with how these students (and most of the others in the class) felt they were required to end a paper written for school: on a tone of moral uplift, showing that they had indeed learned a valuable lesson from this important work of art, and so on. I didn't push this point much; I simply said I was interested less in what these writers agreed on than in how and why they differed in their views of the film, which meant I wanted us to look more closely at what got said in the body of their pieces than in their official conclusions. It's like TV sitcoms, I argued; no matter what, they always end happily, with everybody loving and hugging everybody else, but if you pay attention to what goes on *before* they wrap everything up, you often find both a more tense and interesting view of work and family life. (I think most students took my point, since I read far fewer homilies at the end of their second drafts.)

And what most interested me about these three readings, why I chose them to begin our talk in class, was how each writer defines the boundaries of the scene differently, so that in each of their accounts a different action was emphasized, and a different sort of blame or responsibility is assessed. In her paper on "Radio Raheem's Death," Holly described the strangling of Raheem in detail.

This scene starts out with a racial fight in the street between Radio Raheem, an African American youth who carries around an enormous boom box that symbolizes his power, and Sal, a white, middle-class restaurant owner. People gather around the scuttle as Raheem begins to strangle Sal. This is when the police show up at the scene. Two white policemen pull Raheem off Sal and drag him off into the street. Meanwhile, everyone is screaming in a riotous manner. The police officer, named Gary, with the fair hair and the mustache puts his nightstick around Raheem's neck. Gary then goes through some kind of racial rage and begins to put pressure on Raheem's neck. Everyone watches in terror as they see their friend and neighbor get strangled to death.

Before anyone can stop Gary (and perhaps before he fully knows what he is doing), Raheem falls dead to the ground. Then, as Holly recounts the scene,

[The police] begin to kick him and tell him to get up. When they realized what they had done they picked up Raheem's dead body and put him in the back of a police car. Spike Lee's camera work focuses on Raheem and then out of the back window of the car at people left in the street. . . . They stare into the camera and yell murder and real names of people who were actual fatalities from police brutality cases. . . . That concludes the scene I have chosen.

From this Holly was led to conclude that the "problem . . . in my eyes, is the police brutality and how it is covered up." What bothered Samantha, though, in "Isolating One's Heritage," is the illogic of the riot that follows Raheem's death. She began her account of the scene almost exactly where Holly left off:

As Sal's pizzeria was burning down the crowd suddenly turned around and altered all there attention toward the Korean family across the street persistantely swinging a broom at the people signalling them to stay away from their market. The Korean man was screaming don't touch my store, leave us alone we are the same as you, we are black too. One of the older men in the crowd says he's right there the same as us leave them alone. Instantly the crowd agrees and turns away with agression yet fatigue.

This turn of events troubles Samantha, since it is made clear throughout the film that Sal treats his customers with an affection and respect that the Korean grocer lacks entirely. In trying to explain the actions of the crowd, Samantha goes on to suggest that while Sal is shown as "open-minded" through most of the film, in the end he proves "not willing to change, or 'go along' with the blacks, but the Koreans were." For her the real issue thus comes down to who gets to claim ownership of the neighborhood. "Whatever the case the blacks were still trying to make the point of saying this is our neighborhood, we have lived here for years and you think you can just come in and take over." Underlying the savagery of the riot, then, is the sort of ethnic pride that warrants the use of "violence to receive . . . social justice" — a phrasing that seems to obliquely criticize Malcolm X's famous claim, quoted at the end of the movie, that oppressed peoples have "the right to do what is necessary" in fighting for their freedom. And so while Holly's horror at the cops' brutality led her to see Lee as arguing against the racism of "the system" or "the man," Samantha read the movie instead as indicting the sort of ethnic or racial pride that can quickly devolve into simple racism and violence.

Jim offered yet a third reading of the scene that focused on the verbal duel between Sal and Raheem that leads up to the fight described by Holly and the riot discussed by Samantha. Looking at how Sal shifts suddenly from the role of friendly *pater familias* to screaming racist led Jim to conclude,

> . . . Here you saw Sal's true, hidden feelings come out. Through the entire film you see how Sal gets along with the blacks, but when confronted, he explodes physically and verbally at the blacks. . . . The film illustrates how deep nested and inevitable racism is. Though Sal accepted the blacks and was thankful for their business, that was the extent of it. As people, he didn't really respect them. . . .

And so while Jim agrees with Samantha and Holly in seeing the movie as an attack on racism, he differs with Samantha in viewing Lee's anger as directed largely against *white* racists, and unlike Holly he refuses to sharply distinguish the actions of Sal from those of the cops. In many ways, Jim gives the bleakest reading of the movie, since he sees its critique as directed at one of the most likable characters in it. If Sal is a racist, he seems to imply, then so are we all, and the inevitable result of this will be violence, either to defend "the power" or to fight it.

In leading our talk about these papers, I insisted that at first our goal would simply be to understand and describe (but not yet to evaluate) the readings of the film they offered. I thus asked the class not to compare these three readings yet, to argue right off for one or the other, but instead to think about how you might go about making the best possible case for each. Where else might you go to in the film, for instance, to support Holly's sense that Lee's anger is directed more against the "system" (as represented by the cops) than against white people in general (as represented by Sal and his sons)? Or how might you strengthen Samantha's claim that the "ethnic pride" of blacks is also being critiqued in the film? To have them do so, I broke the class into three groups (of about six or seven students), with each assigned the task of coming up with more evidence for one of these ways of reading the film.

Each of the groups proved able to come up with a striking amount of support for the view of the film they had been asked to discuss. The students who talked about Jim's paper noted several other scenes where Sal could be seen less as friendly than as patronizing; they then remarked that it was, after all, the director of the movie, Spike Lee, who plays Mookie, the character who starts the riot, which would seem to suggest that he has at least some sympathy for such actions; and they also pointed to how the last words of the film literally belong to Malcolm X, in a printed passage that speaks of the possible need for violence in a struggle for justice. In response, the group working with Holly's paper pointed out that in the scenes following the riot we see Sal and Mookie come if not to a reconciliation then at least to an uneasy truce. They also noted that, in the closing shot of the film, we hear the voice of a local radio DJ lamenting the violence that has just taken place and exhorting *political* action instead. Similarly, the group dealing with Samantha's paper had a list of scenes that poked fun (sometimes gentle and sometimes not) at the black residents of the block, and they also noted that the passage by Malcolm X at the end of the movie is preceded by one in which Martin Luther King argues *against* the use of violence. And so by the end of our talk that evening, we had developed not a single collective reading of the film but three distinct and competing views of it. This allowed me to suggest to the class that, in revising their own writings for next week, their task was not to somehow move closer to some ideal or correct understanding of the movie, but to show why, when faced with such an array of competing interpretations, they chose to read it as they did — that our aim was not to reach a consensus about the meaning or value of the text, but to enter into a critical, sustained, and public interchange of views about it.

In *A Rhetoric of Motives*, Kenneth Burke compares the give-and-take of intellectual debate to a "somewhat formless parliamentary wrangle," a "horse-trading" of ideas in which individual critics try to grab support for their own positions through whatever deals, borrowings, and alliances they can strike up with some colleagues, and whatever raids or attacks they can make on the views of others (188). While I prefer this description of intellectual work to Burke's much more often quoted metaphor of an ongoing parlor conversation, I have to admit that there also seems something slightly disreputable about it, and Burke himself points to the temptation, especially among teachers, to give form to such wrangles by placing opposing views in dialectical tension with each other, so their conflicts can then be resolved at some "higher" or "ultimate" level (188–89). The best example of this sort of dialectic can of course be found, as Burke points out, in the dialogues of Plato, which characteristically begin with Socrates facing a diverse set of opinions on a subject (what is piety? what is justice?) and then gradually leading his listeners to a consensus about what can or cannot be known about it. In Book I of *The Republic*, Socrates himself argues for the merit of this approach, saying,

> If we were to oppose him [Thrasymachus, a sophist who is his current foil in the dialogue] . . . with a parallel set speech on the blessings of the just life, then another speech from him in turn, then another from us, then we should have to count and measure the blessings mentioned on each side, and we should need some judges to decide the case. If on the other hand, we investigate the question, as we were doing, *by seeking agreement with each other*, then we ourselves can be both the judges and the advocates. (348b, my italics)

From opposing speeches to agreement, diversity to consensus, wrangle to dialogue — that is the usual progress of teaching. What I have hoped to suggest here is the value of keeping things at the level of a wrangle, of setting up our classrooms so a variety of views are laid out and the arguments for them made, but then trying *not* to push for consensus, for an ultimate view that resolves or explains the various conflicts which can surface in such talk. A problem with much teaching, it seems to me, is that the teacher often serves only too well as both judge and advocate of what gets said, pointing out the weaknesses of some positions while accenting the strengths of others. I'd like to see instead a classroom where student writings function something more like the "set speeches" that Socrates derides, that serve as positions in an argument whose blessings we can count and measure together, but whose final merits we can leave students to judge for themselves. That is, I'd rather have a wrangle, even if it is somewhat formless (or perhaps because it is), that gives students a set of chances to come to their own sense of a text or issue than a dialogue whose course has been charted in advance by their teacher. I don't want no Jesus and I don't want no Socrates either. What I do want is a sort of teaching that aims more to keep the conversation going than to lead it toward a certain end, that tries to set up not a community of agreement but a community of strangers, a public space where students can begin to form their own voices as writers and intellectuals.

Notes

[1] One might argue that there never really is a "we" for whom the language of the university (or a particular discipline) is fully invented and accessible. Greg Meyers, for instance, has shown how two biologists — presumably well-trained scholars long

initiated into the practices of their discipline — had to reshape their writings extensively to make them fit in with "what might be said" in the journals of their own field. Like our students, we too must reinvent the university whenever we sit down to write.

[2] See, for instance, Dell Hymes in *Foundations in Sociolinguistics:* "For our purposes it appears most useful to reserve the notion of community for a local unit, characterized for its members by common locality and primary interaction, and to admit exceptions cautiously" (51).

[3] See, for instance, Bizzell on the need for "emphasizing the crucial function of a collective project in unifying the group" ("What" 222), and Bruffee on the notion that "to learn is to work collaboratively . . . among a community of knowledgeable peers" (646).

[4] Bruce Robbins makes much the same case in "Professionalism and Politics: Toward Productively Divided Loyalties." Fish too seems recently to be moving toward this position, arguing that an interpretive community is an "engine of change" fueled by the interaction and conflict of the various beliefs and practices that make it up. As he puts it, "Beliefs are not all held at the same level or operative at the same time. Beliefs, if I may use a metaphor, are nested, and on occasion they may affect and even alter the entire system or network they comprise" ("Change" 429).

[5] In *The Last Intellectuals,* Russell Jacoby calls on American academics to broaden the sphere of their influence. In "Making Journalism More Public," Jay Rosen both restates this call and provides a useful overview of attempts to theorize a workable notion of the "public."

[6] Readers of her work will, of course, recognize the strong influence of Jacobs on my vision here of an urban counterutopia. In revising this chapter, I was pleased to discover that Iris Marion Young also invokes this passage from Jacobs in order to make a very similar argument to my own for the city as an alternative model of social life. See her *Justice and the Politics of Difference* (226–56).

[7] Of course this scene also offers a kind of nightmare counter to my praise of urban life: the city as the site of violence, anarchy. Again, the risk of diversity will always be conflict, as advocates of organic community are usually quick to point out.

Works Cited

Bangs, Lester. "The Clash." *Psychotic Reactions and Carburetor Dung.* Ed. Greil Marcus. New York: Vintage, 1988. 224–59.

Barthes, Roland. *S/Z.* Trans. Richard Miller. New York: Hill, 1974.

Bartholomae, David. "Inventing the University." *When a Writer Can't Write: Studies in Writer's Block and Other Composing-Process Problems.* Ed. Mike Rose. New York: Guilford, 1985. 134–65.

Bartholomae, David, and Anthony Petrosky. *Facts, Artifacts, and Counterfacts: Theory and Method for a Reading and Writing Course.* Upper Montclair, NJ: Boynton, 1986.

Bizzell, Patricia. "Foundationalism and Anti-Foundationalism in Composition Studies." *Pre/Text* 7 (1986): 37–57.

———. "What Is a Discourse Community?" *Academic Discourse and Critical Consciousness.* Pittsburgh: U of Pittsburgh P, 1992. 222–37.

Brodkey, Linda. *Academic Writing as Social Practice.* Philadelphia: Temple UP, 1987.

Bruffee, Kenneth A. "Collaborative Learning and the 'Conversation of Mankind'." *College English* 46 (Nov. 1984): 635–52.

Burke, Kenneth. *A Rhetoric of Motives.* Berkeley: U of California P, 1969.

Fish, Stanley. "Change." *South Atlantic Quarterly* 86 (1987): 423–44.

Hirsch, E. D., Jr. *Cultural Literacy: What Every American Needs to Know.* Boston: Houghton, 1987.

Hymes, Dell. *Foundations in Sociolinguistics: An Ethnographic Approach.* Philadelphia: U of Pennsylvania P, 1974.

Jacobs, Jane. *The Death and Life of Great American Cities.* 1961. New York: Modern Library, 1993.

Jacoby, Russell. *The Last Intellectuals: American Culture in the Age of Academe.* New York: Basic, 1987.

Plato. *The Republic.* Trans. G. M. A. Grube. Indianapolis: Hackett, 1974.

Porter, James. "Intertextuality and the Discourse Community." *Rhetoric Review* 5 (1986): 34–37.

Pratt, Mary Louise. "Interpretive Strategies/Strategic Interpretations: On Anglo-American Reader Response Criticism." *Boundary* 2.11 (1982–83): 201–31.

Robbins, Bruce. "Professionalism and Politics: Toward Productively Divided Loyalties." *Profession* 85 (1985): 1–9.

Rodriguez, Richard. *Hunger of Memory.* Boston: Godine, 1981.

Rosen, Jay. "Making Journalism More Public." *Communication* 12 (1991): 267–84.

Sennett, Richard. *The Fall of Public Man.* New York: Knopf, 1977.

Swales, John. "Discourse Communities, Genres, and English as an International Language." *World Englishes* 7 (1988): 211–20.

Williams, Raymond. *The Country and the City.* New York: Oxford UP, 1973.

———. *Keywords: A Vocabulary of Culture and Society.* New York: Oxford UP, 1976.

———. *Marxism and Literature.* New York: Oxford UP, 1977.

———. *Second Generation.* New York: Horizon, 1964.

Young, Iris Marion. *Justice and the Politics of Difference.* Princeton: Princeton UP, 1990.

INVENTING THE UNIVERSITY

David Bartholomae

[From *When a Writer Can't Write: Studies in Writer's Block and Other Composing Problems.* Ed. Mike Rose. New York: Guilford, 1985. 134–65.]

Professor of English and chair of the department of English at the University of Pittsburgh, David Bartholomae has been a leading scholar and a widely respected voice in composition studies for nearly two decades. With Anthony Petrosky, he coedited *Facts, Artifacts, and Counterfacts* (1986) and *Ways of Reading* (now in its 4th edition, 1996), two books that have become standards for those studying and teaching composition. Bartholomae has published numerous articles in leading journals and in important collections. He has served as chair of the annual Conference on College Composition and Communication and the second Modern Language Association conference on literacy. He is currently coeditor of the Pittsburgh Series on Composition, Literacy, and Culture published by the University of Pittsburgh Press. His article "The Study of Error" (1980), which is included in Part Five of this book, won the Richard Braddock Award from CCCC in 1981.

In this now classic and often reprinted essay, Bartholomae discusses academic writing situations. He argues that the writing that students do in colleges and universities takes place in a complex context of already ongoing disciplinary discourses. Bartholomae shows that assessing an academic writing situation is more complex than determining purpose and analyzing audience. Instead, students have to learn the languages of the academy, and those languages are embedded in and are the products of a complex academic culture governed in part by disciplinary and institutional conventions. Illustrating his discussion with several student essays, Bartholomae examines ways in which students attempt to join various academic discourse communities. In the process of his analyses, Bartholomae offers several solid suggestions for how teachers can more effectively engage students in purposeful writing projects, initiating them, in a sense, to the business of the academy.

Education may well be, as of right, the instrument whereby every individual, in a society like our own, can gain access to any kind of discourse. But we well know that in its distribution, in what it permits and in what it prevents, it follows the well-trodden battle-lines of social conflict. Every educational system is a political means of maintaining or of modifying the appropriation of discourse, with the knowledge and the powers it carries with it.

> – Foucault, "The Discourse on Language"

Every time a student sits down to write for us, he has to invent the university for the occasion — invent the university, that is, or a branch of it, like History or Anthropology or Economics or English. He has to learn to speak our language, to speak as we do, to try on the peculiar ways of knowing, selecting, evaluating, reporting, concluding, and arguing that define the discourse of our community. Or perhaps I should say the *various* discourses of our community, since it is in the nature of a liberal arts education that a student, after the first year or two, must learn to try on a variety of voices and interpretive schemes — to write, for example, as a literary critic one day and an experimental psychologist the next, to work within fields where the rules governing the presentation of examples or the development of an argument are both distinct and, even to a professional, mysterious.

The students have to appropriate (or be appropriated by) a specialized discourse, and they have to do this as though they were easily and comfortably one with their audience, as though they were members of the academy, or historians or anthropologists or economists; they have to invent the university by assembling and mimicking its language, finding some compromise between idiosyncrasy, a personal history, and the requirements of convention, the history of a discipline. They must learn to speak our language. Or they must dare to speak it, or to carry off the bluff, since speaking and writing will most certainly be required long before the skill is "learned." And this, understandably, causes problems.

Let me look quickly at an example. Here is an essay written by a college freshman, a basic writer:

In the past time I thought that an incident was creative was when I had to make a clay model of the earth, but not of the classical or your everyday model of the earth which consists of the two cores, the mantle and the crust. I thought of these things in a dimension of which it would be unique, but easy to comprehend. Of course, your materials to work with were basic and limited at the same time, but thought help to put this limit into a right attitude or frame of mind to work with the clay.

In the beginning of the clay model, I had to research and learn the different dimensions of the earth (in magnitude, quantity, state of matter, etc.). After this, I learned how to put this into the clay and come up with something different than any other person in my class at the time. In my opinion color coordination and shape was the key to my creativity of the clay model of the earth.

Creativity is the venture of the mind at work with the mechanics relay to the limbs from the cranium, which stores and triggers this action. It can be a burst of energy released at a precise time a thought is being transmitted. This can cause a frenzy of the human body, but it depends on the characteristics of the individual and how they can relay the message clearly enough through mechanics of the body to us as an observer. Then we must determine if it is creative or a learned process varied by the individuals thought process. Creativity is indeed a tool which has to exist, or our world will not succeed into the future and progress like it should.

I am continually impressed by the patience and good will of our students. This student was writing a placement essay during freshman orientation. (The problem set to him was "Describe a time when you did something you felt to be creative. Then, on the basis of the incident you have described, go on to draw some general conclusions about 'creativity.'") He knew that university faculty would be reading and evaluating his essay, and so he wrote for them.

In some ways it is a remarkable performance. He is trying on the discourse even though he doesn't have the knowledge that makes the discourse more than a routine, a set of conventional rituals and gestures. And he does this, I think, even though he *knows* he doesn't have the knowledge that makes the discourse more than a routine. He defines himself as a researcher, working systematically, and not as a kid in a high school class: "I thought of these things in a dimension of . . ."; "had to research and learn the different dimensions of the earth (in magnitude, quantity, state of matter, etc.)." He moves quickly into a specialized language (his approximation of our jargon) and draws both a general, textbook-like conclusion ("Creativity is the venture of the mind at work . . .") and a resounding peroration ("Creativity is indeed a tool which has to exist, or our world will not succeed into the future and progress like it should"). The writer has even, with that "indeed" and with the qualifications and the parenthetical expressions of the opening paragraphs, picked up the rhythm of our prose. And through it all he speaks with an impressive air of authority.

There is an elaborate but, I will argue, a necessary and enabling fiction at work here as the student dramatizes his experience in a "setting" — the setting required by the discourse — where he can speak to us as a companion, a fellow researcher. As I read the essay, there is only one moment when the fiction is broken, when we are addressed differently. The student says, "Of course, your materials to work with were basic and limited at the same time, but thought help to put this limit into a right attitude or frame of mind to work with the clay." At this point, I think, we become students and he the teacher, giving us a lesson (as in, "You take your pencil in your right hand and put your paper in front of you"). This is, however, one of the most characteristic slips of basic writers. It is very hard for them to take on the role — the voice, the person — of an authority whose authority is rooted in scholarship, analysis, or research. They slip, then, into the more immediately available and realizable voice of authority, the voice of a teacher giving a lesson or the voice of a parent lecturing at the dinner table. They offer advice or homilies rather than "academic" conclusions. There is a similar break in the final paragraph, where the conclusion that pushes for a definition ("Creativity is the venture of the mind at work with the mechanics relay to the limbs from the cranium . . .") is replaced by a conclusion which speaks in the voice of an Elder ("Creativity is indeed a tool which has to exist, or our world will not succeed into the future and progress like it should").

It is not uncommon, then, to find such breaks in the concluding sections of essays written by basic writers. Here is the concluding section of an essay written by a student about his work as a mechanic. He had been asked to generalize about "work" after reviewing an on-the-job experience or incident that "stuck in his mind" as somehow significant: "How could two repairmen miss a leak? Lack of pride? No incentive? Lazy? I don't know." At this point the writer is in a perfect position to speculate, to move from the problem to an analysis of the problem. Here is how the paragraph continues, however (and notice the change in pronoun reference):

> From this point on, I take my time, do it right, and don't let customers get under your skin. If they have a complaint, tell them to call your boss and he'll be more than glad to handle it. Most important, worry about yourself, and keep a clear eye on everyone, for there's always someone trying to take advantage of you, anytime and anyplace.

We get neither a technical discussion nor an "academic" discussion but a Lesson on Life.[1] This is the language he uses to address the general question "How could two repairmen miss a leak?" The other brand of conclusion, the more academic one, would have required him to speak of his experience in our terms; it would, that is, have required a special vocabulary, a special system of presentation, and an interpretive scheme (or a set of commonplaces) he could use to identify and talk about the mystery of human error. The writer certainly had access to the range of acceptable commonplaces for such an explanation: "lack of pride," "no incentive," "lazy." Each would dictate its own set of phrases, examples, and conclusions, and we, his teachers, would know how to write out each argument, just as we would know how to write out more specialized arguments of our own. A "commonplace," then, is a culturally or institutionally authorized concept or statement that carries with it its own necessary elaboration. We all use commonplaces to orient ourselves in the world; they provide a point of reference and a set of "prearticulated" explanations that are readily available to organize and interpret experience. The phrase "lack of pride" carries with it its own account for the repairman's error just as, at another point in time, a reference to "original sin" would provide an explanation, or just as, in a certain university classroom, a reference to "alienation" would enable a writer to continue and complete the discussion. While there is a way in which these terms are interchangeable, they are not all permissible. A student in a composition class would most likely be turned away from a discussion of original sin. Commonplaces are the "controlling ideas" of our composition textbooks, textbooks that not only insist upon a set form for expository writing but a set view of public life.[2]

When the student above says, "I don't know," he is not saying, then, that he has nothing to say. He is saying that he is not in a position to carry on this discussion. And so we are addressed as apprentices rather than as teachers or scholars. To speak to us as a person of status or privilege, the writer can either speak to us in our terms — in the privileged language of university discourse — or, in default (or in defiance), he can speak to us as though we were children, offering us the wisdom of experience.

I think it is possible to say that the language of the "Clay Model" paper has come through the writer and not from the writer. The writer has located himself (he has located the self that is represented by the *I* on the page) in a context that is, finally, beyond him, not his own and not available to his immediate procedures for inventing and arranging text. I would not, that is, call this essay an example of "writer-based" prose. I would not say that it is egocentric or that it represents the "interior monologue of a writer thinking and talking to himself" (Flower 63). It is, rather, the record of a writer who has lost himself in the discourse of his readers. There is a context beyond the reader that is not the world but a way of talking about the world, a way of talking that determines the use of examples, the possible conclusions, the acceptable commonplaces, and the key words of an essay on the construction of a clay model of the earth. This writer has entered the discourse without successfully approximating it.

Linda Flower has argued that the difficulty inexperienced writers have with writing can be understood as a difficulty in negotiating the transition between writer-based and reader-based prose. Expert writers, in other words, can better imagine how a reader will respond to a text and can transform or restructure what they have to say around a goal shared with a reader. Teaching students to revise for readers, then, will better prepare them to write initially with a reader in mind. The success of this pedagogy depends upon the degree to which a writer can imagine and conform to a reader's goals. The difficulty of this act of imagination, and the burden of such conformity, are so much at the heart of the problem that a teacher must pause and take stock before offering revision as a solution. Students like the student who wrote the "Clay Model" paper are not so much trapped in a private language as they are shut out from one of the privileged languages of public life, a language they are aware of but cannot control.

Our students, I've said, have to appropriate (or be appropriated by) a specialized discourse, and they have to do this as though they were easily or comfortably one with their audience. If you look at the situation this way, suddenly the problem of audience awareness becomes enormously complicated. One of the common assumptions of both composition research and composition teaching is that at some "stage" in the process of composing an essay a writer's ideas or his motives must be tailored to the needs and expectations of his audience. A writer has to "build bridges" between his point of view and his readers'. He has to anticipate and acknowledge his readers' assumptions and biases. He must begin with "common points of departure" before introducing new or controversial arguments. There is a version of the pastoral at work here. It is assumed that a person of low status (like a shepherd) can speak to a person of power (like a courtier), but only (at least so far as the language is concerned) if he is not a shepherd at all, but actually a member of the court out in the field in disguise.

Writers who can successfully manipulate an audience (or, to use a less pointed language, writers who can accommodate their motives to their readers' expectations) are writers who can both imagine and write from a position of privilege. They must, that is, see themselves within a privileged discourse, one that already includes and excludes groups of readers. They must be either equal to or more powerful than those they would address. The writing, then, must somehow transform the political and social relationships between basic writing students and their teachers.

If my students are going to write for me by knowing who I am — and if this means more than knowing my prejudices, psyching me out — it means knowing what I know; it means having the knowledge of a professor of English. They have, then, to know what I know and how I know what I know (the interpretive schemes that define the way I would work out the problems I set for them); they have to learn to write what I would write, or to offer up some approximation of that discourse. The problem of audience awareness, then, is a problem of power and finesse. It cannot be addressed, as it is in most classroom exercises, by giving students privilege and denying the situation of the classroom, by having students write to an outsider, someone excluded from their privileged circle: "Write about 'To His Coy Mistress,' not for your teacher, but for the students in your class"; "Describe Pittsburgh to someone who has never been there"; "Explain to a high school senior how best to prepare for college"; "Describe baseball to a Martian."

Exercises such as these allow students to imagine the needs and goals of a reader and they bring those needs and goals forward as a dominant constraint in the construction of an essay. And they argue, implicitly, what is generally true about writing — that it is an act of aggression disguised as an act of charity. What they fail to address is the central problem of academic writing, where students must assume the right of speaking to someone who knows Pittsburgh or "To His Coy Mistress" better than they do, a reader for whom the general commonplaces and the readily available utterances about a subject are inadequate. It should be clear that when I say that I know Pittsburgh better than my basic writing students I am talking about a way of knowing that is also a way of writing. There may be much that they know that I don't know, but in the setting of the university classroom I have a way of talking about the town that is "better" (and for arbitrary reasons) than theirs.

I think that all writers, in order to write, must imagine for themselves the privilege of being "insiders" — that is, of being both inside an established and powerful discourse, and of being granted a special right to speak. And I think that right to speak is seldom conferred upon us — upon any of us, teachers or students — by virtue of the fact that we have invented or discovered an original idea. Leading students to believe that they are responsible for something new or original, unless they understand what those words mean with regard to writing, is a dangerous and counterproductive practice. We do have the right to expect students to be active and engaged, but that is more a matter of being continually and stylistically working against the inevitable presence of conventional language; it is not a matter of inventing a language that is new.

When students are writing for a teacher, writing becomes more problematic than it is for the students who are describing baseball to a Martian. The students, in effect, have to assume privilege without having any. And since students assume privilege by locating themselves within the discourse of a particular community — within a set of specifically acceptable gestures and commonplaces — learning, at least as it is defined in the liberal arts curriculum, becomes more a matter of imitation or parody than a matter of invention and discovery.

What our beginning students need to learn is to extend themselves into the commonplaces, set phrases, rituals, gestures, habits of mind, tricks of persuasion, obligatory conclusions, and necessary connections that determine the "what might be said" and constitute knowledge within the various branches of our academic community. The course of instruction that would make this possible would be based on a sequence of illustrated assignments and would allow for successive approximations of academic or "disciplinary" discourse. Students will not take on our peculiar ways of reading, writing, speaking, and thinking all at once. Nor will the command of a subject like sociology, at least as that command is represented by the successful completion of a multiple choice exam, enable students to write sociology. Our colleges and universities, by and large, have failed to involve basic writing students in scholarly projects, projects that would allow them to act as though they were colleagues in an academic enterprise. Much of the written work students do is test-taking, report or summary, work that places them outside the working discourse of the academic community, where they are expected to admire and report on what we do, rather than inside that discourse, where they can do its work and participate in a common enterprise.[3] This is a failure of teachers and curriculum designers who, even if they speak of writing as a mode of learning, all too often represent writing as a "tool" to be used by a (hopefully) educated mind.

Pat Bizzell is one of the most important scholars writing now on basic writers and on the special requirements of academic discourse.[4] In a recent essay, "Cognition, Convention, and Certainty: What We Need to Know about Writing," she argues that the problems of basic writers might be

> better understood in terms of their unfamiliarity with the academic discourse community, combined, perhaps, with such limited experience outside their native discourse communities that they are unaware that there is such a thing as a discourse community with conventions to be mastered. What is underdeveloped is their knowledge both of the ways experience is constituted and interpreted in the academic discourse community and of the fact that all discourse communities constitute and interpret experience. (230)

One response to the problems of basic writers, then, would be to determine just what the community's conventions are, so that those conventions can be written out, "demystified," and taught in our classrooms. Teachers, as a result, could be more precise and helpful when they ask students to "think," "argue," "describe," or "define." Another response would be to examine the essays written by basic writers — their approximations of academic discourse — to determine more clearly where the problems lie. If we look at their writing, and if we look at it in the context of other student writing, we can better see the points of discord when students try to write their way into the university.

The purpose of the remainder of this paper will be to examine some of the most striking and characteristic problems as they are presented in the expository essays of basic writers. I will be concerned, then, with university discourse in its most generalized form — that is, as represented by introductory courses — and not with the special conventions required by advanced work in the various disciplines. And I will be concerned with the difficult, and often violent, accommodations that occur when students locate themselves in a discourse that is not "naturally" or immediately theirs.

I have reviewed five hundred essays written in response to the "creativity" question used during one of our placement exams. (The essay cited at the opening of this paper was one of that group.) Some of the essays were written by basic writers (or, more properly, those essays led readers to identify the writers as "basic writers"); some were written by students who "passed" (who were granted immediate access to the community of writers at the university). As I read these essays, I was looking to determine the stylistic resources that enabled writers to locate themselves within an "academic" discourse. My bias as a reader should be clear by now. I was not looking to see how the writer might represent the skills demanded by a neutral language (a language whose key features were paragraphs, topic sentences, transitions, and the like — features of a clear and orderly mind). I was looking to see what happened when a writer entered into a language to locate himself (a textual self) and his subject, and I was looking to see how once entered, that language made or unmade a writer.

Here is one essay. Its writer was classified as a basic writer. Since the essay is relatively free of sentence level errors, that decision must have been rooted in some perceived failure of the discourse itself.

I am very interested in music, and I try to be creative in my interpretation of music. While in high school, I was a member of a jazz ensemble. The members of the ensemble were given chances to improvise and be creative in various songs. I feel that this was a great experience for me, as well as the other members. I was proud to know that I could use my imagination and feelings to create music other than what was written.

Creativity to me, means being free to express yourself in a way that is unique to you, not having to conform to certain rules and guidelines. Music is only one of the many areas in which people are given opportunities to show their creativity. Sculpting, carving, building, art, and acting are just a few more areas where people can show their creativity.

Through my music I conveyed feelings and thoughts which were important to me. Music was my means of showing creativity. In whatever form creativity takes, whether it be music, art, or science, it is an important aspect of our lives because it enables us to be individuals.

Notice, in this essay, the key gesture, one that appears in all but a few of the essays I read. The student defines as his own that which is a commonplace. "Creativity, to *me*, means being free to express yourself in a way that is unique to you, not having to conform to certain rules and guidelines." This act of appropriation constitutes his authority; it constitutes his authority as a writer and not just as a musician (that is, as someone with a story to tell). There were many essays in the set that told only a story, where the writer's established presence was as a musician or a skier or someone who painted designs on a van, but not as a person removed from that experience interpreting it, treating it as a metaphor for something else (creativity). Unless those stories were long, detailed, and very well told (unless the writer was doing more than saying, "I am a skier or a musician or a van-painter"), those writers were all given low ratings.

Notice also that the writer of the jazz paper locates himself and his experience in relation to the commonplace (creativity is unique expression; it is not having to conform to rules or guidelines) regardless of whether it is true or not. Anyone who improvises "knows" that improvisation follows rules and guidelines. It is the power of the commonplace (its truth as a recognizable, and, the writer believes, as a final statement) that justifies the example and completes the essay. The example, in other words, has value because it stands within the field of the commonplace. It is not the occasion for what one might call an "objective" analysis or a "close" reading. It could also be said that the essay stops with the articulation of the commonplace. The following sections speak only to the power of that statement. The reference to "sculpting, carving, building, art, and acting" attest to the universal of the commonplace (and it attests to the writer's nervousness with the status he has appropriated for himself — he is saying, "Now, I'm not the only one here who's done something unique"). The commonplace stands by itself. For this writer, it does not need to be elaborated. By virtue of having written it, he has completed the essay and established the contract by which we may be spoken to as equals: "In whatever form creativity takes, whether it be music, art, or science, it is an important aspect of *our lives* because it enables *us* to be individuals." (For me to break that contract, to argue that *my* life is not represented in that essay, is one way for me to begin as a teacher with that student in that essay.)

I said that the writer of the jazz paper offered up a commonplace regardless of whether it was "true" or not, and this, I said, was an example of the power of a commonplace to determine the meaning of an example. A commonplace determines a system of interpretation that can be used to "place" an example within a standard system of belief. You can see a similar process at work in this essay.

During the football season, the team was supposed to wear the same type of cleats and the same type socks, I figured that I would change this a little by wearing my white shoes instead of black and to cover up the team socks with a pair of my own white ones. I thought that this looked better than what we were wearing, and I told a few of the other people on the team to change too. They agreed that it did look better and they changed there combination to go along with mine. After the game people came up to us and said that it looked very good the way we wore our socks, and they wanted to know why we changed from the rest of the team.

I feel that creativity comes from when a person lets his imagination come up with ideas and he is not afraid to express them. Once you create something to do it will be original and unique because it came about from your own imagination and if any one else tries to copy it, it won't be the same because you thought of it first from your own ideas.

This is not an elegant paper, but it seems seamless, tidy. If the paper on the clay model of the earth showed an ill-fit between the writer and his project, here the discourse seems natural, smooth. You could reproduce this paper and hand it out to a class, and it would take a lot of prompting before the students sense something fishy and one of the more aggressive ones might say, "Sure he came up with the idea of wearing white shoes and white socks. Him and Billy White-shoes Johnson. Come on. He copied the very thing he said was his own idea, 'original and unique.'"

The "I" of this text, the "I" who "figured," "thought," and "felt" is located in a conventional rhetoric of the self that turns imagination into origination (I made it), that argues an ethic of production (I made it and it is mine), and that argues a tight scheme of intention (I made it because I decided to make it). The rhetoric seems invisible because it is so common. This "I" (the maker) is also located in a version of history that dominates classroom accounts of history. It is an example of the "Great Man" theory, where history is rolling along — the English novel is dominated by a central, intrusive narrative presence; America is in the throes of a great depression; during football season the team was supposed to wear the same kind of cleats and socks — until a figure appears, one who can shape history —Henry James, FDR, the writer of the football paper — and everything is changed. In the argument of the football paper, "I figured," "I thought," "they agreed," and, as a consequence, "I feel that creativity *comes from* when a person lets his imagination come up with ideas and he is not afraid to express them." The story of appropriation becomes a narrative of courage and conquest. The writer was able to write that story when he was able to imagine himself in that discourse. Getting him out of it will be a difficult matter indeed.

There are ways, I think, that a writer can shape history in the very act of writing it. Some students are able to enter into a discourse, but, by stylistic maneuvers, to take possession of it at the same time. They don't originate a discourse, but they locate themselves within it aggressively, self-consciously.

Here is one particularly successful essay. Notice the specialized vocabulary, but also the way in which the text continually refers to its own language and to the language of others.

Throughout my life, I have been interested and intrigued by music. My mother has often told me of the times, before I went to school, when I would "conduct" the orchestra on her records. I continued to listen to music and eventually started to play the guitar and the clarinet. Finally, at about the age of twelve, I started to sit down and to try to write songs. Even though my instrumental skills were far from my own high standards, I would spend much of my spare time during the day with a guitar around my neck, trying to produce a piece of music.

Each of these sessions, as I remember them, had a rather set format. I would sit in my bedroom, strumming different combinations of the five or six chords I could play, until I heard a series which sounded particularly good to me. After this, I set the music to a suitable rhythm, (usually dependent on my mood at the time), and ran through the tune until I could play it fairly easily. Only after this section was complete did I go on to writing lyrics, which generally followed along the lines of the current popular songs on the radio.

At the time of the writing, I felt that my songs were, in themselves, an original creation of my own; that is, I, alone, made them. However, I now see that, in this sense of the word, I was not creative. The songs themselves seem to be an oversimplified form of the music I listened to at the time.

In a more fitting sense, however, I *was* being creative. Since I did not purposely copy my favorite songs, I was, effectively, originating my songs from my own "process of creativity." To achieve my goal, I needed what a composer would call "inspiration" for my piece. In this case the inspiration was the current hit on the radio. Perhaps with my present point of view, I feel that I used too much "inspiration" in my songs, but, at that time, I did not.

Creativity, therefore, is a process which, in my case, involved a certain series of "small creations" if you like. As well, it is something, the appreciation of which varies with one's point of view, that point of view being set by the person's experience, tastes, and his own personal view of creativity. The less experienced tend to allow for less originality, while the more experienced demand real originality to classify something a "creation." Either way, a term as abstract as this is perfectly correct, and open to interpretation.

This writer is consistent and dramatically conscious of herself forming something to say out of what has been said *and* out of what she has been saying in the act of writing this paper. "Creativity" begins, in this paper, as "original creation." What she thought was "creativity," however, she now calls "imitation" and, as she says, "in this sense of the word" she was not "creative." In another sense, however, she says that she *was* creative since she didn't purposefully copy the songs but used them as "inspiration."

The writing in this piece (that is, the work of the writer within the essay) goes on in spite of, or against, the language that keeps pressing to give another name to her experience as a song writer and to bring the discussion to closure. (Think of the quick closure of the football shoes paper in comparison.) Its style is difficult, highly qualified. It relies on quotation marks and parody to set off the language and attitudes that belong to the discourse (or the discourses) it would reject, that it would not take as its own proper location.[5]

In the papers I've examined in this essay, the writers have shown a varied awareness of the codes — or the competing codes — that operate within a discourse. To speak with authority student writers have not only to speak in another's voice but through another's "code"; and they not only have to do this, they have to speak in the voice and through the codes of those of us with power and wisdom; and they not only have to do this, they have to do it before they know what they are doing, before they have a project to participate in and before, at least in terms of our disciplines, they have anything to say. Our students may be able to enter into a conventional discourse and speak, not as themselves, but through the voice of the community. The university, however, is the place where "common" wisdom is only of negative value; it is something to work against. The movement toward a more specialized discourse begins (or perhaps, best begins) when a student can both define a position of privilege, a position that sets him against a "common" discourse, and when he can work self-consciously, critically, against not only the "common" code but his own.

The stages of development that I've suggested are not necessarily marked by corresponding levels in the type or frequency of error, at least not by the type or frequency of sentence level errors. I am arguing, then, that a basic writer is not necessarily a writer who makes a lot of mistakes. In fact, one of the problems with curricula designed to aid basic writers is that they too often begin with the assumption that the key distinguishing feature of a basic writer is the presence of sentence level error. Students are placed in courses because their placement essays show a high frequency of such errors and those courses are designed with the goal of making those errors go away. This approach to the problems of the basic writer ignores the degree to which error is not a constant feature but a marker in the development of a writer. Students who can write reasonably correct narratives may fall to pieces when faced with more unfamiliar assignments. More importantly, however, such courses fail to serve the rest of the curriculum. On every campus there is a significant number of college freshmen who require a course to introduce them to the kinds of writing that are required for a university education. Some of these students can write correct sentences and some cannot, but as a group they lack the facility other freshmen possess when they are faced with an academic writing task.

The "White Shoes" essay, for example, shows fewer sentence level errors than the "Clay Model" paper. This may well be due to the fact, however, that the writer of that paper stayed well within the safety of familiar territory. He kept himself out of trouble by doing what he could easily do. The tortuous syntax of the more advanced papers on my list is a syntax that represents a writer's struggle with a difficult and unfamiliar language, and it is a syntax that can quickly lead an inexperienced writer into trouble. The syntax and punctuation of the "Composing Songs" essay, for example, shows the effort that is required when a writer works against the pressure of conventional discourse. If the prose is inelegant (although I'll confess I admire those dense sentences), it is still correct. This writer has a command of the linguistic and stylistic resources (the highly embedded sentences, the use of parentheses and quotation marks) required to complete the act of writing. It is easy to imagine the possible pitfalls for a writer working without this facility.

There was no camera trained on the "Clay Model" writer while he was writing, and I have no protocol of what was going through his mind, but it is possible to speculate that the syntactic difficulties of sentences like the following are the result of an attempt to use an unusual vocabulary and to extend his sentences beyond the boundaries that would be "normal" in his speech or writing:

> In past time I thought that an incident was creative was when I had to make a clay model of the earth, but not of the classic or your everyday model of the earth which consists of the two cores, the mantle and the crust. I thought of these things in a dimension of which it would be unique, but easy to comprehend.

There is reason to believe, that is, that the problem is with this kind of sentence, in this context. If the problem of the last sentence is a problem of holding together these units — "I thought," "dimension," "unique," and "easy to comprehend" — then the linguistic problem is not a simple matter of sentence construction.

I am arguing, then, that such sentences fall apart not because the writer lacks the necessary syntax to glue the pieces together but because he lacks the full statement within which these key words are already operating. While writing, and in the thrust of his need to complete the sentence, he has the key words but not the utterance. (And to recover the utterance, I suspect, he will need to do more than revise the sentence.) The invisible conventions, the prepared phrases remain too distant for the statement to be completed. The writer must get inside of a discourse he can only partially imagine. The act of constructing a sentence, then, becomes something like an act of transcription, where the voice on the tape unexpectedly fades away and becomes inaudible.

Mina Shaughnessy speaks of the advanced writer as a writer with a more facile but still incomplete possession of this prior discourse. In the case of the advanced writer, the evidence of a problem is the presence of dissonant, redundant, or precise language, as in a sentence such as this: "No education can be *total,* it must be *continuous.*" Such a student, Shaughnessy says, could be said to hear the "melody of formal English" while still unable to make precise or exact distinctions. And, she says, the prepackaging feature of language, the possibility of taking over phrases and whole sentences without much thought about them, threatens the writer now as before. The writer, as we have said, inherits the language out of which he must fabricate his own messages. He is therefore in a constant tangle with the language, obliged to recognize its public, communal nature and yet driven to invent out of this language his own statements (19).

For the unskilled writer, the problem is different in degree and not in kind. The inexperienced writer is left with a more fragmentary record of the comings and goings of academic discourse. Or, as I said above, he often has the key words without the complete statements within which they are already operating.

It may very well be that some students will need to learn to crudely mimic the "distinctive register" of academic discourse before they are prepared to actually and legitimately do the work of the discourse, and before they are sophisticated enough with the refinements of tone and texture to do it with grace or elegance. To say this, however, is to say that our students must be our students. Their initial progress will be marked by their abilities to take on the role of privilege, by their abilities to establish authority. From this point of view, the student who wrote about constructing the clay model of the earth is better prepared for his education than the student who wrote about playing football in white shoes, even though the "White Shoes" paper was relatively error-free and the "Clay Model" paper was not. It will be hard to pry the writer of the "White Shoes" paper loose from the tidy, pat discourse that allows him to dispose of the question of creativity in such a quick and efficient manner. He will have to be convinced that it is better to write sentences he might not so easily control, and he will have to be convinced that it is better to write muddier and more confusing prose (in order that it may sound like ours), and this will be harder than convincing the "Clay Model" writer to continue what he has begun.[6]

Notes

[1] David Olson has made a similar observation about school-related problems of language learning in younger children. Here is his conclusion: "Depending upon whether children assumed language was primarily suitable for making assertions and conjectures or primarily for making direct or indirect commands, they will either find school texts easy or difficult" (107).

[2] For Aristotle there were both general and specific commonplaces. A speaker, says Aristotle, has a "stock of arguments to which he may turn for a particular need."

> If he knows the *topic* (regions, places, lines of argument) — and a skilled speaker will know them — he will know where to find what he wants for a special case. The general topics, or *common*places, are regions containing arguments that are common to all branches of knowledge. . . . But there are also special topics (regions, places, *loci*) in which one looks for arguments appertaining to particular branches of knowledge, special sciences, such as ethics or politics. (154–55)

And, he says "The topics or places, then, may be indifferently thought of as in the science that is concerned, or in the mind of the speaker." But the question of location is "indifferent" *only* if the mind of the speaker is in line with set opinion, general assumption. For the speaker (or writer) who is not situated so comfortably in the privileged public realm, this is indeed not an indifferent matter at all. If he does not have the commonplace at hand, he will not, in Aristotle's terms, know where to go at all.

[3] See especially Bartholomae and Rose for articles on curricula designed to move students into university discourse. The movement to extend writing "across the curriculum" is evidence of a general concern for locating students within the work of the university: see especially Bizzell or Maimon et al. For longer works directed specifically at basic writing, see Ponsot and Deen, and Shaughnessy. For a book describing a course for more advanced students, see Coles.

[4] See especially Bizzell, and Bizzell and Herzberg. My debt to Bizzell's work should be evident everywhere in this essay.

[5] In support of my argument that this is the kind of writing that does the work of the academy, let me offer the following excerpt from a recent essay by Wayne Booth ("The Company We Keep: Self-Making in Imaginative Art, Old and New"):

> I can remember making up songs of my own, no doubt borrowed from favorites like "Hello, Central, Give Me Heaven," "You Can't Holler Down My Rain Barrel," and one about the ancient story of a sweet little "babe in the woods" who lay down and died, with her brother.
>
> I asked my mother, in a burst of creative egotism, why nobody ever learned to sing my songs, since after all I was more than willing to learn *theirs*. I can't remember her answer, and I can barely remember snatches of two of "my" songs. But I can remember dozens of theirs, and when I sing them, even now, I sometimes feel again the emotions, and see the images, that they aroused then. Thus who I am now — the very shape of my soul — was to a surprising degree molded by the works of "art" that came my way.
>
> I set "art" in quotation marks, because much that I experienced in those early books and songs would not be classed as art according to most definitions. But for the purposes of appraising the effects of "art" on "life" or "culture," and especially for the purposes of thinking about the effects of the "media," we surely must include every kind of artificial experience that we provide for one another. . . .
>
> In this sense of the word, all of us are from the earliest years fed a steady diet of art. . . . (58–59)

While there are similarities in the paraphrasable content of Booth's arguments and my student's, what I am interested in is each writer's method. Both appropriate terms from a common discourse (about *art* and *inspiration*) in order to push against an established way of talking (about tradition and the individual). This effort of opposition clears a space for each writer's argument and enables the writers to establish their own "sense" of the key words in the discourse.

[6] Preparation of this manuscript was supported by the Learning Research and Development Center of the University of Pittsburgh, which is supported in part by

the National Institute of Education. I am grateful also to Mike Rose, who pushed and pulled at this paper at a time when it needed it.

Works Cited

Aristotle. *The Rhetoric of Aristotle.* Trans. L. Cooper, Englewood Cliffs: Prentice, 1932.

Bartholomae, D. "Writing Assignments: Where Writing Begins." *Forum.* Ed. P. Stock. Montclair: Boynton/Cook, 1983. 300–312.

Bizzell, P. "The ethos of academic discourse." *College Composition and Communication* 29 (1978): 351–55.

———. "Cognition, Convention, and Certainty: What We Need to Know about Writing." *Pre/text* 3 (1982): 213–44.

———. "College Composition: Initiation into the Academic Discourse Community." *Curriculum Inquiry* 12 (1982): 191–207.

Bizzell, P., and B. Herzberg. "'Inherent' Ideology, 'Universal' History, 'Empirical' Evidence, and 'Context-Free' Writing: Some Problems with E. D. Hirsch's *The Philosophy of Composition.*" *Modern Language Notes* 95 (1980): 1181–1202.

Coles, W. E., Jr. *The Plural I.* New York: Holt, 1978.

Flower, Linda S. "Revising Writer-Based Prose." *Journal of Basic Writing* 3 (1981): 62–74.

Maimon, E. P., G. L. Belcher, G. W. Hearn, B. F. Nodine, and F. X. O'Connor. *Writing in the Arts and Sciences.* Cambridge: Winthrop, 1981.

Olson, D. R. "Writing: The Divorce of the Author from the Text." *Exploring Speaking-Writing Relationships: Connections and Contrasts.* Ed. B. M. Kroll and R. J. Vann. Urbana: National Council of Teachers of English, 1981.

Ponsot, M., and R. Deen. *Beat Not the Poor Desk.* Montclair: Boynton/Cook, 1982.

Rose, M. "Remedial Writing Courses: A Critique and a Proposal." *College English* 45 (1983): 109–28.

Shaughnessy, Mina. *Errors and Expectations.* New York: Oxford UP, 1977.

ANALYZING AUDIENCES

Douglas B. Park

[*College Composition and Communication* 37 (1986): 478–88.]

Douglas Park is professor of English at Western Washington University, where he served as department chair for ten years. He has published articles on composition and rhetoric in several journals; "Analyzing Audiences" continues an article published in *College English* in 1982.

Park recognizes that few teachers agree on how best to teach audience analysis. He offers options for expanded discussions of audience, and he emphasizes that audience analyses will be most successful if students recognize how their writing will function in a reasonable social context. As a result, Park affirms the pragmatic, functional approach to audience analysis that *The Bedford Handbook* promotes.

What do we expect analysis of audience to do for writers? What form should analysis of audience take; or, more precisely, what makes certain kinds of analysis more or less appropriate in given situations?

The centrality of audience in the rhetorical tradition and the detail with which current writing texts provide advice on analyzing an audience might suggest that the answers to such questions are well established. But they clearly are not. Side by side with the growing awareness in recent discussions that audience is a rich and complex concept exists a growing dissatisfaction with traditional audience analysis — those familiar questions about an audience's age, sex, education, and social background that form the core of most proposed heuristics. (See, for instance, Barry Kroll, "Writing for Readers: Three Perspectives on Audience," *CCC*, 35 [May 1984], 172–75; Russell Long, "Writer–Audience Relationships," *CCC*, 31 [May 1980], 221–26; Arthur Walzer, "Articles from the 'California Divorce Project': A Case Study of the Concept of Audience," *CCC*, 36 [May 1985], 155–58.)

The general import of the explicit criticism is that traditional audience analysis is too limited a tool: It works only for persuasive discourse; it seems inapplicable to discourse situations with general audiences about whom specific questions cannot be arrived at. But underneath these criticisms lies a greater uncertainty about the whole subject, characterized on the one hand by a sense that traditional analysis somehow fails altogether to provide what we now expect from audience analysis and on the other by the lack of any other widely shared way of thinking about the subject.

To address this uncertainty, we need to return to first principles and examine just what it is that we do expect audience analysis to accomplish and just how the assumptions behind traditional analysis relate to those expectations. This examination will show why traditional analysis, for all the apparent sanction of tradition, has so little practical rhetorical value for us. More important, it will provide a backdrop for a broader and, I hope, more useful view of what can go into analyzing audiences.

In a broad sense, the purpose of audience analysis is obvious enough: to aid the writer or speaker in understanding a social situation. The advice to "know your audience" carries much of the social meaning of "know" as in knowing who another person is or what that person is like. The advice to "consider your audience" suggests a deliberate weighing of the characteristics of the audience with a view to an appropriate shaping of the discourse. If we look at a set of hypothetical discourses chosen to illustrate a range of different audiences, we can describe more precisely these undifferentiated purposes for analysis. Consider

a legal argument on behalf of an accused embezzler;

a local businessman's letter to City Council protesting a zoning decision;

a grant proposal to develop computer instruction;

a memo from a provost to his university faculty arguing for annual evaluations;

a panel presentation on invention at CCCC;

an article on food in the Pacific Northwest contemplated by a freelance journalist;

an essay on rock and roll contemplated by an English 101 student.

In all but the last two cases, the most obvious specific purpose for analysis will be to understand where a given audience stands in relation to the particular aim and issues at hand. The goal is the immediately strategic one of adapting argument to audience: What are the criteria on which the grant review board makes its decisions? Why are most of the faculty so hostile to annual evaluations? What are the current issues in the discipline's discussions of invention?

In the last two cases above, however, the writers are not yet ready for this sort of strategic analysis. The freelance writer must first choose an audience — a journal such as *Sunset Magazine* — in order to be able to think about rhetorical strategy. The student, in a yet more difficult position, must somehow imagine or invent an audience in a situation where no audience naturally exists. Here the primary purpose of audience analysis becomes not the usual one of providing information about an existing audience but rather a means of actually helping students to discover an audience. And this raises the questions of just how they are to do that. What must they think about to imagine their papers as having or being capable of having an audience?

The special context of the classroom creates a peculiar purpose for audience analysis, one for which it was never intended. It does, however, usefully focus the essential question of what we mean by "having an audience." What is an audience, anyway? — as our baffled students often seem to ask. And this is just a generalized form of a need that all writers experience to understand the identity of the audience that they know they have: What does it mean to be in the situation of addressing a CCCC audience or a grant review board or a City Council? Questions of this sort are, I think, another important part of the meaning of "know your audience." They point to a purpose for analysis which lies underneath the more obvious strategic purpose of determining the audience's responses to particular issues.

Both these purposes for analysis — the fundamental identifying and defining of an audience and the strategic analysis of particular attitudes — involve describing situations, because audience is an inherently situational concept (Lisa Ede, "On Audience and Composition," *CCC*, 30 [October 1979], 294ff.). The notion of accommodating discourse to an audience is one of participating in a dynamic social relationship. And "audience" itself refers to the idea of a collective entity that can exist only in relation to a discourse; it means a group of people engaged in a rhetorical situation. Therefore if we are to identify an audience and say anything useful about it, we will have to speak in terms of the situation that brings it into being and gives it identity.

From this perspective, it becomes easy to see why traditional audience analysis so often seems unsatisfactory. What it does is to take literally the idea of "knowing" an audience as examining a group already assembled and describing any or all of the characteristics that those assembled may happen to have. In so doing it directly addresses neither the situation that has brought the audience into being as an audience nor the particular states of mind that the audience may possess in relation to the issues at hand. It tries rather to describe general traits from which rhetorically useful inferences may be drawn.

> [The elderly] are positive about nothing; in all things they err by an extreme moderation. . . . The rich are insolent and superior. . . . Now the hearer is always receptive when a speech is adapted to his own character and reflects it. (*The Rhetoric of Aristotle*, trans. Lane Cooper [Englewood Cliffs, N.J., Prentice-Hall, 1932], pp. 134–38)

> Different habits . . . and different occupations in life . . . make one incline more to one passion, another to another. . . . With men of genius the most successful topic will be fame; with men of industry, riches; with men of fortune, pleasure. (George Campbell, *The Philosophy of Rhetoric*, 2 vols. [Edinburgh, 1776], 1, 241–42)

It is . . . to begin by recording certain information about an audience and then, on the basis of experience and research, to infer about the audience such matters as knowledge, temperament, attitudes, habits of thought, language preferences or other matters that will enter into their responses to communication. (Theodore Clevenger, Jr., *Audience Analysis* [Indianapolis, Ind.: Bobbs-Merrill, 1966], p. 43)

Clearly, both Campbell and Aristotle envision the possibility of topoi appropriate for various ages and conditions of men. If an assembled audience in a particular situation can be seen to have a salient trait or quality — what classical rhetoric calls the "character" of the audience — then various lines of argument will fit that character more or less effectively. Perhaps most of the City Council are like our letter-writer businessman "men of industry," practical men who will respond best to arguments from "riches." As a general idea — which is how audience analysis usually appears in classical rhetoric (e.g., Quintilian, *Institutio Oratoria*, III, viii, 38) — the notion seems plausible. Certainly in situations involving small, immediate audiences, most of us have had the experience of sensing the overall personality of an audience, or of dominant members in it, and the need to adjust to those qualities in a general and impressionistic way. But inflated to a social-science method of the sort that the modern description suggests, traditional analysis almost completely loses touch with rhetorical usefulness. Aside from the fact that large generalizations about the psychology of age or sex are suspect in any particular application, the accumulation of demographic facts about an audience has no clear goal or limit (Clevenger, pp. 45ff.). All it can do is amass information unlikely to add up to any sort of "character." "The characters of men," admits George Campbell, beating a retreat from the subject, "may be infinitely diversified" (243). One of our industrious business executives may also be a man of genius and education who might therefore be motivated by arguments from fame. Another is perhaps rich and therefore "insolent." Two might be in their 30's, one in his 50's, two in their 60's. Two might have high-school educations, and so on ad infinitum, the writer having no clear way to determine the relevance or weight of any of this information to the task at hand.

Of course the general assumption informing traditional audience analysis as we find it in modern speech communication texts is that it aims at the social traits held in common that shape the responses of the audience as a whole. (See, for instance, Paul Holtzman's *The Psychology of Speakers' Audiences* [Glenview, Ill.: Scott Foresman, 1970], pp. 73–79.) So we can observe that a CCCC audience will share many social traits: most will have advanced degrees in English; most will be between 25 and 65; probably at least half will be women; most will be politically liberal. Certainly all will have modest incomes. But although such facts might well interest a social scientist, they are merely symptoms of the situation that actually gives the audience its identity. If we were to send a speaker to the podium, shanghaied, blindfolded, armed only with the subject and the result of a demographic analysis, our victim would angrily or plaintively want to know, "But who is my audience?" The answer of course is "conferees attending a CCCC panel," a simple identification that compresses for someone in the know a wealth of necessary knowledge about the identity of the audience as an entity assembled for a collective purpose.

Bizarre as the case of the blindfolded speaker may be, it describes exactly the mistaken way in which traditional analysis is used to help students discover audiences by amassing detailed information about people, real or imaginary. "They [students] must construct in imagination an audience that is as nearly a replica as is possible of those many readers who actually exist in the world of reality and who are reading the writer's words" (Fred R. Pfister and Joanne F. Petrick, "A Heuristic Model for Creating a Writer's Audience," *CCC*, 30 [May 1980], 213). Following this principle, discussions commonly suggest as audiences groups with analyzable traits. "Thus a reader might be delineated as being a university administrator, over 40, male, white, etc., or a group of readers might be defined as businessmen in a small [midwestern] community" (Winifred B. Horner, "Speech-Act and Text-Act Theory: 'Theme-ing' in Freshman Composition," *CCC*, 30 [May 1979], 168). But obviously the problem that students face is not one of just visualizing hypothetical real people; it is one of grasping a situation in which real readers could constitute an "audience." In what conceivable situations, for instance, could our student writing about rock and roll be addressing a group of midwestern businessmen?

How then do we go about describing the situations that bring audiences into being and give them their identities? Or to put the question in a more basic way, how is it that discourses of any sort can have audiences? If we look at the most concrete possible image of an audience assembled to hear a speech and ask how they come to be there, the immediate answer will be that a particular occasion has brought them together. This, indeed, is the most common way we tend to think about and characterize audiences, as a particular group assembled to hear a particular speech. But a moment's reflection shows that while an audience assembles only for a particular discourse, the discourse alone cannot bring the audience into being. Lawyers do not defend their clients on street corners; passers-by do not wander into Holiday Inns to hear lectures on teaching composition; freelance journalists do not mimeograph their articles and leave them in mailboxes — unless they have become really desperate.

In brief, an audience can assemble on a particular occasion only because a social setting already exists in which a certain kind of discourse performs a recognized function. Note that the ancient classification of judicial, deliberative, and epideictic discourse follows this principle and amounts, as Chaim Perelman points out, to the identification of three basic audiences (*The New Rhetoric: A Treatise on Argumentation*, trans. John Wilkinson and Purcell Weaver [Notre Dame, Ind.: University of Notre Dame Press, 1969], p. 21). To define other audiences we need simply to amplify the principle to its broadest extent, as follows.

An audience can exist when there is (1) an established social institution or social relationship, a judicial system, a legislative process, an institutional hierarchy, a charitable foundation, a social compact of any sort, a club, a nation, even a friendship between two people; (2) and an evolved and understood function that discourse performs within and for that social relationship. Speech-act theory — and sociolinguistics in general — has taught us to see all discourse as representing action performed within and conditioned by a social situation. We can name these actions in very general terms — making statements, contracts, promises, implications, requests. But it is also important to see that all discourse, especially of the more public or formalized kind, functions in and can be described as part of a social transaction that has defined roles for both writers and readers. If I write a grant proposal, I am making a request, but I am also participating in a highly conventionalized activity evolved to enable the distribution of resources, the manipulation of tax laws, the satisfaction of political and public relations imperatives. I write as the representative of one institution. My audience exists in terms of and reads as representatives of the granting agency.

(3) Finally, for an audience to "assemble," there must be a physical setting. For written discourse, the exact analog to the place of assembly is the means of publication or distribution. Much has been made of the distance between writers and readers as opposed to the closeness of speakers and audience. Walter Ong argues that the readers of written discourse do not form an audience, a "collectivity," as do the listeners to a speech ("The Writer's Audience Is Always a Fiction," *PMLA*, 90 [January 1975], 11). In some senses this must of course be true, but because a written discourse always exists within some larger social setting and reaches its dispersed readers through a given physical means of distribution for an accepted social function, readers of prose are very much part of a collectivity. When I read a memo from the Provost in my office mail or a copy of *Sunset Magazine* in the public mail, I understand that I am participating in a social activity together with others. The major difference between speech and writing in their roles in social settings is that writing has been able to develop a wider range of functions. In the instance of popular journalism, the means of publication has been able to become a social institution in its own right. The reader of a newspaper or a magazine participates in a social relationship that has been largely created by the development of newspapers and magazines themselves.

All these intertwined elements of the social context for discourse define the terms in which the identity of an audience is best understood. This is why when we respond most directly and effectively to the question, "Who is the audience," we always respond in terms of the social institution and function that the discourse serves — a court, members of City Council, a grant review board, the college faculty, CCCC conferees, readers of *Sunset Magazine*. Unspoken but always present in any such simple identification of an audience is the whole complex of the social situation that has brought that audience into being. This unspoken presence is so compressed into the identification that it is easy to take for granted. But a writer who understands the identity of the audience grasps a wealth of tacit and explicit knowledge about the form of the discourse and the way the subject can be treated.

This knowledge informs the obvious rhetorical choices about appropriate formats, matters of tone, diction, stance toward the reader, kinds of allowable openings, structure, evidence, and argument. It also includes more subtle, crucial presuppositions about such things as how much the purpose of the discourse or the writer's own authority can be presumed or needs to be explained and justified. In many cases where the setting is subject specific — e.g., periodical journalism or scholarship — knowledge of the audience's identity also includes a great deal that the audience can be taken to know about the subject at hand. Awareness of the audience's identity provides, in short, all the sense of situation that makes it possible for a writer or speaker to proceed with a sense of being engaged in purposeful communication.

The identity of the audience, as I have described it above, constitutes, therefore, the necessary foundation for audience analysis. It constitutes as well the setting that shapes further considerations of strategy about the specific subject. For example, the lawyer pleading the case before the court will be concerned with the attitudes of the jurors toward the client and the issues of the case. But strategies to play on those attitudes will have to acknowledge the decorum of the courtroom and the jurors' own awareness of their special role as jurors. As Chaim Perelman points out, "It is quite common for members of an audience to adopt attitudes connected with the role they play in certain social institutions" (p. 21). In the case of the audience for the CCCC presentation, almost everything that one can say about their attitudes toward the subject at hand will, as Arthur Walzer suggests, have to be defined in terms of that particular "rhetorical or interpretive community" and in terms of the role that academic audiences are expected to play (p. 157).

To summarize the above discussion, I would suggest that what a writer needs to understand about an audience, what we mean by "knowing" an audience, can be adequately described by two interrelated levels of questions:

I. What is the identity of the audience?
   A. What is the institution or social relationship of writer(s) and audience that the discourse serves (or creates)?
   B. How does the discourse function in that relationship?
   C. What is the physical setting or means of distribution that brings the discourse to the audience and what are the conventions and formats associated with it?
II. How does the audience view the specific subject matter and how may it view the intentions of the discourse?
   A. What is known or can be projected about specific attitudes and knowledge in the audience that affect what the discourse will have to do in order to accomplish its purpose?
   B. To what extent are the audience's attitudes toward subject and purpose affected by or describable by reference to its collective identity as audience?

Although this outline has the appearance of a heuristic, I propose it more as a general framework for thinking about what writers may actually do when they attend to audience. How much, and at what points in the process of composing, such attention may profitably take the form of deliberate analysis of the audience are questions that I hope the above framework may help others to explore further. In particular, I think this framework helps to open a more adequate view of how different kinds of writing situations may require very different kinds of attention to audience. The elements of the audience that I have described above seem in different situations to take on different forms, to claim varying degrees of precedence and to interact in different ways.

For instance, our businessman writing to City Council probably knows the members of the Council well and has several social relationships to them — friend, enemy, fellow member of the Chamber of Commerce, and so on — any of which might be involved explicitly or implicitly in the letter. He has, therefore, a number of ways to conceive of and address his audience. But his attention seems most likely to be concentrated on their individual attitudes and predispositions toward the zoning issues. In the case of the grant proposal, by contrast, the writer's conception of the audience will be necessarily defined by their role as agents of the institution and by the conventions of grant proposals. The means of distribution for the discourse maintains distance, even anonymity, between the writer and the audience. Here, everything that can be said about the audience's attitudes will concern the kinds of argument that this particular granting agency is most responsive to. Yet again, in other kinds of institutional prose, like the provost's memo to the faculty, a piece of discourse may serve more than one function and audience — e.g., the President as well as the faculty. Much of the initial attention to audience will have to fall on actually identifying and defining these multiple audiences and then on juggling issues in recognition of all of them, while perhaps explicitly addressing only one audience. (See C. H. Knoblauch, "Intentionality in the Writing Process: A

Case Study," *CCC,* 31 [May 1980], 153–59. See also Mathes and Stevenson, *Designing Technical Reports* [Indianapolis, Ind.: Bobbs-Merrill, 1976], pp. 9–23.)

In spite of the differences in the attention to audience in the above examples, all are alike in that they aim toward the second level of the audience's specific attitudes and knowledge, and the appropriate strategies to accommodate them. This is so because the general function of the writings is transactional, by which I mean that they work to produce specific actions or responses from an audience who, as members of the institution involved, have an active part to play.

The kinds of attention a writer pays to audience seem likely to alter significantly, in ways that we do not understand at all well, when the function of discourse moves away from the transactional, as it does in the typical periodical essay and in much of what we call discourse written for a general audience. The audience for such discourse is not part of an institution — members of a jury, faculty at University X — within which the discourse performs some function. The audience comes rather to the discourse to participate in the social relationship — a sort of one-sided conversation — that is offered there. Here, understanding the identity of the audience means understanding what readers expect, the nature of the "conversation," the conventions which govern that kind of prose. In particular, it usually means understanding the setting of publication, e.g. *Sunset Magazine,* that ties those conventions to a specific format or to a set of assumed interests and attitudes in readers.

In such discourse, second-level analysis of the audience in relation to the specific subject and purpose often seems almost irrelevant, or so different from the analysis in transactional discourse that we need to find other ways of talking about it. The traditional model sees the writer as assessing and accommodating specific attitudes. The discourse is an instrument of negotiation. But here the writer is in the position of offering readers a social relationship — for entertainment, for intellectual stimulation, for general information — which they may or may not choose to enter.

One familiar way to talk about this very different relationship between discourse and audience is to draw on Walter Ong's idea of the audience as a fiction evoked by the text, a series of roles that the text offers to readers, or a series of presuppositions it makes about readers that the readers can accept or not ("The Writer's Audience Is Always a Fiction," *PMLA,* 90 [January 1975], 9–21; see also Douglas Park, "The Meanings of 'Audience,'" *College English,* 44 [March 1982], 247–57). Accordingly, Russell Long suggests that young writers should not try to analyze their audiences but to ask rather "Who do I want my audience to be?" (Writer–Audience Relationships: Analysis or Invention?" *CCC,* 31 [May 1980], 225).

Although this idea has force, it has remained too undeveloped. Further, it seems clear that all discourse must in some fashion attend to the constraints imposed by the requirements of real audiences. (See Lisa Ede and Andrea Lunsford, "Audience Addressed/Audience Invoked: The Role of Audience in Composition Theory and Pedagogy," *CCC,* 35 [May 1984], 155–71.) Writers, that is to say, can set out to engage readers in conversation only by some appropriate estimate of what they are actually likely to find intelligible, credible, or interesting. In practice, the setting for publication usually yields such information. But it seems probable that what writers work with here is not precise formulations of particular attitudes or states of knowledge but rather an awareness of a range of possible viewpoints. Robert Roth, for example, describes successful student revisions that evolve by appealing to a variety of possible responses from readers, by casting a wider rather than a narrower net ("The Evolving Audience: Alternatives to Audience Accommodation," *CCC*, 38 [February 1987], 47–55). The general aim of such attention to audience might perhaps be described not as fitting discourse to audience but as making it possible for a variety of readers to become an audience.

This survey is too brief to give more than an idea of the range of considerations that can go into audience analysis. But it will do to indicate how the framework I have laid out might be used, and to indicate as well some areas that need more investigation. For teachers of writing, I hope this discussion demonstrates that analysis of audience cannot profitably be seen as a set of all-purpose questions to be tacked on to an assignment to help students invent or identify an audience. To identify an audience means identifying a situation. So the primary issue that our current concern with audience analysis poses for teachers of writing is not how we can help students analyze their audiences but, first, how and to what extent we can help them define situations for their writing. And to this question there are no simple answers.

The most obvious way to define a situation for writing is to pose hypothetical cases — Imagine you are a resident assistant writing a report for the Dean of Students; write an article for *Sports Illustrated* — or to use the composition class for "real" writing such as a letter to the hometown paper. In fact the only way to have an audience analyzable in the detail we usually envision when we speak of audience analysis is to have a situation for writing that includes a concrete setting for "publication." For such assignments, I hope this discussion will facilitate more useful analyses of audience than those evoked by traditional advice.

Most teachers, however, will resist turning their composition courses entirely over to the writing of letters for various occasions. They feel, with good reason, that too much emphasis upon specific and often imaginary situations can lead to crude pretense and mechanical emphasis on format that robs student writing of all genuineness. They want students' writing to be in some elusive but important sense real and self-generated. Unfortunately, this ideal is difficult to reconcile with the obvious need many students have for a clearer sense of audience. Well-meaning advice like, "Be your own audience," while it seems to get at a truth, can leave many students with no way to understand their writing as being for anyone or any purpose at all.

The student who escapes this limbo — perhaps our hypothetical student writing about rock and roll — will do so partly by using various conventions of written prose to evoke the shadow of a situation, by writing like a freelance journalist or a musicologist, or an encyclopedist, or a columnist, or some creative pastiche of these. The very use of a certain recognizable "register" (M. A. K. Halliday and R. Hasan, *Language as Social Semiotic* [London: Longmans, 1976], pp. 65–73) — a way of addressing the readers, of opening the subject, of organizing material, and so on — even though it is accompanied by no identifiable setting for publication, will evoke a sense of the paper's possessing an audience. If the student's paper is sufficiently like other discourse that exists in real settings for publication, then it too will be felt to some extent to have an audience. But such a sense of audience will, I would suggest, always be informed by a grasp of the social function of the prose — that is to say how it works as public discourse, what general kind of thing it offers to readers.

If we are to help students who do not have this grasp on audience, we need to learn more about it ourselves. We need, first of all, to give more attention to defining the social functions of various kinds of public discourse. It is easy enough to see that different composition courses and different teachers have preferences — too often barely conscious or impressionistically defined — for different kinds of audiences. Students in one course may be expected to write like popular journalists about their personal knowledge, in another like apprentice philosophers, in another like informal essayists in the grand tradition. The current trend to center composition courses on the varieties of academic discourse seems especially constructive because it is accompanied by an attempt to understand and make more explicit the nature of such discourse (Walzer, p. 157).

Second, we need to learn more about how different kinds of discourse written for public or "general" audiences actually work rhetorically. Recognizing that the model of audience accommodation which works for transactional prose does not apply well to all discourse situations is a starting point. Doing more to describe the conventions of such prose would also be useful, as for instance in George Dillon's *Constructing Texts* (Bloomington, Ind.: Indiana University Press, 1981). His description of how students fail to understand some of the basic conventions of expository prose gets at a fundamental part of what we mean by a sense of audience. Although it is difficult to say how far such material should be taught directly, my own experience is that students are more receptive to descriptions and discussions of writing conventions as matters of social form and function than they are to descriptions of absolute criteria for good writing.

Finally, we need to keep in mind that the culture of the classroom can be a pervasive influence on a student's ability to understand an audience. In "Collaborative Learning and the 'Conversation of Mankind'" (*College English*, 46 [November 1984], 635–52), Kenneth Bruffee provides a fine account of the way that students can learn through social interaction to internalize and then re-externalize the kind of "conversation" that defines "a community of knowledgeable peers" (p. 642). At this point the discussion may appear to have moved far from analysis of audience, but at its most basic the issue of audience in writing instruction is one of social development and maturation — of student writers learning to see themselves as social beings in a social situation. Only in such a context can the art of rhetoric and of audience analysis have any real meaning or force in our teaching of writing.

PLANNING, DRAFTING, AND REVISING

COMPETING THEORIES OF PROCESS: A CRITIQUE AND A PROPOSAL

Lester Faigley

[*College English* 48 (1986): 527–42.]

Lester Faigley is professor of English and director of the Division of Rhetoric and Composition at the University of Texas at Austin. He has also been a senior fellow at the National University of Singapore and a visiting professor at Pennsylvania State University, the University of Utah, and in the Texas Summer Program at Brasnose College, Oxford University. In 1996, he served as chair of the annual Conference on College Composition and Communication. Faigley has published numerous articles and essays on subjects that range from discourse analysis, text linguistics, and composition theory to travel literature. His 1992 book *Fragments of Rationality: Postmodernity and the Subject of Composition* won the CCCC Outstanding Book Award in 1994.

Through his wide reading about the writing process, Faigley came to see the variety of notions that have been advanced about the process. "Competing Theories of Process" is an effort to sort out those notions and to examine their intellectual backgrounds. Faigley offers an overview of the three prevailing views of composing — the expressive, the cognitive, and the social — and examines the assumptions that each view makes about writers, writing, and the composing process. The article reminds instructors that the choices they make in their course plans and daily classroom practices are informed by an implicit or explicit theory of composing. Faigley's argument is particularly valuable for its suggestive synthesis of the three competing theoretical views.

The recognition of the study of writing as an important area of research within English in North America has also led to a questioning of its theoretical underpinnings. While the teaching of writing has achieved programmatic or departmental status at many colleges and universities, voices from outside and from within the ranks question whether a discipline devoted to the study of writing exists or if those who teach writing simply assume it exists because they share common problems and interests. The convenient landmark for disciplinary historians is the Richard Braddock, Richard Lloyd-Jones, and Lowell Schoer review of the field in 1963, a survey that found a legion of pedagogical studies of writing, most lacking any broad theoretical notion of writing abilities or even awareness of similar existing studies. Contemporary reviewers of writing research point out how much happened in the years that followed, but no development has been more influential than the emphasis on writing as a process. For the last few years, Richard Young's and Maxine Hairston's accounts of the process movement as a Kuhnian paradigm shift have served as justifications for disciplinary status. Even though the claim of a paradigm shift is now viewed by some as an overstatement, it is evident that many writing teachers in grade schools, high schools, and colleges have internalized process assumptions. In the most optimistic visions, writing teachers K–13 march happily under the process banner. Slogans such as "revising is good for you" are repeated in nearly every college writing textbook as well as in many secondary and elementary classrooms. Paradigm, pre-paradigm, or no paradigm, nearly everyone seems to agree that writing as a process is good and "current-traditional rhetoric" is bad. It would seem, therefore, that any disciplinary claims must be based on some shared definition of process.

The problem, of course, is that conceptions of writing as a process vary from theorist to theorist. Commentators on the process movement (e.g., Berlin, *Writing Instruction*) now assume at least two major perspectives on composing, an *expressive view* including the work of "authentic voice" proponents such as William Coles, Peter Elbow, Ken Macrorie, and Donald Stewart, and a *cognitive view* including the research of those who analyze composing processes such as Linda Flower, Barry Kroll, and Andrea Lunsford. More recently, a third perspective on composing has emerged, one that contends processes of writing are social in character instead of originating within individual writers. Statements on composing from the third perspective, which I call the *social view*, have come from Patricia Bizzell, Kenneth Bruffee, Marilyn Cooper, Shirley Brice Heath, James Reither, and authors of several essays collected in *Writing in Nonacademic Settings* edited by Lee Odell and Dixie Goswami.

Before I contrast the assumptions of each of these three views on composing with the goal of identifying a disciplinary basis for the study of writing, I want to raise the underlying assumption that the study and teaching of writing *should* aspire to disciplinary status. In a radical critique of education in America, Stanley Aronowitz and Henry Giroux see the development of writing programs as part of a more general trend toward an atheoretical and skills-oriented curriculum that regards teachers as civil servants who dispense prepackaged lessons. Here is Aronowitz and Giroux's assessment:

> We wish to suggest that schools, especially the colleges and universities, are now battlegrounds that may help to determine the shape of the future. The proliferation of composition programs at all levels of higher education may signal a new effort to extend the technicization process even further into the humanities. . . . The splitting of composition as a course from the study of literature, [sic] is of course a sign of its technicization and should be resisted both because it is an attack against critical thought and because it results in demoralization of teachers and their alienation from work. (52)

While I find their conclusions extreme, their critique provokes us to examine writing in relation to larger social and political issues. Unlike most other Marxist educational theorists, Aronowitz and Giroux do not present a pessimistic determinism nor do they deny human agency. They allow for the possibility that teachers and students can resist domination and think critically, thus leaving open the possibility for a historically aware theory and pedagogy of composing.

I will outline briefly the histories of each of the dominant theoretical views of composing, drawing on an earlier book by Giroux, *Theory and Resistance in Education*, for a critical review of the assumptions of each position.[1] In the concluding section of this essay, however, I reject Aronowitz and Giroux's dour assessment of the study of writing as a discipline. Each of the theoretical positions on composing has given teachers of writing a pedagogy for resisting a narrow definition of writing based largely on "correct" grammar and usage. Finally, I argue that disciplinary claims for writing must be based on a conception of process broader than any of the three views.

The Expressive View

The beginnings of composing research in the mid-1960s hardly marked a revolution against the prevailing line of research; in fact, early studies of composing issues typically were isolated pedagogical experiments similar to those described by Braddock, Lloyd-Jones, and Schoer. One of these experiments was D. Gordon Rohman and Albert Wlecke's study of the effects of "pre-writing" on writing performance, first published in 1964. Rohman and Wlecke maintained that thinking was different from writing and antecedent to writing; therefore, teachers should stimulate students' thinking by having them write journals, construct analogies, and, in the spirit of the sixties, meditate before writing essays. Young cites the Rohman and Wlecke study as one that helped to overturn the current-traditional paradigm. What Young neglects to mention is that Rohman and Wlecke revived certain Romantic notions about composing and were instigators of a "neo-Romantic" view of process. Rohman defines "good writing" as

> that discovered combination of words which allows a person the integrity to dominate his subject with a pattern both fresh and original. "Bad writing," then, is an echo of someone else's combination which we have merely taken over for the occasion of our writing. . . . "Good writing" must be the discovery by a responsible person of his uniqueness within his subject. (107–08)

This definition of "good writing" includes the essential qualities of Romantic expressivism — integrity, spontaneity, and originality — the same qualities M. H. Abram uses to define "expressive" poetry in *The Mirror and the Lamp.*

Each of these expressivist qualities has motivated a series of studies and theoretical statements on composing. We can see the influence of the first notion — integrity — in the transmission of Rohman and Wlecke's definitions of "good" and "bad" writing. In 1969 Donald Stewart argued that the unified aim for writing courses should be writing with integrity. He illustrated his argument with a student paper titled "Money Isn't as Valuable as It Seems" that contained a series of predictable generalities. Stewart criticized the student not for failing to support his generalizations but because he "doesn't believe what he is saying. Worse yet, it is possible that he doesn't even realize he doesn't believe it" (225).[2] The problem with using integrity as a measure of value is obvious in retrospect. Not only is the writer of the paper Stewart reproduces bound by his culture, as Stewart argues, but so too are Stewart's criticisms. Stewart's charges of insincerity are based on the assumption that the student is parroting the antiestablishment idealism of the late sixties. Conversely, career-oriented students of today are so unlikely to write such a paper, that if one started an essay with the same sentences as Stewart's example ("Having money is one of the least important items of life. Money only causes problems and heartaches among one's friends and self."), a teacher likely would assume that the student believed what she was saying, no matter how trite or predictable.

Because the sincerity of a text is finally impossible to assess, a second quality of Romantic expressivism — spontaneity — became important to the process movement primarily through Peter Elbow's *Writing without Teachers,* a book that was written for a broad audience, and that enjoyed great popular success. Elbow adopted Macrorie's method of free writing, but he presented the method as practical advice for writing spontaneously, not as a way of discovering "the truth." Elbow questioned Rohman and Wlecke's separation of thinking from writing, a model he maintained led to frustration. Instead, Elbow urged that we

> think of writing as an organic, developmental process in which you start writing at the very beginning — before you know your meaning at all — and encourage your words gradually to change and evolve. Only at the end will you know what you want to say or the words you want to say it with. (15)

Elbow chose the metaphor of organic growth to describe the operations of composing, the same metaphor Edward Young used to describe the vegetable concept of genius in 1759 and Coleridge borrowed from German philosophers to describe the workings of the imagination (see Abrams 198–225). Coleridge contrasted two kinds of form — one mechanical, when we impress upon any material a predetermined form, the other organic, when the material shapes itself from within. Coleridge also realized the plant metaphor implied a kind of organic determinism. (Tulip bulbs cannot grow into daffodils.) He avoided this consequence by insisting upon the free will of the artist, that the artist has foresight and the power of choice. In much the same way, Elbow qualifies his organic metaphor:

> It is true, of course, that an initial set of words does not, like a young live organism, contain within each cell a *plan* for the final mature stage and all the intervening stages that must be gone through. Perhaps, therefore, the final higher organization in words should only be called a borrowed reflection of a higher organization that is really in me or my mind. (23)

Elbow's point is one of the standards of Romantic theory: that "good" writing does not follow rules but reflects the processes of the creative imagination.

If writing is to unfold with organic spontaneity, then it ought to expose the writer's false starts and confused preliminary explorations of the topic. In other words, the writing should proceed obliquely as a "striving toward" — a mimetic of the writer's actual thought processes — and only hint at the goal of such striving. The resultant piece of writing would then seem fragmentary and unfinished, but would reveal what Coleridge calls a progressive method, a psychological rather than rhetorical organization, unifying its outwardly disparate parts. On the other hand, insofar as a piece of writing — no matter how expressive — is coherent, it must also be mimetic and rhetorical. At times Wordsworth and to a lesser extent Coleridge seem to argue that expressivism precludes all intentionality — as if such meditations as Wordsworth's "Tintern Abbey" and Coleridge's "This Lime-Tree Bower My Prison" weren't carefully *arranged* to seem spontaneous. Peter Elbow's solution to the dilemma of spontaneity comes in *Writing with Power*, where he discusses revision as the shaping of unformed material.

A third quality of Romantic expressivism — originality — could not be adapted directly to current theories of composing because the Romantic notion of originality is linked to the notion of natural genius, the difference between the poet who is born and the poet who is made. The concept of natural genius has been replaced in contemporary expressive theory with an emphasis on the innate potential of the unconscious mind. More limited statements of this position recommend teaching creative writing to stimulate originality.[3] Stronger statements come from those expressive theorists who apply the concept of "self-actualization" from psychoanalysis to writing. Rohman says teachers "must recognize and use, as the psychologists do in therapy, a person's desire to actualize himself" (108). The implication is that personal development aids writing development or that writing development can aid personal development, with the result that better psychologically integrated people become better writers. (Case histories of twentieth-century poets and novelists are seldom introduced in these discussions.) In an essay on meditation and writing James Moffett extends the self-actualization notion introduced by Rohman, saying "good therapy and composition aim at clear thinking, effective relating, and satisfying self-expression" (235).

Giroux, however, would see Moffett's essay as emblematic of what is wrong with the expressive view. Although Giroux grants that expressive theory came as a reaction against, to use his word, the "technicization" of education, he contends the result of the quest for "psychic redemption" and "personal growth" is a turning away from the relation of the individual to the social world, a world where "social practices situated in issues of class, gender, and race shape everyday experience" (219). For Giroux, the expressive view of composing ignores how writing works in the world, hides the social nature of language, and offers a false notion of a "private" self. Before I defend the expressive position against Giroux's attack, I will move on to the cognitive view where Giroux's strongest criticisms center.

The Cognitive View

In addition to promoting expressive assumptions about composing, Rohman and Wlecke helped inspire research that led to the current cognitive view. Several researchers in the late sixties were encouraged by Rohman and Wlecke's mention of *heuristics* and their finding that students who were taught "pre-writing" activities wrote better essays. More important, Rohman and Wlecke's proposal of three linear stages in the writing process stimulated research in response. In 1964 Janet Emig first argued against a linear model of composing, and she redoubled her attack in her 1969 dissertation, later published as an NCTE research monograph. Emig was among the first writing researchers to act on calls for research on cognitive processes issued at the influential 1966 Dartmouth Seminar on English. She observed that high school writers, in contrast to standard textbook advice of the time, did not use outlines to compose and that composing "does not occur as a left-to-right, solid, uninterrupted activity with an even pace" (84). Instead, Emig described composing as "recursive," an adjective from mathematics that refers to a formula generating successive terms. While the term is technically misapplied, since writing processes do not operate this simply, the extent to which it is used by other researchers attests to Emig's influence. Another measure of Emig's influence is that denunciations of Rohman and Wlecke's *Pre-Writing, Writing, Re-writing* model became a trope for introductions of later articles on composing.

In a recent consideration of Emig's monograph, Ralph Voss credits her with developing a "'science consciousness' in composition research" (279). Emig appropriated from psychology more than the case-study approach and think-aloud methodology. Her monograph is a mixture of social science and literary idioms, with one sentence talking about a "sense of closure," the next about "a moment in the process when one feels most godlike" (44). Emig's work was well received because writing researchers wanted to enter the mainstream of educational research. For example, Janice Lauer began a 1970 article directing writing researchers to psychologists' work in problem solving with the following sentence: "Freshman English will never reach the status of a respectable intellectual discipline unless both its theorizers and its practitioners break out of the ghetto" (396). Emig provided not only a new methodology but an agenda for subsequent research, raising issues such as pausing during composing, the role of rereading in revision, and the paucity of substantial revision in student writing. Her monograph led to numerous observational studies of writers' composing behavior during the next decade.[4]

The main ingredient Emig did not give researchers was a cognitive theory of composing. When writing researchers realized Chomsky's theory of transformational grammar could not explain composing abilities, they turned to two other sources of cognitive theory. The first was cognitive-developmental psychology, which James Britton and his colleagues applied to the developing sense of audience among young writers. Britton argued that children as speakers gain a sense of audience because the hearer is a reactive presence, but children as writers have more difficulty because the "other" is not present. Consequently, a child writing must imagine a generalized context for the particular text in all but the most immediate writing situations (such as an informal letter). Britton condemned most school writing assignments for failing to encourage children to imagine real writing situations (see *Development* 63–65). Other researchers probed the notion of developmental stages in writing. Barry Kroll adapted Jean Piaget's concept of *egocentrism* — the inability to take any perspective but one's own — to explain young children's lack of a sense of audience. He hypothesized, like Britton, that children's ability to *decenter* — to imagine another perspective — develops more slowly in writing than in speaking. Andrea Lunsford extended Piaget's stages of cognitive development to college basic writers, arguing that their tendency to lapse into personal narrative in writing situations that call for "abstract" discourse indicates they are arrested in an "egocentric stage."

The second source of cognitive theory came from American cognitive psychology, which has spawned several strands of research on composing. Many college writing teachers were introduced to a cognitive theory of composing through the work of Linda Flower and John R. Hayes. Flower and Hayes' main claims — that composing processes intermingle, that goals direct composing, and that experts compose differently from inexperienced writers — all have become commonplaces of the process movement. Less well understood by writing teachers, however, are the assumptions underlying Flower and Hayes' model, assumptions derived from a cognitive research tradition. Flower and Hayes acknowledge their debt to this tradition, especially to Allen Newell and Herbert A. Simon's *Human Problem Solving,* a classic work that helped define the aims and agenda for a cognitive science research program. Newell and Simon theorize that the key to understanding how people solve problems is in their "programmability"; in other words, how people use "a very simple information processing system" to account for their "problem solving in such tasks as chess, logic, and cryptarithmetic" (870). The idea that thinking and language can be represented by computers underlies much research in cognitive science in several camps, including artificial intelligence, computational linguistics, and cognitive psychology. Newell and Simon's historical overview of this movement credits Norbert Wiener's theory of *cybernetics* as the beginnings of contemporary cognitive science.[5] The basic principle of cybernetics is the *feedback loop,* in which the regulating mechanism receives information from the thing regulated and makes adjustments.

George A. Miller was among the first to introduce cybernetic theory as an alternative to the stimulus-response reflex arc as the basis of mental activity. In *Plans and the Structure of Behavior,* Miller, Eugene Galanter, and Karl Pribram describe human behavior as guided by plans that are constantly being evaluated as they are being carried out in a feedback loop. They theorize that the brain — like a computer — is divided into a *memory* and a *processing unit.* What Miller, Galanter, and Pribram do not attempt to theorize is where plans come from. To fill in this gap, Newell and Simon add to the feedback loop an entity they call the *task environment,* defined in terms of a goal coupled with a specific environment. Newell and Simon claim the resulting loop explains how people think.

If we look at the graphic representation of the Flower and Hayes model in the 1980 and 1981 versions, we can see how closely the overall design follows in the cognitive science tradition. The box labeled *Writing Processes* is analogous to the central processing unit of a computer. In the 1980 version, diagrams representing the subprocesses of composing (*planning, translating,* and *reviewing*) are presented as computer flowcharts. Like Newell and Simon's model of information processing, Flower and Hayes' model makes strong theoretical claims in assuming relatively simple cognitive operations produce enormously complex actions, and like Emig's monograph, the Flower and Hayes model helped promote a "science consciousness" among writing teachers. Even though cognitive researchers have warned that "novice writers cannot be turned into experts simply by tutoring them in the knowledge expert writers have" (Scardamalia 174), many writing teachers believed cognitive research could provide a "deep struc- ture" theory of *the* composing process, which could in turn specify how writing should be taught. Furthermore, the Flower and Hayes model had other attractions. The placement of *translating* after *planning* was compat- ible with the sequence of invention, arrangement, and style in classical rhetoric. It also suited a popular conception that language comes after ideas are formed, a conception found in everyday metaphors that express ideas as objects placed in containers (e.g., "It's difficult to put my ideas into words").[6]

Giroux's response to the cognitive view of composing can be readily inferred. To begin, Giroux would be highly critical of any attempt to dis- cover universal laws underlying writing. Writing for Giroux, like other acts of literacy, is not universal but social in nature and cannot be removed from culture. He would fault the cognitive view for collapsing cultural issues under the label "audience," which, defined unproblematically, is reduced to the status of a variable in an equation. He further would accuse the cognitive view of neglecting the content of writing and downplaying conflicts inherent in acts of writing. As a consequence, pedagogies assum- ing a cognitive view tend to overlook differences in language use among students of different social classes, genders, and ethnic backgrounds.

At this point I'll let Giroux's bricks fly against my windows and use an article on revision I wrote with Steve Witte as a case in point. In this study Witte and I attempt to classify revision changes according to the extent they affect the content of the text. We apply a scheme for describing the structure of a text developed by the Dutch text linguist, Teun van Dijk. What seems obviously wrong with this article in hindsight is the degree to which we assign meaning to the text. Now even van Dijk admits there are as many macrostructures for a text as there are readers. Although our conclusions criticize the artificiality of the experiment and recognize that "revision cannot be separated from other aspects of composing," the intent of the study still suffers from what Giroux sees as a fundamental flaw of cognitivist research — the isolation of part from whole.

The Social View

The third perspective on composing I identified at the beginning of this essay — the social view — is less codified and less constituted at present than the expressive and cognitive views because it arises from several disciplinary traditions. Because of this diversity a comprehensive social view cannot be extrapolated from a collection of positions in the same way I have described the expressive and cognitive views of composing. State- ments that propose a social view of writing range from those urging more attention to the immediate circumstances of how a text is composed to those denying the existence of an individual author. My effort to outline a social view will be on the basis of one central assumption: human language (including writing) can be understood only from the perspective of a society rather than a single individual. Thus taking a social view requires a great deal more than simply paying more attention to the context surrounding a discourse. It rejects the assumption that writing is the act of a private consciousness and that everything else — readers, subjects, and texts — is "out there" in the world. The focus of a social view of writing, therefore, is not on how the social situation influences the individual, but on how the individual is a constituent of a culture.

I will attempt to identify four lines of research that take a social view of writing, although I recognize that these positions overlap and that each draws on earlier work (e.g., Kenneth Burke). These four lines of research can be characterized by the traditions from which they emerge: poststructuralist theories of language, the sociology of science, ethnography, and Marxism.

In the last few years, writing researchers influenced by poststructuralist theories of language have brought notions of discourse communities to discussions of composing. Patricia Bizzell and David Bartholomae, for example, have found such ideas advantageous in examining the writing of college students. Those who believe that meaning resides in the text accuse any other position of solipsism and relativism, but concepts of discourse communities provide an alternative position, offering solutions to difficult problems in interpretative theory. Reading is neither an experience of extracting a fixed meaning from a text nor is it a matter of making words mean anything you want them to in *Alice in Wonderland* fashion. Ambiguity in texts is not the problem for humans that it is for computers — not so much because we are better at extracting meaning but because language is social practice; because, to paraphrase Bakhtin, words carry with them the places where they have been.

This view of language raises serious problems for cognitive-based research programs investigating adults' composing processes. For instance, Bizzell criticizes the separation of "Planning" and "Translating" in the Flower and Hayes model. Even though Flower and Hayes allow for language to generate language through rereading, Bizzell claims the separation of words from ideas distorts the nature of composing. Bizzell cites Vygotsky, whom many cognitive researchers lump together with Piaget, but whose understanding of language is very different from Piaget's. Vygotsky studied language development as a historical and cultural process, in which a child acquires not only the words of language but the intentions carried by those words and the situations implied by them.

From a social perspective, a major shortcoming in studies that contrast expert and novice writers lies not so much in the artificiality of the experimental situation, but in the assumption that expertise can be defined outside of a specific community of writers. Since individual expertise varies across communities, there can be no one definition of an expert writer. David Bartholomae explores the implications for the teaching of college writing. He argues that writing in college is difficult for inexperienced writers not because they are forced to make the transition from "writer-based" to "reader-based" prose but because they lack the privileged language of the academic community. Bartholomae's point is similar to Bizzell's: when students write in an academic discipline, they write in reference to texts that define the scholarly activities of interpreting and reporting in that discipline. Bartholomae alludes to Barthes' observation that a text on a particular topic always has "off-stage voices" for what has previously been written about that topic. Thus a social view of writing moves beyond the expressivist contention that the individual discovers the self through language and beyond the cognitivist position that an individual constructs reality through language. In a social view, any effort to write about the self or reality always comes in relation to previous texts.

A substantial body of research examining the social processes of writing in an academic discourse community now exists in the sociology of science. Most of this research has been done in Britain, but Americans Charles Bazerman and Greg Myers have made important contributions. . . . Research in scientific writing displays many of the theoretical and methodological differences mentioned at the beginning of this section, but this literature taken as a whole challenges the assumption that scientific texts contain autonomous presentations of facts; instead, the texts are "active social tools in the complex interactions of a research community" (Bazerman 3). In the more extreme version of this argument, which follows from Rorty and other pragmatists, science itself becomes a collection of literary forms. Writing about the basis of economics, Donald McCloskey calls statistics "figures of speech in numerical dress" (98). He goes on to say that "the scientific paper is, after all, a literary genre, with an actual author, an implied author, an implied reader, a history, and a form" (105). In contrast, current British research understands a dialectical relationship between external reality and the conventions of a community. A good introduction to this field is Nigel Gilbert and Michael Mulkay's 1984 book, *Opening Pandora's Box.*[7]

A third line of research taking a social view of composing develops from the tradition of ethnography. Ethnographic methodology in the 1970s and 1980s has been used to examine the immediate communities in which writers learn to write — the family and the classroom. These researchers have observed that for many children, the ways literacy is used at home and in the world around them matches poorly with the literacy expectations of the school.[8] The most important of these studies to date is Shirley Brice Heath's analysis of working-class and middle-class families in the Carolina Piedmont. Heath found that how children learn to use literacy originates from how families and communities are structured. Another line of research using ethnographic methodology investigates writing in the workplace, interpreting acts of writing and reading within the culture of the workplace (see Odell and Goswami for examples).

Finally, I include Marxist studies of literacy as a fourth social position on composing. The essential tenet of a Marxist position would be that any act of writing or of teaching writing must be understood within a structure of power related to modes of production. A Marxist critique of the other social positions would accuse each of failing to deal with key concepts such as class, power, and ideology.[9] Giroux finds discourse communities are often more concerned with ways of excluding new members than with ways of admitting them. He attacks non-Marxist ethnographies for sacrificing "theoretical depth for methodological refinement" (98). Indeed, much Marxist scholarship consists of faulting other theorists for their lack of political sophistication.

Toward a Synthesis

At the beginning of this essay I quoted Aronowitz and Giroux's conclusion that the spread of writing programs and, by implication, the process movement itself are part of a general movement toward "atheoretical" and "skills-oriented" education in America. Now I would like to evaluate that claim. If process theory and pedagogy have up to now been unproblematically accepted, I see a danger that it could be unproblematically rejected. Process theory and pedagogy have given student writing a value and authority absent in current-traditional approaches. Each view of process has provided teachers with ways of resisting static methods of teaching writing — methods based on notions of abstract form and adherence to the "rules" of Standard English. Expressive theorists validate personal experience in school systems that often deny it. Cognitive theorists see language as a way of negotiating the world, which is the basis of James Berlin's dialogic redefinition of epistemic rhetoric (*Rhetoric and Reality*). And social theorists such as Heath have found that children who are labeled remedial in traditional classrooms can learn literacy skills by studying the occurrences of writing in the familiar world around them (see *Ways with Words*, chapter 9).

But equally instructive is the conclusion of Heath's book, where she describes how the curriculum she helped create was quickly swept away. It illustrates how social and historical forces shape the teaching of writing — relationships that, with few exceptions, are only now beginning to be critically investigated. If the process movement is to continue to influence the teaching of writing and to supply alternatives to current-traditional pedagogy, it must take a broader conception of writing, one that understands writing processes are historically dynamic — not psychic states, cognitive routines, or neutral social relationships. This historical awareness would allow us to reinterpret and integrate each of the theoretical perspectives I have outlined.

The expressive view presents one of two opposing influences in discourse — the unique character of particular acts of writing versus the conventions of language, genre, and social occasion that make that act understandable to others. The expressive view, therefore, leads us to one of the key paradoxes of literacy. When literacy began to be widespread in Northern Europe and its colonies during the eighteenth and nineteenth centuries, it reduced differences between language groups in those countries and brought an emphasis on standard usage. But at the same time linguistic differences were being reduced, individuals became capable of changing the social order by writing for a literate populace (witness the many revolutionary tracts published during the nineteenth century). Furthermore, modern notions of the individual came into being through the widespread publication of the many literary figures and philosophers associated with the Romantic movement and the later development of psychology as a discipline in the nineteenth century. Current technologies for electronic communications bring the potential for gaining access to large bodies of information from the home, yet at the same time these technologies bring increased potential for control through surveillance of communication and restriction of access. People, however, find ways to adapt technologies for their own interests. In organizations where computer technologies have become commonplace, people have taken advantage of opportunities for horizontal communication on topics of their choice through computer "bulletin boards," which function like radio call-in programs. For example, on ARPANET, the Department of Defense's computer network linking research facilities, military contractors, and universities, popular bulletin boards include ones for science fiction, movie reviews, and even a lively debate on arms control. How the possibilities for individual expression will be affected by major technological changes in progress should become one of the most important areas of research for those who study writing.

In a similar way, historical awareness would enhance a cognitive view of composing by demonstrating the historical origins of an individual writer's goals. The cognitive view has brought attention to how writers compose in the workplace. Many writing tasks on the job can be characterized as rhetorical "problems," but the problems themselves are not ones the writers devise. Writing processes take place as part of a structure of power. For instance, Lee Iacocca's autobiography reveals how writing conveys power in large organizations. Iacocca says he communicated good news in writing, but bad news orally. Surely Iacocca's goals and processes in writing are inseparable from what he does and where he works, which in turn must be considered in relation to other large corporations, and which finally should be considered within a history of capitalism.

Some social approaches to the study of discourse entail historical awareness, but a social view is not necessarily historical. The insight that the learning of literacy is a social activity within a specific community will not necessarily lead us to a desirable end. Raymond Williams observes that the term *community* has been used to refer to existing social relationships or possible alternative social relationships, but that it is always used positively, that there is no opposing term. Yet we know from the sad experiences of the twentieth century that consensus often brings oppression. How written texts become instruments of power in a community is evident in the history of colonial empires, where written documents served to implement colonial power. Some of the earliest recorded uses of writing in Mesopotamia and ancient Egypt were for collecting taxes and issuing laws in conquered territories. Written documents made possible the incident George Orwell describes in "The Hanging" — an essay frequently anthologized but rarely analyzed in writing classes for its political significance. Furthermore, in the effort to identify conventions that define communities of writers, commentators on writing processes from a social viewpoint have neglected the issue of what *cannot* be discussed in a particular community, exclusions Foucault has shown to be the exercise of power.

These questions are not mere matters of ivory-tower debate. The preoccupation with an underlying theory of the writing process has led us to neglect finding answers to the most obvious questions in college writing instruction today: why college writing courses are prevalent in the United States and rare in the rest of the world; why the emphasis on teaching writing occurring in the aftermath of the "literacy crisis" of the seventies has not abated; why the majority of college writing courses are taught by graduate students and other persons in nontenurable positions. Answers to such questions will come only when we look beyond who is writing to whom to the texts and social systems that stand in relation to that act of writing. If the teaching of writing is to reach disciplinary status, it will be achieved through recognition that writing processes are, as Stanley Fish says of linguistic knowledge, "contextual rather than abstract, local rather than general, dynamic rather than invariant" (438).

Notes

[1] Giroux directly criticizes "romantic" and "cognitive developmental" traditions of teaching literacy in *Theory and Resistance in Education*. Bruce Herzberg has extended Giroux's critique to particular composition theorists.

[2] Even more strident attacks on clichés and conventional writing assignments came from Ken Macrorie, who damned "themes" as papers "not meant to be read but corrected" (686), and from William Coles, who accused textbook authors of promoting "themewriting" by presenting writing "as a trick that can be played, a device that can be put into operation . . . just as one can be taught or learn to run an adding machine, or pour concrete" (134–42).

[3] For example, Art Young advocates having students write poems, plays, and stories in writing-across-the-curriculum classes. During the 1920s and 1930s, there were numerous appeals to incorporate creative writing into the English curriculum; see, for example, Lou LaBrant.

[4] For a bibliographic review of cognitive studies of composing, see Faigley, Cherry, Jolliffe, and Skinner, chapters 1–5.

[5] Wiener used the term *cybernetics* — derived from the Greek word for the pilot of a ship — as a metaphor for the functioning mind. He claimed as a precedent James Watt's use of the word *governor* to describe the mechanical regulator of a steam engine. Wiener's metaphor explained the mind as a control mechanism such as an automatic pilot of an airplane. For a historical overview of cybernetics and the beginnings of cognitive science, see Bell.

[6] Reddy discusses some of the consequences of the "conduit" metaphor for our understanding of language.

[7] Gilbert and Mulkay provide a bibliography of social studies of scientific discourse on 194–95.

[8] Heath includes an annotated bibliography of school and community ethnographies in the endnotes of *Ways with Words*.

[9] Richard Ohmann's *English in America* remains the seminal Marxist analysis of American writing instruction.

Works Cited

Abrams, M. H. *The Mirror and the Lamp.* New York: Oxford UP, 1953.

Aronowitz, Stanley, and Henry A. Giroux. *Education under Siege.* South Hadley, MA: Bergin, 1985.

Bartholomae, David. "Inventing the University." *When a Writer Can't Write.* Ed. Mike Rose. New York: Guilford, 1985. 134–65.

Bazerman, Charles. "Physicists Reading Physics: Schema-Laden Purposes and Purpose-Laden Schema." *Written Communication* 2 (1985): 3–23.

Bell, Daniel. *The Social Sciences since the Second World War.* New Brunswick, NJ: Transaction, 1982.

Berlin, James. *Rhetoric and Reality: Writing in American Colleges, 1900–1985.* Carbondale: Southern Illinois UP, 1984.

———. *Writing Instruction in Nineteenth-Century American Colleges.* Carbondale: Southern Illinois UP, 1984.

Bizzell, Patricia. "Cognition, Convention, and Certainty: What We Need to Know about Writing." *PRE/TEXT* 3 (1982): 213–43.

Braddock, Richard, Richard Lloyd-Jones, and Lowell Schoer. *Research in Written Composition.* Urbana: NCTE, 1963.

Britton, James, Tony Burgess, Nancy Martin, Alex McLeod, and Harold Rosen. *The Development of Writing Abilities (11–18).* London: Macmillan, 1975.

Bruffee, Kenneth A. "Collaborative Learning and the 'Conversion of Mankind.'" *College English* 46 (1984): 635–52.

Coleridge, Samuel Taylor. "On Method." *The Portable Coleridge.* Ed. I. A. Richards. New York: Viking, 1950. 339–86.

Coles, William, Jr. "Freshman Composition: The Circle of Unbelief." *College English* 31 (1969): 134–42.

Cooper, Marilyn M. "The Ecology of Writing." *College English* 48 (1986): 364–75.

Elbow, Peter. *Writing without Teachers.* New York: Oxford UP, 1973.

———. *Writing with Power.* New York: Oxford UP, 1981.

Emig, Janet. *The Composing Processes of Twelfth Graders,* NCTE Research Report No. 13. Urbana: NCTE, 1971.

———. "The Uses of the Unconscious in Composing." *College Composition and Communication* 16 (1964): 6–11.

Faigley, Lester, Roger D. Cherry, David A. Jolliffe, and Anna M. Skinner. *Assessing Writers' Knowledge and Processes of Composing.* Norwood, NJ: Ablex, 1985.

Faigley, Lester, and Stephen P. Witte. "Analyzing Revision." *College Composition and Communication* 32 (1981): 400–14.

Fish, Stanley. "Consequences." *Critical Inquiry* 11 (1985): 433–58.

Flower, Linda, and John R. Hayes. "A Cognitive Process Theory of Writing." *College Composition and Communication* 31 (1980): 365–87.

Foucault, Michel. *Power/Knowledge: Selected Interviews and Other Writings, 1972–1977.* Ed. Colin Gordon. New York: Pantheon, 1980.

Gilbert, G. Nigel, and Michael Mulkay. *Opening Pandora's Box: A Sociological Analysis of Scientists' Discourse.* Cambridge: Cambridge UP, 1984.

Giroux, Henry A. *Theory and Resistance in Education.* South Hadley, MA: Bergin, 1983.

Hairston, Maxine. "The Winds of Change: Thomas Kuhn and the Revolution in the Teaching of Writing." *College Composition and Communication* 33 (1982): 76–88.

Hayes, John R., and Linda Flower. "Identifying the Organization of Writing Processes." *Cognitive Processes in Writing: An Interdisciplinary Approach.* Ed. Lee Gregg and Erwin Steinberg. Hillsdale, NJ: Erlbaum, 1980. 3–30.

Heath, Shirley Brice. *Ways with Words.* New York: Cambridge UP, 1983.

Herzberg, Bruce. "The Politics of Discourse Communities." Paper presented at the Conference on College Composition and Communication, New Orleans, March 1986.

Iacocca, Lee. *Iacocca: An Autobiography,* New York: Bantam, 1984.

Kroll, Barry M. "Cognitive Egocentrism and the Problem of Audience Awareness in Written Discourse." *Research in the Teaching of English* 12 (1978): 269–81.

LaBrant, Lou. "The Psychological Basis for Creative Writing." *English Journal* 25 (1936): 292–301.

Lauer, Janice. "Heuristics and Composition." *College Composition and Communication* 21 (1970): 396–404.

Lunsford, Andrea. "The Content of Basic Writers' Essays." *College Composition and Communication* 31 (1980): 278–90.

Macrorie, Ken. "To Be Read." *English Journal* 57 (1968): 686–92.

McCloskey, Donald N. "The Literary Character of Economics." *Daedalus* 113.3 (1984): 97–119.

Miller, George A., Eugene Galanter, and Karl Pribram. *Plans and the Structure of Behavior.* New York: Holt, 1962.

Moffett, James. "Writing, Inner Speech, and Meditation." *College English* 44 (1982): 231–44.

Myers, Greg. "Texts as Knowledge Claims: The Social Construction of Two Biologists' Articles." *Social Studies of Science* 15 (1985): 593–630.

———. "Writing Research and the Sociology of Scientific Knowledge: A Review of Three New Books." *College English* 48 (1986): 595–610.

Newell, Alan, and Herbert A. Simon. *Human Problem Solving.* Englewood Cliffs, NJ: Prentice, 1972.

Odell, Lee, and Dixie Goswami, eds. *Writing in Nonacademic Settings.* New York: Guilford, 1985.

Ohmann, Richard. *English in America: A Radical View of the Profession.* New York: Oxford UP, 1976.

Reddy, Michael J. "The Conduit Metaphor." *Metaphor and Thought.* Ed. Andrew Ortony. Cambridge: Cambridge UP, 1979. 284–324.

Reither, James A. "Writing and Knowing: Toward Redefining the Writing Process." *College English* 47 (1985): 620–28.

Rohman, D. Gordon, "Pre-Writing: The Stage of Discovery in the Writing Process." *College Composition and Communication* 16 (1965): 106–12.

Rohman, D. Gordon, and Alfred O. Wlecke. "Pre-Writing: The Construction and Application of Models for Concept Formation in Writing." U.S. Department of Health, Education, and Welfare Cooperative Research Project No. 2174. East Lansing: Michigan State U, 1964.

Scardamalia, Marlene, Carl Bereiter, and Hillel Goelman. "The Role of Production Factors in Writing Ability." *What Writers Know: The Language, Process, and Structure of Written Discourse.* Ed. Martin Nystrand. New York: Academic, 1982. 173–210.

Stewart, Donald. "Prose with Integrity: A Primary Objective." *College Composition and Communication* 20 (1969): 223–27.

Voss, Ralph. "Janet Emig's *The Composing Processes of Twelfth Graders:* A Reassessment." *College Composition and Communication* 34 (1983): 278–83.

Williams, Raymond. *Keywords: A Vocabulary of Culture and Society.* New York: Oxford UP, 1976.

Young, Art. "Considering Values: The Poetic Function of Language." *Language Connections.* Ed. Toby Fulwiler and Art Young. Urbana: NCTE, 1982. 77–97.

Young, Richard. "Paradigms and Problems: Needed Research in Rhetorical Invention." *Research on Composing: Points of Departure.* Ed. Charles R. Cooper and Lee Odell. Urbana: NCTE, 1978. 29–47.

Acknowledgment: Joseph Alkana, Andrew Cooper, Beth Daniell, Kristine Hansen, Greg Myers, Carolyn Miller, and Walter Reed made helpful comments on earlier drafts of this essay.

PREWRITING TECHNIQUES

Erika Lindemann

[From *A Rhetoric for Writing Teachers* by Erika Lindemann. 3rd ed. New York: Oxford UP, 1995. 105–25.]

A professor of English and current director of the writing program at the University of North Carolina at Chapel Hill, Erika Lindemann also teaches writing courses and courses for writing teachers. Her book *A Rhetoric for Writing Teachers,* now in its third edition, has become a standard text in composition studies. Lindemann has published numerous articles and chapters, and with Gary Tate she coedited *An Introduction to Composition Studies* (1991). Among her numerous professional awards, Lindemann has been recognized by CCCC for her service as the first editor of the Longman and CCCC Bibliographies of Composition and Rhetoric.

Recognizing that "prewriting" activities "help students assess the dimensions of a rhetorical problem and plan its solution," Lindemann suggests that teachers "involve students in several prewriting activities, not just one, for each assignment." Lindemann thinks of prewriting and of invention strategies as "keys of different shapes and sizes that grant access to experience, memory, and intuition." In this chapter from *A Rhetoric for Writing Teachers,* Lindemann presents numerous prewriting activities, including "perception exercises," "brainstorming and clustering," "freewriting," using journals, heuristics, and models. Lindemann helps teachers understand the larger complex rhetorical contexts in which these kinds of activities will be most effective.

This is the first requirement for good writing: truth; not the truth . . . but some kind of truth — a connection between the things written about, the words used in the writing, and the author's real experience in the world he knows well — whether in fact or dream or imagination.

– Ken Macrorie

The prewriting techniques discussed in this chapter help students assess the dimensions of a rhetorical problem and plan its solution. They trigger perceptual and conceptual processes, permitting writers to recall experiences, break through stereotyped thinking, examine relationships between ideas, assess the expectations of their audience, find an implicit order in their subject matter, and discover how they feel about the work.[1] Some prewriting activities enable writers to probe the subject from several perspectives; others help writers assess their relationship to an audience.

Some use pictures, talk, or pantomine to generate ideas, while others ask students to write lists, notes, and scratch outlines.

As a rule, the more time students spend on a variety of prewriting activities, the more successful the paper will be. In working out the possibilities an assignment suggests, students discover what they honestly want to say and address some of the decisions they must make if the paper is to express a message effectively. Writing the first draft becomes easier because some writing — notes, list, freewriting — has already taken place. Drafting also becomes more productive because students are less preoccupied with formulating ideas from scratch and freer to discover new messages as the words appear on the page.

In many composition textbooks, the only prewriting technique discussed is the formal outline. Although writers rarely construct elaborate outlines, informal outlines serve a useful purpose. Outlining can help students shape raw material generated by other prewriting activities. Outlining also can serve revision because when students outline a draft they may discover digressions, inconsistencies, or other organizational problems to work on. Nevertheless, outlining represents only one of many prewriting activities.

Because prewriting is a means to an end, I don't grade the notes, lists, and miscellaneous scratch work my students turn in with their final drafts. I look through the material, however, to discover which students need help generating more support for their topics or making prewriting work more efficiently for them. I also involve students in several prewriting activities, not just one, for each assignment. Sequencing several kinds of prewriting activities encourages students to explore their subjects thoroughly, planning their response to an assignment gradually, moving tentatively but then more confidently toward a first draft. Eventually, students modify and combine in whatever ways work best for them the techniques discussed in this chapter. All of them offer writers places to begin, keys of different shapes and sizes that grant access to experience, memory, and intuition.

Perception Exercises

Thinking games, "conceptual blockbusting," and sense-scrambling activities encourage students to think about how they think. By analyzing the steps they go through to "have ideas" or solve problems, they discover barriers that block perceptions.[2] Much of the material in Chapter 6, including the five-of-hearts exercise, can prompt a discussion of these perceptual, cultural, emotional, and intellectual barriers. To demonstrate these principles, you might ask students to pair up and by turns lead each other blindfolded on a tour of the building or some other familiar place. Deprived of their visual orientations, they can appreciate perceptions gained through other senses: smell, touch, hearing. Students also might discuss pictures, a busy city street for example, and then draw the scene from various perspectives. What would a bird's-eye view of the picture look like? How would you draw it if you were standing at the right-hand side of the picture looking left? After students have compared their drawings and discussed the differences in perspective, the class can move on to other prewriting activities directly relevant to a particular assignment.

For many students, arts and media that don't involve writing offer a comfortable place to begin probing a subject. Pantomime and role-playing encourage students to act out a subject before translating it into written form. Especially when an issue admits several points of view or when an audience may hold diverse opinions about a subject, role-playing clarifies the options students must consider. Assignments involving argumentation can begin with impromptu debates, which might then be worked into brief written dialogues and from there into more formal kinds of discourse. Similarly, students can translate reading assignments, pictures, or music from one medium to another, then to a third and finally to a written form. The assumption behind these activities is that similar principles govern communication in various media. When students practice the "language" of pictorial art, of gesture, and of music, they also learn principles that reinforce their use of the spoken and written word. Furthermore, in responding to cartoons, music, and pantomime, students become more sensitive observers of their world.

Not every piece of writing, of course, finds a convenient beginning in art, music, or drama, but all writing can begin with speech, a comfortable means of expression for most people. As Robert Zoellner and others have suggested, talking out a rhetorical problem helps students define and solve it: "Since students have a greater fluency in speaking than in writing because they practice it more, speaking can be used as a stage prior to writing and can provide the basis for moving through increasingly adequate written versions of a unit of discourse."[3] All students, especially those whose fear of failure makes writing anything, even scratch notes, difficult, need opportunities to explain their plans to themselves or discuss them with other students, a sympathetic teacher, or even a tape recorder. Every assignment should provide several opportunities for students to discuss their work-in-progress with one another.

Brainstorming and Clustering

Brainstorming is an unstructured probing of a topic. Like free association, brainstorming allows writers to venture whatever comes to mind about a subject, no matter how obvious or strange the ideas might be. When the entire class brainstorms a topic, the teacher generally writes on the board whatever words and phrases students call out. When students brainstorm topics on their own, they list whatever details occur to them. As a rule, general or superficial observations head the list, but as students begin to examine the subject more closely, useful and interesting details begin to appear. To be useful, of course, the list must contain abundant raw material.

Sometimes, however, brainstorming yields only rambling, unfocused, or repetitive generalizations. If the teacher has presented the technique as an end in itself, students may conclude, "Okay, she wants a list of 100 details, so I'll give her a list of 100 details." The purpose of brainstorming is neither list making nor reaching a precise number of details. As Donald Murray advises in *A Writer Teaches Writing,* "The teacher must, in such lists as this, begin to encourage honesty, to have the student look into himself and into his subject with candor and vigor. The list also gives the teacher a chance to defeat the cliché and the vague generalization by saying to the student, 'What does that mean? Can you be more specific?' The teacher should praise a student when he gets a good concrete detail which has the ring of reality" (1st ed., p. 78). At least initially, students need guidance in generating *useful* details and enough of them to permit discarding those that seem irrelevant. Students also need reminding that list making serves a larger purpose, to explore the subject thoroughly and discover what makes it interesting or important.

Teachers can go over these lists with individual students in brief conferences during class. An especially rich list can be the subject of whole-class discussion, followed by groups of students reviewing their own lists with one another. What details seem most forceful? In what ways could details be grouped? What patterns have emerged in the list? What dimensions of the subject seemed to attract the writer's interest? What details must be left out at this point if the first draft is to hang together? A discussion along these lines helps students discover organizational possibilities in the raw material and suggests options for developing the paper.

Following such a discussion, students might begin clustering their material, grouping and regrouping items into a diagram such as the one in Figure 7.1. Called "mapping," "clustering," or "webbing," the process of creating such drawings helps writers explore the organizational possibilities in their material. Unlike formal outlines, with their restrictive system of Roman and Arabic numerals and their need for parallelism, cluster diagrams represent provisional representations of the relationships among topics, subtopics, and supporting evidence. If one area of the diagram looks skimpy, additional brainstorming will provide more material (or the writer may abandon it altogether). Heavy branches may need subdividing.

The clusters in Figure 7.1 grew out of a brainstorming session on the topic "campus problems." As it happened, the class creating the diagram eventually abandoned "campus problems" as the topic because the material in some of the subtopics — "alcoholism," "racism," and "apathy" — seemed more interesting. As with most cluster diagrams, any branch could be developed into a new, more detailed diagram. The purpose of clustering is to help a writer discover order in a subject and to transform lists of details into meaningful groupings, some of which eventually may find a place in a first draft.

Freewriting

Freewriting, a technique advocated by Peter Elbow and Ken Macrorie, offers students a risk-free way of getting words onto a page without having to worry about their correctness. Elbow explains the technique this way:

> The idea is simply to write for ten minutes (later on, perhaps fifteen or twenty). Don't stop for anything. Go quickly without rushing. Never stop to look back, to cross something out, to wonder how to spell something, to wonder what word or thought to use, or to think about what you are doing. If you can't think of a word or a spelling, just use a squiggle or else write, "I can't think of it." Just put down something. The easiest thing is just to put down whatever is in your mind. If you get stuck it's fine to write "I can't think of what to say, I can't think what to say" as many times as you want: or repeat the last word you wrote over and over again: or anything else. The only requirement is that you *never* stop. (*Writing without Teachers*, p. 3)

Elbow recommends that students freewrite at least three times a week. Freewritings, he insists, should *never* be graded. Their primary purpose is to get something on paper, and "it's an unnecessary burden to try to think of words and also worry at the same time whether they're the right words" (p. 5). Macrorie advocates freewriting because it produces honest writing, writing that is free from phoniness or pretension. The writer must write fast enough to use "his own natural language without thinking of his expression" (*Telling Writing*, p. 9).

Some teachers do not constrain freewriting in any way; others offer a phrase or the beginning of a sentence to help students get started. Teachers also can sequence freewriting exercises in several ways to move students closer to more formal drafts. For example, after students have completed a freewriting, they may read it aloud or silently to find words, phrases, a sentence or two that seem especially appealing. These words then offer a place to begin a second freewriting. The second freewriting may suggest ideas for a third and so on.

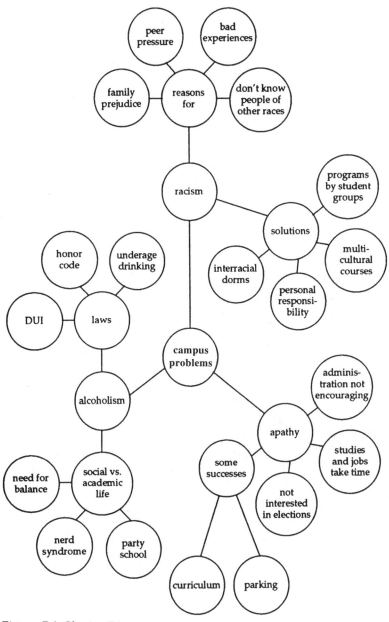

Figure 7.1 Cluster Diagram

Murray sequences freewritings by incorporating student response at each stage.[4] First, students write freely for five minutes or so. Then, working in pairs, they discuss the freewriting by answering a question about it: "What appeared on the page that you didn't expect?" After a few minutes of discussion, students complete a second freewriting and stop to discuss it: "What idea do you want to develop in the next freewriting?" The procedure is repeated six or seven times, a new question guiding the students' discussion after each period of writing. The questions help students focus on what has appeared, on where the composing process is taking them. Teachers and students may substitute their own questions to guide the discussion, focusing on the writing but at the same time leaving students free to let their own language take charge of the page: What is the writing telling you? How do you (the writer) feel about what is appearing on the page? What do you (the reader) need to know that I haven't told you yet?

Freewriting encourages students to overcome their fear of the blank page and their stifling preoccupation with correctness. The technique encourages play with language and uses language as an aid to thinking. A freewriting represents a writer talking out an idea; it is not a polished communication intended for an outside audience. Needless to say, if teachers grade freewritings, they are no longer "free." Threatened by grades, students will shift their attention from generating and developing ideas to editing a finished product.

Journals

Journals, commonplace books, or writer's notebooks have been indispensable tools for many writers, the famous and not so famous. Some journals, like diaries, record experiences and observations meant only to be read by their authors. Other journals, Virginia Woolf's *Writer's Diary* and Ralph Waldo Emerson's *Journals* for example, contain such significant information about an author's life and work that they reach a large public audience. Many professional writers use journals to sketch out, organize, draft, and revise their work before they submit it for publication.

The journal has several uses in a writing class. Many teachers set aside the first few minutes of every class period for journal writing. While the teacher checks the roll, returns papers, or reviews the lesson plan, students use the time to write whatever they want in their journals. The procedure settles the class down to work and gives students daily writing practice. To avoid treating the journal as inconsequential busywork, students should have opportunities to develop the material recorded in their journals into more formal assignments. Journals also can become workbooks for the course. In them, students may practice freewriting, respond to reading assignments, jot down leading ideas in preparation for class discussion, work out plans for papers, complete sentence-combining exercises, work on revisions, experiment with stylistic effects, keep track of spelling demons, and note which writing problems they have conquered and which still need work.

Unaccustomed to writing without some teacher-made assignment in front of them, students may protest that they can't think of anything to write in their journals, or they may devote several entries to deliberately "detached" topics: "I got up at eight, skipped breakfast, and went to class. Nothing much happened today." When this happens, teachers can discuss the difference between simply recording experiences and the more productive activity of reacting to or reflecting on events. They might also suggest that students capture a feeling in words or speculate about some imaginary, "what if" situation. If these open-ended, deliberately vague suggestions don't work, the following list might help, at least until students become comfortable pursuing their own interests.[5]

1. Speculate. Why do you spend so much time in a certain place? Why do you read a certain book or see a particular movie more than once?
2. Sketch in words a person who doesn't know you're watching: a woman studying her reflection in a store window, a spectator at a sports event, a student studying desperately.

3. Record some observations about a current song, book, movie, television program.
4. React to something you've read recently. Was it well written? Why or why not? What strategies did the writer use to get you to like or dislike the piece?
5. Try to capture an incident of night fear — when a bush became a bear, for example — so that a reader might feel the same way you did.
6. Explain an important lesson you learned as a child.
7. If peace were a way of life and not merely a sentiment, what would you have to give up?
8. Describe your idea of paradise or hell.
9. Write a nasty letter complaining about some product that didn't work or some service that was performed poorly.
10. Pretend you're the consumer relations official for the company in number 9. Write a calm, convincing response to your complaint.
11. If you were an administrator in this school, what's the first change you'd make? Why?
12. Tell what season of the year brings the things you like best.
13. You have been given the power to make one person, and only one, disappear. Whom would you eliminate and why?

Most teachers read their students' journals periodically, every few weeks or so. Eventually, they may assign the entire journal a percentage of the final grade; students receive credit simply for writing regularly. Other teachers base the grade for the journal on the quantity of writing it contains, thirty entries receiving an A, twenty to twenty-nine entries earning a B, and so on. Grading individual entries in journals is counterproductive because it discourages provisional thinking and regular practice with writing. Journals offer students a place to write without fear of making mistakes or facing criticism for what they have to say. Comments on journal entries should be positive, encouraging further writing or deeper exploration of an idea: "I felt that way too when my best friend misunderstood what I said." "It must have taken courage to tell your parents this; why not write an entry as if you were telling the story from their point of view?" Students should feel free to write "Do not read" across the top of an entry they don't want anyone else to see or to fold the page over and staple it. A teacher unable to resist temptation should ask students to remove personal entries before the journals are turned in.

When I read a set of journals, occasionally I'll come across an entry full of obscenities. They're meant to shock me. Generally, I ignore them the first time around; if they appear again, I usually discuss the journal with the student. In a fit of frustration, I once asked a student to write another entry defining some of the four-letter words he'd used. He never did. Much more common are the touchingly painful accounts of personal traumas students sometimes share with their English teachers. If I ignore the entry because it makes me uncomfortable, the student will conclude that I can't handle honest, sensitive topics and prefer to read only about "safe," academic subjects. If I write some gratuitous comment in the margin, I belittle the experience. When I discover students working out difficult experiences by writing them down in a journal, I generally encourage them to tackle the problem in several entries. They may have detected an irony in the experience, a weakness or strength in themselves, or a serious flaw in their idealistic notions about people. They need to examine further what they have found, first to understand it for themselves and perhaps later to share it with a larger audience. Precisely because such entries contain honest statements about important problems, they deserve to be treated seriously.

Heuristics

Heuristics derive ultimately from the *topoi* of classical rhetoric. In Book Two of the *Rhetoric,* Aristotle discusses twenty-eight "universal topics for enthymemes on all matters," among them, arguing from opposites, dividing the subject, exploring various senses of an ambiguous term, examining cause and effect. Although the classical *topoi* represent lines of reasoning speakers might pursue to invent arguments, heuristics prompt thinking by means of questions. The questions are ordered so that writers can explore the subject systematically and efficiently, but they also are open-ended to stimulate intuition and memory as well as reason. Most students are already familiar with the heuristic procedure journalists use: Who? What? When? Where? How? These questions help reporters compose effective lead paragraphs in news stories. Conditioned by years of testing, students often think that heuristic questions must have right and wrong answers; they don't. They increase the possibilities for probing a topic thoroughly, and they usually generate provisional answers. Ideally, those tentative answers should lead students to formulate further questions.

In *Writing* (3d ed., pp. 328–29), Elizabeth Cowan Neeld presents a heuristic derived from the categories "definition," "comparison," "relationship," "testimony," and "circumstance." The author encourages students to take the questions one at a time, thoughtfully, replacing the blank with a subject they want to explore and writing brief notes to answer the questions. If students get stuck on a question, they should move on. When they have finished the entire list, they should reread their notes, starring the material that looks promising.

Definition

1. How does the dictionary define _____ ?
2. What earlier words did _____ come from?
3. What do *I* mean by _____ ?
4. What group of things does _____ seem to belong to? How is _____ different from other things in this group?
5. What parts can _____ be divided into?
6. Did _____ mean something in the past that it doesn't mean now? If so, what? What does this former meaning tell us about how the idea grew and developed?
7. Does _____ mean something now that it didn't years ago? If so, what?
8. What other words mean approximately the same as _____ ?
9. What are some concrete examples of _____ ?
10. When is the meaning of _____ misunderstood?

Comparison

1. What is _____ similar to? In what ways?
2. What is _____ different from? In what ways?
3. _____ is superior to what? In what ways?
4. _____ is inferior to what? In what ways?
5. _____ is most unlike what? (What is it opposite to?) In what ways?
6. _____ is most like what? In what ways?

Relationship

1. What causes _____ ?
2. What is the purpose of _____ ?
3. What does _____ happen?
4. What comes before _____ ?
5. What comes after _____ ?

ᴄircumstance

1. Is _____ possible or impossible?
2. What qualities, conditions, or circumstances make _____ possible or impossible?
3. Supposing that _____ is possible, is it also desirable? Why?
4. When did _____ happen previously?
5. Who has done or experienced _____ ?
6. Who can do _____ ?
7. If _____ starts, what makes it end?
8. What would it take for _____ to happen now?
9. What would prevent _____ from happening?

Testimony

1. What have I heard people say about _____ ?
2. Do I know any facts or statistics about _____ ? If so, what?
3. Have I talked with anyone about _____ ?
4. Do I know any famous or well-known saying (e.g., "A bird in the hand is worth two in the bush") about _____ ?
5. Can I quote any proverbs or any poems about _____ ?
6. Are there any laws about _____ ?
7. Do I remember any songs about _____ ? Do I remember anything I've read about _____ in books or magazines? Anything I've seen in a movie or on television?
8. Do I want to do any research on _____ ?

The dramatistic pentad is a heuristic derived from Kenneth Burke's rhetoric of human motives discussed in Chapter 4:

What was done? (act)

Where or when was it done? (scene)

Who did it? (agent)

How was it done? (agency)

Why was it done? (purpose)

Although Burke originally posed these questions to explore the complicated motives of human actions, most composition teachers use the heuristic with a simpler aim in mind: to help students generate descriptive or narrative material. As a prewriting technique, the pentad works well for investigating literary topics, historical or current events, and biographical subjects. The pentad gains additional heuristic power when any two of the five terms are regarded together, as "ratios." Consider, for example, how the act : scene ratio informs the plot of any murder mystery. Or how the act : purpose ratio characterizes what some people call *euthanasia* and others, *murder.*

Another series of questions, adapted from Richard Larson's problem-solving model, suggests ways to engage issues-oriented subjects, the sort teachers often assign for persuasive papers. Students also may find the heuristic useful in sorting through other problems: personal difficulties, writing problems, or the problem posed by a writing assignment.

What is the problem?

Why is the problem indeed a problem?

What goals must be served by whatever action or solution that is taken?

Which goals have the highest priority?

What procedures might attain the stated goals?

What can I predict about the consequences of each possible action?

How do the actions compare with each other as potential solutions to the problem?

Which course of action is best?

In answering these questions, students define the problem, analyze it, formulate several potential solutions, and select the best solution. "In every problem," writes Edward P. J. Corbett, "there are some things that you know or can easily find out, but there is something too that you don't know. It is the *unknown* that creates the problem. When confronted with a problem, you have to take note of all the things you do know. Then, by a series of inferences from the known, you try to form a hypothesis to determine whether your theory leads you to discover the unknown that is causing the problem" (*The Little Rhetoric and Handbook*, p. 44). Teachers too can employ the heuristic to define, analyze, and solve teaching problems or conduct research.

Because most writing teachers also teach literature courses, a heuristic for analyzing, interpreting, and evaluating literature can pose useful questions to guide students' reading or help them explore literary topics. Corbett devised the series of questions shown in Figure 7.2a–c, which have been adapted from *The Little Rhetoric and Handbook* (pp. 186–221).

Obviously, students don't need to answer all of Corbett's questions every time they read a literary work. Routinely dragging the class through each question would be boring busywork. The questions have value insofar as they guide reading, suggest new ideas to explore, or encourage a closer examination of the text. The questions can be broken apart, altered, or culled selectively. At some point, students need to frame their own questions to explain their response to the work.

Because most textbooks devote little attention to audience, students may need help defining for whom they are writing and why. A heuristic for assessing the audience provides such help. Audience analysis not only generates content, depending on what a reader already knows about a subject, but it also encourages writers to think early on about their tone and point of view. The following questions, adapted from Karl R. Wallace's "*Topoi* and the Problem of Invention," ask writers to identify several characteristics of an audience:

How old is the audience?

What is the economic or social condition of the audience?

What is the educational status of the audience?

What general philosophies of government or politics does the audience hold?

What values and beliefs would be common to an audience of this age?

What economic or social values is the audience likely to hold?

What value does the audience place on education, religion, work?

Which of these values — economic, social, political, educational — is most important to the audience? Least important?

In general, how does the audience feel about its heritage or events that happened in the past? That are going on in the present? What hopes for the future does the audience hold?

In general, does the audience expect certain patterns of thought in what it reads? Should I include a lot of data to convince the audience of my point? What authorities would be most convincing? Does the audience need to see the causes and effects of my proposals? Would stories and analogies confuse my readers or encourage them to understand what I

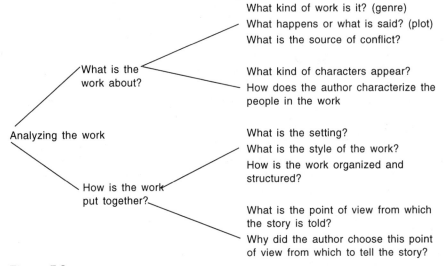

What kind of work is it? (genre)
What happens or what is said? (plot)
What is the source of conflict?

What kind of characters appear?
How does the author characterize the people in the work

What is the setting?
What is the style of the work?
How is the work organized and structured?

What is the point of view from which the story is told?
Why did the author choose this point of view from which to tell the story?

What is the work about?

Analyzing the work

How is the work put together?

Figure 7.2a

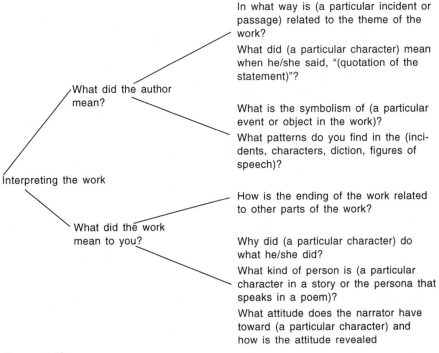

What is the theme of the work?
In what way is (a particular incident or passage) related to the theme of the work?
What did (a particular character) mean when he/she said, "(quotation of the statement)"?

What is the symbolism of (a particular event or object in the work)?
What patterns do you find in the (incidents, characters, diction, figures of speech)?

How is the ending of the work related to other parts of the work?

Why did (a particular character) do what he/she did?
What kind of person is (a particular character in a story or the persona that speaks in a poem)?
What attitude does the narrator have toward (a particular character) and how is the attitude revealed

What did the author mean?

Interpreting the work

What did the work mean to you?

Figure 7.2b

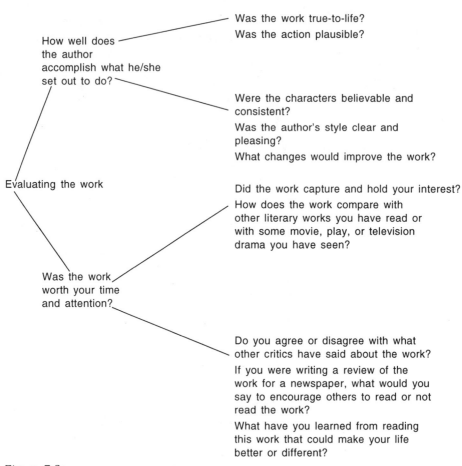

Was the work true-to-life?
Was the action plausible?

How well does
the author
accomplish what he/she
set out to do?

Were the characters believable and
consistent?
Was the author's style clear and
pleasing?
What changes would improve the work?

Evaluating the work

Did the work capture and hold your interest?
How does the work compare with
other literary works you have read or
with some movie, play, or television
drama you have seen?

Was the work
worth your time
and attention?

Do you agree or disagree with what
other critics have said about the work?
If you were writing a review of the
work for a newspaper, what would you
say to encourage others to read or not
read the work?
What have you learned from reading
this work that could make your life
better or different?

Figure 7.2c

want to say? What terms will I need to define, and what terms can I
assume are already understood?

What sorts of issues most frequently make the audience angry or defensive?

What things can I say without antagonizing my audience?

What options do I have for presenting unpopular opinions to my audience?

What is the most convincing appeal I could make? Should I try to convince by being reasonable and logical? Should I appeal to the emotions?
Or should I demonstrate that I am an honest, trustworthy, sympathetic
expert whom the audience can trust?

Have I stereotyped my audience, overlooking individuals who may hold
views that are different from those the rest of my audience believes in?

Am I just saying what my audience wants to hear or am I also saying
what I honestly believe to be true?

After students have grown comfortable with relatively simple prewriting
techniques — brainstorming, clustering, freewriting, answering questions —
they may want to use more elaborate heuristics to probe the subject even
further.[6]

The following heuristic is adapted from Richard Young, Alton Becker, and Kenneth Pike's *Rhetoric: Discovery and Change* (1970) and permits us to examine a subject systematically from several perspectives. Although we customarily consider a subject from only one point of view, tagmemic invention forces us to shift mental gears to see it differently. According to Young, Becker, and Pike, anything — an object, event, concept — can be viewed from three perspectives. We usually regard an oak tree, to use their example, as an isolated, static entity, as a "thing" or particle. But we also could view the oak as a process (wave), as a participant in the natural growth cycle that begins with an acron and ends when the tree rots or is cut into lumber. Or we may regard the tree as a system (field) of roots, trunk, branches, and leaves. These three perspectives — particle, wave, field — permit us to consider the same subject from three angles: as a static entity, as a dynamic process, and as a system.

Furthermore, in order to "know" this oak tree, we must be able to figure out three aspects of its existence (regardless of which perspective we assume):

1. *How is it unique?* As an entity, process, or system, how does it differ from everything else? Young, Becker, and Pike label this aspect "contrast."
2. *How much can it change and still be itself?* How much "variation" is possible in the oak (viewed as entity, process, or system) before it becomes something other than an oak?
3. *How does it fit into larger systems of which it is a part?* What is its "distribution"? In other words, the oak tree not only *is* a system, but it also belongs to other systems. It is affected by a system of seasonal changes; it participates in the ecosystem of the surrounding countryside; it plays a role in an economic system to which lumber production, tourism, and national parks belong.

The six concepts — particle, wave, field, contrast, variation, and distribution — can be arranged to produce a nine-cell chart, often referred to as a *tagmemic grid* or *matrix* (see *Rhetoric: Discovery and Change,* p. 127).

Although the nine-cell matrix can generate enormous amounts of material about a subject, most students need considerable practice using the technique before they find it helpful and comfortable. For this reason, you may prefer to introduce students to a simplified version of the matrix such as the one W. Ross Winterowd includes in *The Contemporary Writer* (p. 94):

The Los Angeles freeway system, for instance, can be viewed

1. *As an Isolated, Static Entity.* We ask, What features characterize it? We can draw a map of it; we can measure its total length; we can count the number of overpasses and underpasses. We can describe it in great detail. In fact, such a description could well demand a number of thick volumes. But the point is that we can view anything as an isolated, static entity and begin to find those features that characterize it.
2. *As One Among Many of a Class.* We ask, How does it differ from others in its class? From this point of view, we would compare the Los Angeles freeway system with others like it. I, for instance, immediately think of the difference between the L. A. freeway system and the turnpikes of the East and Midwest, as well as the German Autobahnen.
3. *As Part of a Larger System.* We ask, How does it fit into larger systems, of which it is a part? The L. A. freeway system would be

worthless if it did not integrate with national, state, and county highway systems; therefore, its place in these larger systems is crucial.

4. *As a Process, Rather Than as a Static Entity.* We ask, How is it changing? In regard to the L. A. freeway system, this question brings up the whole problem of planning for the future, which implies the problem of history, or how the system got to be the way it currently is.

5. *As a System, Rather Than as an Entity.* We ask, What are the parts, and how do they work together? Now we are focusing on the L. A. Freeways as a transportation system, each part of which must integrate and function with the whole.

Models

Discussing models for student writers to emulate is a technique as old as rhetoric itself. For centuries, teachers of rhetoric and composition have asked students to imitate noteworthy essays, aphorisms, fables, speeches, and excerpts from works by great writers. Advocates of the practice believe that it exposes students to important cultural values and helps them develop their sense of style. To imitate an excellent writer, students have to read carefully, analyze the text closely, and then use similar constructions in creating their own texts. Although close imitation is no longer a staple of contemporary writing classes, most writing teachers still present models that illustrate approaches students may take in responding to assignments.

The most common model in today's writing course is the expository essay, perhaps because it is the most frequent form of discourse students write. Despite a long tradition of using essays to teach writing, we ought to question their purpose. What kinds of models are appropriate? In what ways are they helpful? When should they be introduced? How should they be discussed?

First, the models don't always have to be essays. Letters, advertisements, reports, memoranda, newspapers, policy statements, even junk mail, can illustrate rhetorical strategies. Students themselves can bring these materials to class, providing their own examples of the kinds of writing they are practicing.

Second, the models discussed in class don't have to be written by professionals. Good student writing should serve as a model most of the time because it best exemplifies those rhetorical strategies we expect to find in students' papers. Good student writing teaches writers of similar age and experience how to plan their work, how to anticipate problems of organization and language, and how to frame their notions of audience, purpose, subject, and persona. Furthermore, student models have an important advantage over professional models: the author is sitting in the class, a live, present author who can help us sort out intended meanings or points of confusion. Student writing also represents a more realistic, attainable model than the writing of professionals. Students know that they aren't the kind of writer Montaigne or Martin Luther King, Jr., were. Nor do we want them to be. Instead, we want them to use their own voices to express their own messages, to discover their own purposes for writing. From time to time, we may even want to discuss examples of atrocious professional prose to reinforce the notion that students sometimes write better than professionals.

Third, in discussing any model, the focus should be primarily on *how* the writer solves problems. Of course, we also have some responsibility for helping students understand *what* the writer says, for teaching students to read critically and carefully. But we should avoid approaching models, especially those written by professionals, as literary works subject to intense critical analysis. In a writing course, unlike a literature course, models serve not so much as literary artifacts to interpret, but as examples of the rhetorical problems, decisions, and choices student writers confront.

Fourth, most writing teachers introduce models prematurely. The best time to discuss a model is *after* students have already completed some prewriting and perhaps an early draft. That is when they are most likely to appreciate the rhetorical problem an assignment poses and to benefit from discovering how another writer addresses similar difficulties. Students cannot value the strategies a model illustrates if their own writing projects are not yet very far along. After students understand by experience the demands an assignment makes of them, examining a model can be instructive. Then they can know firsthand what options the writer had in presenting a subject, what choices he or she made and perhaps rejected, and how the strategies evident in the model apply to the student's work-in-progress.

The value of a model is what it can teach us about our own writing projects. Consequently, we don't need to belabor their discussion. One or two models for each assignment should be plenty. Most of the time, devoting fifteen to twenty minutes of a class period for their discussion should be adequate if we ask the right questions.

What are the right questions?   Robert Bain's "Framework for Judging" is a good place to begin.[7]

Framework for Judging

1. A writer promises to do something. What does this writer promise to do? Does the writer keep that promise? If not, where and why does she or he fail to do so?
2. What seems to be the writer's attitude toward the reader? Does the writer treat the audience playfully, seriously, with sarcasm? What does the writer's attitude toward the audience say about him/her and his/her subject?
3. Is the writer's attitude toward the subject convincing? Is the writer simply filling space or writing about feelings and ideas that matter? How can we tell?
4. Is there a perceivable order to the presentation? Can we follow and describe that order? If not, where does the writer lose us and why?
5. Has the writer omitted any important details or arguments that would help us understand the piece? Has the writer included details or arguments not connected with the ideas and feelings being discussed?
6. Does each paragraph signal clearly to the reader the direction in which the writer's ideas and feelings are moving? Does each paragraph develop and complete the idea it introduces? If we lose our way in a paragraph, where and why do we get lost?
7. Are the rhythms and patterns of sentences appropriate to the writer's subject and voice? If the sentences seem to be "Dick-and-Jane sentences," how could the writer combine them to break up this pattern? If the sentences are so long that we get lost in them, where could the writer break sentences into shorter units? Does the writer use passive voice excessively? If so, is that usage justified?

8. Is the language of the piece appropriate to the writer's voice and subject? If the writer uses big words, is she or he showing off or trying to help us understand better? Is the language fairly free of clichés, jargon, and worn-out words and phrases? If the writer bends or breaks rules of language, making up new words or running them together, what are some reasons for doing so?

9. Has the writer observed the conventions of grammar, punctuation, spelling, and capitalization? If not, is there a good reason for not doing so?

This sequence of questions places larger rhetorical concerns first, asking students to consider subject, audience, purpose, paragraphs, and sentences before attending to matters of punctuation and usage. Bain's questions also serve several functions. Because the framework helps writers discover what they propose to do and how they intend to go about it, the questions provide an excellent heuristic for planning responses to writing assignments. They also can organize discussions of student writing or some other model. Applied to student or professional models, the framework focuses discussion on *how* the model works, on ways to solve problems in writing. The questions serve revision too. Students can work through them, on their own or in a draft workshop with other students, as they review their drafts. Not all of the questions need answering all of the time. A fifteen-minute class discussion of a student's paper, for example, might cover only the first four sets of questions; a draft workshop early in the term, only the questions in the fourth set.

Eventually, writers must stop generating answers to questions and begin organizing their raw material. They must evaluate what prewriting has yielded, identify hierarchies and classes, assign importance to some ideas and abandon others, and tentatively arrange whatever materials belong in a draft. It's difficult to say when generating material stops and shaping it begins because prewriting, writing, and rewriting don't follow a strict linear sequence. Sometimes prewriting activities generate material that reveals its own implicit organization. Sometimes writers don't discover the best way to organize their material until they've completed two or three drafts. Furthermore, as writers draft and rewrite their work, they often discover "holes" in the discourse. They stop drafting and return to prewriting, generating additional material to fill the gaps.

Most students begin drafting too soon, before they have sufficiently probed the subject, developed their own point of view, and made a commitment to the message. Their papers remain general because they haven't found enough interesting possibilities to pursue in their raw material or have failed to develop meaningful plans and goals to guide subsequent work. To address these problems, we must teach prewriting. We must give students a repertoire of planning strategies that, used in various combinations, will yield abundant raw material. Students need specific instruction in how to use a particular prewriting technique and enough practice with it to gain a sense of its potential. We can give them this practice if we structure writing assignments to move from brainstorming and freewriting to research and note-taking to responding to a heuristic, from role-playing to talking out ideas with classmates to writing them down. We also can collect scratch work and jotted notes from time to time, not merely to ensure that students give adequate time to prewriting, but also to guide them in developing more efficient, effective plans. Students should view these prewriting activities, not as isolated events, but as parts of a process that always looks ahead to drafting and revising. They are ways to let a piece of writing grow, ways to let us find a topic but also to let the topic find us.

Notes

[1] An indispensable bibliographical essay that surveys methods of invention as well as the history of the art is Richard Young, "Recent Developments in Rhetorical Invention," in *Teaching Composition: Twelve Bibliographical Essays,* ed. Gary Tate (Fort Worth: Texas Christian University Press, 1987), pp. 1–38. As Young points out, the term *prewriting* technically denotes the techniques of invention developed by D. Gordon Rohman and Albert O. Wlecke — journals, meditation, and analogy — that emphasize creative thinking and the "self-actualization" of the writer [cf. D. Gordon Rohman and Albert O. Wlecke, *Pre-Writing: The Construction and Application of Models for Concept Formation in Writing* (USOE Cooperative Research Project No. 2174; East Lansing: Michigan State University, 1964)]. However, I use *prewriting* throughout this book as a synonym for "invention," primarily because current usage among writing teachers assigns the term broader meaning than Rohman and Wlecke intended.

[2] James L. Adams, *Conceptual Blockbusting: A Pleasurable Guide to Better Problem Solving* (San Francisco: W. H. Freeman, 1974), is a useful discussion of how to cultivate thinking and problem-solving abilities. The book analyzes barriers to thinking and suggests strategies for breaking through them.

[3] Young, p. 37; cf. Robert Zoellner, "A Behavioral Approach to Writing," *College English* 30 (January 1969), 267–320.

[4] Donald Murray, workshop presentation, South Carolina English Teachers Conference, University of South Carolina, October 21, 1978. See also "The Listening Eye: Reflections on the Writing Conference," *College English* 41 (September 1979), 13–18. "Looping" and "cubing," which also depend on completing series of freewritings, are described in Elizabeth Cowan Neeld, *Writing,* 3d ed. (Glenview, IL: Scott, Foresman, 1990), pp. 20–21, and 315–16, respectively.

[5] Adapted from a list developed by Connie Pritchard, University of South Carolina, Fall 1977. See also Macrorie, *Telling Writing,* pp. 140–51.

[6] See, for example, Richard L. Larson, "Discovery through Questioning: A Plan for Teaching Rhetorical Invention," *College English* 30 (November 1968), 126–34; and Tommy J. Boley, "A Heuristic for Persuasion," *College Composition and Communication* 30 (May 1979), 187–91.

[7] The framework is adapted from Robert A. Bain, "Reading Student Papers," *College Composition and Communication* 25 (October 1974), 307–9.

Works Cited

Burke, Kenneth. *A Rhetoric of Motives.* Berkeley: University of California Press, 1969.

Corbett, Edward P. J. *The Little Rhetoric and Handbook.* 2d ed. Glenview, IL: Scott, Foresman, 1982.

Elbow, Peter. *Writing without Teachers.* New York: Oxford University Press, 1973.

Macrorie, Ken. *Telling Writing.* 4th ed. Upper Montclair, NJ: Boynton/Cook, 1985.

Murray, Donald M. *A Writer Teaches Writing.* 2d ed. Boston: Houghton Mifflin, 1985.

Neeld, Elizabeth Cowan. *Writing.* 3d ed. Glenview, IL: Scott, Foresman/Little, Brown, 1990.

Wallace, Karl R. "*Topoi* and the Problem of Invention." *The Quarterly Journal of Speech* 58 (December 1972): 387–95.

Winterowd, W. Ross. *The Contemporary Writer: A Practical Rhetoric.* 2d ed. New York: Harcourt Brace Jovanovich, 1981.

Young, Richard E., Alton L. Becker, and Kenneth L. Pike. *Rhetoric: Discovery and Change.* New York: Harcourt, Brace and World, 1970.

RIGID RULES, INFLEXIBLE PLANS, AND THE STIFLING OF LANGUAGE: A COGNITIVIST ANALYSIS OF WRITER'S BLOCK

Mike Rose

[*College Composition and Communication* 31 (1980): 389–401.]

Mike Rose is a professor in the Graduate School of Education and Information Studies at UCLA. He has produced important work in remedial reading and writing, writing across the curriculum, the cognition of composing, and the politics of literacy. In addition to many articles and essays, Rose has coedited *Perspectives on Literacy* (1988) and, with Mal Kiniry, *Critical Strategies for Academic Thinking and Writing* (2nd edition, 1993). He has written *Writer's Block: The Cognitive Dimension* (1984), *Lives on the Boundary: The Struggles and Achievements of America's Underprepared* (1989), and most recently *Possible Lives: The Promise of Public Education in America* (1996). In 1991 and 1992, articles that he coauthored won the prestigious Richard Braddock Award. His *Lives on the Boundary* has received the David H. Russell Award for Distinguished Research from the National Council of Teachers of English, the Outstanding Book Award from the Conference on College Composition and Communication, and the Mina P. Shaughnessy Prize from the Modern Language Association. Rose is also the recipient of a Guggenheim Fellowship and the Commonwealth Club of California Award for Literary Excellence.

In this article investigating causes of writer's block, Rose reports on his study of ten undergraduates, five with writer's block and five without. Rose discovered that rigid rules and inflexible plans were a significant cause of writer's block. He argues that stymied writers do not necessarily need more rules and plans, as much previous research has suggested. Rose contends instead that writers may well need different, more flexible plans and rules. He closes the article with several suggestions for helping students who suffer from writer's block.

Ruth will labor over the first paragraph of an essay for hours. She'll write a sentence, then erase it. Try another, then scratch part of it out. Finally, as the evening winds on toward ten o'clock and Ruth, anxious about tomorrow's deadline, begins to wind into herself, she'll compose that first paragraph only to sit back and level her favorite exasperated interdiction at herself and her page: "No. You can't say that. You'll bore them to death."

Ruth is one of ten UCLA undergraduates with whom I discussed writer's block, that frustrating, self-defeating inability to generate the next line, the right phrase, the sentence that will release the flow of words once again. These ten people represented a fair cross-section of the UCLA student community; lower-middle-class to upper-middle-class backgrounds and high schools, third-world and Caucasian origins, biology to fine arts majors, C+ to A– grade point averages, enthusiastic to blasé attitudes toward school. They were set off from the community by the twin facts that all ten could write competently, and all were currently enrolled in at least one course that required a significant amount of writing. They were set off among themselves by the fact that five of them wrote with relative to enviable ease while the other five experienced moderate to nearly immobilizing writer's block. This blocking usually resulted in rushed, often late papers and resultant grades that did not truly reflect these students' writing ability. And then, of course, there were other less measurable but probably more serious results: a growing distrust of their abilities and an aversion toward the composing process itself.

What separated the five students who blocked from those who didn't? It wasn't skill; that was held fairly constant. The answer could have rested in the emotional realm — anxiety, fear of evaluation, insecurity, etc. Or perhaps blocking in some way resulted from variation in cognitive style. Perhaps, too, blocking originated in and typified a melding of emotion and cognition not unlike the relationship posited by Shapiro between neurotic feeling and neurotic thinking.[1] Each of these was possible. Extended clinical interviews and testing could have teased out the answer. But there was one answer that surfaced readily in brief explorations of these students' writing processes. It was not profoundly emotional, nor was it embedded in that still unclear construct of cognitive style. It was constant, surprising, almost amusing if its results weren't so troublesome, and, in the final analysis, obvious: the five students who experienced blocking were all operating either with writing rules or with planning strategies that impeded rather than enhanced the composing process. The five students who were not hampered by writer's block also utilized rules, but they were less rigid ones, and thus more appropriate to a complex process like writing. Also, the plans these non-blockers brought to the writing process were more functional, more flexible, more open to information from the outside.

These observations are the result of one to three interviews with each student. I used recent notes, drafts, and finished compositions to direct and hone my questions. This procedure is admittedly non-experimental, certainly more clinical than scientific; still, it did lead to several inferences that lay the foundation for future, more rigorous investigation: (a) composing is a highly complex problem-solving process[2] and (b) certain disruptions of that process can be explained with cognitive psychology's problem-solving framework. Such investigation might include a study using "stimulated recall" techniques to validate or disconfirm these hunches. In such a study, blockers and non-blockers would write essays. Their activity would be videotaped and, immediately after writing, they would be shown their respective tapes and questioned about the rules, plans, and beliefs operating in their writing behavior. This procedure would bring us close to the composing process (the writers' recall is stimulated by their viewing the tape), yet would not interfere with actual composing.

In the next section I will introduce several key concepts in the problem-solving literature. In section three I will let the students speak for themselves. Fourth, I will offer a cognitivist analysis of blockers' and non-blockers' grace or torpor. I will close with a brief note on treatment.

Selected Concepts in Problem Solving: Rules and Plans

As diverse as theories of problem solving are, they share certain basic assumptions and characteristics. Each posits an *introductory period* during which a problem is presented, and all theorists, from Behaviorist to Gestalt to Information Processing, admit that certain aspects, stimuli, or "functions" of the problem must become or be made salient and attended to in certain ways if successful problem-solving processes are to be engaged. Theorists also believe that some conflict, some stress, some gap in information in these perceived "aspects" seems to trigger problem-solving behavior. Next comes a *processing period,* and for all the variance of opinion about this critical stage, theorists recognize the necessity of its existence — recognize that man, at the least, somehow "weighs" possible solutions as they are stumbled upon and, at the most, goes through an elaborate and sophisticated information-processing routine to achieve problem solution. Furthermore, theorists believe — to varying degrees — that past learning and the particular "set," direction, or orientation that the problem solver takes in dealing with past experience and present stimuli have critical bearing on the efficacy of solution. Finally, all theorists admit to a *solution period,* an end-state of the process where "stress" and "search" terminate, an answer is attained, and a sense of completion or "closure" is experienced.

These are the gross similarities, and the framework they offer will be useful in understanding the problem-solving behavior of the students discussed in this paper. But since this paper is primarily concerned with the second stage of problem-solving operations, it would be most useful to focus this introduction on two critical constructs in the processing period: rules and plans.

Rules

Robert M. Gagné defines "rule" as "an inferred capability that enables the individual to respond to a class of stimulus situations with a class of performances."[3] Rules can be learned directly[4] or by inference through experience.[5] But, in either case, most problem-solving theorists would affirm Gagné's dictum that "rules are probably the major organizing factor, and quite possibly the primary one, in intellectual functioning."[6] As Gagné implies, we wouldn't be able to function without rules; they guide response to the myriad stimuli that confront us daily, and might even be the central element in complex problem-solving behavior.

Dunker, Polya, and Miller, Galanter, and Pribram offer a very useful distinction between two general kinds of rules: algorithms and heuristics.[7] Algorithms are precise rules that will always result in a specific answer if applied to an appropriate problem. Most mathematical rules, for example, are algorithms. Functions are constant (e.g., pi), procedures are routine (squaring the radius), and outcomes are completely predictable. However, few day-to-day situations are mathematically circumscribed enough to warrant the application of algorithms. Most often we function with the aid of fairly general heuristics or "rules of thumb," guidelines that allow varying degrees of flexibility when approaching problems. Rather than operating with algorithmic precision and certainty, we search, critically, through alternatives, using our heuristic as a divining rod — "if a math problem stumps you, try working backwards to solution"; "if the car won't start, check x, y, or z," and so forth. Heuristics won't allow the precision or the certitude afforded by algorithmic operations; heuristics can even be so "loose" as to be vague. But in a world where tasks and problems are rarely mathematically precise, heuristic rules become the most appropriate, the most functional rules available to us: "a heuristic does not guarantee the optimal solution or, indeed, any solution at all; rather, heuristics offer solutions that are good enough most of the time."[8]

Plans

People don't proceed through problem situations, in or out of a laboratory, without some set of internalized instructions to the self, some program, some course of action that, even roughly, takes goals and possible paths to that goal into consideration. Miller, Galanter, and Pribram have referred to this course of action as a plan: "A plan is any hierarchical process in the organism that can control the order in which a sequence of operations is to be performed" (p. 16). They name the fundamental plan in human problem-solving behavior the TOTE, with the initial T representing a *test* that matches a possible solution against the perceived end-goal of problem completion. O represents the clearance to *operate* if the comparison between solution and goal indicates that the solution is a sensible one. The second T represents a further, post-operation, *test* or comparison of solution with goal, and if the two mesh and problem solution is at hand the person *exits* (E) from problem-solving behavior. If the second test presents further discordance between solution and goal, a further solution is attempted in TOTE-fashion. Such plans can be both long-term and global and, as problem solving is underway, short-term and immediate.[9] Though the mechanicality of this information-processing model renders it simplistic and, possibly, unreal, the central notion of a plan and an operating procedure is an important one in problem-solving theory; it at least attempts to metaphorically explain what earlier cognitive psychologists could not —the mental procedures (see pp. 390–91) underlying problem-solving behavior.

Before concluding this section, a distinction between heuristic rules and plans should be attempted; it is a distinction often blurred in the literature, blurred because, after all, we are very much in the area of gestating theory and preliminary models. Heuristic rules seem to function with the flexibility of plans. Is, for example, "If the car won't start, try x, y, or z" a heuristic or a plan? It could be either, though two qualifications will mark it as heuristic rather than plan. (A) Plans subsume and sequence heuristic and algorithmic rules. Rules are usually "smaller," more discrete cognitive capabilities; plans can become quite large and complex, composed of a series of ordered algorithms, heuristics, and further planning "sub-routines." (B) Plans, as was mentioned earlier, include criteria to determine successful goal-attainment and, as well, include "feedback" processes — ways to incorporate and use information gained from "tests" of potential solutions against desired goals.

One other distinction should be made: that is, between "set" and plan. Set, also called "determining tendency" or "readiness,"[10] refers to the fact that people often approach problems with habitual ways of reacting, a predisposition, a tendency to perceive or function in one way rather than another. Set, which can be established through instructions or, consciously or unconsciously, through experience, can assist performance if it is appropriate to a specific problem,[11] but much of the literature on set has shown its rigidifying, dysfunctional effects.[12] Set differs from plan in that set represents a limiting and narrowing of response alternatives with no inherent process to shift alternatives. It is a kind of cognitive habit that can limit perception, not a course of action with multiple paths that directs and sequences response possibilities.

The constructs of rules and plans advance the understanding of problem solving beyond that possible with earlier, less developed formulations. Still, critical problems remain. Though mathematical and computer models move one toward more complex (and thus more real) problems than the earlier research, they are still too neat, too rigidly sequenced to approximate the stunning complexity of day-to-day (not to mention highly creative) problem-solving behavior. Also, information-processing models of problem-solving are built on logic theorems, chess strategies, and simple planning tasks. Even Gagné seems to feel more comfortable with illustrations from mathematics and science rather than with social science and humanities problems. So although these complex models and constructs tell us a good deal about problem-solving behavior, they are still laboratory simulations, still invoked from the outside rather than self-generated, and still founded on the mathematico-logical.

Two Carnegie-Mellon researchers, however, have recently extended the above into a truly real, amorphous, unmathematical problem-solving process — writing. Relying on protocol analysis (thinking aloud while solving problems), Linda Flower and John Hayes have attempted to tease out the role of heuristic rules and plans in writing behavior.[13] Their research pushes problem-solving investigations to the real and complex and pushes, from the other end, the often mysterious process of writing toward the explainable. The latter is important, for at least since Plotinus many have viewed the composing process as unexplainable, inspired, infused with the transcendent. But Flower and Hayes are beginning, anyway, to show how writing generates from a problem-solving process with rich heuristic rules and plans of its own. They show, as well, how many writing problems arise from a paucity of heuristics and suggest an intervention that provides such rules.

This paper, too, treats writing as a problem-solving process, focusing, however, on what happens when the process dead-ends in writer's block. It will further suggest that, as opposed to Flower and Hayes' students who need more rules and plans, blockers may well be stymied by possessing rigid or inappropriate rules, or inflexible or confused plans. Ironically enough, these are occasionally instilled by the composition teacher or gleaned from the writing textbook.

"Always Grab Your Audience" — The Blockers

In high school, *Ruth* was told and told again that a good essay always grabs a reader's attention immediately. Until you can make your essay do that, her teachers and textbooks putatively declaimed, there is no need to go on. For Ruth, this means that beginning bland and seeing what emerges as one generates prose is unacceptable. The beginning is everything. And what exactly is the audience seeking that reads this beginning? The rule, or Ruth's use of it, doesn't provide for such investigation. She has an edict with no determiners. Ruth operates with another rule that restricts her productions as well: if sentences aren't grammatically "correct," they aren't useful. This keeps Ruth from toying with ideas on paper, from the kind of linguistic play that often frees up the flow of prose. These two rules converge in a way that pretty effectively restricts Ruth's composing process.

The first two papers I received from *Laurel* were weeks overdue. Sections of them were well written; there were even moments of stylistic flair. But the papers were late and, overall, the prose seemed rushed. Furthermore, one paper included a paragraph on an issue that was never mentioned in the topic paragraph. This was the kind of mistake that someone with Laurel's apparent ability doesn't make. I asked her about this irrelevant passage. She knew very well that it didn't fit, but believed she had to include it to round out the paper. "You must always make three or more points in an essay. If the essay has less, then it's not strong." Laurel had been taught this rule in high school and in her first college English class; no wonder, then, that she accepted its validity.

As opposed to Laurel, *Martha* possesses a whole arsenal of plans and rules with which to approach a humanities writing assignment, and, considering her background in biology, I wonder how many of them were formed out of the assumptions and procedures endemic to the physical sciences.[14] Martha will not put pen to first draft until she has spent up to two days generating an outline of remarkable complexity. I saw one of these outlines and it looked more like a diagram of protein synthesis or DNA structure than the time-worn pattern offered in composition textbooks. I must admit I was intrigued by the aura of process (vs. the static appearance of essay outlines) such diagrams offer, but for Martha these "outlines" only led to self-defeat: the outline would become so complex that all of its elements could never be included in a short essay. In other words, her plan locked her into the first stage of the composing process. Martha would struggle with the conversion of her outline into prose only to scrap the whole venture when deadlines passed and a paper had to be rushed together.

Martha's "rage for order" extends beyond the outlining process. She also believes that elements of a story or poem must evince a fairly linear structure and thematic clarity, or — perhaps bringing us closer to the issue — that analysis of a story or poem must provide the linearity or clarity that seems to be absent in the text. Martha, therefore, will bend the logic of her analysis to reason ambiguity out of existence. When I asked her about a strained paragraph in her paper on Camus' "The Guest," she said, "I didn't want to admit that it [the story's conclusion] was just hanging. I tried to force it into meaning."

Martha uses another rule, one that is not only problematical in itself, but one that often clashes directly with the elaborate plan and obsessive rule above. She believes that humanities papers must scintillate with insight, must present an array of images, ideas, ironies gleaned from the literature under examination. A problem arises, of course, when Martha tries to incorporate her myriad "neat little things," often inherently unrelated, into a tightly structured, carefully sequenced essay. Plans and rules that govern the construction of impressionistic, associational prose would be appropriate to Martha's desire, but her composing process is heavily constrained by the non-impressionistic and non-associational. Put another way, the plans and rules that govern her exploration of text are not at all synchronous with the plans and rules she uses to discuss her exploration. It is interesting to note here, however, that as recently as three years ago Martha was absorbed in creative writing and was publishing poetry in high school magazines. Given what we know about the complex associational, often non-neatly-sequential nature of the poet's creative process, we can infer that Martha was either free of the plans and rules discussed earlier or they were not as intense. One wonders, as well, if the exposure to three years of university physical science either established or intensified Martha's concern with structure. Whatever the case, she now is hamstrung by conflicting rules when composing papers for the humanities.

Mike's difficulties, too, are rooted in a distortion of the problem-solving process. When the time of the week for the assignment of writing topics draws near, Mike begins to prepare material, strategies, and plans that he believes will be appropriate. If the assignment matches his expectations, he has done a good job of analyzing the professor's intentions. If the assignment *doesn't* match his expectations, however, he cannot easily shift approaches. He feels trapped inside his original plans, cannot generate alternatives, and blocks. As the deadline draws near, he will write something, forcing the assignment to fit his conceptual procrustien bed. Since Mike is a smart man, he will offer a good deal of information, but only some of it ends up being appropriate to the assignment. This entire situation is made all the worse when the time between assignment of topic and generation of product is attenuated further, as in an essay examination.

Mike believes (correctly) that one must have a plan, a strategy of some sort in order to solve a problem. He further believes, however, that such a plan, once formulated, becomes an exact structural and substantive blueprint that cannot be violated. The plan offers no alternatives, no "sub-routines." So, whereas Ruth's, Laurel's, and some of Martha's difficulties seem to be rule-specific ("always catch your audience," "write grammatically"), Mike's troubles are more global. He may have strategies that are appropriate for various writing situations (e.g., "for this kind of political science assignment write a compare/contrast essay"), but his entire approach to formulating plans and carrying them through to problem solution is too mechanical. It is probable that Mike's behavior is governed by an explicitly learned or inferred rule: "Always try to 'psych out' a professor." But in this case this rule initiates a problem-solving procedure that is clearly dysfunctional.

While Ruth and Laurel use rules that impede their writing process and Mike utilizes a problem-solving procedure that hamstrings him, *Sylvia* has trouble deciding which of the many rules she possesses to use. Her problem can be characterized as cognitive perplexity: some of her rules are inappropriate, others are functional; some mesh nicely with her own definitions of good writing, others don't. She has multiple rules to invoke, multiple paths to follow, and that very complexity of choice virtually paralyzes her. More so than with the previous four students, there is probably a strong emotional dimension to Sylvia's blocking, but the cognitive difficulties are clear and perhaps modifiable.

Sylvia, somewhat like Ruth and Laurel, puts tremendous weight on the crafting of her first paragraph. If it is good, she believes the rest of the essay will be good. Therefore, she will spend up to five hours on the initial paragraph: "I won't go on until I get that first paragraph down." Clearly, this rule — or the strength of it — blocks Sylvia's production. This is one problem. Another is that Sylvia has other equally potent rules that she sees as separate, uncomplementary injunctions: one achieves "flow" in one's writing through the use of adequate transitions; one achieves substance to one's writing through the use of evidence. Sylvia perceives both rules to be "true," but several times followed one to the exclusion of the other. Furthermore, as I talked to Sylvia, many other rules, guidelines, definitions were offered, but none with conviction. While she *is* committed to one rule about initial paragraphs, and that rule is dysfunctional, she seems very uncertain about the weight and hierarchy of the remaining rules in her cognitive repertoire.

"If It Won't Fit My Work, I'll Change It" — The Non-blockers

Dale, Ellen, Debbie, Susan, and Miles all write with the aid of rules. But their rules differ from blockers' rules in significant ways. If similar in content, they are expressed less absolutely — e.g., "*Try* to keep audience in mind." If dissimilar, they are still expressed less absolutely, more heuristically — e.g., "I can use as many ideas in my thesis paragraph as I need and then develop paragraphs for each idea." Our non-blockers do express some rules with firm assurance, but these tend to be simple injunctions that free up rather than restrict the composing process, e.g., "When stuck, write!" or "I'll write what I can." And finally, at least three of the students openly shun the very textbook rules that some blockers adhere to: e.g., "Rules like 'write only what you know about' just aren't true. I ignore those." These three, in effect, have formulated a further rule that expresses something like: "If a rule conflicts with what is sensible or with experience, reject it."

On the broader level of plans and strategies, these five students also differ from at least three of the five blockers in that they all possess problem-solving plans that are quite functional. Interestingly, on first exploration these plans seem to be too broad or fluid to be useful and, in some cases, can barely be expressed with any precision. Ellen, for example, admits that she has a general "outline in [her] head about how a topic paragraph should look" but could not describe much about its structure. Susan also has a general plan to follow, but, if stymied, will quickly attempt to conceptualize the assignment in different ways: "If my original idea won't work, then I need to proceed differently." Whether or not these plans operate in TOTE-fashion, I can't say. But they do operate with the operate-test fluidity of TOTEs.

True, our non-blockers have their religiously adhered-to rules: e.g., "When stuck, write," and plans, "I couldn't imagine writing without this pattern," but as noted above, these are few and functional. Otherwise, these non-blockers operate with fluid, easily modified, even easily discarded rules and plans (Ellen: "I can throw things out") that are sometimes expressed with a vagueness that could almost be interpreted as ignorance. There lies the irony. Students that offer the least precise rules and plans have the least trouble composing. Perhaps this very lack of precision characterizes the functional composing plan. But perhaps this lack of precision simply masks habitually enacted alternatives and sub-routines. This is clearly an area that needs the illumination of further research.

And then there is feedback. At least three of the five non-blockers are an Information-Processor's dream. They get to know their audience, ask professors and T.A.s specific questions about assignments, bring half-finished products in for evaluation, etc. Like Ruth, they realize the importance of audience, but unlike her, they have specific strategies for obtaining and utilizing feedback. And this penchant for testing writing plans against the needs of the audience can lead to modification of rules and plans. Listen to Debbie:

> In high school I was given a formula that stated that you must write a thesis paragraph with *only* three points in it, and then develop each of those points. When I hit college I was given longer assignments. That stuck me for a bit, but then I realized that I could use as many ideas in my thesis paragraph as I needed and then develop paragraphs for each one. I asked someone about this and then tried it. I didn't get any negative feedback, so I figured it was o.k.

Debbie's statement brings one last difference between our blockers and non-blockers into focus; it has been implied above, but needs specific formulation: the goals these people have, and the plans they generate to attain these goals, are quite mutable. Part of the mutability comes from the fluid way the goals and plans are conceived, and part of it arises from the effective impact of feedback on these goals and plans.

Analyzing Writer's Block

Algorithms Rather Than Heuristics

In most cases, the rules our blockers use are not "wrong" or "incorrect" — it is good practice, for example, to "grab your audience with a catchy opening" or "craft a solid first paragraph before going on." The problem is that these rules seem to be followed as though they were algorithms, absolute dicta, rather than the loose heuristics that they were intended to be. Either through instruction, or the power of the textbook, or the predilections of some of our blockers for absolutes, or all three, these useful rules of thumb have been transformed into near-algorithmic urgencies. The result, to paraphrase Karl Dunker, is that these rules do not allow a flexible penetration into the nature of the problem. It is this transformation of heuristic into algorithm that contributes to the writer's block of Ruth and Laurel.

Questionable Heuristics Made Algorithmic

Whereas "grab your audience" could be a useful heuristic, "always make three or more points in an essay" is a pretty questionable one. Any such rule, though probably taught to aid the writer who needs structure, ultimately transforms a highly fluid process like writing into a mechanical lockstep. As heuristics, such rules can be troublesome. As algorithms, they are simply incorrect.

Set

As with any problem-solving task, students approach writing assignments with a variety of orientations or sets. Some are functional, others are not. Martha and Jane (see footnote 14), coming out of the life sciences and social sciences respectively, bring certain methodological orientations with them — certain sets or "directions" that make composing for the humanities a difficult, sometimes confusing, task. In fact, this orientation may cause them to misperceive the task. Martha has formulated a planning strategy from her predisposition to see processes in terms of linear, interrelated steps in a system. Jane doesn't realize that she can revise the statement that "committed" her to the direction her essay has taken. Both of these students are stymied because of formative experiences associated with their majors — experiences, perhaps, that nicely reinforce our very strong tendency to organize experiences temporally.

The Plan That Is Not a Plan

If fluidity and multi-directionality are central to the nature of plans, then the plans that Mike formulates are not true plans at all but, rather, inflexible and static cognitive blueprints.[15] Put another way, Mike's "plans" represent a restricted "closed system" (vs. "open system") kind of thinking, where closed system thinking is defined as focusing on "a limited number of units or items, or members, and those properties of the members which are to be used are known to begin with and do not change as the thinking proceeds," and open system thinking is characterized by an "adventurous exploration of multiple alternatives with strategies that allow redirection once 'dead ends' are encountered."[16] Composing calls for open, even adventurous thinking, not for constrained, no-exit cognition.

Feedback

The above difficulties are made all the more problematic by the fact that they seem resistant to or isolated from corrective feedback. One of the most striking things about Dale, Debbie, and Miles is the ease with which they seek out, interpret, and apply feedback on their rules, plans, and productions. They "operate" and then they "test," and the testing is not only against some internalized goal, but against the requirements of external audience as well.

Too Many Rules — "Conceptual Conflict"

According to D. E. Berlyne, one of the primary forces that motivate problem-solving behavior is a curiosity that arises from conceptual conflict — the convergence of incompatible beliefs or ideas. In *Structure and*

Direction in Thinking,[17] Berlyne presents six major types of conceptual conflict, the second of which he terms "perplexity":

> This kind of conflict occurs when there are factors inclining the subject toward each of a set of mutually exclusive beliefs. (p. 257)

If one substitutes "rules" for "beliefs" in the above definition, perplexity becomes a useful notion here. Because perplexity is unpleasant, people are motivated to reduce it by problem-solving behavior that can result in "disequalization":

> Degree of conflict will be reduced if either the number of competing . . . [rules] or their nearness to equality of strength is reduced. (p. 259)

But "disequalization" is not automatic. As I have suggested, Martha and Sylvia hold to rules that conflict, but their perplexity does *not* lead to curiosity and resultant problem-solving behavior. Their perplexity, contra Berlyne, leads to immobilization. Thus "disequalization" will have to be effected from without. The importance of each of, particularly, Sylvia's rules needs an evaluation that will aid her in rejecting some rules and balancing and sequencing others.

A Note on Treatment

Rather than get embroiled in a blocker's misery, the teacher or tutor might interview the student in order to build a writing history and profile: How much and what kind of writing was done in high school? What is the student's major? What kind of writing does it require? How does the student compose? Are there rough drafts or outlines available? By what rules does the student operate? How would he or she define "good" writing? etc. This sort of interview reveals an incredible amount of information about individual composing processes. Furthermore, it often reveals the rigid rule or the inflexible plan that may lie at the base of the student's writing problem. That was precisely what happened with the five blockers. And with Ruth, Laurel, and Martha (and Jane) what was revealed made virtually immediate remedy possible. Dysfunctional rules are easily replaced with or counter-balanced by functional ones if there is no emotional reason to hold onto that which simply doesn't work. Furthermore, students can be trained to select, to "know which rules are appropriate for which problems."[18] Mike's difficulties, perhaps because plans are more complex and pervasive than rules, took longer to correct. But inflexible plans, too, can be remedied by pointing out their dysfunctional qualities and by assisting the student in developing appropriate and flexible alternatives. Operating this way, I was successful with Mike. Sylvia's story, however, did not end as smoothly. Though I had three forty-five minute contacts with her, I was not able to appreciably alter her behavior. Berlyne's theory bore results with Martha but not with Sylvia. Her rules were in conflict, and perhaps that conflict was not exclusively cognitive. Her case keeps analyses like these honest; it reminds us that the cognitive often melds with, and can be overpowered by, the affective. So while Ruth, Laurel, Martha, and Mike could profit from tutorials that explore the rules and plans in their writing behavior, students like Sylvia may need more extended, more affectively oriented counseling sessions that blend the instructional with the psychodynamic.

Notes

[1] David Shapiro, *Neurotic Styles* (New York: Basic Books, 1965).

[2] Barbara Hayes-Ruth, a Rand cognitive psychologist, and I are currently developing an information-processing model of the composing process. A good deal of work has already been done by Linda Flower and John Hayes (see p. 76 of this

article). I . . . recommend . . . their "Writing as Problem Solving" (paper presented at American Educational Research Association, April 1979).

[3] *The Conditions of Learning* (New York: Holt, Rinehart and Winston, 1970), p. 193.

[4] E. James Archer, "The Psychological Nature of Concepts," in H. J. Klausmeier and C. W. Harris, eds., *Analysis of Concept Learning* (New York: Academic Press, 1966), pp. 37–44; David P. Ausubel, *The Psychology of Meaningful Verbal Behavior* (New York: Grune and Stratton, 1963); Robert M. Gagné, "Problem Solving," in Arthur W. Melton, ed., *Categories of Human Learning* (New York: Academic Press, 1964), pp. 293–317; George A. Miller, *Language and Communication* (New York: McGraw-Hill, 1951).

[5] George Katona, *Organizing and Memorizing* (New York: Columbia Univ. Press, 1940); Roger N. Shepard, Carl I. Hovland, and Herbert M. Jenkins, "Learning and Memorization of Classifications," *Psychological Monographs*, 75, No. 13 (1961) (entire No. 517); Robert S. Woodworth, *Dynamics of Behavior* (New York: Henry Holt, 1958), chs. 10–12.

[6] *The Conditions of Learning*, pp. 190–91.

[7] Karl Dunker, "On Problem Solving," *Psychological Monographs*, 58, No. 5 (1945) (entire No. 270); George A. Polya, *How to Solve It* (Princeton: Princeton Univ. Press, 1945); George A. Miller, Eugene Galanter, and Karl H. Pribram, *Plans and the Structure of Behavior* (New York: Henry Holt, 1960).

[8] Lyle E. Bourne, Jr., Bruce R. Ekstrand, and Roger L. Dominowski, *The Psychology of Thinking* (Englewood Cliffs, N.J.: Prentice-Hall, 1971).

[9] John R. Hayes, "Problem Topology and the Solution Process," in Carl P. Duncan, ed., *Thinking: Current Experimental Studies* (Philadelphia: Lippincott, 1967), pp. 167–81.

[10] Hulda J. Rees and Harold E. Israel, "An Investigation of the Establishment and Operation of Mental Sets," *Psychological Monographs*, 46 (1925) (entire No. 210).

[11] Ibid.; Melvin H. Marx, Wilton W. Murphy, and Aaron J. Brownstein, "Recognition of Complex Visual Stimuli as a Function of Training with Abstracted Patterns," *Journal of Experimental Psychology*, 62 (1961), 456–60.

[12] James L. Adams, *Conceptual Blockbusting* (San Francisco: W. H. Freeman, 1974); Edward DeBono, *New Think* (New York: Basic Books, 1958); Ronald H. Forgus, *Perception* (New York: McGraw-Hill, 1966), ch. 13; Abraham Luchins and Edith Hirsch Luchins, *Rigidity of Behavior* (Eugene: Univ. of Oregon Books, 1959); N. R. F. Maier, "Reasoning in Humans. I. On Direction," *Journal of Comparative Psychology*, 10 (1920), 115–43.

[13] "Plans and the Cognitive Process of Writing," paper presented at the National Institute of Education Writing Conference, June 1977; "Problem Solving Strategies and the Writing Process," *College English*, 39 (1977), 449–61. See also footnote 2.

[14] Jane, a student not discussed in this paper, was surprised to find out that a topic paragraph can be rewritten after a paper's conclusion to make that paragraph reflect what the essay truly contains. She had gotten so indoctrinated with Psychology's (her major) insistence that a hypothesis be formulated and then left untouched before an experiment begins that she thought revision of one's "major premise" was somehow illegal. She had formed a rule out of her exposure to social science methodology, and the rule was totally inappropriate for most writing situations.

[15] Cf. "A plan is flexible if the order of execution of its parts can be easily interchanged without affecting the feasibility of the plan . . . the flexible planner might tend to think of lists of things she had to do; the inflexible planner would have his time planned like a sequence of cause-effect relations. The former could rearrange his lists to suit his opportunities, but the latter would be unable to strike while the iron was hot and would generally require considerable 'lead-time' before he could incorporate any alternative sub-plans" (Miller, Galanter, and Pribram, p. 120).

[16] Frederic Bartlett, *Thinking* (New York: Basic Books, 1958), pp. 74–76.
[17] *Structure and Direction in Thinking* (New York: John Wiley, 1965), p. 255.
[18] Flower and Hayes, "Plans and the Cognitive Process of Writing," p. 26.

ON IMPOSED VERSUS IMITATIVE FORM

Richard Fulkerson

[*Journal of Teaching Writing* 7.2 (1988): 143–55.]

Richard Fulkerson teaches at Texas A&M University-Commerce. Among his current administrative duties, he is director of graduate studies in English. He serves on the executive committee of Conference on College Composition and Communication and on the editorial board of *Dialogue*. His articles have appeared in *College Composition and Communication, Rhetoric Review, Informal Logic,* and *Quarterly Journal of Speech*. He is most recently the author of *Teaching the Argument in Writing* (NCTE 1996). An excerpt from that book appears in Part Two of this collection.

Many students, Fulkerson argues, use an "imitative" strategy of writing, organizing papers by "repeating the shape of the materials discussed." These students must be encouraged, however, to take authority in their writing and impose a form that suits the points they wish to make — not merely an imitative form. Fulkerson provides examples of the ways in which students use imitative forms and suggests ways of helping them consider alternatives. By helping students explore alternatives for structuring their writing, instructors also help them understand that writing is a rhetorical act and that composing is a process of choosing and testing options.

In "Confessions of a Former Sailor," a wonderful essay about her own writing process, Professor Sue Lorch tells a traumatic tale from her undergraduate experience in advanced composition. The story is revealing, I think, about some important principles of one of the least understood and least discussed features of writing, the arrangement of a discourse. Lorch's first assignment was to visit the art department and write a descriptive paper about a painting of cows in a field. Lorch, who had always been a "good writer," sailed up, applied the description formula she had been taught, going left to right and top to bottom, and produced a description so thorough it even numbered the spots on the cows. Having never received less than a B on a piece of writing in sixteen years of schooling, she was naturally shocked when her work received an F, an F for being boring.

Since her teacher required that Lorch rewrite the paper, shock became despair. How could she make a description of a boring painting anything but boring? "I tried to imagine what would interest [the professor] — an effective use of colons perhaps, more adjectives, maybe an allusion to a classical myth. What was the name of that cow Jove courted in the form of a bull?" (168).

Finally, she gave up and returned to reexamine the now hated painting. The moment was a revelation. She suddenly saw that one cow had a different look on its face, a look that undercut the surface impression of bucolic bliss. By focusing on that cow and that insight, Lorch rewrote and achieved the painful breakthrough that transformed her writing process for all time. Instead of sailing smoothly down the page, her "progress is now that of a '39 Ford negotiating hard terrain, a Ford operated by a slightly dim twelve-year-old child lacking entirely any experience with stick shift" (170). She does not describe the structure of the revised piece, but she does indicate that it had to be completely redesigned: "My all-purpose sea chart for getting through a description — begin at the upper left of whatever and move clockwise until you come round again to the starting point — was not going to get me where I needed to be" (170). A new form was required.

Structurally Lorch's original paper mirrored the shape of the topic she was writing about. Whatever appeared at the top left of the picture would be discussed first, whatever was in the middle next, etc. In other words, the form of the painting controlled the form of the discourse. That is what I will call "natural" or "imitative" order in discourse. On the other hand, when Lorch rewrote the paper to focus on the importance of that one cow and its odd look, she had to restructure the paper on her own. Whatever form she used, she had to create. This is "imposed" form, form not found in the topic, but chosen by the writer.

Not all topics manifest an inherent shape. Those that do involve either chronology or spatiality. Time and space, the two dimensions of the Newtonian universe, seem also to be the two dimensions of natural form in discourse.

Imposed form in contrast *restructures* the topical material in some significant way. Now imposed form itself has at least two variants. It includes the standard forms we sometimes teach — such as the alternating comparison-contrast structure — the forms of development that Frank D'Angelo presents as conceptual paradigms for various types of writing, what Coleridge called mechanical form. But imposed form also includes the organic form favored by the British Romantics, and by such essayists as Didion, Baldwin, Carlyle, and Emerson.

Having postulated the existence of two broad categories of form, I now offer the Theorem of Student Selected Structure: Whenever possible, students tend to arrange papers by repeating the shape of the materials discussed. In other words, students choose imitative rather than imposed form.

Let me illustrate the Theorem with a personal anecdote. It's the story of one of those times in teaching when what seems like a really good idea at the moment turns into a disaster whose only virtue is that you learn not to do that again. At my university's annual spring symposium in honor of alumnus Sam Rayburn, David Schoenbrun was the featured speaker. All classes were canceled, and we were to "encourage" students to attend.

Now what better way to encourage attendance than to make the speech the subject of a writing assignment? I did not want to ask for anything complex from first-semester freshmen, so I asked them to attend the lecture, then write an account of it as a news story — no critical analysis of the positions taken, just summation of what was said with some attention to what was most important. I explained the 5 W's briefly, devoted at least thirty seconds to inverted pyramidal form, and encouraged them to take notes or even record the session.

When I read the papers, I was aghast. The major problem was structure. As the ritual on such occasions goes, the program had not begun with Schoenbrun but with our student body president, who introduced a regional newscaster, who in turn introduced Schoenbrun. And a good many of my students' papers followed that same order, beginning with the student, then the Dallas newscaster, then Schoenbrun. Of course the papers also mirrored the order of his speech, which had the effect of leaving the most interesting material near the end. My students had enacted what some literary critic once called the fallacy of imitative form.

I was expecting the mechanical imposed form of the journalist's inverted pyramid, but I got imitative chronology. They had written the minutes of the assembly, not news accounts of it.

The students certainly were not at fault — except perhaps in the general sense that they are not very familiar with what a news article sounds like. They had done what students seem to do naturally: they had built their papers in the shape of the material being discussed. But *I* was at fault for providing such an opportunity.

When asked to write a paper based on personal experiences, students also "naturally" seize on chronological order. I often assign students an essay evaluating a teacher they have had, addressed to an appropriate audience, such as the school board or future teachers of that discipline. Unless I take pains to explain the logic of evaluation, they tend to shape the papers by chronicling their experiences with that teacher, beginning with the first day in the classroom, or sometimes even before, with the rumors they had heard. They tend to be quite detailed about the first week or two, and then collapse the rest of the year into a paragraph or so.

Students are in fact ingenious about finding a natural structure, even where one would think it impossible. Last term I spent four weeks teaching research papers. We examined sample papers by other students, stressed use of multiple types of sources, and emphasized locating cognitive dissonance among the sources in order to focus a paper and contribute to the ongoing dialogue on the topic. So I was perplexed at a paper I received with five main points about the effects of teacher personality on elementary students. It had one for each of the five articles the student had located. That particular sort of natural order had seemed so unlikely that I had never warned against it. Later it occurred to me that I had seen exactly the same thing happen in doctoral dissertations in the obligatory review of the literature, which is frequently treated chronologically and exhaustingly. That same term I read such a section that was seventeen paragraphs long. I know its length because it summarized seventeen prior studies, one study per paragraph, in the order of publication.

Why do students tend to seize on natural orders? First, a powerful economy may be at work: natural form is already there, but imposing some alternate form takes extra energy and control of text. Throwing out the form already present and hunting for another seems wasteful.

Second, our textbooks *teach* such orders. When students need to describe a place, person, or object (including Lorch's painting), the books direct them to follow the innate structure of the scene by moving left to right, or top to bottom, etc., although in my experience most published description does not follow such a structure. (Have you ever hunted for such a passage to supplement your textbook?)

Third, the structure our students are most familiar with from media of *all* types may well be chronology. From movies and TV shows, to the literary works we teach, to the U.S. history they study, the majority of the extended discourse they receive is chronologically oriented. Undoubtedly, of course, the urge to hear and tell stories is deeply embedded in the human psyche. Such structure is thus *natural* in the deepest sense of the word.

My second theorem, therefore, is certain to be more controversial: "Natural order is usually ineffective." For mnemonic purposes, we can call it the INS theorem, with INS standing for the "ineffectiveness of natural structure." I base my INS theorem largely on the experience of having read so many ineffective natural-order papers, such as those news stories on David Schoenbrun, papers which could have been presented to a reader clearly and effectively if the same material had merely been reshaped.

I have neither the space nor the inclination to document these theorems directly by comparing alternate versions of student papers. Instead I count on readers having had pedagogical experiences similar to mine that illustrate both points.

I see two explanations for why natural order is less effective than imposed order.

(1) I take it as a given that writing is a purposeful activity. It is also non-algorithmic, meaning no set sequence of steps will guarantee a solution. Consequently, writers are inherently in the business of making choices to achieve their purposes. Certainly not a revolutionary idea.

Writers choose what to include and what to omit; they make stylistic choices, and grammatical choices — and structural choices. The grounds for all these choices ought to be, in the largest sense, rhetorical. That is, the choices should be based on the question "Which of my various options at this point will best help me achieve my purpose for my readers?" Students who follow natural form forfeit the right to make such purposive structural choices. They let the shape of perceived reality deprive them of their privilege to control movement to achieve a goal. They trade freedom for security.[1]

Jack Selzer says this extreme rhetorical view privileges audience-based choices inappropriately. I maintain, however, that whether one is writing science, persuasion, information, evaluation, or a note to the paperboy, audience-based choices *should* be privileged. We write to audiences in order to communicate to them, in order to affect them in some way. Any choice we make that interferes with the audience's reception of that message —whether the choice is in spelling, vocabulary, title, readability level, or structure — is a defective choice, one that *should* have been made otherwise. (See Martin Nystrand's discussion of the principle of "reciprocity" that should operate in discourse.)

I do not wish to oversimplify this matter. Peter Elbow has made a powerful "argument for ignoring audience" in which he asserts — correctly, I think — that "we often do not really develop a strong, authentic voice in our writing till we find important occasions for *ignoring* audience" (55) in order to concentrate on what we need to say. He concludes, however, that "we must nevertheless *revise* with conscious awareness of audience in order to figure out which pieces of writer-based prose are good as they are — and how to discard or revise the rest" (55).

That is my point as well: not that at all moments during writing a student should be conscious of audience, but that *finally* all decisions need to rest on audience — even the decision to retain some natural order discourse.

(2) The second reason for the ineffectiveness of natural order grows from the presumption that discourse is unified, elaborated predication. That is, discourse asserts a claim about a subject (a rheme about a theme, to use the jargon). Natural order focuses on the subject (such as Lorch's painting of the cows), rather than on the claim. Natural order takes whatever noun referent is being discussed — whether it be "pornography," or "my summer vacation," or "the Elizabethan world picture" — locates its spatial or chronological parts and builds the discourse around them, using some variation of a list construction. Natural order thus de-emphasizes the predication and foregrounds the subject.

But the *point* of writing is what the writer predicates.

One useful corollary of the INS theorem applies to writing about writing: in writing about another text, following the structure of that text rarely works. This holds whether one reviews a new textbook, refutes a previous article, or interprets a poem.

My own struggles with textbook reviewing remind me of this point constantly. Inevitably I draft a review that is mainly a summary of the book, with evaluative remarks tied on, clanking like tin cans behind the newlyweds' car. And I defend the structure to myself on the grounds that one major purpose of the review is to tell other teachers what the book includes so they can judge whether it interests them. I maintain that charade through perhaps two drafts before acknowledging that reading even my own summary is boring, that the structure seems childish, mechanical (in the pejorative sense), and lacking in insight. At that point I know I must reconstruct the review, basing it not on the book's structure, but on my own evaluative insights, with supporting detail included but subordinated. In short, I must act on my INS theorem.

Another common example: When students are asked to interpret a poem, they automatically adopt a structure both spatial and chronological: namely, first stanza, second stanza, etc. If asked to analyze a character in a work of fiction, they will typically follow the character through the narrative. If asked to discuss several characters, they will discuss one, then another *seriatim,* often in separate paragraphs.

How often have we asked for more interpretation and less summary from our students? I submit that the problem is frequently not so much quantitative as structural. Following the shape of the work tends to produce summary and bury interpretation.

So far, this has all been personal speculation and pontification. But a fair amount of careful research supports the view that imitative order is generally less effective than imposed order.

The evidence comes from three different sorts of research: cognitive psychology, discourse analysis, and reading research.

Frankly, much of what I have been saying could have been entitled "Footnote to Linda Flower." In her classic "Writer-Based Prose: A Cognitive Basis for Problems in Writing," she asserts that "in its *structure* writer-based prose reflects the associative, narrative path of the writer's own confrontation with her subject" (269). Flower illustrates by comparing two versions of a report, written by students analyzing problems faced by the Oskalossa Brewing Company. When the group first drafted its report, it repeated the order of its own investigation, thus including a great deal of background material about the company that would be unnecessary, in fact counter productive, for the intended audience of company executives.

As Flower points out, such a structure has "an inner logic of its own . . . either a narrative framework or a survey form" (276), what I have been calling chronology or spatiality. But as she further points out, "a narrative obscures the more important logical and hierarchical relations between ideas" (276). This describes much of what our students write when asked to deal with a work of literature, as well as what often happens when they write about their own experiences. Now an argument can be made for the dramatic values of taking a reader through an experience with you — if indeed the experience itself happened to be well structured. Ken Macrorie and others have asserted a natural human "bias toward narrative" (see Dillon 65). But if one wants to make a more complex point about that experience, such as in my earlier example of evaluating a teacher, telling the story in its own order often isn't enough. Even the strict single experience narrative is often improved by using some version of flashback rather than following the natural order of the materials. Narration need not equal chronology.

Suzanne Jacobs used Flower's concept of writer-based prose in a case study of Rudy and his weekly in-class essays in advanced physiology. His teacher regularly gave the class an opening sentence designed to make them focus the ideas in that week's lectures, such as "Muscle cells are cells specialized for contraction" (35). Rudy knew a lot about muscle cells, and his essay retold that information in the order he had learned it — with no attention to the predicate, "specialized for contraction." Jacobs refers in a telling phrase to "the difficulty of fighting against the structure of remembered information" (38). Rudy imitated the order in which the teacher had presented the material. That order had worked for her purposes. But it would not work for his. He produced what we disdainfully call regurgitation. It is information-full, but not well formed.

In an article less well known than Flower's but equally brilliant, entitled "Perceiving Structure in Professional Prose," Gregory Colomb and Joseph Williams categorized the structures of prose in the professions: "There are, we believe, roughly three kinds of large-scale order. The first originates in experience, the second in historical convention, the third in something we will very crudely characterize as logic" (121).

The authors name the type "originating in experience" "iconic order." It is what I have been calling natural or imitative form. The other two types represent varieties of imposed form, a mechanical one imposed by generic conventions, such as the form of a grant application, and an organic one created to help realize the discourse as an argument.

Based on their studies of business prose, Colomb and Williams conclude bluntly, "iconic order characterizes the worst professional prose: the order of information follows the associations of the writer, or the sequence of inquiry the writer engaged in, or the structure of the object under discussion" (122). The INS theorem again.

In a very different sort of study, Richard Haswell examined impromptu essays by 160 writers representing different age groups, ranging from 18-year-old new freshmen in college to working adults age 30 and over already judged by their job supervisors to be competent writers. He discovered fourteen different macro structures and was able to classify them into simple patterns such as partition, seriation, and consequence, or chained patterns made up by joining simple patterns. The important finding for my point is that the simple or unchained patterns could be further divided into symmetrical patterns and asymmetrical patterns. In symmetrical patterns, the parts are "categories of a common class, as in chronology where the parts are all units of time" (404). In asymmetrical patterns such as "consequence" and "problem/solution," different parts are not subdivisions of one class. The five symmetrical patterns he found correspond to what I have been calling "natural" order. Nearly one-fourth of the 128 impromptu essays used "partition" (a natural pattern), but only one of the 32 essays by effective adult writers did (409).

The findings are complex, but in general the mature and effective writers tended to use the more complex asymmetrical and chained patterns, the ones I have been lumping as "imposed" structures. "Asymmetrical construction," Haswell says, "lends itself to the adventurous kind of writing that competent adults favor" (413).

In an earlier related study Aviva Freedman and Ian Pringle compared the abstraction levels of essays written by high school seniors and third-year college students in the same academic subjects. In doing so they created a four part schema in which the two lower parts, the ones showing less use of intellectual abstracting (report and commentary), are written in natural order, while the two higher forms reflect imposed orders. College writers were found to use the forms involving higher level abstraction much more frequently than did the high school students. Thus the use of imposed form was found to correlate with developmental level, a conclusion that seems consistent with Haswell's.

Finally, probably the most elaborate explanation of why imposed structure (what Colomb and Williams call "principled order" and Flower calls "reader-based prose") is generally superior comes from the work of reading researcher Bonnie J. F. Meyer. She categorizes prose structures into five main groups: description, collection (which includes time-order), antecedent/consequent, comparison, and response (which includes such structures as question and answer, and problem-solution) ("Prose Analysis: Purposes, Procedures, and Problems" 11). Her first two structures, description and collection, are simple symmetrical patterns; the other three are asymmetrical. Meyer has done extensive research on how much information readers can recall when texts containing identical information are structured along different lines. (See Meyer and Freedie, "Effects of Discourse Type on Recall.") "Some of our ongoing studies suggest that the descriptive plan is the least effective when people read or listen to text for the purpose of remembering it" ("Reading Research and the Composition Teacher: The Importance of Plans" 41). Meyer's work again suggests the superiority of imposed forms.

In 1980 a national survey of leaders in composition revealed that the inability to organize papers effectively was considered the second most important weakness in student writing, with nearly 70 percent of the 219 respondents identifying it as a "major problem" (Bossone and Larson 12).

If we agree that this is a widespread problem, and we accept the principle that imposed forms are generally superior to imitative forms, what then do we do to help students structure their prose more effectively? On this issue, existing scholarship is much less helpful. Meyer suggests that we ought to teach students conscious use of effective schemata. So does Richard Coe, but he cautions "not by pontificating about form; rather by creating processes that allow them to experience both the constraining and generative powers of forms" ("An Apology for Form" 21). Just what he means by that isn't clear, since in his own pedagogy he begins with description and narration, which he agrees lend themselves to imitative form. He does, at least, have students try out alternate structural versions of the same paper so that they can discover for themselves the effects of alternate patterns (*Form and Substance* 238–41).

It is difficult to teach form directly without returning to the empty formalism for which current-traditional, or product, pedagogies have been widely criticized. Direct teaching of form almost inevitably divorces form from purpose by asking students to locate material suitable for pouring into the mold we have designed rather than imposing whatever form will achieve their purpose.

Instead, I suggest we begin simply by giving students the advice of Leonard Podis that "every paper ought to have a consciously crafted scheme of arrangement" (197) and thus stressing the superiority of imposed form. Then we can follow the lead of a number of teachers who include some discussion of the relevant structural issues when making specific assignments. Jean Jensen, for example, describes an interview assignment for high school students that includes the following directive: "If possible, try to organize by idea rather than by time" (40). Simply telling students not to use the most obvious form might lead them to discover workable alternatives, but probably showing them model interview essays, one organized by time and one done in some other way, would further sensitize them to the general preferability of imposed form. Similarly, Judith and Geoffrey Summerfield discuss at length a personal narrative paper they assign in which students are to "break the hold on chronology" (111) and avoid the natural "bed-to-bed" structure (111). Their chapter includes two versions of a student's autobiographical paper, done six weeks apart. The revision dramatically alters the initial "bed-to-bed" chronological structure (113–21).

Of course, I am assuring that we will teach composition as an extended process — allowing both time for considering alternative structures and opportunities for revisions in which different structures, not just improved surface features, can be tried. And I am assuming that we teach composition from a rhetorical rather than a formalist axiology. In a course based on rhetorical considerations, explicit discussions of natural versus imposed orders would not be out of order.

I already teach writing as a rhetorical process. Maybe in the future I will remember my own advice and spend time discussing preferable structures every time I make a writing assignment. Then, if I am lucky, I won't have to spend my weekends reading papers beginning, "At 9:00 this morning, student body president Martin Solis welcomed a large crowd to the University Auditorium and introduced Gloria Campos, news anchor for WFAA-TV, Dallas. Ms. Campos, in turn, introduced David Schoenbrun. Mr. Schoenbrun opened his speech by saying, . . ."

Note

[1] Obviously in some cases natural order is also the superior rhetorical order — such as in giving directions for carrying out a linear process. I am not opposing *all* natural order, just natural order used without consideration of potentially superior rhetorical alternatives.

Works Cited

Bossone, Richard, and Richard Larson. *Needed Research in the Teaching of Writing.* New York: Center for Advanced Study in Education, The Graduate School and University Center of the City University of New York, 1980.

Coe, Richard. "An Apology for Form; or, Who Took the Form Out of the Process?" *College English* 49 (Jan. 1987): 13–28.

————. *Form and Substance: An Advanced Rhetoric.* New York: John Wiley, 1981.

Colomb, Gregory G., and Joseph M. Williams. "Perceiving Structure in Professional Prose: A Multiply Determined Experience." *Writing in Nonacademic Settings.* Ed. Lee Odell and Dixie Goswami. New York: Guilford, 1985. 87–128.

D'Angelo, Frank. *Process and Thought in Composition.* 2nd ed. Cambridge, Mass.: Winthrop, 1980.

Dillon, George. *Constructing Texts: Elements of a Theory of Composition and Style.* Bloomington: Indiana UP, 1981.

Elbow, Peter. "Closing My Eyes as I Speak: An Argument for Ignoring Audience." *College English* 49 (Jan. 1987): 50–69.

Flower, Linda. "Writer-Based Prose: A Cognitive Basis for Problems in Writing." *College English* 41 (Sept. 1979): 19–37. Rpt. Gary Tate and E. P. J. Corbett, eds. *A Writing Teacher's Sourcebook.* New York: Oxford UP, 1981. 268–92.

Freedman, Aviva, and Ian Pringle. "Writing in the College Years." *College Composition and Communication* 31 (1980): 311–24.

Haswell, Richard. "The Organization of Impromptu Essays." *College Composition and Communication* 37 (Dec. 1986): 402–15.

Jacobs, Susanne. "Composing the In-Class Essay: A Case Study of Rudy." *College English* 46 (January 1984): 34–46.

Jensen, Jean. "The Evolution of a Writing Program." *Teaching Writing: Essays from the Bay Area Writing Project.* Ed. Gerald Camp. Montclair, NJ: Boynton/Cook, 1982. 24–43.

Lorch, Sue. "Confessions of a Former Sailor." *Writers on Writing.* Ed. Tom Waldrep. New York: Random House, 1985. 165–71.

Meyer, Bonnie J. F. "Prose Analysis: Purposes, Procedures, and Problems." *Understanding Expository Text: Theoretical and Practical Handbook for Analyzing Explanatory Text.* Hillsdale, NJ: Lawrence Erlbaum, 1985. 11–64.

————. "Reading Research and the Composition Teacher: The Importance of Plans." *College Composition and Communication* 37 (Feb. 1982): 37–49.

Meyer, Bonnie J. F., and Roy O. Freedle. "Effects of Discourse Type on Recall." *American Educational Research Journal* 21 (Spring 1984): 121–43.

Nystrand, Martin. *The Structure of Written Communication: Studies in Reciprocity between Writers and Readers.* Orlando, FL: Academic Press, Harcourt Brace Jovanovich, 1986.

Podis, Leonard. "Teaching Arrangement: Defining a More Practical Approach." *College Composition and Communication* 31 (May 1980): 197–204.

Selzer, Jack. "A Catalog of Arrangement Considerations and Choices for Writers." Paper presented at CCCC, 1987.

Summerfield, Judith, and Geoffrey Summerfield. *Texts and Contexts: A Contribution to the Theory and Practice of Teaching Composition.* New York: Random House, 1986.

COMPOSING BEHAVIORS OF ONE- AND MULTI-DRAFT WRITERS

Muriel Harris

[*College English* 51 (1989): 174–91.]

Muriel Harris is a professor of English and director of the Writing Lab at Purdue University, where she founded and continues to edit the *Writing Lab Newsletter.* Her articles, book chapters, and conference presentations focus on individualized instruction in writing and the theory, pedagogy, and administration of writing centers. Most recently, she coordinated the development of the Purdue OWL (Online Writing Lab) on the World Wide Web (http://owl.english.purdue.edu). She has also authored several books, including *Teaching One-to-One: The Writing Conference* (1986) and the recently published third edition of the *Prentice Hall Reference Guide to Grammar and Usage* (1997). Harris is widely recognized as an authority on writing centers and Writing Across the Curriculum, and she has won several teaching awards at Purdue University.

Harris suggests that we think of revising behaviors (and thus of revision strategies) as ranging on a continuum from writers who produce only one draft to writers who produce multiple drafts. According to Harris, one writer may exhibit several different revision behaviors, in some instances producing only one draft or doing little revision and in other instances producing multiple drafts and doing extensive revision. The variety of composing and revising behaviors, she contends, is not necessarily attributable to experience or abilities. Harris's approach to understanding revision offers instructors a powerful and flexible explanation of revising, one that accounts more fully for the variety of writing tasks that students encounter and provides them with a variety of effective composing strategies for accomplishing those tasks.

A belief shared by teachers of writing, one that we fervently try to inculcate in our students, is that revision can improve writing. This notion, that revision generally results in better text, often pairs up with another assumption, that revision occurs as we work through separate drafts. Thus, "hand in your working drafts tomorrow and the final ones next Friday" is a common assignment, as is the following bit of textbook advice: "When the draft is completed, a good critical reading should help the writer re-envision the essay and could very well lead to substantial rewriting" (Axelrod and Cooper 10). This textbook advice, hardly atypical, is based on the rationale that gaining distance from a piece of discourse helps the writer to judge it more critically. As evidence for this assumption, Richard Beach's 1976 study of the self-evaluation strategies of revisers and non-revisers demonstrated that extensive revisers were more capable of detaching themselves and gaining aesthetic distance from their writing than were non-revisers. Nancy Sommers' later theoretical work on revision also sensitized us to students' need to re-see their texts rather than to view revision as an editing process at the limited level of word changes.

A logical conclusion, then, is to train student writers to re-see and then re-draft a piece of discourse. There are other compelling reasons for helping students view first or working drafts as fluid and not yet molded into final form. The opportunities for outside intervention, through teacher critiques and suggestions or peer evaluation sessions, can be valuable. And it is equally important to help students move beyond their limited approaches and limiting tendency to settle for whatever rolls out on paper the first time around. The novice view of a first draft as written-in-stone (or fast-drying cement) can preclude engaging more fully with the ideas being expressed. On the other hand, we have to acknowledge that there are advantages in being able, where it is appropriate, to master the art of one-draft writing. When students write essay exams or placement essays and when they go on to on-the-job writing where time doesn't permit multiple drafts, they need to produce first drafts which are also coherent, finished final drafts. Yet, even acknowledging that need, we still seem justified in advocating that our students master the art of redrafting to shape a text into a more effective form.

The notion that reworking a text through multiple drafts and/or visible changes is generally a beneficial process is also an underlying assumption in some lines of research. This had been particularly evident in studies of computer-aided revision, where counts were taken of changes in macrostructure and microstructure with and without word processing. If more changes were made on a word processor than were written by hand, the conclusion was that word processors are an aid to revision. Such research is based on the premise that revision equals visible changes in a text and that these changes will improve the text.

Given this widely entrenched notion of redrafting as being advantageous, it would be comforting to turn to research results for clearcut evidence that reworking of text produces better writing. But studies of revision do not provide the conclusive picture that we need in order to assert that we should continue coaxing our students into writing multiple drafts. Lillian Bridwell's 1980 survey of revision studies led her to conclude that "questions about the relationship between revision and qualitative improvement remain largely unanswered" (199), and her own study demonstrated that the most extensively revised papers "received a range of quality ratings from the top to the bottom of the scale" (216). In another review of research on revision, Stephen Witte cites studies which similarly suggest that the amount of redrafting (which Witte calls "retranscription") often bears little relation to the overall quality of completed texts ("Revising" 256). Similarly, Linda Flower and John Hayes et al., citing studies which also dispute the notion that more re-drafting should mean better papers, conclude that the amount of change is not a key variable in revision and that revision as an obligatory stage required by teachers doesn't necessarily produce better writing. (For a teacher's affirmation of the same phenomenon, see Henley.)

Constricting revision to retranscription (i.e., to altering what has been written) also denies the reality of pre-text, a composing phenomenon studied by Stephen Witte in "Pre-Text and Composing." Witte defines a writer's pre-text as "the mental construction of 'text' prior to transcription" (397). Pre-text thus "refers to a writer's linguistic representation of intended meaning, a 'trial locution' that is produced in the mind, stored in the writer's memory, and sometimes manipulated mentally prior to being transcribed as written text" (397). Pre-texts are distinguished from abstract plans in that pre-texts approximate written prose. As the outcome of planning, pre-text can also be the basis for further planning. In his study Witte found great diversity in how writers construct and use pre-text. Some writers construct little or no pre-text; others rely heavily on extensive pre-texts; others create short pre-texts; and still others move back and forth between extensive and short pre-texts. The point here is that Witte has shown us that revision can and does occur in pre-texts, before visible marks are made on paper. In an earlier paper, "Revising, Composing Theory, and Research Design," Witte suggests that the pre-text writers construct before making marks on paper is probably a function of the quality, kind, and extent of planning that occurs before transcribing on paper. The danger here is that we might conclude that the development from novice to expert writer entails learning to make greater use of pre-text prior to transcribing. After all, in Linda Flower's memorable phrase, pre-text is "the last cheap gas before transcribing text" (see Witte, "Pre-Text" 422). But

Witte notes that his data do not support a "vote for pre-text" ("Pre-Text" 401). For the students in Witte's study, more extensive use of pre-text doesn't automatically lead to better written text. Thus it appears so far that the quality of revision can neither be measured by the pound nor tracked through discreet stages.

But a discussion of whether more or fewer drafts is an indication of more mature writing is itself not adequate. As Maxine Hairston reminds us in "Different Products, Different Processes," we must also consider the writing task that is involved in any particular case of generating discourse. In her taxonomy of writing categories, categories that depict a variety of revision behaviors that are true to the experience of many of us, Hairston divides writing into three classes: first, routine maintenance writing which is simple communication about uncomplicated matters; second, extended, relatively complex writing that requires the writer's attention but is self-limiting in that the writer already knows most of what she is going to write and may be writing under time constraints; and third, extended reflective writing in which the form and content emerge as the writing proceeds. Even with this oversimplified, brief summary of Hairston's classes of writing, we recognize that the matter of when and if re-drafting takes place can differ according to the demands of different tasks and situations as well as the different skills levels of writers.

Many — or perhaps even most — of us may nod in agreement as we recognize in Hairston's classes of writing a description of the different types of writing we do. But given the range of individual differences that exist among writers, we still cannot conclude that the nature of effective revision is always tied to the writing task, because such a conclusion would not account for what we know also exists — some expert writers who, despite the writing task, work at either end of the spectrum as confirmed, consistent one-drafters or as perpetual multi-drafters. That writers exhibit a diversity of revising habits has been noted by Lester Faigley and Stephen Witte in "Analyzing Revision." When testing the taxonomy of revision changes they had created, Faigley and Witte found that expert writers exhibited "extreme diversity" in the ways they revised:

> One expert writer in the present study made almost no revisions; another started with an almost stream-of-consciousness text that she then converted to an organized essay in the second draft; another limited his major revisions to a single long insert; and another revised mostly by pruning. (410)

Similarly, when summarizing interviews with well-known authors such as those in the *Writers at Work: The Paris Review Interviews* series, Lillian Bridwell notes that these discussions reveal a wide range of revision strategies among these writers, from rapid producers of text who do little revising as they proceed to writers who move along by revising every sentence (198).

More extensive insights into a variety of composing styles are offered in Tom Waldrep's collection of essays by successful scholars working in composition, *Writers on Writing*. Here too as writers describe their composing processes, we see a variety of approaches, including some writers who plan extensively before their pens hit paper (or before the cursor blips on their screens). Their planning is so complete that their texts generally emerge in a single draft with minor, if any, editing as they write. Self-descriptions of some experienced writers in the field of composition give us vivid accounts of how these one-drafters work. For example, Patricia Y. Murray notes that prior to typing, she sees words, phrases, sentences, and paragraphs taking shape in her head. Her composing, she concludes, has been done before her fingers touch the typewriter, though as she also notes, she revises and edits as she types (234). William Lutz offers a similar account:

> Before I write, I write in my mind. The more difficult and complex the writing, the more time I need to think before I write. Ideas incubate in my mind. While I talk, drive, swim, and exercise I am thinking, planning, writing. I think about the introduction, what examples to use, how to develop the main idea, what kind of conclusion to use. I write, revise, rewrite, agonize, despair, give up, only to start all over again, and all of this before I ever begin to put words on paper. . . . Writing is not a process of discovery for me. . . . The writing process takes place in my mind. Once that process is complete the product emerges. Often I can write pages without pause and with very little, if any, revision or even minor changes. (186–87)

Even with such descriptions from experienced writers, we are hesitant either to discard the notion that writing *is* a process of discovery for many of us or to typecast writers who make many visible changes on the page and/or work through multiple drafts as inadequate writers. After all, many of us, probably the majority, fall somewhere along the continuum from one- to multi-drafters. We may find ourselves as both one- and multi-drafters with the classes of writing that Hairston describes, or we may generally identify ourselves as doing both but also functioning more often as a one- or multi-drafter. Just as we have seen that at one end of the spectrum there are some confirmed one-drafters, so too must we recognize that at the other end of that spectrum there are some confirmed multi-drafters, expert writers for whom extensive revising occurs when writing (so that a piece of discourse may go through several or more drafts or be re-worked heavily as the original draft evolves). David Bartholomae, a self-described multi-drafter, states that he never outlines but works instead with two pads of paper, one to write on and one for making plans, storing sentences, and taking notes. He views his first drafts as disorganized and has to revise extensively, with the result that the revisions bear little resemblance to the first drafts (22–26). Similarly, Lynn Z. Bloom notes that she cannot predict at the outset a great deal of what she is going to say. Only by writing does she learn how her content will develop or how she will handle the structure, organization, and style of her paragraphs, sentences, and whole essay (33).

Thus, if we wish to draw a more inclusive picture of composing behaviors for revision, we have to put together a description that accounts for differences in levels of ability and experience (from novice to expert), for differences in writing tasks, and also for differences in the as yet largely unexplored area of composing process differences among writers. My interest here is in the composing processes of different writers, more particularly, the reality of those writers at either end of that long spectrum, the one-drafters at one end and the multi-drafters at the other. By one-draft writers I mean those writers who construct their plans and the pre-texts that carry out those plans as well as do all or most of the revising of those plans and pre-texts mentally, before transcribing. They do little or no retranscribing. True one-drafters have not arrived at this developmentally or as a result of training in writing, and they should not be confused with other writers who — driven by deadlines, lack of motivation, insufficient experience with writing, or anxieties about "getting it right the first time" — do little or no scratching out of what they have written. Multi-drafters, on the other hand, need to interact with their transcriptions in order to revise. Independent of how much planning they do or pre-text they compose, they continue to revise after they have transcribed words onto paper. Again, true multi-drafters have not reached this stage developmentally or as a result of any intervention by teachers. This is not to say that we can classify writers into two categories, one- and multi-drafters, because all the evidence we have and, more importantly, our own experience tells us that most writers are not one or the other but exist somewhere between these two ends of the continuum.

However, one- and multi-drafters do exist, and we do need to learn more about them to gain a clearer picture not only of what is involved in different revising processes but also to provide a basis for considering the pedagogical implications of dealing with individual differences. There is a strong argument for looking instead at the middle range of writers who do some writing in single drafts and others in multiple drafts or with a lot of retranscribing as they proceed, for it is very probable that the largest number of writers cluster there. But those of us who teach in the individualized setting of conferences or writing lab tutorials know that we can never overlook or put aside the concerns of every unique individual with whom we work. Perhaps we are overly intrigued with individual differences, partly because we see that some students can be ill-served in the group setting of the classrooms and partly because looking at individual differences gives us such enlightening glimpses into the complex reality of composing processes. Clinicians in other fields would argue that looking at the extremes offers a clearer view of what may be involved in the behaviors of the majority. But those who do research in writing also acknowledge that we need to understand dimensions of variation among writers, particularly those patterned differences or "alternate paths to expert performance" that have clear implications for instruction (Freedman et al. 19). In this case, whatever we learn about patterns of behavior among one- and multi-drafters has direct implications for instruction as we need to know the various trade-offs involved in any classroom instruction which would encourage more single or multiple drafting. And, as we will see when looking at what is involved in being able to revise before drafting or in being able to return and re-draft what has been transcribed, there are trade-offs indeed. Whatever arguments are offered, we must also acknowledge that no picture of revision is complete until it includes all that is known and observed about a variety of revision behaviors among writers.

But what do we know about one- and multi-drafters other than anecdotal accounts that confirm their existence? Much evidence is waiting to be gathered from the storehouse of various published interviews in which well-known writers have been asked to describe their writing. And Ann Ruggles Gere's study of the revising behaviors of a blind student gives us a description of a student writer who does not redraft but writes "first draft/final draft" papers, finished products produced in one sitting for her courses as a master's degree candidate. The student describes periods of thinking about a topic before writing. While she doesn't know exactly what she will say until actually writing it, she typically knows what will be contained in the first paragraph as she types the title. Her attention is not focused on words as she concentrates instead on images and larger contexts. A similar description of a one-drafter is found in Joy Reid's "The Radical Outliner and the Radical Brainstormer." Comparing her husband and herself, both composition teachers, Reid notes the differences between herself, an outliner (and a one-drafter), and her husband, a brainstormer (and a multi-drafter), differences which parallel those of the writers in *Writers on Writing* that I have described.

The descriptions of all of the one- and multi-draft writers mentioned so far offer a fairly consistent picture, but these descriptions do little more than reaffirm their existence. In an effort to learn more, I sought out some one- and multi-drafters in order to observe them composing and to explore what might be involved. Since my intent was not to determine the percentage of one- and multi-drafters among any population of writers (though that would be an interesting topic indeed, as I suspect there are more than we may initially guess — or at least more who hover close to either end of the continuum), I sought out experienced writers who identify themselves as very definitely one- or multi-drafters. The subjects I selected for observation were graduate students who teach composition or communications courses, my rationale being that these people can more easily categorize and articulate their own writing habits. From among the group of subjects who described themselves as very definitely either one- or multi-drafters, I selected those who showed evidence of being experienced, competent writers. Of the eight selected subjects (four one-drafters and four multi-drafters), all were at least several years into their graduate studies in English or communications and were either near completion or had recently completed advanced degrees. All had received high scores in standardized tests for verbal skills such as the SAT or GRE exams; all had grade point averages ranging from B+ to A in their graduate courses; and all wrote frequently in a variety of tasks, including academic papers for courses and journal publications, conference papers, the usual business writing of practicing academics (e.g., letters of recommendation for students, memos, instructional materials for classes, etc.), and personal writing such as letters to family and friends. They clearly earned their description as experienced writers. Experienced writers were used because I also wished to exclude those novices who may, through development of their writing skills, change their composing behaviors, and also those novices whose composing habits are the result of other factors such as disinterest (e.g., the one-drafter who habitually begins the paper at 3 a.m. the night before it's due) or anxiety (e.g., the multi-drafter who fears she is never "right" and keeps working and reworking her text).

The experienced writers whom I observed all confirmed that their composing behaviors have not changed over time. That is, they all stated that their writing habits have not altered as they became experienced writers and/or as they moved through writing courses. However, their descriptions of themselves as one- or multi-drafters were not as completely accurate as might be expected. Self-reporting, even among teachers of writing, is not a totally reliable measure. As I observed and talked with the eight writers, I found three very definite one-drafters, Ted, Nina, and Amy; one writer, Jackie, who tends to be a one-drafter but does some revising after writing; two very definite multi-drafters, Bill and Pam; and two writers, Karen and Cindy, who described themselves as multi-drafters and who tend to revise extensively but who can also produce first draft/final draft writing under some conditions. To gather data on their composing behaviors, I interviewed each person for an hour, asking questions about the types of writing they do, the activities they engage in before writing, the details of what happens as they write, their revision behaviors, the manner in which sentences are composed, and their attitudes and past history of writing. Each person was also asked to spend an hour writing in response to an assignment. The specific assignment was a request from an academic advisor asking for the writers' descriptions of the skills needed to succeed in their field of study. As they wrote, all eight writers were asked to give thinking-aloud protocols and were videotaped for future study. Brief interviews after writing focused on eliciting information about how accurately the writing session reflected their general writing habits and behaviors. Each type of information collected is, at best, incomplete because accounts of one's own composing processes may not be entirely accurate, because thinking-aloud protocols while writing are only partial accounts of what is being thought about, and because one-hour writing tasks preclude observing some of the kinds of activities that writers report. But even with these limitations I observed patterns of composing behaviors that should differentiate one-draft writers from multi-draft writers.

Preference for Beginning with a Developed Focus vs. Preference for Beginning at an Exploratory Stage

Among the consistent behaviors that one-drafters report is the point at which they can and will start writing. All of the four one-drafters expressed a strong need to clarify their thinking prior to beginning to transcribe. They are either not ready to write or cannot write until they have a focus and organization in mind. They may, as I observed Jackie and Ted doing, make some brief planning notes on paper or, as Amy and Nina did, sit for awhile and mentally plan, but all expressed a clearly articulated need to know beforehand the direction the piece of writing would take. For Nina's longer papers, she described a planning schedule in which the focus comes first, even before collecting notes. Ted too described the first stage of a piece of writing as being a time of mentally narrowing a topic. During incubation times before writing, two of these writers described some global recasting of a paper in their minds while the other two expressed a need to talk it out, either to themselves or friends. There is little resorting of written notes and little use of written outlines, except for some short lists, described by Ted as "memory jogs" to use while he writes. Amy explained that she sometimes felt that in high school or as an undergraduate she should have written outlines to please her teachers, but she never did get around to it because outlines served no useful purpose for her. Consistent throughout these accounts and in my observation of their writing was these writers' need to know where they are headed beforehand and a feeling that they are not ready to write — or cannot write — until they are at that stage. When asked if they ever engaged in freewriting, two one-drafters said they could not, unless forced to, plunge in and write without a focus and a mental plan. Ted, in particular, noted that the notion of exploration during writing would make him so uncomfortable that he would probably block and be unable to write.

In contrast to the one-drafters' preference for knowing their direction before writing, the two consistent multi-drafters, Pam and Bill, explained that they resist knowing, resist any attempt at clarification prior to writing. Their preference is for open-ended exploration as they write. They may have been reading and thinking extensively beforehand, but the topic has not taken shape when they decide that it is time to begin writing. Bill reported that he purposely starts with a broad topic while Pam said that she looks for something "broad or ambiguous" or "something small that can grow and grow." As Bill explained, he doesn't like writing about what he already knows as that would be boring. Pam too expressed her resistance to knowing her topic and direction beforehand in terms of how boring it would be. Generally, Bill will do about four or five drafts as he works through the early parts of a paper, perhaps two to four pages, before he knows what he will write about. He and Pam allow for — and indeed expect — that their topic will change as they write. Pam explained: "I work by allowing the direction of the work to change if it needs to. . . . I have to allow things to go where they need to go." When I observed them writing, Pam spent considerable time planning and creating pre-texts before short bursts of transcribing while Bill wrote several different versions of an introduction and, with some cutting and pasting, was about ready to define his focus at the end of the hour. He reported that he depends heavily on seeing what he has written in order to find his focus, choose his content, and organize. Pam also noted that she needs to see chunks of what she has transcribed to see where the piece of discourse is taking her.

The other two writers who characterized themselves as multi-drafters, Karen and Cindy, both described a general tendency to plunge in before the topic is clear. Karen said that she can't visualize her arguments until she writes them out and generally writes and rewrites as she proceeds, but for writing tasks that she described as "formulaic" in that they are familiar because she has written similar pieces of discourse, she can write quickly and finish quickly — as she did with the writing task for this study. Since she had previously written the same kind of letter assigned in this study, she did not engage in the multi-drafting that would be more characteristic, she says, of her general composing behaviors. Cindy, the other self-described multi-drafter, almost completed the task in a single draft, though as she explained with short pieces, she can revert to her "journalistic mode" of writing, having been a working journalist for a number of years. For longer papers, such as those required in graduate courses, her descriptions sound much like those of Bill, Pam, and Karen. All of these writers, though, share the unifying characteristic of beginning to write before the task is well defined in their minds, unlike the one-drafters who do not write at that stage.

Preference for Limiting Options vs. Preference for Open-ended Exploring

Another consistent and clearly related difference between one- and multi-drafters is the difference in the quantity of options they will generate, from words and sentences to whole sections of a paper, and the way in which they will evaluate those options. As they wrote, all four of the one-drafters limited their options by generating several choices and then making a decision fairly quickly. There were numerous occasions in the think-aloud protocols of three of the four one-drafters in which they would stop, try another word, question a phrase, raise the possibility of another idea to include, and then make a quick decision. When Ted re-read one of his paragraphs, he saw a different direction that he might have taken that would perhaps be better, but he accepted what he had. ("That'll do here, OK . . . OK" he said to himself and moved on.) Nina, another one-drafter, generated no alternate options aloud as she wrote.

As is evident in this description of one-drafters, they exhibited none of the agonizing over possibilities that other writers experience, and they appear to be able to accept their choices quickly and move on. While observers may question whether limiting options in this manner cuts off further discovery and possibly better solutions or whether the internal debate goes on prior to transcribing, one-drafters are obviously efficient writers. They generate fewer choices, reach decisions more quickly, and do most or all of the decision-making before transcribing on paper. Thus, three of the four one-drafters finished the paper in the time allotted, and the fourth writer was almost finished. They can pace themselves fairly accurately too, giving me their estimates of how long it takes them to write papers of particular lengths. All four one-drafters describe themselves as incurable procrastinators who begin even long papers the night before they are due, allowing themselves about the right number of hours in which to transcribe their mental constructs onto paper. Nina explained that she makes choices quickly because she is always writing at the last minute under pressure and doesn't have time to consider more options. Another one-drafter offered a vivid description of the tension and stress that can be involved in these last minute, all-night sessions.

While they worry about whether they will finish on time, these one-drafters generally do. Contributing to their efficiency are two time-saving procedures involved as they get words on paper. Because most decisions are made before they commit words to paper, they do little or no scratching out and re-writing; and they do a minimum of re-reading both as they proceed and also when they are finished. The few changes I observed being made were either single words or a few short phrases, unlike the multi-drafters who rejected or scratched out whole sentences and paragraphs. As Nina wrote, she never re-read her developing text, though she reported that she does a little re-reading when she is finished with longer papers. The tinkering with words that she might do then, she says, is counterproductive because she rarely feels that she is improving the text with these changes. (Nina and the other one-drafters would probably be quite successful at the kind of "invisible writing" that has been investigated, that is, writing done under conditions in which writers cannot see what they are writing or scan as they progress. See Blau.)

In contrast to the one-drafters' limited options, quick decisions, few changes on paper and little or no re-reading, the multi-drafters were frequently observed generating and exploring many options, spending a long time in making their choices, and making frequent and large-scale changes on paper. Bill said that he produces large quantities of text because he needs to see it in order to see if he wants to retain it, unlike the one-drafters who exhibit little or no need to examine their developing text. Moreover, as Bill noted, the text he generates is also on occasion a heuristic for more text. As he writes, Bill engages in numerous revising tactics. He writes a sentence, stops to examine it by switching it around, going back to add clauses, or combining it with other text on the same page or a different sheet of paper. For the assigned writing task, he began with one sheet of paper, moved to another, tore off some of it and discarded it, and added part back to a previous sheet. At home when writing a longer paper, he will similarly engage in extensive cutting and pasting. In a somewhat different manner, Pam did not generate as many options on paper for this study. Instead, her protocol recorded various alternative plans and pre-texts that she would stop to explore verbally for five or ten minutes before transcribing anything. What she did write, though, was often heavily edited so that at the end of the hour, she, like Bill, had only progressed somewhat through an introductory paragraph of several sentences. Thus, while Bill had produced large amounts of text on paper that were later rejected after having been written, Pam spent more of her time generating and rejecting plans and pre-texts than crossing out transcriptions.

Writing is a more time-consuming task for these multi-drafters because they expect to produce many options and a large amount of text that will be discarded. Both Bill and Pam described general writing procedures in which they begin by freewriting, and, as they proceed, distilling from earlier drafts what will be used in later drafts. Both proceed incrementally, that is, by starting in and then starting again before finishing a whole draft. Both writers are used to re-reading frequently, partly to locate what Pam called "key elements" that will be retained for later drafts and partly, as Bill explained, because the act of generating more options and exploring them causes him to lose track of where he is.

Because both Bill and Pam seem to be comfortable when working within an as-yet only partially focused text, it would be interesting to explore what has been termed their "tolerance for ambiguity," a trait defined as a person's ability to function calmly in a situation in which interpretation of all stimuli is not completely clear. (See Budner, and Frenkel-Brunswick.) People who have little or no tolerance for ambiguity perceive ambiguous situations as sources of psychological discomfort, and they may try to reach conclusions quickly rather than to take the time to consider all of the essential elements of an unclear situation. People with more tolerance for ambiguity enjoy being in ambiguous situations and tend to seek them out. The relevance here, of course, is the question of whether one-drafters will not begin until they have structured the task and will also move quickly to conclusions in part, at least, because of having some degree of intolerance for ambiguity. This might be a fruitful area for further research.

For those interested in the mental processes which accompany behaviors, another dimension to explore is the Myers-Briggs Type Indicator (MBTI), a measure of expressed preferences (i.e., not performance tasks) in four bipolar dimensions of personality. The work of George H. Jensen and John K. DiTiberio has indicated some relationships between the personality types identified by the MBTI and writing processes. Of particular interest here is that Bill, who had independently taken the MBTI for other reasons, reported that he scored highly in the dimensions of "extraversion" and "perceiving." Extraverts, say Jensen and DiTiberio, "often leap into tasks with little planning, then rely on trial and error to complete the task" (288), and they "often find freewriting a good method for developing ideas, for they think better when writing quickly, impulsively, and uncritically" (289). Perceivers, another type described by Jensen and DiTiberio, appear to share tendencies similar to those with a tolerance for ambiguity, for perceivers "are willing to leave the outer world unstructured. . . . Quickly made decisions narrow their field of vision" (295). Perceiving types tend to select broad topics for writing, like a wide range of alternatives, and always want to read one more book on the subject. Their revisions thus often need to be refocused (296). The similarities here to Bill's writing behaviors show us that while the MBTI is somewhat circular in that the scoring is a reflection of people's self-description, it can confirm (and perhaps clarify) the relationship of writing behaviors to more general human behaviors.

The Preference for Closure vs. Resistance to Closure

From these descriptions of one- and multi-drafters it is readily apparent that they differ in their need for closure. The one-drafters move quickly to decisions while composing, and they report that once they are done with a paper, they prefer not to look back at it, either immediately to re-read it or at some future time, to think about revising it. Ted explained that he generally is willing to do one rereading at the time of completing a paper and sometimes to make a few wording changes, but that is all. He shrugged off the possibility of doing even a second re-reading of any of his writing once it is done because he says he can't stand to look at it again. All of the one-drafters reported that they hardly, if ever, rewrite a paper. This distaste for returning to a completed text can be the source of problems for these one-drafters. Forced by a teacher in a graduate course who wanted first drafts one week and revisions the next week, Nina explained that she deliberately resorted to "writing a bad paper" for the first submission in order to submit her "real" draft as the "revised" paper. Writing a series of drafts is clearly harder for one-drafters such as Nina than we have yet acknowledged.

These one-drafters are as reluctant to start as they are impatient to finish. Although they tend to delay the drafting process, this does not apply to their preparation, which often starts well in advance and is the "interesting" or "enjoyable" part for them. With writing that produces few surprises or discoveries for any of them because the generative process precedes transcription, drafting on paper is more "tedious" (a word they frequently used during their interviews) than for other writers. Said Ted, "Writing is something I have to do, not something I want to do." Even Jackie, who allows for some revising while drafting in order to develop the details of her plan, reported that she has a hard time going back to revise a paper once it is completed. She, like the others, reported a sense of feeling the paper is over and done with. "Done, dead and done, done, finished, done," concluded another of these one-drafters.

On the other hand, the multi-drafters observed in this study explained that they are never done with a paper. They can easily and willingly go back to it or to keep writing indefinitely. Asked when they know they are finished, Bill and Pam explained that they never feel they are "done" with a piece of discourse, merely that they have to stop in order to meet a deadline. As Pam said, she never gets to a last draft and doesn't care about producing "neat packages." Understandably, she has trouble with conclusions and with "wrapping up" at the end of a piece of discourse. Asked how pervasive her redrafting is for all of her writing, Pam commented that she writes informal letters to parents and friends every day and is getting to the point that she doesn't rewrite these letters as much. Bill too noted that he fights against products and hates to finish. As a result, both Bill and Pam often fail to meet their deadlines. Cindy, bored by her "journalistic one-draft writing," expressed a strong desire to return to some of her previously completed papers in order to rewrite them.

Writer-Based vs. Reader-Based Early Drafts

One way of distinguishing the early drafts produced by the multi-drafters for this study from the drafts produced by the one-drafters is to draw upon Linda Flower's distinction between Writer-Based and Reader-Based prose. Writer-Based prose, explains Flower, is "verbal expression written by a writer to himself and for himself. It is the working of his own verbal thought. In its *structure,* Writer-Based prose reflects the associative, narrative path of the writer's own confrontation with her subject" (19–20). Reader-Based prose, on the other hand, is "a deliberate attempt to communicate something to a reader. To do that it creates a shared language and shared context between writer and reader. It also offers the reader an issue-oriented rhetorical structure rather than a replay of the writer's discovery process" (20). Although Flower acknowledges that Writer-Based prose is a "problem" that composition courses are designed to correct, she also affirms its usefulness as a search tool, a strategy for handling the difficulty of attending to multiple complex tasks simultaneously. Writer-Based prose needs to be revised into Reader-Based prose, but it can be effective as a "medium for thinking." And for the multi-drafters observed in this study, characterizing the initial drafts of two of the multi-drafters as Writer-Based helps to see how their early drafts differ from those of the one-drafters.

One feature of Writer-Based prose, as offered by Flower, is that it reflects the writer's method of searching by means of surveying what she knows, often in a narrative manner. Information tends to be structured as a narrative of the discovery process or as a survey of the data in the writer's mind. Reader-Based prose, on the other hand, restructures the information so that it is accessible to the reader. Both the protocols and the written drafts produced by the two confirmed multi-drafters, Bill and Pam, reveal this Writer-Based orientation as their initial way into writing. Bill very clearly began with a memory search through his own experience, made some brief notes, and then wrote a narrative as his first sentence in response to the request that he describe to an academic counselor the skills needed for his field: "I went through what must have been a million different majors before I wound up in English and it was actually my first choice." Pam spent the hour exploring the appropriateness of the term "skills."

In distinct contrast, all four of the one-drafters began by constructing a conceptual framework for the response they would write, most typically by defining a few categories or headings which would be the focus or main point of the paper. With a few words in mind that indicated his major points, Ted then moved on to ask himself who would be reading his response, what the context would be, and what format the writing would use. He moved quickly from a search for a point to considerations of how his audience would use his information. Similarly, Amy rather promptly chose a few terms, decided to herself that "that'll be the focus," and then said, "OK, I'm trying to get into a role here. I'm responding to someone who . . . This is not something they are going to give out to people. But they're going to read it and compile responses, put something together for themselves." She then began writing her draft and completed it within the hour. Asked what constraints and concerns she is most aware of when actually writing, Amy said that she is generally concerned with clarity for the reader. The point of contrast here is that the search process was both different in kind and longer for the multi-drafters. Initially, their time was spent discovering what they think about the subject, whereas the one-drafters chose a framework within a few minutes and moved on to orient their writing to their readers. Because the transformation or reworking of text comes later for the multi-drafters, rewriting is a necessary component of their writing. The standard bit of advice, about writing the introductory paragraph later, would be a necessary step for them but would not be a productive or appropriate strategy for one-drafters to try. For the one-drafters, the introductory paragraph is the appropriate starting point. In fact, given what they said about the necessity of knowing their focus beforehand, the introductory paragraph is not merely appropriate but necessary.

Because the early stages of a piece of writing are, for multi-drafters, so intricately bound up with mental searching, surveying, and discovering, the writing that is produced is not oriented to the reader. For their early drafts, Bill and Pam both acknowledged that their writing is not yet understandable to others. When Pam commented that in her early drafts, "the reader can't yet see where I'm going," she sighed over the difficulties this had caused in trying to work with her Master's thesis committee. If some writers' early drafts are so personal and so unlikely to be accessible to readers, it is worth speculating about how effective peer editing sessions could be for such multi-drafters who appear in classrooms with "rough drafts" as instructed.

Conclusions

One way to summarize the characteristics of one- and multi-drafters is to consider what they gain by being one-drafters and at what cost they gain these advantages. Clearly, one-drafters are efficient writers. This efficiency is achieved by mentally revising beforehand, by generating options verbally rather than on paper, by generating only a limited number of options before settling on one and getting on with the task, and by doing little or no re-reading. They are able to pace themselves and can probably perform comfortably in situations such as the workplace or in in-class writing where it is advantageous to produce first-draft, final-draft pieces of discourse. Their drafts are readily accessible to readers, and they can expend effort early on in polishing the text for greater clarity. But at what cost? One-drafters are obviously in danger of cutting themselves off from further exploration, from a richer field of discovery than is possible during the time in which they generate options. When they exhibit a willingness to settle on one of their options, they may thereby have eliminated the possibility of searching for a better one. In their impatience to move on, they may even settle on options they know could be improved on. Their impulse to write dwindles as these writers experience little or none of the excitement of discovery or exploration during writing. The interesting portion of a writing task, the struggle with text and sense of exploration, is largely completed when they begin to commit themselves to paper (or computer screen). Because they are less likely to enjoy writing, the task of starting is more likely to be put off to the last minute and to become a stressful situation, thus reinforcing their inclination not to re-read and their desire to be done and to put the paper forever behind them once they have finished. And it appears that it is as hard for true one-drafters to suspend the need for closure as it is for multi-drafters to reach quick decisions and push themselves rapidly toward closure.

Multi-drafters appear to be the flip side of the same coin. Their relative inefficiency causes them to miss deadlines, to create Writer-Based first drafts, to produce large quantities of text that is discarded, and to get lost in their own writing. They need to re-read and re-draft, and they probably appear at first glance to be poorer writers than one-drafters. But they are more likely to be writers who will plunge in eagerly, will write and re-write, and will use writing to explore widely and richly. They also are more likely to affirm the value of writing as a heuristic, the merits of freewriting, and the need for cutting and pasting of text. They may, if statistics are gathered, be the writers who benefit most from collaborative discussions such as those in writing labs with tutors. Their drafts are truly amenable to change and available for re-working.

Implications

Acknowledging the reality of one- and multi-drafting involves enlarging both our perspectives on revision and our instructional practices with students. In terms of what the reality of one-drafting and multi-drafting tells us about revision, it is apparent that we need to account for this diversity of revision behaviors as we construct a more detailed picture of revision. As Stephen Witte notes, "revising research that limits itself to examining changes in written text or drafts espouses a reductionist view of revising as a stage in a linear sequence of stages" ("Revising" 266). Revision can and does occur when writers set goals, create plans, and compose pre-text, as well as when they transcribe and re-draft after transcription. Revision can be triggered by cognitive activity alone and/or by interaction with text; and attitudes, preferences, and cognitive make-up play a role in when and how much a writer revises — or is willing to revise — a text.

Yet, while recognizing the many dimensions to be explored in understanding revision, we can also use this diversity as a source for helping students with different types of problems and concerns. For students who are one-drafters or have tendencies toward single drafting, we need to provide help in several areas. They'll have to learn to do more reviewing of written text both as they write and afterwards, in order to evaluate and revise. They will also need to be aware that they should have strategies that provide for more exploration and invention than they may presently allow themselves. While acknowledging their distaste for returning to a draft to open it up again, we also need to help them see how and when this can be productive. Moreover, we can provide assistance in helping one-drafters and other writers who cluster near that end of the spectrum recognize that sometimes they have a preference for choosing an option even after they recognize that it may not be the best one. When Tim, one of the one-drafters I observed, noted at one point in his protocol that he should take a different direction for one of his paragraphs but won't, he shows similarities to another writer, David, observed by Witte ("Pre-Text and Composing" 406), who is reluctant to spend more than fifteen seconds reworking a sentence in pre-text, even though he demonstrates the ability to evoke criteria that could lead to better formulations if he chose to stop and revise mentally (David typically does little revision of written text). This impatience, this need to keep moving along, that does not always allow for the production of good text, can obviously work against producing good text, and it is unlikely that such writers will either recognize or conquer the problem on their own. They may have snared themselves in their own vicious circles if their tendency to procrastinate puts them in a deadline crunch, which, in turn, does not afford them the luxury of time to consider new options. Such behaviors can become a composing habit so entrenched that it is no longer noticed.

As we work with one-drafters, we will also have to learn ourselves how to distinguish them from writers who see themselves as one-drafters because they are not inclined, for one reason or another, to expend more energy on drafting. Inertia, lack of motivation, lack of information about what multiple drafts can do, higher priorities for other tasks, and so on are not characteristic of true one-drafters, and we must be able to identify the writer who might take refuge behind a label of "one-drafter" from the writer who exhibits some or many of the characteristics of one-draft composing and who wants to become a better writer. For example, in our writing lab I have worked with students who think they are one-drafters because of assorted fears, anxieties, and misinformation. "But I have to get it right the first time," "My teachers never liked to see scratching out on the paper, even when we wrote in class," or "I hate making choices, so I go with what I have" are not the comments of true one-drafters.

With multiple-drafters we have other work to do. To become more efficient writers, they will need to become more proficient planners and creators of pre-text, though given their heavy dependence on seeing what they have written, they will probably still rely a great deal on reading and working with their transcribed text. They will also need to become more proficient at times at focusing on a topic quickly, recognizing the difficulties involved in agonizing endlessly over possibilities. In the words of a reviewer of this paper, they will have to learn when and how "to get on with it."

Besides assisting with these strategies, we can help students become more aware of their composing behaviors. We can assist multi-drafters in recognizing that they are not slow or inept writers but writers who may linger too long over making choices. For writers who have difficulty returning to a completed text in order to revise, we can relate the problem to the larger picture, an impatience with returning to any completed task. Granted, this is not a giant leap forward, but too many students are willing to throw in the towel with writing skills in particular without recognizing the link to their more general orientations to life. Similarly, the impatient writer who, like Ted, proclaims to have a virulent case of the "I-hate-to-write" syndrome may be a competent one-drafter (or have a preference for fewer drafts) who needs to see that it is the transcribing stage of writing that is the source of the impatience, procrastination, and irritation. On the other hand, writers more inclined to be multi-drafters need to recognize that their frustration, self-criticism, and/or low grades may be due to having readers intervene at too early a stage in the drafting. What I am suggesting here is that some writers unknowingly get themselves caught in linguistic traps. They think they are making generalizations about the whole act of "writing," that blanket term for all the processes involved, when they may well be voicing problems or attitudes about one or another of the processes. What is needed here is some assistance in helping students define their problems more precisely. To do this, classroom teachers can open conferences like a writing lab tutorial, by asking questions about the student's writing processes and difficulties.

In addition to individualizing our work with students, we can also look at our own teaching practices. When we offer classroom strategies and heuristics, we need to remind our students that it is likely that some will be very inappropriate for different students. Being unable to freewrite is not necessarily a sign of an inept writer. One writer's written text may be just as effective a heuristic for that writer as the planning sheets are for another writer. Beyond these strategies and acknowledgments, we have to examine how we talk about or teach composing processes. There is a very real danger in imposing a single, "ideal" composing style on students, as Jack Selzer found teachers attempting to do in his survey of the literature. Similarly, as Susan McLeod notes, teachers tend to teach their own composing behaviors in the classroom and are thus in danger either of imposing their redrafting approaches on students whose preference for revising prior to transcribing serves them well or of touting their one- or few-draft strategies to students who fare better when interacting with their transcribed text. Imposing personal preferences, observes McLeod, would put us in the peculiar position of trying to fix something that isn't broken. And there's enough of that going around as it is.

Works Cited

Axelrod, Rise B., and Charles R. Cooper. *The St. Martin's Guide to Writing.* New York: St. Martin's, 1985.

Bartholomae, David. "Against the Grain." Waldrep I:19–29.

Beach, Richard. "Self-Evaluation Strategies of Extensive Revisers and Nonrevisers." *College Composition and Communication* 27 (1976): 160–64.

Blau, Sheridan. "Invisible Writing: Investigating Cognitive Processes in Composition." *College Composition and Communication* 34 (1983): 297–312.

Bloom, Lynn Z. "How I Write." Waldrep I:31–37.

Bridwell, Lillian S. "Revising Strategies in Twelfth Grade Students' Transactional Writing." *Research in the Teaching of English* 14 (1980): 197–222.

Budner, S. "Intolerance of Ambiguity as a Personality Variable." *Journal of Personality* 30 (1962): 29–50.

Faigley, Lester, and Stephen Witte. "Analyzing Revision." *College Composition and Communication* 32 (1981): 400–14.

Flower, Linda. "Writer-Based Prose: A Cognitive Basis for Problems in Writing." *College English* 41 (1979): 19–37.

Flower, Linda, John R. Hayes, Linda Carey, Karen Shriver, and James Stratman. "Detection, Diagnosis, and the Strategies of Revision." *College Composition and Communication* 37 (1986): 16–55.

Freedman, Sarah Warshauer, Anne Haas Dyson, Linda Flower, and Wallace Chafe. *Research in Writing: Past, Present, and Future.* Technical Report No. 1. Center for the Study of Writing. Berkeley: University of California, 1987.

Frenkel-Brunswick, Else. "Intolerance of Ambiguity as an Emotional and Perceptual Personality Variable." *Journal of Personality* 18 (1949): 108–43.

Gere, Ann Ruggles. "Insights from the Blind: Composing without Revising." *Revising: New Essays for Teachers of Writing.* Ed. Ronald Sudol. Urbana, IL: ERIC/NCTE, 1982. 52–70.

Hairston, Maxine. "Different Products, Different Processes: A Theory about Writing." *College Composition and Communication* 37 (1986): 442–52.

Henley, Joan. "A Revisionist View of Revision." *Washington English Journal* 8.2 (1986): 5–7.

Jensen, George, and John DiTiberio. "Personality and Individual Writing Processes." *College Composition and Communication* 35 (1984): 285–300.

Lutz, William. "How I Write." Waldrep I:183–88.

McLeod, Susan. "The New Orthodoxy: Rethinking the Process Approach." *Freshman English News* 14.3 (1986): 16-21.

Murray, Patricia Y. "Doing Writing." Waldrep I:225–39.

Reid, Joy. "The Radical Outliner and the Radical Brainstormer: A Perspective on Composing Processes." *TESOL Quarterly* 18 (1985): 529–34.

Selzer, Jack. "Exploring Options in Composing." *College Composition and Communication* 35 (1984): 276–84.

Sommers, Nancy. "Revision Strategies of Student Writers and Experienced Adult Writers." *College Composition and Communication* 31 (1980): 378–88.

Waldrep, Tom, ed. *Writers on Writing. Vol. 1.* New York: Random House, 1985. 2 vols.

Witte, Stephen P. "Pre-Text and Composing." *College Composition and Communication* 38 (1987): 397–425.

———. "Revising, Composing Theory, and Research Design." *The Acquisition of Written Language: Response and Revision.* Ed. Sarah Warshauer Freedman. Norwood, NJ: Ablex, 1985. 250–84.

REVISION STRATEGIES OF STUDENT WRITERS AND EXPERIENCED ADULT WRITERS

Nancy Sommers

[*College Composition and Communication* 31 (1980): 378–88.]

Nancy Sommers is the Sosland Director of Expository Writing at Harvard University. She is widely known for her work on the revision process and on responding to student writing. Sommers currently serves as the series editor for the Prentice Hall Studies in Writing and Culture. Her articles and chapters have appeared in a wide range of scholarly publications. She received the Promising Research Award from NCTE in 1979 and has twice won the Richard Braddock Award from CCCC, in 1983 and in 1993.

This study was among the first to investigate with any methodological rigor the revision process of specific writers, and Sommers's findings caused writing teachers to reconsider how they present revision to their students. *The Bedford Handbook*'s extensive section on revision recognizes implicitly the results of Sommers's research, emphasizing the creative, cyclical, recursive nature of revision.

Although various aspects of the writing process have been studied extensively of late, research on revision has been notably absent. The reason for this, I suspect, is that current models of the writing process have directed attention away from revision. With few exceptions, these models are linear; they separate the writing process into discrete stages. Two representative models are Gordon Rohman's suggestion that the composing process moves from prewriting to writing to rewriting and James Britton's model of the writing process as a series of stages described in metaphors of linear growth, conception — incubation — production.[1] What is striking about these theories of writing is that they model themselves on speech: Rohman defines the writer in a way that cannot distinguish him from a speaker ("A writer is a man who . . . puts [his] experience into words in his own mind" — p. 15); and Britton bases his theory of writing on what he calls (following Jakobson) the "expressiveness" of speech.[2] Moreover, Britton's study itself follows the "linear model" of the relation of thought and language in speech proposed by Vygotsky, a relationship embodied in the linear movement "from the motive which engenders a thought to the shaping of the thought, *first* in inner speech, *then* in meanings of words, and *finally* in words" (quoted in Britton, p. 40). What this movement fails to take into account in its linear structure — "first . . . then . . . finally" — is the recursive shaping of thought by language; what it fails to take into account is *revision*. In these linear conceptions of the writing process revision is understood as a separate stage at the end of the process — a stage that comes after the completion of a first or second draft and one that is temporally distinct from the prewriting and writing stages of the process.[3]

The linear model bases itself on speech in two specific ways. First of all, it is based on traditional rhetorical models, models that were created to serve the spoken art of oratory. In whatever ways the parts of classical rhetoric are described, they offer "stages" of composition that are repeated in contemporary models of the writing process. Edward Corbett, for instance, describes the "five parts of a discourse" — *inventio, dispositio, elocutio, memoria, pronuntiatio* — and, disregarding the last two parts since "after rhetoric came to be concerned mainly with written discourse, there was no further need to deal with them,"[4] he produces a model very close to Britton's conception [*inventio*], incubation [*dispositio*], production [*elocutio*]. Other rhetorics also follow this procedure, and they do so not simply because of historical accident. Rather, the process represented in the linear model is based on the irreversibility of speech. Speech, Roland Barthes says, "is irreversible":

> A word cannot be retracted, except precisely by saying that one retracts it. To cross out here is to add: If I want to erase what I have just said, I cannot do it without showing the eraser itself (I must say: "*or rather . . .*" "*I expressed myself badly . . .*"); paradoxically, it is ephemeral speech which is indelible, not monumental writing. All that one can do in the case of a spoken utterance is to tack on another utterance.[5]

What is impossible in speech is *revision*: Like the example Barthes gives, revision in speech is an afterthought. In the same way, each stage of the linear model must be exclusive (distinct from the other stages) or else it becomes trivial and counterproductive to refer to these junctures as "stages."

By staging revision after enunciation, the linear models reduce revision in writing, as in speech, to no more than an afterthought. In this way such models make the study of revision impossible. Revision, in Rohman's model, is simply the repetition of writing; or to pursue Britton's organic metaphor, revision is simply the further growth of what is already there, the "preconceived" product. The absence of research on revision, then, is a function of a theory of writing which makes revision both superfluous and redundant, a theory which does not distinguish between writing and speech.

What the linear models do produce is a parody of writing. Isolating revision and then disregarding it plays havoc with the experiences composition teachers have of the actual writing and rewriting of experienced writers. Why should the linear model be preferred? Why should revision be forgotten, superfluous? Why do teachers offer the linear model and students accept it? One reason, Barthes suggests, is that "there is a fundamental tie between teaching and speech," while "writing begins at the point where speech becomes *impossible*."[6] The spoken word cannot be revised. The possibility of revision distinguishes the written text from speech. In fact, according to Barthes, this is the essential difference between writing and speaking. When we must revise, when the very idea is subject to recursive shaping by language, then speech becomes inadequate. This is a matter to which I will return, but first we should examine, theoretically, a detailed exploration of what student writers as distinguished from experienced adult writers *do* when they write and rewrite their work. Dissatisfied with both the linear model of writing and the lack of attention to the process of revision, I conducted a series of studies over the past three years which examined the revision processes of student writers and experienced writers to see what role revision played in their writing processes. In the course of my work the revision process was redefined as *a sequence of changes in a composition — changes which are initiated by cues and occur continually throughout the writing of a work.*

Methodology

I used a case study approach. The student writers were twenty freshmen at Boston University and the University of Oklahoma with SAT verbal scores ranging from 450 to 600 in their first semester of composition. The twenty experienced adult writers from Boston and Oklahoma City included journalists, editors, and academics. To refer to the two groups, I use the terms *student writers* and *experienced writers* because the principal difference between these two groups is the amount of experience they had in writing.

Each writer wrote three essays, expressive, explanatory, and persuasive, and rewrote each essay twice, producing nine written products in draft and final form. Each writer was interviewed three times after the final revision of each essay. And each writer suggested revisions for a composition written by an anonymous author. Thus extensive written and spoken documents were obtained from each writer.

The essays were analyzed by counting and categorizing the changes made. Four revision operations were identified: deletion, substitution, addition, and reordering. And four levels of changes were identified: word, phrase, sentence, theme (the extended statement of one idea). A coding system was developed for identifying the frequency of revision by level and operation. In addition, transcripts of the interviews in which the writers interpreted their revisions were used to develop what was called a *scale of concerns* for each writer. This scale enabled me to codify what were the writer's primary concerns, secondary concerns, tertiary concerns, and whether the writers used the same scale of concerns when revising the second or third drafts as they used in revising the first draft.

Revision Strategies of Student Writers

Most of the students I studied did not use the term *revision* or *rewriting.* In fact, they did not seem comfortable using the word *revision* and explained that revision was not a word they used, but the word their teachers used. Instead, most of the students had developed various functional terms to describe the type of changes they made. The following are samples of these definitions:

> *Scratch Out and Do Over Again:* "I say scratch out and do over, and that means what it says. Scratching out and cutting out. I read what I have written and I cross out a word and put another word in; a more decent word or a better word. Then if there is somewhere to use a sentence that I have crossed out, I will put it there."

> *Reviewing:* "Reviewing means just using better words and eliminating words that are not needed. I go over and change words around."

> *Reviewing:* "I just review every word and make sure that everything is worded right. I see if I am rambling; I see if I can put a better word in or leave one out. Usually when I read what I have written, I say to myself, 'that word is so bland or so trite,' and then I go and get my thesaurus."

> *Redoing:* "Redoing means cleaning up the paper and crossing out. It is looking at something and saying, no that has to go, or no, that is not right."

> *Marking Out:* "I don't use the word *rewriting* because I only write one draft and the changes that I made are made on top of the draft. The changes that I made are usually just marking out words and putting different ones in."

> *Slashing and Throwing Out:* "I throw things out and say they are not good. I like to write like Fitzgerald did by inspiration, and if I feel inspired then I don't need to slash and throw much out."

The predominant concern in these definitions is vocabulary. The students understand the revision process as a rewording activity. They do so because they perceive words as the unit of written discourse. That is, they concentrate on particular words apart from their role in the text. Thus one student quoted above thinks in terms of dictionaries, and, following the eighteenth-century theory of words parodied in *Gulliver's Travels,* he imagines a load of things carried about to be exchanged. Lexical changes are the major revision activities of the students because economy is their goal. They are governed, like the linear model itself, by the Law of Occam's razor that prohibits logically needless repetition: redundancy and superfluity. Nothing governs speech more than such superfluities; speech constantly repeats itself precisely because spoken words, as Barthes writes, are expendable in the cause of communication. The aim of revision according to the students' own description is therefore to clean up speech; the redundancy of speech is unnecessary in writing, their logic suggests, because writing, unlike speech, can be reread. Thus one student said, "Redoing means cleaning up the paper and crossing out." The remarkable contradiction of cleaning by marking might, indeed, stand for student revision as I have encountered it.

The students place a symbolic importance on their selection and rejection of words as the determiners of success or failure for their compositions. When revising, they primarily ask themselves: Can I find a better word or phrase? A more impressive, not so clichéd, or less humdrum word? Am I repeating the same word or phrase too often? They approach the revision process with what could be labeled as a "thesaurus philosophy of writing"; the students consider the thesaurus a harvest of lexical substitutions and believe that most problems in their essays can be solved by rewording. What is revealed in the students' use of the thesaurus is a governing attitude toward their writing: that the meaning to be communicated is already there, already finished, already produced, ready to be communicated, and all that is necessary is a better word "rightly worded." One student defined revision as "redoing"; "redoing" meant "just using better words and eliminating words that are not needed." For the students, writing is translating: the thought to the page, the language of speech to the more formal language of prose, the word to its synonym. Whatever is translated, an original text already exists for students, one which need not be discovered or acted upon, but simply communicated.[7]

The students list repetition as one of the elements they most worry about. This cue signals to them that they need to eliminate the repetition either by substituting or deleting words or phrases. Repetition occurs, in large part, because student writing imitates — transcribes — speech; attention to repetitious words is a manner of cleaning speech. Without a sense of the developmental possibilities of revision (and writing in general) students seek, on the authority of many textbooks, simply to clean up their language and prepare to type. What is curious, however, is that students are aware of lexical repetition, but not conceptual repetition. They only notice the repetition if they can "hear" it; they do not diagnose lexical repetition as symptomatic of problems on a deeper level. By rewording their sentences to avoid the lexical repetition, the students solve the immediate problem but blind themselves to problems on a textual level; although they are using different words, they are sometimes merely restating the same idea with different words. Such blindness, as I discovered with student writers, is the inability to "see" revision as a process: the inability to "re-view" their work again, as it were, with different eyes, and to start over.

The revision strategies described above are consistent with the students' understanding of the revision process as requiring lexical changes but not semantic changes. For the students, the extent to which they revise is a function of their level of inspiration. In fact, they use the word *inspiration* to describe the ease or difficulty with which their essay is written, and the extent to which the essay needs to be revised. If students feel inspired, if the writing comes easily, and if they don't get stuck on individual words or phrases, then they say that they cannot see any reason to revise. Because students do not see revision as an activity in which they modify and develop perspectives and ideas, they feel that if they know what they want to say, then there is little reason for making revisions.

The only modification of ideas in the students' essays occurred when they tried out two or three introductory paragraphs. This results, in part, because the students have been taught in another version of the linear model of composing to use a thesis statement as a controlling device in their introductory paragraphs. Since they write their introductions and their thesis statements even before they have really discovered what they want to say, their early close attention to the thesis statement, and more generally the linear model, function to restrict and circumscribe not only the development of their ideas, but also their ability to change the direction of these ideas.

Too often as composition teachers we conclude that students do not willingly revise. The evidence from my research suggests that it is not that students are unwilling to revise, but rather that they do what they have been taught to do in a consistently narrow and predictable way. On every occasion when I asked students why they hadn't made any more changes, they essentially replied, "I knew something larger was wrong, but I didn't think it would help to move words around." The students have strategies for handling words and phrases and their strategies helped them on a word or sentence level. What they lack, however, is a set of strategies to help them identify the "something larger" that they sensed was wrong and work from there. The students do not have strategies for handling the whole essay. They lack procedures or heuristics to help them reorder lines of reasoning or ask questions about their purposes and readers. The students view their compositions in a linear way as a series of parts. Even such potentially useful concepts as "unity" or "form" are reduced to the rule that a composition, if it is to have form, must have an introduction, a body, and a conclusion, or the sum total of the necessary parts.

The students decide to stop revising when they decide that they have not violated any of the rules for revising. These rules, such as "Never begin a sentence with a conjunction" or "Never end a sentence with a preposition," are lexically cued and rigidly applied. In general, students will subordinate the demands of the specific problems of their text to the demands of the rules. Changes are made in compliance with abstract rules about the product, rules that quite often do not apply to the specific problems in the text. These revision strategies are teacher-based, directed toward a teacher-reader who expects compliance with rules — with preexisting "conceptions" — and who will only examine parts of the composition (writing comments about those parts in the margins of their essays) and will cite any violations of rules in those parts. At best the students see their writing altogether passively through the eyes of former teachers or their surrogates, the textbooks, and are bound to the rules which they have been taught.

Revision Strategies of Experienced Writers

One aim of my research has been to contrast how student writers define revision with how a group of experienced writers define their revision processes. Here is a sampling of the definitions from the experienced writers:

> *Rewriting:* "It is a matter of looking at the kernel of what I have written, the content, and then thinking about it, responding to it, making decisions, and actually restructuring it."

> *Rewriting:* "I rewrite as I write. It is hard to tell what is a first draft because it is not determined by time. In one draft, I might cross out three pages, write two, cross out a fourth, rewrite it, and call it a draft. I am constantly writing and rewriting. I can only conceptualize so much in my first draft — only so much information can be held in my head at one time; my rewriting efforts are a reflection of how much information I can encompass at one time. There are levels and agenda which I have to attend to in each draft."

> *Rewriting:* "Rewriting means on one level, finding the argument, and on another level, language changes to make the argument more effective. Most of the time I feel as if I can go on rewriting forever. There is always one part of a piece that I could keep working on. It is always difficult to know at

what point to abandon a piece of writing. I like this idea that a piece of writing is never finished, just abandoned."

Rewriting: "My first draft is usually very scattered. In rewriting, I find the line of argument. After the argument is resolved, I am much more interested in word choice and phrasing."

Revising: "My cardinal rule in revising is never to fall in love with what I have written in a first or second draft. An idea, sentence, or even a phrase that looks catchy, I don't trust. Part of this idea is to wait a while. I am much more in love with something after I have written it than I am a day or two later. It is much easier to change anything with time."

Revising: "It means taking apart what I have written and putting it back together again. I ask major theoretical questions of my ideas, respond to those questions, and think of proportion and structure, and try to find a controlling metaphor. I find out which ideas can be developed and which should be dropped. I am constantly chiseling and changing as I revise."

The experienced writers describe their primary objective when revising as finding the form or shape of their argument. Although the metaphors vary, the experienced writers often use structural expressions such as "finding a framework," "a pattern," or "a design" for their argument. When questioned about this emphasis, the experienced writers responded that since their first drafts are usually scattered attempts to define their territory, their objective in the second draft is to begin observing general patterns of development and deciding what should be included and what excluded. One writer explained, "I have learned from experience that I need to keep writing a first draft until I figure out what I want to say. Then in a second draft, I begin to see the structure of an argument and how all the various subarguments which are buried beneath the surface of all those sentences are related." What is described here is a process in which the writer is both agent and vehicle. "Writing," says Barthes, unlike speech, "develops like a seed, not a line,"[8] and like a seed it confuses beginning and end, conception and production. Thus, the experienced writers say their drafts are "not determined by time," that rewriting is a "constant process," that they feel as if they "can go on forever." Revising confuses the beginning and end, the agent and vehicle; it confuses, *in order to find,* the line of argument.

After a concern for form, the experienced writers have a second objective: a concern for their readership. In this way, "production" precedes "conception." The experienced writers imagine a reader (reading their product) whose existence and whose expectations influence their revision process. They have abstracted the standards of a reader and this reader seems to be partially a reflection of themselves and functions as a critical and productive collaborator — a collaborator who has yet to love their work. The anticipation of a reader's judgment causes a feeling of dissonance when the writer recognizes incongruities between intention and execution, and requires these writers to make revision on all levels. Such a reader gives them just what the students lacked: new eyes to "re-view" their work. The experienced writers believe that they have learned the causes and conditions, the product, which will influence their reader, and their revision strategies are geared toward creating these causes and conditions. They demonstrate a complex understanding of which examples, sentences, or phrases should be included or excluded. For example, one experienced writer decided to delete public examples and add private examples when writing about the energy crisis because "private examples would be less controversial and thus more persuasive." Another writer revised his transitional sentences because "some kinds of transitions are more easily recognized as transitions than others." These examples represent the type of strategic attempts these experienced writers use to manipulate the conventions of discourse in order to communicate to their reader.

But these revision strategies are a process of more than communication; they are part of the process of *discovering meaning* altogether. Here we can see the importance of dissonance; at the heart of revision is the process by which writers recognize and resolve the dissonance they sense in their writing. Ferdinande de Saussure has argued that meaning is differential or "diacritical," based on differences between terms rather than "essential" or inherent qualities of terms. "Phonemes," he said, "are characterized not, as one might think, by their own positive quality but simply by the fact that they are distinct."[9] In fact, Saussure bases his entire *Course in General Linguistics* on these differences, and such differences are dissonant; like musical dissonances which gain their significance from their relationship to the "key" of the composition which itself is determined by the whole language, specific language (parole) gains its meaning from the system of language (langue) of which it is a manifestation and part. The musical composition — a "composition" of parts — creates its "key" as in an overall structure which determines the value (meaning) of its parts. The analogy with music is readily seen in the compositions of experienced writers: Both sorts of composition are based precisely on those structures experienced writers seek in their writing. It is this complicated relationship between the parts and the whole in the work of experienced writers which destroys the linear model; writing cannot develop "like a line" because each addition or deletion is a reordering of the whole. Explicating Saussure, Jonathan Culler asserts that "meaning depends on difference of meaning."[10] But student writers constantly struggle to bring their essays into congruence with a predefined meaning. The experienced writers do the opposite: They seek to discover (to create) meaning in the engagement with their writing, in revision. They seek to emphasize and exploit the lack of clarity, the differences of meaning, the dissonance, that writing as opposed to speech allows in the possibility of revision. Writing has spatial and temporal features not apparent in speech — words are recorded in space and fixed in time — which is why writing is susceptible to reordering and later addition. Such features make possible the dissonance that both provokes revision and promises, from itself, new meaning.

For the experienced writers the heaviest concentration of changes is on the sentence level, and the changes are predominantly by addition and deletion. But, unlike the students, experienced writers make changes on all levels and use all revision operations. Moreover, the operations the students fail to use — reordering and addition — seem to require a theory of the revision process as a totality — a theory which, in fact, encompasses the *whole* of the composition. Unlike the students, the experienced writers possess a nonlinear theory in which a sense of the whole writing both precedes and grows out of an examination of the parts. As we saw, one writer said he needed "a first draft to figure out what to say," and "a second draft to see the structure of an argument buried beneath the surface." Such a "theory" is both theoretical and strategical; once again, strategy and theory are conflated in ways that are literally impossible for the linear model. Writing appears to be more like a seed than a line.

Two elements of the experienced writers' theory of the revision process are the adoption of a holistic perspective and the perception that revision is a recursive process. The writers ask: What does my essay as a *whole* need for form, balance, rhythm, or communication? Details are added, dropped, substituted, or reordered according to their sense of what the essay needs for emphasis and proportion. This sense, however, is constantly in flux as ideas are developed and modified; it is constantly "reviewed" in relation to the parts. As their ideas change, revision becomes an attempt to make their writing consonant with that changing vision.

The experienced writers see their revision process as a recursive process — a process with significant recurring activities — with different levels of attention and different agenda for each cycle. During the first revision cycle their attention is primarily directed toward narrowing the topic and delimiting their ideas. At this point, they are not as concerned as they are later about vocabulary and style. The experienced writers explained that they get closer to their meaning by not limiting themselves too early to lexical concerns. As one writer commented to explain her revision process, a comment inspired by the summer 1977 New York power failure: "I feel like Con Edison cutting off certain states to keep the generators going. In first and second drafts, I try to cut off as much as I can of my editing generator, and in a third draft, I try to cut off some of my idea generators, so I can make sure that I will actually finish the essay." Although the experienced writers describe their revision process as a series of different levels or cycles, it is inaccurate to assume that they have only one objective for each cycle and that each cycle can be defined by a different objective. The same objectives and subprocesses are present in each cycle, but in different proportions. Even though these experienced writers place the predominant weight upon finding the form of their argument during the first cycle, other concerns exist as well. Conversely, during the later cycles, when the experienced writers' primary attention is focused upon stylistic concerns, they are still attuned, although in a reduced way, to the form of the argument. Since writers are limited in what they can attend to during each cycle (understandings are temporal), revision strategies help balance competing demands on attention. Thus, writers can concentrate on more than one objective at a time by developing strategies to sort out and organize their different concerns in successive cycles of revision.

It is a sense of writing as discovery — a repeated process of beginning over again, starting out new — that the students failed to have. I have used the notion of dissonance because such dissonance, the incongruities between intention and execution, governs both writing and meaning. Students do not see the incongruities. They need to rely on their own internalized sense of good writing and to see their writing with their "own" eyes. Seeing in revision — seeing beyond hearing — is at the root of the word *revision* and the process itself; current dicta on revising blind our students to what is actually involved in revision. In fact, they blind them to what constitutes good writing altogether. Good writing disturbs: It creates dissonance. Students need to seek the dissonance of discovery, utilizing in their writing, as the experienced writers do, the very difference between writing and speech — the possibility of revision.

Notes

[1] D. Gordon Rohman and Albert O. Wlecke, "Pre-writing: The Construction and Application of Models for Concept Formation in Writing," Cooperative Research Project No. 2174, U.S. Office of Education, Department of Health, Education, and Welfare; James Britton, Anthony Burgess, Nancy Martin, Alex McLeod, Harold Rosen, *The Development of Writing Abilities* (11–18) (London: Macmillan Education, 1975).

[2] Britton is following Roman Jakobson, "Linguistics and Poetics," in T. A. Sebeok, *Style in Language* (Cambridge, Mass: MIT Press, 1960).

[3] For an extended discussion of this issue see Nancy Sommers, "The Need for Theory in Composition Research," *College Composition and Communication*, 30 (February 1979), 46–49.

⁴ *Classical Rhetoric for the Modern Student* (New York: Oxford University Press, 1965), p. 27.

⁵ Roland Barthes, "Writers, Intellectuals, Teachers," in *Image-Music-Text,* trans. Stephen Heath (New York: Hill and Wang, 1977), pp. 190–191.

⁶ "Writers, Intellectuals, Teachers," p. 190.

⁷ Nancy Sommers and Ronald Schleifer, "Means and Ends: Some Assumptions of Student Writers," *Composition and Teaching,* II (in press).

⁸ *Writing Degree Zero* in *Writing Degree Zero and Elements of Semiology,* trans. Annette Lavers and Colin Smith (New York: Hill and Wang, 1968), p. 20.

⁹ *Course in General Linguistics,* trans. Wade Baskin (New York: McGraw-Hill 1966), p. 119.

¹⁰ Jonathan Culler, *Saussure* (Penguin Modern Masters Series; London: Penguin Books, 1976), p. 70.

Acknowledgment: The author wishes to express her gratitude to Professor William Smith, University of Pittsburgh, for his vital assistance with the research reported in this article, and to Patrick Hays, her husband, for extensive discussions and critical editorial help.

A CONVERSATION ABOUT SMALL GROUPS

Ruth Mirtz

[From *Small Groups in Writing Workshops: Invitations to a Writer's Life* by Robert Brooke, Ruth Mirtz, and Rick Evans. Urbana: NCTE, 1994. 172–84.]

Ruth Mirtz is assistant professor of English and director of the First-Year Writing Program at Florida State University. She has presented her work at CCCC and MLA and published in *Writing on the Edge,* the *ADE Bulletin,* and *Composition Studies.* She continues to do research on small groups in writing classes, and she is also investigating first-year college students' concepts of identity and authority.

The following piece reports on three teachers' uses of small groups in their classes. In this chapter, Mirtz addresses the numerous questions that she and her coauthors have encountered when using small groups. Teachers who are unfamiliar with or skeptical about using groups in their classes will find that this chapter will answer many of their questions, and it offers suggestions for many of the problems they might encounter. The topics that Mirtz addresses include the purposes of groups, strategies for managing groups, and solutions to common problems that occur with groups. Mirtz offers practical advice and explanations, but she consistently and carefully grounds her responses in the larger theoretical contexts that inform contemporary approaches to writing instruction.

In this chapter, I'll start where I think you, our readers, are: in the middle of a course, planning a course, more certain or more confused about what you know about small groups. Just as we try to remember to start where our students are, rather than where we as teachers are, I'll try to begin with immediate questions and specific problems that trouble the people the three of us have talked to about small groups, rather than the types of narratives or descriptions with which we've structured most of this book.

Q: I still am not sure I understand the goals of small-group work in a writing class. How do you rationalize the amount of time spent in small groups in a class that ultimately seeks to improve students' writing, not their oral behavior?

A: What we do and say is largely determined by who we are, who we think we are, who we are trying to be, who we wish we were. Many of these "identity" factors take on a presence in written or spoken discourse. The need for constant direct dialogue in a writing class comes partly from the needs of writers who are trying to construct texts which simultaneously express their selves and relate to other selves, within or without. The second, but no less important, reason is that real learning takes place when one comes to understand the requirements of the role as writer, tries on new roles as writer and reader, and develops meaningfully coordinated or cooperative roles as writer, reader, friend, authority, and whatever else is needed.

Students will translate the difficulties they have finding a workable, comfortable role within our courses into like or dislike for their group members or instructor, feelings of injustice about requirements and evaluations in the course, and so on. They are accustomed to seeing their maturing and learning process (what they often call "real-world learning") as something separate from classroom or academic work.

The transformation that occurs when we see small groups and the writing process as sites of struggles among roles is that students' ability to write and respond well becomes intimately tied to their ability to resolve conflicts and to communicate with group members effectively; that ability is dynamic, constantly changing and adjusting to new situations and ideas. We change how we teach writing by incorporating the whole dimension of small-group dynamics into what we already teach about the process of inventing, revising, and responding.

These goals are the two most important ones for small groups in writing classes for us. Many times, however, small groups are more or less opportunities for (1) getting to know each other and sharing experiences; (2) warming up and reminding students of recent discussions; (3) refocusing the class on questions and issues larger than individual assignments; (4) generating more ideas and reactions faster than a large group; (5) individualizing instruction, especially participation in discussion; and (6) encouraging exposure to diverse perspectives and cultures. All six (certainly not an exhaustive list) subgoals are still sites of the struggles among the roles students take on in writing classes.

Q: I'm confused — your talk about small-group behavior keeps turning into a discussion about response to writing.

A: Because we use small groups in our writing class primarily as a way to get more direct, relevant, and quick response to students' writing, the small-group behavior we are most interested in is that which helps the response become increasingly effective for all the writers' roles students take on in our classes. Also, the structure and guidelines we set up to help small groups get along are basically response rules. Essentially, we believe nearly all small-group behavior in writing classrooms is a response to writing.

Q: I think the small groups in my classes don't work well together because of personality conflicts. If I could find a way to arrange the groups with the right people and personalities together, maybe all the small groups in my class would "work."

A: Personality differences do cause conflicts, but they don't keep us from working together in all sorts of strange situations in the world outside the classroom. Because of the power we have as teachers to move students in and out of groups, we naturally want a way (give Meyers-Briggs tests, for instance) to find out who would get along best with which others.

Outside the classroom, however, one can generally choose the personalities one wants to avoid; students can't do that, short of ignoring a member of their small group. One student may have an overbearing, excessively confrontational way of talking to strangers, while the other students in her group are uncomfortable or even unable to see this student's behavior as valuable. The others may consider her behavior impolite or downright rude. This group is likely to stop responding all together and will certainly have difficulties unless one of the quieter students takes a stronger leadership role and balances the more aggressive personality.

It seems cruel to leave such a group intact, but in our experience, changing groups in order to find compatible personalities only causes a different set of problems. A group with very similar interests and ways of handling communication will often fall into the habit of chatting about their writing instead of responding toward significant revision.

All groups have differences and conflicts, many of which are well below the surface of the conversation and the responding you may observe or participate in. Many of us were taught from childhood to avoid talking about small-group behavior, to not question a group member's words, so even instructors, as members of a group, find that they need more conflict-resolution skills.

Q: Then what do I actually do with a small group which doesn't get along?

A: Ideally, a small group with conflicts which interfere with their ability to respond helpfully to each other's writing will find a way to work through the problems. Realistically, they will need help from their instructor, either in the form of modeling or self-monitoring.

(1) Modeling: the instructor becomes an active part of the group and shows students better ways to handle conflicts, such as asking outright about differences of opinion: "We seem to be disagreeing on this. What shall we do?" or "Since we can't seem to agree on this, let's use one of the guidelines from Tuesday." Most students respond to humor and know how to use humor to break tension. Instructors can show students how they use humor to lighten a conflict while not burying the conflict at the same time ("Gee, if we had some boxing gloves, we could take this outside and settle it like real men").

(2) Self-monitoring: The instructor can ask a small group to write letters to each other about how the group is going and what they'd like to do differently. By focusing on what other things the group could do or on creative alternatives, negative reactions about the current situation can be

diplomatically left out. Reading different versions of what the small group seems to be doing in general ("Describe your small group") can be enlightening for students who don't realize how their behavior is being interpreted and perhaps completely misunderstood. An especially shy student is sometimes perceived as uninterested or indifferent when she is actually desperately trying to get a word into the conversation.

Q: You never directly intervene in a small group?

A: Of course, there are extreme cases when one member is simply out of line, refuses to try to cooperate, and is making everyone completely miserable. So there is a third method for dealing with conflicts:

(3) Intervention: Sometimes the instructor simply needs to take over the leadership of a group and spend significant amounts of time in one group (and simply hope that the other groups will function sufficiently in the interim). Some groups enjoy being labeled the "problem group" or the "slow group" because they garner attention and have a group identity provided for them. Other groups may resent the extra attention the instructor gives one group, but doing a little "floating" during each workshop allows you to explain that some groups need more help than others. Students are generally very alert to what's going on in other groups — they know, for instance, when one group is louder or quieter than other groups, when one group loses members regularly, and so on. If the instructor assumes that all groups have problems from time to time, then she will be talking to the class as a whole regularly about the problems small groups have and how to deal with them.

In rare cases, a student needs to be pulled aside and persuaded individually to resist certain ingrained communication habits, such as incessant teasing and joking or hostile, negative comments. However, giving one of these students the option of not participating in a group is not a good recourse, either, even though a terribly tempting one. This student is exactly the student who needs the time and attention paid to her small-group behavior; if the instructor lets her off the hook, the student's next instructor will merely get the task.

Q: So it really doesn't matter what method I use to form the small groups?

A: We truly suspect that we are overly concerned about how to form small groups. Whether one decides to let the students form their own groups, counts off, or uses some logical device to match or complement students doesn't seem to matter all that much. With any method, in any class, some small groups will work independently and need little modeling or monitoring, and some small groups will need intense attention and help from the instructor. No method that we have heard of will ensure perfectly formed small groups. An instructor should use the method which she is comfortable with, seems fair, and fits in the time frame and flexibility of her plans for the class. For instance, if you want to form small groups on the first day of class, you don't have time to get to know the students, and you may not even have the extra two or three minutes it takes for students to form their own groups; therefore, you'll choose a quick and easy way to form groups.

Q: Your definition of a "good" small group seems to be different than mine. I think a small group works well when they focus on drafts and follow the instructor's instructions; a small group doesn't work when they don't talk, finish early, and use their own ways of organizing themselves and responding to drafts.

A: The way we define our small groups as "working" is unusual. Actually, we are constantly reexamining our definition of a "working" small group (or a "good" small group) within the context of small groups in general. We often worry that a small group isn't "working" because they aren't obediently following directions or because they don't seem to care much for each other, and yet we see those students improving their writing as often and as much as the students in groups that do seem to value each other's writing and enjoy each other's company. What's going on?

"On-task" behavior is a trap, we have found, and just as problematic as defining a "good" student as one who plays our games according to our rules. What appears to be on-task or off-task is often the opposite; what students are learning is more important to us than whether they follow our instructions to the letter. Some groups need larger amounts of seemingly "off-task" talk in order to respond meaningfully to texts. They'll start off talking about the game on Saturday, their plans for the weekend, and half the class period will be gone before they start looking at their drafts. We don't usually worry about this form of procrastination early in the term because it helps students learn about each other, find out what interests other group members, and in general relaxes them enough to be able later to respond helpfully. They'll be the group that can look at one member's draft and make suggestions based on other stories they know the member has stored away or other talents the member has. They will be able to truly "re-envision" their texts and may sometimes have problems deciding which revisions to make and when to stop revising.

The group that seems to be made of "good students" will launch immediately into following exactly the instructions given to them, but suffer from superficial or irrelevant response because they don't know each other well enough to respond helpfully. They will be the group that gives advice too soon rather than response and reactions. They will quickly tire of the responding guidelines, and because they can't use much of the advice they get from their small group, they will rely on the instructor's response solely. They need, as much as the "off-task" group does, to monitor their group behavior and talk about how their group is functioning effectively and not so effectively.

One of the most frustrating aspects of using small groups in composition classrooms is their tendency to come up with their own ways of dealing with things. Sometimes the instructor needs to remind them of the guidelines and instructions because they really are trying to take the easy way out, while other groups are negotiating an effective way to proceed and process their own conflicts. Some groups need monitoring, but not necessarily interference.

We need to constantly examine our own definition of "working" when we talk about small groups: Do we mean following instructions, or working out differences, or helping to improve their writing, or discovering how other writers work, or experimenting with their identity as a writer?

Q: Don't all small groups go through a certain process during the semester? Shouldn't they get through these conflicts as soon as possible and then move on to the real work of the small group? Shouldn't the teacher's job be to push each group through the process as quickly as possible so that they can start working on their texts?

A: We often talk about how we deal somewhat differently with small groups early in the term than at midterm or toward the end of the term. The first few weeks of class are a time when students need more time to get to know each other, find out how each other thinks and acts, and develop functional ways of getting along despite the inevitable conflicts. By midterm, group members should be well-acquainted and ready for more difficult responding and reading tasks, ready to take more risks and experiment more boldly. By the end of term, we hope that all of our students have a rich repertoire of responding and conflict-resolution strategies that will prepare them for any other small-group experiences they have the rest of their lives.

Did you notice how conditional and wishful the last two sentences were? We can be fairly certain about what all students need during the first two or three weeks of class — structure, guidelines, time to get acquainted. But after that, each small group must be treated individually. There are no other reliable "phases" a group will go through, although happily, many groups do follow the process of development (described above). A great deal of social science research is devoted to determining the possible processes and consequently has come up with elaborate theories with fancy diagrams. Whenever we have tried to apply these theories of processes to our students, we find the actual processes much messier, more recursive, and ultimately not much help.

We stress monitoring and modeling all semester, because a small group continues to be a dynamic, constantly renegotiating location for students all semester. Some traditional-age students seem to have less tolerance for stability and routine than older adults and will work at destabilizing some small aspect of the group as soon as they feel bored. And when one student brings a much more personal draft than she has ever brought before (or much more political draft or a draft which responds to another student's draft), the small group must change its ways of responding to be sensitive to the needs of the writer's experiment. Some students are much less sure of their own identities and will need room and space to try out new roles. The student who leads confidently one week may be completely silent the next week. A group which launches into wonderfully directed response to texts one week may need half the class period the next week to talk out and rediscover themselves as peers and friends.

The constant renegotiating that takes place in all groups is what keeps many nonacademic study groups or support groups going for years. The same need makes it difficult for students to change groups during the school term and is why we suggest not changing groups during a normal fifteen- or sixteen-week semester course.

Q: So I shouldn't change the small groups at all during the term?

A: Inevitably we end up moving some members of small groups, but we don't tend to change the groups simply for variety or convenience or because students say they are bored. I often end up shuffling some members the very first day of class, before the students introduce themselves, in order to balance out the number of men and women. When I can avoid it easily, I prefer to have either groups of all women, all men, or two men with two women. The group I try to avoid is the group with a three-to-one ratio, which sometimes places a student at a disadvantage. That's one change I can make easily because I can identify the sexes easily (most of the time). Any other special needs or compatibilities are impossible to learn reliably during the first days of class.

I also change groups to keep the numbers even — three or four in each group. If enrollment changes because of drops or adds, then the small groups may have to be adjusted, but I try to warn students on the first day of class that the possibility exists.

We structure our classes so that there are many opportunities for all the students to meet and work with students besides those in their small groups, even though they may workshop their drafts and papers with the same small group all semester. Our students tell us that they enjoy working with students outside of their small group, but that they feel much more comfortable responding to drafts with a stable long-term group.

Q: What about gender differences? If one of my small groups consists of all women, they inevitably become a support group while my groups of all men become very competitive in appearing "cool" while rebellious.

A: We don't find a support group or a "cool" group as much of a problem as a group which consistently leaves one voice unheard or causes a member too much discomfort to be learning at the same time. Rather than add too many requirements to the ideal group makeup, we work with those groups who have found a real, workable group identity for themselves, to turn that "cool guy" attitude into "cool writer" attitude, or to push the support group to get past its unconditional encouragement. They are not groups in conflict as much as groups with too limited an idea of what their group can be. When we are participating in those groups, the knowledge we point out about their group problems is part of what we are making deliberate, articulate, and changeable in their group behavior.

Q: Even when I have small groups with exactly the same number of members, one group always finishes early. What do I do with them?

A: It may depend on just how early they are finishing. If a group finishes five or six minutes before the other groups, that seems a reasonable amount of time to leave them to their own conversation. Five extra minutes of getting acquainted, especially if the group members didn't pause for socializing before getting started, can only help most groups.

More than five minutes is a good time for a small group to do some writing. An excellent short writing assignment, which I often make a general rule for groups (and which sometimes ensures that they will stretch their responding time in order to finish with the other groups and avoid the extra writing) is to report on what happened in their small group. They might also start writing in their journals for the next entry, either on a suggested topic or on one of their own inspiration.

A group which consistently finishes fifteen or more minutes early needs closer monitoring. They may simply be incredibly efficient, they may have brought spectacularly short texts, or they may be completely lost about how to respond to each other's texts and not really exchanging reactions and ideas. Because my presence as a fellow writer always tends to slow down a group, I often choose to become a part-time member of the group that always finishes too early. And I often say things to them like "Are you sure that's all we can help you with?" or "But you didn't say why you thought the ending was good." I often become the social leader of those groups, too, because sometimes the quick finishers are the group of four shy nontalkers, and they need someone to engage them in conversation.

I think it's important not to "punish" small groups which finish early with the equivalent of "seat work" or expect them to sit there doing nothing, waiting for the other groups. On the other hand, I prefer not to let them leave early either, choosing rather to find a fruitful additional activity which helps them monitor themselves and their group or by modeling the kind of responding which does take time and energy.

Q: What about using small groups not only for workshopping on drafts but for collaborating on group-authored texts or for discussing assigned reading from imaginative or professional writing?

A: We find that the joys and pains of small groups responding to drafts are the same for other kinds of small groups. However, the roles students struggle with change when the goals of the group change. In a collaborative group, more unity is needed in how texts should be written — that is, more of the group members will be forced to take on unfamiliar writerly roles. In a discussion group, the status of the text is often more of a problem, causing students to work out their roles as mass reader or aesthetic critic, for example.

Q: I always thought putting students into small groups was a great way to reduce the load on the teacher.

A: Small groups can reduce the role of the teacher as an absolute authoritarian and can eliminate the need for students to write for a murky "general audience." However, using small groups in a composition class is a tremendous amount of work if the instructor intends for the groups to work as circles of fellow writers and readers.

Some teachers do use the time to mark papers or read the newspaper, but that is not a role which will ensure that the small groups will be successful. We strongly advocate an active role for the instructor during small-group workshops, either as a floating member or as a permanent member of one group. Even then, it often seems (especially to administrators) as though a teacher isn't doing anything when the small groups are meeting during class.

The instructor is constantly monitoring the groups, trying to be in at least two groups during each class session and often speaking in general with all the groups. Sometimes she will sit in on one group while listening to another group nearby. She has to make sure that each group finishes at about the same time. A group which finishes early needs an extra assignment. A group which never finishes on time needs to be pushed to either elect a timekeeper each week or become more aware of the amount of nonessential talking they do. The instructor reads, in addition to the drafts and final papers of each students, reports from each student about the small group and often responds to those additional reports. The instructor is also a fellow writer, and in that role, spends extra time each week keeping her own writing journal or notebook and drafting texts to share with the class. She also disciplines herself to read published texts and recent research in regard not only to composition, but also to small-group behavior and small-group pedagogy.

For some of us, small groups became a pedagogical method when we sought to individualize our instruction more and allow students more self-paced learning. A small group allows a student to work on her own projects at her own speed while still getting the exposure (and some mild pressure) from other students working at different levels and paces. Such individualizing of our instruction takes enormous amounts of time. First, we must keep close track of anywhere from 30 to 100 (or more) students' work separately and also counsel their choices. Then, we must find ways to draw all these separate learners together with issues which most of them have in common, although in many different ways. After more than a decade of teaching, I still find this task overwhelming.

Q: Now you've made it sound like too much work.

A: It's actually a different kind of work than most of us are accustomed to. It's also, fortunately, the kind of work that keeps us challenged as learners ourselves and provoked as teachers. The modeling we do in small groups as expert small-group members keeps us on our toes, because while we can read about research on small groups (or conduct our own), and we can predict what our small groups will do, we are usually called on to model and problem-solve on the spot, as the conflicts come up. When we join the small groups as fellow but expert writers, we get a chance to practice our own craft, to consider ourselves writers for a while.

So if it turns out to be more work, it's the kind of more work we need in order to be good teachers. Not more paperwork or grading, but more interaction with students which lets us learn more about them and about writing and learning processes.

Q: But there's so much to do already in my class, and now I have so many ideas about small-group work. It's the middle of the semester and I've already set out my goals and evaluation process. Where do I start?

A: We agree that an instructor shouldn't, under normal circumstances, suddenly make wholesale changes in a course because a better idea comes along in midstream. But we do hope you start making plans for next semester.

If you have never used small groups or haven't in a while and would like to try a limited experiment at any point in the semester, then here's a suggestion: Begin with a tightly focused, very specific writing and sharing activity which correlates with something your class has been discussing or working on, and ask the students to write an informal description of their writing process on the current assignment. Form small groups to read the descriptions out loud to each other with the rules of no apologies from the writers and no criticism from the listeners. Give the groups time to read out loud and talk about the similarities and differences between the descriptions. Then follow up by asking students to write from three to five minutes about what happened in their small group, to be handed in to you.

The more specific the tasks you give to the groups and the more naturally you can assume they will have no problem with this exercise, the more "in control" and relaxed you may feel. The follow-up responses will let you know what happened and how to adapt your instructions and expectations for the next small-group activity.

Q: Sometimes I think my students don't work well in small-group workshops because they just don't know how to work in small groups, in general. They should learn these skills in high school. Why do I have to teach them?

A: If our students came to us with no skills in small-group work, we would have written a much different book. Instead, our students come as seasoned small-group members of a different kind: they've been active in groups of friends of various sizes, clubs and committees, lab partners, and families. Those groups have provided both positive and negative experiences, though, and we draw on both kinds in college writing classes. Students don't need training in small-group behavior; they need to learn how to reapply what they already know about themselves and how they relate to people in a writing class.

Q: I've had some pretty uncomfortable experiences in small groups, myself. And I was trained to work individually and competitively as a graduate student and as a teacher. Aren't I the least likely person to make small-group work succeed in my classroom?

A: On the contrary, you are probably more sensitive to the level of comfort and discomfort your students are experiencing. For good or ill, instructors take all their educational baggage with them into the classroom. By being aware of the influence of your past experiences, you are well on the way to understanding how you want small groups to work in your own classroom. Plus, you've got some stories about how you don't think small groups should work to tell your students, who can (and should) always regale you with theirs.

Q: I'd like to find out more about small groups. What other books do you suggest?

A: We hope you will first attempt to learn more about small groups from the best source: the small groups in your classroom. Take a few notes while participating in a group. Collect and analyze the short reports your students write about how their small group is going. Look for the metaphors or other kinds of language they use to describe their group. Tape-record one small group which you aren't participating in and promise not to listen to it until after the semester is over — then *do listen to it.* See also the recommended readings in the appendix of this book.

Q: All these practical matters aside, don't you have a social agenda of some kind behind this small-group pedagogy?

A: Like most people, we don't align ourselves with any one social policy or political group. We have been influenced by such diverse thinkers as Paulo Freire, Ann Berthoff, Erving Goffman, Thomas Kuhn, the Sophists of ancient Greece, although we have probably been influenced most about small groups by the thousands of students who told us about what happened in our classrooms. We believe that both individual autonomy and interaction in groups, large and small, are necessary for developing our students' writing processes and facility, as well as their critical acumen and their sense of responsibility toward both themselves and others.

If we were to say we have a social agenda, then it would be the need for society to provide better education for all segments of that society. We believe that small groups are a part of that better education under conditions of equality and opportunity.

HELPING PEER WRITING GROUPS SUCCEED

Wendy Bishop

[*Teaching English in the Two-Year College* 15 (1988): 120–25.]

Wendy Bishop is professor of English at Florida State University. One of the more prolific scholars in composition studies, Bishop has written numerous articles and chapters. In addition, she has authored and edited numerous books, including *Something Old, Something New: College Writing Teachers and Classroom Change* (1990), *Working Words: The Process of Creative Writing* (1992), *The Subject is Writing: Essays by Teachers and Students* (1993), *Colors of a Different Horse: Rethinking Creative Writing, Theory, and Pedagogy* (1994), *Elements of Alternate Style: Essays on Writing and Revision* (1997), *Genre and Writing: Issues, Arguments, Alternatives* (1997), and *Teaching Lives: Essays and Stories* (1997). Currently, she is at work on two textbooks: *Metro: A Guide to Writing Creatively* and *Thirteen Ways of Looking for a Poem: An Introduction to Writing Poetry.*

More and more teachers are establishing writing workshops in their classrooms. In these settings, students work in small groups, collaborating on assignments, sharing works-in-progress, and offering feedback on one another's writing. But establishing and maintaining effective peer writing groups requires serious planning, training, and monitoring on the part of the teacher. Bishop explores causes for successes and failures of peer writing groups and offers practical advice for instructors. Her discussion complements the guidelines for peer reviewers in *The Bedford Handbook.*

An idealized but obtainable writing classroom is one in which students join together in collaborative work and develop their writing abilities in a non-threatening environment. This article explores that concept by reviewing research and by offering a plan for preparing and training students.

Research on Peer Writing Groups

The value of using peer writing groups as a teaching method has at times been overrated and has sometimes been oversimplified. In general, collaborative peer writing groups do benefit the student. The claims for the efficacy of the method are many and various.[1] Beaven, discussing peer evaluation, claims that the collaborative method allows students to develop audience awareness, to check their perceptions of reality, to strengthen their interpersonal skill, and to take risks; the entire process results in improvement in writing and students' ability to revise. Hawkins agrees that students strengthen their interpersonal skills and risk-taking or creative abilities.

Bruffee ("Brooklyn Plan") found that peer tutors and tutees at work in a collaborative environment deal with higher order concerns such as paper focus and development. Researchers like Danis ("Peer Response Groups"), who found that 75 percent of the students in her study correctly identified both major and minor writing problems, and Gere, who felt that student responses did deal with meaning, seem to support Bruffee's contention that students in peer groups do more than simply act as proofreaders of each other's work. Recent research by Gere and Abbott has reaffirmed the power of peer writing groups to stay focused on discussions about writing. Their research also shows that group discussions where teachers are present are significantly different from those where teachers are absent.

Because collaborative learning can be time consuming (Beaven; Abercrombie) for those writing about this method, it is agreed that some training of group members is necessary with emphasis on student-centered discussion rather than teacher/lecture dominated classrooms.

Danis ("Weaving the Web of Meaning") found that students are not always sure of their group role, aren't able to stand back from their own writing, don't know what they want to know, and have a reluctance to offer critical comments. Flynn stated that students lacked critical ability and attributed this to students' tendencies to supply missing information in a paper in order to make sense out of what they were reading. The fact that students need to develop a critical vocabulary with which to discuss their works is supported in Bruffee's articles ("Writing and Reading," "Collaborative Learning"). Clearly, there is a need to introduce writing students to the vocabulary and terminology of the composition community.

When peer groups are fully developed, the method is exciting and rewarding for both student and teacher, but when peer group interactions are underdeveloped or break down, the method is discouraging and group work all too often feels like a matter of luck.

The teacher needs a way to begin to sort out group interaction patterns. George distinguishes among task-oriented, leaderless, and dysfunctional groups. Teachers need to be aware of the attributes of successful groups and learn what can be done to move groups from failure to success, for doing so will enable composition teachers to feel more comfortable using peer writing groups.

Following is a list of causes for group failure or success with the names of researchers or writers who touch on these concerns when discussing peer writing groups.

Causes for Peer Writing Group Failure

- Too much or too little leadership (Hawkins; Elbow; George)
- Poor attendance or participation or preparation of some students, leading to resentment between members (Hawkins; Flynn)
- Unclear group goals; group doesn't value work or works too quickly (Johnson & Johnson *Learning*; Hawkins; George)
- Group doesn't feel confident of group members' expertise or members are afraid to offer criticism (Lagana; Danis; Flynn)
- Group doesn't understand new role of instructor (Ziv)
- Group never develops adequate vocabulary for discussing writing (Danis; Bruffee "Writing and Reading," "Collaborative Learning")
- Group fails to record suggestions or to make changes based on members' suggestions (Ziv; George)

Causes for Peer Writing Group Success

- Group successfully involves all members (Johnson & Johnson *Learning*; Hawkins; Elbow)
- Group works to clarify goals and assignments (Johnson & Johnson; Elbow; Danis)
- Group develops a common vocabulary for discussing writing (Beaven; Bruffee "Writing and Reading," "Collaborative Learning"; Danis)

- Group learns to identify major writing problems such as organization, tone, and focus, as well as minor writing problems such as spelling errors, and so on (Bruffee "Brooklyn Plan"; Danis; Gere; Gere and Abbott)
- Group learns to value group work and to see instructor as a resource which the group can call on freely (Rogers; Danis; Flynn)

Preparing for Peer Writing Groups

Most writers are in agreement: students and teachers need preparation and training for successful peer group work.

Students can work together to discuss readings, to complete exercises, to explore writing invention strategies, and to help members with forming very early drafts.

Teachers who want to use peer writing groups in their classroom should plan ahead and read widely in this area. A teacher should ask several questions:

- Do I understand the theory behind peer writing groups?
- Do I have a clear use for this method in my classroom?
- What are my goals for students when using this method?

The well prepared teacher will acquaint students with concepts of collaborative learning through prepared handouts, class discussion, and continual monitoring of group work. Students need to develop a group identity. To function well, group members must be present, which requires a class attendance policy. I use groups 50 to 75 percent of my available class periods. This percentage allows my students to develop a group identity yet regroup into a class on a regular basis in order to maintain a class identity also.

Classroom communities are formed by the school registrar, academic departments, and the enrolling student. Teachers may divide a class into sets of four to five students, or students may start working collaboratively in pairs and then pairs may be joined. First week diagnostic writings may be used to organize groups with a balance of strong and weak writers. Students may rate themselves on matters such as ability to lead, to help, to take risks, and so on, and groups may be balanced with a member strong in each area. In addition, I group by gender and age.

Groups work best when they are balanced, focused, and comfortable. I let groups work together for at least four sessions, and I rarely leave a group together for an entire semester.

Sometimes a teacher needs to intervene and change group membership (placing an overly dominant member in another, more challenging group, and so on), but often it is wiser to let the group itself solve group problems. Ideally, groups staying together over a long period develop a strong group identity and sense of shared community. Equally, groups that change membership, partially or wholly, are often revitalized and ready to undertake new course challenges with greater enthusiasm.

Choosing a group name can help members identify with their new community. Ordering and clarifying group members' roles, such as monitor and historian and general member, also assures that group work will be carried on in an orderly manner. Group projects should be clearly articulated in handout form or as directions on the chalkboard, and group work should be real work, contributing to each member's writing development.

Reporting on what the group accomplished each session, in the form of historian's notes in a group folder, provides useful artifacts for group self-evaluation and teacher evaluation of the group session.

Training Peer Writing Groups

Peer writing groups need training in two areas: group roles and writing critiquing. A monitor acts as the group caretaker, making sure each member gets time to respond to writing and time to have writing discussed. The historian records group discussions, insuring continuity from session to session. When groups are first formed, handouts to elected members, as well as a handout detailing the responsibilities of a member in general — attendance, support, sharing, and so on — can speed the training in this area.

Teaching each other to talk about writing can be initiated by the teacher, reinforced by the class text, and nurtured by whole class discussion, but it will be brought to fruition in the group itself as members learn to improve their writing. The teacher may begin by teaching the class necessary terminology (concerning writing process and writing analysis) and by training writers and readers to work together through such activities as role playing and reviewing sample essays. Groups can work to answer set questions or can learn to develop their own critical concerns for papers. If composition terms such as prewriting, drafting, revising, focus, organization, and tone are introduced in class discussion, show up on group handouts, are reinforced in peer writing group discussions and recorded in group minutes, such terms will soon become part of the peer group's working vocabulary.

Monitoring Peer Writing Groups

Sometimes the best thing teachers can do is to listen and watch the groups quietly and unobtrusively; sometimes teachers must participate in groups to insure that each group is working efficiently. Teachers should keep records of the groups (a personal journal is a good place to start); teachers can monitor groups by sight (regularly noting what is happening in each by direct observation); by sound (listening to tape recordings of groups at a later date); by direct contact (visits to and participation in groups); and by reviewing group or individual artifacts (learning logs, group weekly reports, group self-evaluations, and questionnaires).

Evaluating Peer Writing Groups

Teachers can determine if students are attaining the goals set for group work. Group folders when examined tell a story of good attendance, completed work, and enlarged understanding. Self-evaluation, on the part of students and teacher, can chronicle success with the method and pinpoint areas for future work and improvement. And most important, gains in individual student writing can be assessed.[2]

Measurements of student growth in collaborative learning techniques and writing in general can be accomplished with pre and post testing in the following areas:

- pre and post written descriptions of what students feel can be accomplished in writing groups
- pre and post written descriptions of student's writing process
- pre and post writing apprehension tests
- pre and post essay samples

Teachers who hope to use peer writing groups should prepare for success. Teachers must become researchers in the classroom. They must plan for the class, train group members, monitor and evaluate them, and, the next semester, begin the process over, refining and developing talents as a group facilitator based on personal observations. These teachers will be willing to experiment, to redefine group failures as steps in a larger process that leads to success, and to have realistic expectations for this holistic teaching method. Before long, those expectations will be met and hopefully surpassed.

Notes

[1] For an in-depth review of research on peer writing groups, see Bishop.

[2] For detailed discussions of methods for evaluating peer writing groups, see Cooper; McAndrew; and Weiner.

Works Cited

Abercrombie, Minnie Louie Johnson. *Aims and Techniques of Group Teaching.* 3rd ed. London: Soc. for Research into Higher Educ. Ltd., 1974.

Beaven, Mary H. "Individualized Goal Setting, Self-Evaluation, and Peer Evaluation." *Evaluating Writing: Describing, Measuring, Judging.* Ed. Charles R. Cooper and Lee Odell. Urbana: NCTE, 1977. 135–56.

Bishop, Wendy. "Research, Theory, and Pedagogy of Writing Peer Groups: An Annotated Bibliography." 1987. Forthcoming in ERIC.

Bruffee, Kenneth A. "The Brooklyn Plan: Attaining Intellectual Growth through Peer Group Tutoring." *Liberal Education* 64 (1978): 447–69.

_____. "Writing and Reading as Collaborative or Social Acts." *The Writer's Mind: Writing as a Mode of Thinking.* Ed. Janet L. Hays and others. Urbana: NCTE, 1983.

———. "Collaborative Learning and the Conversation of Mankind." *College English* 46 (1984): 635–52.

Cooper, Charles. "Measuring Growth in Writing." *English Journal* 64 (1975): 111–20.

Danis, Francine. "Peer-Response Groups in a College Writing Workshop: Students' Suggestions for Revising Compositions." *DAI* 41 (1980): 5008A–5009A.

———. "Weaving the Web of Meaning: Interactions Patterns in Peer-Response Groups." Paper presented at CCCC, San Francisco, March 1982. ERIC ED 214 202.

Elbow, Peter. *Writing with Power.* New York: Oxford UP, 1981.

Flynn, Elizabeth A. "Freedom, Restraint and Peer Group Interaction." Paper presented at CCCC, San Francisco, March 1982. ERIC ED 216 365.

George, Diana. "Writing with Peer Groups in Composition." *College Composition and Communication* 35 (1984): 320–36.

Gere, Anne Ruggles. "Students' Oral Response to Written Composition." Seattle: Washington, 1982. ERIC ED 229 781.

Gere, Anne Ruggles, and Robert D. Abbott. "Talking about Writing: The Language of Writing Groups." *Research in the Teaching of English* 19 (1985): 362–81.

Hawkins, Thom. *Group Inquiry Techniques in Teaching Writing.* Urbana: NCTE, 1976.

Johnson, David W., and Roger T. Johnson. *Learning Together and Alone: Cooperation, Competition, and Individualization.* Englewood Cliffs: Prentice, 1975.

———. "Cooperative Small-Group Learning." *Curriculum Report* 14 (1984): 1–6. ERIC ED 249 625.

Lagana, Jean Remaly. "The Development, Implementation, and Evaluation of a Model for Teaching Composition Which Utilizes Individualized Learning and Peer Grouping." *DAI* 33 (1973): 4063A.

McAndrew, Donald A. "Measuring Holistic and Syntactic Quality in a Semester Writing Course." *The English Record* 29 (1978): 16–17.

Rogers, Carl R. *On Becoming a Person.* Boston: Houghton, 1961.

Weiner, Harvey S. "Collaborative Learning in the Classroom: A Guide to Evaluation." *College English* 48 (1986): 52–61.

Ziv, Nina D. "Peer Groups in the Composition Classroom: A Case Study." Paper presented at CCCC, Detroit, March 1983. ERIC ED 229 799.

RESPONDING TO STUDENT WRITING

RESPONDING TO STUDENT WRITING

Nancy Sommers

[*College Composition and Communication* 33 (1982): 148–56.]

(For biographical information, see page 107.)

This article reports on research Sommers conducted to examine how instructors' responses to student writing actually contributed to subsequent revisions. Her findings, supported with specific examples and extensive observations, revealed discouraging tendencies in teacher responses, and her advice can help teachers avoid these problems. Teachers can apply Sommers's advice to avoid the tendency to attach responses that are too general by following *The Bedford Handbook*'s guidelines for peer reviewers (p. 51), which offer a ready-made list of features to consider while responding to student writing, encouraging text-specific comments that reinforce particular revision strategies.

More than any other enterprise in the teaching of writing, responding to and commenting on student writing consumes the largest proportion of our time. Most teachers estimate that it takes them at least 20 to 40 minutes to comment on an individual student paper, and those 20 to 40 minutes times 20 students per class, times 8 papers, more or less, during the course of a semester add up to an enormous amount of time. With so much time and energy directed to a single activity, it is important for us to understand the nature of the enterprise. For it seems, paradoxically enough, that although commenting on student writing is the most widely used method for responding to student writing, it is the least understood. We do not know in any definitive way what constitutes thoughtful commentary or what effect, if any, our comments have on helping our students become more effective writers.

Theoretically, at least, we know that we comment on our students' writing for the same reasons professional editors comment on the work of professional writers or for the same reasons we ask our colleagues to read and respond to our own writing. As writers we need and want thoughtful commentary to show us when we have communicated our ideas and when not, raising questions from a reader's point of view that may not have occurred to us as writers. We want to know if our writing has communicated our intended meaning and, if not, what questions or discrepancies our reader sees that we, as writers, are blind to.

In commenting on our students' writing, however, we have an additional pedagogical purpose. As teachers, we know that most students find it difficult to imagine a reader's response in advance, and to use such responses as a guide in composing. Thus, we comment on student writing to dramatize the presence of a reader, to help our students to become that questioning reader themselves, because, ultimately, we believe that becoming such a reader will help them to evaluate what they have written and develop control over their writing.[1]

Even more specifically, however, we comment on student writing because we believe that it is necessary for us to offer assistance to student writers when they are in the process of composing a text, rather than after the text has been completed. Comments create the motive for doing something different in the next draft; thoughtful comments create the motive for revising. Without comments from their teachers or from their peers, student writers will revise in a consistently narrow and predictable way. Without comments from readers, students assume that their writing has communicated their meaning and perceive no need for revising the substance of their text.[2]

Yet as much as we as informed professionals believe in the soundness of this approach to responding to student writing, we also realize that we don't know how our theory squares with teachers' actual practice — do teachers comment and students revise as the theory predicts they should? For the past year my colleagues, Lil Brannon, Cyril Knoblach, and I have been researching this problem, attempting to discover not only what messages teachers give their students through their comments, but also what determines which of these comments the students choose to use or to ignore when revising. Our research has been entirely focused on comments teachers write to motivate revisions. We have studied the commenting styles of thirty-five teachers at New York University and the University of Oklahoma, studying the comments these teachers wrote on first and second drafts, and interviewing a representative number of these teachers and their students. All teachers also commented on the same set of three student essays. As an additional reference point one of the student essays was typed into the computer that had been programmed with the "Writer's Workbench," a package of twenty-three programs developed by Bell Laboratories to help computers and writers work together to improve a text rapidly. Within a few minutes, the computer delivered editorial comments on the student's text, identifying all spelling and punctuation errors, isolating problems with wordy or misused phrases, and suggesting alternatives, offering a stylistic analysis of sentence types, sentence beginnings, and sentence lengths, and finally, giving our freshman essay a Kincaid readability score of eighth-grade which, as the computer program informed us, "is a low score for this type of document." The sharp contrast between the teachers' comments and those of the computer highlighted how arbitrary and idiosyncratic most of our teachers' comments are. Besides, the calm, reasonable language of the computer provided quite a contrast to the hostility and mean-spiritedness of most of the teachers' comments.

The first finding from our research on styles of commenting is that *teachers' comments can take students' attention away from their own purposes in writing a particular text and focus that attention on the teachers' purpose in commenting.* The teacher appropriates the text from the student by confusing the student's purpose in writing the text with her own purpose in commenting. Students make the changes the teacher wants rather than those that the student perceives are necessary, since the teachers' concerns imposed on the text create the reasons for the subsequent changes.

We have all heard our perplexed students say to us when confused by our comments: "I don't understand how you want me to change this" or "Tell me what you want me to do." In the beginning of the process there was the writer, her words, and her desire to communicate her ideas. But after the comments of the teacher are imposed on the first or second draft, the student's attention dramatically shifts from "This is what I want to say," to "This is what *you* the teacher are asking me to do."

This appropriation of the text by the teacher happens particularly when teachers identify errors in usage, diction, and style in a first draft and ask students to correct these errors when they revise; such comments give the student an impression of the importance of these errors that is all out of proportion to how they should view these errors at this point in the process. The comments create the concern that these "accidents of discourse" need to be attended to before the meaning of the text is attended to.

It would not be so bad if students were only commanded to correct errors, but, more often than not, students are given contradictory messages; they are commanded to edit a sentence to avoid an error or to condense a sentence to achieve greater brevity of style, and then told in the margins that the particular paragraph needs to be more specific or to be developed more. An example of this problem can be seen in the following student paragraph:

comma needed

wordy — be precise, which Sunday?

Every year [on one Sunday in the middle of January] tens of millions of

word choice

people <u>cancel</u> all events, plans or work to watch the Super Bowl. This

wordy

audience includes [little boys and girls, old people, and housewives and

Be specific — what reasons?

men.] <u>Many reasons</u> have been given to explain why the Super Bowl has

and why   *what spots?*

become so popular t~~h~~at commercial/spots cost up to $100,000.00. <u>One</u>

awkward   *another what?*

<u>explanation is that people</u> like to take sides and root for a team. <u>Another</u>

spelling

is that some people like the pagentry and excitement of the event. These

too colloquial

reasons alone, however, do not explain <u>a happening</u> as big as the Super

Bowl.

(left margin) *you need to do more research.*

(right margin) *This paragraph needs to be expanded in order to be more interesting to the reader.*

In commenting on this draft, the teacher has shown the student how to edit the sentences, but then commands the student to expand the paragraph in order to make it more interesting to a reader. The interlinear comments and the marginal comments represent two separate tasks for this student; the interlinear comments encourage the student to see the text as a fixed piece, frozen in time, that just needs some editing. The marginal comments, however, suggest that the meaning of the text is not fixed, but rather that the student still needs to develop the meaning by doing some more research. Students are commanded to edit and develop at the same time; the remarkable contradiction of developing a paragraph after editing the sentences in it represents the confusion we encountered in our teachers' commenting styles. These different signals given to students, to edit and develop, to condense and elaborate, represent also the failure of teachers' comments to direct genuine revision of a text as a whole.

Moreover, the comments are worded in such a way that it is difficult for students to know what is the most important problem in the text and what problems are of lesser importance. No scale of concerns is offered to a student with the result that a comment about spelling or a comment about an awkward sentence is given weight equal to a comment about organization or logic. The comment that seemed to represent this problem best was one teacher's command to his student: "Check your commas and semicolons and think more about what you are thinking about." The language of the comments makes it difficult for a student to sort out and decide what is most important and what is least important.

When the teacher appropriates the text for the student in this way, students are encouraged to see their writing as a series of parts — words, sentences, paragraphs — and not as a whole discourse. The comments encourage students to believe that their first drafts are finished drafts, not invention drafts, and that all they need to do is patch and polish their writing. That is, teachers' comments do not provide their students with an inherent reason for revising the structure and meaning of their texts, since the comments suggest to students that the meaning of their text is already there, finished, produced, and all that is necessary is a better word or phrase. The processes of revising, editing, and proofreading are collapsed and reduced to a single trivial activity, and the students' misunderstanding of the revision process as a rewording activity is reinforced by their teachers' comments.

It is possible, and it quite often happens, that students follow every comment and fix their texts appropriately as requested, but their texts are not improved substantially or, even worse, their revised drafts are inferior to their previous drafts. Since the teachers' comments take the students' attention away from their own original purposes, students concentrate more, as I have noted, on what the teachers commanded them to do than on what they are trying to say. Sometimes students do not understand the purpose behind their teachers' comments and take these comments very literally. At other times students understand the comments, but the teacher has misread the text and the comments, unfortunately, are not applicable. For instance, we repeatedly saw comments in which teachers commanded students to reduce and condense what was written, when in fact what the text really needed at this stage was to be expanded in conception and scope.

The process of revising always involves a risk. But, too often revision becomes a balancing act for students in which they make the changes that are requested but do not take the risk of changing anything that was not commented on, even if the students sense that other changes are needed. A more effective text does not often evolve from such changes alone, yet the student does not want to take the chance of reducing a finished, albeit inadequate, paragraph to chaos — to fragments — in order to rebuild it, if such changes have not been requested by the teacher.

The second finding from our study is that *most teachers' comments are not text-specific and could be interchanged, rubber-stamped, from text to text.* The comments are not anchored in the particulars of the students' texts, but rather are a series of vague directives that are not text-specific. Students are commanded to "think more about [their] audience, avoid colloquial language, avoid the passive, avoid prepositions at the end of sentences or conjunctions at the beginning of sentences, be clear, be specific, be precise, but above all, think more about what [they] are thinking about." The comments on the following student paragraph illustrate this problem:

Begin by telling your reader what you are going to write about
In the sixties it was drugs, in the seventies it was rock and roll. Now in the

avoid "one of the"
eighties, one of the most controversial subjects is nuclear power. The United

elaborate
States is in great need of its own source of power. Because of environmen-

talists, coal is not an acceptable source of energy. Solar and wind power

be specific   *avoid "it seems"*
have not yet received the technology necessary to use them. It seems that

nuclear power is the only feasible means right now for obtaining self-

sufficient power. However, too large a percentage of the population are

be precise
against nuclear power claiming it is unsafe. With as many problems as the

think more about your reader

United States is having concerning energy, it seems a shame that the

public is so quick to "can" a very feasible means of power. Nuclear energy

should not be given up on, but rather, more nuclear plants should be built.

Thesis sentence needed.

One could easily remove all the comments from this paragraph and rubber-stamp them on another student text, and they would make as much or as little sense on the second text as they do here.

We have observed an overwhelming similarity in the generalities and abstract commands given to students. There seems to be among teachers an accepted, albeit unwritten canon for commenting on student texts. This uniform code of commands, requests, and pleadings demonstrates that the teacher holds a license for vagueness while the student is commanded to be specific. The students we interviewed admitted to having a great difficulty with these vague directives. The students stated that when a teacher writes in the margins or as an end comment, "choose precise language," or "think more about your audience," revising becomes a guessing game. In effect, the teacher is saying to the student, "Somewhere in this paper is imprecise language or lack of awareness of an audience and you must find it." The problem presented by these vague commands is compounded for the students when they are not offered any strategies for carrying out these commands. Students are told that they have done something wrong and that there is something in their text that needs to be fixed before the text is acceptable. But to tell students that they have done something wrong is not to tell them what to do about it. In order to offer a useful revision strategy to a student, the teacher must anchor that strategy in the specifics of the student's text. For instance, to tell our student, the author of the above paragraph, to "be specific," or to "elaborate," does not show our student what questions the reader has about the meaning of the text, or what breaks in logic exist, that could be resolved if the writer supplied information; nor is the student shown how to achieve the desired specificity.

Instead of offering strategies, the teachers offer what is interpreted by students as rules for composing; the comments suggest to students that writing is just a matter of following the rules. Indeed, the teachers seem to impose a series of abstract rules about written products even when some of them are not appropriate for the specific text the student is creating.[3] For instance, the student author of our sample paragraph presented above is commanded to follow the conventional rules for writing a five-paragraph essay — to begin the introductory paragraph by telling his reader what he is going to say and to end the paragraph with a thesis sentence. Somehow these abstract rules about what five-paragraph products should look like do not seem applicable to the problems this student must confront when revising, nor are the rules specific strategies he could use when revising. There are many inchoate ideas ready to be exploited in this paragraph, but the rules do not help the student to take stock of his (or her) ideas and use the opportunity he has, during revision, to develop those ideas.

The problem here is a confusion of process and product; what one has to say about the process is different from what one has to say about the product. Teachers who use this method of commenting are formulating their comments as if these drafts were finished drafts and were not going to be revised. Their commenting vocabularies have not been adapted to revision and they comment on first drafts as if they were justifying a grade or as if the first draft were the final draft.

Our summary finding, therefore, from this research on styles of commenting is that the news from the classroom is not good. For the most part, teachers do not respond to student writing with the kind of thoughtful commentary which will help students to engage with the issues they are writing about or which will help them think about their purposes and goals in writing a specific text. In defense of our teachers, however, they told us that responding to student writing was rarely stressed in their teacher-training or in writing workshops; they had been trained in various prewriting techniques, in constructing assignments, and in evaluating papers for grades, but rarely in the process of reading a student text for meaning or in offering commentary to motivate revision. The problem is that most of us as teachers of writing have been trained to read and interpret literary texts for meaning, but, unfortunately, we have not been trained to act upon the same set of assumptions in reading student texts as we follow in reading literary texts.[4] Thus, we read student texts with biases about what the writer should have said or about what he or she should have written, and our biases determine how we will comprehend the text. We read with our preconceptions and preoccupations, expecting to find errors, and the result is that we find errors and misread our students' texts.[5] We find what we look for; instead of reading and responding to the meaning of a text, we correct our students' writing. We need to reverse this approach. Instead of finding errors or showing students how to patch up parts of their texts, we need to sabotage our students' conviction that the drafts they have written are complete and coherent. Our comments need to offer students revision tasks of a different order of complexity and sophistication from the ones that they themselves identify, by forcing students back into the chaos, back to the point where they are shaping and restructuring their meaning.[6]

For if the content of a text is lacking in substance and meaning, if the order of the parts must be rearranged significantly in the next draft, if paragraphs must be restructured for logic and clarity, then many sentences are likely to be changed or deleted anyway. There seems to be no point in having students correct usage errors or condense sentences that are likely to disappear before the next draft is completed. In fact, to identify such problems in a text at this early first draft stage, when such problems are likely to abound, can give a student a disproportionate sense of their importance at this stage in the writing process.[7] In responding to our students' writing, we should be guided by the recognition that it is not spelling or usage problems that we as writers first worry about when drafting and revising our texts.

We need to develop an appropriate level of response for commenting on a first draft, and to differentiate that from the level suitable to a second or third draft. Our comments need to be suited to the draft we are reading. In a first or second draft, we need to respond as any reader would, registering questions, reflecting befuddlement, and noting places where we are puzzled about the meaning of the text. Comments should point to breaks in logic, disruptions in meaning, or missing information. Our goal in commenting on early drafts should be to engage students with the issues they are considering and help them clarify their purposes and reasons in writing their specific text.

For instance, the major rhetorical problem of the essay written by the student who wrote the first paragraph (the paragraph on nuclear power) quoted above was that the student had two principal arguments running through his text, each of which brought the other into question. On the one hand, he argued that we must use nuclear power, unpleasant as it is, because we have nothing else to use; though nuclear energy is a problematic source of energy, it is the best of a bad lot. On the other hand, he also argued that nuclear energy is really quite safe and therefore should be our primary resource. Comments on this student's first draft need to point out this break in logic and show the student that if we accept his first argument, then his second argument sounds fishy. But if we accept his second argument, his first argument sounds contradictory. The teacher's comments need to engage this student writer with this basic rhetorical and conceptual problem in his first draft rather than impose a series of abstract commands and rules upon his text.

Written comments need to be viewed not as an end in themselves — a way for teachers to satisfy themselves that they have done their jobs — but rather as a means for helping students to become more effective writers. As a means for helping students, they have limitations; they are, in fact, disembodied remarks — one absent writer responding to another absent writer. The key to successful commenting is to have what is said in the comments and what is done in the classroom mutually reinforce and enrich each other. Commenting on papers assists the writing course in achieving its purpose; classroom activities and the comments we write to our students need to be connected. Written comments need to be an extension of the teacher's voice — an extension of the teacher as reader. Exercises in such activities as revising a whole text or individual paragraphs together in class, noting how the sense of the whole dictates the smaller changes, looking at options, evaluating actual choices, and then discussing the effect of these changes on revised drafts — such exercises need to be designed to take students through the cycles of revising and to help them overcome their anxiety about revising: that anxiety we all feel at reducing what looks like a finished draft into fragments and chaos.

The challenge we face as teachers is to develop comments which will provide an inherent reason for students to revise; it is a sense of revision as discovery, as a repeated process of beginning again, as starting out new, that our students have not learned. We need to show our students how to seek, in the possibility of revision, the dissonances of discovery — to show them through our comments why new choices would positively change their texts, and thus to show them the potential for development implicit in their own writing.

Notes

[1] C. H. Knoblach and Lil Brannon, "Teacher Commentary on Student Writing: The State of the Art," *Freshman English News,* 10 (Fall 1981), 1–3.

[2] For an extended discussion of revision strategies of student writers see Nancy Sommers, "Revision Strategies of Student Writers and Experienced Adult Writers," *College Composition and Communication,* 31 (December 1980), 378–388.

[3] Nancy Sommers and Ronald Schleifer, "Means and Ends: Some Assumptions of Student Writers," *Composition and Teaching,* 2 (December 1980), 69–76.

[4] Janet Emig and Robert P. Parker, Jr., "Responding to Student Writing: Building a Theory of the Evaluating Process," unpublished paper, Rutgers University.

[5] For an extended discussion of this problem see Joseph Williams, "The Phenomenology of Error," *College Composition and Communication,* 32 (May 1981), 152–168.

[6] Ann Berthoff, *The Making of Meaning* (Montclair, N.J.: Boynton/Cook Publishers, 1981).

[7] W. U. McDonald, "The Revising Process and the Marking of Student Papers," *College Composition and Communication,* 24 (May 1978), 167–170.

MONITORING STUDENT WRITING:
HOW NOT TO AVOID THE DRAFT

Margie Krest

[*Journal of Teaching Writing* 7.1 (1988): 27–39.]

Margie Krest is an instructor in the Department of Environmental, Population and Organismic Biology at the University of Colorado at Boulder. She has published articles in the *English Journal,* the *Journal of Teaching Writing,* and the *Journal of College Science Teaching.*

In the years since Nancy Sommers's groundbreaking article "Responding to Student Writing" (reprinted on p. 131), instructors have come to understand that student writing improves when students receive meaningful feedback on works-in-progress. Krest describes her strategies for providing this feedback at various stages of the drafting and revising process. She also describes several roles that teachers can adopt when they offer feedback to students. Using drafts from three students, Krest illustrates how her approach can help students make effective revisions.

Monitoring student writing is a challenge because it involves a number of teaching skills, all aimed at effectively guiding students from a first to a final draft. Monitoring is different from evaluating because it does not involve assigning the student a grade or making a final assessment; rather, it helps students direct their attention to aspects of their drafts that they might change to improve their writing. This article is designed to help teachers monitor student writing. In section one, I discuss the rationale for monitoring; in section two, I demonstrate the monitoring procedure on three papers from an English 101 class at the University of Colorado–Denver; in section three, I summarize the major considerations to remember when monitoring writing.

Rationale

When we monitor students' writing with the primary purposes of helping them improve their writing skills and helping them maintain or attain a positive attitude about writing, we must consider a number of important points. The way we phrase our responses to students is just as important as what we actually tell them. And, of course, neither of these can be done in a vacuum. First, we must consider the point in the semester at which a paper is written: what we expect on the first paper should be much less than what we expect on the fifth paper. Second, we must consider the stage of drafting the student is in: what we respond to in a first draft will be different from what we respond to on a third draft. As a general rule, teachers should hold students responsible for implementing skills only after those skills are introduced and discussed in class.

Focus, Development, Organization

Recognizing what to monitor on a student's paper can be simplified when we keep a few major concerns in mind. Instead of approaching a paper looking for problems, we should approach a paper considering how and why communication either failed or succeeded (Lindemann). The question is how to determine what leads to a failure in writing. Certainly sentence structure and mechanics can hinder writing. However, if a student's focus, development and/or organization are not apparent, correcting sentence structure or mechanics will not clarify an idea. Thus, it makes sense to direct our own attention to the paper's focus, development and organization, especially on initial drafts (McDonald; Sommers). Reigstad and McAndrew suggest that teachers divide their own thinking into High Order Concerns (HOCs) and Low Order Concerns (LOCs). HOCs include focus, organization, development and voice. Analyzing these areas only on all initial drafts will first tell us how well the students communicated their ideas, and second, direct the students' attention to these, *as their own* areas of concern on all early drafts.

Style

Determining the point at which we should monitor sentence structure, mechanics, spelling and usage is not difficult when we remember to focus on these only after students have a handle on their HOCs. To simplify monitoring, I make a separate category for sentence structure (variety, subordination, phrasing) calling them "Middle Order Concerns" (MOCs). Once students have focused, organized and developed their content, concentrating on MOCs serves to direct the students' attention to *how* to express ideas (McDonald). When a teacher points out *why* a sentence is awkward and suggests one or two ways to clarify it, students can then work on their own to revise particular sentences. What's more, after students spend class time discussing sentence variety, subordination and coordination and practice using these during class sessions, most students simply need to have their lack of variety or subordination pointed out to them in order to improve their sentences.

Mechanics, Spelling, Usage

As a rule, I rarely spend time responding to individual LOCs such as spelling and mechanics on specific papers when I monitor except when a student asks me to check for a particular pattern of errors (see below). This is not to suggest that LOCs are not important; however, it does say that my emphasis is first on content, then on style, and then on mechanics and spelling (Bridges). Mechanics and spelling are areas for which students can take more responsibility (Hirsch, cited in Lees) once they understand their own pattern of errors (Bridges; Kroll & Schafer; Lindemann; Shaughnessy). That is, instead of students seeing themselves as never knowing how to use a comma, they can begin to see that they omit commas after introductory clauses or use a comma before every coordinating conjunction. Most LOCs, such as mechanics, spelling and usage, can and should be worked on in editing groups in class sessions before the final paper is due but after the student has revised for content and style. Working in mini-groups on a common problem or "error pattern" is effective because group members can work together to isolate and correct a particular error.

Roles

Finally, when we read a student's paper and begin to formulate in our own minds what we want to discuss with the student, it is most important to determine how we will phrase our responses to the student so that we facilitate positive attitudes about writing (Johnston). From the first class session we need to strive to get to know our students and learn to be sensitive to their feelings about who they are as writers.

As we get to know students and develop our own sensitivities to them, we should also be able to assume various roles as teacher (Britton; Calabrese). When I monitor students' writing I assume one of four roles — the partner or trusted adult, the coach, the diagnostician, or the critic:

- As a partner or trusted adult, I give my honest reactions regarding a paper. For example, I might express my own confusion about a certain passage that I do not understand because of a lack of detail or sentence structure; or, I might express my feeling of sadness after reading a certain passage.
- As a coach, I work to direct a student's energies in a certain direction to help him or her accomplish a goal. For me, coaching means asking the writer specific questions. For instance, I might ask a series of questions throughout the paper, all for the purpose of helping the writer answer those questions to find a focus.
- As a diagnostician my role is to analyze or identify what is being said or how something is being said in the paper. For example, I might simply point out that in a particular paragraph, each sentence begins with the subject/verb pattern. I do not praise or criticize this — I simply diagnose or identify it.

- Finally, as a critic, I direct my comments to those areas of the paper that are either "not working" or simply wrong, and *tell* the writer such very openly and directly — much more directly than as a diagnostician. As a critic, a teacher should be sure to explain why something is wrong and refrain from making negative value judgments about the person.

The teacher needs to assume different roles for different students on different papers, during various drafts at various times throughout the semester. In other words, one student may need a partner on a first draft but a critic on a third draft. And another may need a coach on a first draft and a diagnostician on a second. The point is that we need to be *flexible* in our role when monitoring student writing, and this flexibility in our role should coincide with the actual comments that we make. Overall, the role we assume must be determined by (A) the personality of the student and (B) the academic needs of the student because our role as monitor is not only to help students improve their writing but also help them maintain or attain a positive attitude toward writing.

Application

Kay

The following is a copy of Kay's first draft. The assignment, given during the third week of the semester, was to write a one to two page character sketch in which she was to describe a person in terms of a specific quality, trait or characteristic. We spent the class period in which the assignment was given on pre-writing activities specifically relating to the assignment: brainstorming, mapping and free writing about a person. We then discussed how to limit oneself to a single aspect of a person's personality. At this point in the semester, I knew little about Kay or her background in writing. (All student papers in this article are reproduced exactly as written.)

> Up in the morning here we go again, into the shower or maybe not into the shower. washing one face awake. Drawers full of blue shorts, white socks and blue T-shirts. Jocks everwhere thrown all over the place, colors and styles of who only knows what kind. Grabbing one of any kind into the shorts and on goes the T-shit, socks and tennis shoes.
>
> Just a repeat going through the motions, on with the hat and out of the house. Vitamins breakfact some nutrion of that kind. Arriving day to day all jokes aside, Back and forth up and down the floor we go, white lines. red lines up and down I go. Wet like a pig the sweat just pours down his forehead, neck and slowly down the spin.
>
> All the yelling screamin spearing, on this may go however we only know to what extent it really goes, on our mission is to score. As it all ends I must keep in mind in another days time the motion will return

My first response to Kay's paper was in the form of a simple question in our workshop group in class. I asked her what she wanted to get across to us, her audience. Her reply was that she wanted to describe her messy husband in the morning. I then commented that what confused me was the use of different pronouns such as I, one, we, his. I suggested that she focus just on him — what *he* did or thought or where *he* went. Then, I added one additional comment — that it would be nice for me as a reader to have more information that "showed" he was messy.

Obviously, there are many stylistic and mechanical problems in Kay's paper. However, it was important for her to understand that her content was of primary importance in communication. So, she needed to know why her *content* failed to communicate her idea. Because I was merely a member of her workshop group, I responded to her primarily as a partner and a trusted adult, giving my honest responses to her essay.

Kay's second draft contained approximately nine to eleven additional sentences that showed his messiness; she used one "I" pronoun and "he" or "his" in all other places. After reading her second draft, I told her that I was beginning to see how messy he was and that she *had* focused the paper on him. My only suggestion for change was that she might arrange all the information in the order that it happened.

During the remainder of our conference, I talked to Kay about herself. My goal was to understand Kay as a person and learn why she was in school. I wanted to find out why she wrote as she did and the amount of motivation she had to improve her writing. I hoped that in knowing her motivation I would also find out her reaction to criticisms or suggestions so that I could *phrase* my responses accordingly.

Kay was just starting college, 13 years after finishing high school. She always did "awful" in high school but was now training to be an airline stewardess and felt the need to better her education. Kay hated to read. Even at the age of 30, she disliked reading newspapers or magazines. Her only contact with written English was in the form of instructions or mail.

Kay's writing suffered from a lack of exposure to written communication. However, although her skills were very weak, her motivation was very high. Also, she liked the idea of revising her papers and was eager to do so. Kay was not overly sensitive about her writing so I could easily assume the role of a diagnostician and/or critic.

We discussed this third draft several days later.

> Throwing the covers back off the bed, he begins slowly to stroll. Up in the morning, made it once again into the shower or . . . maybe not into the shower he goes. Rubbing his eyes to see clear the view headed straight for the bathroom door. Feeling the running water looking into the fogged mirrors just can't seem to focus a view. Stepped into the shower splashing water all over his body and fact beginning to surface a view. Out of the shower onto the bare floor his feet are stuck to the towel that was left on the floor.
>
> On with the robe and down the stairs he goes, leaving tracks of water dripping from his body onto the floor. Opens the door picking up the newspaper sits at the dining room table, off comes the rubberband and onto the floor. Papers sorted thrown here and thrown there, goes to the kitchen and fixes a bowl of cheerios, dripping milk from the bowl to his mouth realizing the time and away their he goes.
>
> Into the drawers begins the search for daily wear, underwear that are throun hear and there grabbing a pair and on they go. Pulling another drawer open to find a T-shirt, wrinkled and studded no one else would dare, put it on to wear. Sorting through the socks mixed and some matched some long and some short who will ever know. Ties and belts accessories who know where they are, in a pocket or on some slack Lord only knows. Grab a shirt half way hanging on a hook and a pair of slack that are from before. Oh what about his hair a couple of stroked of the comb and out of the door he goes.

Within three drafts, Kay had basically attained a focus (her husband in the morning), given details to support her focus and succeeded at a sense of organization (the order in which he did things in the morning). Kay had made progress with HOCs within three drafts. It became apparent that the next major failure in her communications was due to her lack of proper sentence structure (MOCs). However, marking R.O., Frag. or Awk. beside every sentence would not help Kay in any way. She simply did not understand the function of subjects and verbs in sentences, so the editorial markings would make no sense. First, Kay needed to hear how a correctly written sentence *sounded* when read aloud. She then needed to understand the function of the subject and verb in a sentence so that she could be sure to include them in every sentence she wrote.

I first took a paragraph or two and simply put in subjects and verbs, retaining as much of her own wording as possible. For example:

> He put on the robe and went down the stairs leaving tracks of water dripping from his body onto the floor. He opened the door, picked up the newspaper, and sat at the dining room table. He took off the rubberband and threw it onto the floor. Papers were thrown here and there. He went to the kitchen and fixed a bowl of cheerios. As he read one section of the news and ate his cheerios, milk dripped from his mouth to the bowl. Realizing the time, he went upstairs.

I asked Kay to read this aloud a number of times. We worked on another of her paragraphs, concentrating solely on identifying subjects and verbs in each sentence. I then assigned her exercises in a simple grammar book on sentence fragments and run-ons. We also did some group work in class on how to identify a subject and verb in a sentence and correct run-ons and fragments.

These are the only areas we worked on in this paper. Over a period of two weeks Kay made noticeable progress on the paper and the fact that she still wished to continue writing, knowing that she had numerous hurdles to overcome, encouraged both of us.

Steve

The following is a copy of Steve's third draft. It was the seventh week of the semester, and class discussions had included essay structure, paragraph structure, use of details, methods of organization, and identification and correction of run-ons and fragments. In this assignment he was to write an essay in which he described a person's influence upon him.

> One day while walking through the green and flowered gardens of Kensington park I encountered a man that forever changed my dull view towards music. The man was Bill Wyman the bassest for the Rolling Stones, a legend in the rock music world.
>
> Having met such a renowned person without having heard his work, I decided to listen to some of his bands particular type of music. I went to the largest record store in the city where I found an enormous selection of Rolling Stones albums. I listened to several of their albums and ended up buying my first real rock and roll album. This new album began opening up many new relationships and ideas.
>
> One of the relationships that sprang from my new awakening to rock music was, that I met more musicaly inclined people. They were always interested in playing and listening to different music. An other relationship was that I began participating in a band where I could learn more about musiciams and their instruments. Through these people and the band, I learned how to play the bass guitar as well as recognize different styles and tastes in music. My new friends tastes in music were varied which gave me thoughts of the type of music that excited me. These thoughts led me to choose jazz as the music that I enjoyed listening to. My interest in jazz began with the blues and blossomed into a more progressive instrument style.

> Occasionly I hear different types of jazz that brings back memories of how I had become acquainted with this type of music. Only by having met Bill Wyman would I have eventualy had the influences I did and discovered the music I really liked.

Because it was the seventh week of the semester, I had had some time to get to know Steve. He was 27 years old, had spent four years in the Navy, had worked full time and had just decided to return to school. He had spent much of the semester developing the essay structure and developing details. Steve was a humorous person but extremely sensitive about his writing ability. When given abrupt or negative comments such as "This sentence doesn't make sense" or "I don't understand this at all," his reaction was severe: his facial muscles tightened and he became very discouraged. Consequently, I learned that *how* I phrased my comments to Steve was extremely important. Generally, in order to avoid his interpreting my written responses negatively, I tried to talk so that my tone of voice might convey encouragement or humor. I found that assuming the role of partner or coach relaxed Steve the most while at the same time elicited positive responses.

I began by commenting on the flow of the first sentence and the obvious improvement he had made on paragraphing, noting the different idea each paragraph conveyed. Even though this was his third draft, focus, organization and details in the third paragraph still needed revising so it was on this paragraph that I focused my attention.

I summarized his third paragraph by saying, "This is what I hear you saying in this paragraph. Tell me if I'm correct. Because of Bill, you started listening to music, meeting people interested in music, and really got into jazz." He was excited that I had understood his idea, and the positive feedback encouraged him. My next comment would be an important one for Steve because he would need to understand that the way in which he conveyed these ideas was not clear and detailed. However, knowing Steve, I also knew that I would not need to be blunt because when I simply questioned a statement or suggested another way of saying something, Steve would immediately assume that he didn't get his point across. I started by asking him if "that I met . . . people" and "participating in a band" were "relationships." As he quickly understood that he needed to rephrase his ideas, I voiced my interest in knowing what he meant by such phrases as "musically inclined people" and "different music" and "tastes in music" and a more "progressive instrument style." He began to understand that this paper could use a lot of revision. However, most important for Steve was the fact that he was not devastated or overwhelmed by comments which would discourage him from writing, and he actually became excited at the prospect of revising his content, which he went on to do.

Matt

Approximately eleven weeks into the semester, Matt submitted this paper as his "almost final" draft. In this essay he was to describe and give his own reactions to a situation that he saw but was not involved in. When the paper was submitted, the class had just completed two class sessions on sentence variety (in length and opening) and subordination and coordination of ideas.

> They faced each other. Joe was really mad. He kept yelling and pushing Rob around. Rob repeated, "If you push me again, I'm gonna kill you." Joe did not head this warning. Another shove and Robs head hit the locker. I guess that's when he lost it.

In raged, Rob jumped at Joe, fist flying. I was wondering what provoked this incident. A right hook landed on Joes brow. It looked quite painful. Rob paused and waited for Joes return blow. I don't know why he waited except that they were best friends. Joe, being stunned did not return a punch. I thought it was over, but Rob seemed to desire a punch in the head just to make it even. Again Rob swung and another blow struck and split Joe's lip. Why won't Joe fight back I wondered. By now Joe was being held up by the lockers. I was really mad at both guys. They are best friends. Why are they fighting I though.

I know Rob often jokes around too much. Maybe Joe got fed up with his pranks; however, Rob gave Joe fair warning. Why did Joe want to fight so bad and why isn't he fighting now that he has the chance. Rob continued to pummel Joe's face.

Bleeding from about the eyes and lip, Joe slid to the floor. Some guys pulled Rob off the beaten pile of flesh. Rob quickly ran off somewhere. I asked around and found my hypothesis to be correct. Rob and Joe were having punch wars and Rob hit Joe too hard when Joe didn't expect it. Joe blew up and forced this whole thing. A bunch of questions came to mind. Will they still be friends? Will they see the dean and get suspended? Why didn't some one stop the fight? Why didn't I?

As it turned out the dean did not suspend them because they were best friends and both said they were very sorry. I don't think that really mattered. Sorrow did not help the situation. I wondered how their parents felt. Parents can't win in this situation. The victors parents must be angry at their sons violent agression. And the losers parents must be disappointed in their sons performance. It just proves that fighting serves no purpose for anyone involved.

Matt was 19 years old and interested in writing but overconfident about his writing abilities. In class he quickly responded to discussions on mechanics, grammar and content and could verbalize rules for mechanics and grammar and identify possible problems in essays. However, he did not apply the rules and his insight to his own work. In many ways, it seemed that his overconfidence was his greatest hindrance because he never felt that he was the type of person who needed to revise. Also, Matt often chose not to work on his papers unless someone was very firm with him, pointing out errors directly. "Suggestions" to Matt were merely another way of saying something that he perceived as already well said. Often, encouragement resulted in his working less on his papers because hearing the encouragement, he seemed to consider the weaknesses unimportant.

There are many types of errors on his paper, even though this is his "almost final" draft. His focus and development obviously need to be revised. So, I started by *telling* him that there were three major weaknesses in his content that he needed to work on. One, there were numerous "telling" statements such as "It looked quite painful" rather than "showing" statements; two, there was a paragraphing problem in the fourth paragraph; and three, there was a shift in focus in the last paragraph. Matt understood why these areas were weak and said that he just hadn't taken the time to change them and went on to explain how he would revise them. If when I pointed out to him the weaknesses in his focus and development he could not have told me how and why he would change these, it would have been premature to discuss his style.

However, for Matt, a discussion of style motivated him to place more demands on himself, demands which he knew how to make but too often chose not to. I first asked him to analyze the pattern and length of each sentence in the first two paragraphs, commenting that they did not show application of the skills we had worked on in class. I then had him count the number of coordinating and subordinating ideas. Within a couple of minutes, Matt saw that his first two paragraphs contained many short, choppy sentences and did not give his reader insight into what ideas should be stressed. When I asked him how he might change the situation, he readily rattled off three or four different techniques for sentence opening and sentence combining and illustrated how he would combine his first three sentences. He then took the paper home and revised it. Matt had the skills for being a good writer, but he needed a critic to "encourage" him to use his skills.

Students use and learn from our comments when we monitor their writing rather than simply evaluate their final papers. When students have the opportunity immediately to incorporate ideas and changes into a paper, they understand the value of a particular comment. One student noted this idea quite succinctly in a journal entry: "The more important fact to notice here is that the conference is held *before* the paper is graded. This allows the teacher and student to thoroughly discuss and revise the paper. I believe that everyone should have the right to perfect something to make it the best it can be."

So, as we work to apply the theory behind monitoring writing and help students "make it the best it can be," we must remember four key points: (1) When we respond to student writing, our first concerns must relate to focus, development, organization and voice. (2) Only after students have a handle on these in any given paper should we direct their attention to style. (3) When further revision in these areas is no longer necessary, and students are contemplating their final drafts, we can work with them to help them identify their pattern of errors regarding mechanics and spelling. (4) At each point in our monitoring we must strive to be sensitive to our students as writers so that our comments foster positive attitudes about writing.

Successful monitoring, then, is really a matter of organizing our own expectations for papers and developing our own skills as communicators. As we develop in these areas, our students' writing will develop as well.

Works Cited

Bridges, Charles. "The Basics and the New Teacher," in *Training the New Teacher of College Composition*. Ed. Charles Bridges. Urbana, Ill.: NCTE, 1986.

Britton, James, et al. *The Development of Writing Abilities (11–18)*. London: Macmillan Education LTD, 1975.

Calabrese, Marylyn E. "I Don't Grade Papers Anymore." *English Journal*, 71, 1 (1982): 28–31.

Hirsch, E. D., Jr. *The Philosophy of Composition*. Chicago: University of Chicago Press, 1977.

Johnston, Brian. "Non-Judgmental Response to Students' Writing." *English Journal*, 71, 4 (1982): 50–53.

Kroll, Barry M., and John C. Schafer. "Error-Analysis and the Teaching of Composition." *College Composition and Communication*, 29 (1978): 242–248.

Lees, Elaine O. "Evaluating Student Writing." *College Composition and Communication*, 30 (1979): 370–374.

Lindemann, Erika. *A Rhetoric for Writing Teachers*. New York: Oxford University Press, 1982.

McDonald, W. U., Jr. "The Revising Process and the Marking of Student Papers." *College Composition and Communication*, 24 (1978): 167–170.

Reigstad, Thomas J., and Donald A. McAndrew. *Training Tutors for Writing Conferences*. Urbana, Ill: NCTE, 1984.

Shaughnessy, Mina P. *Errors and Expectations.* New York: Oxford University Press, 1977.

Sommers, Nancy. "Responding to Student Writing." *College Composition and Communication,* 33 (1982): 148–156.

DEMONSTRATING TECHNIQUES FOR ASSESSING WRITING IN THE WRITING CONFERENCE

Richard Beach

[*College Composition and Communication* 37 (1986): 56–65.]

Richard Beach is professor of English education at the University of Minnesota. He is the author of *A Teacher's Introduction to Reader Response Theories* (1993), and he is coauthor of *Teaching Literature in the Secondary School* (1991) and *Journals in the Classroom: Writing to Learn* (1995). He has published numerous book chapters and journal articles on reading, composition research, and teaching literature. He has served as the president of the National Conference on Research in Language and Literacy.

As more classrooms provide environments in which students share and respond to one another's works-in-progress, instructors continue to seek ways to increase and improve on the feedback that writers give each other. Beach argues that students will not necessarily learn to evaluate writing on their own just from reading instructors' responses to their writing. Rather, instructors need to model for students the various strategies for reading and assessing; in essence, students must be taught how to assess.

In a conference, I ask a student to tell me how she feels about her draft. "Oh, I feel pretty good about it," is her response; "maybe it needs a few more details." Having read the draft, I know that it's riddled with more serious problems than lack of details.

How can this student be taught to critically assess her writing? As experienced teachers know, simply telling the students what their problems are and what to do about those problems doesn't help them learn to become their own best readers. It teaches them only how to follow instructions.

Moreover, in giving students "reader-based feedback" — how I respond as a reader — which presumably implies to students that certain problems exist, I must assume that they are capable of defining the implied problem, which is often not the case.

The majority of students who have difficulty assessing their own writing need some instruction in how to assess. Teachers typically demonstrate techniques for assessing writing by discussing rhetorical or logical problems in published and/or students' texts. Unfortunately, students often have difficulty applying this instruction to assessment of problems in their own texts. For these students, a teacher may then need to augment classroom instruction in assessing techniques by demonstrating these techniques in writing conferences — showing them how to assess their own unique problems — and then having them practice this assessing in the conference.

This more individualized approach to teaching assessing in conferences involves the following steps:

1. determining a student's own particular difficulty by analyzing his or her use of certain assessing techniques;
2. demonstrating the stages of assessing: describing, judging, and selecting appropriate revisions;
3. describing the different components of the rhetorical context — purpose, rhetorical strategies, organization, and audience, showing students how each component implies criteria for judging drafts and selecting appropriate revisions;
4. having students practice the technique that was just demonstrated.

Techniques of Assessing

In order to discuss ways of demonstrating different assessing techniques, I propose a model of assessing. As illustrated in the following chart, assessing involves three basic stages: describing, judging, and selecting/testing out revisions. I will briefly define each of these stages and then, for the remainder of this paper, discuss how I demonstrate these techniques in a conference.

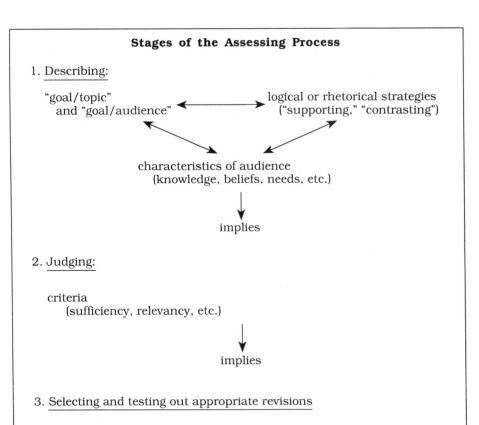

Stages of the Assessing Process

1. Describing:

   "goal/topic" and "goal/audience" ←→ logical or rhetorical strategies ("supporting," "contrasting")

   characteristics of audience (knowledge, beliefs, needs, etc.)

   ↓ implies

2. Judging:

   criteria (sufficiency, relevancy, etc.)

   ↓ implies

3. Selecting and testing out appropriate revisions

As depicted in this chart, each of the first two stages implies a subsequent stage. By *describing* their goals, strategies, or audience, writers have some basis for making judgments about their drafts. For example, a writer describes his strategy — that in the beginning of his story, he is "setting the scene in order to show what a small-town world is like." He describes his audience — noting that the audience probably knows little about that particular setting. Now he can infer appropriate criteria for judging his setting — whether he has included enough information to convey the sense of a "small-town world" to his reader. This judgment, in turn, helps him in the final stage, *selecting appropriate revisions* — in this case, adding more information about the setting.

In demonstrating assessing techniques, I am therefore showing students more than how to use a specific technique. I am also showing them that describing audience implies criteria for judging or that defining a problem implies criteria for selecting revisions. These demonstrations help students appreciate the value of describing and judging in helping them make revisions.

One benefit of a conference is that it provides a forum for students to practice their assessing with a teacher. The teacher can then note instances in which a student is having difficulty and, instead of simply telling the student how to improve her assessing, demonstrate how to assess. The student then has a concrete guide for trying out a certain assessing technique.

Determining Difficulties in Assessing

In order to know which technique to demonstrate, I try to pinpoint a student's difficulty in using a particular technique. I therefore have students begin the conference by giving me their reactions to and sense of the difficulties with their draft, listening carefully for difficulties in describing, judging, or selecting revisions. However, given the brevity of many conferences, I often can't diagnose students' difficulties by relying solely on their comments in the conference. I therefore use guided assessing forms, which students complete prior to the conference.

The questions on these forms are based on the three assessing stages, as listed below:

The Guided Assessing Form

Describing

1. What are you trying to say or show in this section?
2. What are you trying to do in this section?
3. What are some specific characteristics of your audience?
4. What are you trying to get your audience to do or think?

Judging

5. What are some problems you perceive in achieving 1, 2, and 4?

Selecting Appropriate Revisions

6. What are some changes you can make to deal with these problems?

In using the forms, students divide their draft into sections, answering the questions on the form for each section. The students don't necessarily need to begin with the "describing" questions; they may begin by noting problems and then working back to the describing stage.

By reading over the form in the beginning of the conference and by listening to their reactions to the draft, I try to determine a student's particular difficulty in assessing her draft. If, for example, for each of three sections in her draft a student has difficulty describing what she is "trying to say or show," I might conclude that she has difficulty defining her intentions. The fact that she's also had difficulty answering my questions about goals further suggests that inferring intentions is a problem for her.

I then demonstrate how I would identify intentions. Rather than using my own writing, which the student isn't familiar with, I use the student's writing. I adopt the student's role or persona, demonstrating how I, from her perspective, would infer intentions. I stress to the student that while I am showing her how *I* would infer intentions, I am not implying that my approach is the "one correct way." I also *avoid* telling the students what they ought to be saying, for example, by telling them what I think they are "really trying to say." Rather, I am showing students how to do something rather than telling them what to say.

After I demonstrate a certain technique, I then ask the student to make her own inferences. If she continues to have difficulty, I demonstrate that technique further.

All of this requires careful attention to clues suggesting difficulties, as well as a conceptual framework for sorting out and isolating certain strategies. Based on my own experience and research on assessing, I will now discuss how I demonstrate each of the stages of the assessing process — describing, judging, and selecting revisions.

The Describing Stage

The describing stage consists of describing goals for content (What am I trying to say?), audience (What do I want my audience to do or think?), logical or rhetorical strategies (What am I trying to do: supporting, contrasting, shifting to a different point?), and audience characteristics (knowledge, traits, needs, etc.). Writers obviously use goals as criteria for judging whether their text says or does what they want it to say or do. Once they identify their goals, they can detect dissonance between their goals and their text, dissonance that leads to judgments about problems in achieving their goals.

This is not to imply that writers must always articulate their goals in order to assess their writing. Writers often have only a "felt sense" of their intentions without ever articulating them, but they know how to use their unarticulated intentions to determine that something is amiss and to decide what to do about their problems.

In a conference, it is often useful to have students articulate their goals because those goals are necessary for judging, for determining the extent to which those goals have or have not been fulfilled. If students are to be able to make these judgments, they may need help articulating goals.

Difficulties in describing goal/topics and goal/audience. In my research on use of the guided assessing forms, I asked students to describe what they were trying to say or show ("goal/topic") or what they wanted their audience to do or think ("goal/audience") in each of several sections of their draft.[1] Many students in these studies have difficulty stating what it is that they are trying to say or show. They often simply restate their text *verbatim* rather than stating their intended topic or idea. For example, in writing an analysis of citizen participation in the government of her hometown, a student described her draft section as saying that "a lot of citizens in the town don't vote and there often aren't enough candidates to run for local offices," almost a verbatim restatement of what she was saying in the draft. She did not go beyond that restatement to recognize a point of that section, her "goal/topic" — that citizens aren't involved in town government. She also had difficulty identifying her "goal/audience," what she wanted her audience to do or think having read her essay. Because she had difficulty identifying these goals, she had difficulty judging her draft.

To some degree, identifying these goals is difficult, particularly if students don't perceive the purpose for defining goals — to further assess their draft. I therefore try to show students that clearly defining goals helps them in judging their draft.

In demonstrating definitions of goal/topic, I demonstrate the difference between simply restating the content of a section of their draft and recognizing the goal or purpose of that section. In working with the student writing about her local government, I first take her restatement of the text, "that citizens don't vote and there aren't enough candidates" and, playing the role of the "dumb reader," to use Walker Gibson's term, ask the question, "what's the point?" I then infer a goal statement — that the citizens aren't involved — and show her that, in contrast to her restatement, I can use this goal statement to pinpoint disparities between goal and text.

Another problem with students' identifications of goal/topic is that they are often so global that they are not very useful for perceiving disparities between goals and text.[2] For example, in writing an autobiographical narrative about a series of shoplifting incidents, a student states that he was "trying to show what I was like when I was a teenager." This description is too global for assessing what it is he wants to show about this past self. The student needs to identify what the incidents show about his past self.

Having diagnosed the student's goals as too global, I then propose, using his other comments in the conference, a more precise goal statement: "in portraying my shoplifting, I'm trying to show that I was so lonely that I would do anything to be popular with my peers." I then use this inferred goal to review the shoplifting episodes, judging whether or not the descriptions of the student's behavior in each episode convey his need for friendship. Again, I am demonstrating the value of goal statements, particularly precise goal statements.

Difficulties in describing rhetorical or logical strategies. In describing rhetorical or logical strategies, writers are defining what they are doing in their texts — supporting, defining, stating, requesting, contrasting, describing, evaluating, specifying, etc. In naming these strategies, writers go beyond simply summarizing what they are trying to say, to identifying what they are trying to do, conceiving of their text from a functional or pragmatic perspective.

Each of these strategies implies certain criteria for assessing the success or failure of that strategy. By describing these strategies, writers evoke the particular criteria necessary for judging the use of that strategy. Writers then narrow down the criteria in light of their particular goals and the characteristics of their audience. For example, the strategy, supporting, implies the criteria, *sufficiency, relevancy,* or *specificity of support:* do I have enough support? is my support relevant to my thesis? is my support specific enough? Given an audience which the writer assumes knows little about the topic, the writer is particularly concerned about the sufficiency of information — is there enough supportive information for that audience to understand a point? Or, in requesting, as suggested by speech-act theorists, I am concerned about my power, right, or ability to make a request;

my reader's ability to fulfill my request; and my reader's perception of my sincerity in making a request. Given a reader who may doubt my right to make a request, I'm particularly concerned that my request implies that I have the right to make such a request.

For example, the administration at my university has decided to reduce my program, but without giving any clear rationale for the proposed reduction. In writing to the administration requesting some clarification of their rationale, I somewhat cynically anticipate their response — that I have no right to make such a request. In my request, I argue that I have the right to ask for clarification because further reductions would jeopardize my program and my job. I therefore clearly define my affiliation with the program in order to imply my right to make such a request.

Describing strategies and inferring implied criteria is a complicated process that requires a pragmatic perspective on writing — conceiving of writing as doing things rather than simply conveying information. It also requires tacit knowledge of the conditions governing the use of these strategies. It is therefore not surprising that, as our analysis of the assessing forms indicated, many students had difficulty describing their strategies and inferring implied criteria.[3] When asked to describe their strategies, students often had difficulty going beyond describing what they were trying to "say" to inferring what it is they were trying to "do." They frequently restated content — "I am writing about my high school and college courses," rather than inferring strategy — "I am contrasting my high school and college courses." These students, with only a restatement of content, then had difficulty making judgments about their text. Those students who identified a strategy were more likely to make a judgment because they had some basis for making it — for example, whether or not they were able to successfully contrast high school and college courses.

In demonstrating the difference between a summary of content and a description of strategy I again demonstrate how descriptions of strategies can be used to imply criteria. For example, having inferred that the student is contrasting high school and college classes, I then note that "contrasting" implies, among other criteria, the importance of information relevant to the contrast and the validity of the contrast — whether or not the information constitutes valid evidence for a contrast.

Difficulties in describing characteristics of audience. Making inferences about characteristics of audience is also a complex process. There is much debate regarding the conflicting evidence about how much writers actually think about their audience.[4]

I would argue that, rather than conceiving of audience as a unified global construct, writers infer or create specific prototypical characteristics such as what and how much members of an audience know about a topic, what they believe about a topic, and their needs, status, power, attitudes, or expectations. For example, in writing a set of directions for windsurfing, a writer may conceive of her audience as "someone who knows little about windsurfing." Or, in arguing the case for nationalizing the steel industry, a writer conceives of his audience as "someone who is opposed to my belief about nationalization." These conceptions are prototypical because writers often never know, even with familiar audiences, exactly what their audience knows, believes, needs, etc. They must therefore rely on prototypical constructs derived from approximations of their audience.

Writers also derive these characteristics from their defined goals and strategies. In giving a set of directions for windsurfing, a writer knows that she needs to consider what her audience may or may not know about windsurfing, because that characteristic is particularly useful for judging the relevancy and sufficiency of information in her directions. Writers therefore infer these prototypical constructs because, as with decisions about goals and strategies, the constructs imply relevant criteria for judging their writing.

Inferring these characteristics of audience also allows writers to adopt a reader's schema, as they must in order to distance themselves from their text. Having created the construct, "someone who is opposed to nationalizing the steel industry," they can then assess the text from that perspective.

When, in our research, Sarah Eaton and I asked students to infer characteristics of their audience on their assessing form, most of the students made few if any references to specific audience characteristics.[5] Most of their inferences consisted of anticipated emotional responses such as "my reader should like this beginning" or "my audience will be bothered by this section," inferences reflecting an egocentric orientation. They were more concerned with how their audience would react to their writing than with how to adapt their text to their audience.

When I sense that students are having difficulty inferring characteristics of audience, I demonstrate how I infer these characteristics from my description of strategies or goals. For example, in writing her paper about the lack of citizen participation in affairs of her hometown, the student previously cited began her paper by describing the town's government, noting that she's trying to "provide background information in order to set the scene." However, she has difficulty judging her use of this defined strategy — setting the scene — because she has difficulty inferring audience.

Using her description of her "backgrounding" strategy, I note that in giving background information, I need to determine how much her audience may know about her hometown. Once I've isolated the appropriate attribute — knowledge — I create the construct, "someone who knows little about the town." I then use that construct to judge her descriptions of the town.

The Judging Stage

Sensing dissonance. Having described these components of the rhetorical context, writers then judge their text. In judging, a writer needs to sense dissonance between goals and the text, dissonance that serves as an incentive to revise.

However, many students in our research had difficulty sensing dissonance because they had difficulty adopting a reader's perspective. In order to demonstrate ways of sensing dissonance, I go back and describe goals, strategies, characteristics of audience, and intended effects. As instructor, I then review the text from the perspective of a member of an audience with one of these characteristics, for example, "someone who knows little about book publishing." I, as instructor, then cite instances in which I, as a reader, didn't have enough background information to understand the draft. Given my goal, as the writer, of informing my reader about book publishing, I know that, from the reader's perspective, something is amiss.

Applying criteria. Once writers sense the dissonance, they need to specify the reason for the problem, why something is amiss.

Students often have difficulty specifying reasons for their problems. They may say that "this is awkward" or "this doesn't flow"; but these judgments often don't point towards any predicted solutions, because they are too vague. In contrast, judgments such as, "I don't have enough examples to support my thesis," imply some specific directions: add more examples.

One reason students aren't able to specify their reasons is that they simply don't know or don't know how to apply criteria such as sufficiency, relevancy, validity, clarity, appropriateness, or coherence. For example, a student thinks that there is a problem with her extended illustration of an ineffective teaching technique, but she can't define the reason for the problem. I then show her how to define a reason for her problem. Having defined her strategy, *giving examples,* I infer implied criteria — relevancy, sufficiency, or clarity of the information in terms of illustrating the point. I then ask the question — given the goals and characteristics of audience, is this a problem of relevancy, sufficiency, or clarity? I then note that, from my perspective as reader, the illustration is too long. This suggests that sufficiency of information serves as a useful criterion for selecting and testing out appropriate revisions. One can hope that the student will then recognize the value of specifying criteria in order to make revisions.

Selecting and Testing Out Appropriate Revisions

Once writers have defined their problem, they select and test out those revisions that will best solve the problem. A writer may select a certain revision strategy — adding, deleting, modifying, rewording, etc. — and/or formulate the content involved in using that revision strategy ("I will add more information about the appearance of the house").

Difficulties in selecting revisions. Just as writers' descriptions imply judgments, their judgments imply appropriate revisions. If their information is irrelevant, then they need to delete that information or make it more relevant. However, when students in our study were asked to answer the question on the form, "What are you going to do about your problem?" many had difficulty identifying possible revisions because they hadn't clearly defined their problem or the reasons for their problem.[6]

In these instances, I go back to the judging stage and demonstrate how specifying problems and reasons for problems implies revisions.

Difficulties in testing out optional revisions. Once students select a revision, they often assume that that revision will do the job, failing to consider why or how that revision works according to their goals, strategies, and characteristics of audience. For example, in writing about police corruption, a student notes that he wants to add some more examples of police corruption, but he doesn't know why he's adding the examples. I then show him how to review his revisions in terms of his goals, strategies, or audience characteristics. The student then realizes that the additional examples help bolster his charge — his central point — that the police corruption exists in all areas of society. Having reaffirmed his goal, he can test out whether each additional example supports his contention that "corruption is everywhere."

In showing students how to justify their revisions by considering their goals, strategies, or audience characteristics, I am illustrating that in assessing, it is essential to constantly cycle back to conceptions of the rhetorical context in order to reaffirm, clarify, or modify those conceptions in light of their advancing comprehension of that context as they write.

Diagnosing Students' Response to Modeling: Comprehending and Applying

These, then, are some of the techniques of assessing that I demonstrate in the conference. In most cases, I demonstrate no more than one or two of these techniques in any one conference. Otherwise, I end up dominating the conference rather than having the students practice their own assessing. After I complete my demonstration, I ask the students whether or not they understood the technique I was demonstrating. If a student didn't understand the technique, I repeat the demonstration until I am confident that the student not only understood the technique but also could actually employ that technique.

In subsequent conferences, I often find that my demonstrations have benefitted students in that they are able to use these techniques on their own, either in the conferences or on the guided assessing forms. In an attempt to determine the influence of the demonstrations, I conducted a study of one teacher's use of demonstrations with a group of eight college freshman students enrolled in a remedial composition course.[7] I analyzed (1) the transcripts of conferences and the students' assessing forms for evidence of students' use of assessing techniques, and (2) the students' revisions from the beginning to the end of the course. Over time, most of the students demonstrated marked changes, particularly in their ability to describe goals and strategies and to use those descriptions to judge their drafts and make revisions that improved their writing.

If learning to assess drafts is central to learning to revise and improve writing quality, then demonstrating these assessing techniques assumes a central role in composition instruction.

Notes

[1] Richard Beach and Sarah Eaton, "Factors Influencing Self-assessing and Revising of College Freshmen," in Richard Beach and Lillian Bridwell, ed., *New Directions in Composition Research* (New York: Guilford Press, 1984), pp. 149–70.

[2] Beach and Eaton, ibid.

[3] Beach and Eaton, "Factors."

[4] Donald Rubin, Gene Piché, Michael Michlin, and Fern Johnson, "Social-Cognitive Ability as a Predictor of the Quality of Fourth-Graders' Written Narratives," in Richard Beach and Lillian Bridwell, *New Directions;* Brant Burleson and Katherine Rowan, "Are Social-Cognitive Ability and Narrative Writing Skill Related?" *Written Communication* 2 (January 1985), 25–43.

[5] Beach and Eaton, "Factors."

[6] Beach and Eaton, "Factors."

[7] Richard Beach, "The Self-assessing Strategies of Remedial College Students," paper presented at the annual meeting of the American Educational Research Association," New York, 1977.

RANKING, EVALUATING, AND LIKING: SORTING OUT THREE FORMS OF JUDGMENT

Peter Elbow

[*College English* 55 (1993): 187–206.]

Professor of English and director of the writing program at the University of Massachusetts at Amherst, Peter Elbow first gained national fame as author of the classic *Writing without Teachers* (1973). Since then he has been one of the profession's most visible and prolific scholars and teachers. Among his many books, he coedited (with Pat Belanoff and Sheryl Fontaine) *Nothing Begins with N: New Investigations of Freewriting* (1990), and authored *What Is English?* published by the Modern Language Association in 1990. Elbow's many articles and chapters have appeared in a wide range of professional publications. Among his many awards is the CCCC's prestigious Richard Braddock Award, conferred in 1986.

Eventually, students submit their writing for a grade, no matter how much their instructors promote multiple, significant revisions. At that point instructors assess student writing — not to help guide revisions, but to decide how effectively students have achieved their goals or met assignment criteria. Elbow reflects on several alternatives available for assessing student writing, alternatives he characterizes as ranking, evaluating, and liking. He discusses the problems with ranking and the benefits of evaluating, suggesting that teachers do portfolio assessments where possible. He explores, too, the limitations of evaluation and the benefits of evaluation-free zones. Finally, Elbow discusses how simply liking students' writing — enjoying and taking a sincere interest in their work — can help motivate students and foster more effective criticism. Elbow offers several suggestions for teachers who want to explore alternative assessment strategies.

This essay is my attempt to sort out different acts we call assessment — some different ways in which we express or frame our judgments of value. I have been working on this tangle not just because it is interesting and important in itself but because assessment tends so much to drive and control *teaching*. Much of what we do in the classroom is determined by the assessment structures we work under.

Assessment is a large and technical area and I'm not a professional. But my main premise or subtext in this essay is that we nonprofessionals can and should work on it because professionals have not reached definitive conclusions about the problem of how to assess writing (or anything else, I'd say). Also, decisions about assessment are often made by people even less professional than we, namely legislators. Pat Belanoff and I realized that the field of assessment was open when we saw the harmful effects of a writing proficiency exam at Stony Brook and worked out a collaborative portfolio assessment system in its place (Belanoff and Elbow; Elbow and Belanoff). Professionals keep changing their minds about large-scale testing and assessment. And as for classroom grading, psychometricians provide little support or defense of it.

The Problems with Ranking and the Benefits of Evaluating

By ranking I mean the act of summing up one's judgment of a performance or person into a single, holistic number or score. We rank every time we give a grade or holistic score. Ranking implies a single scale or continuum or dimension along which all performances are hung.

By evaluating I mean the act of expressing one's judgment of a performance or person by pointing out the strengths and weaknesses of different features or dimensions. We evaluate every time we write a comment on a paper or have a conversation about its value. Evaluation implies the recognition of different criteria or dimensions — and by implication different contexts and audiences for the same performance. Evaluation requires going *beyond* a first response that may be nothing but a kind of ranking ("I like it" or "This is better than that"), and instead looking carefully enough at the performance or person to make distinctions between parts or features or criteria.

It's obvious, thus, that I am troubled by ranking. But I will resist any temptation to argue that we can get rid of all ranking — or even should. Instead I will try to show how we can have *less* ranking and *more* evaluation in its place.

I see three distinct problems with ranking: it is inaccurate or unreliable; it gives no substantive feedback; and it is harmful to the atmosphere for teaching and learning.

(1) First the unreliability. To rank reliably means to give a *fair* number, to find the single quantitative score that readers will agree on. But readers don't agree.

This is not news — this unavailability of agreement. We have long seen it on many fronts. For example, research in evaluation has shown many times that if we give a paper to a set of readers, those readers tend to give it the full range of grades (Diederich). I've recently come across new research to this effect — new to me because it was published in 1912. The investigators carefully showed how high school English teachers gave different grades to the same paper. In response to criticism that this was a local problem in English, they went on the next year to discover an even greater variation among grades given by high school geometry teachers and history teachers to papers in their subjects. (See the summary of Daniel Starch and Edward Elliott's 1913 *School Review* articles in Kirschenbaum, Simon, and Napier 258–59.)

We know the same thing from literary criticism and theory. If the best critics can't agree about what a text means, how can we be surprised that they disagree even more about the quality or value of texts? And we know that nothing in literary or philosophical theory gives us any agreed-upon rules for settling such disputes.

Students have shown us the same inconsistency with their own controlled experiments of handing the same paper to different teachers and getting different grades. This helps explain why we hate it so when students ask us their favorite question, "What do you want for an A?": it rubs our noses in the unreliability of our grades.

Of course champions of holistic scoring argue that they *can* get agreement among readers — and they often do (White). But they get that agreement by "training" the readers before and during the scoring sessions. What "training" means is getting those scorers to stop reading the way they normally read — getting them to stop using the conflicting criteria and standards they normally use outside the scoring sessions. (In an impressive and powerful book, Barbara Herrnstein Smith argues that whenever we have widespread inter-reader reliability, we have reason to suspect that difference has been suppressed and homogeneity imposed — almost always at the expense of certain groups.) In short, the reliability in holistic scoring is not a measure of how texts are valued by real readers in natural settings, but only of how they are valued in artificial settings with imposed agreements.

Defenders of holistic scoring might reply (as one anonymous reviewer did), that holistic scores are not perfect or absolutely objective readings but just "judgments that most readers will agree are the appropriate ones given the purpose of the assessment and the system of communication."

But I have been in and even conducted enough holistic scoring sessions to know that even that degree of agreement doesn't occur unless "purpose" and "appropriateness" are defined to mean acceptance of the single set of standards imposed on that session. We know too much about the differences among readers and the highly variable nature of the reading process. Supposing we get readings only from academics, or only from people in English, or only from respected critics, or only from respected writing programs, or only from feminists, or only from sound readers of my tribe (white, male, middle-class, full professors between the ages of fifty and sixty). We *still* don't get agreement. We can sometimes get agreement among readers from some subset, a particular community that has developed a strong set of common values, perhaps *one* English department or *one* writing program. But what is the value of such a rare agreement? It tells us nothing about how readers from other English departments or writing programs will judge — much less how readers from other domains will judge.

(From the opposite ideological direction, some skeptics might object to my skeptical train of thought: "So what else is new?" they might reply. "Of *course* my grades are biased, 'interested' or 'situated' — always partial to my interests or the values of my community or culture. There's no other possibility." But how can people consent to give grades if they feel that way? A single teacher's grade for a student is liable to have substantial consequences — for example on eligibility for a scholarship or a job or entrance into professional school. In grading, surely we must not take anything less than genuine fairness as our goal.)

It won't be long before we see these issues argued in a court of law, when a student who has been disqualified from playing on a team or rejected from a professional school sues, charging that the basis for his plight — teacher grades — is not reliable. I wonder if lawyers will be able to make our grades stick.

(2) Ranking or grading is woefully uncommunicative. Grades and holistic scores are nothing but points on a continuum from "yea" to "boo" — with no information or clues about the criteria behind these noises. They are 100 percent evaluation and 0 percent description or information. They quantify the degree of approval or disapproval in readers but tell nothing at all about what the readers actually approve or disapprove of. They say nothing that couldn't be said with gold stars or black marks or smiley-faces. Of course our first reactions are often nothing but global holistic feelings of approval or disapproval, but we need a system for communicating our judgments that nudges us to move beyond these holistic feelings and to articulate the basis of our feeling — a process that often leads us to change our feeling. (Holistic scoring sessions sometimes use rubrics that explain the criteria — though these are rarely passed along to students —and even in these situations, the rubrics fail to fit many papers.) As C. S. Lewis says, "People are obviously far more anxious to express their approval and disapproval of things than to describe them" (7).

(3) Ranking leads students to get so hung up on these oversimple quantitative verdicts that they care more about scores than about learning — more about the grade we put on the paper than about the comment we have written on it. Have you noticed how grading often forces us to write comments to justify our grades? — and how these are often *not* the comment we would make if we were just trying to help the student write better? ("Just try writing several favorable comments on a paper and then giving it a grade of D" [Diederich 21].)

Grades and holistic scores give too much encouragement to those students who score high — making them too apt to think they are already fine — and too little encouragement to those students who do badly. Unsuccessful students often come to doubt their intelligence. But oddly enough, many "A" students also end up doubting their true ability and feeling like frauds — because they have sold out on their own judgment and simply given teachers whatever yields an A. They have too often been rewarded for what they don't really believe in. (Notice that there's more cheating by students who get high grades than by those who get low ones. There would be less incentive to cheat if there were no ranking.)

We might be tempted to put up with the inaccuracy or unfairness of grades if they gave good diagnostic feedback or helped the learning climate; or we might put up with the damage they do to the learning climate if they gave a fair or reliable measure of how skilled or knowledgeable students are. But since they fail dismally on both counts, we are faced with the striking question of why grading has persisted so long.

There must be many reasons. It is obviously easier and quicker to express a global feeling with a single number than to figure out what the strengths and weaknesses are and what one's criteria are. (Though I'm heartened to discover, as I pursue this issue, how troubled teachers are by grading and how difficult they find it.) But perhaps more important, we see around us a deep *hunger to rank* — to create pecking orders: to see who we can look down on and who we must look up to, or in the military metaphor, who we can kick and who we must salute. Psychologists tell us that this taste for pecking orders or ranking is associated with the authoritarian personality. We see this hunger graphically in the case of IQ scores. It is plain that IQ scoring does not represent a commitment to looking carefully at people's intelligence; when we do that, we see different and frequently uncorrelated *kinds* or *dimensions* of intelligence (Gardner). The persistent use of IQ scores represents the hunger to have a number so that everyone can have a rank. ("Ten!" mutter the guys when they see a pretty woman.)

Because ranking or grading has caused so much discomfort to so many students and teachers, I think we see a lot of confusion about the process. It is hard to think clearly about something that has given so many of us such anxiety and distress. The most notable confusion I notice is the tendency to think that if we renounce ranking or grading, we are renouncing the very possibility of judgment and discrimination — that we are embracing the idea that there is no way to distinguish or talk about the difference between what works well and what works badly.

So the most important point, then, is that *I am not arguing against judgment or evaluation*. I'm just arguing against that crude, oversimple way of *representing* judgment — distorting it, really — into a single number, which means ranking people and performances along a single continuum.

In fact I am arguing *for evaluation*. Evaluation means looking hard and thoughtfully at a piece of writing in order to make distinctions as to the quality of different features or dimensions. For example, the process of evaluation permits us to make the following kinds of statements about a piece of writing:

• The thinking and ideas seem interesting and creative.
• The overall structure or sequence seems confusing.
• The writing is perfectly clear at the level of individual sentences and even paragraphs.

- There is an odd, angry tone of voice that seems unrelated or inappropriate to what the writer is saying.
- Yet this same voice is strong and memorable and makes one listen even if one is irritated.
- There are a fair number of mistakes in grammar or spelling: more than "a sprinkling" but less than "riddled with."

To rank, on the other hand, is to be forced to translate those discriminations into a single number. What grade or holistic score do these judgments add up to? It's likely, by the way, that more readers would agree with those separate, "analytic" statements than would agree on a holistic score.

I've conducted many assessment sessions where we were not trying to impose a set of standards but rather to find out how experienced teachers read and evaluate, and I've had many opportunities to see that good readers give grades or scores right down through the range of possibilities. Of course good readers sometimes agree — especially on papers that are strikingly good or bad or conventional, but I think I see difference more frequently than agreement when readers really speak up.

The process of evaluation, because it invites us to articulate our criteria and to make distinctions among parts or features or dimensions of a performance, thereby invites us further to acknowledge the main fact about evaluation: that different readers have different priorities, values, and standards.

The conclusion I am drawing, then, in this first train of thought is that we should do less ranking and more evaluation. Instead of using grades or holistic scores — single number verdicts that try to sum up complex performances along only one scale — we should give some kind of written or spoken evaluation that discriminates among criteria and dimensions of the writing — and if possible that takes account of the complex context for writing: who the writer is, what the writer's audience and goals are, who we are as readers and how we read, and how we might differ in our reading from other readers the writer might be addressing.

But how can we put this principle into practice? The pressure for ranking seems implacable. Evaluation takes more time, effort, and money. It seems as though we couldn't get along without scores on writing exams. Most teachers are obliged to give grades at the end of each course. And many students — given that they have become conditioned or even addicted to ranking over the years and must continue to inhabit a ranking culture in most of their courses — will object if we don't put grades on papers. Some students, in the absence of that crude gold star or black mark, may not try hard enough (though how hard is "enough" — and is it really our job to stimulate motivation artificially with grades — and is grading the best source of motivation?).

It is important to note that there are certain schools and colleges that do *not* use single-number grades or scores, and they function successfully. I taught for nine years at Evergreen State College, which uses only written evaluations. This system works fine, even down to getting students accepted into high quality graduate and professional schools.

Nevertheless we have an intractable dilemma: that grading is unfair and counterproductive but that students and institutions tend to want grades. In the face of this dilemma there is a need for creativity and pragmatism. Here are some ways in which I and others use *less ranking* and *more evaluation* in teaching — and they suggest some adjustments in how we score large-scale assessments. What follows is an assortment of experimental compromises — sometimes crude, seldom ideal or utopian — but they help.

(a) Portfolios. Just because conventional institutions oblige us to turn in a single quantitative course grade at the end of every marking period, it doesn't follow that we need to grade individual papers. Course grades are more trustworthy and less damaging because they are based on so many performances over so many weeks. By avoiding frequent ranking or grading, we make it *somewhat* less likely for students to become addicted to oversimple numerical rankings — to think that evaluation always translates into a simple number — in short, to mistake ranking for evaluation. (I'm not trying to defend conventional course grades since they are still uncommunicative and they still feed the hunger for ranking.) Portfolios permit me to refrain from grading individual papers and limit myself to writerly evaluative comments — and help students see this as a positive rather than a negative thing, a chance to be graded on a body of their best work that can be judged more fairly. Portfolios have many other advantages as well. They are particularly valuable as occasions for asking students to write extensive and thoughtful explorations of their own strengths and weaknesses.

A midsemester portfolio is usually an informal affair, but it is a good occasion for giving anxious students a ballpark estimate of how well they are doing in the course so far. I find it helpful to tell students that I'm perfectly willing to tell them my best estimate of their course grade — but only if they come to me in conference and only during the second half of the semester. This serves somewhat to quiet their anxiety while they go through seven weeks of drying out from grades. By midsemester, most of them have come to enjoy not getting those numbers and thus being able to think better about more writerly comments from me and their classmates.

Portfolios are now used extensively and productively in larger assessments, and there is constant experimentation with new applications (Belanoff and Dickson; *Portfolio Assessment Newsletter; Portfolio News*).

(b) Another useful option is to make a strategic retreat from a wholly negative position. That is, I sometimes do a *bit* of ranking even on individual papers, using two "bottom-line" grades: H and U for "Honors" and "Unsatisfactory." I tell students that these translate to about A or A– and D or F. This practice may seem theoretically inconsistent with all the arguments I've just made, but (at the moment, anyway) I justify it for the following reasons.

First, I sympathize with a *part* of the students' anxiety about not getting grades: their fear that they might be failing and not know about it — or doing an excellent job and not get any recognition. Second, I'm not giving *many* grades; only a small proportion of papers get these H's or U's. The system creates a "non-bottom-line" or "non-quantified" atmosphere. Third, these holistic judgments about best and worst do not seem as arbitrary and questionable as most grades. There is usually a *bit* more agreement among readers about the best and worst papers. What seems most dubious is the process of trying to rank that whole middle range of papers — papers that have a mixture of better and worse qualities so that the numerical grade depends enormously on a reader's priorities or mood or temperament. My willingness to give these few grades goes a long way toward helping my students forgo most bottom-line grading.

I'm not trying to pretend that these minimal "grades" are truly reliable. But they represent a very small amount of ranking. Yes, someone could insist that I'm really ranking every single paper (and indeed if it seemed politically necessary, I could put an OK or S [for satisfactory] on all those middle range papers and brag, "Yes, I grade everything"). But the fact is that I am doing *much less sorting* since I don't have to sort them into five or even twelve piles. Thus there is a huge reduction in the total amount of unreliability I produce.

(It might seem that if I use only these few minimal grades I have no good way for figuring out a final grade for the course — since that requires a more fine-grained set of ranks. But I don't find that to be the case. For I also give these same minimal grades to the many other important parts of my course such as attendance, meeting deadlines, peer responding, and journal writing. If I want a mathematically computed grade on a scale of six or A through E, I can easily compute it when I have such a large number of grades to work from — even though they are only along a three-point scale.)

This same practice of crude or minimal ranking is a big help on larger assessments outside classrooms, and needs to be applied to the process of assessment in general. There are two important principles to emphasize. On the one hand we must be prudent or accommodating enough to admit that despite all the arguments against ranking, there *are* situations when we need that bottom-line verdict along one scale: which student has not done satisfactory work and should be denied credit for the course? which student gets the scholarship? which candidate to hire or fire? We often operate with scarce resources. But on the other hand we must be bold enough to insist that we do far more ranking than is really needed. We can get along not only with fewer occasions for assessment but also with fewer gradations in scoring. If we decide what the *real* bottom-line is on a given occasion — perhaps just "failing" or perhaps "honors" too — then the reading of papers or portfolios is enormously quick and cheap. It leaves time and money for evaluation — perhaps for analytic scoring or some comment.

At Stony Brook we worked out a portfolio system where multiple readers had only to make a binary decision: acceptable or not. Then individual teachers could decide the actual course grade and give comments for their own students — so long as those students passed in the eyes of an independent rater (Elbow and Belanoff; Belanoff and Elbow). The best way to begin to wean our society from its addiction to ranking may be to permit a tiny bit of it (which also means less unreliability) — rather than trying to go "cold turkey."

(c) Sometimes I use an analytic grid for evaluating and commenting on student papers. An example is given in Figure 1.

I often vary the criteria in my grid (e.g. "connecting with readers" or "investment") depending on the assignment or the point in the semester.

Grids are a way I can satisfy the students' hunger for ranking but still not give in to conventional grades on individual papers. Sometimes I provide nothing but a grid (especially on final drafts), and this is a very quick way to provide a response. Or on midprocess drafts I sometimes use a grid in addition to a comment: a more readerly comment that often doesn't so much tell them what's wrong or right or how to improve things but rather tries to give them an account of what is *happening to me* as I read their words. I think this kind of comment is really the most useful thing of all for students, but it frustrates some students for a while. The grid can help

Strong   OK   Weak

			CONTENT, INSIGHTS, THINKING, GRAPPLING WITH TOPIC
			GENUINE REVISION, SUBSTANTIVE CHANGES, NOT JUST EDITING
			ORGANIZATION, STRUCTURE, GUIDING THE READER
			LANGUAGE: SYNTAX, SENTENCES, WORDING, VOICE
			MECHANICS: SPELLING, GRAMMAR, PUNCTUATION, PROOFREADING
			OVERALL [Note: this is not a sum of the other scores.]

Figure 1.

these students feel less anxious and thus pay better attention to my comment.

I find grids extremely helpful at the end of the semester for telling students their strengths and weaknesses in the course — or what they've done well and not so well. Besides categories like the ones above, I use categories like these: "skill in giving feedback to others," "ability to meet deadlines," "effort," and "improvement." This practice makes my final grade much more communicative.

(d) I also help make up for the absence of ranking — gold stars and black marks — by having students share their writing with each other a great deal both orally and through frequent publication in class magazines. Also, where possible, I try to get students to give or send writing to audiences outside the class. At the University of Massachusetts at Amherst, freshmen pay a ten dollar lab fee for the writing course, and every teacher publishes four or five class magazines of final drafts a semester. The effects are striking. Sharing, peer feedback, and publication give the best reward and motivation for writing, namely, getting your words out to many readers.

(e) I sometimes use a kind of modified *contract grading*. That is, at the start of the course I pass out a long list of all the things that I most want students to do — the concrete activities that I think most lead to learning — and I promise students that if they do them *all* they are guaranteed a certain final grade. Currently, I say it's a B — it could be lower or higher. My list includes these items: not missing more than a week's worth of classes; not having more than one late major assignment; *substantive* revising on all major revisions; good copy editing on all final revisions; good effort on peer feedback work; keeping up the journal; and substantial effort and investment on each draft.

I like the way this system changes the "bottom-line" for a course: the intersection where my authority crosses their self-interest. I can tell them, "You have to work very hard in this course, but you can stop worrying about grades." The crux is no longer that commodity I've always hated and never trusted: a numerical ranking of the quality of their writing along a single continuum. Instead the crux becomes what I care about most: the *concrete behaviors* that I most want students to engage in because they produce more learning and help me teach better. Admittedly, effort and investment are not concrete observable behaviors, but they are no harder to judge than overall quality of writing. And since I care about effort and investment, I don't mind the few arguments I get into about them; they seem fruitful. ("Let's try and figure out why it looked to me as though you didn't put any effort in here.") In contrast, I hate discussions about grades on a paper and find such arguments fruitless. Besides, I'm not making fine distinctions about effort and investment — just letting a bell go off when they fall palpably low.

It's crucial to note that I am *not* fighting evaluation with this system. I am just fighting ranking or grading. I still write evaluative comments and often use an evaluative grid to tell my students what I see as strengths and weaknesses in their papers. My goal is not to get rid of evaluation but in fact to emphasize it, enhance it. I'm trying to get students to listen *better* to my evaluations — by uncoupling them from a grade. In effect, I'm doing this because I'm so fed up with students *following* or *obeying* my evaluations too blindly — making whatever changes my comments suggest but doing it for the sake of a grade; not really taking the time to make up their own minds about whether they think my judgments or suggestions really make sense to them. The worst part of grades is that they make students obey us without carefully thinking about the merits of what we say. I love the situation this system so often puts students in: I make a criticism or suggestion about their paper, but it doesn't matter to their grade whether they go along with me or not (so long as they genuinely revise in some fashion). They have to think; to decide.

Admittedly this system is crude and impure. Some of the really skilled students who are used to getting A's and desperate to get one in this course remain unhelpfully hung up about getting those H's on their papers. But a good number of these students discover that they can't get them, and they soon settle down to accepting a B and having less anxiety and more of a learning voyage.

The Limitations of Evaluation and the Benefits of Evaluation-free Zones

Everything I've said so far has been in praise of evaluation as a substitute for ranking. But I need to turn a corner here and speak about the *limits* or *problems* of evaluation. Evaluating may be better than ranking, but it still carries some of the same problems. That is, even though I've praised evaluation for inviting us to acknowledge that readers and contexts are different, nevertheless the very word *evaluation* tends to imply fairness or reliability or getting beyond personal or subjective preferences. Also, of course, evaluation takes a lot more time and work. To rank you just have to put down a number; holistic scoring of exams is cheaper than analytic scoring.

Most important of all, evaluation harms the climate for learning and teaching — or rather *too much* evaluation has this effect. That is, if we evaluate *everything* students write, they tend to remain tangled up in the assumption that their whole job in school is to give teachers "what they want." Constant evaluation makes students worry more about psyching out the teacher than about what they are really learning. Students fall into a kind of defensive or on-guard stance toward the teacher: a desire to hide what they don't understand and try to impress. This stance gets in the way of learning. (Think of the patient trying to hide symptoms from the doctor.) Most of all, constant evaluation by someone in authority makes students reluctant to take the risks that are needed for good learning — to try out hunches and trust their own judgment. Face it: if our goal is to get students to exercise their own judgment, that means exercising an immature and undeveloped judgment and making choices that are obviously wrong to us.

We see around us a widespread hunger to be evaluated that is often just as strong as the hunger to rank. Countless conditions make many of us walk around in the world wanting to ask others (especially those in authority), "How am I doing, did I do OK?" I don't think the hunger to be evaluated is as harmful as the hunger to rank, but it can get in the way of learning. For I find that the greatest and most powerful breakthroughs in learning occur when I can get myself and others to *put aside* this nagging, self-doubting question ("How am I doing? How am I doing?") — and instead to take some chances, trust our instincts or hungers. When everything is evaluated, everything counts. Often the most powerful arena for deep learning is a kind of "time out" zone from the pressures of normal evaluated reality: make-believe, play, dreams — in effect, the Shakespearian forest.

In my attempts to get away from too much evaluation (not from all evaluation, just from too much of it), I have drifted into a set of teaching practices which now feel to me like the *best* part of my teaching. I realize now what I've been unconsciously doing for a number of years: creating "evaluation-free zones."

(a) The paradigm evaluation-free zone is the ten minute, nonstop freewrite. When I get students to freewrite, I am using my authority to create unusual conditions in order to contradict or interrupt our pervasive habit of always evaluating our writing. What is essential here are the two central features of freewriting: that it be private (thus I don't collect it or have students share it with anyone else); and that it be nonstop (thus there isn't time for planning, and control is usually diminished). Students quickly catch on and enter into the spirit. At the end of the course, they often tell me that freewriting is the most useful thing I've taught them (see Belanoff, Elbow, and Fontaine).

(b) A larger evaluation-free zone is the single unevaluated assignment — what people sometimes call the "quickwrite" or sketch. This is a piece of writing that I ask students to do — either in class or for homework — without any or much revising. It is meant to be low stakes writing. There is a bit of pressure, nevertheless, since I usually ask them to share it with others and *I* usually collect it and read it. But I don't write any comments at all — except perhaps to put straight lines along some passages I like or to write a phrase of appreciation at the end. And I ask students to refrain from giving evaluative feedback to each other — and instead just to say "thank you" or mention a couple of phrases or ideas that stick in mind. (However, this writing-without-feedback can be a good occasion for students to discuss the *topic* they have written about — and thus serve as an excellent kick-off for discussions of what I am teaching.)

(c) These experiments have led me to my next and largest evaluation-free zone — what I sometimes call a "jump start" for my whole course. For the last few semesters I've been devoting the first three weeks *entirely* to the two evaluation-free activities I've just described: freewriting (and also more leisurely private writing in a journal) and quickwrites or sketches. Since the stakes are low and I'm not asking for much revising, I ask for *much more* writing homework per week than usual. And every day we write in class: various exercises or games. The emphasis is on getting rolling, getting fluent, taking risks. And every day all students read out loud something they've written — sometimes a short passage even to the whole class. So despite the absence of feedback, it is a very audience-filled and sociable three weeks.

At first I only dared do this for two weeks, but when I discovered how fast the writing improves, how good it is for building community, and what a pleasure this period is for me, I went to three weeks. I'm curious to try an experiment with teaching a whole course this way. I wonder, that is, whether all that evaluation we work so hard to give really does any more good than the constant writing and sharing (Zak).

I need to pause here to address an obvious rejoinder: "But withholding evaluation is not normal!" Indeed, it is *not* normal — certainly not normal in school. We normally tend to emphasize evaluations — even bottom-line ranking kinds of evaluations. But I resist the argument that if it's not normal we shouldn't do it.

The best argument for evaluation-free zones is from experience. If you try them, I suspect you'll discover that they are satisfying and bring out good writing. Students have a better time writing these unevaluated pieces; they enjoy hearing and appreciating these pieces when they don't have to evaluate. And *I* have a much better time when I engage in this astonishing activity: reading student work when I don't have to evaluate and respond. And yet the writing improves. I see students investing and risking more, writing more fluently, and using livelier, more interesting voices. This writing gives me and them a higher standard of clarity and voice for when we move on to more careful and revised writing tasks that involve more intellectual pushing — tasks that sometimes make their writing go tangled or sodden.

The Benefits and Feasibility of Liking

Liking and disliking seem like unpromising topics in an exploration of assessment. They seem to represent the worst kind of subjectivity, the merest accident of personal taste. But I've recently come to think that the phenomenon of liking is perhaps the most important evaluative response for writers and teachers to think about. In effect, I'm turning another corner in my argument. In the first section I argued against ranking — with evaluating being the solution. Next I argued not *against* evaluating — but for no-evaluation zones in *addition* to evaluating. Now I will argue neither against evaluating nor against no-evaluation zones, but for something very different in addition, or perhaps underneath, as a foundation: liking.

Let me start with the germ story. I was in a workshop and we were going around the circle with everyone telling a piece of good news about their writing in the last six months. It got to Wendy Bishop, a good poet (who has also written two good books about the teaching of writing), and she said, "In the last six months, I've learned to *like* everything I write." Our jaws dropped; we were startled — in a way scandalized. But I've been chewing on her words ever since, and they have led me into a retelling of the story of how people learn to write better.

The old story goes like this: We write something. We read it over and we say, "This is terrible. I *hate* it. I've got to work on it and improve it." And we do, and it gets better, and this happens again and again, and before long we have become a wonderful writer. But that's not really what happens. Yes, we vow to work on it — but we don't. And next time we have the impulse to write, we're just a *bit* less likely to start.

What really happens when people learn to write better is more like this: We write something. We read it over and we say, "This is terrible. . . . But I *like* it. Damn it, I'm going to get it good enough so that others will like it too." And this time we don't just put it in a drawer, we actually work hard on it. And we try it out on other people too — not just to get feedback and advice but, perhaps more important, to find someone else who will like it.

Notice the two stories here — two hypotheses. (a) "First you improve the faults and then you like it." (b) "First you like it and then you improve faults." The second story may sound odd when stated so baldly, but really it's common sense. Only if we like something will we get involved enough to work and struggle with it. Only if we like what we write will we write again and again by choice — which is the only way we get better.

This hypothesis sheds light on the process of how people get to be published writers. Conventional wisdom assumes a Darwinian model: poor writers are unread; then they get better; as a result, they get a wider audience; finally they turn into Norman Mailer. But now I'd say the process is more complicated. People who get better and get published really tend to be driven by how much *they* care about their writing. Yes, they have a small audience at first — after all, they're not very good. But they try reader after reader until finally they can find people who like and appreciate their writing. I certainly did this. If someone doesn't like her writing enough to be pushy and hungry about finding a few people who also like it, she probably won't get better.

It may sound so far as though all the effort and drive comes from the lonely driven writer — and sometimes it does (Norman Mailer is no joke). But, often enough, readers play the crucially active role in this story of how writers get better. That is, the way writers *learn* to like their writing is by the grace of having a reader or two who likes it — even though it's not good. Having at least a few appreciative readers is probably indispensable to getting better.

When I apply this story to our situation as teachers I come up with this interesting hypothesis: *good writing teachers like student writing* (and like students). I think I see this borne out — and it is really nothing but common sense. Teachers who hate student writing and hate students are grouchy all the time. How could we stand our work and do a decent job if we hated their writing? Good teachers see what is only *potentially* good, they get a kick out of mere possibility — and they encourage it. When I manage to do this, I teach well.

Thus, I've begun to notice a turning point in my courses — two or three weeks into the semester: "Am I going to like these folks or is this going to be a battle, a struggle?" When I like them everything seems to go better — and it seems to me they learn more by the end. When I don't and we stay tangled up in struggle, we all suffer — and they seem to learn less.

So what am I saying? That we should like bad writing? How can we see all the weaknesses and criticize student writing if we just like it? But here's the interesting point: if I *like* someone's writing it's *easier* to criticize it.

I first noticed this when I was trying to gather essays for the book on freewriting that Pat Belanoff and Sheryl Fontaine and I edited. I would read an essay someone had written, I would want it for the book, but I had some serious criticism. I'd get excited and write, "I really like this, and I hope we can use it in our book, but you've got to get rid of this and change that, and I got really mad at this other thing." I usually find it hard to criticize, but I began to notice that I was a much more critical and pushy reader when I liked something. It's even fun to criticize in those conditions.

It's the same with student writing. If I like a piece, I don't have to pussyfoot around with my criticism. It's when I don't like their writing that I find myself tiptoeing: trying to soften my criticism, trying to find something nice to say — and usually sounding fake, often unclear. I see the same thing with my own writing. If I like it, I can criticize it better. I have faith that there'll still be something good left, even if I train my full critical guns on it.

In short — and to highlight how this section relates to the other two sections of this essay — liking is not the same as ranking or evaluating. Naturally, people get them mixed up: when they like something, they assume it's good; when they hate it, they assume it's bad. But it's helpful to uncouple the two domains and realize that it makes perfectly good sense to say, "This is terrible, but I like it." Or, "This is good, but I hate it." In short, I am not arguing here *against* criticizing or evaluating. I'm merely arguing *for* liking.

Let me sum up my clump of hypotheses so far:

- It's not improvement that leads to liking, but rather liking that leads to improvement.
- It's the mark of good writers to like their writing.
- Liking is not the same as evaluating. We can often criticize something better when we like it.
- We learn to like our writing when we have a respected reader who likes it.
- Therefore, it's the mark of good teachers to like students and their writing.

If this set of hypotheses is true, what practical consequences follow from it? How can we be better at liking? It feels as though we have no choice — as though liking and not-liking just happen to us. I don't really understand this business. I'd love to hear discussion about the mystery of liking — the phenomenology of liking. I sense it's some kind of putting oneself out — or holding oneself open — but I can't see it clearly. I have a hunch, however, that we're not so helpless about liking as we tend to feel.

For in fact I can suggest some practical concrete activities that I have found fairly reliable at increasing the chances of liking student writing:

(a) I ask for lots of private writing and merely shared writing, that is, writing that I don't read at all, and writing that I read but don't comment on. This makes me more cheerful because it's so much easier. Students get *better* without me. Having to evaluate writing — especially bad writing — makes me more likely to hate it. This throws light on grading: it's hard to like something if we know we have to give it a D.

(b) I have students share lots of writing with each other — and after a while respond to each other. It's easier to like their writing when I don't feel myself as the only reader and judge. And so it helps to build community in general: it takes pressure off me. Thus I try to use peer groups not only for feedback, but for other activities too, such as collaborative writing, brainstorming, putting class magazines together, and working out other decisions.

(c) I increase the chances of my liking their writing when I get better at finding what *is* good — or *potentially* good — and learn to praise it. This is a skill. It requires a good eye, a good nose. We tend — especially in the academic world — to assume that a good eye or fine discrimination means *criticizing*. Academics are sometimes proud of their tendency to be bothered by what is bad. Thus I find I am sometimes looked down on as dumb and undiscriminating: "He likes bad writing. He must have no taste, no discrimination." But I've finally become angry rather than defensive. It's an act of discrimination to see what's good in bad writing. Maybe, in fact, this is the secret of the mystery of liking: to be able to see potential goodness underneath badness.

Put it this way. We tend to stereotype liking as a "soft" and sentimental activity. Mr. Rogers is our model. Fine. There's nothing wrong with softness and sentiment — and I love Mr. Rogers. But liking can also be hard-assed. Let me suggest an alternative to Mr. Rogers: B. F. Skinner. Skinner taught pigeons to play ping-pong. How did he do it? Not by moaning, "Pigeon standards are falling. The pigeons they send us these days are no good. When I was a pigeon. . . ." He did it by a careful, disciplined method that involved close analytic observation. He put pigeons on a ping-pong table with a ball, and every time a pigeon turned his head 30 degrees toward the ball, he gave a reward (see my "Danger of Softness").

What would this approach require in the teaching of writing? It's very simple . . . but not easy. Imagine that we want to teach students an ability they badly lack, for example how to organize their writing or how to make their sentences clearer. Skinner's insight is that we get nowhere in this task by just telling them how much they lack this skill: "It's disorganized. Organize it!" "It's unclear. Make it clear!"

No, what we must learn to do is to read closely and carefully enough to show the student little bits of *proto*-organization or *sort of* clarity in what they've already written. We don't have to pretend the writing is wonderful. We could even say, "This is a terrible paper and the worst part about it is the lack of organization. But I will teach you how to organize. Look here at this little organizational move you made in this sentence. Read it out loud and try to feel how it pulls together this stuff here and distinguishes it from that stuff there. Try to remember what it felt like writing that sentence — creating that piece of organization. Do it some more." Notice how much more helpful it is if we can say, "Do *more* of what you've done here," than if we say, "Do something *different* from anything you've done in the whole paper."

When academics criticize behaviorism as crude it often means that they aren't willing to do the close careful reading of student writing that is required. They'd rather give a cursory reading and turn up their nose and give a low grade and complain about falling standards. No one has under-mined behaviorism's main principle of learning: that reward produces learn-ing more effectively than punishment.

(d) I improve my chances of liking student writing when I take steps to get to know them a bit as people. I do this partly through the assignments I give. That is, I always ask them to write a letter or two to me and to each other (for example about their history with writing). I base at least a couple of assignments on their own experiences, memories, or histories. And I make sure some of the assignments are free choice pieces — which also helps me know them.

In addition, I make sure to have at least three conferences with each student each semester — the first one very early. I often call off some classes in order to keep conferences from being too onerous (insisting nevertheless that students meet with their partner or small group when class is called off). Some teachers have mini-conferences with students during class — while students are engaged in writing or peer group meet-ings. I've found that when I deal only with my classes as a whole — as a large group — I sometimes experience them as a herd or lump — as stereo-typed "adolescents"; I fail to experience them as individuals. For me, per-sonally, this is disastrous since it often leads me to experience them as that scary tribe that I felt rejected by when *I* was an eighteen-year-old — and thus, at times, as "the enemy." But when I sit down with them face to face, they are not so stereotyped or alien or threatening — they are just eighteen-year-olds.

Getting a glimpse of them as individual people is particularly helpful in cases where their writing is not just bad, but somehow offensive — perhaps violent or cruelly racist or homophobic or sexist — or frighteningly vacuous. When I know them just a bit I can often see behind their awful attitude to the person and the life situation that spawned it, and not hate their writing so much. When I know students I can see that they are smart behind that dumb behavior; they are doing the best they can behind that bad behavior. Conditions are keeping them from acting decently; something is holding them back.

(e) It's odd, but the more I let myself show, the easier it is to like them and their writing. I need to share some of my own writing — show some of my own feelings. I need to write the letter to them that they write to me — about my past experiences and what I want and don't want to happen.

(f) It helps to work on my own writing — and work on learning to *like* it. Teachers who are most critical and sour about student writing are often having trouble with their own writing. They are bitter or unforgiving or hurting toward their own work. (I think I've noticed that failed PhDs are often the most severe and difficult with students.) When we are stuck or sour in our own writing, what helps us most is to find spaces free from evaluation such as those provided by freewriting and journal writing. Also, activities like reading out loud and finding a supportive reader or two. I would insist, then, that if only for the sake of our teaching, we need to learn to be charitable and to like our own writing.

A final word. I fear that this sermon about liking might seem an invitation to guilt. There is enough pressure on us as teachers that we don't need someone coming along and calling us inadequate if we don't *like* our students and their writing. That is, even though I think I am right to make this foray into the realm of feeling, I also acknowledge that it is dangerous — and paradoxical. It strikes me that we also need to have permission to hate the dirty bastards and their stupid writing.

After all, the conditions under which they go to school bring out some awful behavior on their part, and the conditions under which we teach sometimes make it difficult for us to like them and their writing. Writing wasn't meant to be read in stacks of twenty-five, fifty, or seventy-five. And we are handicapped as teachers when students are in our classes against their will. (Thus high school teachers have the worst problem here, since their students tend to be the most sour and resentful about school.)

Indeed, one of the best aids to liking students and their writing is to be somewhat charitable toward ourselves about the opposite feelings that we inevitably have. I used to think it was terrible for teachers to tell those sarcastic stories and hostile jokes about their students: "teacher room talk." But now I've come to think that people who spend their lives teaching *need* an arena to let off this unhappy steam. And certainly it's better to vent this sarcasm and hostility with our buddies than on the students themselves. The question, then, becomes this: do we help this behavior function as a venting so that we can move past it and not be trapped in our inevitable resentment of students? Or do we tell these stories and jokes as a way of staying stuck in the hurt, hostile, or bitter feelings — year after year — as so many sad teachers do?

In short I'm not trying to invite guilt, I'm trying to invite hope. I'm trying to suggest that if we do a sophisticated analysis of the difference between liking and evaluating, we will see that it's possible (if not always easy) to like students and their writing — without having to give up our intelligence, sophistication, or judgment.

Let me sum up the points I'm trying to make about ranking, evaluating, and liking:

- Let's do as little ranking and grading as we can. They are never fair and they undermine learning and teaching.
- Let's use evaluation instead — a more careful, more discriminating, fairer mode of assessment.
- But because evaluating is harder than ranking, and because too much evaluating also undermines learning, let's establish small but important evaluation-free zones.
- And underneath it all — suffusing the whole evaluative enterprise — let's learn to be better likers: liking our own and our students' writing, and realizing that liking need not get in the way of clear-eyed evaluation.

Works Cited

Belanoff, Pat, and Peter Elbow. "Using Portfolios to Increase Collaboration and Community in a Writing Program." *WPA: Journal of Writing Program Administration* 9.3 (Spring 1986): 27–40. (Also in *Portfolios: Process and Product.* Ed. Pat Belanoff and Marcia Dickson. Portsmouth, NH: Boynton/Cook-Heinemann, 1991.)

Belanoff, Pat, Peter Elbow, and Sheryl Fontaine, eds. *Nothing Begins with N: New Investigations of Freewriting.* Carbondale: Southern Illinois UP, 1991.

Bishop, Wendy. *Something Old, Something New: College Writing Teachers and Classroom Change.* Carbondale: Southern Illinois UP, 1990.

———. *Released into Language: Options for Teaching Creative Writing.* Urbana: NCTE, 1990.

Diederich, Paul. *Measuring Growth in English.* Urbana: NCTE, 1974.

Elbow, Peter. "The Danger of Softness." *What Is English?* New York: MLA, 1990. 197–210.

Elbow, Peter, and Pat Belanoff. "State University of New York: Portfolio-Based Evaluation Program." *New Methods in College Writing Programs: Theory into Practice.* Ed. Paul Connolly and Teresa Vilardi. New York: MLA, 1986. 95–105. (Also in *Portfolios: Process and Product.* Ed. Pat Belanoff and Marcia Dickson. Portsmouth, NH: Boynton/Cook-Heinemann, 1991.)

Gardner, Howard. *Frames of Mind: The Theory of Multiple Intelligences.* New York: Basic, 1983.

Kirschenbaum, Howard, Sidney Simon, and Rodney Napier. *Wad-Ja-Get? The Grading Game in American Education.* New York: Hart, 1971.

Lewis, C. S. *Studies in Words.* 2nd ed. London: Cambridge UP, 1967.

Portfolio Assessment Newsletter. Five Centerpointe Drive, Suite 100, Lake Oswego, Oregon 97035.

Portfolio News. c/o San Dieguito Union High School District, 710 Encinitas Boulevard, Encinitas, CA 92024.

Smith, Barbara Herrnstein. *Contingencies of Value: Alternative Perspectives for Critical Theory.* Cambridge: Harvard UP, 1988.

White, Edward M. *Teaching and Assessing Writing.* San Francisco: Jossey-Bass, 1985.

Zak, Frances. "Exclusively Positive Responses to Student Writing." *Journal of Basic Writing* 9.2 (1990): 40–53.

RESPONDING TO STUDENT WRITING

Erika Lindemann

[From *A Rhetoric for Writing Teachers* by Erika Lindemann. 3rd ed. New York: Oxford UP, 1995. 216–45.]

(For biographical information, see page 55.)

In this chapter, Lindemann situates the practice of responding to student writing in the larger contexts of assessment and evaluation, helping teachers think through the several purposes and methods for responding. Lindemann suggests that teachers think of their assessments and comments as a form of teaching, and describes a step-by-step procedure that teachers can use as they consider how to respond most effectively to student writing. She concludes this chapter with a discussion of alternative assessment methods, as well as with practical advice for "handling the paper load." Lindemann's thoughtful synthesis of current research and practice will help teachers develop effective approaches for assessing and responding to their students' writing.

> The writing teacher must not be a judge, but a physician. His job is not to punish, but to heal.
>
> – Donald M. Murray

The Basics and Testing

The writing teacher's primary responsibility, Charles Cooper maintains, is to guide students through the composing process.

> To do that the teacher will have to be concerned mainly with the *essence* of compositions, rather than the *accidents* of transcriptions, to use Janet Emig's terms. Unfortunately, just as we're learning what to do about the essences, some people are using the talk about basic skills to revive misplaced concern with the accidents; but surely the *most* basic of all the writing skills are matters of persona, audience, and purpose and the word and sentence adjustments the writer makes as he tries to speak with a certain voice to a special audience on a particular topic. ("Responding to Student Writing," p. 32)

Perhaps no words have generated as much controversy among teachers, parents, and the public as "basics," "minimal competence," and "testing." For most people, each word has psychologically comfortable, positive connotations. Who can oppose what is basic? Surely none of us supports *in*competence. And how many of us mathematically inept English teachers would dispute the numbers that experts attach to tests? As a society we've learned to trust statistics. I.Q. scores reveal how smart we are. SAT and ACT scores determine whether or not we may enter college. "Leading economic indicators" tell us our dollars won't buy what they did ten years ago. Insurance figures predict how we're likely to die. Casualty figures released weekly during the Vietnam war told us we were winning.

With similar illogic, many people believe that we can solve educational problems through legislatively mandated competency tests. Test results presumably will tell us if students learn, teachers teach, and the curriculum is sound. "The effectiveness of minimum competency tests," writes

Kenneth Goodman, "depends on the truth of some or all of five propositions:

1. Failure to achieve is due to a lack of school standards.
2. Student failure is largely the result of lack of teacher concern for student success, or teacher mediocrity or both.
3. Solutions for teaching-learning problems are built into current, traditional materials and methods.
4. Test performance is the same as competence; furthermore, existing tests can be used for accurate individual assessment and prediction.
5. If students are required to succeed they will.

None of these propositions, however, is true. ("Minimum Standards: A Moral View," p. 5)

For many educators, going "back to the basics" has become synonymous with going back to the secure good old days, which our selective memories usually recall as having been better than the good old present. In the main, advocates of testing programs are concerned about students, understand the problems teachers face, and want to help solve those problems. Testing students, they believe, will help resolve the literacy crisis.

Many researchers, however, insist that standardized tests aren't valid measures of writing performance. "Although widely used," write Charles Cooper and Lee Odell, "standardized tests measure only editing skills — choosing the best sentence, recognizing correct usage, punctuation, and capitalization" (*Evaluating Writing*, p. viii). Writing teachers, confronted with considerable pressure to submit to accountability-through-testing must educate themselves about the uses and abuses of tests.[1] To support teachers and encourage the responsible use of writing tests, the Conference on College Composition and Communication, a constituent organization of the National Council of Teachers of English, has adopted the following Resolution on Testing and Writing:

RESOLVED: that
1. No student shall be given credit for a writing course, placed in a remedial writing course, exempted from a required writing course, or certified for competency without submitting a piece of written discourse.
2. Responsibility for giving credit, exemption, or accreditation shall rest, not with local administrators or state officials, but with the composition faculty in each institution.
3. Tests of writing shall be selected and administered under the primary control and supervision of representatives of the composition faculty in each institution.
4. Before multiple choice or so-called objective tests are used, the complexities involved in such testing shall be carefully considered. Most important, these tests shall be examined to determine whether they are appropriate to the intended purpose.
5. Before essay tests are used, the complexities of such tests shall be carefully considered. Most importantly, topics shall be designed with great care. Also, readers of the essay tests shall be trained according to principles of statistically reliable holistic and/or analytic reading.
6. The nature and purpose of the test and the various uses of the results shall be clearly explained to all instructors and students prior to the administration of the test.
7. All possible steps shall be taken to educate the universities and colleges, the public and legislatures that, though composition facul-

ties have principal responsibility for helping students develop writing skills, maintenance of these skills is a responsibility shared by the entire faculty, administration, and the public.

8. The officers and Executive Committee of CCCC shall make testing a major concern in the immediate future in order to provide information and assistance to composition instructors affected by a testing situation.

The impulse to assess competence in writing is not solely an educational issue. Nor is it simply a concern of writing teachers. Increasing economic and political pressures will make testing our students' writing abilities a concern well into the twenty-first century. Although high school teachers are thoroughly familiar with the impulse to "teach to the test," many college teachers have yet to discover how large-scale testing programs affect curriculum, soak up an institution's funding for writing courses, and undermine teachers' authority to assign grades. Whenever possible, teachers should involve themselves in these issues so that students, who are rarely consulted, may demonstrate their writing abilities in ways that are educationally sound and so that teachers in other disciplines will assume greater responsibility for having students write.

Describing, Measuring, Judging

The papers in Cooper and Odell's *Evaluating Writing: Describing, Measuring, Judging* (1977) provide a comprehensive discussion of techniques for evaluating students' writing. Because writing evaluations have many uses, the editors caution, "It is critical for teachers . . . to know why they are evaluating before they choose measures and procedures" (p. ix). We may evaluate writing for any one of at least eleven reasons:

Administrative

1. Predicting students' grades in English courses.
2. Placing or tracking students or exempting them from English courses.
3. Assigning public letter or number grades to particular pieces of writing and to students' work in an English course.

Instructional

4. Making an initial diagnosis of students' writing problems.
5. Guiding and focusing feedback to student writers as they progress through an English course.

Evaluation and Research

6. Measuring students' growth as writers over a specific time period.
7. Determining the effectiveness of a writing program or a writing teacher.
8. Measuring group differences in writing performance in comparison-group research.
9. Analyzing the performance of a writer chosen for a case study.
10. Describing the writing performance of individuals or groups in developmental studies, either cross-sectional or longitudinal in design.
11. Scoring writing in order to study possible correlates of writing performance.

(Evaluating Writing, p. ix)

This chapter concerns itself principally with the fourth and fifth purposes for evaluating writing. When we diagnose writing problems (item 4 in the list above), we examine students' work descriptively, not to grade it or to respond with comments that students will read, but to determine simply what strengths and weaknesses characterize the paper. "Joan organizes her paper well and knows how to support her main points," we might note, "but her evidence is skimpy, she constructs paragraphs with only two levels of generality, and she consistently misspells words with *ance/ence* and *able/ible* suffixes." Such diagnostic evaluations permit us to design a course of instruction that enhances Joan's development as a writer. For this reason, many teachers treat the first writing assignment diagnostically. It isn't graded; it's mined for information that helps us plan what to teach.

When we respond to student writing (item 5 in the list above) or encourage students to respond to one another's work, we "guide and focus feedback," helping students understand how a reader perceives the writer's message. Sometimes we provide this feedback in conferences; sometimes we train students to give their classmates good advice. Most of the time, our feedback takes the form of written comments intended to help a student revise a draft or improve a subsequent paper. Writing comments is a form of teaching, a conference on paper. Comments that enhance learning differ from traditional methods of hunting errors and identifying what's wrong with a paper. They also must point out what the student did well, why certain problems undermine effective communication, and how to improve the paper. Comments that teach help students develop effective prewriting, writing, and rewriting strategies. Comments that teach are an open-ended form of evaluation that allows students, guided by responses from their teacher and classmates, to rewrite their drafts or engage the next assignment.

Grading, however, is a closed procedure. Once we assign a grade, we've judged the paper in ways that further revision can't change. Although comments may accompany the grade, most students interpret them not as "feedback" but as justification for the judgment we've made. From the student's perspective a graded paper is "finished," and additional work won't change either the grade or their feelings about succeeding or failing. Grades represent a necessary form of evaluation, but in this chapter we'll discuss some ways in which grades and our written comments can have a less destructive impact than traditional methods promote.[2]

Diagnostic Reading

The best way to assess students' strengths and weaknesses as writers is to examine carefully samples of their work, ideally two short papers with different discourse aims. Written in class during the first week of the course, these writing samples can tell us what students have already mastered and what areas we need to emphasize. Additional diagnostic evaluations at midterm help us identify improvements students have made since the course began, new problems that emerged as students overcame previous weaknesses, and difficulties that we somehow failed to address and that now need a different approach. At the end of the course, diagnostic evaluations help us determine how students' writing has improved and where the course has failed them.

When we examine a paper diagnostically, we're concerned primarily with describing rather than judging or grading it. Although we inevitably compare it to some mental criteria for effective writing, our primary purpose isn't to determine a letter grade. Rather, we want to know how the students write, what they're having trouble with, and why. To demonstrate the procedure, let's examine David's paper, written in forty-five minutes during the second meeting of a first-semester college composition class:

Assignment: Write an essay in which you discuss the way or ways you expect your life to differ from your parents' lives.[3]

> As time changes people's views and outlooks on life change with it. My parents grew up with completely diffrent standards in a completely diffrent time. Because of the time I grew up in, and the time I live in, my life differs greatly from the lives of my parents.
>
> Modern society offers more aid to young people — jobs, school, financial — that my parents could never recieve. Because of this aid my life has been more free than theirs ever was. I have more free time on my hands than they ever did. My parents were, and are, always working to keep and get, the things needed for survival in this life.
>
> Also Because of a higher education than the education of my parents I have diffrent outlooks on life. I have a more well-rounded attitude toward life. I tend to take more things for granted that my parents never would.
>
> We now live in a world of entertainment. My generation has more things in which to occupy their free time that my parents never had.
>
> Because of the time gap separating my parents an I, I have a diffrent lifestyle than they. Lifestyles change with the change of time, and with that so do people's outlook on life.

First we need to look at the assignment. Because it doesn't specify an audience, we shouldn't be surprised to discover that David addresses his composition to his stereotype of the Teacher or to no one in particular. The assignment specifies or implies a mode ("differ" suggests contrast or classification) and a form ("essay"). The topic permits students to draw on personal experience, but it's much too broad. The aim or purpose also may be troublesome because "discuss" can imply "inform," "argue," "explain," and a host of other possibilities. The assignment offers no prewriting help or criteria for success and consequently invites a vague, general response. Given the forty-five-minute time limit, we also can assume that David spent little time prewriting or rewriting the paper.

Indeed, David handled the topic fairly generally. Most of the paragraphs contain only one or two levels of generality. Most of the nouns identify abstractions ("views and outlooks," "modern society," "young people," "well-rounded attitude," "world of entertainment," "lifestyle"). However, David does attempt some classification. He subordinates "jobs, school, financial" to "aid" in paragraph two and identifies in the three body paragraphs three ways his life differs from his parents'. More "aid" gives him free time and freedom from worry; more education gives him different outlooks on life; a world of entertainment occupies his free time. At the same time, David maintains considerable distance between himself, his subject, and his audience, a stance characteristic of most first papers. Although he probably has quite a bit to say about his life, he might not choose to say it here, certainly not in writing, a more discomfiting medium than speech, and not to a stranger, which is how he must regard his English teacher at the beginning of the term.

Although David hasn't generated enough details to develop the paper effectively, it nevertheless has a structure. He's mastered the five-paragraph formula. The first and last paragraphs repeat the idea that "time gaps" separating two generations create different lifestyles and outlooks on life. The three body paragraphs attempt to develop separate subtopics, but the material overlaps, especially when he talks about "free time." David's writing, like that of most first-year students, seems form bound. Form precedes content. David thinks first of the five-paragraph mold and then attempts to find enough material to fill it. He probably needs practice identifying several ways of organizing his work, discovering form *in*, rather than imposing it *on*, the material prewriting generates.

That David stretches himself to find enough to say, a problem prewriting could help him with, also is evident in sentence construction. Students who fear they can't meet a 500-word limit or some self-imposed length requirement often pad their sentences, especially at the end. David does too. The first sentence, for example, might have ended with *change*, but afraid that the paper won't be long enough or that he won't find its message, David adds "with it." Similarly in paragraphs two and three, "in this life" and "toward life" extend sentences that could have closed with *survival* and *attitude* respectively. David writes predominantly simple sentences, but he knows at least one kind of subordination. Four sentences begin with *because*-clauses; the first sentence, with an *as*-clause. He may be avoiding more complex constructions because they'll create additional comma problems; he plays it safe. Risk-free, ungraded sentence-combining exercises might give him greater confidence in varying sentence structures and punctuating them.

Because David writes his way around comma problems, the paper doesn't offer enough evidence to diagnose the logic governing its mispunctuation. Two introductory *because*-clauses are set off; two aren't. The comma in the last sentence correctly separates two independent clauses joined by *and*, but elsewhere, in the first two paragraphs, *and* may govern the misuse of commas. To get at the logic behind these errors, we'd need to discuss the paper with David, asking him why he thinks the misused commas belong there, then pointing out where he's used the comma conventionally and encouraging him to apply what he's done right to the mispunctuated sentences.

A conference with David also might help us understand the logic governing comparisons. David deliberately alternates the conjunction *than* with the relative pronoun *that* to complete comparisons:

That Constructions

Subject + Verb + <u>more</u> aid to young people . . . <u>that</u> my parents could(never)

receive.

Subject + Verb + to take <u>more</u> things for granted <u>that</u> my parents (never)

would.

Subject + Verb + <u>more</u> things . . . <u>that</u> my parents(never)had.

Than Constructions

Clause + Subject + Verb + <u>more</u> free <u>than</u> theirs (ever)was.

Subject + Verb + <u>more</u> free time . . . <u>than</u> they (ever)had.

Also Because of a <u>higher</u> education <u>than</u> the education of my parents.

Subject + Verb + a <u>different</u> lifestyle <u>than</u> they.

In English, we complete comparisons with *than* (or *as*), not *that*. David, however, completes negative comparisons (signaled by *never*) with *that* and positive comparisons (signaled by *ever* or by affirmative phrases and clauses) with *than*. By discussing with him the chart above, we could help him understand two strategies for rewriting the "that constructions": (1) keep *that* but get rid of *more*, or (2) keep *more* but change *that* to *than*.

The paper contains only a few misspellings. *Diffrent* (four times) and *seperating* (once) are logical transcriptions of how most speakers pronounce these words. *An* (for *and*) may not be a "pronunciation spelling" because David spells *and* correctly elsewhere; he probably just left off the *d* as he hurried to finish. In misspelling *receive* as *recieve,* he logically writes "i before e" but forgets (or never confidently learned) "except after c." We might ask him to begin a spelling log, entering these words in one column and their correct spellings in another, so that he can discover which words and sound patterns are likely to give him trouble.[4]

When I analyze a first paper, I make notes about what I've found on a separate sheet kept in each student's folder. Students never see my notes, but I refer to them throughout the term. They help me decide what writing problems each student should work on and permit me to record a student's progress. Because David can't work on everything at once without becoming frustrated, I would select only one or two areas to emphasize as he rewrites this paper or plans the next one. For David (and doubtless other members of the class), careful prewriting would effect the greatest change in future papers. Writing from an overabundance of material would lengthen paragraphs, help him better support generalizations, and perhaps remove the need to pad sentences. Prewriting also might help him find alternative patterns of arrangement in material, reducing his dependence on the five-paragraph model. In the meantime, he can begin a spelling log and practice ungraded sentence-combining exercises to expand his inventory of subordinate constructions and increase his confidence about using commas.

With practice, you can read a paper diagnostically in two or three minutes. At first it helps to describe the features in detail, but after a while, a few brief notes will remind you of problems the student has overcome, new areas to work on, and questions you need more evidence to answer. Diagnostic readings reveal not only what the student has done but also how and why, allowing you to hypothesize about the causes of writing problems. Merely to identify a paper's errors and attach a letter grade is to ignore considerable evidence that can make your teaching more effective and the student's progress surer.

Teaching through Comments

Diagnostic reading is essentially a private response to a composition. We're discussing it with ourselves, explaining its patterns of features and planning a course of instruction for the student. When we write comments, on the other hand, we're communicating with a different audience, the student. As with any communication, purpose governs how we express the message and how our audience is likely to respond. The only appropriate purpose for comments on students' papers is to offer feedback and guide learning. Some comments, however, seem written for other reasons: to damn the paper with faint praise or snide remarks, to prove that the teacher is a superior error hunter, to vent frustration with students, to condemn or disagree with the writer's ideas, to confuse the writer with cryptic correction symbols.[5] Most of us learned how to comment on papers by first surviving and then imitating the responses of teachers to our own work. Few of us, I suspect, looked forward to getting our papers back (except to learn the grade) and could probably sympathize with the following assessment of the experience:

> Confused and angry, he stared at the red marks on his paper. He had awked again. And he had fragged. He always awked and fragged. On every theme, a couple of awks and a frag or two. And the inevitable puncs and sp's. The cw's didn't bother him anymore. He knew that the teacher preferred words like courage and contemptible person to guts and fink. The teacher had dismissed guts and fink as slang, telling students never to use slang in their themes. But he liked to write guts and fink; they meant something to him. Besides, they were in the dictionary. So why couldn't he use them when they helped him say what he wanted to say? He rarely got to say what he wanted to say in an English class, and when he did, he always regretted it. But even that didn't bother him much. He really didn't care anymore.
>
> How do you keep from awking, he asked himself. The question amused him for a moment; all questions in English class amused him for a moment. He knew what awk meant; he looked it up once in the handbook in the back of the grammar book as the teacher told him to. But the illustration didn't help him much. He got more awks, and he quit looking in the handbook. He simply decided that he oughtn't awk when he wrote even though he didn't know how to stop awking.
>
> Why not frag now and then, he wondered for almost thirty seconds. Writers fragged. Why couldn't he? Writers could do lots of things. Why couldn't he? But he forgot the question almost as quickly as it entered his mind. No sense worrying about it, he told himself. You'll only live to frag again.
>
> Damn, he whispered. He knew it had to be damn. He decided that the teacher didn't have the guts to write damn when she was angry with what he wrote. She just wrote dm in the margin. She told the class it meant dangling modifier, but he was sure it meant damn.
>
> Choppy! He spat the word out to no one in particular. He always got at least one choppy. "Mature thoughts should be written in long, balanced sentences," the teacher said once. He guessed his thoughts weren't balanced. Choppy again. But he didn't care anymore. He'd just chop his way through English class until he never had to write again.
>
> He stared at the encircled *and* at the beginning of one of his sentences. The circle meant nothing at first. Then he remembered the teacher's saying something about never beginning sentences with a conjunction. He didn't know why she said it; writers did it. But he guessed that since he wasn't a writer he didn't have that privilege.
>
> The rep staggered him. The teacher had drawn a red line from the red rep to the word commitment. He had used it four times. It fit, he thought. You need commitment if you believe in the brotherhood of man, he argued with himself. Why did she write the red rep? He didn't know. But there were so many things he didn't know about writing.
>
> Why do we have to write anyway, he asked himself. He didn't know. No good reason for it, he thought. Just write all the time to show the teacher that you can't write.
>
> Most of the time he didn't know why he was asked to write on a specific topic, and most of the time he didn't like the topic or he didn't know too

much about it. He had written on the brotherhood of man four times during the last four years. He had doubts about man's brotherhood to man. People really got shook about it only during National Brotherhood Week, he had written once in a theme. The rest of the year they didn't much care about their fellow man, only about themselves, he had written. The teacher didn't like what he said. That teacher, a man, wrote in the margin: "How can you believe this? I disagree with you. See me after class." He didn't show up. He didn't want another phony lecture on the brotherhood of man.

That wasn't the only time a teacher disagreed with what he wrote. One even sent him to the principal's office for writing about his most embarrassing moment even though she had assigned the topic. She told the principal he was trying to embarrass her. But all he did was write about his most embarrassing moment, just as she had told him to. And it was a gas. Another time a teacher told him to write about how a daffodil feels in spring. He just wrote *chilly* on a piece of paper and handed it in. The teacher was furious. But he didn't care. He didn't give a dm about daffodils in spring. He didn't care much about what he did last summer either, but the teacher seemed to.

He looked for the comment at the end of the theme. Trite. Nothing else; just trite. He usually got a trite. It would probably mean a D on his report card, but he didn't care. It was hard for him not to be trite when he wrote on the brotherhood of man for the fourth time in four years. He used all the clichés. The teacher wanted them, he thought. So he gave them to her. But he was never sure just what the teacher wanted. Some kids said they had figured out just what the teachers wanted. They said they knew what kinds of words, what kinds of thoughts, and what kinds of sentences she liked. They said they had her "psyched out"; that's why they got A's. But he didn't have her psyched out, and wasn't going to worry about it anymore.

Every week she told the class to write a theme on some topic, and he knew that she picked out the topics because she liked them. Every week — "Write a theme on such and such." Nothing else — just those instructions. So he gave the topic a few minutes' thought and wrote whatever came to mind. He thought in clichés when he tried to write for her. They were safe, he once thought. But maybe not. Trite again.

He wadded up the brotherhood of man and threw it toward the waste basket. Missed. He always missed — everything.

Drop out, fink, he told himself. Why not? He didn't know what was going on. A dropout. He smiled. Frag, he thought. Can't use dropout all alone. He knew it was a frag. At least he had learned something. The bell rang. No more awks, no more frags, no more meaningless red marks on papers. No more writing about daffodils and the brotherhood of man — until next week. (Edward B. Jenkinson and Donald A. Seybold, "Prologue," *Writing as a Process of Discovery*, pp. 3–6).

As this student's plight reveals, comments that simply point out errors or justify a grade tend to ignore the student who reads them. Formative comments, on the other hand, the kind that support learning, praise what has worked well, demonstrate how or why something else didn't, and encourage students to try new strategies. In an essay describing several approaches to formative evaluation, Mary Beaven defines six assumptions on which to base our written responses to students' writing:

1. Growth in writing is a highly individualistic process that occurs slowly, sometimes over a much longer period of time than the six-, ten-, or even fifteen-week periods teachers and researchers usually allow.

2. Through their evaluatory comments and symbols teachers help to create an environment for writing. Establishing a climate of trust, in which students feel free to explore topics of interest to them without fear that their thoughts will be attacked, is essential.

3. Risk taking, trying new behaviors as one writes, and stretching one's use of language and toying with it are important for growth in writing. As writers break out of old, "safe" composing behaviors, they often make *more* mistakes until they become comfortable with new ways of using language. Teachers must encourage and support this kind of risk taking and mistake making.

4. Goal setting is also an important process in the development of students. Goals need to be concrete and within reach, and students need to see evidence of their progress. Teachers, then, should urge students to work toward a limited number of goals at a time.

5. Writing improvement does not occur in isolation because writing is related to speaking, listening, reading, and all other avenues of communication, including the experience of living. Prewriting activities, responding to literature, class discussion, revisions, developing a sensitivity to self and others, experiences both in and out of the English classroom affect growth in writing.

6. Effective formative evaluation depends on our understanding clearly other procedures that encourage growth in writing: diagnosing what students are able to do; arranging for writing often in many modes; discussing usage, syntactical, and rhetorical deficiencies by working with the students' own writing, not by preteaching rules; giving feedback and encouragement; assessing how much growth individuals have shown, without comparing them to one another and without expecting "mastery" of some uniform class standard.

(Adapted from *Evaluating Writing*, pp. 136–38)

Beaven's assumptions are crucial because much research argues against commenting on students' papers — ever. Surveying this research, George Hillocks concludes: "The results of all these studies strongly suggest that teacher comment has little impact on student writing" (*Research on Written Composition*, p. 165). It makes no difference whether the comments are tape-recorded or written; appear in the margins or at the end of the paper; are frequent or infrequent; are positive, negative, or a mixture of both (though students receiving negative criticism wrote less and developed negative attitudes about themselves as writers and about writing). "Indeed, several [studies] show no pre-to-post gains for *any* groups, regardless of the type of comment" (p. 165). In the face of this evidence, writing teachers must consider whether or not they should even invest their time in commenting on students' work. I believe they should, but only under two circumstances: (1) if the comments are focused, and (2) if students also have opportunities actively to apply criteria for good writing to their own work. The studies Hillocks surveyed "indicate rather clearly that engaging young writers actively in the use of criteria, applied to their own or to others' writing, results not only in more effective revisions but in superior first drafts" (p. 160).

With these assumptions in mind, let's return to David's paper, not to read it diagnostically this time, but to respond to it as we would if we planned to return it to him. I've reproduced the paper twice so that we can compare the responses of two different teachers.

As time changes people's views and outlooks on life change with it. My

Sp
Rep. parents grew up with completely diffrent standards in a completely diffrent

p time. Because of the time I grew up in⊙and the time I live in, my life differs

greatly from the lives of my parents.

Modern society offers more aid to young people — jobs, school, finan-

⫽   **than**   **ever**
Sp   cial — that my parents could never recieve. Because of this aid my life has

                                                            cliché
been more free than theirs ever was. I have more free time on my hands

p than they ever did. My parents were⊙ and are⊙ always working to keep and

get⊙ the things needed for survival in this life.

              b   **I have more education than my parents do**
Also, ⎽Because of a higher education than the education of my parents

                                              cliché
I have diffrent outlooks on life. I have a more well-rounded attitude toward

                              cliché
life. I tend to take more things for granted that my parents never would.

Not a ¶   We now live in a world of entertainment. My generation has more things
awk   **?**
⊙in which to occupy their free time that my parents never had.

Sp   Because of the time gap seperating my parents an I, I have a diffrent

Rep. life⊙tyle than they. Life⊙tyles change with the change of time, and with that

so do people's outlook on life.

Avoid clichés and be more specific.
Proofread for spelling and comma problems.

As time changes people's views and outlooks on life change with it. My

✓✓

Beginning a paper is tough, isn't it? Notice how the sentences
parents grew up with completely diffrent standards in a completely diffrent
in this paragraph repeat one idea three times. Can you tell us
time. Because of the time I grew up in, and the time I live in, my life differs
instead why you think these differences are interesting?
greatly from the lives of my parents.

A good point. Do you have a job? Are you on a scholarship?
Modern society offers more aid to young people — jobs, school, finan-

✓

cial — that my parents could never recieve. Because of this aid my life has

been more free than theirs ever was. I have more free time on my hands

Specifically, what did your parents have to
than they ever did. My parents were, and are, always working to keep and
worry about that you don't?
get, the things needed for survival in this life.

✓

Also Because of a higher education than the education of my parents I
Such as? Can you give some examples of how
✓
have diffrent outlooks on life. I have a more well-rounded attitude toward
your attitude or outlook differs from your parents?
life. I tend to take more things for granted that my parents never would.

What does this phrase mean?   Such as?
We now live in a world of entertainment. My generation has more things in
What do you do with your free time? What did they do?
which to occupy their free time that my parents never had.

✓✓

Because of the time gap seperating my parents an I, I have a diffrent

lifestyle than they. Lifestyles change with the change of time, and with that

so do people's outlook on life.

You have a strong sense of how to organize your paper. You divide the general idea in your first and last paragraph into "aid," "education," and "entertainment," the sub-topics of your three body paragraphs. Your readers will want more specific information about each of these sub-topics. Examples would help us "see" the differences between you and your parents' "outlooks" and "life styles." Before you write your next draft, consider the questions I've written. Go back over the draft, asking of each sentence how? why? in what ways? such as? Then spend at least thirty minutes jotting down examples or incidents that might explain or support each sub-topic. Please log the spelling problems in your journal and bring it to your conference next week. Each check in the margin represents one misspelling in that line of your paper. If you can't account for all of the check marks, I'll be glad to help.

The first set of comments identifies and corrects errors. In addition to placing symbols and abbreviations in the left margin, the teacher underlines misspellings, circles punctuation problems, and rewrites some of David's prose. Comments at the end of the paper address generally what's wrong with the piece and recommend a few changes (but notice the commanding tone of the imperative verbs). For several reasons, this traditional scheme fails to teach writing. First, David may not know what the marginal abbreviations refer to. By frustrating trial and error he may have learned that *P* can mean "passive," "punctuation," "pronoun," "poor phrasing," "point?" — take your pick. *Awk* and its not-so-distant cousin *?* communicate "the teacher didn't like what I said here for some reason." David must puzzle out the reason, guess *why* the phrasing is awkward, and predict as best he can *how* to rewrite it.

Second, the comments don't help David become an independent judge of his own prose. Finding his mistakes underlined again and again, or circled, or corrected, he can easily conclude that he has no responsibility for finding problems he's previously overlooked. The teacher, he believes, will find his mistakes for him. Then, because teachers *always* discover a few errors, he can dismiss the corrections in an effort to protect himself from criticism. Such circular reasoning, which the teacher abets, won't make him a self-sufficient editor.

Third, the comments presuppose that David knew more than in fact he did. They assume that his errors result from carelessness or failure to apply the rules. Perhaps the teacher believes that David overlooked mistakes, didn't proofread his paper, or worse, defied conventions repeatedly discussed in class. David, however, didn't intend to do poorly; he probably wanted to please his teacher and earn a good grade. Except for mistakes prompted by haste, students write errors because they don't know that they *are* writing errors.

Finally, because most of the comments address problems at the level of the word, David is likely to conclude that writing well is largely a matter of "getting the words right." In failing to comment on broader concerns, the teacher promotes the view that purpose, audience, and what a writer wants to say matter very little. The teacher remains an editor, not an "aid-itor," refusing to *respond* to the piece in ways a reader would.

In *Errors and Expectations: A Guide for the Teacher of Basic Writing* (1977), Mina Shaughnessy maintains, "The errors students make . . . no matter how peculiar they may sound to a teacher, are the result not of carelessness or irrationality but of *thinking*" (p. 105). She bases this conclusion on a study of 4,000 essays written between 1970 and 1974 by students entering City College in New York, which had just opened its doors to large numbers of basic writers. She describes and classifies the problems she finds, devoting chapters of her book to problems of handwriting and punctuation; derailed syntax; common errors of tense, inflection, and agreement; spelling errors; vocabulary problems; and errors beyond the level of the sentence. She supports her discussion with copious examples from student papers.

Shaughnessy reads the unique genre called "student writing" in ways that explain how and why errors appear. "Once he grants students the intelligence and will they need to master what is being taught," she argues, "the teacher begins to look at his students' difficulties in a more fruitful way: he begins to search in what students write and say for clues to their reasoning and their purposes, and in what *he* does for gaps and misjudgments" (p. 292). Although errors may appear to us unconventional ways of using language, they are logical; they reflect unique rules and hypotheses students devise to attempt communication. Errors also are regular; they occur in deliberate, often ingenious patterns.

Instead of isolating mistakes in line after line of a student's work, Shaughnessy encourages us to examine the paper systematically for *patterns* of error, reconstructing the student's unique grammar and formulating hypotheses to explain why or how the patterns developed. What a student does right also may explain the pattern, especially when errors seem partially under control or result from mislearning or misapplying some textbook pronouncement. Whenever our own logic, the logic of the fluent writer, prevents us from discovering the rationale behind a pattern of errors, we must seek an explanation for it by discussing the evidence with the student.[6]

As the second teacher, I responded to David's paper differently. Notice that I didn't mark everything. That doesn't mean I overlooked problems; instead, I chose to address only a few manageable ones. Because David can't work on everything at once, he needs some help defining priorities. Some teachers may feel irresponsible in not marking every mistake, but with practice those pangs of guilt will diminish. Or we can redirect them by helping students log their own errors, signaled by checks in the margin. The purpose of our comments, remember, isn't to compete with other teachers in an error-hunting contest but to guide students' learning. Just as a class meeting organizes discussion around one or two topics, so too limiting the scope of our comments makes learning more efficient.

Second, the comments don't label problems; rather, they emphasize how and why communication fails. The questions create a kind of dialogue between David and me. In answering them, David must reread what he's written, eventually learning to ask similar questions of subsequent drafts. If the comments balance praise and criticism, David is more likely to read them and understand what strategies seem to have worked well. To keep lines of communication open, students can submit their own questions or comments about what concerns them, letting us know how carefully they are evaluating their work and what kinds of suggestions might help most.

Finally, in view of the research Hillocks surveyed, comments belong on students' drafts, not on final versions. If comments are to have any effect, students need opportunities to incorporate them. Commenting on drafts encourages and guides further revision. It also ensures that comments remain focused on the work-in-progress, not on the grade a student's work eventually receives.

Responding to papers in ways that enhance learning is as time-consuming as locating errors, more so until the procedure becomes comfortable and each student's problems more familiar. Although we obviously can't approach every paper in the same way, the following procedure offers some suggestions for planning written comments much as we prepare classes: (1) assess what the student needs to learn (steps 1–2), (2) plan what to teach and how (steps 3–4), (3) conduct the lesson (steps 5–10), and (4) keep notes to evaluate learning and plan future lessons (step 11).

Teaching through Comments

1. Read the paper through without marking on it.
2. Identify one or two problems. In deciding what to teach this time, view the paper descriptively, not to judge it, but to discover what the text reveals about decisions the writer made. You may want to ask yourself the following questions:

a. Was the student committed to the assignment?
b. What did the student intend to do? What was the purpose for writing?
c. How did the writer define the audience for the piece?
d. How thoroughly did the student probe the subject?
e. How are paragraphs arranged?
f. What are the most frequent types of sentences?
g. What patterns of errors in spelling, punctuation, grammar, and usage does the paper contain? In what contexts do the errors appear? What makes them similar?

Examining scratch notes and earlier drafts also helps reconstruct how the student created the final draft.

3. Formulate tentative hypotheses to explain the problem you want to focus on. You can assume that there's a logic to what appears on the page, even if it isn't your logic. Try to define that logic so that your comments can turn it around or modify it. For example, "I disliked the story because it's ending confused me" assumes (logically but unconventionally) that 's marks the possessive pronoun just as it does most nouns. Students who put commas in front of every *and* may be misapplying the rule for punctuating series or conjoining independent clauses; they need to learn that a "series" of two coordinated subjects or verbs doesn't need the comma. Merely labeling the error "misplaced comma" doesn't teach students *why* and *how* your logic and theirs differ.

4. Examine what the student has done well. Can this evidence help the student solve a problem elsewhere in the paper? How can the student's strengths be used to repair weaknesses?

5. Now you are ready to begin commenting on the paper. You have examined the evidence, decided what you want to teach, and identified specific examples of the problem (and perhaps its solution) on which to base your lesson.

6. Questions can call attention to troublespots, but avoid questions that prompt simple "yes" or "no" answers. Preface questions with *why, how,* or *what* so that students must reexamine the paper and become conscious critics of their own prose ("How often have you used this kind of sentence in this paragraph?"). Avoid imperatives ("Proofread more carefully"), which identify problems but don't help students learn *how* to solve them.

7. Avoid labeling problems *unless* you also give students a way of overcoming them. If something is "unclear" or "awkward," let students know the source of your confusion ("Do you mean . . . or . . . ?"). Refer to other sections of the paper that illustrate a strategy worth repeating ("You're using abstract words here; why not give me another example as you did in paragraph 2?"). Eschew, when you can, Latinate grammatical terms, abbreviations, and private symbols. They may be clear to you — after all, you've marked hundreds of papers with them — but they might mystify the student.

8. Make praise work toward improvements. Students need to know how a reader responds to their work, but they're rarely fooled by token praise. Avoid "good" or "I like this" unless you add a noun ("Good sentence variety here") or *because* ("I like these details because they help me see Uncle Max"). Remember to commend students for progress they've made.

9. Avoid doing the student's work. Rewriting an occasional sentence can give students a model to imitate, *if* you make it clear what principle the model illustrates. Circled or underlined words (and

most marginal symbols) simply locate and label errors; the student probably didn't "see" the problem and needs practice proofreading and editing. A better strategy for handling surface errors might be to place a check in the margin next to the line in which a misspelled word or punctuation problem occurs. Then ask the student to examine the entire line, locate the problem, and determine how to eliminate it. Students who can't find the error on their own should feel free to ask you what the check means. Students may log these errors and their corrections in their journals so that they develop a sense of what they're overlooking. Logs can be discussed briefly in conference to identify patterns in the errors and work out strategies for anticipating them in future papers.

10. Write out a careful endnote to summarize your comments and to establish a goal for the next draft. Endnotes can follow a simple formula:

   a. Devote at least one full sentence to commending what you can legitimately praise; avoid undercutting the praise with *but* ("I like your introduction, *but* the paper is disorganized)."

   b. Identify one or two problems and explain why they make understanding the piece difficult.

   c. Set a goal for the student to work toward in the next draft.

   d. Suggest specific strategies for reaching the goal ("In your next draft, do this: . . . ").

   Traditional endnotes address a paper's weaknesses, but if you want to see the strengths repeated, praise them when you find them. Silence tells students nothing. Traditional endnotes also omit goals and offer few explicit suggestions for reaching them. Including goals and strategies gives the endnote a teaching function, helps redirect a writer's energies, and reduces the amount of trial-and-error learning students must go through to improve their writing. Subsequent papers are more likely to show improvement if you explicitly define what you think needs work and how to go about it. Your suggestions also will encourage students to see connections between what they discuss in class and what they practice in their assignments, between problems they've encountered in one draft and solutions worth trying in the next.

   Setting goals and offering specific solutions to writing problems can be difficult at first, especially if you don't know what to suggest to address the problem you see. But with practice, you'll find yourself developing a repertoire of goals and strategies to adapt to individual papers. State each goal positively, perhaps mentioning problems in previous papers that now have been solved or pointing to specific strengths in this paper. Instead of writing "This paper shows little thought," write "In planning your next paper, spend fifteen minutes freewriting; then fill a page with notes on your subject and decide how to group them under three or four headings." Not, "Your sentences are hopeless"; rather, "You've made considerable progress in organizing the whole essay. Now it's time to work on sentences. Read this draft aloud to hear where sentences could be combined or made less wordy. Your ideas will come across more forcefully if you avoid passive voice verbs and sentences that begin with *There are* and *It is*." Phrase the goal in language that encourages students to experiment and take risks. Avoid prescribing additional goals until students have reached those you've already given them.

11. Write yourself a note to chart the student's progress, a reminder you can keep in the student's folder. Describe briefly what areas no longer seem to be problems, what problems you addressed this

time, and what needs attention later on. If this draft enabled you to teach a principle of paragraphing, remind yourself to evaluate the next paper in light of the paragraph-goal you set. If you also noticed sentence problems this time around, a note will remind you to set a sentence-goal when paragraphs begin to look stronger.

At first reading these eleven steps seem cumbersome, but after some practice, the procedure saves time. Writing teachers expect to spend many hours commenting on papers. We do this work conscientiously because we believe that students will read what we've written and will profit from our advice. Too often, however, they don't, and consequently, we resent having devoted so much energy to an apparently pointless task. One advantage of the procedure described above is that students *will* read what we've written. They'll expect us to say "bad" things, but they'll discover that we've said "good" things about their work too. They'll read about their weaknesses as they search for comments praising the paper. Second, the procedure offers specific help with weaknesses, especially in the goal-setting endnote. If the endnote explains *how* to tackle a problem, students will attempt the strategy we've suggested at least once. If we then praise the attempt, or even notice that the writer tried something new, he or she may try it again. Focused feedback, not diffuse comments, makes learning efficient. Third, the procedure saves us time because it focuses on only one or two problems. With practice, we can develop a mental repertoire of endnotes addressing specific problems. Although the long endnote on page 183 may appear to have taken considerable time to write, it didn't. I would like my students to think so, but I drew on a stock endnote I've used many times, simply modifying it to fit the particular paper I was commenting on.

Self-evaluation

Students also must have a role in evaluating their work. They should respond to their own writing and that of other classmates for several reasons. Good writers are proficient in addressing varied audiences. Students develop this proficiency not only by writing for others but also by gaining responses to their work from audiences other than the teacher. Furthermore, because composing is highly idiosyncratic, students learn new strategies for solving writing problems by explaining their decisions to other students and hearing how they have negotiated the demands of a similar assignment. As students become progressively more independent and self-confident, their responses to one another's work become more incisive. They learn constructive criticism, close reading, and collaboration.

Writing workshops, discussed in Chapter 12, offer one way of encouraging students to respond to one another's writing. Self-evaluation encourages students to assess their own compositions. As Mary Beaven suggests, "Self-evaluation strengthens students' editing abilities, giving them control over decisions that affect their own writing growth as they learn to trust their own criteria of good writing" (*Evaluating Writing*, p. 153). Self-evaluation typically requires students to answer questions designed to elicit information about their work. Students submit their answers when they turn in a draft or final version. Although self-evaluation questions should change with each assignment to reflect the work students are doing, Beaven (p. 143) offers the following questions as a starting point:

1. How much time did you spend on this paper?
2. (After the first evaluation) What did you try to improve, or experiment with, on this paper? How successful were you? If you have questions about what you were trying to do, what are they?

3. What are the strengths of your paper? Place a squiggly line beside those passages you feel are very good.
4. What are the weaknesses, if any, of your paper? Place an *X* beside passages you would like your teacher to correct or revise. Place an *X* over any punctuation, spelling, usage, etc., where you need help or clarification.
5. What one thing will you do to improve your next piece of writing? Or what kind of experimentation in writing would you like to try? If you would like some specific information related to what you want to do, write down your questions.
6. (Optional) What grade would you give yourself on this composition? Justify it.

Self-evaluation benefits teachers as well as students. The answers to self-evaluation questions tell us what concerns students. As they become more aware of what they wanted to do and where a paper fails to realize their intentions, we can offer help, acting less like a judge and more like an experienced, trusted advisor. We discover how students perceive the composing process, what sorts of risks they're taking, and when to encourage and applaud growth. Self-evaluation realizes an important goal in a writing course: to help students become self-sufficient writers. As Beaven urges, students must have opportunities to decide for themselves "what they are going to learn, how to go about that learning process, and how to evaluate their own progress" (p. 147). Beaven recommends that students evaluate their own papers from the beginning of the course. Initially, we can comment on the quality of their assessment, modifying the goals they've set for themselves or suggesting alternatives when students seem headed in unprofitable directions. Later in the course, as students gain confidence in recognizing the qualities of good writing, we can give them more responsibility for evaluating, even grading, their work.

If answering a long list of questions begins to bore students, teachers can shift to other methods of self-evaluation. Some teachers, for example, ask students to write a paragraph or two describing the major strengths and weaknesses of a draft or final paper. These notes also might explain how students defined their purpose and audience or comment on organizational and stylistic goals that received special attention. Many teachers find these statements surprisingly perceptive and extremely useful in composing their own responses to students' work. They encourage an ongoing dialogue about writing between teacher and student.

Atomistic Evaluation

Measures of writing performance can be grouped into two categories: atomistic and holistic measures. Atomistic measures evaluate some part of the composing process, or certain features of the written product, or a skill presumed to correlate with writing ability. When teachers or administrators place students into writing courses on the basis of a vocabulary test such as the Verbal portion of the Scholastic Aptitude Test (SAT), they assume that a knowledge of words correlates with skills needed to write well. For some students it does; for others it doesn't. Students may score well on vocabulary tests yet produce ineffective compositions; they may score poorly on the test and write well. One reason is that composing involves much more than skill with words.

Editing, mechanics, and usage tests also are atomistic measures. They reveal whether or not students recognize conventions of edited American English. But because composing requires the ability to generate discourse, not merely to analyze it, editing tests can tell us only about some of the skills students use when they write. Tests of syntactic maturity are atomistic too. They enable us to evaluate the length and complexity of sentences and reveal what types of coordination and subordination students achieve in their writing.[7] This information is useful in planning instruction that enlarges students' repertoire of syntactic options. Nevertheless, because they focus primarily on the ability to construct sentences, such tests assess only one of many skills important to composing.

Atomistic measures aren't "bad" tools for evaluating student performance. They measure what they were designed to measure. Because they evaluate some activities required in composing or assess particular features in the product, they isolate problems we can help students overcome. They're misused when we mistake the part for the whole, when we ask atomistic measures to tell us everything we need to know about our students' writing ability. Writing assessments are invalid when procedures intended to evaluate only one aspect of composing are presumed to indicate "writing ability."

Holistic Evaluation

Holistic measures assume that all the features of a composition or all the skills that comprise writing ability are related, interdependent. When we grade papers holistically, we assert that their rhetorical effectiveness lies in the combination of features at every level of the discourse, that the whole is greater than the sum of its parts. Charles Cooper describes the procedure this way:

> Holistic evaluation of writing is a guided procedure for sorting or ranking written pieces. The rater takes a piece of writing and either (1) matches it with another piece in a graded series of pieces or (2) scores it for the prominence of certain features important to that kind of writing or (3) assigns it a letter or number grade. The placing, scoring, or grading occurs quickly, impressionistically, after the rater has practiced the procedure with other raters. The rater does not make corrections or revisions in the paper. Holistic evaluation is usually guided by a holistic scoring guide that describes each feature and identifies high, middle, and low quality levels for each feature. (*Evaluating Writing*, p. 3)

As most teachers know, if six of us were to assign individual numbers or letter grades to the same paper, all of us might evaluate it differently. How then does holistic, "impressionistic" scoring represent an improvement over traditional methods? First of all, holistic scoring is a group activity that requires readers to agree beforehand on the criteria that will determine the ranking of papers. The readers agree to match their impressions of any particular paper to preselected model papers, a scoring guide, or a list of features that define each rank.[8] Second, before readers begin scoring the papers, they practice the procedure, using sample papers written on the same topics by the same kinds of students as those whose work they will score later. The practice session allows raters to "calibrate" themselves to the models, scoring guide, or list of features. When raters consistently agree on what rankings the sample papers should have, the actual scoring can begin. During the scoring session, each student's paper is read at least twice, by two different raters, and assigned a number or letter ranking. When raters disagree on a score, the paper is read by a third reader or given to a panel that determines the score. Because raters don't stop to mark the paper, to correct or revise the student's work, they can score a large number of papers in a short time, "spending no more than two minutes on each paper" (p. 3). And because they have practiced matching each paper against predetermined criteria, they "can achieve a scoring reliability as high as .90 for individual writers" (p. 3).

Holistic evaluation assumes, first, that written discourse communicates a complete message to an audience for a particular purpose. Consequently, "holistic evaluation by a human respondent gets closer to what is essential in such a communication than frequency counts [of errors or of word or sentence elements] do" (p. 3). Rather than single out a few features in the piece, as atomistic measures require, holistic scores recognize all the decisions students make in writing the paper.

Second, holistic measures are flexible. Working together, English teachers can define criteria consistent with a particular course or writing program. Designing and trying out the procedure requires careful work, but once the scale is in place, readers can score large numbers of papers quickly and reliably. Because raters make no comments on the papers, holistic evaluations provide no feedback for students; that is, the scores serve an administrative, not an instructional, purpose and usually help teachers make decisions about placement or final grades.

Third, holistic evaluation removes much of the subjective static that unavoidably interferes with placement and grading decisions. Although we all try to evaluate our students' work objectively, our judgments are always influenced to some degree by factors that have nothing to do with writing. Students who misbehave in class, whose socioeconomic or racial backgrounds differ from ours, whose handwriting is poor, whose past performance has already branded them as D or F students, or whose papers happen to be near the bottom of the stack may receive lower grades than their actual writing ability warrants. However, when papers are coded so that students' names don't appear, when at least two teachers must agree on the score, when all of us in the writing program participate, judgments become considerably more objective and consistent. Furthermore, in developing specific, uniform criteria to guide our scoring, we must discuss, as a faculty, what constitutes "good writing" and how the school's composition program develops the writing abilities of its students. Such questions lie at the center of all writing instruction, and working out the answers together improves both the program and our teaching.

What works for teachers works for students too. Teachers who are themselves trained in holistic scoring can teach their students to score one another's work. They give students the responsibility for assigning grades. The teacher's training is crucial; without it, teachers undermine the procedure, give responsibility with one hand while taking it away with another, and promote irresponsible grading practices. Once trained, however, teachers can help students develop a scoring guide for each assignment, explicitly defining with the class what constitutes a successful response to the assignment. The scoring guide, developed early in the students' work on an assignment, functions to clarify what the assignment requires and may serve as a revision checklist when students discuss their drafts with classmates. When students turn in their final papers, they omit their names and identify the paper with a number the teacher has assigned or with the last four digits of their social security number.

Having collected the papers, the teacher reads them quickly (without marking them), selecting two or three sample papers that meet the criteria for scores at different points in the scale established by the scoring guide. These sample papers become models discussed with the class during the practice session. During the practice session, which must be held on the same day that students score one another's papers, the students review the scoring guide again and then rate the models. The teacher discusses the ratings with the class, allowing students to "calibrate" themselves to the scoring guide. When students reach consensus on what rankings the models should have, the actual scoring begins.

During the scoring session, each student's paper receives two readings, by two different students who assign it a score that most closely matches the criteria defined by the scoring guide. To make two readings of each student's work possible, teachers may swap papers across groups (if the class is divided into permanent workshop groups) or they may require students to submit two copies of the final draft. When student raters disagree on a score by more than one point, as sometimes happens, the teacher acts as the third reader to resolve the conflict. If necessary, the teacher can convert the scores into letter grades by fiat or by discussing with the class the range of scores an assignment receives.

Because very young children can reliably score one another's work, older students, some of whom will be teachers themselves in a few years, can certainly manage the responsibility. Those who will raise the most static about the procedure tend to be students who have made good grades by learning over the years to "please the teacher." If the teacher no longer gives the grades, these students must adjust their usual definitions of success to "please the reader," an audience of classmates. Students trained to use holistic scoring rapidly learn what it means to write for a reader because they tend to see much more writing than they would in a teacher-graded class. They also become confident about how to improve their own work and offer better advice to classmates about their drafts. Letting students score one another's compositions realizes a teacher's conviction that students can learn to recognize good writing, in their own work and in the work of others, and can take active responsibility for their own learning. Teachers who share this conviction can release their control over grades and teach students to assess one another's writing carefully.

Handling the Paper Load

Both theory and practice suggest that students should write more than they do, in English classes and in other disciplines. But the size of our classes and other demands on our time work against us. Our students' work deserves a thoughtful response, but thoughtful responses take time. How can we keep up with the paper load? The question is one that both experienced and inexperienced teachers ask. Fortunately, those who ask it most have developed some of the best answers.

High school teachers, who usually teach 130 to 150 students a day, know many ways to keep students writing while simultaneously encouraging constructive responses from an interested reader.[9] They understand two important principles: the "reader" need not always be the teacher, and the writing need not always receive *written* responses.

We sometimes underestimate the value of ungraded writing assignments. Freewritings, journal entries, sentence-combining problems, and brief paragraphs can give students almost daily writing practice. They may serve several purposes: to summarize the main points of class discussion, to react to a reading assignment, to work out possibilities for future papers. We don't have to respond to these writings as we do to drafts or finished papers. Students can simply add them to their folders for review later, or they can exchange papers for a five-minute response from classmates. Or, we can collect them, skim them, and assign them a daily grade or write a few words at the top of the page. Or, we may respond orally in class by asking a few students to read their work aloud.

On longer, graded assignments, we can use other methods to save time without diminishing the quality of instruction. Many teachers find conference teaching successful. Student-teacher conferences can occur at any time during composing and offer teachers an excellent way to provide feedback when it is most useful, during planning, drafting, or rewriting. Conferences are most effective when teachers listen carefully and allow students to set the agenda. Students should begin the conference, perhaps by reading and commenting on a draft or by explaining what pleases and puzzles them most about the project they are working on. The teacher then responds to the comments, addressing the student's agenda first before raising other issues. The student ends the conference by reacting to the teacher's suggestions and summarizing what strategies will shape the next draft.

Another way to handle the paper load involves asking students to build portfolios of multiple drafts and final versions of several assignments.[10] Portfolios are collections of students' work assembled over time. They originated in fine arts departments, where students customarily select their best paintings, photographs, or drawings to submit for a grade. Although portfolios are relatively new to writing programs, they have several functions. Some institutions now use portfolios of high school writing to determine a student's placement in college writing courses. Other schools have substituted portfolios for competency exams, replacing a one-time test with writing completed in several disciplines throughout the first three years of college. The most common use of writing portfolios is the class portfolio, a collection of work students submit at the end of a single writing course.

Class portfolios permit teachers to assign a great deal of writing. Students keep all of their drafts and final versions in a folder, bring it to class and conferences, and produce an impressive quantity of work. At the end of the term (and sometimes also at midterm), students revise some of these writings yet again and submit the portfolio for a grade. Most teachers who use portfolios define some of the work that must be in the folder, let students choose the rest, and ask them to write a self-evaluation that comments on the entire collection. For example, the teacher might require four papers: a persuasive essay, an analysis of an academic text, any paper the student wishes to include, and a letter describing the contents of the portfolio and chronicling the student's development as a writer. For one of these assignments, perhaps the "student's choice," all drafts and scratchwork must accompany the final draft.

Throughout the term, students work on these assignments, just as they would in a traditional class. Teachers may write comments on drafts and discuss them in conference. Classmates also can offer feedback in writing workshops. If midterm grades are necessary, students may submit two pieces from their portfolios-in-progress at that time for grading. But they also may revise the papers again before the completed portfolio is due.

Regardless of what goes into the portfolio, teachers must define in advance what they expect it to include and how they will evaluate it. Individual pieces of writing do not receive grades; instead, teachers read the entire portfolio holistically, assigning a single comprehensive grade for all of the work. For this reason, they must develop a scoring guide in advance of receiving the portfolios, a difficult task because the portfolio comprises, by design, a diversity of writing. Although individual teachers can develop their own scoring guide independently, most teachers define the nature of the portfolio and the criteria used to judge it collaboratively. They reach consensus about what all of their students' portfolios will contain, develop a common scoring guide, and organize themselves into a review panel to evaluate one another's students' portfolios.

Portfolios demand a great deal of reading time at the end of the term and raise questions about reliably scoring such a diverse body of work; nevertheless, they have clear advantages. A carefully designed scoring guide can increase reliability, and because readers assess the portfolio as a whole, not individual papers, evaluating portfolios takes less time than grading and commenting on final drafts. Moreover, portfolios remain the best way of evaluating students' growth in writing over time. When drafts and scratchwork are included, they can document the composing process, especially rewriting. Portfolios also demonstrate to students that writing is process. Most students take greater pride and pleasure in preparing their portfolios than they do in writing individual papers for the teacher to grade. Plagiarism is virtually unheard of; while it may be tempting to cheat on one assignment, a portfolio contains so much material that must be genuine that students will find it difficult to copy someone else's work. Teachers also find their collaboration in a portfolio project rewarding. In defining the portfolio's contents and devising the standards by which it will be judged, teachers must articulate the goals of their writing courses, a conversation that reinforces convictions about the best practices for teaching writing. Portfolio projects encourage teachers to support one another in setting standards and designing courses, decisions that foster collegiality and give teachers ownership of their work.

All of these methods — in addition to class discussions of students' papers, self-evaluations, and peer responses — encourage students to write frequently, to have their work read by a variety of audiences, and to share the authority for evaluating writing. Teachers unwilling to share that authority face at least two unpleasant consequences. They feel obligated to mark too many papers (or to assign too little writing), and worse, they prevent their students from learning what the standards for effective writing are. Sharing responsibility for the paper load not only keeps us sane; it's also good teaching.

Notes:

[1] For a comprehensive discussion of issues surrounding assessment, see Edward M. White, *Teaching and Assessing Writing*, 2d ed. (The Jossey-Bass Higher Education Series; San Francisco: Jossey-Bass, 1994).

[2] Although experienced teachers seem to have internalized the criteria for A, B, C, D, and F papers, beginning teachers may want a more explicit discussion of grades than they will find in this chapter. I recommend the practical advice William F. Irmscher gives in Chapter 13, "Evaluation," in *Teaching Expository Writing* (New York: Holt, Rinehart and Winston, 1979), pp. 142–78.

[3] The assignment appears among the "Placement Essay Topics" in Mina F. Shaughnessy, *Errors and Expectations: A Guide for the Teacher of Basic Writing* (New York: Oxford University Press, 1977), p. 295.

[4] An excellent discussion of types of misspellings and their causes appears in Shaughnessy, Chapter 5.

[5] A revealing study of initial and terminal comments in a sample of 3,000 papers is Robert J. Connors and Andrea A. Lunsford, "Teachers' Rhetorical Comments on Student Papers," *College Composition and Communication* 44 (May 1993), 200–223: "The teachers whose comments we studied seem often to have been trained to judge student writing by rhetorical formulae that are almost as restricting as mechanical formulae. The emphasis still seems to be on finding and pointing out problems and deficits in the individual paper, not on envisioning patterns in student writing habits or prompts that could go beyond such analysis" (p. 218). See also Chris M.

Anson, ed., *Writing and Response: Theory, Practice, and Research* (Urbana, IL: NCTE, 1989).

[6] Beyond Shaughnessy's work, teachers will find helpful Elaine O. Lees, "Evaluating Student Writing," *College Composition and Communication* 30 (December 1979), 370–74; and David Bartholomae, "The Study of Error," *College Composition and Communication* 31 (October 1980), 253–69.

[7] For a description of the procedure developed by Kellogg W. Hunt, see his "A Synopsis of Clause-to-Sentence Length Factors," *English Journal* 54 (April 1965), 300, 305–9; and Kellogg W. Hunt, "Early Blooming and Late Blooming Syntactic Structures," in *Evaluating Writing*, pp. 91–104.

[8] For a description of holistic scoring using sample student papers as models, see Edward M. White, *Assigning, Responding, Evaluating: A Writing Teacher's Guide*, 2d ed. (New York: St. Martin's Press, 1990). Primary Trait Scoring, developed to score the essays for the National Assessment of Educational Progress, uses an elaborate scoring guide, described by Richard Lloyd-Jones, "Primary Trait Scoring," in *Evaluating Writing*, pp 33–66. The best known "analytic scale" appears in Paul B. Diederich, *Measuring Growth in English* (Urbana, IL: NCTE, 1974). The prominent features of a piece of writing receive weighted numerical values, "ideas" and "organization" receiving greater weight than "handwriting" and "spelling." Diederich also constructs an attractive argument for involving the entire English faculty in evaluating writing performance so that bias doesn't unduly affect students' final grades.

[9] See the collection of practical essays compiled by the NCTE Committee on Classroom Practices in Teaching English, *How to Handle the Paper Load* (Urbana, IL: NCTE, 1979); for a valuable discussion of responding to student writing in conferences, see Donald M. Murray, *A Writer Teaches Writing*, 2d ed. (Boston: Houghton Mifflin, 1985), especially Chapter 8.

[10] For a discussion of portfolios and their uses, see *Portfolios: Process and Product*, ed. Pat Belanoff and Marcia Dickson (Portsmouth, NH: Boynton/Cook, 1991); and *New Directions in Portfolio Assessment: Reflective Practice, Critical Theory, and Large-Scale Scoring*, ed. Laurel Black, Donald A. Daiker, Jeffrey Sommers, and Gail Stygall (Portsmouth, NH: Boynton/Cook, 1994).

Works Cited

Beaven, Mary H. "Individualized Goal Setting, Self-Evaluation, and Peer Evaluation." In *Evaluating Writing: Describing, Measuring, Judging.* Ed. Charles R. Cooper and Lee Odell. Urbana, IL: NCTE, 1977. Pp. 135–56.

Cooper, Charles R. "Responding to Student Writing." In *The Writing Processes of Students.* Ed. Walter T. Petty and Patrick J. Finn. Buffalo: State University of New York, 1975. Pp. 31–39.

Cooper, Charles R., and Lee Odell, eds. *Evaluating Writing: Describing, Measuring, Judging.* Urbana, IL: NCTE, 1977.

Goodman, Kenneth. "Minimum Standards: A Moral View." In *Minimum Competency Standards: Three Points of View.* N.P.: International Reading Association, 1978. Pp. 3–5.

Hillocks, George, Jr. *Research on Written Composition: New Directions for Teaching.* Urbana, IL: ERIC Clearinghouse on Reading and Communication Skills and the National Conference on Research in English, 1986.

Jenkinson, Edward B., and Donald A. Seybold. *Writing as a Process of Discovery: Some Structured Theme Assignments for Grades Five through Twelve.* Bloomington: Indiana University Press, 1970.

Shaughnessy, Mina. *Errors and Expectations: A Guide for the Teacher of Basic Writing.* New York: Oxford University Press, 1977.

PARAGRAPHS

From PARAGRAPHING FOR THE READER
Rick Eden and Ruth Mitchell

[*College Composition and Communication* 37 (1986): 416–30.]

Rick Eden is a writer/analyst at the RAND Corporation. He has published articles and reviews in several journals, and he has taught a wide variety of composition and rhetoric courses. Ruth Mitchell is author of *First Steps* (1990) and *Testing for Learning* (1991).

The following excerpt is the introduction and first part of Eden and Mitchell's article "Paragraphing for the Reader," in which they react to the prevalent method of teaching paragraphing found in many textbooks. Arguing that teaching students formulas for constructing paragraphs is ineffective, they demonstrate convincingly that we should teach writers to make paragraphing decisions in light of "purpose, audience, and rhetorical stance," always attending to readers' expectations.

The teaching of paragraphs needs a revolution. Classroom instruction offers patterns and precepts which cannot be applied to the ordinary process of writing and which, moreover, are unsupported by current research. Researchers in English like Braddock, Meade and Ellis, and Knoblauch report findings which directly contradict the textbooks' platitudes:[1] Paragraphs in admired professional writing do not necessarily contain topic sentences, they rarely follow prescribed patterns, and they seem essentially accidental, invented as the writer composes.

We have found that textbooks do not heed these warnings. Students perceive a strange disjunction between the paragraphs they read and those they are asked to write in class. Too often the latter are miniature five-element themes — introductory and concluding sentences, with three intervening sentences connected by "therefore" and "in addition."

We believe that paragraphing is best presented to student writers as an important signaling system, based on signals of two sorts, visual and substantive. To readers, the strip of indented white space separating paragraphs indicates both connection and discontinuity. It heightens their attention. To the writer, marking paragraphs offers opportunity for manipulating the reader's focus. Strategically paragraphed prose not only streamlines a message but also molds and shapes it to achieve the writer's purpose.

We shall argue for a reader-oriented theory of the paragraph.[2] In order to paragraph effectively, a writer needs to know, not the five, ten, fifteen, or twenty most common paragraph patterns that current theories enumerate, but how indentions affect the reader's perception of prose discourse. Knowing how readers perceive prose, the writer can arrange his text to mesh with their perception.

Our argument proposes (and, we hope, proves) two main theses:

1. Paragraphs depend for their effectiveness on the exploitation of psycholinguistic features — that is, of the reader's conventional ex-

pectations and perceptual patterns. For example, readers treat the first sentence of a paragraph as the orienting statement necessary for them to understand the rest, regardless of whether the writer so intended. Thus a paragraph does not "need" a topic sentence: Every paragraph has one, willy-nilly. The question for the writer is not "Where shall I put my topic sentence?" but "Do I want this initial statement to direct the reader's understanding of the paragraph?" A good deal of our argument will explicate and extend these psycholinguistic features and their consequences.

2. Paragraphing is not part of the composing but of the editing process. To think about paragraphs too early may invoke the blocking mechanisms that Mike Rose has described in "Rigid Rules, Inflexible Plans, and the Stifling of Language: A Cognitivist Analysis of Writer's Block" (*College Composition and Communication,* 41 [December 1980], 389–400) [p. 72 in this book]. Current paragraph theory has assumed that paragraphing is part of the process of generating, whereas it properly belongs with revision. It refines and shapes material already on the page.

Our argument is divided into four parts. In the first part we explain the reader's expectations of paragraphs and point out research which has clarified these expectations. Part Two demonstrates the strengths and weaknesses of the most popular current model of paragraph structure, the scheme devised by Francis Christensen to explain paragraph structure according to levels of generality. In Part Three an extended example demonstrates the power of rhetorical paragraphing. In Part Four we lay out pedagogical implications of our reader-oriented theory.[3]

1

Paragraphing for the reader means meeting the reader's expectations. These expectations are unconscious and remain so unless repeatedly disappointed. Some are rooted in cognition itself, in the reader's patterns of perception and comprehension. Others are rooted in rhetorical convention, in current practices of formatting prose.

What are these expectations?

1. Readers expect to see paragraphs when they read a piece of extended prose. They expect to see regularly spaced indentions. This is only an expectation about the appearance of the page. How frequently readers expect the indentions to appear — i.e., how long they expect the average paragraph to run — will vary according to several factors, including the size and genre of the text as a whole. Readers conventionally expect a book on philosophy to have many very long paragraphs, some filling entire pages. They do not expect the same from a modern narrow-column newspaper. Reading typescript, they need relief upon encountering pages unbroken by indentions — too many such pages make a coffee break irresistible.

   This initial, visual expectation — that prose will be indented at regular intervals — is conventional, and it changes as continually as other social conventions. In the nineteenth century, for instance, readers expected newspapers virtually to eschew indentions. The other expectations, which follow, are derived from human cognitive processes and are thus universal.

2. Readers expect paragraphs to be unified simply because they perceive them as units. Readers expect the paragraph's formal unity to signal substantive unity and they infer one from the other as they half-find and half-fashion significance in the text.

3. Readers expect the initial sentences of a paragraph to orient them, to identify the context in which succeeding sentences are to be understood. Readers accept the initial sentences as instructions for integrating what they are about to read with what they have just read.

   These instructions do little good if readers receive them only as they finish reading a paragraph: To work effectively the instructions must appear initially. People understand material most readily when it is presented to them in a top-down fashion, with details and reasons preceded by orienting statements.[4]

4. Readers expect to find at each paragraph's peripheral points something which merits special attention, because readers naturally attend to endpoints. As they read a paragraph, their attention is greatest as they begin and end. This is simply a fact about perception —a principle of peripherality.[5] We shall show that it has implications for the rhetorical organization of paragraphs.

5. Readers expect paragraphs to be coherent, both internally and externally. The demand for external coherence is implied by the expectation for unity. To distinguish external from internal coherence, we will term the latter "cohesiveness." The reader expects each paragraph to cohere internally as well as externally, to contain a sensible sequence of thought within itself as well as to continue one begun in previous paragraphs.

Current rhetorics teach various strategies, such as repeating words and structures and supplying transitional words and phrases, to help the writer make the text cohere for the reader, and it is important that writers learn them. However, important as these strategies are in practice, in theory they have nothing to do with paragraphing. Readers expect paragraphs to be cohesive only because they expect all prose, all discourse, to be so. Rhetorics would have to teach these strategies even if we did not conventionally organize prose into paragraphs.

The same is true of the many plans of development — compare/contrast, topic/comment, question/answer, and so on — that rhetorics teach as ways to organize paragraphs internally. These patterns also have nothing inherent to do with the practice of indention. They are characterized in some texts as "types" of paragraphs simply because paragraphs provide conveniently sized forums in which to discuss, illustrate, and practice them. Francis Christensen made this point twenty years ago, but no one seems much to have heeded him:

> These methods [of paragraph development] are real, but they are simply methods of development — period. They are no more relevant to the paragraph than, on the short side, to the sentence or, on the long side, to a run of several paragraphs or to a paper as long as this or a chapter. They are the topoi of classical rhetoric. They are the channels our minds naturally run in whether we are writing a sentence or a paragraph or planning a paper. (*Notes toward a New Rhetoric*, 2nd ed. [New York: Harper & Row, 1978], p. 77)

Not many researchers have investigated how paragraphing influences the reader's interpretation of the text, but during the 1960s Koen, Becker, and Young performed a series of experiments which support our characterization of the reader's expectations.[6] They established that paragraphs are both visual and structural units. A writer sets up a paragraph by framing it with white space. He unifies its structure with three kinds of internal markers, representing the three systems which interact to produce cohesion. The lexical system depends on reiterated nouns and pronouns producing a chain of references over several sentences. These are the lexical markers. The grammatical system is signaled by inflections, the grammatical markers. The rhetorical system consists of expository patterns or modes of development — topic and illustration, for example. Its markers consist of so-called "collocational sets," that is, words whose meanings cluster round a general topic. Formal markers — such as conjunctions and transitional words and phrases — permitted subjects in Koen, Becker, and Young's experiments to recognize the systems even in nonsense passages. When prose is well paragraphed, these markers permit readers to predict paragraph boundaries in unindented passages.

The experimenters established an important principle: reparagraphing — i.e., moving indention points — is not only typographical but also substantive. Because the visual breaks direct the reader's attention, changing them changes the reader's interpretation of the text. They thus showed that paragraphs have a psychological as well as a physical reality. Their results pointed toward a reader-oriented theory of the paragraph.

More recent research, conducted by David Kieras, a psychologist at the University of Arizona, also supports our reader-oriented approach. His work corroborates our characterization of the reader's expectations for initial, orienting material. Kieras has found that "information appearing first in the passage has more influence on the reader's perception of the main idea compared to the very same information appearing later in the passage" ("How Readers Abstract Main Ideas from Technical Prose: Some Implications for Document Design," paper presented at a Document Design Center Colloquium, American Institute for Research, Washington, D.C., 17 November 1980, p. 6). These results led him to endorse the initial placement of orienting sentences: "the topic sentence of a passage really should be first, because that is where a reader expects to find the important information" (p. 7). A paragraph which violates this expectation may remain comprehensible, of course, especially if the content is familiar to the reader, but it takes longer to read and demands more work of the reader, who must revise his notion of the paragraph's main point as he proceeds.

Paragraphing is as complex as the reader's pattern of comprehension and expectation. A writer who understands these complexities commands a powerful and flexible rhetorical resource. With paragraphs, writers can shape their text so as to influence its reading. Indeed, paragraphing offers the prose writer the poet's privileges. Prose writers cannot govern the placement of sentences — where they begin and end depends on layout design, choice of typeface, size of page, and so on. But they can choose where the white indentions will indicate paragraphs. That choice offers them opportunity and responsibility, the opportunity to manipulate the reader's attention and the responsibility to do so effectively. To paragraph well, writers must exploit and reinforce the visual impact of indentions. They must provide the unity and cohesion that the paragraph's visual form promises.

Current text-oriented writing theory and pedagogy misrepresent paragraphing by oversimplifying it. Text-centered approaches abbreviate the writing process; they treat the text rather than the reader as its end point. This oversimplification creates unnecessary complications in the form of poorly motivated prescriptions (e.g., for unity) and fossilized taxonomies.

The inadequacy of these taxonomies is evident to anyone who has tried to learn or teach them. They are not and cannot possibly become exhaustive. They can't list every type of paragraph, every strategy for paragraphing. Thus, they don't give the student the flexibility he will need to handle unanticipated rhetorical demands. Nor can the taxonomies help us to evaluate paragraphs: It's impossible to know whether a paragraph which doesn't fall under one of the types is a poor paragraph or a new species.

Formal definitions of the paragraph also vitiate much research and pedagogy. Too many researchers and rhetoricians take the paragraph to be a conveniently sized, self-contained piece of prose — a sort of latter-day *chreia*. Roger C. Schank, for instance, in a paper entitled "Understanding Paragraphs" (Technical Report, Instituto per gli studi semantici e cognitivi, Castagnola, Switzerland, 1974), investigates the structures of inferences in what he calls paragraphs but what are in fact "short stories." Sharing Schank's misconception of the paragraph as a self-contained rhetorical form, composition instructors often ask students to "write a paragraph" when they mean a short story, summary, or writing sample.

Inflexible formal definitions also lie behind the frequent proscription against the one-sentence paragraph. Although student writers are commonly denied this tool by edict, any attentive reading of effective prose will demonstrate its usefulness and its frequent occurrence. A one-sentence paragraph packs a double punch: It has the normal emphasis of a sentence as well as the visual emphasis of a paragraph.

By taking into account the reader's needs, we can clear up the current muddle of principles and patterns in our theories and our texts. We can't make paragraphing appear simple, because it isn't, but we can make its complexities appear sensible and well motivated. . . .

Notes

The authors wish to thank the following colleagues who generously gave their time to criticize earlier versions of this paper: Molly Faulkner, Connie Greaser, Carol Hartzog, Richard Lanham, Alan Purves, Mike Rose, Mary Vaiana, and Joseph Williams.

[1] Richard Braddock, "The Frequency and Placement of Topic Sentences in Expository Prose," *Research in the Teaching of English*, 8 (Winter 1974), 287–302. Richard A. Meade and W. Greiger Ellis, "Paragraph Development in the Modern Age of Rhetoric," *English Journal*, 59 (February 1970), 219–26; C. H. Knoblauch, "Some Formal and Nonformal Properties of Paragraphs and Paragraph Sequences," a paper delivered in session B-12, "Revisiting the Rhetoric of the Paragraph," Conference on College Composition and Communication, Dallas, Texas, March 1981.

[2] Ruth Mitchell and Mary Vaiana Taylor laid out a reader-oriented model for composition in their article "The Integrative Perspective: An Audience-Response Model for Writing," *College English*, 41 (November 1979), 247–70. The present essay offers an extension and specific application of their model.

[3] There is a considerable history to the paragraph, documented in James R. Bennett, Betty Brigham, Shirley Carson, John Fleischauer, Turner Kobler, Foster Park, and Allan Thies, "The Paragraph: An Annotated Bibliography," *Style*, 9 (Spring 1977), 107–18. Paul C. Rodgers claimed that Alexander Bain first systematically formulated paragraph theory ("Alexander Bain and the Rise of the Organic Paragraph," *Quarterly Journal of Speech*, 51 [December 1965], 399–403). His view was modified by Ned A. Shearer ("Alexander Bain and the Genesis of Paragraph Theory," *Quarterly Journal of Speech*, 58 [December 1972], 408–17). Shearer claimed that Bain had unacknowledged predecessors and furthermore derived his paragraph theory from the unity of the sentence: a paragraph was a larger sentence, a sentence a smaller paragraph.

[4] Top-down processing means proceeding from an orienting statement to details. It applies to all units of prose larger than the sentence. A top-down arrangement presents the reader with a thesis statement which allows him to understand why he is being told what follows. But composing processes . . . often proceed bottom-up — they don't begin with an orienting statement but end with one. The conse-

quences of top-down processing for paragraph comprehension have been investigated by Perry Thorndyke in "Cognitive Structures in Comprehension and Memory of Narrative Discourse," *Cognitive Psychology*, 9 (January 1977), 77–110, and by Bonnie Meyer in *The Organization of Prose and Its Effects on Memory* (Amsterdam: North-Holland, 1975). Perhaps the most striking example of dependence on top-down processing is supplied by J. D. Bransford and M. K. Johnson, "Considerations of Some Problems of Comprehension," in W. G. Chase, ed., *Visual Information Processing* (New York: Academic Press, 1973). They found that experimental subjects could not understand or remember the following passage, which does not identify its orienting topic:

> The procedure is actually quite simple. First you arrange things into different groups depending on their makeup. Of course, one pile may be sufficient, depending on how much there is to do. If you have to go somewhere else due to lack of facilities, that is the next step, otherwise, you are pretty well set. It is important not to overdo any particular endeavor. That is, it is better to do too few things at once than too many. . . .

Readers must be told first that the passage describes washing clothes. Without that information, they cannot make sense of it.

⁵ The principle of peripherality is well established in cognitive psychology. For a discussion of the literature see J. A. McGeoch and A. L. Irion, *The Psychology of Human Learning* (New York: Longmans Green, 1952).

⁶ Frank Koen, Alton Becker, and Richard Young, "The Psychological Reality of the Paragraph, Part I," *Studies in Language and Language Behavior*, 4 (February 1967), University of Michigan; rpt. in *Technical Communication: Selected Publications by the Faculty*, Department of the Humanities, College of Engineering, University of Michigan, 1977. This article is not listed in the *Style* bibliography of the paragraph cited in note 3.

AN APPETITE FOR COHERENCE:
AROUSING AND FULFILLING DESIRES
Kristie S. Fleckenstein

[*College Composition and Communication* 43 (1992): 81–87.]

Kristie S. Fleckenstein is a lecturer in the Department of English at the University of Missouri-Kansas City. Her research interests include affect and imagery in reading and writing. Her articles have appeared in the *Journal of Advanced Composition*, the *English Journal*, *Teaching English in the Two-Year College*, and *College Composition and Communication*. Most recently, her essay "Images, Words, and Narrative Epistemology" appeared in *College English* (December 1996).

Fleckenstein suggests that coherence is so difficult to teach, in part, because it is as much a "reader-based phenomenon as it is a writer-based creation." She describes a sequence of classroom activities that help students see their writing from a reader's perspective. Fleckenstein also includes examples from her students' work to illustrate how her suggestions help students become more effective at perceiving coherence (or incoherence) in their own writing. She suggests activities for individuals, peer groups, and the whole class.

The American Dream is to lose weight quickly and to keep it off without going hungry. But that's all it is: a dream. Wouldn't it be great if you could lose weight by swallowing a pill? The truth is no diet aid or diet pill will take excess weight off unless a person takes in less calories than he/she burns. Some pill packets even suggest a 1,200-calorie-a-day diet program for weight loss. How effective and safe are these diet products, though? Every year seems to bring a new drug for weight loss, and every year Americans seem to spend millions of dollars on diet aids that are ineffective and may even be dangerous.

Wouldn't it be great if you could lose weight by swallowing a pill? The American dream is to lose weight quickly and to keep it off without going hungry. Some pill packets even suggest a 1,200-calorie-a-day diet program for weight loss. But that's all it is: a dream. The truth is no diet aid or diet pill will take excess weight off unless a person takes in fewer calories than he/she burns. Yet every year seems to bring a new drug for weight loss, and every year Americans seem to spend millions of dollars on diet aids that are ineffective and may even be dangerous.

These two introductory paragraphs, so similar but so different, demonstrate the "before" and "after" texts created by Shelly, a struggling writer in an introductory college composition course. Beyond one or two minor stylistic changes and the omission of a single sentence, the two paragraphs are identical, save in the arrangement of the sentences. And that revision in order is the difference between a coherent introductory paragraph and an incoherent introductory paragraph.

Helping students create coherent texts is one of the most difficult jobs that composition teachers have. Part of that difficulty lies in the fact that coherence is as much a reader-based phenomenon as it is a writer-based creation. As Robert de Beaugrande and Wolfgang Dressler point out in *Introduction to Text Linguistics*, writers may provide the linguistic cues, but it is the readers who fill the gaps between ideas by building relationships that bridge ideas, and who thereby create their sense of order (Longman, 1981). Form is not a product, but a process, Kenneth Burke says, "an arousing and fulfillment of desires," "the creation of an appetite in the mind of the auditor, and the adequate satisfying of that appetite" (qtd. in Sonja Foss, Karen Foss, and Robert Trapp, *Contemporary Perspectives on Rhetoric*, Waveland, 1985, 162).

No wonder it is difficult for inexpert — and expert — writers to create coherent texts, both locally, at the sentence and paragraph levels, and globally, at the full-text level. To judge the success or failure of a particular passage requires the writer to step out of his or her shoes as a writer and examine the passage as a reader. Writers need to perceive the desires or expectations their texts arouse in their projected readers and then check to see if those desires are satisfied. Such a difficult role reversal is not easy to achieve, especially for students previously taught that form, for instance the five-paragraph form, is imposed on content or for those students taught to write without a consideration of their readers.

A method that helps writers shift perspectives involves getting them outside their texts. The technique requires students to examine what they do as readers to create coherent meaning, apply those discoveries to an incoherent text, then examine their own in-progress essays for problems with coherence.

The first part of this classroom strategy demonstrates that coherence is not "in the text," but something that readers create with the aid of cues provided by the writer. Begin this process by offering students the following brief passage, instructing them to read it, noting any words or sentences they don't understand, and then, if possible, to summarize it:

> Sally first tried setting loose a team of gophers. The plan backfired when a dog chased them away. She then entertained a group of teenagers and was delighted when they brought their motorcycles. Unfortunately, she failed to find a Peeping Tom listed in the Yellow Pages. Furthermore, her stereo system was not loud enough. The crabgrass might have worked, but she didn't have a fan that was sufficiently powerful. The obscene phone calls gave her hope until the number was changed. She thought about calling a door-to-door salesman but decided to hang up a clothesline instead. It was the installation of blinking neon lights across the street that did the trick. She eventually framed the ad from the classified section.

Most students are unable to create a coherent meaning out of this passage, although they understand all the words and most of the sentences. They merely can't weave the disparate ideas into any understandable pattern. So the next step is to discuss the reasons for their difficulty. For instance, three sentences that commonly confuse my students are (1) "The crabgrass might have worked, but she didn't have a fan that was sufficiently powerful"; (2) "She thought about calling a door-to-door salesman but decided to hang up a clothesline instead"; and (3) "She eventually framed the ad from the classified section." During full-class discussions, my students complain that they can't connect crabgrass to fans in the first sample sentence. They point to a similar problem between door-to-door salesman and clothesline. Finally, in the last sample sentence, students say that they don't know what ad Sally refers to.

Following a discussion of reading frustrations, provide students with the following sentence: "Sally disliked her neighbors and wanted them to leave the area." Students discover that this sentence provides them a context to draw from. Now, they can use their background knowledge about human motivation, neighborhood irritations, and offensive strategies to build relationships within and between sentences. Thus, they are able to relate crabgrass and fan by filling the gaps with the cause-effect knowledge (1) that crabgrass is the bane of the suburbanite's lawn and (2) that the fan was meant to infest the neighbor's lawn with crabgrass. Door-to-door salesmen and clotheslines are connected in an additive relationship as ploys designed to irritate the neighbors, and the ad, associated with Sally's implied goal of driving her neighbors out, is the real estate ad announcing the sale of the neighbor's home.

These observations serve as a basis for the discovery that coherent meaning results from the relationships we as readers build between ideas. If we can't build relationships by bridging the gaps between ideas — ideas such as crabgrass and fans — we create no coherent sense of the text.

The orienting statement about Sally's sentiments can also be used to demonstrate that readers approach a text with an array of expectations already cued (including the expectation that the text confronting us is coherent). Then, as we read, we are guided by those expectations, or appetites, and sample the text to satisfy or revise those appetites. By discussing the expectations the first sentence elicits, students discover how those expectations become predictions, hypotheses, and guesses which they validate or revise as they read.

The next step of this strategy is to move students from a contemplation of themselves as readers to practical work as peer editors. Sharing and revising an incoherent text helps effect this shift from reader to writer. Using an overhead projector, project an incoherent paragraph, but separate each sentence with three to four lines of space. With a sheet of paper, cover everything except the first sentence. Ask students to write down (a) what they think the idea of the sentence is, (b) what they think will come next, and (c) what they think the entire essay will concern. Uncover the second sentence and ask the students to decide if this sentence is consistent with their expectations. Discuss differences in opinion, but without attempting to arrive at any premature closure. Then, with the first two sentences as a basis, ask students to again write down what they think the essay will be about and what will come next. Continue predicting and discussing those predictions throughout the paragraph. As the last step in the exercise, have the students pool their observations and decide, as a class, how best to revise the paragraph so that it achieves a greater sense of coherence. Ask students to make specific suggestions for revisions: what to rearrange, add, or delete.

Following this whole-class work, divide the students into small groups, pass out copies of a second paragraph, and ask each group to read, analyze, and suggest changes for that paragraph, just as they had done for the first one. Finally, ask students to take the first one or two paragraphs of their current essays-in-progress and "stretch them out" — separate each sentence by three or four lines of space — and bring them to share with their peer partners for an analysis of paragraph coherence.

During the third stage of this experience with coherence, students apply to *each other's papers* the techniques they applied previously as a group. The sample below illustrates a typical interchange between writer and peer partner. I have selected this particular interaction for a variety of reasons. First, both the writer, Trish, and the peer editor, Terry, were average writers from a developmental college writing class. Second, this sample reflects Trish's work with her first complete, formal draft of her first essay. Finally, I chose this sample because Terry did not follow the precise instructions provided in class; however, he still produced valuable reactions and advice for Trish. For instance, students were asked to (a) jot down the focus of the sentence under analysis, (b) jot down what they expect next, and (c) jot down what they expect from the entire essay. Terry frequently failed to include his expectations and the focus; instead, he explained why the sentence under examination did or did not meet his expectations, and he provided on-the-spot advice. Terry's success as a peer editor illustrates that the effectiveness of the strategy is not a product of its exact application.

1. In high school I had been in the printing class for about 3 and 1/2 years.
   a. The sentence is about printing class.
   b. Your essay's about printing class.

2. When we started out, there were 6 or 7 black students in a class that was predominately white and hispanic.
   a. It's about the kids in the class.
   b. The sentence doesn't correspond with the previous sentence. I am a bit confused.
   c. The paper is still about printing class.

3. As the years progressed and I was in my junior year there was one black student left: me.
   a. This should have been your second sentence because it corresponds with the first sentence.
   b. The problems she had in her class because she was the only black person.

   c. The essay's going to be about the problem that she had for being black.

4. I had become extremely talented with lithographic photography, which is making negatives of line copy (words), halftone pictures (regular pictures into dot form), and the PMT process (taking drawn art and making it usable for printing).

   a. This sentence doesn't fit because you started talking about being the only black and then you start explaining what you did in the class. The reader is like, the only black and so what?

   b. Being the only black gave these advantages of learning how to work the many different equipments.

   c. Learning how to work the equipment in the printing class.

5. Due to the fact I was working with light sensitive film a lot, I was in the darkroom, which is away from the rest of the class, and where I am hardly seen.

   a. This sentence doesn't fit. What does light sensitive film have to do with equipment or being the only black? About now I am confused.

   b. The sentence is about her class work.

   c. I'm not sure what the paper will be about. Discrimination in the printing class? her work?

6. This made the class look as if it was all white and hispanic, and gave the impression to the customers as well.

   a. This sort of follows because she's still talking about working out of sight, but what customers is she talking about?

   b. The customers gave all the credit to the white students.

   c. The discrimination from the printing class.

7. When I was seen in the class room, which was rare, and a customer would walk in, they would be shocked to see me.

   a. This sentence fits and your essay is starting to make sense. I think it is about being discriminated by your printing class.

8. It was then I realized the subtle prejudice of my printshop teacher, Mr. H—.

   a. I finally got the connection in your last sentence and the topic of the essay is clearer.

   Suggestions for Revision I finally figured out your topic, but I still can't make all the sentences fit. Maybe you should explain about your print class and the customers. Why were you in the same class for 3 years? Maybe take out the sentence on what you did in class. I don't know how to fit it in. Can you combine the ideas in the first three sentences? Or start out with your first sentence, add a couple of sentences about the class, then explain that by your junior year you were the only black? Then say you were out of sight a lot?

Trish revised her first paragraph into the following:

In high school I had been in a printing class for about 3 and 1/2 years. The class was a production class, which meant that students could take it for a number of years and that we learned about printing by doing jobs for customers. When I started out as a freshman, there were about 6 or 7 other black students in a predominately white and hispanic class, but by my junior year I was the only black student left. Also, because I was working with light sensitive film much of the time, I was in the darkroom, away from the class and hardly seen. Customers had the impression that the class was all white and hispanic. When customers saw me in the class room, which was rare, they would be shocked. It was then that I realized the subtle prejudice of my printshop teacher, Mr. H—.

With Terry's help, Trish was able to revise her first paragraph into a much tighter introduction, one that consistently cued her topic for the entire paper and one that maintained greater unity between ideas.

Beyond the value of this technique as a revision tool, it also helps students achieve more writing control. For instance, one pedagogical goal in any writing class is to wean our students from dependence on our judgment and to foster reliance on their own judgment. This strategy for creating coherence facilitates that movement, in that it provides what Carl Bereiter and Marlene Scardamalia call executive controls: a method of determining when the composing process derails and a procedure for correcting the derailment (*The Psychology of Written Composition*, Erlbaum, 1987). This strategy does that; it can be effectively wielded by writers without access to peer partners or with less-than-satisfactory peer partners, as the following example demonstrates. The three sample paragraphs below are from the first, second, and final drafts of a paper by a writer in a developmental freshman composition class. Tina, whose peer partner frustrated her with an inconsistent performance, applied the strategy herself, as she worked through several versions of her introduction.

> *Draft I:* Remember if you don't follow your dreams, you'll never know what's on the other side of the rainbow; you'll never know what you can find at the top of the mountain; you'll never know your journey's best. By being a pushover, you let people dictate what you can and cannot do. Letting people run over you, or pushing your thoughts aside and not caring how you feel, you'll never know what you're capable of in terms of success but the failures you possess will always carry with you. Of course the failure is being afraid to speak and tell somebody or anybody how you truly feel. By bottling up your personal frustrations that you have problems saying aloud, your insides are going to explode. That explosion can be dangerous or even fatal that you get to the point of going out and killing that person who pushes you around or develop a high blood pressure which will eventually result in a heart attack. On the other hand, you can let your frustrations out and let that weak point of your character work to your advantage. Believe me, the second choice is safer and more productive.

> *Draft II:* For all of you pushovers out there, never let anyone tell you what to do or what's impossible for you. Remember, if you don't follow your dreams, you'll never know what's on the other side of the rainbow or what's at the top of the mountain. So always speak up for what you believe in, because if you don't do it for yourself, no one will. If you continue to be a pushover, a sucker for the rest of your life, you'll be a rug for the rest of your life. People will continue to step all over you. Believe me. I know. I was once a pushover myself. A pushover. An opponent who is easy to defeat or a victim who is capable of no effective resistance. Do not and I repeat do not subject yourself to that despicable low-life group called: the suckers.

> *Draft III:* Pushover. An opponent who is easy to defeat or a victim who is capable of no effective resistance. Do not, and I repeat, do not subject yourself to that despicable, low-life group called the suckers. If you continue to be a sucker for the rest of your life, you'll be a rug for the rest of your life. People will continue to step all over you. Believe what I am saying. I was once a pushover myself.

Although Tina's introduction still has problems, it does reflect a tighter focus and greater coherence than do her previous two efforts.

This way to help students perceive incoherence in their writing also possesses peripheral benefits. First, it emphasizes the importance of reading in writing. To be good writers, students must also be good readers. The focus of discussions can switch easily from the students' writing process to an examination of specific cues that can help readers create the relationships the writers seemingly have in mind. Second, the strategy also offers a productive way to introduce transitions and cohesive ties as linguistic cues that signal to readers an underlying relationship. This method centers students' attention on the underlying relationship of the transitional word cues, not on the word itself. Finally, students can examine the texts of professional writers, tracing shifts and noting how these writers ensure smooth bridges between ideas, gaining a greater sense of the rhetorical conventions that govern discourse. Again, this fosters the students' growth as readers, as well as writers.

Shelly's, Trish's, and Tina's revisions are hardly problem free, but each demonstrates the increasingly effective coherence this strategy promotes. Perhaps the most rewarding outgrowth of this technique is watching students gain confidence in their own ability to create meaningful texts and to create meaning from texts without a teacher's continued intercession.

CHOOSING FORMATS AND DOCUMENT DESIGN

Many students in composition courses are pursuing business or technical careers, and they need help writing in those fields. Further, as more and more students grow familiar with word processing and desktop publishing software, they have the technology to design documents for a variety of situations, in a variety of fields.

Part One of the handbook offers a concise discussion of writing for business and professional purposes, emphasizing that effective communication is direct, clear, and appropriate for the situation. Further, with the new emphasis on document design, the handbook recognizes that effective communication entails more than clear writing; students and teachers must also be conscious of the visual rhetoric of the page. Few teachers of first-year composition have formal training in teaching business or technical writing or in the principles of document design. The selections that follow address several questions that teachers might consider as they attempt to incorporate these issues into their courses.

- What is visual rhetoric? How do the rhetorical features of a document's design relate to the rhetorical features of its text? How can teachers help students integrate writing processes and document design?
- How does teaching business writing compare to teaching other kinds of writing?
- What can teachers of first-year composition courses do to prepare students for the kinds of writing they will have to do in business and professional situations?

THE TROUBLE WITH EMPLOYEES' WRITING
MAY BE FRESHMAN COMPOSITION
Elizabeth Tebeaux

[*Teaching English in the Two-Year College* (1988): 9–19.]

Elizabeth Tebeaux, a professor of English, teaches undergraduate and graduate courses in technical communications at Texas A&M University. She has published widely on technical writing, including articles, chapters, and textbooks. Tebeaux authored *Design and Business Communications: The Process and the Product* (1990) and, with Tom Pearsall, *Reporting Technical Information* (8th ed., 1994). She has also published articles in *Written Communication, Issues in Writing, Journal of Business and Technical Communication,* and the *Technical Communications Quarterly.*

Because many students do not take any writing courses after freshman composition, they may find themselves underprepared for jobs that require them to write for a variety of specific purposes. Tebeaux describes her experience as a writing consultant in business and government, observing that many problems employees have in their writing result from writing strategies they learned in first-year composition courses. Tebeaux suggests changes in the design of composition courses — changes that will help students become more effective writers in the "real world." Her argument makes explicit the vital connections between what we ask students to do in writing classrooms and what those same students will do when they write at work.

In the past two decades, programs in rhetoric and composition have expanded in size as well as in range of studies offered. Yet literacy still remains a serious national problem, and business and industry continue to report problems in their employees' ability to write effectively. A number of large corporations are attempting to handle the problem in one of two ways: (1) by developing in-house writing courses that are included as part of company training programs; and (2) by hiring college writing teachers to design and to teach in-house writing courses. After having taught eleven workshops for three large corporations during the past three years and having served as a writing consultant to a large county government for two additional years, I have observed a number of employee writing problems that are traceable to writing strategies learned in freshman composition. While my findings will certainly not be new to technical writing teachers, my purpose here is to share these findings with teachers of freshman composition.

During this five-year period, I have worked with approximately 250 writers in either business organizations or county government. I found that 218 of 250 participants (87 percent) reported that traditional freshman composition was the only writing instruction they had received in college. Of that 250, 91 percent held at least one college degree, and 31 percent had a master's degree. Participants had been out of college 2 to 26 years, although most had been out of college fewer than 10 years. Those who had not earned a four-year degree had completed two years of junior college. Nearly all of these writers (234) reported that they had taken one or two courses in freshman composition. Only 37 reported having taken any kind of course in professional, technical, or business writing, although a course in business letter writing was the most frequent professional writing course mentioned. Forty-four participants reported that spelling, usage, and punctuation errors were marked in some courses in their major field of study. But the most revealing statement was that 87 percent of the employee-participants said that what they knew about how to write they gained in freshman composition.

Designing the Organizational Short Course

Prior to beginning the short courses, I asked employee-participants (all were there because they knew they needed help) to complete a background questionnaire (from which I derived the information given above) and to submit two samples of writing that they knew had been ineffective or that their supervisors had deemed "bad." To each example they submitted, they were asked to answer the following questions:

1. How did you determine that this piece of writing is "bad" writing?
2. Why did you write it the way you did?
3. What was the purpose of the document? What were the circumstances that led to your writing this document?

Prior to planning each workshop, which consisted of four two-hour settings, I examined these samples and discussed them with the manager who had retained me to design the workshop. Based on the problems discovered in analyzing the samples and talking to each manager, I designed an instructional approach to deal efficiently with the problems. The kinds of problem reports employees submitted were similar to Figure 1. Basically, this memorandum looks just like a freshman essay. The opening

Figure 1. *Original Sample*

Company Policy on Interduct

The Company's previous position has been not to place interduct direct buried for fiber optic cable. This directive reemphasizes this policy and explains why it is still in effect.

There has recently been a company pursuing sales of interduct for this purpose, stating that their interduct will allow placing of fiber optic cable. Several demonstrations were held that showed the duct being buried and a similar size cable being pulled into the duct with some success.

A recent real life trial of this direct buried interduct was very unsuccessful. It was found that after placing the interduct and allowing the ground to settle for several days, the interduct conformed to the high and low spots in the trench. When these numerous small bends are introduced into the interduct, it becomes impossible to pull more than 400 to 600 feet of fiber optic cable into the interduct before the 600-pound pulling tension is exceeded.

Interduct itself offers little or no advantage as protection to a direct buried fiber optic cable. In fact, it has a negative advantage, in that it will allow the cable to be pulled and fibers shattered or cracked for much greater distances.

As a result of this trial and previous recommendation, there should be no interduct placed for direct buried.

Please direct further questions to H. L. Rogers at 6727. We will appreciate your cooperation in enforcing this matter.

---

paragraph states the purpose. The second and third paragraphs provide support, and the final paragraph concludes by asking for the reader's cooperation.

From the perspective of a reader in an organization who is inundated with routine paperwork like this, the report reveals a number of problems that make it "bad" writing:

- Lack of clearly revealed organization;
- Lack of deductive presentation strategy that gives the reader the main information first;
- Lack of visual presentation techniques for revealing organization and content;
- Lack of analysis of the reader's needs concerning the topic being discussed.

During the workshop, participants were asked to analyze and then revise the two reports they knew to be poorly written. After reviewing the report in Figure 1 with the four problem areas in mind, the writer admitted that the main information he wanted to emphasize was not easy to find, much less remember. But after studying visual presentation techniques, the rationale for deductive organization, and the importance of designing any writing with the readers' needs dictating the organization and the visual design, the engineer who wrote Figure 1 submitted the revision in Figure 2.

The most striking aspect of the revision is the effective way in which the writer has visually displayed the information. Through use of visual strategies, the readers have various options for reading the report: they can read the boldface subject line and overview sentence for each reason given and be able to grasp the essential meaning of the report. Or, they can read the subject line, the opening paragraph, the overview sentence for each supporting point, and perhaps as much detail pertaining to each point as they deem necessary. Note, too, that the revision contains more specific reasons for not using interduct than the original version. During analysis of the sample, the writer stated that in designing the message deductively, and in listing each reason for not using interduct, he discovered, in his original, that he had failed to provide all reasons for not using interduct. Thus, the revision is not only visually effective, it is more complete.

Another sample (Figure 3) illustrates the same problems as the previous one; i.e., the report looks like an essay. The report opens with a paragraph stating the thesis. The second and third paragraphs elaborate on that thesis. The final sentence reiterates the thesis statement.

After the discussion on the importance of deductive organization, visual display of information, and the importance of designing writing with readers' needs in mind, the writer stated that she could now see why the MISS Worksheets were not being corrected and/or returned. First, she had not anticipated her readers' needs, particularly that they would not know how to deal with the Profiles and Worksheets. Second, she had not given a date by which she wanted the materials returned to her and additional information that would help readers respond as she wished them to. Third, she had not organized the instructions and presented them on the page so that they could be easily followed. As a result, most profiles had not been returned; she had received numerous calls asking for clarification; several profiles that had been returned were incorrect or had notes attached indicating that the reader was not sure if changes had been done correctly.

In revising her original, the writer places important information first, establishes hierarchies of key information with headings, uses these head-

Figure 2. *Revised Sample*

TO: Harlan Stevenson, Manager — Customer Services, BIRMINGHAM

SUBJECT: Company Policy: Interduct shall not be placed for buried lightweight cable.

Contrary to the alleged claims of some overzealous vendors, the above policy remains unchanged.

A field trial was recently conducted where the interduct was buried and cable placement was attempted several days later. The negative observations were as follows:

1. **Cable lengths are reduced between costly splices.**

   The interduct conformed to the high and low spots in the trench. These numerous bends introduced added physical resistance against the cable sheath during cable pulling. Even with application of cable lubricant, the average length pulled was 500 feet before the 600 pound pulling tension was exceeded.

2. **Maintenance liability is increased.**

   Due to shorter cable lengths, the number of splices increases. As the number of splices increases, maintenance liability increases.

3. **Added material costs are counterproductive.**

   Interduct, while adding 16% to the material cost, offers little or no mechanical protection to buried fiber optic cable. In fact, when an occupied interduct was pulled at a 90 degree angle with a backhoe bucket, the fibers were not broken only at the place of contact, as would have been with a direct buried cable. Instead, due to the stress being distributed along the interduct, the fibers shattered and cracked up to 100 feet in each direction.

4. **Increased labor costs are unnecessary.**

   In about the same amount of time required to place interduct, the fiber optic cable could be placed. The added 28% of labor hours expended to pull cable after the interduct is placed cannot be justified.

Please insure that this policy is conveyed to and understood by your construction managers. If you have questions, please call me at 817 334-2178.

                                        John Doe
                                        Corporate Engineering Manager

---

ings to guide inclusion of information that will make verification easier for readers, and displays all information so that it is visually accessible.

In analyzing the revision by emphasizing the reader's response, other employees observed that the revision was easy to see, easy to follow. In addition, the importance of the message was now apparent.

The essay technique, as applied to short reports and memoranda, the most commonly written documents in business organizations, was apparent in nearly every employee's submission. In fact, the most common answer to Question 2 on the Trouble Analysis Sheet — Why did you write this document the way you did? — yielded some version of the following answers on over 200 samples:

1. this is the way we were taught to write in college;
2. this is the only way I have ever written anything;
3. I don't know any other way to write.

Figure 3.   *Original Sample*

MISS

Employee Profiles and Employee Worksheets

The purpose of the following is to explain how the MISS Employee Profiles and Employee Worksheets are to be verified. Your group's worksheets are attached.

The Employee Profiles need to be verified for accuracy before they are filed in the employee's Personal History File. If a change needs to be made that was our error, mark the profile and return it with the Worksheet so that a new profile can be generated. If you are making a change, mark the profile and have it signed and concurred and return both the profile and the Employee Worksheet. After the Employee Profile has been verified, please return the Employee Worksheet to me for my records.

Please note that only information that appeared on the Worksheet was keyed into the MISS data base. Information other than what is on the worksheet is furnished by other data bases. For example, the title is generated by the title code. The title code suffix is generated by the job evaluation number. There have been problems with the title suffix being incorrect. If this is the only correction, please note this on the Employee Profile and worksheet. Please advise me by attaching a note to the employee worksheet when you return it to me. Also, please verify that any other information that may appear to be incorrect is not due to a recent change on payroll records.

If you have problems, please contact me at 6512.

Jane Doe
MISS Administrator

Given the fact the employees in business have too much to read, that they seldom read all of any document, that they "skim" or "search" read most routine writing, participants soon realized why documents, like Figure 3, were not being read or not being read correctly. That is, because of lack of deductive organization to give the reader the "news" immediately and visual presentation technique to reveal organization and content, the memorandum was not "readable"[1] in the sense that the intended audience did not find the document easy to access and process. The revision, Figure 4, however, was deemed a document that would be read because it is visually accessible. You can see organization and content at a glance.

The final assignment required participants to revise some kind of document, usually a policy, which I selected from each organization's policy binder. Like the reports that participants brought to the workshop, many policies too often were not clearly organized and were too visually dense to be read quickly. Figure 5 is one vacation policy statement that participants were asked to revise.

After having revised two of their own reports, participants yielded interesting versions of policies. Figure 6 is one revision of the policy shown in Figure 5. It is concise and clear mainly because it is visually accessible.

Analysis of Samples — Implications for Basic Composition

The opportunity I have had to observe the writing problems and the writing instruction backgrounds of these employees has led me to several

Figure 4. *Revised Sample*

TO: Jane Doe

FROM: MISS Administrator

SUBJECT: Procedures for Reviewing MISS Employee Profiles by

May 22, 1986

If any information is inaccurate on the attached MISS profiles, please return those for correction within the next two weeks.

Each employee should have a MISS profile placed in his/her history file. The profile will replace the SW-1006 in the near future. In addition, all departments within Fabrico's five-state area will be pulling MISS profiles to fill vacancies within their departments.

Procedures for Reviewing MISS Employee Profiles

1. If a change is required because information was keyed incorrectly, mark the profile and return it with the worksheet. A new profile will be sent to you.
2. If you are making a change, mark the profile and have it signed and concurred at the next higher level. Return both the profile and the worksheet. A new profile will be sent to you for review.
3. After the profile has been verified, please return the worksheet to me for my records.

Incorrect Information That May Appear on the MISS Employee Profile

The information that appeared on the worksheet shows the only items that were keyed into MISS. The MISS data base is merged with other data bases to produce the profile.

1. Incorrect title — The title is generated by the title code from the MERT data base. Please check this code on the last PCR and allow one week for the PCR to be worked.
2. Incorrect title code suffix — The title code suffix is generated by the JE number from the Atlanta job evaluation data base. Please note an incorrect title suffix on the worksheet and profile, as I will be working with Atlanta on this problem.
3. Incorrect payroll information — Please allow one week for the last PCR submitted to be worked and merged with new data.

Please call me if you have any questions about how to make changes.

---

initial conclusions which I believe are worth sharing with other composition teachers:

(1) If my experience during the past five years is even partially representative of the kinds of problems many employee writers are experiencing, then, more than likely there are many other employees who are attempting to write at work by applying techniques learned in freshman composition to the kinds of writing they are required to do on the job. Yet, traditional freshman composition, as it is usually taught, does not provide adequate preparation for writing at work. While the goal of freshman composition has traditionally been to help students write better in school, too many students and even faculty within English departments and other college departments have assumed that "good writing" is "good writing," and that the student who writes well in school will write well on the job. Too many

Figure 5. *Original Policy*

Joint Practice 27: Vacation Days for Management

General

The purpose of this Joint Practice is to outline the vacation treatment applicable to Management employees.

Eligibility

Vacations with pay shall be granted during the calendar year to each management employee who shall have completed six months' employment since the date employment began. Vacation pay will not be granted if the employee has been dismissed for misconduct. Vacation allowed will be determined according to the following criteria: (a) One week's vacation to any such management employee who has completed six months or more but less than twelve months of service. (b) Two weeks' vacation to any such management employee who has completed twelve months of service but who could not complete seven years of service within the vacation year. Two weeks will be allowed if the employee initially completes six months' service and twelve months' service within the same vacation year. (c) Three weeks' vacation to any management employee who could complete seven or more but less than fifteen years' service within the vacation year and to District level who shall have completed six months' employment within the vacation year. (e) Five weeks' vacation to any management employee who completes twenty-five or more years of service within the vacation year and to Department head level and higher management who shall have completed a period of six months' employment within the vacation year.

The criteria described above are Net Credited Service as determined by the Employees' Benefit Committee. Where eligibility for a vacation week under (a) or (b) above first occurs on or after December 1 of a vacation year, the vacation week may be granted in the next following vacation year if it is completed before April 1 and before the beginning of vacation for the following year. When an authorized holiday falls in a week during which a management employee is absent on vacation, an additional day off (or equivalent time off with pay) may be taken in either the same calendar year or prior to April 1 of the following calendar year. When the additional day of vacation is Christmas Day, it may be granted immediately preceding the vacation or prior to April 1 of the following calendar year.

---

people outside the ranks of technical writing teachers are unaware of the differences between writing in academe and writing in nonacademic settings. English teachers assume, perhaps too optimistically, that what we teach in freshman composition and in writing across the curriculum programs will automatically transfer to nonacademic settings.

(2) Even though technical and business communication programs have grown steadily in the past decade,[2] they are apparently not reaching enough students. In other words, freshman composition is still the main and only "writing instruction" for many students.

(3) Well-meaning faculty in non-English disciplines are not "teaching writing" by assiduously marking errors in spelling, usage, and punctuation and implying that mechanically correct writing is good writing. The problems I found — the previous samples illustrate these — were not mechanical ones; they stemmed from:

Figure 6. *Revised Policy*

Joint Practice 27: Vacation Time Allowed Management Employees

The following schedule describes the new vacation schedule approved by the company. This schedule is effective immediately and will remain in effect until a further update is issued.

Vacation Eligibility

1. Vacation with pay shall be granted during the calendar year to each management employee who has completed 6 months' service since the date of employment. Employees who have been dismissed for misconduct will not receive vacation with pay.

Net Credited Service	*Eligible Weeks*
6 mos.–12 mos.	1
12 mos.–7 yrs.	2
7 yrs.–15 yrs. and to District Level with 6 mos. service	3
15 yrs.–25 yrs. and to Division Level with 6 mos. service	4
25 yrs. or more and to Department Head or higher management with 6 mos. service	5

Net Credited Service is determined by the Employee Benefits Committee

2. If eligibility occurs on or after December 1 of a vacation year,
   • vacation may be granted in the next following year if it is taken before April 1.

3. If an authorized holiday falls in a vacation week,
   • an additional day may be taken in either calendar year or before April 1 of the following year.

4. If the additional day of vacation is Christmas day,
   • it may be taken immediately preceding the vacation or before April 1 of the following year.

- failing to determine what the audience needed to know so that the writer's purpose (to instruct, persuade, or inform) was achieved;
- failing to organize deductively to reveal the main information first to readers who have more to read than they can and will read carefully;
- failing to use visual design to produce documents that are visually accessible and therefore easy to read;
- failing to understand the importance of creating a visually accessible document and believing that messages that are important to the writer will be important to the reader, and therefore, will be read thoroughly.

The most common problem attributed by any supervisor to the employees attending the workshops was not mechanics; it was lack of clarity and "getting the point across,"[3] both of which, my experience suggests, can be corrected to a great extent by using deductive organization of information and visual design to reveal hierarchies, or levels, of information. Even in original samples that contained a large number of comma splices and nonstandard usage, participants during peer review of each other's work did not think that the main "problem" was mechanics. Employees, in skim- or search-reading routine documents, read holistically. They are looking for answers to the following questions: What is this? Why am I getting this? What am I supposed to do now? The effectiveness of the routine business document is determined by how quickly the reader can answer these questions, not by the mechanical correctness of the content. Correctness becomes an issue if problems in usage, sentence construction, or punctuation hinder the audience's ability to find and process the message.

Reorienting Freshman Composition — Five Recommendations

I am not suggesting that freshman composition be replaced by courses in technical or business writing. Students clearly need the preparation that freshman composition gives them for writing in college. I am suggesting, however, that we need to impress our freshman students and our colleagues in other disciplines with the importance of a course in professional writing to prepare these students for writing in nonacademic contexts. We need to emphasize to students and colleagues that writing at work is not like writing in the classroom and that students need preparation in both areas.

There are, however, some changes that could be implemented in freshman composition programs to make our basic composition courses more relevant to students after they leave school without damaging the basic mission of freshman composition:

(1) Visual design strategies — presenting content in visually effective ways — need to be introduced in composition.[4] Much of the writing in the world of work (brochures, technical reports, articles for publication, advertisements) uses visual rhetoric in making messages persuasive and clear. Why pretend any longer that visual appeal is not an important rhetorical device? Students need to be introduced, even in freshman composition, to basic concepts in producing visually accessible, visually pleasing documents. They need to understand that visual accessibility (one aspect of the difficult area of readability) is as crucial a quality in writing as coherence, unity, and structure. They also need to understand that teachers are the only people who are committed to reading everything students write, that in a work context audiences will read a document only if they believe it will benefit them and if it is easy to access and understand.

(2) The importance of deductive writing in developing "reader-based" prose needs to be emphasized more in freshman composition. In learning to write research papers, students should be taught that placing the conclusions after the introduction is an acceptable organizational method. Students should also be required to use clearly worded informative headings throughout research papers. Doing so enforces the point that developing the outline into headings and subheadings helps the reader follow the presentation and helps the writer organize the discussion, eliminate irrelevant information, and generally "stay on track."

(3) The essay needs to be deemphasized as the main, if not the sole, teaching form in freshman composition. (How many people ever write essays after they graduate from college?) Students may benefit from studying effectively designed sets of instructions, which incorporate visual design. Students may also benefit from writing instructions and then evaluating them for clarity and visual access during peer review.

(4) Freshman composition should be redefined as Introduction to Writing, to emphasize to our colleagues in other disciplines and to our freshmen that students need more than an introduction to writing to prepare them for the writing they will do after college. We need to explain to students throughout freshman composition how writing in school differs from writing at work, that the standards of "good" writing will ultimately change, that they cannot write on the job the way they have written in the

classroom. More freshman composition texts, such as *Four Worlds of Writing*,[5] would be helpful in giving students a perspective on how writing is used beyond the classroom.

(5) To develop competencies that will be valuable outside academic writing, the paradigm in freshman composition needs to be integrated with the paradigm in technical writing. That is, in every writing course, students should have to write for specifically defined audiences; students should have a purpose to achieve with that audience; they should learn to deal with tone, voice, organization, and visual presentation commensurate with that purpose. But ultimately, students need to understand that these common rhetorical elements control all writing, whether it is expressive, referential, literary, or informative.[6]

Conclusion

Much of the published scholarship that fills the pages of rhetoric and composition journals underscores the problem I continue to confront in teaching industrial short courses: little concern is expressed for the usefulness of freshman composition after college, for the differences in which writing in school differs from writing at work, for designing writing curricula to ensure that writing instruction is relevant during students' college years and afterward in nonacademic settings. Basic composition theory, in its emphasis on expressive discourse, continues to foster the traditional goals of writing as learning and writing as thinking, with little attention to ways by which these competencies can be sustained and applied in nonacademic writing environments. The problem, I suspect, stems from the fact that few composition teachers, unless they also teach technical writing, understand, or even care about the relevance of their instruction. However, my consulting experience suggests that we should care and that achieving relevance is not only possible but necessary if our composition instruction is to provide any long-lasting solution to the literacy problem.

Notes

[1] For useful approaches to the design of readable texts, see the following essays in *New Essays in Technical and Scientific Communication: Research, Theory, Practice,* ed. Paul V. Anderson, R. John Brockmann, Carolyn R. Miller (Farmingdale: Baywood, 1983): Lester Faigley and Stephen P. Witte, "Topical Focus in Technical Writing," (pp. 59–68); Jack Selzer, "What Constitutes a 'Readable' Style?" (pp. 71–89); Thomas N. Huckin, "A Cognitive Approach to Readability," (pp. 90–98). Also, Daniel B. Felker, ed. *Document Design: A Review of the Relevant Research* (Washington, DC: American Institutes for Research, 1979): Chapters 1, 2, and 4; Lee Odell and Dixie Goswami, *Writing in Nonacademic Settings* (New York: Guilford, 1985), Chapters 2 and 3.

[2] William E. Rivers, "The Current Status of Business and Technical Writing Courses in English Departments," *ADE Bulletin* 82 (Winter 1985): 50–54.

[3] A number of studies suggest the paramount importance of clarity as the most desirable quality in employee writing: Donna Stine and Donald Skarzenski, "Priorities for the Business Communication Classroom: A Survey of Business and Academe," *Journal of Business Communication* 16 (Summer 1979): 15–30; Robert R. Bataille, "Writing in the World of Work: What Our Graduates Report," *CCC* 32 (Oct. 1982): 276–280; Lester Faigley and Thomas P. Miller, "What We Learn from Writing on the Job," *College English* 44 (Oct. 1982): 567–569; Gilbert Storms, "What Business School Graduates Say about the Writing They Do at Work: Implications for the Business Communication Course," *ABCA Bulletin* 46 (Dec. 1983): 13–18; Carol Barnum and Robert Fischer, "Engineering Technologists as Writers: Results of a Survey," *Technical Communication* 31 (Second Quarter, 1984): 9–11.

[4] The Document Design Center has generated a number of studies on visual design which are available for purchase through DDC. However, only two articles in

rhetoric and composition journals have yet dealt with the importance of visual rhetoric as a pedagogical consideration: Robert J. Conners, "*Actio:* A Rhetoric of Manuscripts," *Rhetoric Review* 2.1 (Sept. 1983): 64–73; and Stephen Bernhardt, "Seeing the Text," *CCC* 37 (Feb. 1986): 66–78.

⁵ Janice M. Lauer and others, *The Four Worlds of Writing* (New York: Harper, 1985).

⁶ For a discussion of linking all writing, see Harry P. Kroitor and Elizabeth Tebeaux, "Bringing Literature Teachers and Writing Teachers Closer Together," *ADE Bulletin* 78 (Summer 1984): 28–34.

THE SHAPE OF TEXT TO COME:
THE TEXTURE OF PRINT ON SCREENS
Stephen A. Bernhardt

[*College Composition and Communication* 44 (May 1993): 151–75.]

Stephen A. Bernhardt is associate professor of English at New Mexico State University in Las Cruces, where he teaches a wide range of courses in the English department, especially within the graduate programs in technical and professional communication. His current research interests include workplace communication, scientific and technical writing, and computers and language. He has published numerous articles and chapters on technical communication, and he regularly serves as a consultant and workplace trainer for several major corporations.

Most first-year college students use sophisticated word processing programs and are technologically literate, navigating the multimedia texts available on the World Wide Web. For these students, "texts" are more than books. Bernhardt recognizes this "monumental transformation" of texts, "as the medium of presentation shifts from paper to screen," and he suggests that writing teachers should "constantly appraise the broad drifts in the shape of text — to anticipate what now constitutes and what will soon constitute a well-formed text." Recognizing that "electronic text does not create a totally new rhetoric but depends for its design on the strategies of paper texts," Bernhardt identifies "nine dimensions of variation that help map the differences between paper and on-screen text. Screen-based text tends to exploit these dimension to a greater degree than does paper text." Bernhardt argues that teachers need to understand these transformations and consider them "as we teach our students strategies for reading and writing text in a new age."

Changes in the technology of text invariably trigger changes in the shape of text. Texts are undergoing monumental transformation as the medium of presentation shifts from paper to screen. We need to constantly appraise the broad drifts in the shape of text — to anticipate what now constitutes and what will soon constitute a well-formed text. We need to think about how readers interact with text — what they do with it and how. We need to anticipate where text is going: the shape of text to come.

This paper suggests some of the dimensions of change in how text is structured on the page and on the screen. It is necessarily speculative, since the topic is just beginning to receive systematic attention (Bolter; Brockmann; Horton; Kostelnick; Merrill; Rubens, "A Reader's View" and "Online Information"; Rubens and Krull; Special Issue of *Visible Language* 1984).

We have a good theoretical understanding and a highly developed practical art of the rhetoric and text structure of paper documents, and this praxis exerts a strong shaping influence over texts produced via electronic media. We are in a state of rapid evolution, with heavy borrowing on the history of text on paper, applied sometimes appropriately and sometimes inappropriately to the new medium. Because electronic text does not create a totally new rhetoric but depends for its design on the strategies of paper texts, the starting point in this analysis is not "How do screen-based texts differ categorically or essentially from their paper-based counterparts?" but "What is a framework for understanding dimensions of variation in texts across the two media?"

This paper uses a text analytical approach to identify nine dimensions of variation that help map the differences between paper and on-screen text. Screen-based text tends to exploit these dimensions to a greater degree than does paper text.

To a relatively greater extent, then, on-screen text tends to be:

Situationally Embedded: The text doesn't stand alone but is bound up within the context of situation — the ongoing activities and events that make the text part of the action.

Interactive: The text invites readers to actively engage with it — both mentally and physically — rather than passively absorb information.

Functionally Mapped: The text displays itself in ways that cue readers as to what can be done with it.

Modular: The text is composed and presented in self-contained chunks, fragments, blocks.

Navigable: The text supports reader movement across large pools of information in different directions for different readers and purposes.

Hierarchically Embedded: The text has different levels or layers of embedding; text contains other texts.

Spacious: The text is open, unconstrained by physicality.

Graphically Rich: The text exploits and integrates graphic display to present information and facilitate interaction.

Customizable and Publishable: The text is fluid, changing, dynamic; the new tools of text make every writer a publisher.

As academics with a commitment to certain kinds of discourse, we may not see as desirable all of these developments in the ways text is structured, but they appear to be inevitable. We need first to understand the directions that computers are taking written language, and then to consider these changes as we teach our students strategies for reading and writing text in a new age.

Situationally Embedded Text

When people voice doubts about whether computers will take the place of books, they are generally expressing doubts about readers' tolerance for extended reading on screen. Reading from screens tends to slow people down and fatigue them, in part because the contrast of print on page is much better than that of text on screen. But when reading is viewed as a sub-task within a larger task environment, the issue of fatigue is not so critical. Extended reading will continue to rely on print, while other functional sorts of reading will rely on screen-based text.

Screen-based text differs from paper text in many ways, and not just because the two media are different. We use text on screens under different conditions and for different purposes than we do paper texts, and it is these differences in use and purpose that will ultimately determine the key points of difference between the two media (Barton and Barton, "Simplicity"; Duchastel).

A real virtue of paper text is its detachment from the physical world. We can read on planes or in the car; we can put books in our backpacks or leave them at home. We can pick up a book or magazine or a newspaper and read in every imaginable situation, no matter what else is going on about us. In fact, reading allows us to escape the immediate situation, to enter other worlds.

In comparison with paper text, screen-based text tends to be more tightly embedded in the context of situation; it is more likely to be bound up as a part of ongoing activities. Reading screen-based text is often integrated with other forms of action — learning to use software, constructing texts from separate files, or searching a database. A reader might search for relevant text, retrieve information in the form of procedures or syntax, and then return to the task environment. In such situations, reading becomes a second-level activity, resorted to when the higher-level task activity hits a snag.

This kind of task-oriented reading stands in contrast to, say, reading imaginative literature or magazines, where readers enter a world of text that impinges little on their real-time situation. Readers of screen-based text are not so much *readers* as *doers* or *seekers;* they read to find out how to do something or to retrieve some bit of information. People tend to read screen-based text to play games or to program; they read-to-write, or read-to-operate, or read-to-look-up. We don't really have language for this kind of reading — it's more like *using* text than *reading* it. Such reading-to-do is more like making raids on print than having extended engagements with a writer's ideas or arguments. It is driven by the pragmatic situation; it is exploitative; it is manipulative (see both Sticht and Redish).

The shape of screen-based text is influenced heavily by one specific development: *help systems* — those word files that attempt to rescue computer users who encounter difficulties. Nobody reads this kind of text in anything like linear order, but many users make incursions on it as they struggle to work with their machines, reading bits and pieces as needed. The help text is simply part of the machine.

But reading that is situationally integrated with other activities is typical not just of help systems for using computers. The electronic writing classrooms of Project Jefferson at the University of Southern California (Chignell and Lacy; Lynch) or Project Athena's Educational Online System at MIT (Barrett, "Introduction," *Society*) exist to support not so much reading activities as writing activities: researching, keeping track of information, drafting and revising text, sharing text through collaboration, or sharing texts and notes with others in the class. Pieces of text get used, copied, borrowed, annotated, clipped, revised, and passed around in the interest of some governing activity — in this case, the improvement of writing. Text is read throughout the process, but reading is not the primary or ultimate goal. The computer structures an environment, where the writer, a set of texts, and a group of people interact in desirable ways. The screen-based text is interwoven with the larger activity of producing work in a group setting. Text is inseparable from the situation.

Such applications of technology take reading and writing beyond simple interaction with the computer; the computer scaffolds social interaction within an electronic environment. In his Introduction to *The Society of Text*, Barrett describes the use of computers to structure interaction (as opposed to modeling cognition) in MIT's Athena-supported network:

> [T]he internal workings of the mind were not mapped to the machine; instead, we conceived of the classroom as a "mechanism" for interaction and collaboration and mapped those social processes to the computer. In essence, we textualized the computer: we made it enter, and used it to support, the historical, social processes that we felt defined the production of texts in any instructional or conferencing environment. (xv)

In such situations of use, text is embedded within systems — it is not separate like a book or a magazine. Its texture is shaped by both the machine and the instrumental purposes and social interactions to which the text is put. Screen-based text becomes part of a physical system that governs where it can be used, who can access it, what is needed to access it, and so on. Text is inseparable from the machine.

Notice how different this tends to make screen-based text from paper text. While books are self-contained, portable, and usable within almost any situation, screen-based text becomes dependent on a larger techno-logical and social environment, to be used under delimited circumstances, typically as an integral part of other ongoing events. This is an important contrast in the pragmatics of paper vs. screen, underscored by the contrast of *text-intensive* books vs. *situationally embedded* screen-based language.

Interactive Text

It is commonplace to characterize the reader's role in a text as being active or transactive, constructive or constitutive. In this view, readers construct or reconstruct a text in their own image, bringing as much to a text as they take from it. When we talk in these ways, we often have in mind private encounters with text in physically inactive settings. We are talking primarily about mental processes, or language processes, or some-times social processes, but not necessarily physical processes.

It is useful to view the reading of electronic text in similar terms, only more so, or at least, more variously so. Readers of on-screen text interact physically with the text. Through the mouse, the cursor, the touch screen, or voice activation, the text becomes a dynamic object, capable of being physically manipulated and transformed. The presence of the text is height-ened through the virtual reality of the screen world: readers become par-ticipants, control outcomes, and shape the text itself.

Figure 1 presents a screen from the Perseus project, a HyperCard ap-plication developed at Harvard and Brown Universities as an Annenberg/CPB project (Harward). The project is designed to help undergraduates understand the classical Greek world and its literature. The particular module, from "Visualizing Aristophanes," helps students visualize a staged production of a Greek play.

In the Perseus model, learning is highly interactive and manipulative: students use the mouse to assign roles, to position and move characters

Selectable,
moveable chorus

Get other information,
read other texts

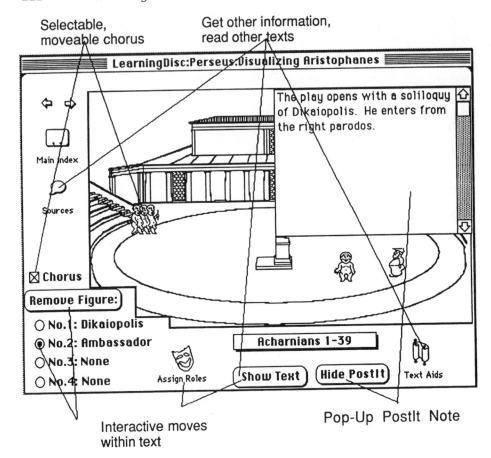

Figure 1. Interactive Screen Text: The reader interacts in multiple ways with the text by making selections, moving characters on the stage, requesting help or commentary, going to related texts, or popping up PostIt notes. From Perseus Project, hypermedia educational software under development at Harvard and Brown Universities; screen captured from Apple Learning Disk (CD-ROM). © 1988 Apple Computer, Cupertino, California.

on stage, and to block out the plays scene by scene. The on-screen text reflects the active, participatory style of learning, with active, imperative verb/object commands around the perimeter of the stage drawing: Remove Figure, Show Text, Hide PostIt, and Assign Roles. Certainly, there is reading going on here — continuously — but it is fully integrated with other sorts of actions: planning scenes; reading text, translations, and commentary; checking necessary background, source, or related information; visualizing the interaction of characters as the drama unfolds; and actually moving figures about in physical space.

Here, the Perseus designers take active, constructive reading into the arena of physical manipulation and sensory visualization. They take advantage of what we have long known from learning psychology — that as opposed to learners who passively attempt to learn information, learners who are active readers, who engage with material in multi-modal capacities, are likely to remember more, to remember it longer, and to remember it more accurately. Perseus forces readers to be physically and mentally present, to interpret options, to make selections, and to construct textual, visual, and metaphoric worlds. Such materials take computer-based texts and computer-based learning well beyond simple page turning by giving readers control of flexible, interactive engagements with the text.

As Perseus suggests, reading text on screen tends to be a much more behaviorally interactive process than reading text on paper (Duchastel). The parallel activities of reading and writing create the interaction. Screen readers are actively engaged with screen text, as they key in information, or capture text from one file and move it somewhere else, or annotate or add to existing information in a file. A similar interactivity is sometimes sought in books, as writers try to engage the reader in solving problems, considering scenarios, or attempting various learning activities while reading the text. However, writers of print material cannot *force* the interaction, they can only *invite* it; readers can play along or skim past the problem sets, brain teasers, or tutorial activities. Writers of on-screen text can *force* interaction, making it necessary for the reader to do something physical in order to get to the next step.

The contrast in interactivity distinguishes other genres as well. Consider printed novels and their screen counterparts: text-based "novels" or adventure games. Readers of novels are constrained by the linearity of the text. While there are fundamental differences in how readers respond to a text, the book presents the same face to each reader, and the choices of approach are very limited. One might choose to read the ending first or to peek at various chapters, but these are fairly impoverished choices. A reader of a text-based electronic novel or adventure game, in contrast, has to make constant decisions about where to go, what to do, who to follow or question. In doing so, the reader is forced to construct not just a mental representation of the work, but a physical representation as well (the succession of screens), through concrete manipulations of the text. Out of many possible physical constructions of the text, the reader creates one, a particular chronological and experiential ordering of the text, a reading that belongs to no other reader.

I am not holding up increased interactivity as a goal of print and I am not suggesting that, for example, electronic novels are richer or more satisfying than print novels. Such is clearly not the case. However, we should not underestimate the developing genre of electronic novel: writers are discovering new forms of literary textuality and engaging in some very interesting experiments. (See, for example, the special issue of *Writing on the Edge,* with its accompanying hypernovellas on disk.) In these experiments, authors engage readers in new forms of interaction, encourage readers to take control over the text, and blur the lines separating author and reader. We need to be alert to interactivity as a deeply interwoven feature of electronic texts, one we are just beginning to exploit.

Functionally Mapped Text

Text, whether on page or on screen, performs a function of some sort: informing, directing, questioning, or posing situations contrary to fact. Such functional variation is often expressed linguistically through the grammatical systems of mood (indicative, imperative, interrogative, subjunctive). Readers can also usually make some rhetorical determination as to what a chunk of text is doing — whether it is making a generalization, committing a vow, stating a fact, offering an example or definition, offering metacommentary on the text itself, or some other text act. In many printed texts, such functional variation is mapped semantically — one interprets the functional roles of various chunks of text by inferring purpose from the meaning of the words or phrases. Often, semantic or rhetorical function shifts are mapped by cohesive devices, phrases like "for example," or "to consider my next point." When text shifts from one function to another, the rhetorical tension at the boundary tends to demand some kind of signal, and the language is rich in such signal systems (Bernhardt, "Reader").

Both sorts of text — print and screen-based — also use visual cues of layout and typography to signal functional shifts. The visual system maps function onto text, signaling to the reader how the text is to be read and acted upon. Thus tutorial writers (print or online) might use a numbered list of action steps, with explanations indented below each action, or they might use a double-column playscript format, with actions on the left and results or explanations on the right. Boldface or other typographical signals might highlight actions, while parentheses or italics might signal incidental commentary. The visual structuring that functionally differentiates text is reinforced by syntactic cues that highlight the action being performed — imperative or declarative grammatical structures, sequence cues like *next* or enumeratives, and explanatory phrases like "to complete the installation" or "pressing the return key enters the value."

When language is onscreen, readers must be able to distinguish different functions:

- Some language cues interaction with the system: how to manage files, execute commands, or control the display.
- Other language cues navigation: where one is, how to move around, or how to get help.
- Still other language offers system messages, showing that errors have occurred or that the system is currently processing some command. Some language simply reminds readers of the system status or default settings.
- And some language is informative/ideational.

The tight interworking of text and action leads to frequent system requests for action that the reader must interpret and respond to correctly (from the system's point of view). These functional discriminations are not unique to electronic text, but they tend to be much more important to efficient reading, and they tend to demand highly planned and carefully structured formatting decisions on the part of the writer.

Figure 2 shows rich functional mapping in a screen from Project Jefferson, a HyperCard "electronic writing notebook" developed to support writing instruction at the University of Southern California (Chignell and Lacy).

Numerous buttons exist on this screen — places to click with the mouse that execute some move or operation. The screen is full of things to do, not just things to read. Icons initiate procedures and help readers recognize the hot spots on the screen. The escape hatches — **HELP** and **QUIT** — are signaled both iconically and verbally to show the reader that something can actually be done with the icons. The tabs, representing possible moves to other text space, are boxed and use a font that contrasts with the primary text, suggesting that they are active buttons. Within extended passages, words in bold print signal other places to go and things to do — in this case, accessing additional information and glossary definitions. Arrows signal movement — hot spots that take the reader forward or backward in the text, at normal pace or fast, using an easily understood analogy to tape recorder controls.

Not all areas of the screen are equal, and functional mapping tends to be richest on the borders — in the peripheral areas a biologist would call

**Hot links to definitions
and cases**

**Orienting
information**

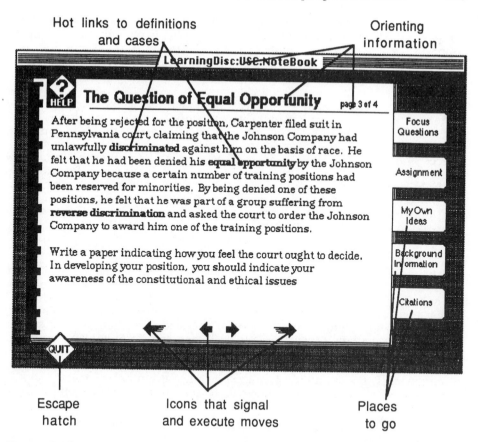

**Escape
hatch**

**Icons that signal
and execute moves**

**Places
to go**

Figure 2. This screen shows rich functional mapping, with icons, bolded terms, index tabs, help and quit buttons — all signaling things to do and places to go. Screen from Project Jefferson, HyperCard stack under development at the University of Southern California; screen captured from Apple Learning Disk (CD-ROM), © 1988, Apple Computer, Cupertino, California.

ecotonic. There is always a rich diversity and abundance of life on the edges of systems. On screens, the language is the richest, there is the most going on, there is the greatest range of things to do around the edges, on the perimeters. It is on the edge that we recognize where we are, what we can do, where we can go, or how we can get out.

Increasingly, various programs are adapting consistent functional mapping of options. With pull-down menus, for example, available options often appear in a regular or bolded black font, while program options that are not currently available are shown in a shadowy, gray font. A simple, efficient cue such as this can greatly help readers use the functional mapping of programs they have never seen before. As readers become increasingly sophisticated and as interfaces coalesce around predictable design strategies, readers will develop their skills to the point where they efficiently and correctly recognize text-as-information versus text-as-signal-that-something-can-be-done-with-it.

Unlike paper texts, screens offer a dynamic medium for mapping text in highly functional ways. Relying largely on visual cuing, readers acquire knowledge of how to do things with words and images. The traditional cues of paper texts — margins, indents, paragraphs, page numbers — appear impoverished next to the rapidly expanding set of cues that facilitate functional writing and reading on screen.

Modular Text

Most texts reflect some modularity of structure: a text is composed of other texts. Books have chapters or individual articles; magazines have articles, sidebars, letters-to-the-editors, advertisements, tables of contents, and so on. Many forms of print are in some way or another compositions, pieces of text positioned with other pieces of text, and often the individual modules are very different in type or function. A newspaper, for example, with its large pages, allows many modules of several sorts to be composed on the same page, and readers can efficiently scan large amounts of information. And the direction in popular newspapers, such as *USA Today,* is toward modularization, with pages composed of short, self-contained, highly visual exposition. An encyclopedia, too, is composed of many individual modules, each of which constitutes a text that can stand on its own.

The movement of text from paper to computer screen encourages further modularization of text structure. The screen is a window on a text base — only so much can be seen at one time. Just as an 8 1/2" by 11" sheet of paper to some extent determines the shape of printed text (titles, headings, white space, line length, indentations), the size and shape of the screen constrains the shape of electronic text. The screen, or a window contained within the screen, becomes the structural unit of prose, with text composed in screen-size chunks, no matter what their subject or function. In such systems, text is highly localized. Reader attention is arrested at the level of idea grouping — the single topic that is represented on a single screen.

Because text is fragmented and localized, on-screen text has problems with local cohesion. Closely related ideas must frequently be separated by screen boundaries. Even lists of strictly parallel, coordinate information must often bridge screen divisions, and the break from one screen to the next presents a larger gap than that from one page to the next. Consider that in a book, even when chunks of information must be broken at page boundaries, there is a 50% chance that the boundary will be at facing pages. And print layout can be manipulated to keep related information on one page. The problem is more difficult with small screen dimensions and strictly modular text fragments. Each module must, to some extent, stand on its own, interpretable without close logical cohesion with other screens. The writer must assume that a reader can arrive at a given screen from practically anywhere, so there can be no assumption that the reader has built up a model of the logical relations of the text from processing pages in a linear order.

It might be argued that since screen text can easily be scrolled, text need not be fragmented into screen-size modules. While it is true that most windows allow scrolling of text that is longer than a screen, scrolling is inherently unsatisfactory. When text must be scrolled to be viewed, readers hesitate, not knowing whether to scroll down or skip the text. And while a reader can quickly skim a stack of information if each card is completely contained within the window, it is time-consuming and ultimately wasteful to have to scroll to see if text should be read.

Also, when text is not composed in screen-size bites, readers tend to lose their places and become disoriented. An example of this occurs with the ERIC CD-ROM indexes on Silver Platter (Figure 3).

```
implementation, and evaluation. The final chapter includes a summary and
recommendations. The 12 appendixes, which constitute more than half of the
report, include the pre- and posttests, personal data and summative reaction
questionnaires, the task analysis, a skills and interests questionnaire,
project PERT and Gantt charts, screen design prototypes, and a user's guide.
Tables and figures appear throughout. Field test data are also included. (26
references) (GL)

                                                            19 of 29
AN: ED308829
AU: Morrison,-Gary-R.; And-Others
TI: Reconsidering the Research on CBI Screen Design.
PY: 1989
NT: 20 p.; In: Proceedings of Selected Research Papers presented at the
Annual Meeting of the Association for Educational Communications and
Technology (Dallas, TX, February 1-5, 1989). For the complete proceedings,
see IR 013 865.
PR: EDRS Price - MF01/PC01 Plus Postage.
AB: Two variables that designers should consider when developing
```

MENU: Mark Record   Select Search Term   Options   Find   Print   Download

Press ENTER to Mark records for PRINT or DOWNLOAD

Figure 3. Screen from ERIC CD-ROM Silver Platter. Notice how the scrolling interferes with reading, because top of screen is not top of module. The text also has a homogeneity problem, because the lack of typographic cues leads to a homogeneous visual surface and attendant reading difficulties. Screen from ERIC (Educational Resources Clearinghouse) CD-ROM Silver Platter. Boston: Silver Platter, 1986–91.

The *Page Up* and *Page Down* keys are used to move through lists of references, but these commands take the reader across the boundaries of individual entries. Readers (at least this reader) constantly lose track of whether entries have been read or not, since top-of-screen is not also top-of-page. Information that identifies titles or authors is frequently separated visually from other important text (such as abstracts or keywords), and a given type of information (such as title or author) is never in the same place on the screen. The whole system feels jumpy and erratic, and a general sense of disorientation prevails. The problem is alleviated to some extent through the use of *Control-Page Down*, which takes the browser to the top of each entry. But then text is missed that does not fit on a screen. Thus, with document databases containing huge numbers of entries that must be browsed quickly, avoiding scrolling text modules is preferable.

Where the purpose for reading is to explore as well as search and retrieve information (as in encyclopedias), scrollable windows can provide for extended passages of text. Figure 4 presents another screen from the Perseus Project.

Notice the two scroll bars, one in the left window with the primary text (in Greek) of *Acharnians*, the other in the right window with running commentary. The reader can scroll down through either text window, reading both primary text and commentary in parallel. The two windows are modules in a much larger document database that contains other plays, with associated commentary, information on sources, maps, models, diagrams, and so on. Here, the anticipated purposes and styles of readers determine an appropriate use of scrolling text modules.

Modular text does have its advantages. One distinct advantage is that the same text base can serve multiple audiences and multiple purposes for reading (Walker). When texts are composed in screen size chunks, the same modular text fragments can be used to build different documents or

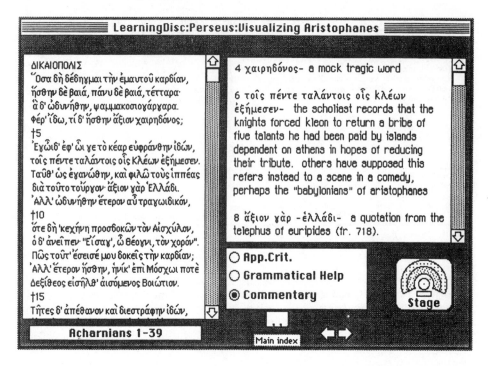

Figure 4. Modular Text. Scrolling text in the two main windows allows for side-by-side primary text in Greek with commentary in English. Note that other text modules are available at the click of a mouse—Applied Criticism and Grammatical Help. From Perseus Project, hypermedia educational software under development at Harvard and Brown Universities; screen captured from Apple Learning Disk (CD-ROM). © 1988, Apple Computer, Cupertino, California.

different paths through a document. Novice and expert tracks, for example, can be structured out of the same set of information. Texts of various sorts can be *compiled* instead of *written,* constructed out of interchangeable parts. Both the WordPerfect and the Microsoft Word manuals are examples of highly modular writing, with topics arranged alphabetically under headings, so the manuals work simultaneously as alphabetically-organized tutorials and reference volumes. Each page has predictable information in predictable slots. Such a book can be written in any order, and modules can be revised as needed without much effect on the other modules. And a modular approach can work well in both paper and electronic media. (Although, of course, a printed manual needs careful adaptation to work well as an online manual.)

Whatever we may wish for, modular text is definitely the shape of text to come. For many pragmatic uses of screen-based text (such as online help), highly localized, non-sequential, fragmented pieces of text work find. Such modularization leads to tremendous economy — a single piece of text can be written once, but read and used many times, by various writers and readers, for various purposes. It is well suited to mass storage on CD-ROM disks and to search-and-retrieve operations using keywords or browsers.

We might speculate on the effects of modularity. Will readers become less tolerant of extended arguments and reasoning? Will all texts disintegrate into fragments — a chopped up hash of language — with texts of 75-

words-or-less dominating the presentation of information? Will we stop thinking of reading as an extended, engrossing transaction with a text and its author and think of reading, instead, as gleaning or grazing across a range of *textbits?* Yes and no. Some of us will continue to engage with extended, lengthy, integrated text for certain purposes under certain conditions. And all of us will be exposed to increasing quantities of textbits — bits that are skimmed and scanned, compiled and com-positioned, presented through various text databases that help us organize and exploit the information explosion.

Hierarchical, Layered, Embedded Text

To a limited extent, printed text can achieve a special sort of modularization through layered or embedded effects. Within passages of text, semantic cues signal that information is peripheral, or supportive, or explanatory, or defining. Parentheses, footnotes, asides, and facsimile or boxed text all allow writers to escape the immediately present text, to move down or across a level in the text hierarchy, to assign a different status to information, to put it next to or below the predominant text level. In longer printed texts, writers can assemble glossaries, indexes, information on authors, prefaces, notes on the edition, or notes to specific groups of readers. These devices give print some texture of hierarchy, indicating that not all information is on the same level. Readers can pursue the mainline text, but they can also read peripheral or supporting information that has a status other than mainline. Texts digress.

Books, however, are imperfectly suited to hierarchical or embedded text. They essentially are a flat medium, meant to be read in linear fashion. Readers can escape linearity; they can jump around or use different sections of a text in different ways. (For a provocative presentation of ways that texts can escape two dimensions, see Tufte). The programmed textbooks that reflected behavioristic models of learning, such as Joseph C. Blumenthal's *English 2600,* were one attempt to escape the linearity of print. These books took learners on various tracks through the text. Short quizzes over material would assess learner knowledge and then send the learner to appropriate pages for explanation and practice. Advanced learners would speed along on the advanced track. Such books were always a little odd. The habits of approaching text in linear fashion were too ingrained on learners. As one worked through such texts, one wondered what was being skipped and whether learning was being accurately evaluated.

Unlike books, computers *are* well suited to nonlinear text. *Nonlinear text* is, in fact, probably the best definition of the kind of text generated by the rapidly expanding technologies of hypertext. Hypertext programs allow texts of various sorts to be combined into large text bases, allowing readers to move freely across various sorts of information in nonlinear ways.

Though two-dimensional, screens offer the compelling illusion of depth. In a windowing environment, active files and various kinds of text can be displayed and stacked up on the screen. Somewhere behind an active file, help can exist, to be called with a simple command or click of the mouse. Glossaries can exist behind words, levels of explanation and example can exist below the surface of the text. Text can be put on clipboards or pushed out to the side of the work area. Information can be present without being visible except through subtle reminders: a shaded term suggesting a connection to another text, a dog-eared page icon pointing toward a personal annotation on a file, a pull-down bar offering access to other texts. The reader can be in two (or more) places at once, with a definition popped up alongside an unknown text or with a palette of shading patterns placed alongside a graphic. The desktop can be stacked with open files — multiple applications running simultaneously — each with its own text in its own screen areas.

Paper text must embed signals of hierarchy within the linear text itself or in some remote location, such as a table of contents. But electronic text can actually be hierarchically or loosely structured, and it can show its structure schematically or in full detail. A screen-based technical manual, for example, can have a cascading design, with top-level screens offering statements of purpose, scope, and audience definition. At a next level of detail, overviews of steps in a process can be offered. Each step can be exploded to show detailed procedures, and behind the detailed procedures other sorts of information can reside — troubleshooting advice, specifications, or code (Herrstrom and Massey). Such hypertext features essentially allow text to escape linearity — there need not be a Chapter One because there need not be a declared linear order of information. Text can be loosely structured, built by association, linked in networks or multidimensional matrices.

Linguists have long noted that syntax is deeply recursive. Sentences can contain sentences, clauses can contain multiple other clauses, and phrases can themselves contain clauses, so that, in effect, lower-level units within a hierarchy can contain higher-level ones. With electronic text, what is true at the syntactic level — the recursion that gives language extreme structural flexibility — is true at the discourse level. Like Chinese boxes, text can be nested within text, and huge texts can reside within tiny fragments. With the combination of both hierarchical subordination and lateral links from any point to any point, hypertext offers greatly expanded possibilities for new structures characterized by layering and flexibility.

Navigable Text

Readers of all text must navigate; they must find their ways through sometimes large or diffuse collections of information. And they have developed navigational strategies for print — using signposts such as tables of contents, indexes, headings, headers, pagination, and so on. Print readers can flip around in a text, scan very quickly, size up the whole, and generally learn from physical and directional cues where they are in the text and where information they need is likely to be.

Imagine your own strategies for reading a newspaper: how it is you decide what to read and how much of it, how your eyes work the page, how quickly and efficiently you take in information. There are highly developed skills operating here, and it shouldn't be too surprising that the early forms of teletext news, presented as a simple scrolling panel of information, did not enjoy much acceptance since they did not allow readers to exercise existing, efficient strategies for using print. People do not want to read extended text on screen, especially when the machine controls the content and the pace. Readers want control.

Books are highly evolved forms: what they do, they do well. A reader can come to a book with highly evolved strategies for getting information from print, but users of computer systems are often handicapped by not having useful, productive strategies for approaching computer-based text. They are often frustrated when they apply learned strategies from print or from other software, only to find that one system doesn't work the same way another one does. Because the screen lacks the total physical presence of a printed text, screen readers have difficulty sizing up the whole, getting a full sense of how much information is present and how much has been viewed. One knows immediately where one is in a book, but it is often difficult to maintain the same intelligence in screen-based text. And so readers of on-screen text have a difficult time navigating. They must read through a window onto a text, and that window limits what the reader sees at any one time. The window is a flat, two-dimensional space, and it is notoriously difficult to know exactly where one is, where one has been, or where one is going. And when an on-screen text is complicated by multiple windows and multiple active files, levels of embedded texts, or a hypermedia environment, navigation poses significant threats to coherence.

A critical threat to the usefulness of on-screen text is the *homogeneity problem* (Nielsen 299). Text on a computer screen tends to be uniform; because of consistent display fonts, spacing, margins, color, design, and size of text modules, it all starts to look the same. Contrast a book with a newspaper or a shopping list to get a sense of the variation in surface that print presents and it becomes clear why on-screen readers are frequently lost in textual space. The challenge of designing text on screens rests in large part on overcoming the machine's tendency toward a homogeneous surface.

Many initial attempts to provide navigation aids for screen-based text are analogically borrowed from paper text. Menus are something like tables of contents, except that when one makes a decision about where to go for information, the page turning is automatic. Indexes look similar in both media and work equally well if designed well. Still borrowing on paper cues, screen headers and footers — as well as titles on menus, pop-up windows, or text modules — can tell readers of screen text where they are, much as one can tell in many books what chapter or what article one is reading by looking to a title or a page header. Screens can be paginated (borrowing even the term *page* for *screen*), often in the form *Page 3 of 6*, but also iconically as in PageMaker documents, with sets of tiny, numbered pages on the lower left of the screen that can be clicked on to move through the document. Readers need a sense of how much they have viewed and what is left in the set of related screens they are scanning.

In Figure 4 on page 228, notice how much of the screen is devoted to navigation. Titles at the top of the screen show one's place in the overall system, and line numbers on the text itself help locate the reader. The bull's eye on *Commentary* suggests the current location, with targets on *App. Crit.* and *Grammatical Help* suggesting there are other places one could be (critical commentary or grammatical help in understanding the primary text). The index is always available, as are arrows for moving forward or backward. If the student wants to exit to the graphic stage — effectively moving from text to performance — the link is there. The environment is rich with cues for locating oneself in textual space and for navigating to new areas.

While some navigation aids are borrowed from print, other navigation options work best only within electronic media. Graphical browsers (looking like cluster diagrams) can offer readers a visualization of the structure of information, so that one can see at a glance the scope and nature of large collections of information. The information contained in a large text base is mapped onto a network representation — with key terms constituting nodes and lines showing relationships among the nodes. Each node represents a group of related information. Like electronic menus and indexes, such browsers offer more than a cue to structure; they facilitate interaction with the text base. Readers can point and click their way from one node to another, explode a node to explore sub-nodes, and so build mental models of the structure of information in interactive, highly intuitive ways. Books might provide similar browsers, such as timelines or the *Encyclopaedia Britannica's* Topicon, but these devices simply do not have the fluid or interactive qualities of electronic browsers.

Ties, or links, or buttons — hot spots in the text that link one screen or term with other screens or terms in the text base — work much better in screen-based text than in paper texts. Some books achieve a limited level of such linking through, for example, endnotes or references to appendices, but the general mechanism is much better suited to electronic text. (Students of mine have read and used Joseph Williams's *Style* for months without recognizing that bold-faced terms are defined in the glossary.) The links in screen-based text announce themselves by their typography or visual character; clicking on a link takes one immediately to some related text. The links can be visually distinguished by function — links from an index to relevant text, from a term to a glossary definition, from a menu to a chosen activity, from an overview to more detailed information, and so on. Links serve as *anchors* to a given screen; one is anchored to the screen icon while going off for an exploratory cruise. For navigating large text bases, the single device of links with anchors in a present screen provides a powerful control over text that cannot be approached within paper texts.

Standard navigation devices are quickly emerging, so that screen readers can bring learned strategies to new interfaces and new texts. In many programs, the perimeter of the screen is defined as a wayfinding area, containing cues about where one currently is (as in the title on the screen) and about where one can currently go (as represented primarily in the choices of active icons). Having worked with a few programs that use similar devices, readers come to expect the icons to be active — to respond to a point-and-click. They realize, too, that cues will generally allow them to determine where they are and where they can go. They relate to the home menu — the familiar, top-level screen that offers a breakdown of wayfinding options at the broadest level. Such screens constitute *landmarks* to the navigator — familiar, easily recognizable locations. Readers come to expect to be able to do certain things, and well-designed systems use the navigational knowledge readers have naturally acquired through interaction with other programs, just as book designers offer readers an index, or a page number, or a chapter title.

Spacious Text

Print is constrained by sheer physical bulk. Consider the constraint of bulk on the compact *Oxford English Dictionary*, with its print compressed to the point of practical illegibility to the naked eye, crammed onto pages full of abbreviations and omitted information. Or consider the sheer bulk of paper documentation necessary to run a complex piece of machinery — an aircraft carrier or an airplane. The sheer weight of paper makes a strong argument for online information. The tons of paper documentation that burn the precious fuel supply of a submarine have a negligible weight in electronic form. The same physicality that makes books easy to use — portable, handy, laptop — makes them impossible to use as systems grow larger and more complex, and as the need for documentation increases proportionately (or geometrically).

No similar physical constraint shapes electronic text. The result is a spaciousness in both the amount of information that can be recorded and in the design of information display. Steven Jobs can include the *Oxford English Dictionary* and Shakespeare's plays in the NEXT computer's memory — no problem. The price of memory has been decreasing quickly while new technologies increase storage limits. Large stacks of information can be duplicated for the price of a disk; huge quantities of information can reside on a single compact disk. A CD-ROM disk might hold 550,000 pages of text with 1,000 characters per page. But it weights only ounces, fits into your pocket, and will soon be replaced by more compact storage media.

Writers of paper texts are always contained by length (as I am here!): writing is a process of selection, cutting, paring away at what is non-essential or redundant. Paper text forces absurdities upon writers — squeezing text into narrow margins and using smaller fonts to keep the overall page count within limits. But screens introduce the luxury of open space. There is no demand to run unrelated text together in the interest of saving page space. If a writer hasn't much to say about something, space can be left blank without worrying about cost. The effect on prose is liberating, freeing it from the economic constraints of inscription.

Graphically Rich Text

Print is a graphic medium; it displays its meanings in the spread of ink on page (Bernhardt, "Seeing the Text"). Writers of printed text have many options at their disposal to make texts visually informative: white space, font sizes, line spacing, icons, non-alphabetic characters like bullets and daggers, margins, and the whole range of pictorial displays — graphs, charts, drawings, etc. The use of computers for word processing has heightened our awareness of the graphic component of meaning. Both student writers and experts have at their command a wide range of graphic tools and an expanding base of research and aesthetic insight to guide the design of text on page (see Barton and Barton, "Trends"). Wholly new products — desktop publishing and graphics software — give authorial control over text/graphic integration. More than ever before, writers are page designers; they are com-position specialists.

Electronic text extends visual composition by offering a surface with more graphic potential and greatly augmented options for text/graphic display and integration. Some of these display options are shared by print and screen-based text. White space (though often not white), space breaks, and margins actively signal divisions within a text, showing what goes with what and where the boundaries are. Bullets and numbered lists cue sequences of information. Font sizes and varieties, headings, color, boldface and italics show hierarchies within a text, cuing subordinate and superordinate relations. Headings, text shape, and callouts in the margins can provide filters for readers, tracking them toward or through various information paths so that each reader is guided to appropriate text for the task at hand.

But screen-based text goes beyond print in its visual effects. Readers can zoom in and out on screen text, editing graphics at the pixel level or looking at facing pages in page-preview mode, with Greeked text downplaying verbal meanings in favor of a visual gestalt that allows writers to evaluate design. Sequences can be animated, procedures can be demonstrated. Text can flash or take on spot color or be outlined or presented in inverse video. With CD-ROM integration, video, voice, or musical sequences can be part of a text, achieving effects that print can only struggle to suggest. Exploded diagrams, so important to technical writing, can actually explode, and readers can view technical illustrations at varying levels of detail, with high resolution on close-up shots of delicate mechanisms (Jong). Readers can travel in virtual space, examining an object such as a building or an automobile from various perspectives, moving around the object in three-dimensional CAD space.

Screen-based text takes information in iconic, visually metaphoric directions. We know people learn about complicated systems best when they have organizing metaphors. Electronic information allows us to exploit metaphors, so that the screen is a *window* onto a *desktop* and information is kept in *files.* We use *control panels,* complete with *gauges, switches, bells,* and *alarm clocks.* We relate easily to the icons of control, throwing text into the *garbage can* or moving icons for pages (representing files) from one location to another.

We seem to adapt easily to metaphoric designs. Figure 5, the drawing palette from DrawPerfect, is thoroughly iconic and metaphoric.

We use *palettes* to choose colors and patterns and use *brushes, pencils,* and *erasers* to draw objects. We enter a metaphoric world, one reliant on the objective correlates of an artist's workspace and tools. The knowledge and manipulation is visual, physical, and immediate; it exploits powerful, metaphoric knowledge based on the screen's correspondence to other objects and activities. At its best, the interface is intuitive, and we move easily from one application to the next, relying on our sense of metaphor to identify similar functions and to make guesses, building a visual, interpretive intelligence as we go along. Once one knows how to read a book, one can pick up any book from any publisher. We are getting closer to such intuitive convenience in software applications and interface design.

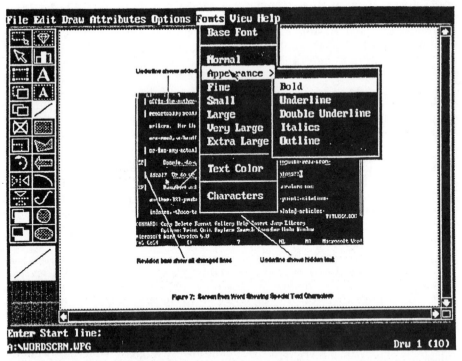

Figure 5. Screen from DrawPerfect, published by WordPerfect. This screen is thoroughly metaphorical and iconic, relying on a system of visual cues related to the tools of drawing and painting. Notice the rich environment on the periphery: things to do and places to go. The pull-down, point-and-click menu interface represents the convergence of design around a single standard. Screen from DrawPerfect 1.1 © 1991 WordPerfect Corporation, Orem, Utah.

One striking fact about the interface in the DrawPerfect palette, a DOS program, is its similarity to applications on the Macintosh. DrawPerfect represents the convergence of design around mouse-driven, point-and-click, windowed, pop-up interfaces. It is the product of rapid evolution and reflects the dominance of a single, strong design model over many applications from many different companies. The convergence on a design standard is a wonderful convenience, since the reader can make an easy transition from one application to the next, from one system to the next, relying on learned strategies for interacting with on-screen text. (Conversely, it is the points of divergence, when the program looks like a Macintosh application but doesn't work like one, that drive people crazy.)

Of course, the phosphor glow of screen text causes its share of problems. We are subjected to flicker, glare, and electronic interference. The screen image suffers, and so we do, from non-optimal light conditions. Our eyes complain of fatigue from attempting to maintain focus on a curved screen. We are hampered by screen size and resolution. But that same phosphor offers a fluid, dynamic medium, with many more options than print has for displaying information and exploiting visual intelligence.

Customizable, Publishable Text

Little can be done by the reader of paper text to customize the text itself. The few customizing devices are well exploited: turning down the corner of a page or leaving a bookmark or a self-stick note, writing notes in the margin, or highlighting and underlining passages. Such modest adaptations of the static text to the uses of an individual reader make the book more valuable to the owner but less valuable to other readers.

Electronic text, in contrast, benefits from being infinitely more fluid, expansive, and adaptable to individual uses. Readers can annotate without the boundaries of hard copy. Text on screens can be changed — that is one of its essential properties. Lines can be written between the lines, notes can be appended to the text itself or as pop-up annotations behind the screen. Figure 6, from Microsoft Word 5.0 for the IBM PC, shows some of the ways text on screen can be adapted to individual preferences.

This particular passage is the result of collaboration that involved passing the disk with the text back and forth with my collaborator with Word's revision marks turned on. These marks show up on the screen, and they can then be accepted or rejected, printed or suppressed during printing. Revision bars on the left margin signal edits and additions, while the codes in the same margin signal the style tags on blocks of text (either can be suppressed). Struck-through text signals deletions even while the deleted text is present; hidden text (dotted underline) allows commentary so authors and editors can talk to each other below the surface of the text.

I just wrote (or "spoke") metaphorically about authors and editors "talking" to each other below the surface of the text, but it need not be read as metaphor. The Macintosh extends the media of textual metacommentary in wholly new ways by offering voice "post-its" — little sound bites that can be attached to files. The reader clicks on the sound button and hears the voice of the author: "Note that I changed the figures here to give you some budget flexibility" or "Don't let George know I'm telling you about the meeting." Here's a new form of textual presence — the author present in voice, embedded in the textual surface. These tools — ones that introduce multiple voices, allowing editing and commentary at various levels and in various modes — are recognizably wonderful tools for writers, who respond to the fluidity of the text, but they work correspondingly well for readers,

Underline shows added text   **Line through shows deleted text**

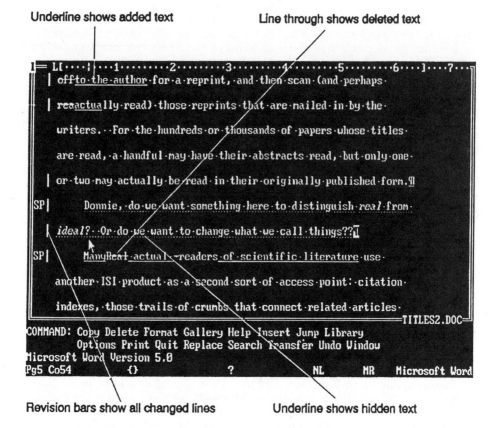

Revision bars show all changed lines   **Underline shows hidden text**

Figure 6. Screen from Word 5.0. The text is individualized, with comments from one coauthor to the other in hidden text and the history of passback edits represented by strikethroughs, revision bars in the left margin, and underlined text. Screen from Word 5.0 © 1989 Microsoft Corporation, Redmond, Washington.

whose interaction with the text is not restricted to mental activities but can be executed physically within the text itself.

The display of the text itself can be customized. Readers can reduce screen clutter by suppressing the display of rulers, spaces, returns, mark-up language, stylebars, borders, and menus. Or readers can show properties of screen text — with every space and return signaled in a fashion that has no print equivalent. (In Figure 6, note the dot between words and the paragraph symbol at the end of each paragraph.) Readers can decide the level of on-screen prompting they want, with menus and help cues displayed or suppressed. Background colors, screen borders, audio messaging, cursor speed — any number of features of the display can be set to individual parameters. Individual user profiles can be stored that automatically adjust the parameters based on predetermined settings. This means the "same" text can display itself differently, depending on the preferences of individual readers.

Screen-based text has the potential to adapt to individual users automatically by keeping histories on users and responding in intelligent ways to likely scenarios based on what a particular user has done in the past. Individualized glossaries, dictionaries, macros, indexes, authoring levels, search procedures, bookmarks, and stylesheets all give the readers of screen-based text real ownership of their texts. Readers own the text because they can do what they want with it; they can make it their own, unlike any other reader's texts.

The controls over fluid, customizable text are shared by the system designer and the user. Systems can be made sensitive to user context, providing help based on best guesses about where the user is in the program and what sort of help might be needed. Shortcuts that allow individual control can be built into the system. For example, many programs offer novice and expert paths, with menus and on-screen prompts for new users. Such prompting speeds learning for new users. But power users want menus and cues suppressed — they know what they need to do and want to do it in the fewest number of keystrokes. Good design allows both types of user to coexist.

The control over the shape of text that microcomputers grant users leads inevitably toward not just customizable but publishable text. Just as the printing press eventually put books into everyone's hands, desktop publishing systems put the printing press into everyone's hands. Anyone can now design, display, and print work that is potentially indistinguishable from professionally printed work.

Traditionally, much of the cost of print has been in the production stage — the human and machine costs of typesetting, paper, binding, and distribution. Longer length or fancier graphics meant higher prices. The high production cost per unit for books and magazines made copies fairly expensive, but highly portable and accessible to anyone who could read. With screen-based text, however, much of the cost of production is shifted from the printer to the author and the audience. It is cheap and easy to duplicate disks. And disks (whether floppy or hard) hold immense quantities of information in a small format, so issues of length are no longer so important to overall cost. A disk can hold graphics and animated sequences, color diagrams and fancy fontography, interactive tutorials and reference materials. Once the information is coded to the disk, reproduction is a simple, inexpensive matter.

But the more complicated the on-screen text, the higher the overhead demands on authors and readers. Instead of printers needing high-priced equipment and expensive materials to produce fancy texts, writers need high-priced equipment to author texts, and readers now need high-priced equipment to run the disk. And whereas there never were compatibility problems between readers and books, there are now multiple and vexing problems of matching hardware and software.

Once printed, paper text is fairly static. It presents the same face to all readers, so that my copy of a book looks just like yours. In contrast to the static quality of paper text, on-screen text is fluid and customizable, updatable and expandable. These qualities lead to multiple versions, to individually adapted texts, and give an elasticity to electronic text that changes the nature of publication. And with the advent of desktop publishing, the movement from screen-based text to paper is eased, so even print loses its static quality. A writer can produce papers or books in multiple versions, easily redesigned and updated. Print is no longer permanent, because the cost and effort of updating editions is negligible. The fluidity of the screen has begun to overcome the static inertia of print.

The Shape of Text to Come

The shape of text changes as it moves from paper to screen. On-screen text is eminently interactive, closely embedded in ongoing action in real-time settings. It borrows heavily on the evolved strategies readers possess for interacting with printed texts, but provides a more fluid, changeable medium, so that the text itself becomes an object for manipulation and change.

As texts change, we will develop new strategies for reading and writing. Text bases will grow, becoming huge compilations of information stored on disk with no corresponding printed versions. It will feel natural to move through large pools of information, and we will rely on learned strategies for knowing where we are, where we want to go, and what we want to do when we get there. We will develop new sorts of reading skills, ones based around text that is modular, layered, hierarchical, and loosely associative. We will demand control over text — over its display, its structure, and its publication.

We are now at a point of transition of the sort described by Ong, similar to transitions from orality to literacy or from handwritten manuscripts to printed. The computer is becoming increasingly dominant as a primary medium for presenting and working with texts. As we take control of computer-based texts, the existing lines between reading and writing will tend to blur into a single notion of use (Slatin). Texts will have multiple authors and grow incrementally as readers individualize and structure text for their own uses. The presence of screens will become increasingly common, a part of our daily lives, close at hand in a variety of situations.

As with the interrelation of spoken and written media, so between paper and screen-based text: we will see crossbreeding, with the uses and forms of one medium shaping the uses and forms of the other, so that as the predominance of and our familiarity with screen-based text increases, the dimensions of variation discussed here will have a greater and greater shaping influence on paper text. But the real potential for full exploitation of these dimensions of variation lies in text on screens. It is the dynamic, fluid, graphic nature of computer-based text that will allow full play of these variables in shaping the texture of print on screens.

Works Cited

Barton, Ben F., and Marthalee S. Barton. "Simplicity in Visual Representation: A Semiotic Approach." *Journal of Business and Technical Communication* 1 (1987): 9–26.

———. "Trends in Visual Representation." *Technical and Business Communication: Bibliography Essays for Teachers and Corporate Trainers.* Ed. Charles Sides. Urbana: NCTE, 1989. 95–135.

Barrett, Edward, ed. *The Society of Text: Hypertext, Hypermedia, and the Social Construction of Knowledge.* Cambrdige: MIT P, 1989.

Bernhardt, Stephen A. "The Reader, the Writer, and the Scientific Text." *Journal of Technical Writing and Communication* 15.2 (1985): 163–74.

———. "Seeing the Text." *College Composition and Communication* 37 (Feb. 1986): 66–78.

Bolter, Jay David. *Writing Space: The Computer, Hypertext, and the History of Writing.* Hillsdale: Erlbaum, 1991.

Brockmann, R. John. *Writing Better Computer User Documentation: From Paper to Hypertext.* Version 2. New York: Wiley, 1990.

Chignell, Marc H., and Richard M. Lacy. "Project Jefferson: Integrating Research and Instruction." *Academic Computing* 3 (Oct. 1988): 12–17, 40–45.

Duchastel, Philippe C. "Display and Interaction Features of Instructional Texts and Computers." *British Journal of Educational Technology* 19.1 (1988):58–65.

Harward, V. Judson. "From Museum to Monitor: The Visual Exploration of the Ancient World." *Academic Computing* 2 (May/June 1988): 16–19, 69–71.

Herrstrom, David S., and David G. Massey. "Hypertext in Context." Barrett 45–58.

Horton, William. *Designing and Writing Online Documentation: Help Files to Hypertext.* New York: Wiley, 1990.

Jong, Steven. "The Challenge of Hypertext." *Proceedings of the 35th International Technical Communication Conference.* Washington: Society for Technical Communication, 1988. 30–32.

Kostelnick, Charles. "Visual Rhetoric: A Reader-Oriented Approach to Graphics and Design." *Technical Writing Teacher* 16 (Winter 1989): 77–88.

Lynch, Anne. "Project Jefferson and the Development of Research Skills." *Reference Services Review* (Fall 1989): 91–96.

Merrill, Paul F. "Displaying Text on Microcomputers." *The Technology of Text.* Ed. David Jonassen. Vol. 2. Englewood Cliffs: Educational Technology Publications, 1982. 401–13.

Nielsen, Jakob. "The Art of Navigating through Hypertext." *Communications of the ACM* 33 (March 1990): 296–310.

Ong, Walter J. *Orality and Literacy: The Technologizing of the Word.* London: Methuen, 1982.

Redish, Janice. "Writing in Organizations." *Writing in the Business Professions.* Ed. Myra Kogen. Urbana: NCTE, 1989. 97–124.

Rubens, Philip M. "Online Information, Hypermedia, and the Idea of Literacy." Barrett 3–20.

———."A Reader's View of Text and Graphics: Implications for Transactional Text." *Journal of Technical Writing and Communication* 16.1/2 (1986): 73–86.

Rubens, Philip M., and Robert Krull. "Application of Research on Document Design to Online Displays." *Technical Communication* (4th Quarter 1985): 29–34.

Slatin, John M. "Reading Hypertext: Order and Coherence in a New Medium." *College English* 52 (Dec. 1990): 870–83.

Sticht, Thomas. "Understanding Readers and Their Uses of Text." *Designing Usable Texts.* Ed. Thomas M. Duffy and Robert M. Waller. Orlando: Academic Press, 1985. 315–40.

Tufte, Edward R. *Envisioning Information.* Cheshire, CT: Graphics Press, 1990.

Visible Language. Special issue on adaptation to new display technologies. 18.1 (Winter 1984).

Walker, Janet H. "Authoring Tools for Complex Document Sets." Barrett 132–47.

Writing on the Edge. Special issue on hypertext. 2.2 (Spring 1991).

PART TWO

CRITICAL THINKING

The idea of promoting and enabling critical thinking has gained considerable credibility over the past two decades, but thinking critically has always been a part of the rhetorical tradition. Critical analyses of rhetorical situations, purposeful and judicious choices of argumentative strategies, careful construction of reasonable arguments — these are only a few of the contemporary approaches to teaching composition that encourage writers to develop their critical thinking faculties. Although *The Bedford Handbook*'s approach to writing invites student to exercise their critical thinking skills throughout the composing process, this new section of the *Handbook* focuses specifically on the more prominent dimensions of critical thinking.

The following three readings address two necessary components for developing critical consciousness: careful, critical reading and responsible argumentation.

- How can teachers help students develop critical reading skills? How can teachers help students approach their reading (and writing) as though they were engaging authors and readers in a conversation?
- How can teachers help students think of argumentation as a deliberative and generative process?
- How can teachers help students expand their understanding of "argument" to include not only confrontation and conflict but also critical inquiry, sustained deliberation, and responsible cooperation?

CONVERSATIONS WITH TEXTS: READING IN THE TEACHING OF COMPOSITION

Mariolina Salvatori

[*College English* 58 (April 1996): 440–54.]

Associate professor of English at the University of Pittsburgh, Mariolina Salvatori teaches and does research in the areas of hermeneutics, composition, literacy, and pedagogy. She is particularly interested in exploring the transactions of knowledge, and the relations between teachers, students, and texts that different theories of reading make possible. She has published numerous articles and chapters on composition and teaching, and she has written on twentieth-century Italian literature, literary perceptions of the aging, and the immigrant experience. Her most recent book is *Pedagogy: Disturbing History, 1819–1929* (1996).

Engaging students in active critical thinking helps them think of reading and writing as conversation with readers and writers. In this article, Salvatori builds on the notion of critical reading as conversing with a text, observing that readers have the "tremendous responsibility of giving a voice, and therefore a sort of life, to the text's argument." Writers have "the responsibility of writing a text that asks (rather than answers) questions, that proposes (rather than imposes) arguments, and that therefore makes a conversation possible." In a teacher-student relationship, teachers have a responsibility to converse with students' writing; but students have a responsibility to make that conversation possible. After providing a brief historical context, Salvatori traces the theoretical connections between reading and writing, and then she offers an example of how she teaches the interconnectedness of reading and writing.

The art of dialectic is not the art of being able to win every argument. . . . Dialectic, as the art of asking questions, proves itself only because the person who knows how to ask questions is able to persist in his questioning. . . . The art of questioning . . . i.e. the art of thinking . . . is called 'dialectic,' for it is the art of conducting a real conversation. . . . To conduct a conversation means to allow oneself to be conducted by the object to which the partners in the conversation are directed. It requires that one does not try to out-argue the other person, but that one really considers the weight of the other's position . . .

     – Hans-Georg Gadamer, *Truth and Method* (330)

Here Gadamer is writing about face-to-face conversations; but he does so in order to articulate the rules and the workings of other inaudible conversations, those that readers make happen as they read. Gadamer theorizes reading as a "hermeneutical conversation with a text" — a conversation that can only begin and be sustained if and when the reader/interlocutor reconstructs and critically engages the "question," or the argument, that the text itself might have been occasioned by or be an answer to. He writes, "Texts . . . have to be *understood,* and that means that one partner in the hermeneutical conversation, the text, is expressed only through the other partner, the interpreter" (349; emphasis added). This view of reading enables us to imagine a text's argument not as a position to be won and defended by one interlocutor at the expense of another, but rather as a "topic" about which interlocutors generate critical questions that enable them to reflect on the meaning of knowledge and on different processes of knowledge formation. Thus a text's argument can function as a fulcrum that brings parties (reader and text) together. But for this to happen a reader must accept and carry out the tremendous responsibility of giving a voice, and therefore a sort of life, to the text's argument. Although Gadamer does not point it out explicitly, a corollary to the reader's responsibility is the writer's responsibility, the responsibility of writing a text that asks (rather than answers) questions, that proposes (rather than imposes) arguments, and that therefore makes a conversation possible. And although Gadamer's subjects are expert readers and writers, what he has to offer those of us who teach as yet inexperienced readers and writers is, I believe, very valuable. Gadamer's emphasis on the reader's responsibility, for example, makes me think of the tremendous and delicate responsibility I have as reader of my students' arguments. But it also makes me think of the corollary to my responsibility, a student's responsibility to write argument in ways that allow a reader to converse with it. To teach students to assume and to exercise this responsibility is indeed very difficult. Nevertheless, I will suggest, they can learn to exercise this sophisticated practice of writing in the process of learning to understand and to appreciate the effects of writing on themselves as readers.

What follows is an argument on behalf of the theoretical and practical appropriateness of using "reading" as a means of teaching "writing." The word "argument" has multiple resonances here: my essay enters an ongoing argument or debate about the place of reading in the composition classroom (see for instance Gary Tate's and Erika Lindemann's recent essays in *College English*), and the arguments of texts are at the same time central to the particular understanding of reading and of teaching reading that I propose.

Historical Context

In 1974, in *Teaching Composing: A Guide to Teaching Writing as a Self-Creating Process*, William E. Coles argued against the use of reading in the composition classroom. He wrote:

> So we decided to get rid of everything that teachers and students alike are tempted to look at writing from behind or through or under. The anthology went; so did the standard plays, novels, poems.(2)

I remember, when I read these lines for the first time in the early 1980s, how struck I was by what seemed a peculiar and arbitrary decision. In 1992, in the process of composing a paper to be delivered at the Conference on College Composition and Communication, I returned to Coles's text and for reasons that have to do with the kind of work I had done in the interim — mainly, my historical research in pedagogy, and my work with hermeneutics and the phenomenology of reading — I was able to read and to respond to this passage differently. In that paper (of which this essay is a revision) I myself returned to a subject that, though central to my intellectual formation as a compositionist, and central to my undergraduate and graduate teaching, I had not written about for some time. The paper was my attempt to understand which theoretical and institutional forces had led first to the separation and subsequently to the integration of the activities of reading and writing in the composition classroom. Focusing on the juncture of the theoretical and the institutional gave me a vantage point from which I was able to conjecture and to reconstruct the "argument" that had led Coles to make what had seemed to me such an iconoclastic gesture. This time, rather than judging Coles's statement as a blanket and arbitrary indictment of the presence of "reading" in composition classrooms, I began to see in his gesture a specific denunciation of what reading had been reduced to within *the teaching of composition* (but also within the teaching of literature, which problematically was and remains the model for much of the teaching of reading done in composition classrooms). I began to see that what Coles was indicting was a particularly enervated, atrophied kind of reading. A reading immobilized within textbooks, and reduced therein to sets of disparate simplifying practices that, separated from the various theories that motivate them, turn into meaningless and arbitrary exercises: reading for "the main idea," for "plot," for "argument," for "point of view," for "meaning," for "message" — interchangeably and without knowing what for. Or reading texts, especially literary texts, as inscrutable and unquestionable "models" of style or rhetorical strategies. Or as "blueprints" for linguistic theories, or political programs, or philosophies of language. I began to see, *through* Coles, the effects of practices that restrain students and teachers from asking questions of a text other than the ones the textbooks have already "gridded." I began to see, *with* Coles, why the kind of writing that these texts and their "facilitating" questions would foster could be nothing but "canned" or "theme" writing. This I understood to be the "problem" of reading that Coles was attacking, and for which he proposed, as a "pharmakon," getting rid of anthologies, plays, novels, poems, and replacing them with the text of the assignments and of the writing that students did in response to them.

Considering the position of composition in the academy in 1974, both inside and outside departments of English; considering the available work force of teachers of composition at the time; considering that the services of composition were in growing demand; considering the perceived need for compositionists to define their discipline on their own terms — considering all this, Coles's apparently "disciplinarian" act can be read, perhaps, as a stern act of self-discipline. That act, set in motion by a confluence of institutional needs, theoretical positions, and programmatic divisions, had a lasting influence. Moreover, in complex ways, it encouraged or catalyzed other compositionists' felt need for a theory and practice of the reading-writing relation that would include the teacher's reading of student writing.

In the 1980s, Coles's move was challenged by some compositionists who shared his concern for student writing as the center of attention in the composition classroom. Rather than turning away from reading, however, these compositionists turned *to* theories of reading that seemed to offer fresh perspectives.

A 1985 essay by John Clifford and John Schilb, "Composition Theory and Literary Theory," reviewed the work of literary theorists who made it possible to imagine the teaching of literature and composition, reading and writing, as interconnected disciplines. Clifford and Schilb assessed the influence of reader-response poststructuralist theories and rhetoric and examined the work of those compositionists and literary critics who, they argued, offered ways of thinking about reading and writing that would elide programmatic and disciplinary separations (to name a few: Susan Miller, Richard Lanham, Ross Winterowd, Wayne Booth, Nancy Comley and Robert Scholes, and Terry Eagleton). Though remarkably different from one another, these theorists share a concern with *acts* rather than *facts* of reading (Ray). Instead of being seen as an intrusion onto the field of composition, or a pretext for paying attention to something other than students' writing, as in the thinking of the 1970s, reading, re-seen in the 1980s through new theories and practices, was now appealed to as a means of "bridging the gap" between the two activities and disciplines, a way of paying attention to reading and writing *differently*. But, I wish to argue, to set the two arguments side by side is to realize what either position may in debate unwittingly end up obscuring: that "the question of reading in the teaching of composition" is not merely the question of whether reading should or should not be used in the composition classroom. The issue is *what kind of reading* gets to be theorized and practiced. (Even if it were true that certain aspects of reading would always remain mysterious, teachers would still need to attend most closely to those aspects of reading which are not cloaked but can be made visible.) This issue cannot be critically and reflexively engaged apart from the following interconnected questions: (1) Which theories of reading are better suited to teaching reading and writing as interconnected activities? (2) What is the theoretical justification for privileging that interconnectedness? (3) How can one teach that interconnectedness?

Theories of Reading and Writing as Interconnected Activities

Not all theories of reading are suited to uncovering and enacting the interconnectedness of reading and writing. Among those least suited to doing so are those that construct writers as visionary shapers of meanings, and their works as venerable repositories for those meanings (such theories generally discourage or consider inappropriate a reader's critical response to a text, particularly the response of an inexperienced reader); theories that construct as mysterious and magical the complicated processes of thinking on which writing imposes provisional order and stability (I am thinking here of critics/theorists as different as Benedetto Croce and Georges Poulet); and theories with unquestioned and unquestionable interpretive frames reducing texts to various thesis statements — cultural, political, religious, and so on. What I find objectionable in these theories is that they make it possible to cover over the processes by which knowledge and understanding are produced. By making it impossible to recapture and learn from the complex processes that have given a written text its particular shape, these theories, in different ways and for different reasons, simultaneously glorify reading and proclaim its unteachability. In classrooms where these theories of reading are unreflexively performed *for* students, where reading materials are used as mere pretexts for writing exercises, a *student's* reading of those materials may become *secondary* in at least two ways: it may become less important than the writing it produces; it may be constructed as needing to rely on a series of simplifying practices generated by somebody else. Such uses of reading as a means of teaching writing can indeed be arbitrary, questionable, even counterproductive.

In contrast with these notions about reading are theories that posit the possibility and the advantages of exploring the complex processes by which "reading" gives a voice to an otherwise mute "writing"; theories that turn texts and readers into "interlocutors" of each other; theories that interrogate rather than mystify the "naturalness," the mystery; and the interpretive "framing" both of the reading and of the writing processes. Such theories make it possible to claim not only that reading can be taught, but also that it can be taught as an opportunity to investigate knowledge-producing practices. Rather than divining a text's meaning or making a text subservient to preestablished significations, such theories construct reading as an activity by means of which readers can engage texts responsibly and critically. *Responsibly*, that is, in ways that as far as possible make *those* texts speak, rather than speak *for* them or make them speak *through* other texts. And *critically* — in ways, that is, that demand that readers articulate a reflexive critique both of the argument they attribute to those texts and of the argument they compose as they respond to those texts. (Among theorists of reading who, in different ways, provide such possibilities are Hans-Georg Gadamer, Wolfgang Iser, M. M. Bakhtin, and Paul de Man.) However, it does not follow that these theories automatically and necessarily lead to their own rigorous enactment.

Two of the texts that in the 1980s advocated a programmatic and theoretical rapprochement of reading and writing and their attendant domains of expertise and performance — literature and composition — demonstrate what I would call a perplexing inattentiveness to moving from theorizing the interconnectedness of reading and writing to making it visible and teaching it. The texts are *Composition and Literature: Bridging the Gap*, edited by Winifred Bryan Horner, and *Writing and Reading Differently*, edited by Douglas Atkins and Michael Johnson. With a few notable exceptions (the essays by Sharon Crowley, Barbara Johnson, and Jasper Neel in *Writing and Reading Differently*), in these volumes reading and writing as interconnected activities are constructed as something that teachers do either *to* and *for* their students or for themselves and equally enlightened others — rather than something teachers do *with* their students to open up the areas of investigation that this particular focus makes possible. The interconnectedness of reading and writing (that virtual, provisional interaction between two extremely complex, invisible, imperceptible processes that can nevertheless be used to test and to foreground each other's moves) tends to be constructed as something either obvious or authorized by such an illustrious tradition — from Plato to Derrida — as not to require much explanation or articulation.

The advantages for the teaching of writing that this understanding of reading promises are ultimately invalidated. Teaching the reading/writing interconnection becomes another kind of hermetic performance, one that hides rather than reveals the processes of cognition that should be the subject of investigation and reflection. Paradoxically, these two texts end up reconfiguring the very situation that Coles was trying to avoid — approaching students' writing, and reading, "from behind or through or under" something else. Perhaps, though, what I perceive as a regrettable shortcoming of otherwise praiseworthy projects can serve an important function: it can remind us that although certain theories of reading *are* more conducive than others to teaching reading and writing as interconnected activities, to foreground and to teach — rather than just to understand — that interconnectedness is a highly constructed, unnatural, obtrusive activity — one that requires a particular kind of training that historically our educational systems and traditions have neither made available nor valorized.

Theoretical Justifications for Focusing on the Interconnectedness of Reading and Writing

I wish to suggest at least two justifications for privileging this interconnectedness. First, insofar as reading is a form of thinking (Gadamer calls it "an analogue for thinking"), written accounts of it, however approximate, can provide us with valuable insights into the ways we think. Second, learning to recapture in one's writing that imperceptible moment when our reading of a text began to attribute to it — began to produce — a particular "meaning" makes it possible to consider what leads us to adopt and to deploy certain interpretive practices. In other words, although the processes that constitute our reading and writing are essentially invisible, those processes are, in principle, accessible to analysis, scrutiny, and reflection. "The ways we think" need neither be kept shrouded in mystery, nor be reduced, in the interest of demystifying the reading process, to a bunch of technical, predictive, or authoritarian formulas. The possibility of gaining access to these processes by no means implies that they can be completely controlled or contained. Nor should they be. But through such access one might learn to account for, however approximately, and to understand, however imperfectly, how certain meanings, certain stories, certain explanations, certain interpretive frames come to be composed or adopted. Expert readers and writers have developed a kind of introspective reading that allows them to decide — as they read and as they write — when to pursue, when to revise, when to abandon a line of argument, and when to start afresh. They have devised a method of reading that, in Coleridge's words, functions as "a way or path of transit" that allows their minds "to classify" and "to appropriate" the events, the images, the thoughts they think as they read. Part of the challenge confronting us as teachers is to learn how to make it possible — within the time and institutional constraints that bind us — for students to learn to perform this kind of introspective reading. To think about reading and the teaching of reading in these terms — to think of reading, that is, as an analogue for thinking about one's own and others' thinking, about how one's thinking ignites and is ignited by the thoughts of others, justifies the presence of reading in composition classrooms not as a pretext but as a context for writing.

Teaching the Interconnectedness of Reading and Writing

It is one thing to say that, even to articulate how, reading and writing are interconnected (as most of the authors featured in *Bridging the Gap* and *Writing and Reading Differently* do); and it is another to imagine and to develop teaching practices that both enact and benefit from that interconnectedness. This approach to teaching, one that requires teachers' and students' relentless attention and reflexivity, is difficult both to initiate and to sustain. Over the years, as a teacher of both composition and literature, I have learned to deploy certain teaching strategies that simultaneously enable and force me and my students to reflect on the moves we make as readers, writers, and thinkers. I do not consider these strategies as mere applications or implementations of somebody else's theories, and as I proceed to describe some of them I do not offer them as such. Nor — an important caveat — can these strategies be lifted out of the theoretical framework I have articulated here and seen as transportable tips or prescriptions; like all strategies, they make sense, that is, are plausible and justifiable, only within the particular approach to teaching that my understanding of "the act of reading" and its connections with writing calls for. I think of these strategies as means a teacher has of exposing (that is, of making visible as well as making available to reflection and critique — her own and others') the *nexus* between the theory she espouses and the practices that theory demands.

To foreground and to exploit the interconnectedness of reading and writing, I make a point of framing reading and writing activities (formal assignments, in-class writings, journals) that ask students first to write their response to a text, second to construct a reflective commentary on the moves they made as readers and the possible reasons for them, and third to formulate an assessment of the particular text their reading produced (an adaptation of Ann E. Berthoff's double-entry journal). By means of this triadic (and recursive) sequence, I try to teach readers to become conscious of their mental moves, to see what such moves produce, and to learn to revise or to complicate those moves as they return to them in light of their newly constructed awareness of what those moves did or did not make possible. This "frame" is my attempt to imagine strategies that enact what Gadamer sees as the three pivotal and interconnected phases of reading — *erkennen, wiedererkennen,* and *berauserkennen.* It is important to note that this frame is not a "grid." Insofar as readers bring their own "presuppositions of knowledge" to the texts they read, the situations they find themselves in, and the experiences they live, and insofar as those presuppositions of knowledge will differ from one person to another, readers' readings of a text will vary.

Initially, my assignments generate considerable resistance on the part of students, mainly because they are not accustomed to performing this kind of introspective reading. When I ask of a point they made, "what made you think that?" or "how did you come to that conclusion?" they often hear reproach in my questions, in spite of my repeated efforts to explain my rationale for this approach. Occasionally students do readily learn to hear my questions as I intend them. But often they don't, and in this case I try to be extremely sensitive to any clues they offer that might make it possible for me to develop a strategy that answers the need of the moment. Here is an example.

Several years ago, one of the first times I taught Charlotte Perkins Gilman's "The Yellow Wall-Paper," I was temporarily silenced by a female student's defense of "the doctor." She was very articulate about all that the doctor had said and done, and she had come to the conclusion that the text made an argument for men's (as opposed to women's) inclination for science (medicine), and for what women had to lose when they did not abide by men's counsel. As I tried to collect myself enough to formulate a question that might make her reflect on what she had just said and why, the book in front of her caught my attention. It was highlighted, rather sparsely. I picked it up, flipped through it, and in a rare moment of extraordinary clarity I noticed that what she had marked in the text, what she had chosen to pay attention to, was everything in the text that had to do with "the doctor." She had paid little or no attention to anything else. I asked to be shown how other students had marked the text. Many had left it untouched (their reasons varied from not wanting to mark their books so that they could sell them to assuming that putting pen to page would interrupt their concentration, arrest their speed). Others had highlighted it, some methodically, others erratically. What became evident to me was that "making a mark" on a text (Bartholomae and Petrosky) was a way of reading they had been taught *not* to perform. (A historical antecedent for my attempt to read the marks on the page as traces of a method could be found in the Renaissance "adversaria" [see Sherman].)

The rest of the period was spent first discussing the marks in the text as indicating what a reader chooses to be attentive to as she or he reads a text and then focusing on three representative samples: one by the student who mainly paid attention to the character of the doctor; one by a student who chose to focus on the narrator; and one by a student who, after an initial rather random system of marking the text, focused on the various characters' responses to the wallpaper. That class made it possible for me to turn a rather mechanical "study habit" — the highlighting of a text — into a strategy, one that can make "visible" the number and the intricacy of strands in a text's argument that a reader (or an interlocutor) pays attention to, and that can show how the selection, connection, and weaving of those strands affects the structuring of the argument a reader constructs. Like any strategy, this is not effective by itself. It is a tool to be used at the appropriate moment, more as a commentary on an incipient awareness of what it means to read an argument than as a means of instructing a reader how to pay attention to somebody else's argument.

A less local strategy, one less contingent on a particular context, is the assignment of what I call the "difficulty paper." (My article "Towards a Hermeneutics of Difficulty" articulates a theoretical framework for such an assignment; note also that Dave Bartholomae and Anthony Petrosky have developed a sequence of assignments around the generative force of difficulty.) Before we discuss a text collectively, I ask students to write a detailed one-page description of any difficulty the text they have been assigned to read might have posed for them. I photocopy what I consider a representative paper and distribute it for class discussion. Then, what I try to do is guide the discussion toward an assessment of the kind of reading that names a particular feature of a text as "difficult." Does difficulty arise because a reader's expectations blind her to a text's clues? Or because the method of reading a reader is accustomed to performing will not work with this particular text? Is it exacerbated when inexperienced readers assume that difficulties are an indictment of their abilities rather than characteristic features of a text? I have repeatedly relied on this kind of assignment, not as a means to expose my students' inadequacies, but as a reflexive strategy that eventually allows them to recognize that what they perceive as "difficult" is a feature of the text demanding to be critically engaged rather than ignored. What is remarkable about this approach is that students' descriptions of difficulties almost inevitably identify a crucial feature of the text they are reading and contain *in nuce* the interpretive move necessary to handle them. They might say for example that they had "difficulty" with a text because it presented different and irreconcilable positions on an issue — their "difficulty" being in fact an accurate assessment of that text's argument.

The focus on difficulty can also be profitably used as a means of directing students' attention to the assignments by means of which many teachers suggest a possible reading of a text. Students can be asked to reflect on the kind of argument that the assignment's frame invites readers to construct about the text — and the kinds of arguments that it simultaneously closes off. Thus the focus will be not only on the difficulty of doing justice to a complex text, but also on the difficulty of adequately representing the complexity of one's response to a complex text. This exercise can help foster habits of rigorous attention to one's reading of others' positions and to one's re-presentations of them; and it can teach students (and remind teachers) to read assignments as more than sets of injunctions.

There are many ways of encouraging students to practice recursive and self-monitoring readings, and they will vary according to context, the rapport that teachers can establish with their students, the configuration of the group, the "feel" of the classroom . . . I am partial to those that can contribute to making what is imperceptible — thinking — at least dimly perceptible. Let's assume, for example, that a student writer has begun to compose a reading of a text (whether in response to an assignment, or to the "difficulty paper" instructions, or as a response of his own) that the teacher thinks might benefit from a second, more attentive reading. Perhaps the student has produced a hasty generalization or an inaccurate conclusion or an overbearingly biased and unexamined pre-understanding that made her oblivious to a text's argument. To ask that student to account for the steps she took to compose that reading, to ask her to actually *mark* which places in the text she "hooked up with" and which she merely scanned, can yield a dramatic visualization of how much of a text's argument can be erased because of preestablished conclusions or inattentiveness to the construction of that argument. Another way of putting students in a position to see the limits and the possibilities of how they choose to structure an argument is to set up a comparative analysis of two or three different papers. Focusing on the papers' introductory moves as simultaneously points of entry into a text (reading) and tentative beginnings for the arguments they will formulate (writing) helps to illuminate what difference it makes to begin a discussion of a text *there* rather than *elsewhere,* or to begin, say, with a question rather than an evaluative comment. It also helps teachers avoid interventions that focus on mistakes, on deficiencies, on what's wrong with this or that way of thinking.

The strategies I have cursorily described here represent some of the ways I choose to participate in and respond to my students' reading/ thinking/writing activities. What is significant about these strategies is that they function simultaneously as heuristic devices for students (through them they learn how to perform certain reflexive moves) and as constant reminders to me that as a teacher I must demonstrate in my reading of my students' words the responsiveness and the responsibility with which I expect them to engage texts. (This does not mean that I am always successful in doing so.) It is also significant that these strategies deliberately foreground "moments of reading" to show how these determine the writing students produce, and that they privilege places that can serve as points of critical reflection on the connection between reading and writing.

Countering Objections

I want now to turn to two of the most frequently articulated academic objections to the theory and practice of reading/writing interconnectedness I have outlined. I find these objections compelling and challenging, so much so that I keep returning to them to assess how they can help me understand better the assumptions about reading that subtend them. Insofar as for the past ten years these objections have consistently complicated and forced me to reexamine my positions on reading, on writing, on teaching, on education, I cannot exclude them from an argument of which they are such an integral part.

Using the names of the programs in my department whose theoretical orientations these objections could be said to represent, I will call them the "creative writing" and the "cultural studies" positions. What follows is a composite sketch of these objections that I have gleaned from three graduate courses I teach — the "Seminar in the Teaching of Composition," "Literacy and Pedagogy," and "Reception Theories." These courses lend themselves extremely well to engaging the issue of the intellectual and programmatic division of which the question of reading in the teaching of composition is both a cause and a consequence.

In the name of (a version of) "creativity" that is constructed as *being,* and *needing to remain,* beyond analysis, some of the representatives of the "creative writing" position articulate their opposition to the rigorous introspection that the interconnectedness of reading and writing requires. When as a group we grope for ways of describing not only *what* happens when we read, but also *how* it is that we tend to construct one and not another critical response to a text, some of the graduate students who align themselves with the "creative writing" position seem willing to engage the first but not the second line of inquiry. Their descriptions of reading are often magical, mysterious. They recollect, lyrically and convincingly, scenes of instruction within which — as children or adolescents — they taught themselves to read, with passion and imagination as their motives and guides. In response to questions about the context that favored their auto-didacticism, some will describe households replete with books and talk about books — a kind of oasis of family discourse that "naturally" fostered a love of reading and writing. Others, however, will describe settings that are exactly the opposite, within which they performed a sort of heroic, individually willed — and therefore "natural" in quite a different sense of the word — form of self-education.

My aim in interrogating these moving accounts is not to devalue them or discredit their veracity, but to point out that these notions of reading may lead to approaches to teaching that are potentially elitist and exclusionary. (I develop this argument in "Pedagogy and the Academy," and more fully in *Pedagogy: Disturbing History.*) What happens when students show little cultural, emotional, or intellectual predisposition for this mystical love of reading? What kinds of responses will they write to a text they did not *love* reading? How can a teacher teach her students to perform a kind of reading that she has herself learned to perform mysteriously and magically? It is significant, I think, that when some of the readers who describe their reading processes as dream-like or intuitive are asked to read back those processes so as to gain insight into their habitual cognitive strategies, they often declare their suspicion of a process they name "critical dissecting."

The "cultural studies" position, on the other hand, objects to the focus on critical self-reflexivity as "nostalgic, reactionary, humanistic," and ultimately an ineffective educational practice. Such a focus, it is claimed, on the one hand can foster the illusion of human beings as independent, self-relying subjectivities; on the other hand, it can disseminate a pernicious account of knowledge-formation, one that exploits self-reflexivity, or a focus on method, as a tactic of avoidance, derailment, deflection. A teacher's commitment to enacting ways of reading that make it both possible and necessary for readers to reflect on and to be critically aware of how arguments — their own and others' — are constructed becomes within this critique a structured avoidance of more substantial issues. According to this critique, to focus, for example, on *how* John Edgar Wideman in "Our Time," or Alice Walker in "In Search of Our Mothers' Gardens," or Gloria Steinem in "Ruth's Song (Because She Could Not Sing It)" construct their narratives, is potentially a way of avoiding the ideological issues of race, class, and gender.

Insofar as it does not reduce "critical reflexivity" to an intentionally depoliticizing attention to form, the cultural studies position provides a salutary warning. Insofar as it does not reduce it to a version of necrophilia, the creative writing position on critical self-reflexivity as a potential blockage to action — creative or political — is compelling. But why is it that at their most oppositional, these and other critiques of self-reflexivity are predicated on a construction that turns it into an unnecessary, arbitrary, or stultifying practice?

What is so disturbing and uncomfortable about critical reflexivity? Why do the critical questioning and the introspective analysis it requires generate such suspicion and anxiety? How are we to read these responses? Do they indicate that the project of teaching reading and writing as interconnected activities is unreasonable, utopian, oblivious to the material circumstances within which it is to be carried out? Should we decide, as Coles did in the 1970s, that it might be opportune to scale down this project of reading in the composition classroom from reading the interconnectedness of reading and writing to the reading of the assignments and student papers? (What does this suggest about teachers' and students' ability to engage this task?) Does my critique of the ways most "integrationists" in the 1980s carried out the project of eliding the schism between reading and writing, literature and composition, confirm the wisdom of Coles's solution?

I see how it might be possible to answer all these questions in the affirmative. And I become despondent. My current historical work in pedagogy, work that I undertook to understand what as a foreigner I found puzzling and disturbing, namely the separation of reading from writing, the proliferation of specialized programs within departments, the reduction of pedagogy from a philosophical science to a repertoire of "tips for teaching," shows that our educational system has consistently opted for simplifying solutions every time it has been confronted with the inherent and inescapable complexity of educational issues. What I find disturbing is that decisions often made for teachers, without the participation of teachers, are subsequently read as indictments of teachers' inadequate intellectual and professional preparation. (One of the most frequently voiced reservations to my project is that "it is too difficult" to carry it out without sacrificing writing to reading.) We cannot afford not to come to terms with the consequences of these streamlining interventions. We need to acknowledge that, for reasons whose complexity we cannot deny but that we can certainly call into question, our scheme of education has consistently and repeatedly skirted the responsibility of nurturing one of the most fundamental human activities — critical self-reflexivity.

Every time I teach reading and writing as interconnected activities, I begin by declaring, by making visible, my teaching strategies and by exposing their rationale. And yet every time it is a struggle for students to see this approach to teaching not as a cynical tendency to tear apart and to discredit the ways they read and write, as an exercise in dissection, or as a paralyzing threat, but rather, the way it is meant, as an attempt at promoting engagement in the kind of self-reflection and self-awareness that they are so often expected to demonstrate but are so seldom given an opportunity to learn.

In *On Literacy*, Robert Pattison argues that the project of developing the critical mind requires "another kind of training not generally available in the American scheme of education" (176). I agree with him, and I believe that we can and must find ways of providing that kind of training even within institutional environments that are opposed to it. Let me suggest that teaching reading and writing as interconnected activities, teaching students how to perform critically, and self-reflexively, those recuperative acts by means of which they can conjecture an argument and can establish a responsible critical dialogue with it, as well as with the text they compose in response to it, might be an approach appropriate to developing the critical mind — an approach that might mark the difference between students' participating in their own education and their being passively led through it.

Works Cited

Atkins, Douglas G., and Michael L. Johnson, eds. *Writing and Reading Differently: Deconstruction and the Teaching of Composition and Literature*. Lawrence, KS: U of Kansas P, 1985.

Bakhtin, M. M. *The Dialogic Imagination: Four Essays by M. M. Bakhtin*. Ed. Michael Holquist. Trans. Caryl Emerson and Michael Holquist. Austin: U of Texas P, 1981.

Bartholomae, David, and Anthony Petrosky. *Ways of Reading: An Anthology for Writers*. 2d ed. Boston: Bedford Books, 1990.

Clifford, John, and John Schilb. "Composition Theory and Literary Theory." *Perspectives on Research and Scholarship in Composition*. Ed. Ben W. McClelland and Timothy R. Donovan. New York: Modern Language Association, 1985.

Coleridge, Samuel Taylor. "On Method." *The Portable Coleridge*. Ed. I. A. Richards. New York: Viking, 1950.

Coles, William E. *Teaching Composing: A Guide to Teaching Writing as a Self-Creating Process*. Rochelle Park, NY: Hayden, 1974.

De Man, Paul. *Blindness and Insight: Essays in the Rhetoric of Contemporary Criticism*. Minneapolis: U of Minnesota P, 1983.

Gadamer, Hans-Georg. *Truth and Method*. New York: Continuum, 1975.

———. *Philosophical Hermeneutics*. Trans. and ed. David E. Linge. Berkeley: U of California P, 1976.

Horner, Winifred Bryan, ed. *Composition and Literature: Bridging the Gap*. Chicago: U of Chicago P, 1983.

Iser, Wolfgang. *The Act of Reading: A Theory of Aesthetic Response*. Baltimore: Johns Hopkins UP, 1978.

———. *The Fictive and the Imaginary: Charting Literary Anthropology*. Baltimore: Johns Hopkins UP, 1993.

Lindemann, Erika. "Freshman Composition: No Place for Literature." *College English* 55 (March 1993): 311–16.

———. "Three Views of English 101." *College English* 57 (March 1995): 287–302.

Pattison, Robert. *On Literacy: The Politics of the Word From Homer to the Age of Rock*. New York: Oxford UP, 1982.

Salvatori, Mariolina. "Towards a Hermeneutics of Difficulty." *Audits of Meaning: A Festschrift in Honor of Ann E. Berthoff.* Ed. Louise Z. Smith. Portsmouth, NH: Boynton/Cook, 1988.

———. "Pedagogy and the Academy: 'The Divine Skill of the Born Teacher's Instincts.'" *Pedagogy in the Age of Politics: Writing and Reading (in) the Academy.* Ed. Patricia A. Sullivan and Donna J. Qualley. Urbana: NCTE, 1994.

———. *Pedagogy: Disturbing History, 1819–1929.* Pittsburgh: U of Pittsburgh P, 1996.

Ray, William. *Literary Meaning: From Phenomenology to Deconstruction.* New York: Basil Blackwell, 1984.

Sherman, William. *John Dee: The Politics of Reading and Writing in the English Renaissance.* Amherst: U of Massachusetts P, 1995.

Tate, Gary. "A Place for Literature in Freshman Composition." *College English 55* (March 1993): 317–21.

———. "Notes on the Dying of a Conversation." *College English 57* (March 1995): 303–309.

MOMENTS OF ARGUMENT: AGONISTIC INQUIRY AND CONFRONTATIONAL COOPERATION

Dennis A. Lynch, Diana George, and Marilyn M. Cooper

[*College Composition and Communication* 48 (February 1997): 61–84.]

Dennis A. Lynch is an assistant professor of rhetoric and composition, director of writing programs, and a member of the graduate committee at Michigan Technological University. Most recently, his work has appeared in *Rhetoric Review.* Diana George is an associate professor in the Department of Humanities at MTU, where she teaches courses in composition pedagogy and theory, cultural studies and composition, visual representation, popular culture, and British literature. She has published many articles and chapters in composition studies, and is the author of *Reading Culture* (1995). Marilyn Cooper is an associate professor of English and director of Graduate Teaching Assistant Education at MTU. She, too, has published widely in composition studies, and her work has most recently appeared in the *Journal of Advanced Composition.*

Students often have difficulty developing responsible arguments that employ the fullest range of critical thinking strategies. Too often, the kind of argumentation that students learn and use is one that reduces complex issues to artificial dualities, which Deborah Tannen describes as "two and only two, diametrically opposed positions." Recognizing that this view of argument will not prepare "students to participate in serious deliberations on issues that face all of us every day," the authors of this article explore "a way of reconceiving argument that includes both confrontational and cooperative perspectives, a multifaceted process that includes moments of conflict and agonistic positioning as well as moments of understanding and communication." Their explanations and descriptions are useful, and help teachers "to see argumentation as a crucial social responsibility — an activity that requires us to position ourselves within complicated and interconnected issues."

Writing teachers have been teaching argument for decades. As a profession, we have taken generations of students through the laws of logic, the etiquette of dispute, and the lessons of preparedness only to receive in return the same stale and flat arguments on the big issues: abortion rights, gun control, affirmative action, and others just as large and just as canned. In their writings, our students fall easily into one of two camps: for or against. They cling to their original positions as if those were sacred to home, country, and spiritual identity. Too frequently absent from these debates is any real knowledge of the issue at hand as anything more than a pointless argument among people who do not care very much about the outcome — except that it is always better, in the classroom as in many other arenas, to be on the winning rather than the losing side.

We don't blame our students. Schooled, as so many of us are lately, on the heated but shallow public debates raging on such television programs as *Firing Line* and *Crossfire,* or the broadside attacks of Rush Limbaugh, or even the sleepy This-Side-Then-That-Side interviews of *MacNeil/Lehrer Newshour,* our students merely follow their models. Students have learned to argue vigorously and even angrily, but not think about alternatives, or listen to each other, or determine how their position may affect others, or see complexities, or reconsider the position they began with, or even to make new connections across a range of possible disagreements. Louis Menand points out that "[o]ne of the techniques we've perfected for screaming at one another — as the linguist Deborah Tannen has recently been complaining — is to divide every discussion, 'Crossfire'-style, into two, and only two, diametrically opposed positions, and to have the representatives of each side blast away at each other single-mindedly until interrupted by a commercial" (76). Hardly a style that will generate new, productive lines of action.

Iris Marion Young locates one source of this pattern of public discourse in what she calls interest-group pluralism. All debates over public policy in our society, she argues, are reduced to debates over the distribution of wealth, income, and material goods, and interest groups are formed to ensure that particular interests get their fair share. "Public policy dispute is only a competition among claims, and 'winning' depends on getting others on your side" (72). This distributive paradigm forces even arguments for ending nonmaterially based oppression and dominance to look like arguments to attain the selfish desires of a particular interest group. Thus, for example, arguments for affirmative action programs appear not as attempts to change unconscious stereotypes that underlie biased hiring practices but as attempts to get more jobs for minorities. Young concludes, "This process that collapses normative claims to justice into selfish claims of desire lacks the element of public deliberation that is a hallmark of the political. A politicized public resolves disagreement and makes decisions by listening to one another's claims and reasons, offering questions and objections, and putting forth new formulations and proposals, until a decision can be reached" (72–73).

What we want to work out in this essay is a way of understanding and teaching argument that prepares students to participate in serious deliberations on issues that face all of us every day. It sometimes seems, in

recent arguments over argument, that we must choose between two contrasting styles of argument, competitive or collaborative, but such a decision is unnecessarily abstract and ignores the historical development of
thought about argument and its role in social democratic processes. Throughout most of this century, as Andrea Lunsford and Lisa Ede argue (39), we
have steadily moved away from argumentation as competition and contest.
Since I. A. Richards defined rhetoric as the study of misunderstanding
(thereby bringing rhetoric closer to hermeneutics), the prevailing sentiment
has been in favor of a more cooperative conception of rhetoric. The ultimate aim of rhetoric should be communication, not persuasion, we are
told. And later, the idea that rhetoric is epistemic and the correlate notions
of rhetoric as inquiry and of writing to learn have continued the same
general effort to expand rhetoric's horizons while diminishing or eliminating altogether the nasty clash of individual intentions that marks much
traditional rhetorical practice and its theory.

More recently, though, some rhetoricians have begun to suspect that the
whole point of argumentation is being lost in our talk about cooperation
and collaboration, that we are losing the value of challenging, opposing,
and resisting "the interplay of social, cultural and historical forces" that
structure our lives (Bizzell, *Discourse* 284). Susan Jarratt, for example,
calls for composition instructors to rethink their objections to agonistic
rhetoric and conflict-based pedagogy. She acknowledges that, at this historical juncture, those who advocate a "nurturing, nonconflictual composition classroom" may feel uneasy with her suggestion ("Feminism" 120).
Indeed, as bell hooks points out (*Talking Back* 53), students may not leave
the class feeling all that comfortable, either. Nevertheless, Jarratt and
others (among them Bizzell, Bauer, Berlin, and Fitts and France) continue
to argue that teachers should take a stronger, less nurturing, and more
confrontational role in the classroom — especially if the aim is to prepare
students to take action in a bureaucratized world that resists change.

Peter Elbow has argued that we neutralize potential hostility by emphasizing the believing game over the doubting game. While this position
encourages students to listen to each other and to think about alternatives, Jarratt points out that it also leaves unexamined the social origins
of difference and untouched the existing structures of privilege and authority ("Feminism" 116–17). Students — as well-schooled in the ideology of
pluralism as in the habits of popular debate — are eager to grant the right
of everyone to their own opinion. A theoretical openness to other perspectives is, though, easily reversed in practice, especially when the situatedness
of perspectives within established power structures is ignored, as when
whites insist that blacks, or men insist that women, be more open to and
accepting of their perspectives.

What we are seeking is a way of reconceiving argument that includes
both confrontational and cooperative perspectives, a multifaceted process
that includes moments of conflict and agonistic positioning as well as
moments of understanding and communication. We want to see argument
as agonistic inquiry or as confrontational cooperation, a process in which
people struggle over interpretations together, deliberate on the nature of
the issues that face them, and articulate and rearticulate their positions
in history, culture, and circumstance. And thus we join with Jarratt in
hoping for writing courses where "instructors help their students to see
how differences emerging from their texts and discussions have more to do
with those contexts than they do with an essential and unarguable indi-
viduality" ("Feminism" 121). Such a conception can remove argument from
the (televised) boxing ring and return it not to the private domestic sphere

but to the many ambiguous public spaces — meeting rooms, hallways, cafeterias, and, yes, classrooms — where it has a chance to become more productive. The question that confronts us now is, what exactly might such a conception of argument look like? What kind of activity are we trying to suggest by the admittedly difficult (if not oxymoronic) expressions "agonistic inquiry" and "confrontational cooperation"?

A New Articulation

Before we describe two different courses in which we attempted to put into practice our understanding of how argument might best be approached in first-year composition, we would like to briefly articulate the theoretical perspective that emerged as we tried to find a new paradigm for the teaching of argument.

Our concern from the start was that, without knowledge of the history behind an issue or those affected or potentially affected by it, or of the complex material causes and potential real effects of the decisions being made, classrooms could easily drive students back into a narrower kind of arguing. Jarratt, in "Feminism and Composition," shows her awareness of such a potential problem when she argues for a distinction between "eristic wrangling" and "disputation." Wrangling takes place, according to Jarratt, between people who position themselves from the start as enemies, whereas disputation acknowledges that conflict also plays a role among friends who argue with one another out of good will. Disputation, which draws on the "ability to move into different positions," should then open up the space needed for more considered judgments and disagreements.

However, the point of Jarratt's distinction often seems on the edge of slipping away, for instance, when she quotes bell hooks urging us to establish in the classroom ". . . an atmosphere where [students] may be afraid or see themselves at risk" ("Feminism" 120). If we emphasize the fear and the risk, we can see the aggressive and agonistic qualities of traditional debate returning to the classroom, together with its narrowness and simplicity. The weight placed by Jarratt on conflict, on the necessary emergence of real differences, and especially on the need for students who have been disempowered to become more "self-assertive" in the classroom may push students toward strategies of simplification as a matter of survival. But if instead we emphasize, as Jarratt later does, a classroom "in which students argue about the ethical implications of discourse on a wide range of subjects and, *in so doing, come to identify their personal interests with others*, understand those interests as implicated in a large communal setting, and advance them in a public voice" ("Feminism" 121, emphasis added), then we hear an echo of John Gage and what we have called a cooperative rhetoric of inquiry.

In an essay that in some interesting ways anticipates Jarratt's position, "An Adequate Epistemology For Composition," Gage suggests that we might clarify our disagreements over the best way to teach argument by attending to the epistemological bases of the modes of argumentation we are considering. Toward this end, he offers his own distinction among three views of argument. The first two views disconnect rhetoric from knowledge — either skeptically or positivistically — and turn it into an artifice or a vehicle. An argument, under both of these views, becomes a mere formal exercise. In the first case, unencumbered by any sense of truth or right, one concentrates on learning and employing those forms that will help one to win or survive. In the second case, one has recourse to rhetorical forms because ideas — truths — still need to be embodied and communicated: argument thus becomes a mere vehicle for leading an audience to a truth known independently of the rhetorical process. The third view, in contrast to the other two, connects rhetoric to dialectic and to the social production of knowledge, and, as we might expect, Gage associates this view with Aristotle:

> From this perspective, rhetoric aims at knowledge, or makes it available. Rather than producing persuasion without reference to truth, rhetoric aims at producing mutual understandings and therefore becomes the basis for inquiry into sharable truths. "The function of rhetoric," Aristotle asserted, "is to deal with things about which we deliberate, but for which we have no rules." ("Adequate Epistemology" 153–55)

Gage thus seeks to contain the eristic impulses within argumentation by linking argument to the production of knowledge — though disagreeing, people cooperate to make connections in the construction of "sharable truths." This is not knowledge in the modernist sense — objective and time-less truth — but a knowledge that is true only insofar as it emerges from the social, cooperative process of argumentation.

People argue, according to Gage, in order to negotiate conflicts and differences. We do not argue in order to express our inner selves or as a fun exercise, though we can approach argument in this way if we so choose. The primary function of argument, therefore, the one Young argues is necessary for public deliberation and that Gage would have us consider as teachers of writing, is to get something done in the world, including the academic world. And given the kinds of issues we tend to discuss in the academic world, according to Gage, we cannot and should not expect to rely on truths or independent formal guarantees that would render the negotiation process mechanical and easy. All we can do is come together (in some fashion), articulate our differences, listen, try hard to understand, acknowledge how thoroughgoing the differences may be, and — and here is Gage's main contribution, as he sees it — not just formulate reasons that defend our initial position, but reformulate those very positions through a process of argument ("Adequate Epistemology" 162). In other words, the real conflicts are already there at the outset of a disagreement, in the way we define the issues and set up our purposes, and thus when teachers ask students to establish their position *before* they interact with those with whom they disagree, teachers inadvertently push students to reproduce their disagreements rather than moving towards negotiated and temporary resolutions of disagreements.

Gage's approach to argument perhaps sounds closer than it probably is to the work of Jarratt, Bizzell, and others who have been critical of a humanist tradition (with its connections to Aristotle) and who look instead to postmodern theories or look behind Aristotle to the sophists. Yet even so, a lingering concern might remain for many who would read (or reread) Gage's work in the present context of composition studies: careful as he is to emphasize the thoroughly social and dialectical nature of his approach to argument, his account still lacks a fully social and political dimension. This is perhaps most visible in his characterization of conflict. When Gage sets his students up to argue with one another, the aim that he assumes will govern their efforts *is* to negotiate conflict — but the conflicts he imag-ines are what he calls "conflicts of knowledge." What is at stake in any argumentative situation for Gage is the current state of one's knowledge or beliefs, and even though he is careful to stress that people, not ideas, are in conflict — the "real people" that he reaches for in his account of argu-ment often seem at the last minute to gently dissolve into mere place holders for the ideas they are committed to. The effect is especially appar-ent when one recalls that the conflicts our students experience are reflected in the structure of our social, political, and economic conditions — and thus are not contained in the minds of individual students. Put otherwise, the social production of knowledge that Gage so engagingly argues for remains a mostly abstract and intellectual affair because the extent to which his students enter into their arguments already positioned unequally itself remains unquestioned.

But if we hesitate to embrace the limited sense of "social" in Gage's social rhetoric of inquiry, neither are we fully satisfied with Jarratt's pedagogy of "productive conflict." In this regard, we intend our provisional and somewhat playful notion of "agonistic inquiry" to delineate an activity that is a social process of negotiating, not "conflicts of knowledge," so much as conflicts of positioning and power — conflicts in which students can discern that something is at stake, someone is affected, and someone has been silenced for reasons that can be determined.

Indeed, the differences among Gage's, Jarratt's, and our positions can perhaps better be seen in the manner in which we each describe the kind of risks we anticipate our students will face in our classrooms. In Gage's contribution to *What Makes Writing Good,* for instance, he asks his students to "risk committing yourself, if only for the time being, to an idea," and he sees such a commitment as a risk because it "means that there will be people who will not agree with you" (100). To argue is to commit yourself, not to others, but to an idea, and to be committed to an idea ensures that you will run into conflicts and disagreements with others. The risk for students, in other words, is that by connecting with an idea they will isolate themselves, which of course is what has motivated Gage's argument from the start: by risking disagreement, we stand to recoup our loss on another level, that of the social production of knowledge.

The strong focus on knowledge that Gage adopts thus threatens to hold students within a temporary state of isolation while they carefully work and rework their thesis-statements. True enough, the consideration a student gives to her opponent's position overcomes some of the effects of that isolation — but only certain intellectual effects. The fact that argumentative activity has been cut off from that which differentiates us — especially from our histories, our cultures, our various positions of power within institutions and social practices — all serves to decrease the chance that our students will feel or find new connections with those affected by an issue, especially with those whose "interests" are not readily observable within the issue as it has been divided up and handed to us historically. The possibility that traditional argumentation, even reconfigured as a rhetoric of inquiry, might still isolate students more than it connects them is finally what led Lester Faigley, in part, to explore the potential of networked classrooms — in spite of or perhaps because of their admitted messiness: "while electronic discourse explodes the belief in a stable, unified self, it offers a means of exploring how identity is multiply constructed and how agency resides in the power of connecting with others and building alliances" (199). We believe that argumentation can and should be approached in a manner that will allow this form of agency to emerge in the classroom, rather than be constrained by a particular epistemological model.

The risk Jarratt's students face is similar to the one Gage anticipates, though it is tinged with a much stronger sense of loss or threat. She also asks her students to accept the risk of encountering disagreement, to risk a public display of difference, but she anticipates much more in such a risk — much more struggle, tension, confusion, anger, embarrassment, condescension, reprisal, intractability. When Jarratt calls for a renewed commitment to "serious and rigorous critical exchange" between students, and also between teachers and students, we sense that her aim is not just to get her students to reconsider a few beliefs or opinions. Her aim is to position students in a manner that will challenge who they are — positions they might enjoy or suffer. The risk of not being connected with others, of learning that others disagree with you, thus becomes intensified for Jarratt's students, increasing the likelihood that disagreement will turn into direct challenge.

Because we are sympathetic to Jarratt's concerns — especially regarding the "unequal positioning" some people enjoy over others when arguing within institutional settings — we appreciate the urge to intensify the risks her students might experience in her classroom and the desire to make differences and disagreements more real and more risky. From our perspective, though, the risk is not merely that your social position and identity may be challenged, or not merely that someone may disagree with your intellectual position, or not even that you may lose the argument; the risk is also that you may become different than you were before the argument began. Serious argumentation requires a willingness to see things differently and to be changed in and through the dialogic process. As Gage points out, argumentation enables us to reformulate our positions through our interactions with those with whom we are in conflict; as Jarratt emphasizes, those positions are not just intellectual ones but positions of power and identity that come out of real histories.

This kind of change is not easy. In *Teaching to Transgress*, bell hooks acknowledges the pain in this process and the consequent need for teachers to show compassion:

> There can be, and usually is, some degree of pain involved in giving up old ways of thinking and knowing and learning new approaches. I respect that pain. And I include recognition of it now when I teach, that is to say, I teach about shifting paradigms and talk about the discomfort it can cause. (43)

Eloise Buker points out that the change we go through in order to understand another person or perspective is "often accomplished only through struggle," and the threat of struggle always carries with it the reflex action of retrenchment, a retreat back into isolation and defended difference. We believe that students will risk such changes only when argumentation is perceived as a social activity through which they, first and foremost, *connect* with others.

We have seen that aspects of the kind of argumentation to which we have been pointing can be found within both Gage's and Jarratt's fully articulated positions: Gage moves us toward an understanding of rhetoric as something that requires us to connect and interact with those with whom we disagree; and Jarratt insists that when we do so we must squarely confront the differences among us. Yet the pressure each puts on argumentation — as the production of knowledge (finding a sharable thesis) or as the last hope in a world of unspeakable injustices — tends to obscure these insights and thus to reduce, rather than to enhance, the chance that students will experience how argument can facilitate our "ability to move into different positions," generate new relations with others, and thus change both the inner and outer landscapes of our initial disagreements and conflicts.

Our quest to develop a new approach to teaching argumentation began, however, not with these theoretical considerations but rather developed as we together designed courses that tried to instantiate a revised sense of argument as inquiry. The two courses we describe below differ from each other in outline and content, but each course takes as its primary goal to engage students in a kind of writing that moves beyond the "opposing viewpoints," disputatious, display type of argumentation. Both courses avoid, as much as possible, rushing students to defend sides or to decide on a position. Instead, we sought to give students more time to learn and think about the issues they were engaging, with the idea in mind that in the process they will recognize that the positions we take — especially the first, easy positions that we have "accepted" — usually have been socially, culturally, and historically determined and, not coincidentally, usually have unforeseen consequences for others, others whose positions are often not even represented by the manner in which the issues are handed down to us ("pro and con").

At the same time, we wanted students to have the chance to discover that complex issues have the potential to involve us in unexpected alliances through which we can open ourselves to new possibilities and responsibilities. What we are about to offer, we acknowledge, is not so much a specific method of teaching argument that can be followed, step by step, as an approach, or a loose affiliation of approaches. Our discussion is instead meant as a part of an ongoing project we share with others to rethink the role of argument in the writing curriculum, especially as we attempt to answer the demand that our writing courses help prepare students to deal with the real conflicts that face all of us in society today.

What's Wrong with the Washington Redskins?

> What the government did to the Cherokee Indians was cruel and unusual punishment. No one should be forced off their land and then forced to travel hundreds of miles. On top of this one third of their population died along the way. Even though this type of thing would never happen in modern day, we can look back now and critique the action of the government. I feel sorry for the Indians, but if the government had not done this, America would not be what it is today. If Indians still owned most of the United States, America would be a third world country.

The first-year MTU student whose work is excerpted above is not exceptional in his assessment that bad things just happen on the road to progress. This is the sort of comment that is normal in many courses, at least in Michigan's Upper Peninsula, that deal with issues of American Indian rights or the history of westward expansion. This student was not taking such a course, however. He was in a second term composition course and was asked to write a short response to a passage from *The Education of Little Tree*. That he chose to stake out a position is less interesting to us, in our discussion of argument, than is the sense we have that he feels that there is no real issue at hand. History is history. Bad things happen to good people. Let's get on with our lives. The course we will describe in the next few pages was designed partially in response to that easy way in which first-year students often seem to dismiss the many issues that surround them daily, in the news, in classes, in work situations, even in the most mundane kinds of arenas — like what to name a football team.

In this writing course, which focused on the issue of using Indian mascot names and logos for sports teams, we began working essentially from argument out: we asked students to read and to summarize two extremely opposed positions presented in two articles: "Indians Have Worse Problems," by syndicated columnist Andy Rooney, and "Crimes Against Humanity," by Cherokee activist and critic Ward Churchill. Many students found Rooney's arguments (even such claims as "American Indians were never subjected to the same kind of racial bias that blacks were," or, "While

American Indians have a grand past, the impact of their culture on the world has been slight") as reasonable, even persuasive. By contrast, many were offended by Ward Churchill's charge that "the use of native names, images and symbols as sports team mascots and the like is, by definition, a virulently racist practice" (43). But by far, the most consistent response of the class, an honors section, was that the question of Indian mascot names was a non-issue. Several students, for example, wrote that demonstrations over mascot names were publicity stunts from a radical group of Indians who did not represent the majority. Moreover, the class made the charge that this issue was just another example of PC at work. Why should anyone care what a team calls itself?

It seemed to us that this was a good start for the approach to argument we had in mind. The question, "Why should anyone care?" was precisely the kind of question we wanted students to ask — and answer. Yet, at this moment in the course we also had to contend with the fact that our students were oscillating in their relation to the issue, oscillating between disengaging from the issue — calling it PC and a non-issue — and throwing themselves into a heated defense of using Indian mascot names. Clearly Ward Churchill's charges had threatened something very close to them, perhaps their loyalties to school, team, tradition, even national identity. Since team and school mascot names function to unite students' and fans' identities, in effect building both public and private loyalties, the issue of changing the name of a team can easily become tied to those and other loyalties. Such an issue threatens to polarize students as they take sides and doggedly defend their "camp" — which is precisely the behavior we had hoped to avoid. That attachment to "what is" over a willingness to debate "what might be the implications of" accounts, at least in part, for the sort of positioning we see in the passage above. To that student, America is fine as it is. This is his country. If anything else had happened, we would have some other, some less developed country — a country not his. Loyalty is a complicated bit of the puzzle of human reasoning.

What is more, an issue like the mascot one seems, for many students, to hit at political loyalties. As we noted above, by the second day of this assignment, students were already dismissing its relevance as simply another "PC debate." This turn was perhaps inevitable, for, as Gerald Graff points out, "In literature and the humanities, cultural nationalism has been the main organizing principle since the romantic period, when the doctrine became established that the quality of a nation's language and literature was the touchstone of its greatness as a nation" (151). This kind of loyalty plays itself out easily enough every time we bring cultural studies, cultural critique, or a multicultural agenda to the writing class. Such an agenda threatens nationalism. As Graff reminds us, "The rule seems to be that any politics is suspect except that kind that helped us get where we are, which by definition does not count as politics" (156). Thus, our students' easy initial acceptance of Rooney's column and their discomfort with Churchill's article. They found Rooney abrasive but acceptable and Churchill merely abrasive. (We might add here that both are openly abrasive.)

This is, of course, a paradoxical predicament for a class given over to the study of argumentation. The presumed goal is to critically examine not just one's beliefs but the decisions that are being made in our communities. The more those decisions touch students' loyalties, though, the more likely students are to retrench, not listen to others, resort to quips, and as a result lose sight of the complexity of the issue under consideration. We chose this moment of oscillation, then, to ask the students to write out (in their notebooks) their own position in this debate. Then we asked them to put that position statement away and to start a different kind of work.

At the end of the term, when they did share with their instructor that initial notebook entry, students' own inability to see any issue worth discussing here was clear. The most common reaction was anger: Indians, one student wrote, just "have to have something to cry about." They should, "GROW UP, STOP CRYING, AND GET ON WITH LIFE!" Others echoed that attitude. One admitted that when she thought of Indians, she got a picture of fat, lazy drunkards who live off the government. The class, as a whole, certainly gave the impression that they felt those arguing over mascot names were "making a big deal out of nothing." They didn't understand why anyone could get upset over such a topic. And, they felt that American Indians were simply holding onto a past they no longer had a right to. One student, for example, wrote that he lives in Keweenaw Bay, where one band of Ojibway is located, and he resents the fact that the Indians there can haul "thousands of pounds of lake trout from Keweenaw Bay with motorized boats, instead of canoes and commercially made nets, instead of hand woven ones." A few stated very simply that Indian people ought to assimilate and get it over with. Many agreed with the student who said, during class discussion, that the Indians have lost the big battle, and they have to understand what it means to lose. The instructor, by contrast, was not convinced that her students knew the many consequences of "losing." The class seemed comfortable with the status quo, unwilling to poke around into an argument they wished had never been brought up in the first place.

These vigorously negative stereotypes might surprise a few readers who see more romanticized images as the current media stereotype, especially from such recent popular programs and films as *Northern Exposure, Dr. Quinn: Medicine Woman, Pocahontas, Dances with Wolves,* and *The Last of the Mohicans,* to name a few. Jeffrey Hanson and Linda Rouse explain this kind of contradictory stereotyping of American Indians as common. They discovered that, although the students they studied reported that most of the information they have about American Indians came from the media, the stereotype they eventually formed depended on where they were living. If they lived in areas where American Indians were not a visible minority and were not competing for resources, the stereotype tended to be overwhelmingly positive and romanticized. If they lived in a region (such as South Dakota, Wisconsin, or Minnesota), where Indian people did constitute a visible minority and might compete for resources, the stereotypes were severely negative. Our students' responses to this issue are typical of the kinds of responses Rouse and Hanson discovered among students living in this part of the country.

For this section of the term, then, the class sometimes angrily argued that we had entered into a silly, even meaningless debate. They claimed no interest in and, several of them, no knowledge of the ways each side might argue their position. And, yet, when asked to list arguments from both sides of the discussion, students found it much easier to outline the position represented by Rooney than that represented by Churchill. For the instructor, that meant that either Rooney's position was the position most available in the popular press, or that students' own loyalties or stereotypes were interfering with their ability to understand other positions.

The next step in this assignment, then, was to begin investigating the many issues, questions, and concerns that surround the arguments set forth in Rooney's and Churchill's articles. In an attempt to get students beyond polarized debate, we asked them not to look for more arguments for or against using Indian mascot names. Instead, we wanted them to ask different questions — questions that would direct their attention more broadly to the people involved in the discussion, what matters to those people, and how the debate got to the Rooney-Churchill level. Then we asked them to start looking for some possible answers to these questions: Why would anyone argue over something as seemingly harmless as a name? Why does anyone think it is an issue at all? Obviously, it wasn't just an issue with Indian people, or Andy Rooney, the Cleveland Indian fans, and others would not be so resolute in their determination to keep what they considered theirs. The argument came from somewhere, and it was about something more than naming teams. Where did it come from? What was it about? Our first strategy, then, was to ask students to question the concepts they were using (the significance of naming), to situate the issue historically (how did the problem develop?), and to find analogous problems from the past in order to resist coming to closure too quickly.

For the next six weeks, the students did research that might have seemed far afield of the initial argument. Goaded by Rooney's assertion that American Indians had contributed little to contemporary culture, they learned and wrote about separate Indian cultures. In response to Churchill's question of why it seems so much easier these days to use Indian names in ways we would not use other group names, they did research on reservation schools and acculturation — along the way learning what Richard Henry Pratt meant when he declared it a necessity that "[t]he Indian must die as an Indian in order to live as a man." During this part of the course, several students did work on stereotyping and its effects. As a result, one student compared the arguments over Indian mascot names and symbols to arguments in the sixties and seventies when a number of African American stereotyped product names and logos were changed. Another student ran across articles detailing the controversy over Crazy Horse Malt Liquor and was prompted by that controversy to learn more about Crazy Horse. He had heard the name all his life and knew nothing of the man. The student who shouted in all caps to Indian people to GROW UP! found there was much more to get over than he had anticipated. After watching *In the White Man's Image,* this student wrote,

> After watching the tape on the Indian school, I was shocked when I heard an Indian voice say that after the school, they wanted to be good and live in wood houses and settle down. They taught the Indians that their old ways were bad. I think this is horrible. It helps to destroy the heritage of the Indians.

In his paper, he acknowledged the truth that most team supporters quite honestly do not intend to demean Indian people with mascot names, but he pointed out that the intention is not necessarily the effect. He quoted Indian activist and songwriter John Trudell who told the class, "There are a million ways to put a people down and using their names and rituals is just one way." What this student did, then, was to try to understand why some people might defend the status quo while others see it as "a virulently racist practice" (Churchill).

At the end of the term, students wrote about the experience of using argument as a tool of intellectual inquiry. In portfolio cover letters, most said they had not really changed their initial position on the argument (though now most simply said that if a name offends the group named, it ought to be dropped), and they still thought the argument was a trivial one. What had changed, however, was why they thought it trivial. In the process of questioning the issue — what matters? why does naming seem both so serious and so trivial? — they felt they had discovered other, more significant (historically and culturally informed) issues within this one.

They weren't ready to give either Andy Rooney or Ward Churchill the nod in terms of who they thought had "won" this debate, but they did see something much more profound embedded within the terms of the debate. One student wrote that, far from learning to keep his opinion to himself (as he had been taught to do in high school), this work had taught him that he had to more carefully understand his position and its consequences. He wrote, "[t]he research I did for essay 3 made me want tò run and tell the world how I felt about the mascot issue. So I did. I was rewarded when upon reading my paper in front of the class, everyone seemed interested in it." This was the student who had done his work on Crazy Horse.

We should add that these students did not feel compelled to take the Indians' side in this debate, either. Despite fears expressed by some that introducing political dispute into the classroom is a way of forcing students to accept the instructor's politics, our experience has been that such acceptance is neither easy nor likely. For example, in this course, one student who began the class angrily declaring that Indians had to accept the fact that they were the ones who lost, wrote.

> I feel I have succeeded in showing that one of the reasons that this topic is an issue is that the American mainstream and the Indians are two separate cultures. The two most important things that I have learned from this course [are] that it is all right to think for yourself and form educated opinions . . . [and] that you have to look at every issue from many different perspectives .

He remained steadfast in his belief that the only way for this issue to be resolved would be for Indian people to accept assimilation as a goal (a position that certainly did not reflect the instructor's politics), but he no longer thought of assimilation as an easy or natural consequence of having lost the big battle. He had, in other words, uncoupled his conclusion that Indians must accept assimilation from the myth of the big battle and reconnected it to his emerging thoughts about culture and cultural conflicts. What he makes of that achievement may well take years to fully realize.

It is true that what these students ended up writing might look less like argument, as we have come to know it, and more (depending on the student's choice of topic) like analysis. And, yet, the course does not avoid argument, either. The kind of assignment we have been describing acknowledges the flat debate then leaves it alone. At the same time, the assignment leads students to an understanding that a more complex argument might be made possible through ongoing inquiry. Too many classroom strategies, too many textbooks, insist that students learn to take hold of and argue a position long before they understand the dimensions of a given issue. We would much rather our students learn to resist doggedly defending their position too soon in the discussion. That is not to suggest that students do not hold positions very early in this process. Certainly, they do, and they most likely want to defend and keep intact those positions. We won't deny that. For the students in this class, however, their initial position statements were never used during whole-class discussion. Those early statements remained theirs to do with as they pleased. Primarily, students seemed to use them as a starting point for their research or as a way to identify questions within the broader topic of the course. As their instructors, we were more interested (and we believe the class was, too) in what students learned about the issues surrounding this debate than which side they initially took in it. Moreover, we were interested in helping students realize the complications embedded in discussions on even seemingly uncomplicated issues like what to name a football team.

A River Runs Through It

> Eventually, all things merge into one, and a river runs through it. The river was cut by the world's great flood and runs over rocks from the basement of time. On some of the rocks are timeless raindrops. Under the rocks are the words, and some of the words are theirs. I am haunted by waters.
>
> – Norman MacLean, *A River Runs Through It* (113)

Generally speaking, water is not a topic people in the upper midwest spend a lot of time thinking about, much less arguing about. Except in bad winters when water mains freeze, we don't worry much about where our water is coming from and whether we will have enough. So, when we announced to a first-year writing class that the topic we would be focusing on for the quarter was water resources, they were distinctly nonplused. But a few weeks into the course, many of them wrote comments like the following:

> Before entering HU 101, water resources rated just as high as the Royal Family on my list of importance. Now, after reading a few articles on the subject, I think about it quite often. What amazes me most about water resource management is its complexity.

Like the rivers of North America, the issue of water resources flows through a complex array of political positions and priorities in our society. From the James Bay hydroelectric project in Quebec to the California aqueduct, from the draining of the Everglades to proposals for a pipeline to pump Alaskan water to Texas, the questions of who owns the water in North America and how it should be used are the concern of agribusiness, golfers, small farmers, white-water rafters, mining companies, American Indians, fishermen, electrical companies, environmentalists, and urban residents, among others, and the conflicting demands of these interests result in strange and shifting alliances among groups who are often opposed on other issues. In arguing in this arena, students find it hard to locate preconstructed positions they can accept and argue for. Instead, they must sort through and negotiate competing concerns in order to construct a position they feel is justified and they want to defend.

Of course, any issue, including water resources, can be cast in the point-counterpoint argument mode: America's Rivers — Should we dam them for power or let them run free? When differences of opinion are polarized and sensationalized in this way, the emphasis in argument shifts from the issue to the skills and personalities of the combatants and the formal structures of argumentation. And while these are always a part of argument, and contribute a lot to the enjoyment some people find in argument, focusing on stark controversies at the expense of the complexities of an issue is also a way of evading or covering up the painful and complex problems that face us and that we must resolve if we want to have a society that's worth living in. We wanted to show students that arguments do matter, that the positions they take matter to them in their daily lives, and that argument serves a useful function in society, the function of helping us all make better decisions, together. We called the kind of writing they would be doing deliberative discourse, not to take the focus off the differences that lead to disputation but to emphasize that such differences are legitimate and deeply felt and must be talked about in a serious way.

We were again, in this course, concerned to not push students prematurely into taking a position on issues they knew little about and thus cared little about. Certainly, the aim of argument is to influence specific decisions in a specific context, to recommend a particular course of action, and certainly it is the pressure imposed by the need for specific decisions — should we enact NAFTA? should we raise the sales tax or the income tax to finance public schools? — that sometimes leads us to simplify what we know are complicated issues and to wrangle over them heatedly. But this is only one moment in the activity of arguing, and in many ways the end of argument. To see this moment as the whole of argumentative writing is to risk seeing all decisions as final, all positions as absolute or even natural, to see argument, paradoxically, as somehow antithetical to change.

It takes time to learn about an issue, to learn what you really think about it and how it affects your life and the lives of others. On the first day, we talked about all the ways water was important to us: in raising crops and in otherwise providing us with food; in mining resources; in manufacturing products; in disposing of waste; in transporting people and products; in providing electrical power; in providing habitats for other species, recreational opportunities, and spiritual relaxation; and in simply sustaining our lives. We then handed out the assignments for the course. We asked them to write four related papers in which they were to construct a position they believed in on a specific issue of their choice involving water resources. The assignments were designed to give students a chance to reflect on their ideas and arguments as they wrote and read and discussed and rewrote; in essence, the first three papers were simply drafts, albeit "good" drafts, steps in the process of developing a carefully considered argument for a carefully constructed position in the fourth and final paper.

The first assignment asked them simply to explore the general issue of water resources and their reactions to it, to find what aspects of this issue interested them. Some of the questions we asked them to think about in this paper were: What aspects of this issue relate to your interests and plans and how do they relate? What experiences have you had that shape how you feel about this issue? What aspects of the issue do you find interesting at this point and why? What surprised you in what we have read and discussed? What else would you like to find out about this issue? The purpose here was for them to find some way to connect to the issue, whether intellectually, experientially, or emotionally.

Many of our midwestern students who personally experienced the decline of farming in this region were struck by one of Marc Reisner's conclusions in *Cadillac Desert:* "In a West that once and for all made sense, you might import a lot more meat and dairy products from states where they are raised on rain, rather than dream of importing those states' rain" (517). One student who grew up on a farm in Michigan explained that his stepfather had committed suicide when the price of milk declined and he couldn't repay his bank loans. His experience clearly affected how he responded to much of the material we looked at in the course: he was especially sympathetic to the plight of the long-term small rancher in Nevada who lost his water to the newly irrigated large farms down the valley, to the situation of the olive farmer in California who was put out of business by Prudential Insurance's cornering the market with their five-thousand acre farm near Bakersfield, and to the Hispanic farmers in *The Milagro Beanfield War* in their fight against the developers.

Other students found less heart-rending personal connections to the issues involving water. A student who lived on a lake investigated the state laws that allowed the owner of the water rights of the lake to manipulate the water level to maximize the hydroelectric power his dam could produce. A student with a passion for golf looked into water conserving designs for the abundant golf courses in western deserts. Some students were simply moved by a question of fairness: several wrote about the treatment of the Cree Indians by the developers of the James Bay hydroelectric project. And others were interested in the technological problems involved, like the students who wrote about new methods of irrigation and power generation. The students' level of commitment to the issue — and then to the position they constructed — thus varied in strength and nature, but all understood that deliberative discourse required some kind of commitment on their part.

The second assignment asked students to begin to stake out a position they found persuasive on a specific issue, although we cautioned them to discuss *all* the positions that they found persuasive and to explain how these positions might conflict with one another and how these conflicts might be resolved. We also emphasized, both in the instructions and in comments on their drafts, that this paper was only the beginning of the process of constructing a position, that they would next need to look at the position they had stated and think about such things as whether it really represented what they believed in, what sort of actions would follow from this position, whether they really found these actions to be possible and desirable, and what questions their position raised that they would need to investigate further.

When one student, a very skilled writer, handed in the first draft of this second paper, he told the instructor he had the outline of his final paper, and all he would have to do in the rest of the course was to add in a little more information from the library. He had formulated a logical problem-solution argument: since irrigated farming in the west made no economic sense, the government should buy out western agricultural concerns and subsidize the development of more agriculture in the midwest and east. When we suggested that there were a couple of serious problems with his solution, namely that the federal government most assuredly did not have the money in these times of national debt to finance such a plan, and that people who had lived and farmed in the west for generations might not appreciate having their livelihoods eliminated in this way, he said that he was ignoring these aspects of the situation for the purposes of his argument. We said that a solution that wouldn't work isn't a solution at all, that there was more to taking a position than constructing a clear thesis and a logically argued paper.

He seemed somewhat taken aback; clearly, this strategy of quickly taking stock of the issue and offering a novel and definitive solution had worked well for him in past writing courses. We pressed our questions because we wanted to push him (and the other students) beyond the form of argument that ignores real conflicts by turning them into abstract problems to be solved or managed. In his second draft of the second paper and in the third paper, he analyzed the complexities of the situation more thoroughly. He discovered that financial incentives for more efficient use of water by farmers could and were being paid for by urban water users in the west rather than the federal government. He discovered that zoning, the establishment of agricultural districts, and cluster residential development were possible solutions to the increasing pressure of development that drives up the property values of agricultural land beyond the levels where farming is economically feasible in the midwest.

The third assignment asked students to reconsider their initial positions from the point of view of someone who would not agree with them. We told students that the reason to look at opposing positions when constructing an argument was not so much to anticipate and counter objections as it was to learn more about the issue and thus to make your own position more reasonable and practical, to take into account not only your own interests and desires and experiences but also those of others.

We had a chance to make this point clearer one day in another class that was similarly structured but focused on a different topic. A female student stated unequivocally that it was essential that one parent in a family not work so that someone would be home when the kids got back from school; a male student countered that both his parents worked and that he had not suffered at all from coming home to an empty house. The two debated this issue rather heatedly for about five minutes with the rest of the class throwing in encouraging comments or reactions. She argued that she would have felt insecure and unloved in his position; he countered that he developed a strong sense of independence and still felt close to his parents because of the time they did find to spend together. When he finally said it was clear he couldn't win this argument because she always had something to say in response, we instead asked the class to look at what had happened differently, not as simply an argument to be won or lost but as an opportunity to learn about different perspectives — to learn that your experiences and needs are not necessarily the same as those of others and that there are benefits and drawbacks to the differing decisions made by parents.

In composing this third assignment we reminded ourselves that the risk in argument is not that you may lose but rather that you may change. We asked them to think about the concerns of someone who held a position that they did not find to be persuasive and explain why someone might hold this position. Then we asked them to discuss what they might learn from this position: What beliefs and feelings did they find they could sympathize with, even if they did not agree with them? What experiences did they learn about that might help them see new aspects of the issue? How did some of the concerns expressed relate to some of their concerns? We asked these questions knowing full well that our students were in the midst of working and reworking their relations to the world around them and that our questions might contribute to that work by asking them to connect with others' concerns and needs. We also knew full well the rhetorical force of the questions we asked; thoughtfully pursued, these questions could and did prompt changes in our students.

The student who was so concerned with the plight of small farmers began his writing by adamantly opposing corporate farming, but he really did not know why he opposed corporate farming — except that it put small traditional farmers out of business and he thought that this was unfair. In the course of his work on his papers, he came across a statement by René Dubos in an essay by Edward Abbey ("farming as a way of life is a self-sustaining, symbiotic relationship between man and earth") that gave him a way of talking about the difference in attitude toward the land and toward their work he felt between traditional small farmers and corporate agribusinesses. But at the same time, he developed an understanding of the place of corporate farming in the economic system of the country. In a statement he wrote at the end of the course, he explained:

> My position on the topic of water at first was corporate farms are no good and we shut them down completely. As we read articles and wrote papers I slowly learned how complex our economic system is. I didn't realize all the jobs that would be lost and how it would affect California's economic system. Also I finally realized the fact that corporate farms just didn't appear out of nowhere. They developed over time. . . . The corporate farms that should be kept after and be taxed super high are conglomerates like Pru-

dential, [which] would possibly force them to sell their land to people who care and respect the land and soil. These are the corporate farms that don't care for the land and if the land becomes worthless they just buy land somewhere else and they say "oh well we lost a couple of acres of land we can just write it off as a loss." I guess I'm still against corporate farms but mostly only them being owned by conglomerates.

The student who lived on a lake came to sympathize with the owner of the water rights' desire to make a living through the sale of hydroelectric power, and he connected this situation to that of a western water dispute between a rancher and alfalfa farmers. Instead of recommending government regulation, as he had started out doing, he argued instead that people need to learn to work together so that all can make a living and be satisfied that their water is being used efficiently.

The last assignment asked students to pull together all that they had learned from writing and rewriting the first three papers, from their readings, and from our work in class. By then they had all learned a lot — and so had we — not only about the specific issue they had been researching and analyzing, but also about different attitudes toward water issues in general and different concerns that needed to be taken into account. They had lots of their own writing to read over and reflect on, to revise and reuse. They had, in short, a good place from which to begin constructing a thoughtful and informed argument. Constructing a position, we told them, means sorting through for yourself the various questions and problems and values involved in an issue and coming to a decision you can stand up for.

What this sequence of assignments allowed students to do, then, was to take some time with a single issue, to really think about it, to investigate what was involved, to respond to it in more than one way, to make assertions about it and then reconsider those assertions, to risk changing how they thought about the things that mattered to them and what they might do in the future. And students did, for the most part, change their thinking about the issues they dealt with, although, as with the students in the course discussing mascot names, they did not simply shift sides or take on the instructor's position. Despite a great deal of skepticism expressed by the instructor, the golf aficionado still argued that the desert was a good place to situate golf courses, as long as they were correctly designed. The student who first proposed that western agriculture be abandoned still argued in his final paper that we must reverse the trend toward dependence on western agriculture, but the solution he offered was much more complex — and much more realistic. In a statement about his paper, he observed, "I initially thought that farming in the desert was completely ludicrous and had no place in crop production. I've since learned that, if done correctly, irrigating farming can be a part of American farming for a long time." In his paper, he argued that "irrigating farmers in the American southwest are going to have to adapt to their regions pending water shortages," and that "planned rural developments" in the midwest "are needed to ensure that these lands remain available for farming." Almost all of the students in this class arrived at extremely complex positions, often so complex that they had to struggle hard to express them in any coherent way. But also, more importantly, students developed positions that mattered to them and that dealt with real world problems in a realistic way.

Pushing students to develop positions that take into account the complexities of real world issues not only moves argumentative writing into a more serious realm, away from display or eristic debate, it also gives them a sense of how their academic work can connect with and help them understand their everyday lives. One of the number of students who wrote about the impact of the James Bay hydroelectric project on the lifestyle of the Cree Indians attended a local round table discussion about sustainable development as part of her preparation for writing her final paper. What she learned there was more than just support for her position: "When I went to the Round Table Meeting on Monday night my thoughts about this paper strengthened even more. My feelings were really true, they weren't made up by reading about the subject in magazine articles."

Asking students to research issues and to learn from people they disagree with does not prevent them from taking strong positions, though it does result in positions that are more reasonable and thoughtful. Their work is a form of collaborative inquiry, but it is still argument, too, in that it negotiates serious differences and recommends a course of action. We also found that bringing conflicts into the classroom does not necessarily mean turning the classroom into a site of conflict. When students are aware that the differences of opinion between them exist in a broader arena — that these differences are not just their own opinions but arise from historical, social, and cultural conditions — they do not feel they need to argue so fiercely and single-mindedly, and they can take the time to listen to other voices and rethink their positions.

By Way of a Conclusion

Perhaps the most frustrating, though not surprising, thing we learned from our two courses was that the very things we set out to resist — two-sided issues, the rush to assert a thesis, and the concentration on forms — returned again and again, if we were not careful. Just as so many argument readers tell students that pro-and-con arguments are too facile and yet go on to organize their chapters in terms of pro-and-con (or speak in ways that assume students "want to take a side"), we found ourselves worrying whether our students' "positions" were clear enough, or whether they had a controversial enough "thesis." Even our examples betray the obvious, namely, that once you ask students to write through their interest in an issue, the assumption becomes that they will have a position that stands against, is differentiated from, someone else's position. And it is easier to grasp one's position, think it through, and present it to others if it is conceived in terms of an opposition.

We thus saw (and tried to understand) the forces that drove us and our students to simplify and to formalize the argumentative situation, and this is why, in the first course, we were not concerned that the papers we received did not all look argumentative. We understood that the initial disagreement (between Rooney and Churchill) would contextualize, for them and for their readers, their effort to answer questions that seemed only tangentially related to the disagreement. Their research did not preclude argument; it was infused with the initial sense of argument, and, what is most important, their answers served to modify the initial simplicity of the disagreement.

In the second class, on water resources, similar doubts arose. Although we asked students to articulate their "positions," the decision to see their positions as solutions to problems, together with the scrutiny given the solutions offered (and together with the relatively "untopical" nature of the issue), encouraged students to reconfigure the conflicts, to bring in other perspectives, other complications, which then served to decenter the original disagreement in a fresh (and more complex) direction. Thus, in one case the issue shifted from "irrigated farming in the western states: yes or no?" to "how can we tilt the balance of farming back to the midwestern states (which have a natural supply of water) in a manner that increases the efficiency of western farming and discourages the selling off of good farm land to developers in the midwest?"

In our approach to argument, we share concerns with both cooperative and neosophistic rhetorics. Although we too want to teach the conflicts, at the same time we do not want to turn the classroom into the place where conflicts between students or between students and teachers erupt — not because we are reticent to allow emotion or turmoil into our classrooms, and not because we think all classrooms should be nurturing, but because we suspect, for now at any rate, that the desire to see results in the form of "critical action," when pressed too single-mindedly, may backfire and reduce a much needed understanding of the complexity of those conflicts. Wanting to have something to say and (desperately) needing to have something to say in self-defense can be productive under certain circumstances. But when arguments are entered into hastily, the complexity of the issues is often lost, and with it (we might add) the basis for introducing important, higher level concepts such as ideology, multiple subjectivity, and contingent foundations.

Neither do we wish to ignore or banish the different experiences and commitments that students bring with them into the classroom, for the expression and investigation of these differences is crucial to understanding the complexities of the problems we want to do something about. Conflicts have histories and are embedded in more or less permanent power structures; decisions affect different people differently and have consequences that go beyond immediate situations; differences are rarely (if ever) brought permanently into consensus. What is important, to our minds, in teaching students to deal with conflict is that they experience the process of constructing a complex, historically knowledgeable position in light of what matters to, and what will result for, those affected by the positions taken.

If we believe that the writing classroom is a place to engage in serious intellectual inquiry and debate about the questions that trouble our everyday lives, we need to think again about our approach to argument. We need to see argumentation as a crucial social responsibility — an activity that requires us to position ourselves within complicated and interconnected issues. We need to see it as a complex and often extended human activity, or, rather, as an array of human activities, including institutionalized formal debate, legal trials, shouting matches that threaten to end in fistfights, conversational games of one-upsmanship, disagreements among friends, and extended deliberations within a community over what course of action to pursue. We need to see it not just as a matter of winning or losing but as a way to connect with others which may lead to change, not only in the world but also in ourselves. But, most of all, we need to see it as a means of coming to decisions, a way of getting things done in the world, that includes moments of agonistic dispute, moments of inquiry, moments of confrontation, and moments of cooperation.

Works Cited

Bauer, Dale M. "The Other 'F' Word: The Feminist in the Classroom," *College English* 52 (1990): 385–97.

Berlin, James. *Rhetorics, Poetics, and Cultures*. Urbana: NCTE, 1996.

Bizzell, Patricia. *Academic Discourse and Critical Consciousness*. Pittsburgh: U of Pittsburgh P, 1992.

———. "Power, Authority, and Critical Pedagogy." *Journal of Basic Writing* 10 (1991): 54–70.

Buker, Eloise A. "Rhetoric in Postmodern Feminism: Put-Offs, Put-Ons, and Political Plays." *The Interpretive Turn: Philosophy, Science, Culture.* Ed. David R. Hiley, James F. Bohman, and Richard Shusterman. Ithaca: Cornell UP, 1991. 218–45.

Churchill, Ward. "Crimes Against Humanity." *Z Magazine* March 1993: 43–48.

Elbow, Peter. "The Doubting Game and the Believing Game." *Writing Without Teachers.* New York: Oxford UP, 1973. 147–91.

Faigley, Lester. *Fragments of Rationality: Postmodernity and the Subject of Composition.* Pittsburgh: U of Pittsburgh P, 1992.

Fitts, Karen and Alan W. France, eds. *Left Margins: Cultural Studies and Composition Pedagogy.* New York: State U of New York P, 1995.

Gage, John. "John Gage's Assignment." *What Makes Writing Good: A Multiperspective.* Ed. William E. Coles, Jr., and James Vopat. Lexington: Heath, 1985. 98–105.

———. "An Adequate Epistemology for Composition: Classical and Modern Perspectives." *Essays on Classical Rhetoric and Modern Discourse.* Ed. Robert J. Connors, Lisa S. Ede, and Andrea A. Lunsford. Carbondale: Southern Illinois UP, 1984. 152–70.

Graff, Gerald. *Beyond the Culture Wars: How Teaching the Conflicts Can Revitalize American Education.* New York: Norton, 1993.

Hanson, Jeffery R., and Linda P. Rouse. "Dimensions of Native American Stereotyping." *American Indian Culture and Research Journal* 11 (1987): 33–58.

hooks, bell. *Talking Back: Thinking Feminist, Thinking Black.* Boston: South End, 1989.

———. *Teaching to Transgress: Education as the Practice of Freedom.* New York: Routledge, 1994.

Jarratt, Susan C. *Rereading the Sophists: Classical Rhetoric Refigured.* Carbondale: Southern Illinois UP, 1991.

———. "Feminism and Composition: The Case for Conflict." *Contending With Words: Composition and Rhetoric in a Postmodern Age.* Ed. Patricia Harkin and John Schilb. New York: MLA, 1991. 105–24.

Lunsford, Andrea A., and Lisa S. Ede. "On Distinctions between Classical and Modern Rhetoric." *Essays on Classical Rhetoric and Modern Discourse.* Ed. Robert J. Connors, Lisa S, Ede, and Andrea A. Lunsford. Carbondale: Southern Illinois UP, 1984. 37–50.

MacLean, Norman. *A River Runs Through It.* New York: Pocket, 1992.

Menand, Louis. "The War of All against All." *The New Yorker* (14 March 1994): 74–85.

Pratt, Richard H. "Remarks on Indian Education." *Americanizing the American Indians: Writings by the "Friends of the Indian" 1880–1900.* Ed. Francis Paul Prucha. Cambridge: Harvard UP, 1973. 277–80.

Reisner, Marc. *Cadillac Desert.* New York: Viking, 1986.

Rooney, Andy. "Indians Have Worse Problems." *Chicago Tribune* 14 March 1991: 14, 92.

Rouse, Linda P., and Jeffery R. Hanson. "American Indian Stereotyping, Resource Competition, and Status-based Prejudice." *American Indian Culture and Research Journal* 15 (1991): 1–17.

Young, Iris Marion, *Justice and the Politics of Difference.* Princeton: Princeton UP, 1990.

APPROACHES TO THE STUDY OF ARGUMENT

Richard Fulkerson

[From *Teaching Argument in Writing.* Urbana: NCTE, 1996. 10–17, 136–38.]

(For biographical information, see page 83.)

Fulkerson's book synthesizes an impressive range of material related to argumentation. Combining a modern version of classical stasis theory with Toulmin's model of argument and with informal logic, Fulkerson's discussions are accessible and meant for class-room writing teachers. In the excerpts reprinted here, Fulkerson offers an overview of the study of argument and describes the characteristics of an effective argument. Fulkerson suggests that writing teachers do not need to devote extensive time to distinguishing between "formal" and "informal" logic or "induction" and "deduction" as forms of reasoning. Instead, he suggests that they think of argumentation as a process used to "forge agreement among disparate voices." Fulkerson discusses nine characteristics that "constitute the best description of a 'good argument' within the public, civic, [or] dialectical context[s]" in which students will be participating. Fulkerson wants teachers and students to think of argumentation as "the chief cognitive activity by which a democracy, a field of study, a corporation, or a committee functions."

Logic is often defined as "the systematic study of argument," but logic now comes in two different varieties: formal and informal. These terms are not unchallenged: To a "formal logician" there is no such thing as a logic that isn't formal. And to some informal logicians, formal logic is seen as essentially useless. Moreover, since informal logic is anything but casual, perhaps it should be "nonformal" (Stephen Toulmin's term is "substantive" logic).

Formal logic is the study of valid and invalid argument forms. The study goes back to Aristotle's *Prior* and *Posterior Analytics.* It has a long, interesting, and complex history, although it did not actually change much until early in the twentieth century (see Kneale and Kneale). Traditional formal logic was concerned specifically with the reasoning form known as the syllogism. The syllogism consists of two statements called premises, which share a common term and a prescribed grammatical structure (involving two nouns and a linking verb), plus a conclusion with that same grammatical structure. If the syllogism is formally correct, the truth of the two premises would guarantee the truth of the conclusion; it doesn't matter what specific content it has — at least it doesn't matter to a logician, who is concerned with validity, not substance. In the early twentieth century, Bertrand Russell introduced a new and much more complex version of formal logic in his and Alfred North Whitehead's *Principia Mathematica,* a sort of logic known as symbolic logic, which includes yet another sort called predicate logic. Neither of these is ever seen outside the pages of logic textbooks, math books, and a few books on the intricacies of computer programming, so they need not concern us here. Readers who are interested in symbolic logic, which looks more like algebra than anything else, may consult any of a number of textbooks, including the ancestor of all contemporary logic books, Irving Copi's *Introduction to Logic,* now in its ninth edition (with Carl Cohen).

It is fairly common for college writing textbooks to introduce some of the paraphernalia of traditional formal logic, usually an abbreviated (and misleading) discussion of the syllogism (see my "Technical Logic, Comp-Logic, and the Teaching of Writing"). I take the position that English teachers need to understand syllogistic reasoning. But I also maintain they should not, repeat *not*, bring syllogisms and their attendant terms into the writing classroom. Doing so isn't useful, it is likely to be confusing, and it takes up a good deal of time.

Ever since Aristotle, it has also been traditional to distinguish deductive from inductive reasoning, with deductive reasoning being the only sort that can be reduced to formalisms. (So formal logicians actually study only deductive logic. They aren't concerned with induction, which they see as dubious reasoning based on messy substantive matters, argument in which even the truth of the premises doesn't guarantee the conclusion.)

Authors of composition textbooks often feel that they need to explain the deduction/induction distinction. Deduction *can* be distinguished from induction. But the distinction is both difficult and unnecessary, and English textbooks that make it generally do it badly, once more illustrating Pope's maxim about the dangers of "little knowledge":

[Scene: a freshman composition class, meeting at an early period, say, 9 a.m. After checking the roll, collecting daily journals, answering a question or two, the teacher begins.]

Teacher: OK, now what was the main subject of the reading assignment for today?

Class: Induction and deduction.

Teacher: Good. And what did your text say they were?

1st Student: [Reading] "Inductive reasoning proceeds from a number of cases to a generalized conclusion: deductive reasoning proceeds from the application of a general principle to a particular case and then to a particular conclusion."

Teacher: OK, that is *exactly* what it says. Now in your own words, what does that mean?

2nd Student: It means that in induction you go from specific instances to a general conclusion, but in deduction you go from the general to the particular.

Teacher: [Not sure of whether they understand or of how to find out without just stating it himself. Inspiration strikes, and he writes two brief paragraphs on the board.] OK, look at these paragraphs; this one starts by claiming that "Honors students are sometimes lazy." Then it develops with three examples. The second gives the same three examples, but puts the main point at the end: "Clearly, even honors students are sometimes lazy."

Class: Yeah, that's it. The first is deductive reasoning; the second is inductive.

Teacher: That's what I suspected. You are confusing the *order* of presentation of an argument with the *type* of reasoning. The reasoning in these paragraphs is identical; both show induction.

2nd Student: But that's what the book said! "Inductive reasoning proceeds from a number of particular cases to a generalized conclusion." That's what your second paragraph does, but the first one is just the opposite. It *has* to be deduction.

The conversation continues, in circles mostly, for the rest of the period. Ironically, the students have just reasoned very well from the definition given in the textbook. They have applied the definition to the teacher's sample paragraphs and come out with a conclusion, in almost classical syllogistic form. The fact that the conclusion is wrong, though validly derived, merely indicates the problems with the book's definition.

The teacher in our scene above is quite correct that, despite the common use of the phrase "going from" in textbook definitions, the order of presentation is irrelevant to the type of argument involved. Whether one presents the premises first and follows with the conclusion or the conclusion first and follows with the premises (or some other combination), the same set of premises and conclusions will always be the same argument. That is one major difference between logical structure and rhetorical structure. Diagraming an argument can help solve this problem since it gets around the question of the order in which the discourse is presented.

But even if it is solved, other problems remain. The general-to-specific distinction, for instance, can be anything but clear. Consider the following argument as an example: "Most college students are in favor of abortion rights, yet abortion rights are immoral, so colleges need to offer courses in which the rights of the fetus are stressed." The word "so" marks off the conclusion for us, and there are clearly two premises, but which is more general, the premise "abortion rights are immoral" or the claim "colleges need to offer courses in which the rights of the fetus are stressed"? I suggest that the whole concept of general and specific is simply inapplicable here (the concepts may apply to noun categories, but not to propositions). If one is defining induction and deduction on the basis of generality and specificity of the premises and claim, then neither definition fits this argument at all.

Furthermore, even logicians use the word "induction" in two rather different senses. In sense one, induction means drawing a conclusion about a group of phenomena by examining a carefully chosen sample of the group and then generalizing from the sample. This is the sort of reasoning we are all familiar with from opinion polls and various statistical studies of causation. And it is probably what most of the English textbook authors have in mind when they define induction. But in sense two — the more important one in logic — "induction" refers to any argument in which the premises are offered as providing some reason to accept the conclusion but not as a guarantee. (It is only in this latter sense that the duality inductive/deductive takes in all of argumentation. If "induction" is used to mean "generalizing from a sample," then the induction/deduction pairing leaves no room for arguments by authority or arguments by sign, among others.)

For instance, suppose someone argued that "John is a senior, and the seniors are dismissed today to rehearse for graduation, so John is probably in the auditorium now." The adverbial hedge "probably" warns a reader: the arguer is not proposing that her premises guarantee her conclusion, but merely that they make it probable. To a logician, such an argument is inductive. Yet, since it moves from a general principle ("the seniors are all at rehearsal in the auditorium") to a specific application, it surely looks like a deductive argument — specifically, a syllogism — to many.

The following attempt to make the distinction, from Rorabacher's *Assignments in Exposition,* is typical:

> In induction we analyze particular instances to establish a general truth, but in deduction we begin with a general truth and from it "deduce," or

> derive, knowledge of a particular instance. Inductively, we progress from the parts to the whole; deductively, from the whole to the parts. (195)

If Rorabacher is defining *induction* and *deduction* as types of reasoning, as the context implies, then her analysis is inaccurately oversimple as explained above. But some teachers and texts have appropriated the terms *induction* and *deduction* to refer not to types of reasoning, but to *orders* of presenting material. Thus a block of discourse that begins with its point and then provides supporting detail is called "deductively ordered," and the same block with the point moved to the end becomes "inductively ordered." Nothing is inherently wrong with this usage. In fact, Fahnestock and Secor have said,

> Here perhaps is the only legitimate use of the terms "inductive" and "deductive" in written argument. They can be used to describe the organization of arguments, the deductive setting out the thesis at the beginning and the inductive disclosing it at the end. ("Teaching Argument" 30)

Using the terms to refer to patterns of presentation rather than to the type of argument presented is perhaps theoretically acceptable, but it is more than a little confusing to students and teachers alike.

A simple solution to these and other problems is not to use the terms "deduction" or "induction" at all. In teaching composition, one gains virtually nothing by them. Since deductive reasoning always requires a universal premise of some sort, and we live in a world of very few universals, students are almost never going to be reasoning deductively anyway. As Aristotle pointed out, the things we argue over are contingent matters. Even in his practical logic textbook, Michael Scriven, one of the leaders of the informal logic movement, tells students,

> You don't need to memorize the terms "inductive" and "deductive"; we mention them only because you may run across them in some of your background reading. A slight juggling of the premises (by adding some unstated ones) and the conclusions can always convert an inductive argument into a deductive one without any essential loss of the "point of the argument," so the distinction isn't one you would want to build very much on; and, to make matters worse, some of the most respected professional logicians in the country today think there aren't any pure examples of deductive argument anyway. (34; also, see Weddle)

Four "Approaches" to Argumentation

Basically, there are four common nonformal approaches to argumentation, and I intend to synthesize at least three of them.

(1) The classical rhetorical approach to argument will be familiar to most composition teachers. It stresses the use of argument to make decisions in a "democracy," especially decisions in law courts and in public forums. It emphasizes certain formulaic elements (which together make up the "classical oration"), and its key source is (once again) Aristotle, who gave us the still important distinction among ethos, pathos, and logos as modes of persuasion, and the much discussed enthymeme as a pattern of reasoning paired with the example. Only implicit in Aristotle, but developed at length by later classical rhetoricians, was the doctrine of stasis theory.

(2) Aristotle is also the origin of an indirect approach to argumentation, fallacy theory. In *On Sophistical Refutations,* Aristotle wrote the first of a good many works in which various unfair (but often effective) argumentative moves were named and defined. To Aristotle, these were ways of arguing that smacked of sophistry. To this day, most introductory logic text-

books, and many composition books, both high school and college alike, include a longer or shorter list of fallacies, complete with elegant Latin names, definitions, and illustrations. This approach to argument is useful, but since it is negative, it is not terribly helpful by itself. It seems to presume that any argument lacking the identified fallacies is a good argument, which isn't true — any more than writing free from grammatical errors is good writing.

(3) In 1958, British philosopher Stephen Toulmin, distressed over what he called the "crude muddle" of deduction and induction, proposed a system of analyzing all arguments that has become known as the Toulmin model. It has not been widely adopted in the field of logic, but soon found fertile ground in speech communication, where it came to dominate argument textbooks. During the past decade, it has also been integrated into a host of composition texts and occasionally hailed as a major breakthrough. The model itself is problematic in some senses, but it provides a useful set of terms for discussing various features of simple arguments.

(4) The newest theory of argumentation is the "pragma-dialectical" approach being developed at the University of Amsterdam by the leaders of the International Society for the Study of Argument (ISSA). This approach presumes that all argument goes on between two (or more) discussants who are engaged in a mutual, synchronous interaction aimed at resolving an issue. That is where the "dialectical" comes from. The approach also borrows from speech-act theory and linguistics the idea that all messages have semantic, syntactic, and pragmatic dimensions. And in this view, argument theory focuses on the pragmatic dimensions of argumentative messages, on what the messages do as acts, as much as what they assert. As an act, a message may request a definition, offer a definition, introduce evidence, retract an earlier statement, grant an opponent's proposition, etc. So far, most of the pragma-dialectical approach has been applied to finding exact conditions for describing with precision fallacious moves in simple and artificial argumentative dialogues. The system is relatively cumbersome and not without theoretical objections. Moreover, in large measure, it is an attempt to systematize what argument analysts do more intuitively when they use a rhetorical approach and examine an argument within its context of audience and situation. It will not be used in the remainder of this monograph, partly because it seems, so far, to apply only to face-to-face oral exchanges, but those who are interested may consult Walton or any of the works of van Eemeren and Grootendorst.

In what follows, I shall argue that writing teachers need to know both syllogistic logic and fallacy theory but should not teach them. I will instead propose an adaptation of classical argumentation as the most fruitful approach to teaching students to write good arguments or to read argumentative texts effectively, and I will leave the classroom use of the Toulmin system as an open question.

A Philosophy of Argumentation

By an "argument" I mean a full discourse designed to establish a position by rational support (although not to the exclusion of pathos and ethos). An argument then is a textual product. It is composed of levels of sub-arguments going all the way down to specific factual evidence. By "argumentation" I will mean a process, either the internal process a writer goes through in constructing that text, a process in which she may well argue with herself before settling on a position, or the collective procedure in which a group of arguers interact in order to use their arguments to forge agreement among disparate voices.

As I perceive argumentation, it is the chief cognitive activity by which a democracy, a field of study, a corporation, or a committee functions. It is the overt sign of human rationality (see Billig's *Arguing and Thinking*). And it is vitally important that high school and college students learn both to argue well and to critique the arguments of others. In a postmodern world, what we call *knowledge* is the result of extended argumentation. Some of that argumentation is agonistic or adversarial — as when we have two lawyers or teams of lawyers make the best arguments for opposing positions. Unfortunately, this is probably the more common image our students come up with when told to write an argument. They participate in what Lakoff and Johnson have called one of the dominant metaphors of our culture, "argument-as-war" (4). They see an issue as two-sided, and the goal as presenting their own view in a way that will defeat their opponents.

But I want students to see argument in a larger, less militant, and more comprehensive context — one in which the goal is not victory but a good decision, one in which all arguers are at risk of needing to alter their views, one in which a participant takes seriously and fairly the views different from his or her own. If agonistic argument is displayed in the courtroom, the larger context I am suggesting (sometimes called *irenic*) is displayed in the jury room and by appellate judges. It is crucial that students learn to participate effectively in argumentation as a cooperative, dialectical exchange and a search for mutually acceptable (and contingent) answers, not just in English, and not just in schools. (See Crusius for a Heideggerian elaboration of this viewpoint.)

So What Makes a Good Argument?

In answer to the perennial student complaint, "I just don't know what you want," I am sometimes tempted to reply, "All I want is a good argument." But as the previous pages perhaps indicate, outside of the confines of formal logic, it isn't at all simple to tell someone what a good argument is. It isn't a formally valid argument; nor is it an argument free from fallacies; nor is it an argument that cites lots of authorities; and it is of no help to students to tell them that it shows analysis, synthesis, and critical thinking.

The best "answer" I know was provided by an informal logician, Trudy Govier, of the University of Calgary, in the course of answering the question, "Are there two sides to every question?" In her essay of the same name, Govier constructs an excellent argument that there aren't two sides to all (probably most) arguments: sometimes there is only one (credible) "side"; much more often there are multiple "sides." Consequently, the common model of "objectivity" used on many editorial pages and news shows like "The News Hour with Jim Lehrer" is misguided; having two equally biased and opposite positions presented is no guarantee of fairness or even clarity. The likely result is confusion, extremism, and finally a profound conservatism. (Since "both sides" seem to have strong arguments, we might just as well leave things as they are.)

Govier ends her article by giving a list of nine characteristics of what she calls a "fair and balanced account," which does not mean that a position isn't taken (see Govier, "Are There Two Sides" 53). These nine characteristics constitute the best description of a "good argument," within the public, civic, dialectical context I have been presuming, that I have seen. So I offer them here as a conclusion:

1. The language used is relatively neutral. (Example: a speaker opposing religion in public schools refers to religious people as believers or adherents, not as bigots or fanatics.)

Failure to follow this guideline involves one in the fallacy of *argumentum ad populum,* either by use of scare words or of glittering generalities.

2. Facts that would tend to support an interpretation or evaluation different from that of the speaker or writer are acknowledged. Their apparent impact is either recognized or argued against and accounted for. . . .

Failure here means that one is suppressing evidence, that the author's ethos is actually weak, and that he or she is more interested in winning than in reaching the best dialectically negotiated viewpoint.

3. The point is acknowledged where expert opinion is cited and the relevant experts differ from each other. Either the case developed does not depend entirely on citing expert opinion or good reasons for selecting particular experts are given. Those experts whose views are not accepted are not attacked on irrelevant personal grounds.

Obviously, failure here involves a combination of the *argumentum ad verecundiam* and the *argumentum ad hominem.*

4. Controversial interpretations of events or texts, explanations for which there are plausible alternatives, disputable predictions, estimations, or value judgments are acknowledged as such. Reasons for them are given and, where appropriate, the impact on the analysis of making another such judgment is recognized.

We live in a complicated world. Argumentative issues are by their nature contingent. What we seek is not "the truth," but a warranted belief (Dewey 7).

5. The speakers or writers do not insidiously introduce their own special point of view as being the one the audience would naturally adopt. (Example: If a feminist is speaking in favor of equal pay for work of equal value, the speaker does not refer to the audience as "we in the feminist movement.")

6. Sources are indicated and, where practically feasible, quoted so that they may be checked in contexts where this is sufficiently important.

Not to do so is to commit a variety of the *ad verecundiam* argument, not to mention to plagiarize.

7. Arguments are careful and well reasoned, not fallacious.

The previous ten chapters of [*Teaching Argument in Writing*] have been devoted to what makes an argument careful and well reasoned: satisfying the STAR criteria, providing a prima facie case for whatever stasis is being argued, being aware of one's data, warrant, and other features of the Toulmin model.

8. Where time and space permit, alternative positions are stated, explained, and considered. Reasons are given as to why these positions are seen to be less satisfactory than the one advocated. Alternative positions are fairly and accurately represented and described in nonprejudicial language. People holding them are described accurately, politely, and respectfully.

In dyadic communication, the arguer shows his or her own awareness and fairness by considering alternative positions, critiquing them fairly, not engaging in straw man attacks, and not ignoring the contexts of argument.

9. The point is acknowledged where evidence and reasons offered are less than rationally compelling. An explanation is given as to why the position taken nevertheless seems the most nearly correct or appropriate in the context.

For many of the issues we must argue, there is no rationally compelling set of arguments. As Perelman and Olbrechts-Tyteca put it, "Only the existence of an argumentation that is neither compelling nor arbitrary can give meaning to human freedom, a state in which a reasonable choice can be exercised" (514).

All of this is probably too much to expect from our high school or undergraduate writing students, but it nevertheless remains a valuable ideal to aim for — whether in our classes or in our own scholarship. [*Teaching Argument*] has itself certainly been an argument. In it I hope I have come close to satisfying Govier's criteria.

Works Cited

Aristotle, *Aristotle's Prior and Posterior Analytics*. Ed. W. D. Rose. New York: Garland, 1980.

——. *On Sophistical Refutations*. Ed. and trans. D. J. Furley and E. S. Forster. Cambridge, MA: W. Heineman, 1965.

Billig, Michael. *Arguing and Thinking: A Rhetorical Approach to Social Psychology*. New York: Cambridge UP, 1987.

Copi, Irving M., and Carl Cohen. *Introduction to Logic*. 9th ed. New York: Macmillan, 1994.

Crusius, Timothy W. *A Teacher's Introduction to Philosophical Hermeneutics*. Urbana, IL: NCTE, 1991.

Dewey, John. *Logic: The Theory of Inquiry*. New York: Henry Holt, 1938.

Fahnestock, Jeanne, and Marie Secor. "Teaching Argument: A Theory of Types." *College Composition and Communication* 34 (Feb. 1983): 20–30.

Fulkerson, Richard. "Technical Logic, Comp-Logic, and the Teaching of Writing." *College Composition and Communication* 39 (Dec. 1988): 436–52.

Govier, Trudy. "Are There Two Sides to Every Question?" *Selected Issues in Logic and Communication*. Ed. Trudy Govier. Belmont, CA: Wadsworth, 1988. 43–54.

Lakoff, George, and Mark Johnson. *Metaphors We Live By*. Chicago: U of Chicago P, 1980.

Perelman, Chaim, and L. Olbrechts-Tyteca. *The New Rhetoric: A Treatise on Argumentation*. Trans. John Wilkinson and Purcell Weaver. Notre Dame, IN: U of Notre Dame P, 1969.

Rorabacher, Louise E., and Georgia Dunbar. *Assignments in Exposition*. 6th ed. New York: Harper, 1979.

Scriven, Michael. *Reasoning*. New York: McGraw, 1976.

Weddle, Perry. "Inductive, Deductive." *Informal Logic* 22 (Nov. 1979): 1–5.

Whitehead, Alfred North, and Bertrand Russell. *Principia Mathematica*. New York: Cambridge UP, 1927.

CLEAR SENTENCES AND WORD CHOICE

Parts Three and Four of *The Bedford Handbook* offer students easy-to-understand advice about how to solve sentence-level problems, supplemented with examples that model revision possibilities. In these discussions *The Handbook* emphasizes the rhetorical impact of sentence structure and word choice, helping students understand the importance of making careful choices as they revise and edit their work.

The articles that follow will help teachers consider several alternatives for teaching students about sentences and word choice:

- How can teachers help students enlarge their repertoire of options for composing and revising sentences in the contexts of their larger rhetorical situations?
- How can teachers help students develop an awareness of sexist or discriminatory language, and how can they help students avoid using it?

TEACHING ABOUT SENTENCES

Erika Lindemann

[From *A Rhetoric for Writing Teachers*, 3rd ed. New York: Oxford UP, 1995. 158–69.]

(For biographical information, see p. 55)

Writers compose and revise sentences within larger rhetorical contexts, and effective writers make conscious choices about sentences based on their understanding of their rhetorical situation. Lindemann suggests that "[t]he goal of our teaching should be to enlarge the student's repertoire of sentence options and rhetorical choices." Synthesizing several decades of important scholarly work on syntax and discourse analysis, she offers three approaches, each one meant to help students "apply what they're learning about sentences to composing." Lindemann suggests that teachers help students recognize that readers bring a number of expectations to sentences. She also suggests that students regularly practice combining (and decombining) sentences, preferably ones from their own work in progress. As a third technique for teaching sentences, she describes how teachers can use Christensen's "generative rhetoric" to help students explore alternative sentence constructions and to help "students attend to the ways sentences express relationships among ideas." Lindemann's chapter provides teachers with theoretically consistent advice that they can apply to their work with students.

> A sentence should read as if its author, had he held a plow instead of a pen, could have drawn a furrow deep and straight to the end.
>
> – Henry David Thoreau

All of us have an intuitive understanding of sentence structures and their use. We've all been talking in sentences since childhood, rarely stopping to consider whether or not our speech represents a "complete thought," contains a subject and predicate, or shows "dependent" and "independent" clauses. Our sentences, most of which we've never heard or said before, get the message across. All native speakers *do* know what a sentence is; they can create complex sentences without knowing the names for the constructions they produce.

If that's so, why spend time in a writing class on sentences? To be sure, some types of sentence instruction do not use classtime productively. Too much time spent analyzing someone else's sentences gives students too little practice generating their own. Too much attention to labeling sentence types or classifying phrases and clauses may teach terminology — *what* to call a construction — but not writing — *how* to create it. Although human beings have an intuitive competence for creating sentences, many student writers need practice translating competence into fluent performance.

A major reason why "performing" written sentences is difficult stems from differences between speech and writing. Spoken communication, which may be highly elliptical, generally succeeds without complicated syntax. Gestures, facial expressions, and the habit of taking turns reinforce the message. Although high school and college students are capable of writing complicated sentences, they're unaccustomed to using their entire syntactic repertoire, especially if they habitually write as they talk. Second, writing sentences presents considerable risk. Every word added to a sentence increases the possibility of misspellings, punctuation mistakes, or other other errors that jeopardize students' grades. Short, simple sentences are safest. Third, some students have trouble with sentences because they can't depend on the eye or ear to help them identify prose rhythms. If they read poorly, rarely read for pleasure, converse infrequently with adults, or passively watch a great deal of television, they may have difficulty imagining comfortable options for sentences. Television commercials, for example, are usually scripted in sentence fragments, a style that may influence our students' "ear" for sentences to a greater extent than we realize. Finally, writing sentences requires punctuation marks that have few equivalents in speech. Yes, we pause for longer or shorter periods as we speak, but writing indicates "pauses" with a confusing array of symbols, with commas, dashes, colons, semicolons, periods, and other marks. Conversely, we don't "speak" apostrophes. Performing written sentences, then, requires confidence in manipulating symbols that have no true counterparts in spoken English.

For these reasons, students need risk-free opportunities to practice sentences, especially complex sentences. Such practice should take place in the context of composing longer stretches of discourse. When students study and practice sentences, they must be able to apply what they're learning *about* sentences to composing. They must translate knowledge into performance. Instead of analyzing sentences in a textbook, we can help students discover what kinds of sentences their own writing contains. Instead of drilling students on punctuation rules, we can encourage them to practice unfamiliar constructions and address the punctuation problems as they arise. Instead of discussing sentence patterns students have already mastered, we can help them practice types they may be avoiding for fear of making mistakes in punctuation or subject-verb agreement. The goal of our teaching should be to enlarge the student's repertoire of sentence options and rhetorical choices.

One relatively simple way to discuss sentences involves talking about readers. Readers expect sentences to conform to conventional punctuation, but they have other expectations as well.[1] Readers expect the most important information in a sentence to appear at the beginning and at the end. The beginning of a sentence names the actors and either establishes a context for information to come or links the sentence to the one before it by providing transitional, old information. The end of the sentence stresses new information. Information buried in the middle gets the least attention. Putting important information in the right slot helps readers follow along. What is "important" depends on the context in which the sentence appears. That is, writers do not compose individual sentences; they put sentences together into paragraphs and larger units of discourse. In reading the following student's paragraph, notice which words Roger has put in the most emphatic positions, the beginning and end of the sentence:

> In some cultures, <u>it is</u> the men who are more conscious of nonverbal communication than *the women are*. <u>That is</u> not true *in North America.* In our culture <u>it seems</u> that of both groups the women are more aware of body language, voice tone, and *other nonverbal messages.* <u>This was brought</u> to my attention by *a man*, but <u>it was</u> only after I became more sensitive myself that *I really believed him.*

Although Roger's paragraph is about men's awareness of nonverbal communication, *men, I* (Roger), or *nonverbal communication* rarely appear in emphatic sentence positions. The paragraph's implicit story of how Roger "became more sensitive" never gets told. Discussing such a paragraph with students shows them how to reorder sentence elements so that important information appears where a reader expects to find it. Roger's revised paragraph is more specific, shows better sentence variety, and also makes more effective use of sentence positions to advance the story of what Roger learned:

> While <u>men</u> in some cultures are more conscious than women of *nonverbal communication,* <u>I haven't always been</u>. *I learned* from my girlfriend's brother that body language, tone of voice, and gestures are less important to me than *they are to my girlfriend.* Through his advice, <u>I learned</u> *what my girlfriend's signals meant.* For example, <u>I realized</u> that when she leaned back in her chair, *she was saying, "I'm upset."* By watching my girlfriend's nonverbal messages, <u>I became</u> *more sensitive* to them.

In addition to discussing how readers regard sentences, two other techniques for teaching sentences in the context of composing are popular with writing teachers: sentence combining and generating cumulative sentences. Both techniques can increase the "syntactic fluency" of students' writing. At the same time, writing teachers must guard against the exaggerated claims of some proponents of these techniques, especially of sentence combining. Kellogg Hunt, for example, suggests structuring an entire writing course around sentence combining: "In every sense, sentence combining can be a comprehensive writing program in and of itself, for at least one semester. It is nonsense, rather than common sense, to suggest that sentence combining can't be the one and only instructional strategy, at least for one term."[2] Nonsense or not, many writing teachers and researchers *do* express misgivings about the efficacy of sentence combining as the sole instructional method in a writing course and have doubts about the syntactic gains attributed to sentence-combining practice. Some of these gains, in fact, may result from instruction in semantics and rhetoric that accompanies discussions of sentence-combining problems. More important, because composing involves more than mastering sentences, no single instructional method, including sentence combining or work with cumulative sentences, will transform poor writers into accomplished ones. Although both techniques have advantages, neither should become the exclusive focus of a writing class.

Sentence Combining

Generative-transformational theory suggests that we transform sentences intuitively by adding to, deleting from, or rearranging sentence elements. Sentence combining applies this principle to writing instruction.[3] As Charles Cooper explains, sentence-combining problems "confront the student with sentences more complex than ones he would be likely to write at that point in his development; they ask the student to write out fully-formed sentences and they provide him the content of the sentences so that his attention can remain focused on the *structural* aspects of the problem."[4] To combine the following sentences, for example, students would insert information from the indented sentence into the first sentence:

The canary flew out the window.
> The canary is yellow.

Student's response: The yellow canary flew out the window.

Some sentence-combining problems offer clues about which words to add or delete:

SOMETHING made her angry.
> She read something in the note. (what)

Student's response: What she read in the note made her angry.

Multiple embeddings are also possible:

My friends and I enjoy SOMETHING.
We race our bicycles around the paths in the park. (racing)
> Our bicycles are lightweight.
> Our bicycles are ten-speed.
> The paths are narrow.
> The paths are winding.

Student's response: My friends and I enjoy racing our lightweight, ten-speed bicycles around the narrow, winding paths in the park.

Exercises that contain transformation cues require students to combine the sentences in a specified way. Cued exercises can give students confidence in generating syntactic structures that they may be avoiding. The cues show students *how* to combine the sentences, providing a repertoire of connectives that hold phrases and clauses together. As students work through the exercises, teachers can introduce terminology and whatever punctuation conventions a particular transformation requires.

Open-ended exercises, which offer no cues, may be more difficult for some students, but they permit more choices and encourage students to consider the rhetorical effects of possible combinations:

The national debt concerns Americans.
The national debt grows eight thousand dollars every second.
The national debt totals nearly four trillion dollars.

Possible student responses, each of which achieves a different rhetorical effect: The national debt concerns Americans because it grows eight thousand dollars every second and totals nearly four trillion dollars.

The national debt, a concern for Americans, grows eight thousand dollars every second and totals nearly four trillion dollars.

The national debt, growing eight thousand dollars every second and totaling nearly four trillion dollars, concerns Americans.

Americans are concerned about the national debt, which grows eight thousand dollars every second and totals nearly four trillion dollars.

Because the national debt grows eight thousand dollars every second and totals nearly four trillion dollars, it concerns Americans.

When students combine sentences in as many ways as they know how, read them aloud, and discuss which versions they like best, they're not only exercising syntactic muscles but also making rhetorical choices. Like professional writers, students develop an eye and ear for prose rhythms. "In addition to playing with transformations and making their choices," writes William Strong, "professional writers also seem to spend considerable time hearing the way sentences fit together to make up the 'melody' of their writing. They listen for the dips and swaying curves of some phrases, the hard, rhythmic, regular punch of others. They sensitize themselves to avoid sentences where meaning is almost obscured within the lengthy confines of the sentence itself; they study those sentences where pause, and momentary reflection, have their impact" (*Sentence Combining*, p. xv).

Discussing sentence-combining exercises also helps students become confident about punctuation. My own students shun participial modifiers, appositives, and relative clauses because they aren't sure how to use commas to set them off. They avoid introductory adverb clauses for similar reasons. Students who have learned to be careful about commas understandably "write around" the problem. Sentence-combining exercises illustrate how punctuation organizes sentence elements for a reader and offer risk-free opportunities to solve punctuation problems that have baffled students for years. Sometimes an exercise exposes a punctuation rule misunderstood in a previous English class. A former student of mine consistently placed commas behind words such as *because, since,* and *if* when they began a sentence: "Because, I didn't have a car I couldn't date Susan." When I asked him why he thought the comma belonged there, he explained, "My English teacher told me to set off *because* words; she called them 'introductory' something-or-other." Doubtless, his teacher encouraged him to set off the entire introductory clause, but the student had heard only part of the rule. He solved the problem by practicing a few sentence-combining exercises. My student's problem also illustrates another point; grammatical terminology sometimes creates punctuation problems. Sentence combining allows teachers to dispense with terminology altogether or, if they wish, to name constructions *after* students have practiced them.

Other students may need practice "decombining" sentences. Older students sometimes attempt such extraordinarily complicated sentences that the syntax gets twisted. They may be writing to please teachers who implicitly praise "long" sentences; nevertheless, they develop a style that obscures ideas in hopelessly convoluted syntax. Here's an example from a first-year college student's paper:

The things that people go to the pharmacist for sometimes are just to get the pharmacist to prescribe them something for their illness, and he can not do any prescribing for anyone for medicine.

Prepositions are part of the problem here, but Kenny loses his reader by piling too much information into one sentence. When he read the sentence out loud, he said it sounded "weird," but he didn't know how to revise it.

I asked him to "decombine" the sentence, breaking it into simple sentences. We came up with the following two lists, which reproduce the simple sentences embedded in his original:

   People go to the pharmacist for things.
   People go to the pharmacist sometimes.
   People just get the pharmacist to do SOMETHING. (to)
     The pharmacist prescribes them something for their illness.

and

   He cannot do any SOMETHING. (–ing)
   He prescribes for anyone.
   He prescribes medicine.

At this point, Kenny could understand why the sentence seems "weird." It lacks a single focus. Two or three subjects — "people," "pharmacist," and perhaps "things" — vie for attention. Recombining the sentences to emphasize only one subject, "people" or "pharmacist," might yield the following options:

"People" Sentences

1. People sometimes go to the pharmacist, who cannot prescribe medicine for anyone, just to get him to prescribe something for their illness.
2. Sometimes people go to the pharmacist just to get him to prescribe medicine for their illness, something he cannot do.

"Pharmacist" Sentences

1. The pharmacist cannot prescribe medicine for anyone's illness, even though people sometimes ask him to.
2. Although people sometimes ask the pharmacist to prescribe medicine for their illness, he cannot write prescriptions.

The two-step decombining and recombining procedure now gives Kenny several sentences to choose from in revising his paper.

Decombining and recombining sentences can help students untangle, tighten, and rewrite sentences too complex for a reader to follow easily. After a while, students also discover which transformations create convoluted sentences. For Kenny, beginning sentences with noun clauses and piling up infinitives creates problems. For other students, passive constructions or beginning sentences with "There are" and "It is" tangle the syntax. Different kinds of sentence-combining exercises help students detect and solve these problems.

To improve their skill in manipulating sentence structures, students need regular sentence-combining practice over a long period, ideally two or three times a week throughout the entire course of instruction. The exercises can begin as early as the fourth grade and increase in complexity through college. Inundating students with sentence-combining problems, however, turns a means into an end. Assigning too many problems too frequently bores students, who begin to regard the exercises as busywork. Because the exercises focus only on sentences, not longer stretches of discourse, and because the content of the sentences is predetermined, not invented by the student, sentence combining should supplement, not replace, students' own writing.

All the same, sentence combining has several advantages. Used correctly, the technique *does* increase students' syntactic fluency. Teachers can assign the exercises as individual homework or as in-class group-work, students pooling their intuitive linguistic resources to solve the problems. Teachers can design their own exercises, use those available in published textbooks, or best of all, glean them from students' papers. Grading the work is inappropriate because it attaches risks to the exercises. To be effective, sentence-combining must remain risk free, a way of experimenting with syntactic structures students avoid for fear of making low marks. Some teachers post or pass out answers for the problems so that students can check their sentences against the key.

Besides increasing the complexity of students' sentences, the exercises have other advantages. They demonstrate how to construct sentences without resorting to grammatical terms or singling out errors in students' papers. They permit us to avoid terminology altogether or introduce it after students understand how to perform a particular transformation. They offer plenty of examples for describing punctuation, mechanics, and conventions of edited American English in the context of writing, not isolated from it. And because students will combine sentences in many interesting ways, the exercises allow us to discuss rhetorical choices, differences in emphasis that might work more effectively in some contexts than in others. Open-ended exercises work especially well in this regard. They help students discover, not the one "right" sentence, but a range of options. Students also can apply the technique to their own drafts, rewriting sentences to emphasize ideas differently, change the focus, coordinate or subordinate material, and achieve sentence variety.

Cumulative Sentences

In *Notes toward a New Rhetoric* (1978), Francis Christensen expresses considerable dissatisfaction with traditional methods of teaching sentences. "We need," he says, "a rhetoric of the sentence that will do more than combine the ideas of primer sentences. We need one that will *generate* ideas" (p. 26). Instead of teaching sentences based on rhetorical classifications (loose, balanced, and periodic sentences) or grammatical categories (simple, compound, complex, and compound-complex sentences), Christensen offers an alternative method, generative rhetoric. It's a rhetoric that generates ideas, not words. According to Christensen, students don't need to write longer, more complex sentences simply to produce more words; rather, the sentence-as-form encourages writers to examine the ideas expressed by the words, to sharpen or add to them, and then to reproduce the idea more effectively. The "cumulative sentence," the heart of Christensen's generative rhetoric, compels writers to examine their thoughts, the meanings words convey. Consequently, generative rhetoric serves prewriting as well as rewriting.

Christensen bases his generative rhetoric on four principles derived from his study of prose style and the works of contemporary authors. He maintains, first, that "composition is essentially a process of addition"; nouns, verbs, or main clauses serve as a foundation or base to which we add details, qualifications, new meanings. Second, Christensen's "principle of modification" suggests that we can add these new meanings either before or after some noun, verb, or base clause. The "direction of movement" for the sentence changes, depending on where we've added modifiers and new meaning. When modifiers appear before the noun, verb, or base clause (which Christensen calls the "head" of the construction), the sentence "moves" forward. Modifiers placed after the noun, verb, or base clause move the sentence backward because they require readers to relate the new details, qualifications, and meanings *back* to the head appearing earlier in the sentence. Christensen's third principle states that, depending on the meanings of the words we add, the head becomes either more concrete or less so. The base word or clause together with one or more modifying additions expresses several "levels of generality or abstraction." Finally, Christensen's "principle of texture" describes and evaluates a writer's style. He characterizes style as relatively "dense" or "plain," depending on the number and variety of additions writers make to nouns, verbs, and base clauses.

We don't need to explain Christensen's four principles to students before asking them to create cumulative sentences. Native speakers form such sentences naturally. When I introduce my class to cumulative sentences, I begin by asking students to add words and phrases to the following sentence, written on the blackboard: "The horse galloped." I provide a base clause and deliberately ask the class to "load the pattern," a practice that Christensen would condemn but that gives me a starting point. After students suggest additions to the sentence for three to five minutes, it might look like the following monstrosity: "Because Farmer Brown didn't notice the swarm of bees in the apple tree and hadn't tightened the cinch on the old, brown leather saddle securely, the horse galloped off through the orchard, throwing the startled rider to the ground, terrified by the bees buzzing around his head, until he reached the weathered board fence, where he stopped."

Although the sentence is unwieldy, students seem pleased to discover that they *can* compose complicated sentences like this one. Initially, quantity not quality intrigues them. That's fine for now; we'll get to quality soon enough (and fix that misplaced modifier). Generally, students add material at the end of the base clause first. Then, prompted by prewriting questions — Who? What? When? Where? How? Why? — they begin to place modifiers at the beginning or in the middle of the sentence: appositives, participial constructions, relative clauses, adverb and adjective constructions. After they have created the sentence, we discuss the kinds of grammatical structures and relationships the sentence expresses as well as punctuation problems we have encountered. Finally, we assess its rhetorical effectiveness, concluding that writing long sentences per se isn't a virtue and that our example needs revising. So, we tighten it, rearranging and deleting elements, reading versions aloud to evaluate their rhythm, and finally, imagining the larger context of the paragraph in which revised versions of our sentence might appear. Although the sample sentence enables us to take up several grammatical, rhetorical, and mechanical concerns, we will explore them in detail for several class meetings.

In one class period, for example, we might examine the kinds of additions that expand the base clause, discussing sentences from students' papers or a reading assignment. Although I avoid grammatical terms, Christensen uses them. In contrast to traditional methods, however, he limits the number of modifiers added to base clauses to only seven grammatical constructions:

PP	Prepositional phrase
NC	Noun cluster (appositives)
VC	Verb cluster (present and past participles, infinitives)
Abs	Absolute construction (a participial construction with its own subject)
Adv	Adverb clauses
AC	Adjective clauses
Rel	Relative clauses

Each of these additions adjusts the meaning of the base clause (or other clauses added to the base). "The main or base clause," Christensen explains, "is likely to be stated in general or abstract or plural terms. With the main clause stated, the forward movement of the sentence stops: The writer instead of going on to something new shifts down to a lower level of generality or abstraction or to singular terms, and goes back over the same ground at this lower level" (p. 29).

If we indent and number the levels of generality in the sample sentence discussed earlier, it looks like this:

> 2 Because Farmer Brown didn't notice the swarm of bees/ . . . and (Adv)
>> 3 in the apple tree (PP)
> 2 (because he) hadn't tightened the cinch/. . . securely, (Adv)
>> 3 on the old, brown leather saddle (PP)
1 the horse galloped off
> 2 through the orchard, (PP)
> 2 throwing the startled rider (VC)
>> 3 to the ground (PP)
> 2 terrified (VC)
>> 3 by the bees (PP)
>>> 4 buzzing around his head, (VC)
> 2 until he reached the weathered board fence, (Adv)
>> 3 where he stopped. (Rel)

Christensen calls this a four-level sentence. The base clause is always numbered "level 1," regardless of where it appears in the sentence. All of the level-2 additions modify "horse" and "galloped off," words in the base or level-1 clause. The level-3 modifiers refer back to and elaborate elements of level-2 constructions; level-4 modifiers particularize elements in level 3. Indenting each level helps students see what kinds of additions have been made and where they appear (before, after, or as the slash indicates, in the middle of a group of words). The diagram also reveals whether or not groups of words are grammatically similar or parallel, and how they relate to one another by qualifying or elaborating material elsewhere in the sentence. It's not necessary that students always label the modifiers correctly or number the levels the same way. What's important is seeing how the parts of the sentence work together.

Although our Farmer Brown sentence contains four levels, it is uncharacteristically "dense." Most high school and college students write one-, or at best, two-level sentences. Their "texture" is thin or plain. They resemble lists of information that have no shape because the writer hasn't figured out what relationship the details have to some larger idea. Here's an example of a one-level sentence, written by Maria, a first-year college student who is describing an advertisement.

1 The background is a dull, white film while
1 the caption shows black type.

Because Maria had practiced expanding sentences with level-2 and -3 modifiers, she knew how and where to improve the sentence with details. Here's her revision:

> 2 Cloudy and misty, (AC)
1 the background looks like a soft, white film,
> 2 draped behind bold, black type, (VC)
>> 3 which catches the reader's eye. (Rel)

Out of context, this revision may sound flowery, but it demonstrates the generative power of Christensen's cumulative sentence. In reviewing her first sentence, Maria was able to generate additional details about the background and caption, features of the advertisement she wanted to discuss. Her revised sentence is longer — not necessarily a virtue — but it also relates the details instead of merely listing them. It subordinates the "bold, black type" of the caption (level 2) to the background (level 1).

Generative rhetoric helps students attend to the ways sentences express relationships among ideas.

1 The cumulative sentence in unskillful hands is unsteady,

   2 allowing a writer to ramble on, (VC)

      3 adding modifier after modifier, (VC)

         4 until the reader is almost overwhelmed (Adv)

         5 because the writer's central idea is lost. (Adv)

Cumulative sentences are not merely multilevel constructions that string together modifiers one after another. Students also must control the placement of modifiers, drawing them out of ideas in the base clause. They must see the idea again, sharpen the image, the object, the action. In exploring the implications of what they've said, they will generate or reinvent additional meanings to express. At the level of the sentence, the new meanings become cumulative modifiers. At the level of the paragraph and whole discourse, as we've already seen, the generative principles of Christensen's rhetoric can shape new sentences, paragraphs, and sections.

Notes

[1] See Joseph M. Williams, *Style: Ten Lessons in Clarity and Grace*, 3d ed. (Glenview, IL: Scott, Foresman, 1989). I also draw on unpublished material developed by George Gopen, Duke University.

[2] Kellogg W. Hunt, "Anybody Can Teach English," in *Sentence Combining and the Teaching of Writing*, ed. Donald A. Daiker, Andrew Kerek, and Max Morenberg (Conway, AR: L & S Books, 1979), p. 156. Although I disagree with Hunt, I recommend this collection of essays for those who want to know more about sentence combining. I also recommend Stephen P. Witte's review of the book in *College Composition and Communication* 31 (December 1980), 433–37, which discusses some of the reservations writing teachers have about sentence-combining research. For a comprehensive, though dated, bibliography on the theory and practice of sentence combining, see Max Morenberg and Andrew Kerek, "Bibliography on Sentence Combining: Theory and Practice, 1964–1979," *Rhetoric Society Quarterly* 9 (Spring 1979), 97–111. A useful summary of research on sentence combining is George Hillocks, Jr., *Research on Written Composition: New Directions for Teaching* (Urbana, IL: ERIC Clearinghouse on Reading and Communication Skills and the National Conference on Research in English, 1986), pp. 141–51.

[3] Frank O'Hare, *Sentence Combining: Improving Student Writing without Formal Grammar Instruction* (NCTE Research Report No. 15; Urbana, IL: NCTE, 1973), reviews research on the relationship between grammar study and improvement in writing and describes his own investigation. O'Hare's study demonstrates that written and oral sentence-combining exercises helped seventh graders "write compositions that could be described as syntactically more elaborated or mature" and "better in overall quality" (p. 67).

[4] Charles Cooper, "An Outline for Writing Sentence-Combining Problems," *English Journal* 62 (January 1973). The next three sample problems appear in Cooper.

Work Cited

Christensen, Francis, and Bonniejean Christensen. *Notes toward a New Rhetoric*. 2d ed. New York: Harper & Row, 1978.

From *THE HANDBOOK OF NONSEXIST WRITING*

Casey Miller and Kate Swift

[From *The Handbook of Nonsexist Writing.* 2nd ed. New York: Harper, 1988. 1–9.]

Freelance writers and editors Casey Miller and Kate Swift have published as partners since 1970. Over the years, their work on sexism and language has been published widely, and *The Handbook of Nonsexist Writing* has been the standard recommended text on the topic since its first appearance in 1980.

In the following selection, the introduction to their book, Miller and Swift argue forcefully for continued efforts to change sexist language. The balance of the book exposes the widespread sexism in language, provides historical analyses of sexist usage, and offers practical suggestions for avoiding sexist language. *The Bedford Handbook*'s expanded discussion of sexist language, including the helpful chart on page 268, testifies to the continued concern about sexism and language.

Introduction: Change and Resistance to Change

When the first edition of *The Handbook of Nonsexist Writing* appeared in 1980, efforts to eliminate linguistic sexism had already gained support from a wide assortment of national and local organizations, both public and private. Guidelines for nonsexist usage had been issued by most major textbook publishers, and professional and academic groups ranging from the Society of Automotive Engineers to the American Psychological Association were developing their own guidelines, as were such diverse public institutions as the City of Honolulu and the University of New Hampshire. Churches and synagogues were struggling with the problems of perception raised by traditional male-oriented language; librarians were rethinking the wording of catalog entries; and groups as varied as philanthropic foundations, political councils, and consumer cooperatives were recasting their charters, bylaws, application forms, and other materials in gender-neutral terms. Advertising copy had begun to acknowledge that bankers, insurance agents, scientists, consumers at every level, farmers, and athletes are female as well as male.

By the mid-eighties the movement toward nonsexist usage had gained so much momentum that researchers who studied its impact by analyzing three recently published American dictionaries of new words were prepared to state, in the cautious phraseology of scholarship, that their results showed "a trend toward nonsexism" in written language. The data, they said, "provided a judgment of the efficacy of feminists' efforts toward nonsexist vocabulary," and they ventured the opinion that the "importance and justice of the subject have been recognized."

During the same period, a marked increase occurred in academic research into language use and its relation to women, and the number of books and articles on the subject addressed to the general public continues to grow. So extensive is this outpouring, in fact, that a newsletter established in 1976 to report on activities in the field grew in only ten years from a 4-page pamphlet to a 64-page periodical called *Women and*

Language. Not all this interest has been on the side of linguistic reform, of course; opposition to the concept of nonsexist language continues and in some quarters has stiffened. But during the past ten years, some of the most influential opponents of linguistic change have been persuaded that the problem is not going to disappear as obligingly as ground fog on an autumn morning.

The increased use of nonsexist language by those in major channels of communication provides a graphic demonstration of the mysterious ways in which reality affects language and is, in turn, affected by it. For as women become more prominent in fields from which they were once excluded, their presence triggers questions of linguistic equity that, once having been asked and answered, bring new visibility to women. How does one refer to a woman who is a member of Congress, or address a woman who sits on her country's highest court or is its chief of state? What does one call a woman who flies in space? Superficial as such questions may seem, their existence brings into focus a new awareness of women's potential. When *Time* magazine named Corazon Aquino its "Woman of the Year," it paid tribute to her extraordinary achievements and, at least by implication, made two other statements: (1) the year's most newsworthy person need not be a man, and (2) some of the connotations once assumed to be communicated only by the word *man* are now attaching themselves to the word *woman.* Still to come, however, is widespread acceptance of a gender-inclusive term that, in such a context, would concentrate attention on the person's newsworthiness rather than on the irrelevant factor of gender.

Notable among recent acknowledgments of the need for more even-handed usage was the change of policy adopted by the *New York Times* regarding titles of courtesy. First the *Times* stopped prefixing women's names with honorifics in both headlines and sports stories — thereby including women under the same rubric it had followed for years with respect to men. Then the newspaper dropped its ban on the courtesy title *Ms.* because, as an Editor's Note explained, "The *Times* now believes that 'Ms.' has become part of the language." Since the *Times* moves to a majestic beat, it is not about to rush headlong into the unqualified adoption of a nonsexist lexicon, but the recognition of *Ms.* wasn't its first move in that direction, and each day brings new evidence that it was not intended to be its last.

As individuals and the media gradually work out the logic involved in each new linguistic quandary, the presence of women in government and business and in the arts and professions becomes more and more apparent. Which is not to say that as women gain positive linguistic visibility they magically gain recognition and respect. But something "magical" does happen whenever people — singly or as a class — begin to sense their potential as fully integrated members of society, and it is this "magic" that using nonsexist language helps to bring about.

One subtle, and therefore particularly harmful, linguistic practice that has not changed much in the last few years is the use of common-gender terms as though they automatically refer only to males. When a member of Congress says on a televised news program, "Any politician would have trouble running against a woman," or a newspaper reports that a man "went berserk . . . and murdered his neighbor's wife," the effect is to make women irrelevant. Politicians become, once again, an all-male breed, and a woman, denied even the identity of "neighbor," is relegated instead to that of "neighbor's wife."

The reason the practice of assigning masculine gender to neutral terms is so enshrined in English is that every language reflects the prejudices of the society in which it evolved, and English evolved through most of its history in a male-centered, patriarchal society. We shouldn't be surprised, therefore, that its vocabulary and grammar reflect attitudes that exclude or demean women. But we are surprised, for until recently few people thought much about what English — or any other language for that matter — was saying on a subliminal level. Now that we have begun to look, some startling things have become obvious. What standard English usage says about males, for example, is that they are the species. What it says about females is that they are a subspecies. From these two assertions flow a thousand other enhancing and degrading messages, all encoded in the language we in the English-speaking countries begin to learn almost as soon as we are born.

Many people would like to do something about these inherited linguistic biases, but getting rid of them involves more than exposing them and suggesting alternatives. It requires change, and linguistic change is no easier to accept than any other kind. It may even be harder.

At a deep level, changes in a language are threatening because they signal widespread changes in social mores. At a level closer to the surface they are exasperating. We learn certain rules of grammar and usage in school, and when they are challenged it is as though we are also being challenged. Our native language is like a second skin, so much a part of us we resist the idea that it is constantly changing, constantly being renewed. Though we know intellectually that the English we speak today and the English of Shakespeare's time are very different, we tend to think of them as the same — static rather than dynamic. Emotionally, we want to agree with the syndicated columnist who wrote that "grammar is as fixed in its way as geometry."

One of the obstacles to accepting any kind of linguistic change — whether it concerns something as superficial as the pronunciation of *tomato* or as fundamental as sexual bias — is this desire to keep language "pure." In order to see change as natural and inevitable rather than as an affront, we need perspective, and to gain perspective it helps to take a look at some of the changes that have already taken place in English.

To start with, if it were true that "grammar is as fixed in its way as geometry," we would still, in the twentieth century, be speaking Old English, the earliest version of the tongue we know today: Our vocabulary would be almost totally different; we would still be altering a word's form to change the meaning of a sentence instead of shifting words about — as in "Dog bites man," "Man bites dog" — to do the same thing; and we would still have "grammatical" rather than "natural" gender. The last change is important because the gender assigned to nouns and pronouns in Old English, as in most modern European languages, often had no relationship to sex or its absence. The word for "chair," for example, was masculine; the word for "table" was feminine; and the word of "ship" was neuter. In modern English we match gender with sex. That is, we reserve feminine and masculine gender for human beings and other sex-differentiated animals or, in flights of fancy, for nonliving things (like ships) onto which we project human associations. At least theoretically all other English nouns and pronouns are neuter or, in the case of agent-nouns like *teacher* and *president,* gender-neutral.

Greatly as these grammatical simplifications invigorated English, some of its special richness comes from the flexibility of its vocabulary. The English lexicon is a kind of uninhibited conglomeration put together over the centuries from related Indo-European languages and, though far less frequently, from languages as unrelated to English as Chinese, Nahuatl, and Yoruba.

Yet despite the hospitality of English to outside as well as internal influences, many people, including many language experts, become upset when confronted with new words or grammatical modifications they happen not to like. H. W. Fowler, whose widely used *Dictionary of Modern English Usage* was first published in 1926, deplored such "improperly formed" words as *amoral, bureaucrat, speedometer, pacifist,* and *coastal,* terms so commonly used today we take them for granted. His scorn for *electrocute* (formed by analogy to *execute*) pushed him beyond compassion or reason. The word, he wrote, "jars the unhappy latinist's nerves much more cruelly than the operation denoted jars those of its victims" (an emotional excess Sir Ernest Gowers, editor of the current edition of Fowler, mercifully deleted).

Lexicographers are less judgmental. In compiling dictionaries, they try to include as many commonly used words as space allows, whether the words are "properly formed" or not. Dictionaries, however, cannot help but lag behind actual usage, so they are not always reliable indicators of new or altered meanings. Merriam-Webster's Collegiate Dictionary (10th edition) defines *youth* as (among other things) "a young person; *esp:* a young male between adolescence and maturity." Essentially the same definition appears in several other current dictionaries, and some people continue to use the word in that limited sense. When film director Martha Coolidge approached a Hollywood producer about making a "low-budget youth picture," he is reported to have said, "No gays or women; it's a male subject." Actually the accepted meaning of *youth* is shifting faster than the producer realized or dictionaries can keep up with. Under the headline "Stolen Horse Is Found by Relentless Searcher," a news story in the *New York Times* referred to the horse's owner, a sixteen-year-old girl, as a youth: "After Rocky was stolen . . . the youth called every stable and horse handler she could find" and "the youth's parents brought a trailer . . . for the trip home." Though the term may once have been anomalous when used of a young woman, today it is a recognized common-gender noun, and the next round of dictionaries will no doubt add their authority to the change.

Changes in usage often occur slowly and imperceptibly, but some take place seemingly overnight. Such was the case in the 1960s when *black* replaced *Negro.* How the change occurred and something of the power of the words was described by Shirley Chisholm:

> A few short years ago, if you called most Negroes "blacks," it was tantamount to calling us niggers. But now black is beautiful, and black is proud. There are relatively few people, white or black, who do not recognize what has happened. Black people have freed themselves from the dead weight of albatross blackness that once hung around their necks. They have done it by picking it up in their arms and holding it out with pride for all the world to see. . . . [A]nd they have found that the skin that was once seen as symbolizing their chains is in reality their badge of honor.

Although a few people are still reluctant to accept this use of *black,* the balance has clearly shifted in its favor, and the familiar alternatives *Negro, colored,* and *Afro-American* are heard less often.

Ironically, those who deal with words professionally or avocationally can be the most resistant to linguistic changes. Like Fowler, they may know so much about etymology that any deviation from the classical pattern of word formation grates on their ears. Or having accepted certain rules of grammar as correct, they may find it impossible to acknowledge that those particular rules could ever be superseded.

What many people find hardest to accept is that a word which used to mean one thing now means another, and that continuing to use it in its former sense — no matter how impeccable its etymological credentials — can only invite misunderstanding. When the shift in meaning happened centuries ago, no problem lingers. One may be fully aware that *girl* once meant "a young person of either sex" (as it did in Chaucer's time) and yet not feel compelled to refer to a sexually mixed group of children as girls. When the change happens in one's lifetime, recognition and acceptance may be harder.

The word *intriguing* is such a case. Once understood to mean "conniving" or "deceitful" (as a verb, *intrigue* comes through the French *intriguer,* "to puzzle," from the Latin *intricare,* "to entangle"), *intriguing* now means "engaging the interest to a marked degree," as Webster's Third New International Dictionary noted over three decades ago. People still make statements like "They are an intriguing pair" with the intention of issuing a warning, but chances are the meaning conveyed is "They are a fascinating pair," because that is how a new generation of writers and speakers understands and uses the word. In one sense precision has been lost; in another it has only shifted.

The transformation of *man* over the past thousand years may be the most troublesome and significant change ever to overtake an English word. Once a synonym for "human being," *man* has gradually narrowed in meaning to become a synonym for "adult male human being" only. Put simply in the words of a popular dictionary for children, "A boy grows up to be a man. Father and Uncle George are both men." These are the meanings of *man* and *men* native speakers of English internalize because they are the meanings that from infancy on we hear applied to everyday speech. Though we may later acquire the information that *man* has another, "generic" meaning, we do not accept it with the same certainty that we accept the children's dictionary definition and its counterparts: A girl does not grow up to be a man. Mother and Aunt Teresa are not men; they are women.

To go on using in its former sense a word whose meaning has changed is counterproductive. The point is not that we should recognize semantic change, but that in order to be precise, in order to be understood, we must. The difference is a fundamental one in any discussion of linguistic bias, for some writers think their freedom of expression and artistic integrity are being compromised when they are asked to avoid certain words or grammatical forms. Is it ever justifiable, for example, for publishers to expect their authors to stop using the words *forefathers, man,* and *he* as though they were sex-inclusive? Is this not unwarranted interference with an author's style? Even censorship?

No, it is not. The public counts on those who disseminate factual information — especially publishers of textbooks and other forms of nonfiction, and those who work in the mass media — to be certain that what they tell us is as accurate as research and the conscientious use of language can make it. Only recently have we become aware that conventional English usage, including the generic use of masculine-gender words, often obscures the actions, the contributions, and sometimes the very presence of women. Turning our backs on that insight is an option, of course, but it is an option like teaching children that the world is flat. In this respect, continuing to use English in ways that have become misleading is no different from misusing data, whether the misuse is inadvertent or planned.

The need today, as always, is to be in command of language, not used by it, and so the challenge is to find clear, convincing, graceful ways to say accurately what we want to say. . . .

PART FIVE

GRAMMATICAL SENTENCES

Part V of *The Bedford Handbook,* "Grammatical Sentences" helps students apply rules for grammar and usage as they revise. The handbook keeps these rules in perspective, presenting them in an accessible format that helps students, whatever their backgrounds, to make their writing more effective.

Since Mina Shaughnessy's seminal work on "basic writing" introduced composition specialists to error analysis (*Errors and Expectations,* 1977), instructors have become more attuned to the problems that many students have with sentence grammar and standard usage. We now understand that many students experience conflicts and struggles with issues of grammar and usage that are more fundamental than problems with correctness. Their personal and cultural identities are related inextricably to their use of language.

The following selections present a dialogue about grammar, usage, and error, offering instructors an expanded perspective from which they can consider questions fundamental to the relation of grammar and composition.

- What is error analysis? How can it help students recognize and solve problems with grammar and usage? How can we make error analysis productive for students?
- What are the relations between language and identity? How can we help students learn to use standard edited English without asking them to abandon cultural values? How can we help students understand the implications of choosing or resisting to conform?

CONFLICT AND STRUGGLE:
THE ENEMIES OR PRECONDITIONS OF BASIC WRITING?

Min-Zhan Lu

[*College English* 54 (1992): 887–913.]

Min-Zhan Lu is an associate professor of English at Drake University, where she teaches composition, literary and cultural criticism, and autobiography. She has published numerous articles in journals such as the *Journal of Basic Writing,* the *Journal of Education,* and *College English.* Much of her work in composition relates to the use of cultural dissonance in teaching.

In this and other recent essays, Lu challenges prevailing views of basic writing. Up to now, many composition theorists have seen the "conflict and struggle" that basic writers experience while learning conventions of standard English as negative — something to be overcome. Lu contests this assumption, arguing that teachers should consider the productive, creative, and positive potential of conflict. "We need to find ways of foregrounding conflict and struggle," Lu asserts, "not only in the generation of meaning and authority, but also in the teaching of conventions of 'correctness' in syntax, spelling, and punctuation, traditionally considered the primary focus of Basic Writing instruction."

Harlem taught me that light skin Black people was better look, the best to suceed, the best off fanicially etc this whole that I trying to say, that I was brainwashed and people aliked.

    I couldn't understand why people (Black and white) couldn't get alone. So as time went along I began learned more about myself and the establishment.

       – Sample student paper, Shaughnessy, *Errors and Expectations* 278

. . . Szasz was throwing her. She couldn't get through the twelve-and-a-half pages of introduction. . . .

    One powerful reason Lucia had decided to major in psychology was that she wanted to help people like her brother, who had a psychotic break in his teens and had been in and out of hospitals since. She had lived with mental illness, had seen that look in her brother's eyes. . . . The assertion that there was no such thing as mental illness, that it was a myth, seemed incomprehensible to her. She had trouble even entertaining it as a hypothesis. . . . Szasz's bold claim was a bone sticking in her assumptive craw.

       – Mike Rose, *Lives on the Boundary* 183–84

In perceiving conflicting information and points of view, she is subjected to a swamping of her psychological borders.

       – Gloria Anzaldúa, *Borderlands/La Frontera: The New Mestiza* 79

In the Preface to *Borderlands,* Gloria Anzaldúa uses her own struggle "living on borders and in margins" to discuss the trials and triumphs in the lives of "border residents." The image of "border residents" captures the conflict and struggle of students like those appearing in the epigraphs. In perceiving conflicting information and points of view, a writer like Anzaldúa is "subjected to a swamping of her psychological borders" (79). But attempts to cope with conflicts also bring "compensation," "joys," and "exhilaration" (Anzaldúa, Preface). The border resident develops a tolerance for contradiction and ambivalence, learning to sustain contradiction and turn ambivalence into a new consciousness — "a *third* element which is *greater* than the sum of its *severed parts*": "a mestiza consciousness" (79–80; emphasis mine). Experience taught Anzaldúa that this developing consciousness is a source of intense pain. For development involves struggle which is "inner" and is played out in the outer terrains (87). But this new consciousness draws energy from the "continual creative motion that keeps breaking down the unitary aspect of each new paradigm" (80). It enables a border resident to act on rather than merely react to the conditions of her or his life, turning awareness of the situation into "inner changes" which in turn bring about "changes in society" (87).

Education as Repositioning

    Anzaldúa's account gathers some of the issues on which a whole range of recent composition research focuses, research on how readers and writers necessarily struggle with conflicting information and points of view as they reposition themselves in the process of reading and writing. This research recognizes that reading and writing take place at sites of political as well as linguistic conflict. It acknowledges that such a process of conflict and struggle is a source of pain but constructive as well: a new consciousness emerges from the creative motion of breaking down the rigid boundaries of social and linguistic paradigms.

Compositionists are becoming increasingly aware of the need to tell and listen to stories of life in the borderlands. The CCCC Best Book Award given Mike Rose's *Lives on the Boundary* and the Braddock Award given to Glynda Hull and Mike Rose for their research on students like Lucia attest to this increasing awareness. *College Composition and Communication* recently devoted a whole issue (February 1992) to essays which use images of "boundary," "margin," or "voice" to re-view the experience of reading and writing and teaching reading and writing within the academy (see also Lu, "From Silence to Words"; Bartholomae, "Writing on the Margins"; and Mellix). These publications and their reception indicate that the field is taking seriously two notions of writing underlying these narratives: the sense that the writer writes at a site of conflict rather than "comfortably inside or powerlessly outside the academy" (Lu, "Writing as Repositioning" 20) and a definition of "innovative writing" as cutting across rather than confining itself within boundaries of race, class, gender, and disciplinary differences.

In articulating the issues explored by these narratives from the borderlands, compositionists have found two assumptions underlying various feminist, marxist, and poststructuralist theories of language useful: first, that learning a new discourse has an effect on the re-forming of individual consciousness; and second, that individual consciousness is necessarily heterogeneous, contradictory, and in process (Bizzell; Flynn; Harris; Lunsford, Moglen, and Slevin; Trimbur). The need to reposition oneself and the positive use of conflict and struggle are also explored in a range of research devoted to the learning difficulties of Basic Writers (Bartholomae, "Inventing"; Fox; Horner; Hull and Rose; Lu, "Redefining"; Ritchie; Spellmeyer; Stanley). Nevertheless, such research has had limited influence on Basic Writing instruction, which continues to emphasize skills (Gould and Heyda) and to view conflict as the enemy (Schilb, Brown). I believe that this view of conflict can be traced in the work of three pioneers in Basic Writing: Kenneth Bruffee, Thomas Farrell, and Mina Shaughnessy. In what follows, I examine why this view of conflict had rhetorical power in the historical context in which these pioneers worked and in relation to two popular views of education: education as acculturation and education as accommodation. I also explore how and why this view persists among Basic Writing teachers in the 1990s.

Although Bruffee, Farrell, and Shaughnessy hold different views on the goal of education, they all treat the students' fear of acculturation and the accompanying sense of contradiction and ambiguity as a *deficit*. Even though stories of the borderlands like Anzaldúa's suggest that teachers can and should draw upon students' perception of conflict as a constructive resource, these three pioneers of Basic Writing view evidence of conflict and struggle as something to be dissolved and so propose "cures" aimed at *releasing* students from their fear of acculturation. Bruffee and Farrell present students' acculturation as inevitable and beneficial. Shaughnessy promises them that learning academic discourse will not result in acculturation. Teachers influenced by the work of these pioneers tend to view all signs of conflict and struggle as the *enemy* of Basic Writing instruction. In perpetuating this view, these teachers also tend to adopt two assumptions about language: 1) an "essentialist" view of language holding that the essence of meaning precedes and is independent of language (see Lu, "Redefining" 26); 2) a view of "discourse communities" as "discursive utopias," in each of which a single, unified, and stable voice directly and completely determines the writings of all community members (Harris 12).

In the 1970s, the era of open admissions at CUNY, heated debate over the "educability" of Basic Writers gave these views of language and of conflict exceptional rhetorical power. The new field of Basic Writing was struggling to establish the legitimacy of its knowledge and expertise, and it was doing so in the context of arguments made by a group of writers — including Lionel Trilling, Irving Howe, and W. E. B. DuBois — who could be viewed as exemplary because of their ethnic or racial backgrounds, their academic success, and the popular view that all Basic Writers entering CUNY through the open admissions movement were "minority" students. The writings of Bruffee, Farrell, and Trilling concur that the goal of education is to acculturate students to the kind of academic "community" they posit. Shaughnessy, on the other hand, attempts to eliminate students' conflicting feelings towards academic discourse by reassuring them that her teaching will only "accommodate" but not weaken their existing relationship with their home cultures. Shaughnessy's approach is aligned with the arguments of Irving Howe and W. E. B. DuBois, who urge teachers to honor students' resistance to deracination. Acculturation and accommodation were the dominant models of open admissions education for teachers who recognized teaching academic discourse as a way of empowering students, and in both models conflict and struggle were seen as the enemies of Basic Writing instruction.

This belief persists in several recent works by a new generation of compositionists and "minority" writers. I will read these writings from the point of view of the border resident and through a view of education as a process of repositioning. In doing so, I will also map out some directions for further demystifying conflict and struggle in Basic Writing instruction and for seeing them as the preconditions of all discursive acts.

Education as Acculturation

In *Errors and Expectations,* Mina Shaughnessy offers us one way of imagining the social and historical contexts of her work: she calls herself a trailblazer trying to survive in a "pedagogical West" (4). This metaphor captures the peripheral position of Basic Writing in English. To other members of the profession, Shaughnessy notes, Basic Writing is not one of their "'real' subjects"; nor are books on Basic Writing "important enough" either to be reviewed or to argue about ("English Professor's Malady" 92). Kenneth Bruffee also testifies to feeling peripheral. Recalling the "collaborative learning" which took place among the directors of CUNY writing programs — a group which included Bruffee himself, Donald McQuade, Mina Shaughnessy, and Harvey Wiener — he points out that the group was brought together not only by their "difficult new task" but also by their sense of having more in common with one another than with many of their "colleagues on [their] own campuses" ("On Not Listening" 4–5).

These frontier images speak powerfully of a sense of being *in* but not *of* the English profession. The questionable academic status of not only their students (seen as "ill-prepared") but also themselves (Basic Writing was mostly assigned to beginning teachers, graduate students, women, minorities, and the underemployed but tenured members of other departments) would pressure teachers like Shaughnessy and Bruffee to find legitimacy for their subject. At the same time, they had to do so by persuading both college administrators who felt "hesitation and discomfort" towards open admissions policies and "senior and tenured professorial staff" who either resisted or did not share their commitment (Lyons 175). Directly or indirectly, these pioneers had to respond to, argue with, and persuade the "gatekeepers" and "converters" Shaughnessy describes in "Diving In." It is in the context of such challenges that we must understand the key terms the pioneers use and the questions they consider — and overlook — in establishing the problematics of Basic Writing.

One of the most vehement gatekeepers at CUNY during the initial period of open admissions was Geoffrey Wagner (Professor of English at City College). In *The End of Education,* Wagner posits a kind of "university" in which everyone supposedly pursues learning for its own sake, free of all "worldly" — social, economic, and political — interests. To Wagner, open admissions students are the inhabitants of the "world" outside the sort of scholarly "community" which he claims existed at Oxford and City College. They are dunces (43), misfits (129), hostile mental children (247), and the most sluggish of animals (163). He describes a group of Panamanian "girls" taking a Basic Writing course as "abusive, stupid, and hostile" (128). Another student is described as sitting "in a half-lotus pose in back of class with a transistor strapped to his Afro, and nodding off every two minutes" (134). Wagner calls the Basic Writing program at City a form of political psychotherapy (145), a welfare agency, and an entertainment center (173). And he calls Shaughnessy "the Circe of CCNY's remedial English program" (129). To Wagner, Basic Writers would cause "the end of education" because they have intellects comparable to those of beasts, the retarded, the psychotic, or children, and because they are consumed by non-"academic" — i.e., racial, economic, and political — interests and are indifferent to "learning."

Unlike the "gatekeepers," Louis Heller (Classics Professor, City College) represents educators who seemed willing to shoulder the burden of converting the heathens but disapproved of the ways in which CUNY was handling the conversion. Nonetheless, in *The Death of the American University* Heller approaches the "problems" of open admissions students in ways similar to Wagner's. He contrasts the attitudes of open admissions students and of old Jewish City College students like himself:

> In those days ["decades ago"] there was genuine hunger, and deprivation, and discrimination too, but when a child received failing marks no militant parent group assailed the teacher. Instead parent and child agonized over the subject, placing the responsibility squarely on the child who was given to know that *he* had to measure up to par, not that he was the victim of society, a wicked school system, teachers who didn't understand him, or any of the other pseudosociological nonsense now handed out. (138)

According to Heller, the parents of open admissions students are too "militant." As a result, the students' minds are stuffed with "pseudosociological nonsense" about their victimization by the educational system. The "problem" of open admissions students, Heller suggests, is their militant attitude, which keeps them from trying to "agonize over the subject" and "measure up to par."

Wagner predicts the "end of education" because of the *"arrival* in urban academe of *large,* indeed *overwhelming, numbers* of *hostile* mental children" (247; emphasis mine). As the titles of Heller's chapters suggest, Heller too believes that a "Death of the American University" would inevitably result from the "Administrative Failure of Nerve" or "Capitulation Under Force" to "Violence on Campus" which he claims to have taken place at City College. The images of education's end or death suggest that both Wagner and Heller assume that the goal of education is the acculturation of students into an "educated community." They question the "educability" of open admissions students because they *fear* that these students would not only be hostile to the education they promote but also take it over — that is, change it. The apocalyptic tone of their book titles suggests their fear that the students' "hostile" or "militant" feelings towards the existing educational system would weaken the ability of the "American University" to realize its primary goal — to acculturate. Their writings show that their view of the "problems" of open admissions students and their view of the goal of education sustain one another.

This view of education as a process of acculturation is shared by Lionel Trilling, another authority often cited as an exemplary minority student (see, for example, Howe, "Living" 108). In a paper titled "The Uncertain Future of the Humanistic Educational Ideal" delivered in 1974, Trilling claims that the view of higher education "as the process of initiation into membership" in a "new, larger, and more complex community" is "surely" not a "mistaken conception" (*The Last Decade* 170). The word "initiation," Trilling points out, designates the "ritually prescribed stages by which a person is brought into a community" (170–71). "Initiation" requires "submission," demanding that one "shape" and "limit" oneself to "*a* self, *a* life" and "preclude any other kind of selfhood remaining available" to one (171, 175; emphasis mine). Trilling doubts that contemporary American culture will find "congenial" the kind of "initiation" required by the "humanistic educational ideal" (171). For contemporary "American culture" too often encourages one to resist any doctrine that does not sustain "a multiplicity of options" (175). And Trilling admits to feeling "saddened" by the unlikelihood that "an ideal of education closely and positively related to the humanistic educational traditions of the past" will be called into being in contemporary America (161).

The trials of "initiation" are the subject of Trilling's short story "Notes on a Departure." The main character, a young college professor about to leave a university town, is portrayed as being forced to wrestle with an apparition which he sometimes refers to as the "angel of Jewish solitude" and, by the end of the story, as a "red-haired comedian" whose "face remained blank and idiot" (*Of This Time* 53, 55). The apparition hounds the professor, often reminding him of the question "'What for?' Jews did not do such things" (54). Towards the end of the story, the professor succeeds in freeing himself from the apparition. Arriving at a state of "readiness," he realizes that he would soon have to "find his *own* weapon, his *own* adversary, his *own* things to do" — findings in which "this red-haired figure . . . would have *no* part" (55; emphasis mine).

This story suggests — particularly in view of Trilling's concern for the "uncertain future" of the "humanistic educational ideal" in the 1970s — that contemporary Americans, especially those from minority cultural groups, face a dilemma: the need to combat voices which remind them of the "multiplicity of options." The professor needs to "wrestle with" two options of "selfhood." First, he must free himself from the authority of the "angel"/ "comedian." Then, as the title "Notes on a Departure" emphasizes, he must free himself from the "town." Trilling's representation of the professor's need to "depart" from the voice of his "race" and of the "town" indirectly converges with the belief held by Wagner and Heller that the attitudes "parents" and "society" transmit to open admissions students would pull them away from the "university" and hinder their full initiation — acculturation — into the "educated" community.

Read in the 1990s, these intersecting approaches to the "problems" of "minority" students might seem less imposing, since except perhaps for

Trilling, the academic prestige of these writers has largely receded. Yet we should not underestimate the authority these writers had within the academy. As both the publisher and the author of *The End of Education* (1976) remind us within the first few pages of the book, Wagner is not only a graduate of Oxford but a full professor at City College and author of a total of twenty-nine books of poetry, fiction, literary criticism, and sociology. Heller's *The Death of the American University* (1973) indicates that he has ten years' work at the doctoral or postdoctoral level in three fields, a long list of publications, and years of experience as both a full professor of classics and an administrator at City College (12). Furthermore, their fear of militancy accorded with prevalent reactions to the often violent conflict in American cities and college campuses during the 1960s and 70s. It was in the context of such powerful discourse that composition teachers argued for not only the "educability" of open admissions students but also the ability of the "pioneer" educators to "educate" them. Bruffee's and Farrell's eventual success in establishing the legitimacy of their knowledge and expertise as Basic Writing teachers, I believe, comes in part from a conjuncture in the arguments of the two Basic Writing pioneers and those of Wagner, Heller, and Trilling.

For example, Thomas Farrell presents the primary goal of Basic Writing instruction as acculturation — a move from "orality" to "literacy." He treats open admissions students as existing in a "residual orality": "literate patterns of thought have not been interiorized, have not displaced oral patterns, in them" ("Open Admissions" 248). Referring to Piaget, Ong, and Bernstein, he offers environmental rather than biological reasons for Basic Writers' "orality" — their membership in "communities" where "orality" is the dominant mode of communication. To Farrell, the emigration from "orality" to "literacy" is unequivocally beneficial for everyone, since it mirrors the progression of history. At the same time, Farrell recognizes that such a move will inevitably be accompanied by "anxiety": "The *psychic strain* entailed in moving from a highly oral frame of mind to a more literate frame of mind is *too great* to allow rapid movement" (252; emphasis mine). Accordingly, he promotes teaching strategies aimed at "reducing anxiety" and establishing "a supportive environment." For example, he urges teachers to use the kind of "collaborative learning" Bruffee proposes so that they can use "oral discourse to improve written discourse" ("Open Admissions" 252–53; "Literacy" 456–57). He reminds teachers that "highly oral students" won't engage in the "literate" modes of reasoning "unless they are shown how and reminded to do so often," and even then will do so only "gradually" ("Literacy" 456).

Kenneth Bruffee also defines the goal of Basic Writing in terms of the students' acculturation into a new "community." According to Bruffee, Basic Writers have already been acculturated within "local communities" which have prepared them for only "the narrowest and most limited" political and economic relations ("On Not Listening" 7). The purpose of education is to "reacculturate" the students — to help them "gain membership in another such community" by learning its "language, mores, and values" (8). However, Bruffee believes that the "trials of changing allegiance from one cultural community to another" demand that teachers use "collaborative learning" in small peer groups. This method will "create a *temporary transition* or 'support' group that [one] can join *on the way*" (8; emphasis mine). This "transition group," he maintains, will offer Basic Writers an arena for sharing their "trials," such as the "uncertain, nebulous, and protean thinking that occurs in the process of change" and the "painful process" of gaining new awareness ("On Not Listening" 11; "Collaborative Learning" 640).

Two points bind Bruffee's argument to Farrell's and enhance the rhetorical power of their arguments for the Wagners, Hellers, and Trillings. First, both arguments assume that the goal of education is acculturation into a "literate" community. The image of students who are "changing allegiance from one cultural community to another" (Bruffee), like the image of students "moving" from "orality" to "literacy" (Farrell), posits that "discourse communities" are discrete and autonomous entities rather than interactive cultural forces. When discussing the differences between "orality" and "literacy," Farrell tends to treat these "discourses" as creating coherent but distinct modes of thinking: "speaking" vs. "reading," "clichés" vs. "explained and supported generalizations," "additive" vs. "inductive or deductive" reasoning. Bruffee likewise sets *"coherent* but *entirely* local communities" against a community which is "broader, highly diverse, *integrated*" ("On Not Listening" 7; emphasis mine). Both Farrell and Bruffee use existing analyses of "discourse communities" to set up a seemingly non-political hierarchy between academic and non-academic "communities." They then use the hierarchy to justify implicitly the students' need to be acculturated by the more advanced or broader "community." Thus, they can be construed as promising "effective" ways of appeasing the kind of "hostility" or "militancy" feared in open admissions students. The appeal of this line of thinking is that it protects the autonomy of the "literate community" while also professing a solution to the "threat" the open admissions students seem to pose to the university. Farrell and Bruffee provide methods aimed at keeping students like Anzaldúa, Lucia, and the writer of Shaughnessy's sample paper from moving the points of view and discursive forms they have developed in their home "communities" into the "literate community" and also at persuading such students to willingly "move" into that "literate community."

Second, both Bruffee and Farrell explicitly look for teaching methods aimed at reducing the feelings of "anxiety" or "psychic strain" accompanying the process of acculturation. They thus present these feelings as signs of the students' still being "on the way" from one community to another, i.e., as signs of their failure to complete their acculturation or education. They suggest that the students are experiencing these trials only because they are still in "transition," bearing ties to both the old and new communities but not fully "departed" from one nor comfortably "inside" the other. They also suggest that these experiences, like the transition or support groups, are "temporary" (Bruffee, "On Not Listening" 8). In short, they sustain the impression that these experiences ought to and will disappear once the students get comfortably settled in the new community and sever or diminish their ties with the old. Any sign of heterogeneity, uncertainty, or instability is viewed as problematic; hence conflict and struggle are the enemies of Basic Writing instruction.

This linkage between students' painful conflicts and the teacher's effort to assuage them had rhetorical power in America during the 1970s because it could be perceived as accepting rather than challenging the gatekeepers' and converters' arguments that the pull of non-"academic" forces — "society" (Wagner), "militant parents" (Heller), and minority "race" or "American culture" at large (Trilling) — would render the open admissions students less "educable" and so create a "problem" in their education. It feeds the fear that the pulls of conflicting "options," "selfhoods," or "lives" promoted by antagonistic "communities" would threaten the university's ability to acculturate the Basic Writers. At the same time, this linkage also offers a "support system" aimed at releasing the gatekeepers and converters from their fear. For example, the teaching strategies Farrell promotes, which explicitly aim to support students through their "psychic strain," are also aimed at gradually easing them into "interiorizing" modes of thinking privileged by the "literate community," such as "inductive or deductive" reasoning or "detached, analytic forms of thinking" ("Literacy" 455, 456). Such strategies thus provide a support system for not only the students but also the kind of discursive utopia posited by Trilling's description of the "humanistic educational ideal," Heller's "American University," and Wagner's "education." Directly and indirectly, the pedagogies aimed at "moving" students from one culture to another support and are supported by gatekeepers' and converters' positions towards open admissions students.

The pedagogies of Bruffee and Farrell recognize the "psychic strain" or the "trials" experienced by those reading and writing at sites of contradiction, experiences which are depicted by writers like Trilling ("Notes on a Departure"), Anzaldúa, and Rose and witnessed by teachers in their encounters with students like Lucia and the writer of Shaughnessy's sample paper. Yet, for two reasons, the approaches of Bruffee and Farrell are unlikely to help such students cope with the conflicts "swamping" their "psychological borders." First, these approaches suggest that the students' primary task is to change allegiance, to "learn" and "master" the "language, mores, and values" of the academic community presented in the classroom by passively internalizing them and actively rejecting all points of view or information which run counter to them (Bruffee, "On Not Listening" 8). For the author of Shaughnessy's sample student paper, this could mean learning to identify completely with the point of view of authorities like the Heller of *The Death of the American University* and thus rejecting "militant" thoughts about the "establishment" in order to "agonize over the subject." For Lucia, this could mean learning to identify with the Trilling of "Notes on a Departure," viewing her ability to forget the look in her brother's eyes as a precondition of becoming a psychologist like Szasz. Yet students like Lucia might resist what the classroom seems to indicate they must do in order to achieve academic "success." As Rose reminds us, one of the reasons Lucia decided to major in psychology was to help people like her brother. Students like these are likely to get very little help or guidance from teachers like Bruffee or Farrell.

Secondly, though Bruffee and Farrell suggest that the need to cope with conflicts is a temporary experience for students unfamiliar with and lacking mastery of dominant academic values and forms, Rose's account of his own education indicates that similar experiences of "confusion, anger, and fear" are not at all temporary (Rose 235–36). During Rose's high school years, his teacher Jack MacFarland had successfully helped him cope with his "sense of linguistic exclusion" complicated by "various cultural differences" by engaging him in a sustained examination of "points of conflict and points of possible convergence" between home and academic canons (193). Nevertheless, during Rose's first year at Loyola and then during his graduate school days, he continued to experience similar feelings when encountering texts and settings which reminded him of the conflict between home and school. If students like Rose, Lucia, or the writer of Shaughnessy's sample paper learn to view experiences of conflict — exclusion, confusion, uncertainty, psychic pain or strain — as "temporary," they are also likely to view the recurrence of those experiences as a reason to discontinue their education. Rather than viewing their developing ability to sustain contradictions as heralding the sort of "new mestiza consciousness" Anzaldúa calls for (80), they may take it as signaling their failure to "enter" the academy, since they have been led to view the academy as a place free of contradictions.

Education as Accommodation

Whereas the gatekeepers and converters want students to be either barred from or acculturated into academic culture, Irving Howe (Distinguished Professor of English, Graduate Center of CUNY and Hunter College), another City graduate often cited by the public media as an authority on the education of open admissions students (see Fiske), takes a somewhat different approach. He believes that "the host culture, resting as it does on the English language and the literary traditions associated with it, has . . . every reason to be *sympathetic* to the *problems* of those who, from choice or necessity, may *live with* the *tension of biculturalism*" ("Living" 110; emphasis mine).

The best way to understand what Howe might mean by this statement and why he promotes such a position is to put it in the context of two types of educational stories Howe writes. The first type appears in his *World of Our Fathers,* in which he recounts the "cultural bleaching" required of Jewish immigrants attending classes at the Educational Alliance in New York City around the turn of this century. As Eugene Lyons, one immigrant whom Howe quotes, puts it, "We were 'Americanized' about as gently as horses are broken in." Students who went through this "crude" process, Lyons admits, often came to view their home traditions as "alien" and to "unconsciously resent and despise those traditions" (234). Howe points out that education in this type of "Americanization" exacted a price, leaving the students with a "nagging problem in self-perception, a crisis of identity" (642). Read in the context of Howe's statement on the open admissions students cited above, this type of story points to the kind of "problems" facing students who have to live with the tension between the "minority subcultures" in which they grow up and a "dominant" "Western" "host culture" with which they are trying to establish deep contact through education ("Living" 110). It also points to the limitations of an educational system which is not sympathetic to their problems.

The "Americanization" required of students like Eugene Lyons, Howe points out, often led Jewish students to seek either "a full return to religious faith or a complete abandonment of Jewish identification" (642). But Howe rejects both such choices. He offers instead an alternative story — the struggle of writers like himself to live with rather than escape from "the tension of biculturalism." In *A Margin of Hope,* he recounts his long journey in search of a way to "achieve some equilibrium with that earlier self which had started with childhood Yiddish, my language of naming, and then turned away in adolescent shame" (269). In "Strangers," Howe praises Jewish writers like Saul Bellow and the contributors to *Partisan Review* for their attitudes towards their "partial deracination" (*Selected Writings* 335). He argues that these writers demonstrated that being a "loose-fish" (with "roots loosened in Jewish soil but still not torn out, roots lowered into American soil but still not fixed") is "a badge" to be carried "with pride" (335). Doing so can open up a whole "range of possibilities" (335), such as the "forced yoking of opposites: gutter vividness and university refinement, street energy and high-culture rhetoric" Howe sees these writers achieving (338). This suggests what Howe might mean by "*living with* the tension of biculturalism." The story he tells of the struggle of these Jewish writers also proves that several claims made in the academy of the earlier 1970s, as Howe points out, are "true and urgent": 1) students who grow up in "subcultures" can feel "pain and dislocation" when trying to "connect with the larger, cosmopolitan culture"; 2) for these students, "there must always be some sense of 'difference,' even alienation"; 3) this sense of difference can "yield moral correction and emotional enrichment" ("Living" 110). The story of these writers also suggests that when dealing with students from "subcultures," the dominant culture and its educational system need, as Howe argues, to be more "sympathetic to" the pain and alienation indicated by the first two claims, and at the same time should value more highly the "infusion of vitality and diversity from subcultures" that the third claim suggests these students can bring (110).

Howe believes that the need for reform became especially urgent in the context of the open admissions movement, when a large number of "later immigrants, newer Americans" from racial as well as ethnic "subcultures" arrived at CUNY ("A Foot"). He also believes that, although the dominant culture needs to be more "responsive" and "sympathetic" towards this body of students, it would be "a dreadful form of intellectual condescension — and social cheating" for members of the "host culture" to dissuade students from establishing a "deep connection" with it. The only possible and defensible "educational ideal" is one which brings together commitments to "the widespread diffusion of learning" and to the "preservation of the highest standards of learning" ("Living" 109).

However, as Howe himself seems aware throughout his essay, he is more convinced of the need to live up to this ideal than certain about how to implement it in the day-to-day life of teaching, especially with "the presence of large numbers of ill-prepared students in our classroom" ("Living" 110, 112). For example, the values of "traditionalism" mean that teachers like Howe should try to "preserve" the "English language and the literary traditions" associated with "the dominant culture we call Western" (109, 110). Yet, when Howe tries to teach *Clarissa* to his students, he finds out that he has to help students to "transpose" and "translate" Clarissa's belief in the sanctity of her virginity into their "terms." And he recognizes that the process of transposing would "necessarily distort and weaken" the original belief (112). This makes him realize that there is "reason to take seriously the claim" that "a qualitative transformation of Western culture threatens the survival of literature as we have known it" (112).

Although Howe promotes the images of "loose-fish" and "partial deracination" when discussing the work of Jewish writers, in his discussion of the education of "ill-prepared" students, he considers the possibility of change from only one end of the "tension of bi-culturalism" — that of "Western culture." His essay overlooks the possibility that the process of establishing a deep connection with "Western culture," such as teaching students to "transpose" their "subcultural" beliefs into the terms of "Western culture," might also "distort and weaken" — *transform* — the positions students take towards these beliefs, especially if these beliefs conflict with those privileged in "Western culture." In fact, teachers interested in actively honoring the students' decisions and needs to "live with the tension of bi-culturalism" must take this possibility seriously (see Lu, "Redefining" 33).

In helping students to establish deep connections with "Western culture," teachers who overlook the possibility of students' changing their identification with "subcultural" views are likely to turn education into an accommodation — or mere tolerance — of the students' choice or need to live with conflicts. This accommodation could hardly help students explore, formulate, reflect on, and enact strategies for coping actively with conflicts as the residents of borderlands do: developing a "tolerance for" and an ability to "sustain" contradictions and ambiguity (Anzaldúa 79). Even if teachers explicitly promote the image of "partial deracination," they are likely to be more successful in helping students unconsciously "lower" and "fix" their roots into "Western culture" than in also helping them keep their roots from being completely "torn out" of "subcultures."

Two recurring words in Howe's essay, "preserve" and "survival," suggest a further problematic, for they represent the students as "preservers" of conflicting but unitary paradigms — a canonical "literary tradition" and "subcultures" with "attractive elements that merit study and preservation" ("Living" 110). This view of their role might encourage students to envision themselves as living at a focal point where "severed or separated pieces merely come together" (Anzaldúa 79). Such perceptions might also lead students to focus their energy on "accommodating" their thoughts and actions to rigid boundaries rather than on actively engaging themselves in what to Anzaldúa is the resource of life in the borderlands: a "continual creative motion" which breaks entrenched habits and patterns of behavior (Anzaldúa 79). The residents of the borderlands act on rather than react to the "borders" cutting across society and their psyches, "borders" which become visible as they encounter conflicting ideas and actions. In perceiving these "borders," the mestizas refuse to let these seemingly rigid boundaries confine and compartmentalize their thoughts and actions. Rather, they use these "borders" to identify the unitary aspects of "official" paradigms which "set" and "separate" cultures and which they can then work to break down. That is, for the mestizas, "borders" serve to delineate aspects of their psyches and the world requiring change. Words such as "preserve" and "survival," in focusing the students' attention on accommodation rather than change, could not help students become active residents of the borderlands.

The problematics surfacing from Howe's writings — the kind of "claims" about students from "subcultures" that he considers "true and urgent," the kind of "problems" he associates with students living with the tension of conflicting cultural forces, and the questions he raises as well as those he overlooks when discussing his "educational ideal" — map the general conceptual framework of a group of educators to whose writings I now turn. The writings of Leonard Kriegel, another member of the CUNY English faculty, seem to address precisely the question of how a teacher might implement in the day-to-day teaching of "remedial" students at City College the educational ideal posited by Howe.

In *Working Through: A Teacher's Journey in the Urban University*, Kriegel bases his authority on his personal experience as first a City undergraduate and then a City professor before and during the open admissions movement. Kriegel describes himself as a "working-class Jewish youth" — part of a generation not only eager to "get past [its] backgrounds, to deodorize all smells out of existence, especially the smells of immigrant kitchens and beer-sloppy tables," but also anxious to emulate the "aggressive intellectualism" of City students (32, 123). Kriegel maintains that in his days as a student, there existed a mutual trust between teachers and students: "My teachers could assume a certain intelligence on my part; I, in turn, could assume a certain good will on theirs" (29).

When he was assigned to teach in the SEEK program, Kriegel's first impression was that such a mutual trust was no longer possible. For example, when he asked students to describe Canova's *Perseus Holding the Head of Medusa*, a student opened his paper, "When I see this statue it is of the white man and he is holding the head of the Negro" (176). Such papers led Kriegel to conclude that these students had not only "elementary" problems with writing but also a "racial consciousness [which] seemed to obscure everything else" (176). Yet working among the SEEK students gradually convinced Kriegel that the kind of mutual trust he had previously enjoyed with his teachers and students was not only possible but necessary. He discovered that his black and Puerto Rican students "weren't very different from their white peers": they did not lack opinions and they did want in to the American establishment (175, 178). They can and do trust the "good will" of the teacher who can honestly admit that he is a product of academic culture and believes in it, who rids himself of the "inevitable white guilt" and the fear of being accused of "cultural colonialism," and who permits the students to define their needs in relation to the culture rather than rejecting it for them (180). Kriegel thus urges teachers to "leave students alone" to make their own choices (182).

Kriegel's approach to his journey falls within the framework Howe establishes. The university ought to be "*responsive* to the needs and points of view of students who are of *two minds* about what Western culture offers them" ("Playing It Black" 11; emphasis mine). Yet, when summarizing the lessons he learned through SEEK, Kriegel implies that being "responsive" does not require anything of the teacher other than "*permit[ting]* the student *freedom of choice,* to let him take what he felt he needed and let go of what was not important to him" (*Working Through* 207; emphasis mine). Kriegel ultimately finds himself "mak[ing] decisions based on old values" and "placing greater and greater reliance on the traditional cultural orientation to which [he] had been exposed as an undergraduate" (201–2). The question he does not consider throughout his book is the extent to which his reliance on "old values" and "traditional cultural orientation" might affect his promise to accommodate the students' freedom of choice, especially if they are of "two minds" about what Western culture offers them. That is, he never considers whether his teaching practice might implicitly disable his students' ability to exercise the "freedom" he explicitly "permits" them.

Kriegel's story suggests that business in the classroom could go on as usual so long as teachers openly promise students their "freedom of choice." His story implies that the kind of teaching traditionally used to disseminate the conventions of the "English language or literary tradition" is politically and culturally neutral. It takes a two-pronged approach to educational reform: 1) explicitly stating the teacher's willingness to accommodate — i.e., understand, sympathize with, accept, and respect — the students' choice or need to resist total acculturation; 2) implicitly dismissing the ways in which particular teaching practices "choose" for students — i.e., set pressures on the ways in which students formulate, modify, or even dismiss — their position towards conflicting cultures (for comparable positions by other City faculty, see Volpe and Quinn). This approach has rhetorical currency because it both aspires to and promises to deliver the kind of education envisioned by another group of minority writers with established authority in 1970s America, a group which included black intellectuals W. E. B. DuBois and James Baldwin. Using personal and communal accounts, these writers also argue for educational systems which acknowledge students' resistance to cultural deracination. Yet, because their arguments for such an educational reform are seldom directly linked to discussion of specific pedagogical issues, teachers who share Kriegel's position could read DuBois and Baldwin as authorizing accommodation.

For example, in *The Education of Black People,* DuBois critiques the underlying principle of earlier educational models for black students, such as the "Hampton Idea" or the Fisk program, which do not help students deal with what he elsewhere calls their double-consciousness (12, 51). Instead, such models pressure students to "escape their cultural heritage and the body of experience which they themselves have built-up." As a result, these students may "meet *peculiar frustration* and in the end be unable to achieve success in the new environment or fit into the old" (144; emphasis mine).

DuBois's portrayal of the "peculiar frustration" of black students, like Howe's account of the "problems" of Jewish students, speaks powerfully of the need to consider seriously Howe's list of the "claims" made during the open admissions movement ("Living" 110). It also supports Howe's argument that the dominant culture needs to be more "sympathetic" to the "problems" of students from black and other ethnic cultures. DuBois's writings offer teachers a set of powerful narratives to counter the belief that students' interests in racial politics will impede their learning. In fact, DuBois's life suggests that being knowledgeable of and concerned with racial politics is a precondition to one's eventual ability to "force" oneself "in" and to "share" the world with "the owners" *(Education 77)*.

At the same time, DuBois's autobiography can also be read as supporting the idea that once the teacher accepts the students' need to be interested in racial politics and becomes "sympathetic to" — acknowledges — their "peculiar frustration," business in the writing classroom can go on as usual. For example, when recalling his arrival at Harvard "in the midst of a violent controversy about poor English among students," DuBois describes his experiences in a compulsory Freshman English class as follows:

> I was at the point in my intellectual development when the content rather than the form of my writing was to me of prime importance. Words and ideas surged in my mind and spilled out with disregard of exact accuracy in grammar, taste in word or restraint in style. I knew the Negro problem and this was more important to me than literary form. I knew grammar fairly well, and I had a pretty wide vocabulary; but I was bitter, angry and intemperate in my first thesis. . . . Senator Morgan of Alabama had just published a scathing attack on "niggers" in a leading magazine, when my first Harvard thesis was due. I let go at him with no holds barred. My long and blazing effort came back marked "E" — not passed. *(Autobiography 144)*

Consequently, DuBois "went to work at" his English and raised the grade to a "C." Then, he "*elected* the best course on the campus for English composition," one which was taught by Barrett Wendell, "then the great pundit of Harvard English" (144–45; emphasis mine).

DuBois depicts his teacher as "fair" in judging his writing "technically" but as having neither any idea of nor any interest in the ways in which racism "scratch[ed] [DuBois] on the raw flesh" (144). DuBois presents his own interest in the "Negro problem" as a positive force, enabling him to produce "solid content" and "worthy" thoughts. At the same time, he also presents his racial/political interest as making him "bitter, angry, and intemperate." The politics of style would suggest that his "disregard of exact accuracy in grammar, taste in word or restraint in style" when writing the thesis might have stemmed not only from his failure to recognize the importance of *form* but also from the particular constraints this "literary form" placed on his effort to "spill out" bitter and angry *contents* against the establishment. Regard for "*accuracy* in grammar, *taste* in word or *restraint* in style" would have constrained his effort to "let go at [Senator Morgan] with no holds barred" (emphasis mine). But statements such as "style is *subordinate* to content" but "*carries* a message further" suggest that DuBois accepts wholeheartedly the view that the production of "something to say" takes place before and independent of the effort to "say it well" (144; emphasis mine). Nor does DuBois fault his teachers for failing to help him recognize and then practice ways of dealing with the politics of a "style" which privileges "restraint." Rather, his account suggests only that writing teachers need to become more understanding of the students' racial/political interests and their tendency to view "the Negro problem" as more important than "literary form." Thus, his account allows teachers to read it as endorsing the idea that once the teachers learn to show more interest in what the students "have to say" about racism, they can continue to teach "literary form" in the way DuBois's composition teachers did.

Neither do the writings of James Baldwin, whom Shaughnessy cites as the kind of "mature and gifted writer" her Basic Writers could aspire to become (*Errors* 197), provide much direct opposition to this two-pronged approach to reform. In "A Talk to Teachers" (originally published in the *Saturday Review*, 21 December 1963), Baldwin argues that "any Negro who is born in this country and undergoes the American educational system runs the risk of becoming schizophrenic" (*Price* 326; see also *Conversations* 183), thus providing powerful support for Howe's call for sympathy from the dominant culture. Baldwin does offer some very sharp and explicit critiques of the view of literary style as politically innocent. In "If Black English Isn't a Language, Then Tell Me, What Is?" Baldwin points out that "the rules of the language are dictated by what the language must convey" (*Price* 651). He later explains that standard English "was not designed to carry those spirits and patterns" he has observed in his relatives and among the people from the streets and churches of Harlem, so he "had to find a way to bend it [English]" when writing about them in his first book (*Conversations* 162). These descriptions suggest that Baldwin is aware of the ways in which the style of one particular discourse mediates one's effort to generate content or a point of view alien to that discourse. Yet, since he is referring to his writing experience *after* he has become what Shaughnessy calls a "mature and gifted writer" rather than to experience as a student in a writing classroom, he does not directly challenge the problematics surfacing in discussions of educational reform aimed at accommodation without change.

The seeming resemblances between minority educators and Basic Writers — their "subculture" backgrounds, the "psychic woe" they experience as a result of the dissonance within or among cultures, their "ambivalence" towards cultural bleaching, and their interest in racial/class politics — make these educators powerful allies for composition teachers like Shaughnessy who are not only committed to the educational rights and capacity of Basic Writers but also determined to grant students the freedom of choosing their alignments among conflicting cultures. We should not underestimate the support these narratives could provide for the field of Basic Writing as it struggled in the 1970s to establish legitimacy for its knowledge and expertise. I call attention to this support because of the intersection I see between Shaughnessy's approach to the function of conflict and struggle in Basic Writing instruction and the problematics I have sketched out in discussing the writings of Howe, Kriegel, DuBois, and Baldwin.

Like Howe and DuBois, Shaughnessy tends to approach the problems of Basic Writers in terms of their ambivalence toward academic culture:

> College both beckons and threatens them, offering to teach them useful ways of thinking and talking about the world, promising even to improve the quality of their lives, but threatening at the same time to take from

them their distinctive ways of interpreting the world, to assimilate them into the culture of academia without acknowledging their experience as outsiders. (*Errors* 292)

Again and again, Shaughnessy reminds us of her students' fear that mastery of a new discourse could wipe out, cancel, or take from them the points of view resulting from "their experience as outsiders." This fear, she argues, causes her students to mistrust and psychologically resist learning to write. And she reasons that "if students understand why they are being asked to learn something and if the reasons given *do not conflict* with deeper needs for self-respect and loyalty to their group (whether that be an economic, racial, or ethnic group), they *are disposed* to learn it" (*Errors* 125; emphasis mine).

Shaughnessy proposes some teaching methods towards that end. For example, when discussing her students' difficulty developing an "academic vocabulary," she suggests that students might resist associating a new meaning with a familiar word because accepting that association might seem like consenting to a "linguistic betrayal that threatens to wipe out not just a word but the reality that the word refers to" (*Errors* 212). She goes on to suggest that "if we consider the formal (rather than the contextual) ways in which words can be made to shift meaning we are closer to the kind of practical information about words BW students need" (212). Shaughnessy's rationale seems to be that the "formal" approach (in this case teaching students to pay attention to prefixes and suffixes) is more "practical" because it will help students master the academic meaning of a word *without* reminding them that doing so might "wipe out" the familiar "reality" — the world, people, and meanings — previously associated with that word.

However, as I have argued elsewhere, the "formal" approach can be taken as "practical" only if teachers view the students' awareness of the conflict between the home meaning and the school meaning of a word as something to be "dissolved" at all costs because it will make them less "disposed to learn" academic discourse, as Shaughnessy seems to believe (Lu, "Redefining" 35). However, the experiences of Anzaldúa and Rose suggest that the best way to help students cope with the "pain," "strain," "guilt," "fear," or "confusions" resulting from this type of conflict is not to find ways of "releasing" the students from these experiences or to avoid situations which might activate them. Rather, the "contextual" approach would have been more "practical," since it could help students deal self-consciously with the threat of "betrayal," especially if they fear and want to resist it. The "formal approach" recommended by Shaughnessy, however, is likely to be only a more "practical" way of preserving "academic vocabulary" and of speeding the students' internalization of it. As Rose's experiences working with students like Lucia indicate, it is exactly because teachers like him took the "contextual" approach — "encouraging her to talk through opinions of her own that ran counter to these discussions" (Rose 184–85) — that Lucia was able to get beyond the first twelve pages of Szasz's text and learn the "academic" meaning of "mental illness" posited by Szasz, a meaning which literally threatens to wipe out the "reality" of her brother's illness and her feelings about it.

Shaughnessy's tendency to overlook the political dimensions of the linguistic choices students make when reading and writing also points to the ways in which her "essentialist" view of language and her view of conflict and struggle as the enemies of Basic Writing instruction feed on one another (Lu, "Redefining" 26, 28–29). The supposed separation between language, thinking, and living reduces language into discrete and autonomous linguistic varieties or sets of conventions, rules, standards, and codes rather than treating language as a site of cultural conflict and struggle. From the former perspective, it is possible to believe, as Shaughnessy seems to suggest when opting for the "formal" approach to teaching vocabulary, that learning the rules of a new "language variety" — "the language of public transactions" — will give the student the "ultimate freedom of deciding how and when and where he will use which language" (*Errors* 11, 125). And it makes it possible for teachers like Shaughnessy to separate a "freedom" of choice in "linguistic variety" from one's social being — one's need to deliberate over and decide how to reposition oneself in relationship to conflicting cultures and powers. Thus, it might lead teachers to overlook the ways in which one's "freedom" of cultural alignment might impinge on one's freedom in choosing "linguistic variety."

Shaughnessy's approach to Basic Writing instruction has rhetorical power because of its seeming alignment with positions taken by "minority" writers. Her portrayal of the "ambivalent feelings" of Basic Writers matches the experiences of "wrestling" (Trilling) and "partial deracination" (Howe), "the peculiar frustration" (DuBois), and "schizophrenia" (Baldwin) portrayed in the writings of the more established members of the academy. All thus lend validity to each other's understanding of the "problems" of students from minority cultures and to their critiques of educational systems which mandate total acculturation. Shaughnessy's methods of teaching demonstrate acceptance of and compassion towards students' experience of the kind of "dislocation," "alienation," or "difference" which minority writers like Howe, DuBois, and Baldwin argue will always accompany those trying by choice or need to "live with" the tensions of conflicting cultures. Her methods of teaching also demonstrate an effort to accommodate these feelings and points of view. That is, because of her essentialist assumption that words can express but will not change the essence of one's thoughts, her pedagogy promises to help students master academic discourse without forcing them to reposition themselves — i.e., to re-form their relation — towards conflicting cultural beliefs. In that sense, her teaching promises to accommodate the students' need to establish deep contact with a "wider," more "public" culture by "releasing" them from their fear that learning academic discourse will cancel out points of view meaningful to their non-"academic" activities. At the same time, it also promises to accommodate their existing ambivalence towards and differences from academic culture by assuming that "expressing" this ambivalence and these differences in academic "forms" will not change the "essence" of these points of view. The lessons she learns from her journey in the "pedagogical West" thus converge with those of Kriegel, who dedicates his book to "Mina Shaughnessy, who knows that nothing is learned simply." That is, when discussing her teaching methods, she too tends to overlook the ways in which her methods of teaching "linguistic codes" might weaken her concern to permit the students freedom of choice in their points of view. Ultimately, as I have argued, the teaching of both Shaughnessy and Kriegel might prove to be more successful in preserving the traditions of "English language and literature" than in helping students reach a self-conscious choice on their position towards conflicting cultural values and forces.

Contesting the Residual Power of Viewing Conflict and Struggle as the Enemies of Basic Writing Instruction: Present and Future

The view that all signs of conflict and struggle are the enemies of Basic Writing instruction emerged partly from a set of specific historical conditions surrounding the open admissions movement. Open admissions at CUNY was itself an attempt to deal with immediate, intense, sometimes violent social, political, and racial confrontations. Such a context seemed to provide a logic for shifting students' attention *away* from conflict and struggle and *towards* calm. However, the academic status which pioneers like Bruffee, Farrell, and Shaughnessy have achieved and the practical, effective *cures* their pedagogies seem to offer have combined to perpetuate the rhetorical power of such a view for Basic Writing instruction through the 1970s to the present. The consensus among the gatekeepers, converters, and accommodationists furnishes some Basic Writing teachers with a complacent sense that they already know all about the "problems" Basic Writers have with conflict and struggle. This complacency makes teachers hesitant to consider the possible uses of conflict and struggle, even when these possibilities are indicated by later developments in language theories and substantiated both by accounts of alternative educational experiences by writers like Anzaldúa and Rose and by research on the constructive use of conflict and struggle, such as the research discussed in the first section of this essay.

Such complacency is evident in the works of compositionists like Mary Epes and Ann Murphy. Epes's work suggests that she is aware of recent arguments against the essentialist view of language underlying some composition theories and practices. For example, she admits that error analysis is complex because there is "a crucial area of overlap" between "*encoding*" (defined by Epes as "controlling the visual symbols which represent meaning on the page") and "*composing* (controlling meaning in writing)" (6). She also observes that students are most likely to experience the "conflict between composing and decoding" when the "norms of the written code" are "in conflict" with "the language of one's nurture" (31). Given Epes's recognition of the conflict between encoding and composing, she should have little disagreement with compositionists who argue that learning to use the "codes" of academic discourse would constrain certain types of meanings, such as the formulation of feelings and thoughts towards cultures drastically dissonant from academic culture. Yet, when Epes moves from her theory to pedagogy, she argues that teachers of Basic Writers can and ought to treat "encoding" and "composition" as two separate areas of instruction (31). Her rationale is simple: separating the two could avoid "exacerbating" the students' experience of the "conflict" between these activities (31). The key terms here (for me, at any rate) are "exacerbating" and "conflict." They illustrate Epes's concern to eliminate conflict, disagreement, tension, and complexity from the Basic Writing classroom (cf. Horner).

Ann Murphy's essay "Transference and Resistance" likewise demonstrates the residual power of the earlier view of conflict and struggle as the enemies of Basic Writing instruction. Her essay draws on her knowledge of the Lacanian notion of the decentered and destabilized subject. Yet Murphy argues against the applicability of such a theory to the teaching of Basic Writing on the ground that Basic Writers are not like other students. Basic Writers, Murphy argues, "may need centering rather than decentering, and cognitive skills rather than (or as compellingly as) self-exploration" (180). She depicts Basic Writers as "shattered and destabilized by the social and political system" (180). She claims that "being taken seriously as *adults* with something of value to say can, for many Basic Writing students, be a *traumatic* and *disorienting* experience" (180; emphasis mine). Murphy's argument demonstrates her desire to eliminate any sense of uncertainty or instability in Basic Writing classrooms. Even though Murphy is willing to consider the implications of the Lacanian notion of individual subjectivity for the teaching of other types of students (180), her readiness to separate

Basic Writing classrooms from other classrooms demonstrates the residual power of earlier views of conflict and struggle.

Such a residual view is all the more difficult to contest because it is supported by a new generation of minority educators. For example, in "Teacher Background and Student Needs" (1991), Peter Rondinone uses his personal experiences as an open admissions student taking Basic Writing 1 at CCNY during the early 70s and his Russian immigrant family background in the Bronx to argue for the need to help Basic Writers understand that "in deciding to become educated there will be times when [basic writers] will be forced to . . . reject or *betray* their family and friends in order to succeed" ("Teacher" 42). Rondinone's view of how students might best deal with the conflict between home and school does not seem to have changed much since his 1977 essay describing his experience as a senior at City College (see Rondinone, "Open Admissions"). In his 1991 essay, this time writing from the point of view of an experienced teacher, Rondinone follows Bruffee in maintaining that "learning involves shifting social allegiances" ("Teacher" 49). My quarrel with Rondinone is not so much over his having opted for complete deracination (for I honor his right to choose his allegiance even though I disagree with his choice). I am, however, alarmed by his unequivocal belief that his choice is the *a priori* condition of his academic success, which reveals his conviction that conflict can only impede one's learning.

Shelby Steele's recent and popular *The Content of Our Character* suggests similar assumptions about experiences of cultural conflict. Using personal experiences, Steele portrays the dilemma of an African-American college student and professor in terms of being caught in the familiar "trap": bound by "two equally powerful elements" which are "at odds with each other" (95). Steele's solution to the problem of "opposing thrusts" is simple: find a way to "unburden" the student from one of the thrusts (160). Thus, Steele promotes a new, "peacetime" black identity which could "release" black Americans from a racial identity which regards their "middle-class" values, aspirations, and success as suspect (109).

To someone like Steele, the pedagogies of Bruffee, Farrell, and Rondinone would make sense. In such a classroom, the black student who told Steele that "he was not sure he should master standard English because then he 'wouldn't be black no more'" (70) would have the comfort of knowing that he is not alone in wanting to pursue things "all individuals" want or in wishing to be drawn "into the American mainstream" (71). Furthermore, he would find support systems to ease him through the momentary pain, dislocation, and anxiety accompanying his effort to "unburden" himself of one of the "opposing thrusts." The popular success of Steele's book attests to the power of this type of thinking on the contemporary scene. Sections of his book originally appeared in such journals as *Harper's, Commentary,* the *New York Times Magazine,* and *The American Scholar.* Since publication of the book, Steele has been touted as an expert on problems facing African-American students in higher education, and his views have been aired on PBS specials, *Nightline,* and the *MacNeil/Lehrer News Hour,* and in *Time* magazine. The popularity of his book should call our attention to the direct and indirect ways in which the distrust of conflict and struggle continues to be recycled and disseminated both within and outside the academy. At the same time, the weight of the authority of the Wagners and Hellers should caution us to take more seriously the pressures the Rondinones and Steeles can exert on Basic Writing teachers, a majority of us still occupying peripheral positions in a culture repeatedly swept by waves of new conservatism.

But investigating the particular directions taken by Basic Writing pioneers when establishing authority for their expertise and the historical contexts of those directions should also enable us to perceive alternative ways of conversing with the Rondinones and Steeles in the 1990s. Because of the contributions of pioneers like Bruffee, Farrell, and Shaughnessy, we can now mobilize the authority they have gained for the field, for our knowledge as well as our expertise as Basic Writing teachers. While we can continue to benefit from the insights into students' experiences of conflict and struggle offered in the writings of all those I have discussed, we need not let their view of the cause and function of such experiences restrict how we view and use the stories and pedagogies they provide. Rather, we need to read them against the grain, filling in the silences left in these accounts by re-reading their experiences from the perspective of alternative accounts from the borderlands and from the perspective of new language and pedagogical theories. For many of these authors are themselves products of classrooms which promoted uncritical faith in either an essentialist view of language or various forms of discursive utopia that these writers aspired to preserve. Therefore, we should use our knowledge and expertise as compositionists to do what they did not or could not do: re-read their accounts in the context of current debates on the nature of language, individual consciousness, and the politics of basic skills. At the same time, we also need to gather more oppositional and alternative accounts from a new generation of students, those who can speak about the successes and challenges of classrooms which recognize the positive uses of conflict and struggle and which teach the process of repositioning.

The writings of the pioneers and their more established contemporaries indicate that the residual distrust of conflict and struggle in the field of Basic Writing is sustained by a fascination with cures for psychic woes, by two views of education — as acculturation and as accommodation — and by two views of language — essentialist and utopian. We need more research which critiques portrayals of Basic Writers as belonging to an abnormal — traumatized or underdeveloped — mental state and which simultaneously provides accounts of the "creative motion" and "compensation," "joy," or "exhilaration" resulting from Basic Writers' efforts to grapple with the conflict within and among diverse discourses. We need more research analyzing and contesting the assumptions about language underlying teaching methods which offer to "cure" all signs of conflict and struggle, research which explores ways to help students recover the latent conflict and struggle in their lives which the dominant conservative ideology of the 1990s seeks to contain. Most of all, we need to find ways of foregrounding conflict and struggle not only in the generation of meaning or authority, but also in the teaching of conventions of "correctness" in syntax, spelling, and punctuation, traditionally considered the primary focus of Basic Writing instruction.

Author's Note: *Material for sections of this essay comes from my dissertation, directed by David Bartholomae at the University of Pittsburgh. This essay is part of a joint project conducted with Bruce Horner which has been supported by the Drake University Provost Research Fund, the Drake University Center for the Humanities, and the University of Iowa Center for Advanced Studies. I gratefully acknowledge Bruce Horner's contributions to the conception and revisions of this essay.*

Works Cited

Anzaldúa, Gloria. *Borderlands/La Frontera: The New Mestiza.* San Francisco: Aunt Lute, 1987.

Baldwin, James. *Conversations with James Baldwin.* Ed. Fred L. Standley and Louis H. Pratt. Jackson: UP of Mississippi, 1989.

———. *The Price of the Ticket.* New York: St. Martin's, 1985.

Bartholomae, David. "Inventing the University." *When a Writer Can't Write: Studies in Writer's Block and Other Composing Process Problems.* Ed. Mike Rose. New York: Guilford, 1985. 134–65.

———. "Writing on the Margins: The Concept of Literacy in Higher Education." *A Sourcebook for Basic Writing Teachers.* Ed. Theresa Enos. New York: Random, 1987. 66–83.

Bizzell, Patricia. "Beyond Anti-Foundationalism to Rhetorical Authority: Problems Defining 'Cultural Literacy.'" *College English* 52 (Oct. 1990): 661–75.

Brown, Rexford G. "Schooling and Thoughtfulness." *Journal of Basic Writing* 10.1 (Spring 1991): 3–15.

Bruffee, Kenneth A. "On Not Listening in Order to Hear: Collaborative Learning and the Rewards of Classroom Research." *Journal of Basic Writing* 7.1 (Spring 1988): 3–12.

———. "Collaborative Learning: Some Practical Models." *College English* 34 (Feb. 1973): 634–43.

DuBois, W. E. B. *The Autobiography of W. E. B. DuBois: A Soliloquy on Viewing My Life from the Last Decade of Its First Century.* New York: International, 1968.

———. *The Education of Black People: Ten Critiques 1906–1960.* Ed. Herbert Aptheker. Amherst: U of Massachusetts P, 1973.

Epes, Mary. "Tracing Errors to Their Sources: A Study of the Encoding Processes of Adult Basic Writers." *Journal of Basic Writing* 4.1 (Spring 1985): 4–33.

Farrell, Thomas J. "Developing Literacy: Walter J. Ong and Basic Writing." *Journal of Basic Writing* 2.1 (Fall/Winter 1978): 30–51.

———. "Literacy, the Basics, and All That Jazz." *College English* 38 (Jan. 1977): 443–59.

———. "Open Admissions, Orality, and Literacy." *Journal of Youth and Adolescence* 3 (1974): 247–60.

Fiske, Edward B. "City College Quality Still Debated after Eight Years of Open Admission." *New York Times* 19 June 1978: A1.

Flynn, Elizabeth. "Composing as a Woman." *College Composition and Communication* 39 (Dec. 1988): 423–35.

Fox, Tom. "Basic Writing as Cultural Conflict." *Journal of Education* 172.1 (1990): 65–83.

Gould, Christopher, and John Heyda. Literacy Education and the Basic Writer: A Survey of College Composition Courses." *Journal of Basic Writing* 5.2 (Fall 1986): 8–27.

Harris, Joseph. "The Idea of Community in the Study of Writing." *College Composition and Communication* 40 (Feb. 1989): 11–22.

Heller, Louis G. *The Death of the American University: With Special Reference to the Collapse of City College of New York.* New Rochelle, NY: Arlington House, 1973.

Horner, Bruce. "Re-Thinking the 'Sociality' of Error: Teaching Editing as Negotiation." *Rhetoric Review* 11.1 (Fall 1992): 172–99.

Howe, Irving. "A Foot in the Door." *New York Times* 27 June 1975: 35.

———. "Living with Kampf and Schlaff: Literary Tradition and Mass Education." *The American Scholar* 43 (1973–74): 107–12.

———. *A Margin of Hope: An Intellectual Autobiography.* New York: Harcourt, 1982.

———. *Selected Writings 1950–1990.* New York: Harcourt, 1990.

———. *World of Our Fathers.* New York: Harcourt, 1976.

Hull, Glynda, and Mike Rose. "'This Wooden Shack Place': The Logic of an Unconventional Reading." *College Composition and Communication* 41 (Oct. 1990): 287–98.

Kriegel, Leonard. "Playing It Black." *Change* Mar./Apr. 1969: 7–11.

————. *Working Through: A Teacher's Journey in the Urban University.* New York: Saturday Review, 1972.

Lu, Min-Zhan. "From Silence to Words: Writing as Struggle." *College English* 49 (Apr. 1987): 433–48.

————. "Redefining the Legacy of Mina Shaughnessy: A Critique of the Politics of Linguistic Innocence." *Journal of Basic Writing* 10.1 (Spring 1991): 26–40.

————. "Writing as Repositioning." *Journal of Education* 172.1 (1990): 18–21.

Lunsford, Andrea A., Helene Moglen, and James Slevin, eds. *The Right to Literacy.* New York: MLA, 1990.

Lyons, Robert. "Mina Shaughnessy." *Traditions of Inquiry.* Ed. John Brereton. New York: Oxford UP, 1985. 171–89.

Mellix, Barbara. "From Outside, In." *Georgia Review* 41 (1987): 258–67.

Murphy, Ann. "Transference and Resistance in the Basic Writing Classroom: Problematics and Praxis." *College Composition and Communication* 40 (May 1989): 175–87.

Quinn, Edward. "We're Holding Our Own." *Change* June 1973: 30–35.

Ritchie, Joy S. "Beginning Writers: Diverse Voices and Individual Identity." *College Composition and Communication* 40 (May 1989): 152–74.

Rondinone, Peter. "Teacher Background and Student Needs." *Journal of Basic Writing* 10.1 (Spring 1991): 41–53.

————. "Open Admissions and the Inward 'I'." *Change* May 1977: 43–47.

Rose, Mike. *Lives on the Boundary.* New York: Penguin, 1989.

Schilb, John. "Composition and Poststructuralism: A Tale of Two Conferences." *College Composition and Communication* 40 (Dec. 1989): 422–43.

Shaughnessy, Mina. "Diving In: An Introduction to Basic Writing." *College Composition and Communication* 27 (Oct. 1976): 234–39.

————. "The English Professor's Malady." *Journal of Basic Writing* 3.1 (Fall/Winter 1980): 91–97.

————. *Errors and Expectations: A Guide for the Teacher of Basic Writing.* New York: Oxford UP, 1977.

Spellmeyer, Kurt. "Foucault and the Freshman Writer: Considering the Self in Discourse." *College English* 51 (Nov. 1989): 715–29.

Stanley, Linda C. "'Misreading' Students' Journals for Their Views of Self and Society." *Journal of Basic Writing* 8.1 (Spring 1989): 21–31.

Steele, Shelby. *The Content of Our Character: A New Vision of Race in America.* New York: St. Martin's, 1990.

Trilling, Lionel. *The Last Decade: Essays and Reviews, 1965–75.* Ed. Diana Trilling. New York: Harcourt, 1979.

————. *Of This Time, Of That Place, and Other Stories.* Selected by Diana Trilling. New York: Harcourt, 1979.

Trimbur, John. "Beyond Cognition: The Voices in Inner Speech." *Rhetoric Review* 5 (1987): 211–21.

Volpe, Edmond L. "The Confession of a Fallen Man: Ascent to the DA." *College English* 33 (1972): 765–79.

Wagner, Geoffrey. *The End of Education.* New York: Barnes, 1976.

From THE STUDY OF ERROR

David Bartholomae

[*College Composition and Communication* 31 (1980): 253–69.]

(For biographical information, see page 19.)

Bartholomae wrote this article in response to instructors who felt that students' errors were signs that they couldn't write. He opens his article by surveying then current (1980) attitudes about "basic writing," the various pedagogies that instructors have adopted when confronted with "basic writers," and the results of their attempts. He argues for further research into "basic writing" and the concurrent perceptions of errors apparently inherent to basic writers. Aligning his argument with Mina Shaughnessy's groundbreaking work in *Errors and Expectations*, Bartholomae proposes error analysis as a method to better understand how writers develop and learn. The excerpt that follows begins at that point, with Bartholomae explaining error analysis and demonstrating its effectiveness with a study of one of his students' assignments in progress.

Error analysis begins with a theory of writing, a theory of language production and language development, that allows us to see errors as evidence of choice or strategy among a range of possible choices or strategies. They provide evidence of an individual style of using the language and making it work; they are not a simple record of what a writer failed to do because of incompetence or indifference. Errors, then, are stylistic features, information about *this* writer and *this* language; they are not necessarily "noise" in the system, accidents of composing, or malfunctions in the language process. Consequently, we cannot identify errors without identifying them in context, and the context is not the text, but the activity of composing that presented the erroneous form as a possible solution to the problem of making a meaningful statement. Shaughnessy's taxonomy of error, for example, identifies errors according to their source, not their type. A single type of error could be attributed to a variety of causes. Donald Freeman's research, for example, has shown that "subject-verb agreement . . . is a host of errors, not one." One of his students analyzed a "large sample of real world sentences and concluded that there are at least eight different kinds, most of which have very little to do with one another."[1]

Error analysis allows us to place error in the context of composing and to interpret and classify systematic errors. The key concept is the concept of an "interlanguage" or an "intermediate system," an idiosyncratic grammar and rhetoric that is a writer's approximation of the standard idiom. Errors, while they can be given more precise classification, fall into three main categories: errors that are evidence of an intermediate system; errors that could truly be said to be accidents, or slips of the pen as a writer's mind rushes ahead faster than his hand; and, finally, errors of language transfer, or, more commonly, dialect interference, where in the attempt to produce the target language, the writer intrudes forms from the "first" or "native" language rather than inventing some intermediate form. For writers, this intrusion most often comes from a spoken dialect. The error analyst is primarily concerned, however, with errors that are evidence of some intermediate system. This kind of error occurs because the writer *is* an active, competent language user who uses his knowledge that language is rule-governed, and who uses his ability to predict and form analogies, to construct hypotheses that can make an irregular or unfamiliar language more manageable. The problem comes when the rule is incorrect or, more properly, when it is idiosyncratic, belonging only to the language of this writer. There is evidence of an idiosyncratic system, for example, when a student adds inflectional endings to infinitives, as in this sentence, "There was plenty the boy had to *learned* about birds." It also seems to be evident in a sentence like this: "This assignment calls on *choosing* one of my papers and making a last draft out of it." These errors can be further subdivided into those that are in flux and mark a fully transitional stage, and those that, for one reason or another, become frozen and recur across time.

Kroll and Schafer, in a recent *CCC* article, argue that the value of error analysis for the composition teacher is the perspective it offers on the learner, since it allows us to see errors "as clues to inner processes, as windows into the mind."[2] If we investigate the pattern of error in the performance of an individual writer, we can better understand the nature of those errors and the way they "fit" in an individual writer's program for writing. As a consequence, rather than impose an inappropriate or even misleading syllabus on a learner, we can plan instruction to assist a writer's internal syllabus. If, for example, a writer puts standard inflections on irregular verbs or on verbs that are used in verbals (as in "I used to runned"), drill on verb endings will only reinforce the rule that, because the writer is overgeneralizing, is the source of the error in the first place. By charting and analyzing a writer's errors, we can begin in our instruction with what a writer *does* rather than with what he fails to do. It makes no sense, for example, to impose lessons on the sentence on a student whose problems with syntax can be understood in more precise terms. It makes no sense to teach spelling to an individual who has trouble principally with words that contain vowel clusters. Error analysis, then, is a method of diagnosis.

Error analysis can assist instruction at another level. By having students share in the process of investigating and interpreting the patterns of error in their writing, we can help them begin to see those errors as evidence of hypotheses or strategies they have formed and, as a consequence, put them in a position to change, experiment, imagine other strategies. Studying their own writing puts students in a position to see themselves as language users, rather than as victims of a language that uses them.

This, then, is the perspective and the technique of error analysis. To interpret a student paper without this frame of reference is to misread, as for example when a teacher sees an incorrect verb form and concludes that the student doesn't understand the rules for indicating tense or number. I want, now, to examine error analysis as a procedure for the study of errors in written composition. It presents two problems. The first can be traced to the fact that error analysis was developed for studying errors in spoken performance.[3] It can be transferred to writing only to the degree that writing is like speech, and there are significant points of difference. It is generally acknowledged, for example, that written discourse is not just speech written down on paper. Adult written discourse has a grammar and rhetoric that is different from speech. And clearly the activity of producing language is different for a writer than it is for a speaker.

The "second language" a basic writer must learn to master is formal, written discourse, a discourse whose lexicon, grammar, and rhetoric are learned not through speaking and listening but through reading and writing. The process of acquisition is visual not aural. Furthermore, basic writers do not necessarily produce writing by translating speech into print (the way children learning to write would); that is, they must draw on a memory for graphemes rather than phonemes. This is a different order of memory and production from that used in speech and gives rise to errors unique to writing.

Writing also, however, presents "interference" of a type never found in speech. Errors in writing may be caused by interference from the act of writing itself, from the difficulty of moving a pen across the page quickly enough to keep up with the words in the writer's mind, or from the difficulty of recalling and producing the conventions that are necessary for producing print rather than speech, conventions of spelling, orthography, punctuation, capitalization, and so on. This is not, however, just a way of saying that writers make spelling errors and speakers do not. As Shaughnessy pointed out, errors of syntax can be traced to the gyrations of a writer trying to avoid a word that her sentence has led her to, but that she knows she cannot spell.

The second problem in applying error analysis to the composition classroom arises from special properties in the taxonomy of errors we chart in student writing. Listing varieties of errors is not like listing varieties of rocks or butterflies. What a reader finds depends to a large degree on her assumptions about the writer's intention. Any systematic attempt to chart a learner's errors is clouded by the difficulty of assigning intention through textual analysis. The analyst begins, then, by interpreting a text, not by describing features on a page. And interpretation is less than a precise science.

Let me turn to an example. This is part of a paper that a student, John, wrote in response to an assignment that asked him to go back to some papers he had written on significant moments in his life in order to write a paper that considered the general question of the way people change:

> This assignment call on chosing one of my incident making a last draft out of it. I found this very differcult because I like them all but you said I had to pick one so the Second incident was decide. Because this one had the most important insight to my life that I indeed learn from. This insight explain why adulthood mean that much as it dose to me because I think it alway influence me to change and my outlook on certain thing like my point-of-view I have one day and it might change the next week on the same issue. So in these frew words I going to write about the incident now. My exprience took place in my high school and the reason was out side of school but I will show you the connection. The situation took place cause of the type of school I went too. Let me tell you about the situation first of all what happen was that I got suspense from school. For thing that I fell was out of my control sometime, but it taught me alot about respondability of a growing man. The school suspense me for being late ten time. I had accummate ten dementic and had to bring my mother to school to talk to a conselor and Prinpicable of the school what when on at the meet took me out mentally period.

One could imagine a variety of responses to this. The first would be to form the wholesale conclusion that John can't write and to send him off to a workbook. Once he had learned how to write correct sentences, then he could go on to the business of actually writing. Let me call this the "old style" response to error. A second response, which I'll call the "investigative approach," would be to chart the patterns of error in this particular text. Of the approximately 40 errors in the first 200 words, the majority fall under four fairly specific categories: verb endings, noun plurals, syntax, and spelling. The value to pedagogy is obvious. One is no longer teaching a student to "write" but to deal with a limited number of very specific kinds of errors, each of which would suggest its own appropriate response. Furthermore, it is possible to refine the categories and to speculate on and organize them according to cause. The verb errors almost all involve "s" or "ed" endings, which could indicate dialect interference or a failure to learn the rules for indicating tense and number. It is possible to be even more precise. The passage contains 41 verbs; only 17 of them are used incorrectly. With the exception of four spelling errors, the errors are all errors of inflection and, furthermore, these errors come only with regular verbs. There are no errors with irregular verbs. This would suggest, then, that when John draws on memory for a verb form, he gets it right; but when John applies a rule to determine the ending, he gets it wrong.

The errors of syntax could be divided into those that might be called punctuation errors (or errors that indicate a difficulty perceiving the boundaries of the sentence), such as

Let me tell you about the situation first of all that happen was that I got suspense from school. For thing that I fell was out of my control sometime, but it taught me alot about respondability of a growing man.

and errors of syntax that would fall under Shaughnessy's category of consolidation errors,

This insight explain why adulthood mean that much as it dose to me because I think it alway influence me to change and my outlook on certain thing like my point-of-view I have one day and it might change the next week on the same issue.

One would also want to note the difference between consistent errors, the substitution of "situation" for "situation" or "suspense" for "suspended," and unstable ones, as, for example, when John writes "cause" in one place and "because" in another. In one case John could be said to have fixed on a rule; in the other he is searching for one. One would also want to distinguish between what might seem to be "accidental" errors, like substituting "frew" for "few" or "when" for "went," errors that might best be addressed by teaching a student to edit, and those whose causes are deeper and require time and experience, or some specific instructional strategy.

I'm not sure, however, that this analysis provides an accurate representation of John's writing. Consider what happens when John reads this paper out loud. I've been taping students reading their own papers, and I've developed a system of notation, like that used in miscue analysis,[4] that will allow me to record the points of variation between the writing that is on the page and the writing that is spoken, or, to use the terminology of miscue analysis, between the expected response (ER) and the observed response (OR). What I've found is that students will often, or in predictable instances, substitute correct forms for the incorrect forms on the page, even though they are generally unaware that such a substitution was made. This observation suggests the limits of conventional error analysis for the study of error in written composition.

I asked John to read his paper out loud, and to stop and correct or note any mistakes he found. Let me try to reproduce the transcript of that reading. I will italicize any substitution or correction and offer some comments in parentheses. The reader might first go back and review the original. Here is what John read:

> This assignment calls on *choosing* one of my incident making a last draft out of it. I found this very difficult because I like them all but you said I *had* to pick one so the Second incident was decide*d on.* Because (John goes back and rereads, connecting up the subordinate clause.) So the second incident was decided on because this one had the most important insight to my life that I indeed learn*ed* from. This insight explains why adulthood *meant* that much as it dose to me because I think it always influences me to change and my outlook on certain things like my point-of-view I have one day and it might change the next week on the same issue. (John goes back and rereads, beginning with "like my point-of-view," and he is puzzled but he makes no additional changes.) So in these *few* words *I'm* going to write about the incident now. My experience took place *because* of the type of school I went to (John had written "too.") Let me tell you about the situation (John comes to a full stop.) first of all what happen*ed* was that I got *suspended* from school (no full stop) for things that I *felt* was out of my control sometime, but it taught me a lot about *responsibility* of a growing man. The school *suspended* me for being late ten times. I had *accumulated* (for "accumate") ten *demerits* (for "dementic") and had to bring my mother to school to talk to a counselor and *the Principal* of the school (full stop) what *went* on at the meet*ing* took me out mentally (full stop) period (with brio).

I have chosen an extreme case to make my point, but what one sees here is the writer correcting almost every error as he reads the paper, even though he is not able to recognize that there *are* errors or that he has corrected them. The only errors John spotted (where he stopped, noted an error and corrected it) were the misspellings of "situation" and "Principal," and the substitution of "chosing" for "choosing." Even when he was asked to reread sentences to see if he could notice any difference between what he was saying and the words on the page, he could not. He could not, for example, see the error in "frew" or "dementic" or any of the other verb errors, and yet he spoke the correct form of every verb (with the exception of "was" after he had changed "thing" to "things" in "for things that I *felt* was out of my control") and he corrected every plural. His phrasing as he read produced correct syntax, except in the case of the consolidation error, which he puzzled over but did not correct. It's important to note, however, that John did not read the confused syntax as if no confusion were there. He sensed the difference between the phrasing called for by the meaning of the sentence and that which existed on the page. He did not read as though meaning didn't matter or as though the "meaning" coded on the page was complete. His problem cannot be simply a syntax problem, since the jumble is bound up with his struggle to articulate this particular meaning. And it is not simply a "thinking" problem — John doesn't write this way because he thinks this way — since he perceives that the statement as it is written is other than that which he intended.

When I asked John why the paper (which went on for two more pages) was written all as one paragraph, he replied, "It was all one idea. I didn't want to have to start all over again. I had a good idea and I didn't want to give it up." John doesn't need to be "taught" the paragraph, at least not as the paragraph is traditionally taught. His prose is orderly and proceeds through blocks of discourse. He tells the story of his experience at the school and concludes that through his experience he realized that he must accept responsibility for his tardiness, even though the tardiness was not his fault but the fault of the Philadelphia subway system. He concludes that with this realization he learned "the responsibility of a growing man." Furthermore John knows that the print code carries certain conventions for ordering and presenting discourse. His translation of the notion that "a paragraph develops a single idea" is peculiar but not illogical.

It could also be argued that John does not need to be "taught" to produce correct verb forms, or, again, at least not as such things are conventionally taught. Fifteen weeks of drill on verb endings might raise his test scores, but they would not change the way he writes. He *knows* how to produce correct endings. He demonstrated that when he read, since he was reading in terms of his grammatical competence. His problem is a problem of performance, or fluency, not of competence. There is certainly no evidence that the verb errors are due to interference from his spoken language. And if the errors could be traced to some intermediate system, the system exists only in John's performance as a writer. It does not operate when he reads or, for that matter, when he speaks, if his oral reconstruction of his own text can be taken as a record of John "speaking" the idiom of academic discourse.[5]

John's case also highlights the tremendous difficulty such a student has with editing, where a failure to correct a paper is not evidence of laziness or inattention or a failure to know correct forms, but evidence of the tremendous difficulty such a student has objectifying language and seeing it as black and white marks on the page, where things can be wrong even though the meaning seems right.[6] One of the hardest errors for John to spot, after all my coaching, was the substitution of "frew" for "few," certainly not an error that calls into question John's competence as a writer. I can call this a "performance" error, but that term doesn't suggest the constraints on performance in writing. This is an important area for further study. Surely one constraint is the difficulty of moving the hand fast enough to translate meaning into print. The burden imposed on their patience and short-term memory by the slow, awkward handwriting of many inexperienced writers is a very real one. But I think the constraints extend beyond the difficulty of forming words quickly with pen or pencil.

One of the most interesting results of the comparison of the spoken and written versions of John's text is his inability to *see* the difference between "frew" and "few" or "dementic" and "demerit." What this suggests is that John reads and writes from the "top down" rather than the "bottom up," to use a distinction made by cognitive psychologists in their study of reading.[7] John is not operating through the lower level process of translating orthographic information into sounds and sounds into meaning when he reads. And conversely, he is not working from meaning to sound to word when he is writing. He is, rather, retrieving lexical items directly, through a "higher level" process that bypasses the "lower level" operation of phonetic translation. When I put *frew* and *few* on the blackboard, John read them both as "few." The lexical item "few" is represented for John by either orthographic array. He is not, then, reading or writing phonetically, which is a sign, from one perspective, of a high level of fluency, since the activity is automatic and not mediated by the more primitive operation of translating speech into print or print into speech. When John was writing, he did not produce "frew" or "dementic" by searching for sound/letter/ letter correspondences. He drew directly upon his memory for the look and shape of those words; he was working from the top down rather than the bottom up. He went to stored print forms and did not take the slower route of translating speech into writing.

John, then, has reached a stage of fluency in writing where he directly and consistently retrieves print forms, like "dementic," that are meaningful to him, even though they are idiosyncratic. I'm not sure what all the implications of this might be, but we surely must see John's problem in a new light, since his problem can, in a sense, be attributed to his skill. To ask John to slow down his writing and sound out words would be disastrous. Perhaps the most we can do is to teach John the slowed down form of reading he will need in order to edit.

John's paper also calls into question our ability to identify accidental errors. I suspect that when John substitutes a word like "when" for "went," this is an accidental error, a slip of the pen. Since John spoke "went" when he read, I cannot conclude that he substituted "when" for "went" because he pronounces both as "wen." This, then, is not an error of dialect interference but an accidental error, the same order of error as the omission of "the" before "Principal." Both were errors John corrected while reading (even though he didn't identify them as errors).

What is surprising is that, with all the difficulty John had identifying errors, he immediately saw that he had written "chosing" rather than "choosing." While textual analysis would have led to the conclusion that he was applying a tense rule to a participial construction, or overgeneralizing from a known rule, the ease with which it was identified would lead one to conclude that it was, in fact, a mistake, and not evidence of an approximative system. What would have been diagnosed as a deep error now appears to be only an accidental error, a "mistake" (or perhaps a spelling error).

In summary, this analysis of John's reading produces a healthy respect for the tremendous complexity of transcription, for the process of recording meaning in print as opposed to the process of generating meaning. It also points out the difficulty of charting a learner's "interlanguage" or "intermediate system," since we are working not only with a writer moving between a first and a second language, but a writer whose performance is subject to the interference of transcription, of producing meaning through the print code. We need, in general, to refine our understanding of performance-based errors, and we need to refine our teaching to take into account the high percentage of error in written composition that is rooted in the difficulty of performance rather than in problems of general linguistic competence.

Let me pause for a moment to put what I've said in the context of work in error analysis. Such analysis is textual analysis. It requires the reader to make assumptions about intention on the basis of information in the text. The writer's errors provide the most important information since they provide insight into the idiosyncratic systems the writer has developed. The regular but unconventional features in the writing will reveal the rules and strategies operating for the basic writer.

The basic procedure for such analysis could be outlined this way. First the reader must identify the idiosyncratic construction; he must determine what is an error. This is often difficult, as in the case of fragments, which are conventionally used for effect. Here is an example of a sentence whose syntax could clearly be said to be idiosyncratic.

> In high school you learn alot for example Kindergarten which I took in high school.[8]

The reader, then, must reconstruct that sentence based upon the most reasonable interpretation of the intention in the original, and this must be done *before* the error can be classified, since it will be classified according to its cause.[9] Here is Shaughnessy's reconstruction of the example given above: "In high school you learn a lot. For example, I took up the study of Kindergarten in high school." For any idiosyncratic sentence, however, there are often a variety of possible reconstructions, depending on the reader's sense of the larger meaning of which this individual sentence is only a part, but also depending upon the reader's ability to predict how this writer puts sentences together, that is, on an understanding of this individual style. The text is being interpreted, not described. I've had graduate students who have reconstructed the following sentence, for example, in a variety of ways:

> Why do we have womens liberation and their fighting for Equal Rights ect.
> to be recognized not as a lady but as an Individual.

It could be read, "Why do we have women's liberation and why are they fighting for Equal Rights? In order that women may be recognized not as ladies but as individuals." And, "Why do we have women's liberation and their fight for equal rights, to be recognized not as a lady but as an individual?" There is an extensive literature on the question of interpretation and intention in prose, too extensive for the easy assumption that all a reader has to do is identify what the writer would have written if he wanted to "get it right the first time." The great genius of Shaughnessy's study, in fact, is the remarkable wisdom and sympathy of her interpretations of student texts.

Error analysis, then, involves more than just making lists of the errors in a student essay and looking for patterns to emerge. It begins with the double perspective of text and reconstructed text and seeks to explain the difference between the two on the basis of whatever can be inferred about the meaning of the text and the process of creating it. The reader/researcher brings to bear his general knowledge of how basic writers write, but also whatever is known about the linguistic and rhetorical constraints that govern an individual act of writing. In Shaughnessy's analysis of the "kindergarten" sentence, this discussion is contained in the section on "consolidation errors" in the chapter on "Syntax."[10] The key point, however, is that any such analysis must draw upon extra-textual information as well as close, stylistic analysis.

This paper has illustrated two methods for gathering information about how a text was created. A teacher can interview the student and ask him to explain his error. John wrote this sentence in another paper for my course:

> I would to write about my experience helping 1600 childrens have a happy christmas.

The missing word (I would *like* to write about . . .) he supplied when reading the sentence aloud. It is an accidental error and can be addressed by teaching editing. It is the same kind of error as his earlier substitution of "when" for "went." John used the phrase, "1600 childrens," throughout his paper, however. The conventional interpretation would have it that this is evidence of dialect interference. And yet, when John read the paper out loud, he consistently read "1600 children," even though he said he did not see any difference between the word he spoke and the word that was on the page. When I asked him to explain why he put an "s" on the end of "children," he replied, "Because there were 1600 of them." John had a rule for forming plurals that he used when he wrote but not when he spoke. Writing, as we rightly recognized, has its own peculiar rules and constraints. It is different from speech. The error is not due to interference from his spoken language but to his conception of the "code" of written discourse.

The other method for gathering information is having students read aloud their own writing, and having them provide an oral reconstruction of their written text. What I've presented in my analysis of John's essay is a method for recording the discrepancies between the written and spoken versions of a single text. The record of a writer reading provides a version of the "intended" text that can supplement the teacher's or researcher's own reconstruction and aid in the interpretation of errors, whether they be accidental, interlingual, or due to dialect interference. I had to read John's paper very differently once I had heard him read it.

More importantly, however, this method of analysis can provide access to an additional type of error. This is the error that can be attributed to the physical and conceptual demands of writing rather than speaking; it can be traced to the requirements of manipulating a pen and the requirements of manipulating the print code.[11]

In general, when writers read, and read in order to spot and correct errors, their responses will fall among the following categories:

1. overt corrections — errors a reader sees, acknowledges, and corrects;
2. spoken corrections — errors the writer does not acknowledge but corrects in reading;
3. no recognition — errors that are read as written;
4. overcorrection — correct forms made incorrect, or incorrect forms substituted for incorrect forms;
5. acknowledged error — errors a reader senses but cannot correct;
6. reader miscue — a conventional miscue, not linked to error in the text;
7. nonsense — In this case, the reader reads a nonsentence or a nonsense sentence as though it were correct and meaningful. No error or confusion is acknowledged. This applies to errors of syntax only.

Corrections, whether acknowledged or unacknowledged, would indicate performance-based errors. The other responses (with the exception of "reader miscues") would indicate deeper errors, errors that, when charted, would provide evidence of some idiosyncratic grammar or rhetoric.

John "miscues" by completing or correcting the text that he has written. When reading researchers have readers read out loud, they have them read someone else's writing, of course, and they are primarily concerned with the "quality" of the miscues.[12] All fluent readers will miscue; that is, they will not repeat verbatim the words on the page. Since fluent readers are reading for meaning, they are actively predicting what will come and processing large chunks of graphic information at a time. They do not read individual words, and they miscue because they speak what they expect to see rather than what is actually on the page. One indication of a reader's proficiency, then, is that the miscues don't destroy the "sense" of the passage. Poor readers will produce miscues that jumble the meaning of a passage, as in

Text: Her wings were folded quietly at her sides.
Reader: Her wings were floated quickly at her sides.

or they will correct miscues that do not affect meaning in any significant way.[13]

The situation is different when a reader reads his own text, since this reader already knows what the passage means and attention is drawn, then, to the representation of that meaning. Reading also frees a writer from the constraints of transcription, which for many basic writers is an awkward, laborious process, putting excessive demands on both patience and short-term memory. John, like any reader, read what he expected to see, but with a low percentage of meaning-related miscues, since the meaning, for him, was set, and with a big percentage of code-related miscues, where a correct form was substituted for an incorrect form.

The value of studying students' oral reconstruction of their written texts is threefold. The first is as a diagnostic tool. I've illustrated in my analysis of John's paper how such a diagnosis might take place.

It is also a means of instruction. By having John read aloud and, at the same time, look for discrepancies between what he spoke and what was on the page, I was teaching him a form of reading. The most dramatic change in John's performance over the term was in the number of errors he could spot and correct while rereading. This far exceeded the number of errors he was able to eliminate from his first drafts. I could teach John an editing procedure better than I could teach him to be correct at the point of transcription.

The third consequence of this form of analysis, or of conventional error analysis, has yet to be demonstrated, but the suggestions for research are clear. It seems evident that we can chart stages of growth in individual basic writers. The pressing question is whether we can chart a sequence of "natural" development for the class of writers we call basic writers. If all nonfluent adult writers proceed through a "natural" learning sequence, and if we can identify that sequence through some large, longitudinal study, then we will begin to understand what a basic writing course or text or syllabus might look like. There are studies of adult second language learners that suggest that there is a general, natural sequence of acquisition for adults learning a second language, one that is determined by the psychology of language production and language acquisition.[14] Before we can adapt these methods to a study of basic writers, however, we need to better understand the additional constraints of learning to transcribe and manipulate the "code" of written discourse. John's case illustrates where we might begin and what we must know.[15]

Notes

[1] Donald C. Freeman, "Linguistics and Error Analysis: On Agency," in Donald McQuade, ed., *Linguistics, Stylistics and the Teaching of Composition* (Akron, Ohio: L & S Books, 1979), pp. 143–44.

[2] Kroll and Schafer, "Error Analysis and the Teaching of Composition," *CCC,* 29 (October 1978), 243–48.

[3] In the late sixties and early seventies, linguists began to study second language acquisition by systematically studying the actual performance of individual learners. What they studied, however, was the language a learner would speak. In the literature of error analysis, the reception and production of language is generally defined as the learner's ability to hear, learn, imitate, and independently produce *sounds.* Errors, then, are phonological substitutions, alterations, additions, and subtractions. Similarly, errors diagnosed as rooted in the mode of production (rather than, for example, in an idiosyncratic grammar or interference from the first language) are errors caused by the difficulty a learner has hearing or making foreign sounds. When we are studying written composition, we are studying a different mode of production, where a learner must see, remember, and produce marks on a page. There may be some similarity between the grammar-based errors in the two modes, speech and writing (it would be interesting to know to what degree this is true), but there should be marked differences in the nature and frequency of performance-based errors.

[4] See Y. M. Goodman and C. L. Burke, *Reading Miscue Inventory: Procedure for Diagnosis and Evaluation* (New York: Macmillan, 1972).

[5] Bruder and Hayden noticed a similar phenomenon. They assigned a group of students exercises in writing formal and informal dialogues. One student's informal dialogue contained the following:

What going on?
It been a long time . . .
I about through . . .
I be glad . . .

When the student read the dialogue aloud, however, these were spoken as

What's going on?
It's been a long time . . .
I'm about through . . .
I'll be glad . . .

See Mary Newton Bruder and Luddy Hayden, "Teaching Composition: A Report on a Bidialectal Approach," *Language Learning*, 23 (June 1973), 1–15.

[6] See Patricia Laurence, "Error's Endless Train: Why Students Don't Perceive Errors," *Journal of Basic Writing*, I (Spring 1975), 23–43, for a different explanation of this phenomenon.

[7] See, for example, J. R. Frederiksen, "Component Skills in Reading" in R. R. Snow, P. A. Federico, and W. E. Montague, eds., *Aptitude, Learning, and Instruction* (Hillsdale, N.J.: Erlbaum, 1979); D. E. Rumelhart, "Toward an Interactive Model of Reading," in S. Dornic, ed., *Attention and Performance VI* (Hillsdale, N.J.: Erlbaum, 1977); and Joseph H. Denks and Gregory O. Hill, "Interactive Models of Lexical Assessment during Oral Reading," paper presented at Conference on Interactive Processes in Reading, Learning Research and Development Center, University of Pittsburgh, September 1979.

Patrick Hartwell argued that "apparent dialect interference in writing reveals partial or imperfect mastery of a neural coding system that underlies both reading and writing" in a paper, "'Dialect Interference' in Writing: A Critical View," presented at CCCC, April 1979. This paper is available through ERIC. He predicts, in this paper, that "basic writing students, when asked to read their writing in a formal situation, . . . will make fewer errors in their reading than in their writing." I read Professor Hartwell's paper after this essay was completed, so I was unable to acknowledge his study as completely as I would have desired.

[8] This example is taken from Shaughnessy, *Errors and Expectations: A Guide for the Teacher of Basic Writing* (New York: Oxford University Press, 1977), p. 52.

[9] Corder refers to "reconstructed sentences" in "Idiosyncratic Dialects and Error Analysis."

[10] Shaughnessy, *Errors and Expectations*, pp. 51–72.

[11] For a discussion of the role of the "print code" in writer's errors, see Patrick Hartwell, "'Dialect Interference' in Writing: A Critical View."

[12] See Kenneth S. Goodman, "Miscues: Windows on the Reading Process," in Kenneth S. Goodman, ed., *Miscue Analysis: Applications to Reading Instruction* (Urbana, Ill.: ERIC, 1977), pp. 3–14.

[13] This example was taken from Yetta M. Goodman, "Miscue Analysis for In-Service Reading Teachers," in Kenneth S. Goodman, ed., *Miscue Analysis*, p. 55.

[14] Nathalie Bailey, Carolyn Madden, and Stephen D. Krashen, "Is There a 'Natural Sequence' in Adult Second Language Learning?" *Language Learning*, 24 (June 1974), 235–243.

[15] This paper was originally presented at CCCC, April 1979. The research for this study was funded by a research grant from the National Council of Teachers of English.

PART SIX

ENGLISH AS A SECOND LANGUAGE

Part VI of *The Bedford Handbook*, "ESL Trouble Spots," recognizes that increasing numbers of composition students acquired English as a second language, and it focuses on areas of English grammar that typically cause difficulty for nonnative speakers. The purpose of this section of the handbook is to provide students with rules they need to edit their writing and to augment those rules with practical explanations and examples that relate specifically to ESL students.

Instructors encountering ESL students should recognize that language interference in student writing does not necessitate remedial exercises and drills. Instead, instructors should consider ESL problems in a developmental context: Writers make mistakes as they attempt to master conventions in a new language. Further, instructors must understand that ESL writers operate within several competing cultural contexts, and their home cultures may be governed by assumptions radically different from those that they encounter in and out of our classrooms. These differing cultural assumptions affect fundamentally the ways that ESL writers acquire and use English, especially in their writing, which is a social action. Because of the complexities associated with teaching ESL writers, instructors often feel ill equipped to help such students in writing classes. The following selections address questions that arise as a result of that uncertainty:

- What should instructors expect from ESL students? What kinds of culturally conditioned behaviors and expectations do ESL students bring to our classrooms?
- How should instructors construct courses and conduct composition classes for ESL writers?
- How do cultural differences — many of which create fundamental conflicts for students and teachers — affect student writing and student behavior? How can teachers help students negotiate among these apparent conflicts?

CLASSROOM EXPECTATIONS AND BEHAVIORS
Ilona Leki

[From *Understanding ESL Writers: A Guide for Teachers* by Ilona Leki. Portsmouth, NH: Boynton, 1990. 47–57.]

Professor of English Ilona Leki is director of English as a Second Language at the University of Tennessee. Widely recognized as an authority in teaching ESL, Leki has published numerous articles and chapters. She is also the author of *Academic Writing: Techniques and Tasks*, Second Edition (1995), and she coedited (with Joan Carson) *Reading in the Composition Classroom: Second Language Perspectives* (1993).

In this chapter from *Understanding ESL Writers,* Leki offers an overview of the various expectations and behaviors that ESL students bring to the classroom, including their ideas about course work, evaluation, and student-instructor relations. Instructors who are conscious of ESL students' expectations can help make those students' learning experiences more effective and beneficial.

Most of the time ESL students are not traumatized, just surprised, surprised at the receptions they get here and surprised at some of the customs and behaviors they encounter in U.S. classrooms. International students are often hurt and insulted by American ignorance of, and disinterest in, their home countries. American undergraduates are notorious for such geographical gaffs as placing Canada on a map of Texas; Malaysia may as well be in outer space. One international student was upset to learn that his American classmate had never heard of Thailand. African students are asked if people live in houses in Africa. French students have been asked if they have refrigerators in France.

All this is disheartening coming from college students, but international students have more serious problems to face. Although many faculty members are interested in international students and friendly toward them, in disciplines and perhaps parts of the country where there are many non-natives enrolled as students, these students sometimes encounter hostility from their teachers. Certain professors build a reputation of disliking international students in their classes and of automatically giving them lower grades. How prevalent such a practice is probably cannot be determined, but certainly students believe it happens.

Students have reported other behavior on the part of some professors which is, at the very least, unbelievably insensitive, perhaps racist. One student's content-area teacher took his paper and tore it into pieces, telling the student to learn English before turning in a paper. Another student reports:

> Right at the beginning the professor said that I could not pass the course. He said, "As long as you have a Japanese mind, you can not pass 111." When he said this I thought I could not survive sometimes. I have had a Japanese mind for 30 years how can I change it? I felt so depressed. The teacher said that he had had a Korean student who had taken 111 three times in order to pass. He compared me to the Korean saying that it would take me at least that long. I felt like he thought all Asians were the same — Korean Japanese there's no difference. This felt like racial discrimination to me. (Newstetter et al., 1989)

International students fare as badly in the community. A student from Hong Kong claims that he is regularly overcharged for purchases in his conservative Southeastern community and that residual, confused resentments from the war in Vietnam cause locals to automatically take him for Vietnamese and discriminate against him. (His hilarious and ingenious solution to this problem was to announce that he was not foreign; he was just from California, a location probably as distant and exotic to many of these local residents as any place in Southeast Asia!)

Classroom Expectations

Different national groups and different individuals bring different expectations to the classroom, but many students express surprise at the same aspects of post-secondary classroom culture in the United States. Many of the surprises are pleasant. Some international students come from educational systems in which famous scholars and researchers deliver lectures to several hundred students at once, never getting to know any of them personally, or even speaking to them individually. These students are pleased to find that many of their professors here are approachable, informal, and friendly, that they set up office hours when students are welcome to discuss concerns privately. Some students are also thrilled with the flexibility of the U.S. university system and with the diversity of completely unexpected classes available, like typing or various physical education classes.

On the other hand, ESL students often remark on the apparent lack of respect for teachers here, shown in the casual clothes, sandals, even shorts, that their native classmates wear to class or in the eating and drinking that may go on in some classes. The whole teaching environment is disturbingly casual to some students. Teachers sit on the front desk while lecturing, students interrupt lectures to question or dispute what the teacher has said, teachers sometimes say they do not know the answer to a question. Any of these behaviors may jolt the expectations of non-native students.

Even something as simple as what students and teachers call each other can create confusion. Some international students feel uncomfortable calling teachers by names and prefer to use only titles, addressing their instructors simply as "Doctor" without using a name or using a first name, as in "Professor Ken," or simply using "Teacher." Students from the People's Republic of China tend to address their professors by their last names only: "Good morning, Johnson." By the same token, of course, they may expect to be addressed by their family names only and feel uncomfortable being addressed by their given names, an intimacy reserved for only a few very close family members. Even husbands and wives may refer to each other by their family names. Many of the international names are difficult for linguistically provincial Americans to pronounce, and students often resort to taking on English names while they are here. One Jordanian student writes that his name has been spelled and pronounced in so many different ways that he now responds to anything even vaguely resembling Najib: Jeeb, Nick, Nancy.

Many international university students also have a hard time adjusting to what they see as being treated like high school students. They are amazed to find teachers demanding daily attendance, assigning homework, and policing the class by testing periodically to make sure they have done the homework. These students may come from a system in which students may choose to take advantage of class lectures or not, as long as they pass a comprehensive, end-of-the-year exam. Quite a different attitude toward student responsibilities from our own!

In some countries, students may take pre-departure classes or U.S. culture classes which may cover some of the areas of difference between educational practices at home and abroad and thereby help students prepare for their experiences. But these courses cannot cover every encounter the students may have. One international student, for example, took a multiple choice test here for the first time. Having had no previous experience with this form of testing, the student assumed that multiple choice meant choosing more than one answer per item (Stapleton, 1990). Other students come from educational systems in which competing theories are presented only in order to explain the correct theory. The students are confused when they realize that their professor here assumes none of the theories is entirely correct (Krasnick, 1990). It is important to keep in mind that in addition to learning subject matter in a class, ESL students are also often learning a whole new approach to learning itself.

Classroom Behaviors

It should not come as a surprise to us, then, that these students will not always do what we expect in our classes. International students have stood up when the teacher entered the room; others have insisted on erasing the blackboard after class for the teacher. A student of mine, misconstruing the idea of office hours, complained that he had come by my office, hoping to find me by chance for a conference at 5:00 P.M. Saturday afternoon. That student said he waited for me for an hour!

Some students have a difficult time with the style of class participation they observe. While U.S. teachers may consider class participation an important sign that the students are paying attention, some ESL students will never participate unless specifically called on. They may be especially reluctant to volunteer answers to questions since they may feel that by doing so they are humiliating their classmates who cannot answer the question. A Japanese proverb says something like, "The nail that sticks up gets hammered down." Compare that to our own, "The squeaky wheel gets the oil."

ESL students may also react badly to teacher requests for opinions, especially opinions in conflict with those expressed by the teacher. Such requests may be viewed as evidence of teacher incompetence (Levine, 1983, cited in Scarcella, 1990, 94), and many ESL students are trained specifically *not* to hold opinions differing from those of their teachers. By the same token, ESL students may expect teachers to know the answers to any question they may have; these students may become embarrassed and lose confidence in teachers who honestly state that they do not know an answer but will find out. In one case, an Iranian student whose chemistry teacher had made such a statement dropped the class, explaining that he did not see the point in trying to learn from someone who did not know. In Iran, he explained, a professor would sooner fabricate an answer than admit to not knowing.

Many other types of assumptions come into conflict in culturally mixed classes. In an article on attitudes toward time, Levine (1985) describes a problem familiar to ESL teachers — ESL students' flexible attitude toward deadlines. This professor describes his first day teaching at a university in Brazil. Fearing he will be late for his first class, he asks several people the correct time and gets different answers from everyone he asks, answers differing by twenty minutes! Some of the casual strollers he asks are, he later realizes, students in the very class he was in such a rush to get to on time. Once in class, he notices students coming in fifteen minutes, thirty minutes, even an hour late, and none of them act embarrassed or chagrined or apologetic. And when the class period is over, none of them get up to leave, willing instead to stay on another fifteen, or thirty, minutes or whatever it takes to get their business done. People in many other countries are simply not driven by the clock in the way people in the United States are. As a result, even though ESL students usually know of the U.S. reputation for, they might say, fanatic devotion to punctuality, these students sometimes just cannot bring themselves to conform to class starting times and paper deadline dates. Their priorities are such that they may be unable to refuse to help a friend in need even if their term papers are due tomorrow. In one 8:00 A.M. class of mine, students from Greece, Zaire, and Palestine arrived in class every single day from five to fifteen minutes late; on the other hand, a group of students from the People's

Republic of China arrived every single day from five to fifteen minutes early!

Traditional gender roles may also create problems for ESL students. For some of these students, their experience in the United States will be the first time they have been in a mixed-sex classroom. This alone may be intimidating for them. But in addition, in some parts of the world, women are expected not to speak in the presence of males at all, clearly posing a special problem of classroom participation for these students. Even if women students do not have this additional burden placed on them, they, and males from these cultures, may feel awkward working in groups together and, if given the choice, may choose to work only in groups of the same sex.

It is also the case that some of these students, particularly the males, may never have had a female professor and may need some time to adjust themselves to that new experience. ESL professionals also cite instances in which gender prejudices make male ESL students unable to take female authority figures, including teachers, as seriously as they would males. But general respect for authority and for teachers in particular apparently overrides these prejudices for the most part. These problems occur with very few students and far less often in English-speaking countries than in the students' home countries.

Language

Language obviously creates misunderstandings. Even though ESL students may be paying careful attention to what is going on, they may actually understand only a portion of what they hear. New ESL teachers consistently register surprise at their own overestimation of how much their students understand of classroom management talk. Numbers in particular may be difficult, for example, the page numbers of reading assignments. These students may need to have directions repeated even when they claim to have understood. In fact, for students from some cultures where it seems to be taken for granted that all credit for students' learning belongs to the teacher, it may be utterly useless to ask if they understand. For cultural and linguistic reasons, they may always claim to understand even when they don't, either hesitant to bring further attention to themselves by their failure to understand or reluctant to imply that the teacher has not made a point clearly enough.

Sometimes the confusion arises because, for some cultural groups, nodding the head, which indicates agreement or at least understanding to English speakers, may merely indicate that the listener is continuing to listen, while perhaps not understanding the content of what is being said at all (Scarcella, 1990). For some Arabs, blinking the eyes indicates agreement, a gesture unlikely even to be noticed by uninformed native English speakers, and for some Indians, the gesture used is tilting the head to the side in a movement that resembles the English gesture indicating doubt! (This gesture looks like the one which might be accompanied in English by "Oh well" and a shrug.)

Some languages are spoken with a great deal more intonation or emphasis than is usual for English. If students from those language backgrounds have not learned to imitate English oral delivery style well, they may come off sounding more vehement or emotional than they intend. Other students, many Asians, for example, may seem excruciatingly shy because of the longer pauses they customarily take before answering a question put to them. An English speaker may perceive a Vietnamese speaker as not participating in a conversation because the Vietnamese speaker takes so long to reply; the Vietnamese speaker, however, may perceive a series of friendly questions as a barrage implying impatience and not permitting appropriately reflective answers (Robinson, 1985, cited in Scarcella, 1990, 103).

Another aspect of the problems caused by language, even for students who are fairly proficient in English, may occur when a student tries to make a point. The rules for turn-taking vary among languages. A person speaking English is expected to heed verbal and kinetic cues indicating that the listener is now ready to speak, cues like taking a breath or making a sound toward the end of the speaker's sentence. Non-native students may inappropriately interrupt a speaker because turn-taking is handled differently in those students' cultures and they may not yet know the correct signals to send in this culture. In some cultures, interrupting a speaker may not be rude; it may be a sign of listener attentiveness intended to show the listener's involvement in the interaction. But it is also entirely possible that while the speaker is speaking, the non-native student is rehearsing what she or he planned to say and simply has to begin speaking before the planned sentence slips away.

Language-based confusion also arises unexpectedly and in ways impossible to guard against. One example is [an] Asian student . . . who interpreted the comment "It's a shame you didn't have more time to work on this paper" to mean "You should be ashamed of this paper."

The confusion may also be on the teacher's part. Oral English proficiency, for example, including accents, can be extremely misleading. ESL students who have learned English in an environment which precluded much contact with spoken English may speak with accents very difficult to understand but may write quite well. Conversely, particularly with immigrant students, the students' oral English may sound quite native-like but their written English may be a problem. They may be quite proficient at BICS [Basic Interpersonal Communicative Skills] but may have had little experience with CALP [Cognitive Academic Language Proficiency], the language of the academy. In either case, accents cannot be equated one way or the other with proficiency.

Grades and Exams

One very important area in which cultural assumptions may differ and cause friction is evaluation. Some of these students are under tremendous pressure to get good grades either because their financial support depends on maintaining a certain average or because their pride or family honor requires excellent performance. In addition, in many countries around the world, exam results are extremely important, determining much more absolutely than we may be used to here a student's admission to certain types of educational tracks or to certain prestigious schools and ultimately to a desirable job and life style. Even exams taken at age five or six can set children on the road to a comfortable, financially secure future or to a lifetime of factory work. Students from these countries take exams extremely seriously.

Further complicating the exam issue is the fact that it is taken for granted in some countries that friends and relatives have the right to call upon each other for any help they need, and that that call must be answered. Some students feel as much obliged to share exam answers or research papers as they would to share their notes of that day's class or to share their book with a classmate. (See Kuehn, Stanwyck, and Holland,

1990, for a discussion of ESL students' attitudes towards cheating.) Knowledge may be thought of more as communal, less as individual property. The moral obligation to share, to cooperate, to help a friend or relative makes far more pressing demands on some of these students than the obligation our culture may wish to impose of individual work and competition. In other words, what we call cheating is not particularly uncommon or shocking for some of these students. It simply does not carry the onus it does here.

In places where personal relationships have more weight than they do here and adherence to impersonal rules has less weight, bureaucrats and others in authority often have a great deal more flexibility to act than they might here. As a result, arguing, persuading, and bargaining for a better deal is a part of human interaction. That includes, of course, bargaining with teachers for better grades. In situations where students are pleading for higher grades, the justification is nearly always the same: not that the student actually did better, not that the teacher's judgment was wrong, not that the student does not deserve the lower grade, but that the student *needs* a higher grade and that it is in the teacher's power to *help*. When the teacher refuses to help, the student may go away hurt and confused, personally wounded at the teacher's indifference to the student's plight. These are very painful experiences both for the student and for the teacher, but particularly for non-ESL teachers who may not understand that the student (and the teacher as well, obviously) is operating according to another set of culturally determined rules about personal interactions. Non-ESL teachers may well come to resent international students for putting them in such tense, embarrassing situations and making them feel guilty about sticking to their decisions.

In these awful confrontations, it is also not unheard of for students to exhibit more emotion than most U.S. post-secondary teachers are accustomed to dealing with. Men in other cultures, for example, are permitted to cry under a much wider range of circumstances than is permitted here. Unrestrained sobbing is sometimes a student's response to the sadness of failure or defeat.

Body Language and Socio-linguistic Snags

Other conflicting cultural styles may be less dramatic but also disconcerting. Latin American and Arab students may sit or stand too close during conferences; Vietnamese students may feel uncomfortable with a friendly pat on the shoulder; Japanese students may not look at the teacher when addressed. During a discussion of body language, I asked a class of international students whether they noticed that people use eye contact differently in the United States from the way it is used in their home countries. Several students strongly felt that this was the case. When asked to elaborate, a man from El Salvador complained that Americans refused to look him in the eye, as if they were lying, insincere, or hiding something, and a woman from Japan claimed that Americans made her feel uneasy because they seemed to insist on staring at her when they spoke, right in the eye instead of somewhere at the base of the throat, as she was accustomed to doing!

Cultural differences can cause other complications which are not strictly linguistic. One of the experiences Americans abroad often complain about is suffering the injustice of having someone butt in line and be served out of order while those in line continue to wait. But in many other cultures, people assume that those who are waiting in line are in no particular hurry and don't mind not being waited on next. If they did mind, they would be aggressively demanding attention by pushing to the front of the line and stating their desire. Students from these places, then, may feel quite comfortable crowding the teacher after class and demanding attention while other students patiently await their turns.'

Other embarrassing moments may occur as a result of socio-linguistic differences among cultures. One of these areas concerns the tacit rules which govern topics of conversation. Teachers may feel intruded upon by questions which are completely normal in the students' cultures: In Asia: Are you married? How old are you? In the Arab world: How much did that cost? Do you have sons? In Eastern Europe: How much money do you make? How much do you weigh? (Wolfson, 1989). The reaction to such questions may be outrage unless we realize that the question of what is appropriate to talk about is a part of the linguistic system of a language that must be learned just as verb tenses must be learned. Just as the questions above may strike us as inappropriate, others take offense at different questions. Muslim students, for example, are offended by questions like "Why don't you drink?" or "Have you ever kissed your boyfriend?" (Wolfson, 1989). Unfortunately, socio-linguistic rules are not visible as rules, are taken for granted, and are assumed to be universal. As a result, while grammatical errors may be ignored, socio-linguistic errors brand the non-native as rude and offensive.

Notions of modesty about achievements also differ among cultures. Writing teachers may find it difficult, for example, to learn whether a writing assignment went well for given students. When asked how well they did on an assignment, Asian students invariably say they did not do a good job, that they are not good students, while Arab students seem to always reply that their paper is very good, that everything went exceedingly well.

ESL students may actually behave in ways that strike us as unusual, unexpected, or even inappropriate, but difficulties may also arise as we simply misinterpret what appears to be ordinary, recognizable behavior. The Japanese, for example, have an aversion for direct disagreement and instead of saying no to a suggestion may hedge, preferring to indicate vaguely that the decision must be postponed or further studied (Christopher, 1982, cited in Wolfson, 1989, 20). As a result, an English speaker may not recognize that the Japanese speaker has said no and may assume that the Japanese speaker really is still debating the issue. The Japanese apparently do not even like to say the word "no"; when asked whether she liked Yoko Ono, one Japanese student replied, "Yes, I hate her."

Finally, the offices of ESL teachers are often crowded with Chinese paper cuttings, Korean fans, Latin American *mulas,* and pieces of Arabic brass. Non-ESL colleagues of mine with ESL students in their classes have sometimes expressed concern that these gifts look like bribes and have wondered whether or not to accept them from their students. But this type of gift-giving is an accepted part of many cultures, and ESL students often give their teachers small gifts as tokens of respect and gratitude with no baser intentions in mind at all.

Students may misinterpret us as well or feel confused about how to interpret our signals correctly. While they may be happy to learn, for example, that professors have office hours, they may feel unsure about whether or not they are actually invited to take advantage of them. Students may be confused if the decision of whether or not to come by the office during office hours is left up to them and may conclude that an offhand invitation to come by if they have problems, an invitation which does not *urge* or order the student to come by, is not sincere.

Conclusion

It takes some time for international students to determine exactly what their relationship with a professor is. Many of them come from cultures, such as China, in which teachers are highly respected but also are expected to behave more like mentors, to involve themselves in the students' lives, to know about them as people, and to guide them closely in moral, personal, or educational decisions. These students may then be disappointed to find this is not usually the case here.

Clearly, there is a great deal of room for both misunderstanding and resentment during confrontations involving different cultural styles. For the most part, it is the international students, outnumbered as they are, who will have to make the greater part of the adjustment to accommodate U.S. classroom expectations. But an awareness of some of these students' expectations on the part of their U.S. instructors can certainly make the adjustment easier for all. Anticipating some of the behaviors of culturally mixed groups can help us be more tolerant of them and perhaps at the same time less hesitant about pointing out, if necessary, the inappropriateness of some of these behaviors within the culture of the U.S. college classroom.

References

Krasnick, H. 1990. Preparing Indonesians for graduate study in Canada. *TESL Reporter* 23: 33–36.

Kuehn, P., D. J. Stanwyck, and C. L. Holland. 1990. Attitudes toward "cheating" behaviors in the ESL classroom. *TESOL Quarterly* 24: 313–317.

Levine, R., with E. Wolff. 1985. Social time: The heartbeat of a culture. *Psychology Today* 19 (March): 28–37.

Newstetter, W., T. Shoji, N. Mokoto, and F. Matsubara. 1989. From the inside out. Student perspectives on the academic writing culture. Paper presented at the Conference on Culture, Writing, and Related Issues in Language Teaching, Atlanta, Georgia.

Scarcella, R. 1990. *Teaching language minority children in the multicultural classroom.* Englewood Cliffs, NJ: Prentice-Hall.

Stapleton, S. 1990. From the roller coaster to the round table: Smoothing rough relationships between foreign students and faculty members. *TESL Reporter* 23 (April): 23–25.

Wolfson, N. 1989. *Perspectives: Sociolinguistics and TESOL.* New York: Newbury House.

TAILORING COMPOSITION CLASSES TO ESL STUDENTS' NEEDS

Ann Schlumberger and Diane Clymer

[*Teaching English in the Two-Year College* 16 (May 1989): 121–28.]

A faculty member at Pima County Community College and the University of Arizona, Tucson, Ann Schlumberger has taught writing from the elementary school to the college level for more than twenty years. With Diane Clymer, Schlumberger wrote "Teacher Education through Teacher Collaboration," a chapter in *Richness in*

Writing: Empowering ESL Students (1989). The article included here resulted from Schlumberger's and Clymer's ESL teaching experiences and their recognition that fellow teachers regularly have questions about how to teach writing to ESL students.

Composition teachers encounter ESL students in several different contexts, and Schlumberger and Clymer offer practical advice that applies to any of them. Arguing that learning a language and learning to write are analogous, Schlumberger and Clymer advocate using a process methodology with ESL writers instead of reverting to product-oriented approaches. They explain clearly why and how their four general recommendations for teaching ESL writers will contribute to a more effective pedagogy. Their bibliography will help instructors explore these four recommendations further.

During the past decade, two-year colleges have been providing education to growing numbers of nonnative speakers of English. These English-as-a-second-language students are attracted to two-year campuses for the same reasons as other students: Open enrollment policies provide them with access to postsecondary education, relatively low tuition and fees make education feasible, and the faculty emphasis on teaching rather than research assures students of the personal and academic support necessary to sustain their studies. In addition, many of these students see the two-year college as a low-risk environment in which to improve their English.

Quite often it is the English composition teacher — with little or no background in teaching ESL — who is charged with helping the students realize this goal. Beyond urging novice ESL teachers to subscribe to the *TESOL Quarterly* (the ESL professional journal), this article offers four general recommendations for accommodating composition instruction to the needs of ESL learners. These suggestions are applicable (1) to classes of ESL students sharing the same first language, (2) to classes with students of different first languages, and (3) to classes made up of both ESL and native English speakers. Also included is a bibliography of suggested readings for teachers who wish to increase their knowledge of ESL pedagogy.

Recommendation 1

Make holistically graded papers a part of the procedure for placing ESL students in composition courses. Placement by objective grammar tests can mask the linguistic facility of ESL students who have grown up in the United States, while misrepresenting the productive skills of foreign ESL students. International students, in particular, can often recognize correct grammatical forms far better than they can use them in their own writing.

While misuse of grammar is often the most salient feature of ESL compositions, holistic scoring permits teachers to assess content, development, organization, and diction as well. When ESL students are literate in their first language, their English writing samples often reflect the rhetorical conventions of their first language. For instance, an argument which is artfully conceived by Korean standards will probably seem confusingly indirect to native English speakers. The repetitious, emphatic language of essays written by Arabic students, while satisfying the phatic purpose of Arabic discourse, will probably be judged redundant hyperbole by an English reader, who wonders when the students will stop repeating themselves and start developing support for their claims.

To minimize misplacement in classes, we further recommend correlating the holistic rating scale with the entrance criteria for courses in the curriculum. When graders are familiar with the sequence of courses, they expedite the placement process by thinking in terms of "This student would benefit from asking _____." In addition, the training session for holistic grading is a useful means of familiarizing new or part-time faculty with the expectations for student performance at different levels of the curriculum. In particular, part-time faculty, who are often hired to teach the same one or two courses each semester, appreciate the experiential overview that participating in a holistic grading session can provide.

At the University of Arizona, ESL students have thirty minutes to write an argumentative placement essay on their choice from three thesis statements. Two teachers independently rate each essay on a scale of 1 to 4; a two-point discrepancy results in the paper's being evaluated by a third reader. Awarding a 1 indicates placement in the preparatory composition course. A 2 indicates the teacher thinks the student can pass the first semester of ESL composition; a 3 indicates that the student will probably do well in that course, and 4 suggests placement in a native-speaker section of freshman composition.

Recommendation 2

Organize courses around thematic units. May Shih describes such "content-based" academic writing courses as "composition courses organized around sets of readings on selected topics" (p. 632). One of the advantages to this format is that recursive encounters with a topic allow both native and nonnative speakers of English to gradually amass a body of material to think and write about. By examining a topic from different perspectives over time, the students' lexical knowledge increases even as their intellectual understanding of the subject deepens: The result is greater fluency. Shih points out that content-based composition instruction enables students to develop the cognitive, evaluative skills needed for work in all academic disciplines.

Teachers of ESL composition students need to remember that developing native-speaker fluency in a foreign language takes time; it is the result of prolonged exposure to the way the language is used in many different contexts. Yet, as Anne Raimes has noted, complete mastery of syntax and expression is not a prerequisite for instruction in English rhetoric ("Composition"). Beginning ESL writing students should not be restricted to grammar drills, sentence combining exercises, and the construction of isolated paragraphs.

Several approaches are possible when designing thematic units. First, since people write best about subjects they know and care about, the choice of unit themes should take into account the students' experiences as well as their writing skills and academic needs. For example, students in a preparatory composition class who have recently arrived in the United States and are just beginning their studies do well reading, discussing, and writing about experiences with language, paralingual communication, and cultural differences — topics which are relevant to their positions as newcomers in a foreign culture. From these personal experiences, they can extract generalizations or inferences that become the focus for expository prose, the type of writing predominant in an academic setting. For instance, a Vietnamese student, reacting in her journal to the informality of American greetings, might develop an essay that classifies and explores the significance of the modes of address used by Vietnamese. Student experiences also yield material for writing personal essays popular in composition classes for native speakers. However, it is important to realize that some ESL students may have traumatic pasts that they do not care to reminisce about.

Another way to ensure that students explore topics that interest them is to enlist their help in selecting thematic units. In some ESL freshman composition classes, students review the table of contents of their anthology of readings and write a proposal to their teacher in which they state the sections of the text they would like the class to cover. Since some international students have been told by their governments what they must study, these students in particular enjoy an opportunity to exercise their freedom of choice. Some semesters an entire class might be in agreement about what they want to read, and they choose to write their papers on the same general topic (such as education or technology). Other semesters, students have divided into interest groups to discuss related readings, to collect copies of library articles to augment their knowledge of a subject, and to garner suggestions for their papers.

At times, however, teachers will want to preserve their control over the choice of theme and materials in order to ensure that students approach one theme from different rhetorical perspectives. For example, in a second-semester freshman composition course, students read essays, poems, short stories, and two short novels — all relating to an overall theme, such as heroism or family and community. Each semester, the teachers of this course agreed on a common theme and the major novels to be studied. Their consensus allowed them to work together in collecting relevant short pieces and developing materials to supplement the literature. The supplementary compilation was copied and sold in the bookstore with the works of fiction. Although many teachers may prefer to work with a thematically arranged reader, using a compilation allows flexibility in the choice of materials, enables teachers to change the thematic focus of their courses frequently, and incidentally, prevents students from plagiarizing the previous semester's papers.

Recommendation 3

Reduce the assigned number of formal, polished essays. As a consequence of the shift in composition instruction from a product to a process orientation, many ESL composition teachers have decreased the number of formal papers they require of students. Instead, students are given more opportunities for revision and for informal, exploratory writing to discover topics. Just as students increase their reading rate and comprehension by extensive reading, so do they gain fluency in writing by extensive writing on a topic. Fluency is more important than correctness of expression in the early stages of the writing process because students are writing to discover ideas, to incorporate new information from a variety of sources, and to explore connections. Eventually, some of this extensive writing evolves into the initial drafts for three or four intensive writing projects, which can culminate in formal, polished essays of 800 to 2500 words.

One advantage of a multidraft approach is that it encourages teachers to vary their responses to student writing according to a paper's stage of development. Vivian Zamel cautions against the dangers of responding to all student writing "as if it were a final draft" (p. 79). When teachers read exploratory writing or early drafts of students' papers, their first concern should be ideas. Extensive correcting of grammar at this point makes it difficult for students to jettison sentences or change passages that do not contribute effectively to ideas that are being developed. ESL composition teachers should de-emphasize mechanics and expression until later stages of revision — a more appropriate time to consider correctness of grammar and niceties of expression.

When marking mechanical errors, we suggest restraint, lest the number of marks overwhelm both ESL students and their teachers. Chastain recommends targeting for correction a maximum of three types of errors per paper. The teacher labels the grammatical structures involved, explains the mistakes, and models correct forms. Thereafter, the student is held accountable for eliminating these errors in papers. Errors are selected for remediation on the basis of their frequency in a paper, their disruption of the text, and their focus in class instruction.

Homburg describes a useful system for classifying mechanical errors according to their serious, irritating, or negligible effects on text comprehensibility. One does not have to be an expert in linguistics to realize that syntax problems severe enough to obscure meaning are more of a concern for teachers than consistent misuse of the definite article or the occasional omission of -s endings on third person verb forms. In fact, composition teachers with experience conducting basic writing classes for native English speakers will recognize some of the same sorts of errors in the work of their ESL students. However, to help teachers understand the ways in which ESL students' native language and background influence their production of English prose, our bibliography includes articles contrasting linguistic and rhetorical features of other languages with those of English. When teachers feel they do not have the resources to interpret the problems a student is having with the language, they may want to consult someone who has specialized training in teaching ESL.

Recommendation 4

Encourage ESL students to develop and use all four language skills in the composition classroom: writing, listening, speaking, and reading. Research supports such a holistic approach to language learning, indicating that instruction and practice in other aspects of language reinforce writing skills.

A standard means of integrating language skills in English classes has been to require students to present oral reports on a topic they have researched and written about. This is a useful practice, but we have found that the spontaneous, informal conversations carried on during small group work are even more beneficial to ESL students' written and oral language development. Long and Porter enumerate the positive effects of group work: It (1) increases opportunities for language practice, (2) improves the quality of student communication, (3) helps individualize instruction, (4) promotes a positive affective environment, and (5) motivates learners (pp. 208–12). From a pedagogical and from a language acquisition perspective, collaborative learning makes sense. Nevertheless, sometimes teachers who have successfully employed peer collaboration in their other classes fear that ESL students' cultural reservations or lack of oral proficiency will cause group work to fail.

We have not found this to be the case. In fact, group activities and peer editing contribute significantly to the invention, drafting, and revision cycles of student writing. We do, though, recommend multilingual groupings, when possible, to ensure the use of English as the medium of discussion. And, as is true for native English speakers, teachers have to explain clearly the rationale for group work since many students will be unfamiliar with this technique. Teachers also need to structure group activities carefully, providing clear directives to the groups and allowing them sufficient time to complete the assigned task. Occasionally misunderstandings develop during peer editing exchanges, but tact, humor, and lessons in the polite subjunctive can help with students who have difficulty expressing or accepting criticism.

Direct instruction in reading also has an important place in the ESL composition curriculum. Indeed, the current literature focuses on the close relationship between reading and writing. We always model for our students how to skim, scan, and annotate a text. In-class previewing of assigned readings is particularly important. The ESL composition teacher — to an even greater extent than the basic writing teacher — cannot assume that students will understand what they read. All students need knowledge of the topic assigned (an issue discussed in the section on thematic units), but ESL students, in particular, may need supplemental background information to help them understand a reading.

One method of previewing a text with students is to have them scan it for words that seem to be important to the text's meaning. These are put on the board, and the teacher uses them to elicit student predictions about what the assigned reading will be about. Idioms, expressions, and difficult vocabulary can thus be explained in a way that highlights the fact that reading, like writing, involves the construction of meaning.

Fraida Dubin stresses the importance of students' knowing "the whole context of a selection so that significant clues to meaning are not overlooked" (p. 157). Echoing the writing teacher's concern for audience, Dubin recommends that ESL students be made aware of the conventions and characteristics of different text types: scholarly prose for experts, popular culture texts for the general public, and nonacademic nonfiction for the educated audience (pp. 155–57).

Students also benefit from direction in how to elaborate on what they read. We have designed an exercise to promote reading/writing connections in ESL freshman composition classes. Whenever students have an assigned reading, they are required to explore, in brief paragraph-length passages, insights or questions that occur to them as they read. The teacher later reads and responds to the content of these informal compositions while modeling active involvement with a text. This exercise ensures that students are prepared for class discussions, and for making connections beyond the literal level of the text. Some of these connections, when explored further, can be the source of ideas which eventually mature into a formal essay.

Conclusion

Composition teachers with a firm grounding in process methodology are in an excellent position to assist ESL students in developing language skills, even though such teachers are not language specialists *per se.* Obviously, a background in linguistics is very valuable to the teacher of ESL composition classes, but current theories of teaching composition complement the current theories in language acquisition.

Stephen D. Krashen, a widely cited theorist on language acquisition, identifies in *The Input Hypothesis: Issues and Implications* (New York: Longman, 1985) two recursive processes in gaining competence in a language: *acquisition* and *learning.* During acquisition, the learner is exposed to "comprehensible input," developing fluency in a language with emphasis on understanding and communicating ideas, not on grammatical correctness. This parallels the early phases of the writing process when the student's focus is comprehending and generating content. Then, during what Krashen calls the learning process ("a conscious process that results in 'knowing about' language"), learners begin to monitor their output, consciously shaping it according to rhetorical, syntactic, and morphological conventions. This process is quite similar to that which student writers engage in as they revise and edit their compositions. What has been discovered about learning a language is applicable to learning to write and vice versa. The analogous nature of these two activities should provide encouragement and reassurance to composition teachers newly assigned to teach ESL classes.

A Bibliography for Tailoring Composition Classes to ESL Students' Needs

CURRICULUM DESIGN

Farr, Marcia, and Harvey Daniels. "Writing Instruction and Nonmainstream Students." *Language Diversity and Writing Instruction.* Urbana, Ill.: NCTE, 1986. 43–85.

Johnson, Donna M., and Duane H. Roen, ed. *Richness in Writing: Empowering ESL Students.* In press.

Long, Michael H., and Patricia A. Porter. "Group Work, Interlanguage Talk, and Second Language Acquisition." *TESOL Quarterly* 19 (1985): 207–28.

Mackay, Sandra, ed. *Composing in a Second Language.* Rowley, Mass.: Newbury, 1984.

Raimes, Ann. "Composition: Controlled by the Teacher, Free for the Student." *On TESOL '76* (1977): 183–94.

———. "Teaching ESL Writing: Fitting What We Do to What We Know." *The Writing Instructor* 5 (1986): 153–65.

Shih, May. "Content-Based Approaches to Teaching Academic Writing." *TESOL Quarterly* 20 (1986): 617–48.

Spack, Ruth. "Literature, Reading, Writing, and ESL: Bridging the Gaps." *TESOL Quarterly* 19 (1985): 703–25.

Watson-Reekie, Cynthia B. "The Use and Abuse of Models in the ESL Writing Class." *TESOL Quarterly* 16 (1982): 5–14.

RESPONDING TO PAPERS

Brown, H. Douglas. "Interlanguage." *Principles of Language Learning and Teaching.* 2nd ed. Englewood Cliffs: Prentice, 1987. 169–97.

Chastain, Kenneth. "Composition: Toward a Rationale and a System of Accountability." *Toward a Philosophy of Second Language Learning.* Boston: Heinle, 1980. 67–74.

Homburg, Taco Justus. "Holistic Evaluation of ESL Compositions: Can It Be Validated Objectively?" *TESOL Quarterly* 18 (1984): 87–105.

Zamel, Vivian. "Responding to Student Writing." *TESOL Quarterly* 19 (1985): 79–101.

CULTURAL ASPECTS OF WRITING

Connor, Ulla, and Robert B. Kaplan, ed. *Writing across Languages: Analysis of L2 Text.* Reading, Mass.: Addison-Wesley, 1987.

Derrick-Mescua, Maria, and Jacqueline L. Gmuca. "Concepts of Unity and Sentence Structure in Arabic, Spanish, and Malay." 1985. ERIC ED 260 590.

Hinds, John. "Contrastive Rhetoric: Japanese and English." *Text* 3 (1983): 183–96.

Kaplan, Robert B. "Cultural Thought Patterns in Intercultural Education." *Language Learning* 16 (1966): 1–20.

Lay, Nancy. "Chinese Language Interference in Written English." *Journal of Basic Writing* 1 (1975): 50–61.

Mohan, Bernard A., and Winnie Au-Yeung Lo. "Academic Writing and Chinese Students: Transfer and Developmental Factors." *TESOL Quarterly* 19 (1985): 515–34.

Ostler, Shirley E. "Writing Problems of International Students in the College Composition Classroom." *The Writing Instructor* 5 (1986): 177–89.

Rizzo, Betty, and Santiago Villafane. "Spanish Influence on Written English." *Journal of Basic Writing* 1 (1975): 62–71.

Thompson-Panos, Karyn, and Maria Thomas-Ruzic. "The Least You Should Know about Arabic: Implications for the ESL Writing Instructor." *TESOL Quarterly* 17 (1983): 609–21.

READING

Carrell, Patricia L. "The Effects of Rhetorical Organization on ESL Readers." *TESOL Quarterly* 18 (1984): 441–69.

Carrell, Patricia L., Joanne Devine, and David Eskey, ed. *Interactive Approaches to Second Language Reading.* Cambridge: Cambridge UP, 1988.

Dubin, Fraida, David E. Eskey, and William Grabe, eds. *Teaching Second Language Reading for Academic Purposes.* Reading, Mass.: Addison-Wesley, 1986. 127–60.

HOW TO TAME A WILD TONGUE

Gloria Anzaldúa

[From *Borderlands/La Frontera: The New Mestiza* by Gloria Anzaldúa. San Francisco: Aunt Lute, 1987. 53–64.]

Chicana writer Gloria Anzaldúa grew up in southwest Texas, the borderland between the United States and Mexico. In addition to *Borderlands/La Frontera,* Anzaldúa coedited *This Bridge Called My Back: Writings by Radical Women of Color* (1983) and edited *Haciendo Caras: Making Face/Making Soul* (1990).

ESL problems in the composition class may appear most often as difficulties with conventions and grammatical rules, but those problems are manifestations of larger, more fundamental challenges facing ESL writers, challenges involving their home cultures, and their individual identities. In this chapter from *Borderlands/La Frontera,* Anzaldúa tells of the complexities of growing up a Chicana in the "borderland" between the United States and Mexico. In this piece, as in other selections from *Borderlands,* Anzaldúa's prose shifts in language and style in a way that can be confusing. But these shifts have the valuable effect of helping readers understand what it is like to live on linguistic and cultural borderlands. Anzaldúa reminds us of the necessity to respect all cultures.

"We're going to have to control your tongue," the dentist says, pulling out all the metal from my mouth. Silver bits plop and tinkle into the basin. My mouth is a motherlode.

The dentist is cleaning out my roots. I get a whiff of the stench when I gasp. "I can't cap that tooth yet, you're still draining," he says.

"We're going to have to do something about your tongue," I hear the anger rising in his voice. My tongue keeps pushing out the wads of cotton, pushing back the drills, the long thin needles. "I've never seen anything as strong or as stubborn," he says. And

I think, how do you tame a wild tongue, train it to be quiet, how do you bridle and saddle it? How do you make it lie down?

> Who is to say that robbing a people of
> its language is less violent than war?
> – RAY GWYN SMITH[1]

I remember being caught speaking Spanish at recess — that was good for three licks on the knuckles with a sharp ruler. I remember being sent to the corner of the classroom for "talking back" to the Anglo teacher when all I was trying to do was tell her how to pronounce my name. "If you want to be American, speak 'American.' If you don't like it, go back to Mexico where you belong."

"I want you to speak English. *Pa' hallar buen trabajo tienes que saber hablar el inglés bien. Qué vale toda tu educación si todavía hablas inglés con un* 'accent,'" my mother would say, mortified that I spoke English like a Mexican. At Pan American University, I and all Chicano students were required to take two speech classes. Their purpose: to get rid of our accents.

Attacks on one's form of expression with the intent to censor are a violation of the First Amendment. *El Anglo con cara de inocente nos arrancó la lengua.* Wild tongues can't be tamed, they can only be cut out.

Overcoming the Tradition of Silence

> *Ahogadas, escupimos el oscuro.*
> *Peleando con nuestra propia sombra*
> *el silencio nos sepulta.*

En boca cerrada no entran moscas. "Flies don't enter a closed mouth" is a saying I kept hearing when I was a child. *Ser habladora* was to be a gossip and a liar, to talk too much. *Muchachitas bien criadas,* well-bred girls don't answer back. *Es una falta de respeto* to talk back to one's mother or father. I remember one of the sins I'd recite to the priest in the confession box the few times I went to confession: talking back to my mother, *hablar pa' 'tras, repelar. Hociona, repelona, chismosa,* having a big mouth, questioning, carrying tales are all signs of being *mal criada.* In my culture they are all words that are derogatory if applied to women — I've never heard them applied to men.

The first time I heard two women, a Puerto Rican and a Cuban, say the word "*nosotras,*" I was shocked. I had not known the word existed. Chicanas use *nosotros* whether we're male or female. We are robbed of our female being by the masculine plural. Language is a male discourse.

> And our tongues have become
> dry   the wilderness has
> dried out our tongues   and
> we have forgotten speech.
> – IRENA KLEPFISZ[2]

Even our own people, other Spanish speakers *nos quieren poner candados en la boca.* They would hold us back with their bag of *reglas de academia.*

Oyé como ladra: el lenguaje de la frontera

> *Quien tiene boca se equivoca.*
> – Mexican saying

"*Pocho,* cultural traitor, you're speaking the oppressor's language by speaking English, you're ruining the Spanish language," I have been accused by various Latinos and Latinas. Chicano Spanish is considered by the purist and by most Latinos deficient, a mutilation of Spanish.

But Chicano Spanish is a border tongue which developed naturally. Change, *evolución, enriquecimiento de palabras nuevas por invención o adopción* have created variants of Chicano Spanish, *un nuevo lenguaje. Un lenguaje que corresponde a un modo de vivir.* Chicano Spanish is not incorrect, it is a living language.

For a people who are neither Spanish nor live in a country in which Spanish is the first language; for a people who live in a country in which English is the reigning tongue but who are not Anglo; for a people who cannot entirely identify with either standard (formal, Castilian) Spanish nor standard English, what recourse is left to them but to create their own language? A language which they can connect their identity to, one capable of communicating the realities and values true to themselves — a language with terms that are neither *español ni inglés,* but both. We speak a patois, a forked tongue, a variation of two languages.

Chicano Spanish sprang out of the Chicanos' need to identify ourselves as a distinct people. We needed a language with which we could communicate with ourselves, a secret language. For some of us, language is a homeland closer than the Southwest — for many Chicanos today live in the Midwest and the East. And because we are a complex, heterogeneous people, we speak many languages. Some of the languages we speak are

1. Standard English
2. Working class and slang English
3. Standard Spanish
4. Standard Mexican Spanish
5. North Mexican Spanish dialect
6. Chicano Spanish (Texas, New Mexico, Arizona, and California have regional variations)
7. Tex-Mex
8. *Pachuco* (called *caló*)

My "home" tongues are the languages I speak with my sister and brothers, with my friends. They are the last five listed, with 6 and 7 being closest to my heart. From school, the media, and job situations, I've picked up standard and working class English. From Mamagrande Locha and from reading Spanish and Mexican literature, I've picked up Standard Spanish and Standard Mexican Spanish. From *los recién llegados,* Mexican immigrants, and *braceros,* I learned the North Mexican dialect. With Mexicans I'll try to speak either Standard Mexican Spanish or the North Mexican dialect. From my parents and Chicanos living in the Valley, I picked up Chicano Texas Spanish, and I speak it with my mom, younger brother (who married a Mexican and who rarely mixes Spanish with English), aunts, and older relatives.

With Chicanas from *Nuevo México* or *Arizona* I will speak Chicano Spanish a little, but often they don't understand what I'm saying. With most California Chicanas I speak entirely in English (unless I forget). When I first moved to San Francisco, I'd rattle off something in Spanish, unintentionally embarrassing them. Often it is only with another Chicana *tejano* that I can talk freely.

Words distorted by English are known as anglicisms or *pochismos.* The *pocho* is an anglicized Mexican or American of Mexican origin who speaks Spanish with an accent characteristic of North Americans and who distorts and reconstructs the language according to the influence of English.[3] Tex-

Mex, or Spanglish, comes most naturally to me. I may switch back and forth from English to Spanish in the same sentence or in the same word. With my sister and my brother Nune and with Chicano *tejano* contemporaries I speak in Tex-Mex.

From kids and people my own age I picked up *Pachuco*. *Pachuco* (the language of the zoot suiters) is a language of rebellion, both against Standard Spanish and Standard English. It is a secret language. Adults of the culture and outsiders cannot understand it. It is made up of slang words from both English and Spanish. *Ruca* means girl or woman, *vato* means guy or dude, *chale* means no, *simón* means yes, *churro* is sure, talk is *periquiar*, *pigionear* means petting, *que gacho* means how nerdy, *ponte águila* means watch out, death is called *la pelona*. Through lack of practice and not having others who can speak it, I've lost most of the *Pachuco* tongue.

Chicano Spanish

Chicanos, after 250 years of Spanish/Anglo colonization, have developed significant differences in the Spanish we speak. We collapse two adjacent vowels into a single syllable and sometimes shift the stress in certain words such as *maíz/maiz*, *cohete/cuete*. We leave out certain consonants when they appear between vowels: *lado/lao*, *mojado/mojao*. Chicanos from South Texas pronounce *f* as *j* as in *jue* (*fue*). Chicanos use "archaisms," words that are no longer in the Spanish language, words that have been evolved out. We say *semos*, *truje*, *haiga*, *ansina*, and *naiden*. We retain the "archaic" *j*, as in *jalar*, that derives from an earlier *h* (the French *halar* or the Germanic *halon* which was lost to standard Spanish in the sixteenth century), but which is still found in several regional dialects such as the one spoken in South Texas. (Due to geography, Chicanos from the Valley of South Texas were cut off linguistically from other Spanish speakers. We tend to use words that the Spaniards brought over from Medieval Spain. The majority of the Spanish colonizers in Mexico and the Southwest came from Extremadura — Hernán Cortés was one of them — and Andalucía. Andalucians pronounce *ll* like a *y*, and their *d*'s tend to be absorbed by adjacent vowels: *tirado* becomes *tirao*. They brought *el lenguaje popular, dialectos y regionalismos*.) [4]

Chicanos and other Spanish speakers also shift *ll* to *y* and *z* to *s*.[5] We leave out initial syllables, saying *tar* for *estar*, *toy* for *estoy*, *hora* for *ahora* (*cubanos* and *puertorriqueños* also leave out initial letters of some words). We also leave out the final syllable such as *pa* for *para*. The intervocalic *y*, the *ll* as in *tortilla*, *ella*, *botella*, gets replaced by *tortia* or *tortiya*, *ea*, *botea*. We add an additional syllable at the beginning of certain words: *atocar* for *tocar*, *agastar* for *gastar*. Sometimes we'll say *lavaste las vacijas*, other times *lavates* (substituting the *ates* verb endings for the *aste*).

We used anglicisms, words borrowed from English: *bola* from ball, *carpeta* from carpet, *máchina de lavar* (instead of *lavadora*) from washing machine. Tex-Mex argot, created by adding a Spanish sound at the beginning or end of an English word such as *cookiar* for cook, *watchar* for watch, *parkiar* for park, and *rapiar* for rape, is the result of the pressures on Spanish speakers to adapt to English.

We don't use the word *vosotros/as* or its accompanying verb form. We don't say *claro* (to mean yes), *imagínate*, or *me emociona*, unless we picked up Spanish from Latinas, out of a book, or in a classroom. Other Spanish-speaking groups are going through the same, or similar, development in their Spanish.

Linguistic Terrorism

> *Deslenguadas. Somos los del español deficiente.* We are your linguistic night-
> mare, your linguistic aberration, your linguistic *mestisaje*, the subject of your
> *burla.* Because we speak with tongues of fire we are culturally crucified. Ra-
> cially, culturally, and linguistically *somos huérfanos* — we speak an orphan
> tongue.

Chicanas who grew up speaking Chicano Spanish have internalized the
belief that we speak poor Spanish. It is illegitimate, a bastard language.
And because we internalize how our language has been used against us by
the dominant culture, we use our language differences against each other.

Chicana feminists often skirt around each other with suspicion and
hesitation. For the longest time I couldn't figure it out. Then it dawned on
me. To be close to another Chicana is like looking into the mirror. We are
afraid of what we'll see there. *Pena.* Shame. Low estimation of self. In
childhood we are told that our language is wrong. Repeated attacks on our
native tongue diminish our sense of self. The attacks continue throughout
our lives.

Chicanas feel uncomfortable talking in Spanish to Latinas, afraid of
their censure. Their language was not outlawed in their countries. They
had a whole lifetime of being immersed in their native tongue; generations,
centuries in which Spanish was a first language, taught in school, heard
on radio and TV, and read in the newspaper.

If a person, Chicana or Latina, has a low estimation of my native tongue,
she also has a low estimation of me. Often with *mexicanas y latinas* we'll
speak English as a neutral language. Even among Chicanas we tend to
speak English at parties or conferences. Yet, at the same time, we're afraid
the other will think we're *agringadas* because we don't speak Chicano
Spanish. We oppress each other trying to out-Chicano each other, vying to
be the "real" Chicanas, to speak like Chicanos. There is no one Chicano
language just as there is no one Chicano experience. A monolingual Chicana
whose first language is English or Spanish is just as much a Chicana as
one who speaks several variants of Spanish. A Chicana from Michigan or
Chicago or Detroit is just as much a Chicana as one from the Southwest.
Chicano Spanish is as diverse linguistically as it is regionally.

By the end of this century, Spanish speakers will comprise the biggest
minority group in the United States, a country where students in high
schools and colleges are encouraged to take French classes because French
is considered more "cultured." But for a language to remain alive it must
be used.[6] By the end of this century English, and not Spanish, will be the
mother tongue of most Chicanos and Latinos.

So, if you want to really hurt me, talk badly about my language. Ethnic
identity is twin skin to linguistic identity — I am my language. Until I can
take pride in my language, I cannot take pride in myself. Until I can accept
as legitimate Chicano Texas Spanish, Tex-Mex, and all the other languages
I speak, I cannot accept the legitimacy of myself. Until I am free to write
bilingually and to switch codes without having always to translate, while
I still have to speak English or Spanish when I would rather speak Spanglish,
and as long as I have to accommodate the English speakers rather than
having them accommodate me, my tongue will be illegitimate.

I will no longer be made to feel ashamed of existing. I will have my voice:
Indian, Spanish, white. I will have my serpent's tongue — my woman's
voice, my sexual voice, my poet's voice. I will overcome the tradition of
silence.

My fingers
move sly against your palm
Like women everywhere, we speak in code. . . .
    – MELANIE KAYE/KANTROWITZ[7]

"Vistas," corridos, y comida: My Native Tongue

In the 1960s, I read my first Chicano novel. It was *City of Night* by John Rechy, a gay Texan, son of a Scottish father and a Mexican mother. For days I walked around in stunned amazement that a Chicano could write and could get published. When I read *I Am Joaquín*[8] I was surprised to see a bilingual book by a Chicano in print. When I saw poetry written in Tex-Mex for the first time, a feeling of pure joy flashed through me. I felt like we really existed as a people. In 1971, when I started teaching High School English to Chicano students, I tried to supplement the required texts with works by Chicanos, only to be reprimanded and forbidden to do so by the principal. He claimed that I was supposed to teach "American" and English literature. At the risk of being fired, I swore my students to secrecy and slipped in Chicano short stories, poems, a play. In graduate school, while working toward a Ph.D., I had to "argue" with one adviser after the other, semester after semester, before I was allowed to make Chicano literature an area of focus.

Even before I read books by Chicanos or Mexicans, it was the Mexican movies I saw at the drive-in — the Thursday night special of $1.00 a carload — that gave me a sense of belonging. *"Vámonos a las vistas,"* my mother would call out and we'd all — grandmother, brothers, sister, and cousins — squeeze into the car. We'd wolf down cheese and bologna white bread sandwiches while watching Pedro Infante in melodramatic tearjerkers like *Nosotros los pobres,* the first "real" Mexican movie (that was not an imitation of European movies). I remember seeing *Cuando los hijos se van* and surmising that all Mexican movies played up the love a mother has for her children and what ungrateful sons and daughters suffer when they are not devoted to their mothers. I remember the singing-type "westerns" of Jorge Negrete and Miquel Aceves Mejía. When watching Mexican movies, I felt a sense of homecoming as well as alienation. People who were to amount to something didn't go to Mexican movies, or *bailes,* or tune their radios to *bolero, rancherita,* and *corrido* music.

The whole time I was growing up, there was *norteño* music sometimes called North Mexican border music, or Tex-Mex music, or Chicano music, or *cantina* (bar) music. I grew up listening to *conjuntos,* three- or four-piece bands made up of folk musicians playing guitar, *bajo sexto,* drums, and button accordion, which Chicanos had borrowed from the German immigrants who had come to Central Texas and Mexico to farm and build breweries. In the Rio Grande Valley, Steve Jordan and Little Joe Hernández were popular, and Flaco Jiménez was the accordion king. The rhythms of Tex-Mex music are those of the polka, also adapted from the Germans, who in turn had borrowed the polka from the Czechs and Bohemians.

I remember the hot, sultry evenings when *corridos* — songs of love and death on the Texas-Mexican borderlands — reverberated out of cheap amplifiers from the local *cantinas* and wafted in through my bedroom window.

Corridos first became widely used along the South Texas/Mexican border during the early conflict between Chicanos and Anglos. The *corridos* are usually about Mexican heroes who do valiant deeds against the Anglo oppressors. Pancho Villa's song, *"La cucaracha,"* is the most famous one. *Corridos* of John F. Kennedy and his death are still very popular in the

Valley. Older Chicanos remember Lydia Mendoza, one of the great border *corrido* singers who was called *la Gloria de Tejas*. Her *"El tango negro,"* sung during the Great Depression, made her a singer of the people. The ever-present *corridos* narrated one hundred years of border history, bringing news of events as well as entertaining. These folk musicians and folk songs are our chief cultural mythmakers, and they made our hard lives seem bearable.

I grew up feeling ambivalent about our music. Country-western and rock-and-roll had more status. In the fifties and sixties, for the slightly educated and *agringado* Chicanos, there existed a sense of shame at being caught listening to our music. Yet I couldn't stop my feet from thumping to the music, could not stop humming the words, nor hide from myself the exhilaration I felt when I heard it.

There are more subtle ways that we internalize identification, especially in the forms of images and emotions. For me food and certain smells are tied to my identity, to my homeland. Woodsmoke curling up to an immense blue sky; woodsmoke perfuming my grandmother's clothes, her skin. The stench of cow manure and the yellow patches on the ground; the crack of a .22 rifle and the reek of cordite. Homemade white cheese sizzling in a pan, melting inside a folded *tortilla*. My sister Hilda's hot, spicy *menudo*, *chile colorado* making it deep red, pieces of *panza* and hominy floating on top. My brother Carito barbequing *fajitas* in the backyard. Even now and 3,000 miles away, I can see my mother spicing the ground beef, pork, and venison with *chile*. My mouth salivates at the thought of the hot steaming *tamales* I would be eating if I were home.

Si le preguntas a mi mamá, "¿Qué eres?"

> Identity is the essential core of who
> we are as individuals, the conscious
> experience of the self inside.
>   – GERSHEN KAUFMAN[9]

Nosotros los Chicanos straddle the borderlands. On one side of us, we are constantly exposed to the Spanish of the Mexicans, on the other side we hear the Anglos' incessant clamoring so that we forget our language. Among ourselves we don't say *nosotros los americanos, o nosotros los españoles, o nosotros los hispanos*. We say *nosotros los mexicanos* (by *mexicanos* we do not mean citizens of Mexico; we do not mean a national identity, but a racial one). We distinguish between *mexicanos del otro lado* and *mexicanos de este lado*. Deep in our hearts we believe that being Mexican has nothing to do with which country one lives in. Being Mexican is a state of soul — not one of mind, not one of citizenship. Neither eagle nor serpent, but both. And like the ocean, neither animal respects borders.

> *Dime con quien andas y te diré quien eres.*
> (Tell me who your friends are and I'll tell you who you are.)
>   – Mexican saying

Si le preguntas a mi mamá, "¿Qué eres?" te dirá, *"Soy mexicana."* My brothers and sister say the same. I sometimes will answer *"soy mexicana"* and at others will say *"soy Chicana"* o *"soy tejana."* But I identified as *"Raza"* before I ever identified as *"mexicana"* or "Chicana."

As a culture, we call ourselves Spanish when referring to ourselves as a linguistic group and when copping out. It is then that we forget our predominant Indian genes. We are 70–80 percent Indian.[10] We call ourselves Hispanic[11] or Spanish-American or Latin American or Latin when linking ourselves to other Spanish-speaking peoples of the Western hemisphere and when copping out. We call ourselves Mexican-American[12] to signify we are neither Mexican nor American, but more the noun "American" than the adjective "Mexican" (and when copping out).

Chicanos and other people of color suffer economically for not acculturating. This voluntary (yet forced) alienation makes for psychological conflict, a kind of dual identity — we don't identify with the Anglo-American cultural values and we don't totally identify with the Mexican cultural values. We are a synergy of two cultures with various degrees of Mexicanness or Angloness. I have so internalized the borderland conflict that sometimes I feel like one cancels out the other and we are zero, nothing, no one. *A veces no soy nada ni nadie. Pero hasta cuando no lo soy, lo soy.*

When not copping out, when we know we are more than nothing, we call ourselves Mexican, referring to race and ancestry; *mestizo* when affirming both our Indian and Spanish (but we hardly ever own our Black) ancestry; Chicano when referring to a politically aware people born and/or raised in the United States; *Raza* when referring to Chicanos; *tejanos* when we are Chicanos from Texas.

Chicanos did not know we were a people until 1965 when Cesar Chavez and the farmworkers united and I *Am Joaquín* was published and *la Raza Unida* party was formed in Texas. With that recognition, we became a distinct people. Something momentous happened to the Chicano soul — we became aware of our reality and acquired a name and a language (Chicano Spanish) that reflected that reality. Now that we had a name, some of the fragmented pieces began to fall together — who we were, what we were, how we had evolved. We began to get glimpses of what we might eventually become.

Yet the struggle of identities continues, the struggle of borders is our reality still. One day the inner struggle will cease and a true integration take place. In the meantime, *tenémos que hacer la lucha. ¿Quién está protegiendo los ranchos de mi gente? ¿Quién está tratando de cerrar la fisura entre la india y el blanco en nuestra sangre? El Chicano, si, el Chicano que anda como un ladrón en su propia casa.*

Los Chicanos, how patient we seem, how very patient. There is the quiet of the Indian about us.[13] We know how to survive. When other races have given up their tongue we've kept ours. We know what it is to live under the hammer blow of the dominant *norteamericano* culture. But more than we count the blows, we count the days the weeks the years the centuries the aeons until the white laws and commerce and customs will rot in the deserts they've created, lie bleached. *Humildes* yet proud, *quietos* yet wild, *nosotros los mexicanos-Chicanos* will walk by the crumbling ashes as we go about our business. Stubborn, persevering, impenetrable as stone, yet possessing a malleability that renders us unbreakable, we, the *mestizas* and *mestizos,* will remain.

Notes

[1] Ray Gwyn Smith, *Moorland Is Cold Country,* unpublished book.

[2] Irena Klepfisz, "*Di rayze aheym*/The Journey Home," in *The Tribe of Dina: A Jewish Women's Anthology,* Melanie Kaye/Kantrowitz and Irena Klepfisz, eds. (Montpelier, VT: Sinister Wisdom Books, 1986), 49.

[3] R. C. Ortega, *Dialectología Del Barrio*, trans. Hortencia S. Alwan (Los Angeles, CA: R. C. Ortega Publisher & Bookseller, 1977), 132.

[4] Eduardo Hernandéz-Chávez, Andrew D. Cohen, and Anthony F. Beltramo, *El Lenguaje de los Chicanos: Regional and Social Characteristics of Language Used by Mexican Americans* (Arlington, VA: Center for Applied Linguistics, 1975), 39.

[5] Hernandéz-Chávez, xvii.

[6] Irena Klepfisz, "Secular Jewish Identity: Yidishkayt in America," in *The Tribe of Dina*, Kaye/Kantrowitz and Klepfisz, eds., 43.

[7] Melanie Kaye/Kantrowitz, "Sign," in *We Speak in Code: Poems and Other Writings* (Pittsburgh, PA: Motheroot Publications, Inc., 1980), 85.

[8] Rodolfo Gonzales, *I Am Joaquín/Yo Soy Joaquín* (New York, NY: Bantam Books, 1972). It was first published in 1967.

[9] Gershen Kaufman, *Shame: The Power of Caring* (Cambridge, MA: Schenkman Books, Inc., 1980), 68.

[10] John R. Chávez, *The Lost Land: The Chicano Images of the Southwest* (Albuquerque, NM: University of New Mexico Press, 1984), 88–90.

[11] "Hispanic" is derived from *Hispanis* (*España*, a name given to the Iberian Peninsula in ancient times when it was a part of the Roman Empire) and is a term designated by the U.S. government to make it easier to handle us on paper.

[12] The Treaty of Guadalupe Hidalgo created the Mexican–American in 1848.

[13] Anglos, in order to alleviate their guilt for dispossessing the Chicano, stressed the Spanish part of us and perpetrated the myth of the Spanish Southwest. We have accepted the fiction that we are Hispanic, that is Spanish, in order to accommodate ourselves to the dominant culture and its abhorrence of Indians. Chávez, 88–91.

PUNCTUATION AND MECHANICS

The parts of *The Bedford Handbook* on punctuation and mechanics, continuing the emphasis of the two preceding parts, present rules in the context of how they affect writers' goals. Students typically encounter these rules only when they have broken them, and too often instructors ask students to learn them through exercises, drills, and rote memorization. The handbook's presentation of the use and application of these rules suggests that students should avoid the counterproductive approach of trying to apply all of the rules every time they write. Instead, students should consider applying particular rules at appropriate stages of the revision process.

Writing teachers regularly face the challenge of convincing students to attend to rules and conventions. No matter what approach teachers use when presenting these rules to writers, the following selections will challenge standard perceptions about teaching the basics and force teachers to consider their answers to the following questions:

- How can teachers invite students to think about rules (such as those for punctuation or spelling) differently?
- Students have covered punctuation and mechanics in one form or another throughout their education. When traditional teaching methods seem to be ineffective or counterproductive, how can teachers question them? What alternatives can they explore? Why?

WHAT GOOD IS PUNCTUATION?

Wallace Chafe

[Center for the Study of Writing Occasional Paper No. 2. Berkeley: Center for the Study of Writing, 1985. ERIC ED 292 120.]

A professor in the Department of Linguistics at University of California–Santa Barbara, Wallace Chafe is coauthor (with Jane Danielewicz) of "Properties of Spoken and Written Language," a chapter in *Comprehending Oral and Written Language* (1987). His most recent work is *Discourse, Consciousness, and Time: The Flow and Displacement of Conscious Experience in Speaking and Writing* (1994). An expanded version of the selection that follows appeared in *Written Communication* in 1988 under the title "Punctuation and the Prosody of Written Language."

Both articles resulted from Chafe's research on the differences between speaking and writing. He suggests that instructors consider supplementing their presentation of punctuation rules by teaching students to relate punctuation to the "sound of written language." This would encourage students to be more conscious of punctuation as a stylistic option that can contribute to the effectiveness of their writing.

There are few people whose heart will skip a beat at the thought of punctuation. For sheer excitement, punctuation ranks well below spelling, which at least lends itself to interesting games and contests. At best, it seems to be a necessary evil. Since it is present in all normal English writing, anyone who is going to write English needs to learn to use it in an acceptable way, but it is seldom mentioned as an important ingredient of good writing. Interestingly, in the early nineteenth century those in the printing profession believed they knew more about how to punctuate than their authors did. A book called *The Printers' Manual* published in London in 1838 "laments the ignorance of most writers in the art of punctuation and fantasizes about a world in which authors turn in manuscripts with no punctuation at all, leaving that chore to the professional competence of the compositors" (Shillingsburg, 1986, p. 60).

Even if we might now be willing to admit that punctuation is not exactly in a class with setting type, and that authors are best allowed to have some control over it, it continues to suffer from a popular reputation as something that is arbitrary, unmotivated, and governed by rules that make no particular sense. In short, it is in a class with "grammar." Perhaps it is even a part of grammar, but certainly not one of the more interesting parts.

There is a centuries old debate over whether, or to what extent, punctuation is in fact determined by grammar, or whether its primary function is rather to signal the "prosody" — the patterns of pitch and stress and hesitations — that authors have in mind when they write and that readers attribute to a piece of writing. Prosody is an obvious property of *spoken* language, where it takes only a moment of listening to confirm the presence of pitch changes, stresses, and hesitations. But what could it mean to say that these same features are present in written language too? Is not writing something that we see, rather than hear?

Some who have reflected on their own personal experiences in reading and writing have concluded that written language does actually involve a mental image of sound. Just as people can imagine what some familiar piece of music sounds like, readers and writers seem to be able to imagine how writing sounds. Eudora Welty, in her autobiographical book *One Writer's Beginnings,* put it this way: "Ever since I was first read to, then started reading to myself, there has never been a line read that I didn't *hear.* As my eyes followed the sentence, a voice was saying it silently to me. . . . My own words, when I am at work on a story, I hear too as they go, in the same voice that I hear when I read in books. When I write and the sound of it comes back to my ears, then I act to make my changes. I have always trusted this voice." If we can assume that Welty's observations capture something real and important, then the ways writers manage prosody can have an important effect on their writing.

To return to the debate over whether punctuation reflects grammar or whether it has more to do with the prosody of this inner voice, one reason for the inconclusiveness of the debate is the fact that, in the majority of cases, prosody and grammar support each other. Whether the period at the end of a sentence means, "This is the end of a sentence" (signaling something grammatical), or whether it means, "This is where there is a falling pitch and a pause" (signaling something prosodic) may be difficult to decide, since usually both things are true. There are some cases, to be sure, where grammar dictates the presence or absence of punctuation, whereas prosody does the reverse. When one looks at such cases in actual writing, one finds that sometimes grammar has its way, sometimes prosody. There is no clear answer to which predominates, but it is prosody that gives expression to that inner voice.

If we listen a little more carefully to spoken language and its prosody, we find that it is typically produced in brief spurts, each showing a coherent pitch contour and usually followed by a pause. (For more on these spurts and their significance, see Chafe, 1987a.) It is of some interest that these spoken "intonation units" are nicely reflected in the punctuation units of much good writing. (By "punctuation unit" I mean the stretches of language that are separated by punctuation marks.) Notice how Herman Melville used commas, semicolons, and periods to create this effect in *Moby Dick*. I have written the punctuation units on separate lines to emphasize their nature:

1. The prodigious strain upon the mainsail had parted the weather-sheet,
2. and the tremendous boom was now flying from side to side,
3. completely sweeping the entire after part of the deck.
4. The poor fellow whom Queequeg had handled so roughly,
5. was swept overboard;
6. all hands were in a panic;
7. and to attempt snatching at the boom to stay it,
8. seemed madness.
9. It flew from right to left,
10. and back again,
11. almost in one ticking of a watch,
12. and every instant seemed on the point of snapping into splinters.

This example typifies much nineteenth-century writing by including instances of punctuation that are not in accord with grammatically based rules. Most obvious is the fact that the commas and the ends of lines 4 and 7 separate a subject from a predicate, where conventional grammar would not countenance such a separation. But if one thinks of how this passage *sounds* as one reads it to oneself, and presumably as Melville imagined it to himself, the punctuation quite plausibly reflects his prosodic intentions.

Other literature, however, provides us with many examples where punctuation, or the lack of it, seems not to reflect the way the writing sounds. Take, for example, the following long unpunctuated sequence from James Agee's *A Death in the Family*, where a reader may have some difficulty restraining the impulse to insert a few prosodic boundaries:

> He has been dead all night while I was asleep and now it is morning and I am awake but he is still dead and he will stay right on being dead all afternoon and all night and all tomorrow while I am asleep again and wake up again and go to sleep again and he can't come back home again ever any more but I will see him once more before he is taken away.

Doubtless Agee was trying to achieve an effect of breathlessly tumbling, silent ideas. That kind of effect, however, is possible only in writing, and it removes writing from the link with spoken prosody that is so clear in Melville.

The Melville and Agee examples were produced about a hundred years apart, but we can easily find examples of contemporary writing that differ in similar ways. To illustrate with two extremes, there is a marked contrast between the punctuation of the text of a recent automobile advertisement in *Time:*

> Town road.
> The longest straightaway on the course.
> The 16-valve,
> intercooled,
> turbocharged engine,
> capable of doing 130 and more on a test track,
> reaches its mandated maximum of 35 mph and purrs nicely along at that speed.

and the punctuation of a recent scholarly article regarding "paleodemography":

> Persons familiar with the problems inherent in the estimation of demographic parameters for living human groups characterized by small size and a lack of census records should scarcely be surprised to find that paleodemography is controversial.

We can see, then, that writers of different periods as well as of different contemporary styles use punctuation in different ways. Is this because their prosodic intentions are so different, or is it because they differ in the degree to which they make use of punctuation to express their intentions? Both factors undoubtedly play a role, but I will focus here on the second: the assertion that styles of writing are distinguished by the degree to which their punctuation captures the prosody of the inner voice.

Putting things in this way implies that we can have some independent knowledge of the prosody of inner voice, so that we can compare it with a writer's punctuation in order to determine whether that punctuation expresses it well or badly. But how can we know about the inner voice except through punctuation? One way to make it overt might be through reading aloud. In a sense, reading aloud turns written language into spoken language, giving it a prosody that anyone can hear. To see what a systematic investigation along these lines would offer, we listened to tape recordings of a number of people reading aloud various passages of different styles (see Chafe, 1987b, for further details). It was found that they divided the passages into intonation units much like those of normal speech, regardless of how the passages had been punctuated. For example, the Agee passage was divided in the following way by most oral readers:

> He has been dead all night,
> while I was asleep,
> and now it is morning,
> and I am awake,
> but he is still dead,
> and he will stay right on being dead,
> all afternoon,
> and all night,
> and all tomorrow,
> while I am asleep again,
> and wake up again,
> and go to sleep again,
> and he can't come back home again,
> ever any more.
> But I will see him once more,
> before he is taken away.

The average length of these intonation units was just under five words. Five or six words is the typical length for intonation units in ordinary spoken English.

If oral readers create intonation units much like those of speech, regardless of how a passage was punctuated, they show us the degree to which an author punctuated in a spoken-like way. Thus, the automobile advertisement quoted above could be said to be very spoken-like in its punctuation, whereas the Agee passage was very unspoken-like in this respect. Reading aloud can also show associations between specific punctuation marks and specific pitch contours. For example, periods are almost always read aloud as falling pitches (suggesting the end of a declarative sentence), whereas commas are usually read aloud as nonfalling pitches (suggesting that more is to follow).

But it is not necessarily the case that people read something aloud the same way they read it to themselves. Reading aloud is subject to various constraints, both physical and psychological. A speaker has to breathe, for example, and there is a practical limit on how fast one can say something. There seem also to be some mental limitations on the speed with which one can process speech. The inner voice of written language may be freer of these constraints, with the result that more can be included in a written punctuation unit than in a spoken intonation unit. We asked some other readers, instead of reading these passages aloud, to "repunctuate" them, that is, to insert their own punctuation into versions from which the original punctuation had been removed. These repunctuated versions showed us the extent to which the authors had punctuated in ways their readers regarded as appropriate. They also provided clues as to how readers chose between the dictates of grammar and prosody.

The difference between those who read the passages and those who repunctuated them can be illustrated with a brief excerpt from Henry James (taken from *The Turn of the Screw*). James wrote at one point:

We were to keep our heads if we should keep nothing else —

Most of the people who read this little excerpt aloud, in spite of the fact that they were looking at the original punctuation, inserted a prosodic boundary after the word "heads." That is, they read it as if the punctuation had been:

We were to keep our heads, if we should keep nothing else —

In splitting this fragment into two six-word segments, these oral readers were adhering to the five- or six-word limit of spoken intonation units. But the silent readers who repunctuated this passage, even though they did not see the original punctuation, agreed with James: Most of them left the passage whole.

Why did both James and his silent readers prefer a punctuation unit twelve words long, twice the normal length of a spoken intonation unit? They probably were not just being slaves to punctuation rules. In another study writers were found to insert commas before subordinate clauses about 40 percent of the time (Chafe, 1984). Probably it is relevant that very little in this excerpt was "new," in the sense of information being brought up for the first time. Just before this James had written:

. . . we were of a common mind about the duty of resistance to extravagant fancies.

To then write "we were to keep our heads" was to repeat the idea of a "resistance to extravagant fancies," clarifying it and reinforcing it by wording it in a different way. And then to add "if we should keep nothing else" was only to emphasize the resolve by saying that this was the one essential thing to do. The passage in question does little more than strengthen an idea that had already been expressed in the passage before it. In writing, it seems that passages which express little in the way of new information can be all of a piece. Silent readers can absorb them without the need to split them apart. Speakers, locked into the more rigid requirements of spoken language, are more comfortable with a prosody that keeps things shorter. If, among the silent readers, some wish to follow a more leisurely pace, they are free in this example to interpret the conjunction "if " as a prosodic boundary in their own inner prosody. But neither James nor most of his readers saw any need to make this option explicit by inserting a comma.

What does such a study suggest with regard to the teaching of writing? Above all, it suggests how important it is for writers to pay attention to their inner voices. Good writers, whether or not they realize it, *listen to what they write.* They listen while they are writing, and even more importantly they listen while they are reading what they wrote in order to make changes. Paying attention to the sound of written language is absolutely essential to the effective use of punctuation.

It may be a little harder to be a writer these days than it was in the days of Thoreau and Melville. Then, writers were skilled in imagining how something would sound if it were read aloud, and they punctuated accordingly. The trick was to use punctuation marks as if they were stage directions for effective oral presentation. Whether or not these authors specifically intended their works to be read aloud, they punctuated as if that were their intention.

Reading aloud is not so much in fashion any more, nor is punctuation that is based on what reading aloud would sound like. If, as is currently assumed, most reading is going to take place silently and rapidly, more language can be assimilated within single acts of comprehension. A result is the current tendency for longer punctuation units, and for leaving more of a prosodic interpretation up to the reader, allowing the grammar to give prosodic options. This is the style often referred to nowadays as "open" punctuation.

Contemporary writing actually exhibits a broad variety of punctuation styles, so that accomplished writers need to be able to punctuate in ways that are appropriate to whatever kinds of writing they may be doing. An advertising copy writer who punctuated like a professor would soon be out of work, and a professor who punctuated like a nineteenth-century novelist would find journal editors deleting commas right and left.

Students, in addition to being sensitized to their inner voices, will benefit from knowing the range of punctuating options that are available, and from being shown, through examples, what is most appropriate to one style and another. They can learn from practice in writing advertising copy as well as the more academic kinds of exposition, and from experimenting with fiction that mimics the very different punctuation styles of, say, Melville and Agee. At the same time, developing writers need to know that there are certain specific rules for punctuating that violate the prosody of their inner voices, and that simply have to be learned. These arbitrary rules are few in number and well defined, and to learn them need be no burden. The rules themselves may be appropriate to some styles and not to others. For example, the rule against placing a comma between a subject and predicate, violated so often by nineteenth-century writers, was also safely ignored by the person who wrote the following for the outside of a cereal box:

> Two cups of Quaker 100% Natural Cereal mixed with a little of this and a little of that, make the best cookies you've tasted in years.

The bottom line is that punctuation contributes substantially to the effectiveness of a piece of writing, and that its successful use calls for an awareness of something that is, for this and other reasons, essential to good writing: a sensitivity to the sound of written language.

References

Chafe, Wallace. 1984. "How People Use Adverbial Clauses." *Proceedings of the Tenth Annual Meeting of the Berkeley Linguistics Society.*

Chafe, Wallace. 1987a. "Cognitive Constraints on Information Flow." In Russell Tomlin (ed.), *Coherence and Grounding in Discourse.* Amsterdam: John Benjamins.

Chafe, Wallace. 1987b. "Punctuation and the Prosody of Written Language." Technical Report No. 11, Center for the Study of Writing, Berkeley.

Shillingsburg, Peter L. 1986. *Scholarly Editing in the Computer Age: Theory and Practice.* Athens: University of Georgia Press.

Welty, Eudora. 1983. *One Writer's Beginnings.* New York: Warner Books.

SPELLING INSTRUCTION IN THE WRITING CENTER

Linda Feldmeier White

[*The Writing Center Journal* 12 (Fall 1991): 34–47.]

Linda Feldmeier White is associate professor of English and chair of the Department of English and Philosophy at Stephen F. Austin State University. Before becoming chair, she directed the Writing Center for more than ten years, and she has served as chair of the Texas Association of Writing Centers. White teaches composition and eighteenth-century British literature, and she is currently working on an analysis of the discourse of learning disabilities.

Though this article is addressed primarily to writing center tutors, the advice that White offers will be useful for classroom teachers, too, especially as more use one-to-one conferencing strategies to help students with their writing. Following a short overview of recent research on the development of spelling ability and a brief summary of the connections (or lack of) between spelling and English orthography, White describes a four-lesson sequence she uses to help college students improve their spelling. Beginning with a lesson in which students explore the affective dimensions of being labeled a "poor speller," White moves to strategies for self-assessment that help students recognize error patterns and learn to proofread effectively. Following this, students learn how to use the various tools available to them, including dictionaries and spelling checkers. The sequence ends with a lesson in "how English spelling works," an understanding of the system of spelling. White concludes that students can learn to spell, but not by memorizing or by having teachers mark every spelling error. She recommends that teachers use a cognitivist approach to teaching spelling rather than a behaviorist approach.

Despite the advent of computerized spelling checkers, being a poor speller is still a significant burden for a writer. Spelling errors are stigmatizing, considered a mark of illiteracy both in academia and in business. Occasions for spelling errors are far more frequent than are opportunities for other errors, and misspellings are more noticeable. Relatively few readers respond to comma splices or dangling participles, but virtually everyone reacts to "dosen't" or "stuped" or "thair." For the poor speller, writing, particularly in impromptu situations, is a gamble; spelling errors always threaten to sabotage the communication. Since spelling instruction is usually not part of the first-year composition curriculum — even in a basic writing course, only some students will be poor spellers — assistance with spelling problems should become a regular part of a writing center program; it may be the only resource available to students who need help.

While text-based or programmed instruction is the easiest form of assistance to offer, it is generally ineffective. In a 1984 *Writing Center Journal* article, I.Y. Hashimoto and Roger Clark analyze the shortcomings of college spelling texts, which teach phonics and syllabification, and have students memorize rules and exceptions — despite research findings that question the efficacy of these methods. Textbooks oversimplify; there is little match between the activities they provide and the actual problems writers face in controlling spelling during the process of composing ("Texts" 1–3).

Rather than depend on textbooks, a writing center needs a staff member who is familiar enough with research on how spelling proficiency develops to analyze students' difficulties and to offer a short course or workshop on spelling improvement that treats spelling problems as part of the writing process. For those who would like to develop such a course, this article provides a brief introduction to recent research in spelling, suggestions for further reading, and a description of a writing center spelling workshop.

The Nature of English Orthography

Much has been made of the difficulty of English spelling, of the confusion caused by the fact that it is not based on a simple sound-to-symbol correspondence. George Bernard Shaw insisted that English spelling is so unpredictable that *fish* might be spelled *ghoti: gh* as in *rough, o* as in *women,* and *ti* as in *solution.* Other proponents of spelling reform attack the capriciousness of English spelling as the root cause of illiteracy. Research conducted at Stanford University during the mid-sixties demonstrated that English orthography is neither entirely predictable, nor as random as Shaw and the spelling reformists claim. Hanna maintains that, "contrary to traditional viewpoints, the orthography is far from erratic. It is based upon relations between phonemes and graphemes — relationships that are sometimes complex in nature but which, when clarified, demonstrate that American-English orthography, like that of other languages, is largely systematic" (Hanna et al. 83). Shaw's bizarre representation of *fish* actually serves to illustrate the regularity of English spelling; *ghoti,* even for a poor speller, is not a reasonable hypothesis for fish because it ignores rules of position and stress that are part of the system. It is true that *gh* represents the sound of *f* in *rough,* but it never represents that sound at the beginning of a word, and the letters *ti* are an alternative to *sh* only in medial positions. In the Stanford experiments, researchers discovered that a computer programmed with rules for phonetics, position, and stress was able to generate the correct spellings of approximately 49 percent of a core vocabulary of 17,000 words. As might be expected, the computer could not be programmed to predict such spellings as *eye, pizza, one, two, guitar, does.* Nor could researchers devise an algorithm to spell long vowel phonemes correctly. In words like *pail, break, pale, bay, they,* and *weigh,* no phonetic or positional rule governs the choice entirely, although some patterns are more common than others.

The fact that English spelling is not entirely phonetically regular does not mean that it is chaotic; rather, it is based on other patterns and principles. The most significant way English spelling deviates from phonetic correspondences is in reflecting the meaning and derivation of words. The past tense marker *–ed,* for example, is pronounced in three different ways, as in *stopped, begged,* and *loaded.* But since the three sounds have the same meaning, they are spelled *–ed.* English spelling also retains the history of the language. Words that have similar roots are spelled the same way, reflecting lexical relationships even where pronunciation has changed over time. The *g* in *sign* is phonetically puzzling but predictable because of the semantic relationships among *sign, signal, signature, resignation,* and the like.

In sum, English orthography is fairly complex. Its base is alphabetic; there are many one-to-one sound-to-symbol correspondences. There are also more complicated patterns, involving rules of position and stress. A part of English spelling is not predictable and does require exposure and memorization. And a large part of spelling ability is closely tied to knowing what words mean.

The Development of Spelling Ability

How this system is learned is still the subject of speculation among cognitive psychologists. Researchers disagree on such basic issues as whether our spelling memories consist of a single template for each word or multiple representations of the same word (Brown 488). In *Cognitive Processes in Spelling,* Uta Frith notes that "the most tantalising question still open is how spelling ability is learned and improved . . . . research results are mostly not yet at a stage where they can be applied" (5). However, what is known about language learning discredits the behaviorist approach that underlies most spelling instruction. The dominant mode of instruction in spelling, as Hashimoto and Clark's review of textbooks shows, is to drill students on rules, as if they were computers needing to be reprogrammed ("Texts" 1–3).

Persistent as it is, this approach is flawed. Teaching spelling rules assumes that a writer at the point of composition will sort through the rules he or she knows, select the most appropriate one, and then apply it, in order to generate one correct spelling. This model does not describe what proficient spellers do. The sheer number of rules that need to be mastered, along with their complexity, makes their use impractical. J. N. Hook's *Spelling 1500,* for example, consists of 85 units, including one on words ending in *–yze* or *–ize,* another on *–ery* or *–ary,* two on dropping final *e,* two on keeping final *e,* four on words ending in *–ence* or *–ent,* and so on. Roloff and Snow (109) need four rules to clarify the choice between *–able* and *–ible* — four rules to make one choice in one set of words. It has been argued that poor spellers need rules as an aid because they cannot do what proficient spellers do, but the proposed crutch seems more baggage than tool. The conscious application of rules is practical only if it happens rarely and with very few rules. The rules are accurate, perhaps even elegant, providing as they do an explicit formulation of complex patterns. But they are not useful. The conscious application of rules does not account for our production of correct spellings.

What does account for the proficiency in spelling that many English speakers acquire is the same language-learning mechanism that allows toddlers to master spoken language. According to current psycholinguistic theory, learning to spell, like all language learning, is not a simple matter of memorization or stimulus-and-response reinforcement, but a consequence of our innate ability to discern patterns as a function of experience with language.

Some of the most important advances in understanding this process have been made by linguist Charles Read, reading specialist Edmund Henderson, and several of Henderson's doctoral candidates, whose research is based on observing what they call "creative" or "invented" spellings, the spellings devised by preschoolers and first-graders who have not yet learned to read. These invented spellings, which represent the child's hypotheses about reasonable ways to represent speech sounds, provide a fascinating body of data on how the human brain masters the complexities of language.

One of the early stages of invented spelling is phonetic spelling, in which children match the sound they hear with the letter of the alphabet that has the same sound in its name, for example, *are* is spelled R, *you* is U, *rescue* is RESQ, *eighty* is ATE. At this stage, children make phonetic distinctions in their spelling that adults no longer hear because they are literate, more in tune with graphemic realities than with phonetic ones. Read found that children who invent spellings write CHROK or CHRAC for *truck*, AS CHRAY for *ashtray*, CHRIBLS for *troubles*, CHRIE for *try*, JRAGIN for *dragon*, JRIV for *drive*. These spellings look random to an adult, to whom it is axiomatic that *truck* begins with a *t*, drive with a *d*. That perception is based on reading, not hearing. The initial sounds in *truck* and *tick* are not identical; the *t* in *truck* is an affricate, similar to the initial sound in *chuck*. Because the affrication of *t* next to *r* is predictable, the difference between the initial sounds of *tick* and *truck* is not represented in our orthography. Nor are the initial sounds of *dragon* and *dive* identical, as the invented spelling of JRAGIN recognizes. On the basis of their experience with print, literate adults are convinced that both sounds are the same; non-readers hear and represent the difference.

Another revealing characteristic of invented spelling is the treatment of nasalized vowels in words like *angry* and *hunt*. Children's invented spellings often omit the *n* before consonants, but not the *n* before vowels: MOSTR *(monster)*, PLAT *(plant)*, AD *(and)*, AGRE *(angry)*, NUBRS *(numbers)*. Phonetically, these spellings are accurate; the sound of a nasalized vowel is not identical to the sound that begins *not* or *never*. Similarly, invented spellings are more phonetically accurate than standard spellings in placing vowels in stressed syllables but not in unstressed syllables: LITL *(little)*, CANDL *(candle)*, WAGN *(wagon)*, and EVN *(even)*, and in representing intervocalic flaps as voiced rather than unvoiced: LADR *(letter)*, WOODR *(water)*, BEDR *(better)*, PREDE *(pretty)* (Read, *Categorization* 52–64).

These examples illustrate what it means to have tacit knowledge and how it is that we can learn things about spelling that we are not explicitly taught. Literate speakers who think that *dragon* and *dive* begin with the same sound (or that *no* and *own* have the same sounds) are following spelling rules. Because the rules are not conscious, they feel they are observing a simple sound-to-symbol correspondence. The patterns found in invented spellings show that children have already mentally organized speech sounds. If they had not, their creations would be random. Children abstract and categorize the sounds they hear without being taught to do so. The same ability is the basis for learning standard spelling except that in learning to spell, the relevant experience is exposure to written rather than to spoken language. Children learning to spell are not blank slates on which knowledge is inscribed. Rather, the task of learning standard spellings is one of replacing tacit knowledge of phonetic patterns with tacit knowledge of graphemic patterns.

Given sufficient exposure to print, this transfer takes place in a normal developmental sequence. As children learn to read, their invented spellings begin to change. For example, at first they make a spelling distinction that matches the three different sounds of the past tense marker. But gradually these different spellings begin to disappear as children internalize the concept that spelling represents meaning as well as sound (Read, *Categorization* 65–68). Typical growth toward standard spelling can be seen in these successive approximations: MOSTR, MONSTOR, MONSTER; ATE, EIGTY, EIGHTY; LUVATR, AELUVATER, ELEVATOR; LFT, ALAFAT, ELEFANT, ELEPHANT (Gentry and Henderson 117; Henderson, *Learning* 34).

This research has important pedagogical implications. Since spelling is not an isolated, mechanical skill, it is best learned as part of a curriculum that engages children in worthwhile reading and writing activities; children who are involved in reading and writing will search for and find order in written language in the same way they find order in spoken language when they learn to speak. Learning to spell is a gradual process of mastering complex patterns and depends less on memorization than on experience:

> Correct spelling is not learned by sheer memory nor is it learned mechanically from rules. Our research suggests instead that some underlying abstract orderings are gradually acquired as a function of developing intellectual maturity and a prolonged experience with written language. . . . Knowledge of this kind can be conceived of only as tacit knowledge; it cannot be taught directly or expressed concretely at any of its stages. (Henderson, *Learning* 95–96)

The research also suggests that two facets of traditional instruction do more to hinder than aid the development of spelling ability. The first, an overemphasis on phonetics, gives students misleading information. Children who have difficulty spelling a word are often told to listen more carefully and spell the sounds they hear. In truth, they are listening carefully and need to learn to abstract further, to stop attending to some phonetic differences, in order to categorize sounds the way the written system does. "When children spell PUP (or POP, or whatever) for *pump*, there is probably nothing wrong with their hearing . . . they do not regard the 'missing' sound as being the same as that at the beginning of *my*. Furthermore, they do not immediately alter their spelling when you pronounce the word as 'pummmp'" (Read, *Categorization* 115–116). Instead of telling students to listen more carefully, teachers should help them make the transition from attending to phonetic patterns to attending to graphemic ones.

Instruction also fails when it insists too early on correct spellings and thereby short circuits the process of experimentation that allows the child to make the patterns of written English his or her own (Gentry 7–10). Teachers fear that leaving spelling errors uncorrected will reinforce bad habits. Again, the behaviorist model is deceptive. As they gain experience, children self-correct their limited or incorrect generalizations in the same way that they learn to say "went" rather than "goed" as they master grammar. Mistakes are best seen as necessary experiments. Too early an attempt to be correct forces a child to depend on rote memorization and direct copying, which are inefficient ways to learn.

Teaching Spelling to College Students

Why learning to spell is effortless for some and tortuous for others is not entirely clear. If all poor spellers were poor readers, their difficulties could be explained by their lack of experience, since spelling knowledge is so closely related to the development of other reading and writing skills. But many poor spellers are quite literate. Uta Frith's hypothesis is most convincing. She believes that there are two different but equally effective strategies for reading. One type of reader uses full cues, absorbing details as he or she makes global predictions. The other type of reader relies on partial cues; since written language is redundant, it is possible to determine meaning without absorbing letter-by-letter detail. Readers who develop the latter strategy are more likely to have difficulty with spelling (505–507).

It is also not clear to what extent remediation is possible, or whether disabilities are innate or learned. Not all spelling disabilities are incurable; as case studies show, some are simply the result of poor teaching (Gentry 11–25; Henderson, *Learning* 135). On the other hand, neither intelligence nor effort guarantees success. Richard Gentry's history as a poor speller, which he recounts in *Spel . . . Is a Four-Letter Word,* is instructive. Gentry made perfect scores on spelling tests throughout his elementary school career, winning third place in a county spelling bee in eighth grade. His test-taking expertise was the result of many hours devoted to memorizing word lists. His writing, flawed with misspellings like "becase" and "stoped," belied his success (5–6; 42–43). And although he is now an expert on how spelling is learned, he remains a poor speller, as does Henderson (Gentry 25; Henderson, *Learning* 32).

Given these uncertainties, it is unreasonable for a college-level remedial program to attempt to transform poor spellers into good ones. Remedial instruction for children can teach them how to learn so that they can profit from the years of experience that are still ahead. College students no longer have years of schooling ahead and need immediate help in dealing with their spelling problems. Thus, a more reasonable goal for remediation in college is to enable poor spellers to cope with their difficulty. Such a goal is not pessimistic; there are many things poor spellers can learn that will improve their writing performance.

At the writing center that I direct, spelling instruction is offered in a four-session workshop. The first lesson of the workshop is affective: through discussion, students are encouraged to see that being a poor speller is a frustrating but not insurmountable problem. This lesson is necessary because the emotional legacy of being a poor speller is a significant barrier to learning. Poor spelling seems to win a disproportionate share of scorn from which few poor spellers escape unscathed. Gentry, a model of diligent pursuit of spelling knowledge, tells an ironic story about being berated by a college professor for making so many spelling errors on an exam essay; according to the professor, anyone so intelligent who couldn't spell must be lazy (5). A fellow writing center director who is a poor speller recalls being so angry about spelling during her college years that she refused to proofread, preferring to take lower grades than to confront her errors. All of the students I have worked with in spelling workshops have had similar experiences. It is important for them to hear that a poor speller is not necessarily unintelligent, illiterate, or morally defective.

One way to structure this discussion is to have students apply a problem-solving heuristic to spelling. In problem analysis, one identifies and contextualizes the problem, analyzes its causes, and evaluates alternative solutions to find the most promising. In helping students to identify why spelling is a problem, I note that some apparent problems are not worth solving, that it is best to see problems in context to determine whether they interfere with important goals. Given this prompt, students begin to redefine spelling problems as writing problems. It doesn't take long to establish that misspellings are problems because they bother readers, who (perhaps wrongly but nonetheless inevitably) then misjudge the writer's intelligence or carefulness. Students also begin to consider how spelling interferes with composing. They realize, some for the first time, that the coherence of their arguments suffers when they pause to look up or try to remember a spelling and that their syntax suffers when they recast a sentence to avoid words they don't know. Their speculations about the causes of their problems with spelling are predictable: some suspect dyslexia; others complain that English spelling is impossible; most blame their teachers. When the discussion turns to possible solutions, students are at a loss. Most have had no instruction in spelling beyond having their errors marked and being told to use a dictionary. These problem-solving sessions are unusually energetic, perhaps because students have had few opportunities to talk non-judgmentally about spelling. Students are eager to share their experiences and eager for suggestions. It is salutary for them to have the opportunity to discuss their problems with others who share them.

Another major focus of the workshop is to provide the opportunity for self-assessment. Since most poor spellers are ashamed of their inadequacy, spelling is generally an area they have avoided examining; they know that they can't spell, but they know little about the specific nature of their difficulties. As part of the workshop, they begin to explore their habits and skills: what percentage of words they typically misspell, whether they misspell words in the same or different ways, what words they misspell. An important part of this assessment is having students analyze their spelling errors, classifying them according to type. The chapter on spelling in Mina Shaughnessy's *Errors and Expectations* provides a model for this analysis, although I have found a simplified version with fewer categories more practical than the one Shaughnessy gives. Students collect their errors (from essays, journals, notebooks, etc.) and enter them on a chart in which each error is classified according to type, for example, long vowel sound, short vowel sound, missing letter, silent -*e*, homophone, double consonant. As Shaughnessy points out, poor spellers are often convinced that their errors are "infinite and unpredictable." Cataloguing their own errors not only gives them insight into how the spelling system works, but helps them to see that their errors form patterns and thus are not unmanageable (175–177). A further application of error analysis is described by Hashimoto and Clark. Their students take a spelling inventory containing high-frequency vocabulary and then use the misspelled words thus identified to create personalized dictionaries. By using their own dictionaries when they write, students become more familiar with words that are likely to be problems for them and so find them easier to recognize ("Program" 34–35).

Above all, poor spellers need to find out whether they can proofread for spelling errors. I ask students to take an ungraded draft and mark the words that they think are misspelled; we can then calculate whether they doubt too much or too little. Some students who initially identify their problem as being unable to discern spelling errors in a draft find that they are good at it. That they have not made this discovery previously is not, I think, a sign of dishonesty or laziness, but a consequence of the way writing instruction is organized. So much writing is done under time constraints that poor spellers get a great deal of experience in finding out that they don't catch mistakes. Each time they get a paper back with spelling errors marked by someone else, that conviction is reinforced. Although my evidence for this assertion is anecdotal, I believe that the reason many poor spellers don't proofread is that they don't know that they can; their experience has convinced them not to try. Once they find out that they can proofread, they do. Teaching students how to proofread has been responsible for the spelling workshop's most impressive successes: in the space of a few weeks, some students reduce the number of errors in a paper from ten or fifteen to two or three. Unhappily, others find that they do not proofread efficiently. Usually, the problem is not that they fail to identify words that are misspelled but that they doubt everything. I once observed a workshop participant spend two hours proofreading a 500-word paper. That even with such extraordinary effort he failed to correct some of his errors is understandable: two hours spent at such a tedious task is likely to make one's attention lapse.

Students also need instruction in using the tools that can help them deal with being poor spellers. Word processors with spelling checkers and pocket-sized electronic dictionaries are a great boon to a poor speller if he or she becomes proficient in their use. Students need practice in using spelling checkers and need to become aware of their limitations: computers cannot diagnose homophone errors; they sometimes flag words that are not incorrect; their use requires the ability to select the correct spelling from a list of choices; the correct choice may not appear in the list. Students also need instruction in using dictionaries; typically, they have no plan for what to do if a word is not where they expect to find it. How can you look up a word, they ask, if you don't know how it is spelled? Their frustration with dictionaries stems from and reinforces their conviction that spelling is impossible. The strategy of considering possible alternative spellings needs to be introduced and practiced. Group brainstorming sessions are productive. ("If you think a word is spelled with an *e,* and it isn't, what are some other possibilities?" If *else* isn't under 'elce' where else could you look?" "What other spellings of 'atention' are possible?")

Mnemonic devices, like those described in Harry Shefter's *Six Minutes a Day to Perfect Spelling,* are another tool for poor spellers. Although Shefter's spelling program is ill-founded — he overemphasizes the extent to which spelling ability depends on memorization — his suggestions for how to memorize are more efficient than the serial rehearsal strategies that students often use. Shefter recommends learning to spell by using visualization, associative recall, and practice tracings to make the spelling of a word automatic (9–28). The utility of these devices is more limited than Shefter admits, but they do provide quick results and are thus useful in learning unfamiliar terms in preparation for an exam or for gaining control over a small number of words.

Finally, students need a better understanding of how English spelling works. Henderson provides word sorting tasks that help students explore the patterns of written English. In one exercise, for example, students are asked to first sort a list of words containing *oi-* or *oy-* (*soil, toy, rejoice, boycott,* etc.) and then determine which pattern occurs more frequently in the middle of words and which at the end (*Teaching* 53–70). Workshop students also explore the principle that spelling is related to meaning by examining word pairs like *miracle* and *miraculous, medical* and *medicine, narrate* and *narrative,* and by practicing using lexical relationships to solve spelling problems. One student with whom I worked on a draft, Luke, had spelled *competition* as "compitition." I explained that unstressed syllables generally give no phonetic clue to how the vowel is spelled, but that sometimes a related word will. Luke supplied *compete* as having the same meaning and changed the *i* to an *e*. We had gone on to discuss other issues in the draft when Luke looked at another paragraph, pointed to his spelling of "challanging" and asked, tentatively, if the word were related to the name of the space shuttle, which, being a NASA buff, he knew how to spell. The connection between "Challenger" and "challenging" may seem obvious, but some students' experiences either don't lead them to make the discovery or don't make it relevant to the problem of how to spell a word. Thus, the importance of studying patterns is that it helps to demystify spelling. Most poor spellers seem to be working from the underlying hypothesis that spelling is phonetic. Viewed from this perspective, the way words are spelled seems a bewildering array of irregularities and exceptions. Understanding that there is a system to spelling does not solve all spelling problems, but it does make students less confused and discouraged; spelling no longer seems impossible.

For those students who are interested, the writing center also offers semester-long tutorials on the spelling system. Student and tutor work through the eighth-grade volume of Henderson's elementary school spelling series. I do not, however, try to convince students to engage in an extended course of study. In part, this decision is pragmatic; in the past, many students who have begun spelling programs have discontinued them when their course assignments became pressing. But my main reason for favoring the workshop approach is that I am not sure that a longer course of study would actually return greater benefit. With beginners, long-term, formal word study might produce the tacit knowledge of the system that good spellers intuit. But college students are not beginners, and it may not be possible for an adult to actually re-structure the way he or she organizes word knowledge. Despite the grandiose claims of many remedial spelling texts, I have never met anyone who reports having been transformed from a poor speller into a good one. I have met poor spellers whose written work does not reveal their disability. But they do not have the same facility in transcription that good spellers take for granted. They are successful writers who have learned to cope with being poor spellers. Producing such writers is the goal of the workshop.

Conclusion

Teaching spelling to college students is more rewarding than one might expect. Spelling, like other "basic" skills, appears simple only when it is unexamined; watching poor spellers make discoveries is fascinating. And spelling research is interesting for the light it sheds on teaching writing. The literature on teaching spelling provides some of the clearest examples of the difference between behaviorist and cognitivist paradigms and of the special problems teachers face when much of their own knowledge of a subject is tacit. Picture the teacher confronted with a child who spells truck with a "ch." A teacher with a commonsense understanding of language uninformed by linguistic research might easily err. One wonders how many poor spellers have been created by formal education. The most successful students may be those who learn to ignore instruction when it conflicts with experience, to act on the hypothesis that one's teachers mean well but often don't tell the truth.

Perhaps fewer college students would need remedial instruction in spelling if more teachers applied psycholinguistic research on how spelling is learned. But saner methods of instruction seem unlikely in this era of measurement and accountability. The pressure to document achievement will keep teachers marking first- and second-graders' spelling errors and testing their ability to memorize. The demand for spelling instruction in the writing center is likely to continue.

Works Cited

Note: The single best overview of research and theory on the development of spelling ability is Edmund Henderson's *Learning to Read and Spell.* Also recommended as introductory readings are Gentry's *Spel . . . Is a Four-Letter Word,* the two articles by Hashimoto and Clark, Dobie's "Orthographical Theory and Practice" and Anderson's response, and Uta Frith's chapter in *Cognitive Processes in Spelling.* Additional references of interest to writing center teachers are listed below under "Works Consulted." Useful literature on teaching spelling at the college level is not easy to find, since most psychological research is too narrowly focused and most spelling pedagogy is designed for young children.

Brown, Alan S. "Encountering Misspellings and Spelling Performance: Why Wrong Isn't Right." *Journal of Educational Psychology* 80 (1988): 488–494.

Frith, Uta, ed. *Cognitive Processes in Spelling.* New York: Academic Press, 1980.

Frith, Uta. "Unexpected Spelling Problems." Frith, *Cognitive Processes in Spelling* 495–515.

Gentry, J. Richard. *Spel . . . Is a Four-Letter Word.* Portsmouth, NH: Heinemann, 1987.

Gentry, J. Richard and Edmund Henderson. "Three Steps to Teaching Beginning Readers to Spell." Henderson and Beers, eds. *Developmental and Cognitive Aspects of Learning to Spell: A Reflection of Word Knowledge.* Newark, DE: International Reading Association, 1980 112–119.

Hanna, Paul R., Richard F. Hodges, and Jean S. Hanna. *Spelling: Structures and Strategies.* Boston: Houghton Mifflin, 1971.

Hashimoto, I. Y. and Roger Clark. "College Spelling Texts: The State of the Art." *The Writing Center Journal* 5.1 (1984): 1–13.

———."A Spelling Program for College Students." *Teaching English in the Two-Year College* 11 (1984): 34–38.

Henderson, Edmund. *Houghton Mifflin Spelling.* Boston: Houghton Mifflin, 1988.

———. *Learning to Read and Spell: The Child's Knowledge of Words.* DeKalb: Northern Illinois UP, 1981.

———. *Teaching Spelling.* Boston: Houghton Mifflin, 1985.

Henderson, Edmund and James Beers, eds. *Developmental and Cognitive Aspects of Learning to Spell: A Reflection of Word Knowledge.* Newark, DE: International Reading Association, 1980.

Hook, J. N. *Spelling 1500: A Program.* New York: Harcourt Brace, 1976.

Read, Charles. *Children's Categorization of Speech Sounds in English.* Urbana, IL: NCTE, 1975.

———. *Children's Creative Spelling.* London: Routledge & Kegan Paul, 1986.

Roloff, Joan G. and Roslyn Snow. *Spelling.* Encino: Glencoe, 1980.

Shaughnessy, Mina P. *Errors and Expectations: A Guide for the Teacher of Basic Writing.* New York: Oxford UP, 1977.

Shefter, Harry. *Six Minutes a Day to Perfect Spelling.* New York: Pocket Books, 1976.

Works Consulted

Anderson, Kristine F. "The Development of Spelling Ability and Linguistic Strategies." *Reading Teacher* 39 (1985): 140–147.

———. "Using a Spelling Survey to Develop Basic Writers' Linguistic Awareness: A Response to Ann B. Dobie." *Journal of Basic Writing* 6.2 (1987): 72–78.

Buck, Jean. "A New Look at Teaching Spelling." *College English* 38 (1977): 703–706.

Dobie, Ann B. "Orthographical Theory and Practice, Or How to Teach Spelling." *Journal of Basic Writing* 5.2 (1986): 41–48.

———. "Orthography Revisited: A Response to Kristine Anderson." *Journal of Basic Writing* 7.1 (1988): 82–83.

Groff, Patrick. "The Implications of Developmental Spelling Research: A Dissenting View." *Elementary School Journal* 86 (1986): 317–323.

McClellan, Jane. "A Clinic for Misspellers." *College English* 40 (1978): 324–29.

Ormrod, Jeanne Ellis. "Learning to Spell: Three Studies at the University Level." *Research in the Teaching of English* 20 (1986): 160–173.

Templeton, Shane. "Synthesis of Research on the Learning and Teaching of Spelling." *Educational Leadership* 43.6 (1986): 73–78.

PART NINE

RESEARCHED WRITING

The Bedford Handbook recognizes the essential connections between research and much of the writing students will do in school and beyond. Typically, the research paper occupies a central position in freshman writing courses. But as the content and the focus of writing courses have become more interdisciplinary, instructors across the curriculum have recognized the need to incorporate more assignments that require research. The selections that follow focus on several questions worth posing about research writing:

- What do instructors mean by "research" in the context of writing courses? How do we define research (for our students and for ourselves)? How do our different definitions of research affect our writing courses and our teaching?
- If many instructors see the traditional research paper as dysfunctional, what alternative forms of research writing can replace the traditional model?
- How can instructors help students be more critical about the results of their research, and how can students use those results more effectively? How can instructors help students take control of the research instead of letting the research take control of them?
- How can instructors help students understand and avoid plagiarism?

RESEARCH AS A SOCIAL ACT
Patricia Bizzell and Bruce Herzberg

[*The Clearing House* 60 (1987): 303–6.]

Patricia Bizzell is a professor of English and director of the honors program at the College of the Holy Cross, where she directed the writing program for ten years, founded the peer tutoring workshop, and started the writing across the curriculum program. A frequent speaker at professional meetings, Bizzell has published many articles on basic writing, writing across the curriculum, and rhetorical theory in such journals as *College English, College Composition and Communication, PRE/TEXT*, and *Rhetoric Review*, and in the anthology *Contending with Words* (1991). She is also the author of *Academic Discourse and Critical Consciousness* (1992), a collection of her articles. Bruce Herzberg is a professor of English at Bentley College, where he is director of the expository writing program and the writing across the curriculum program. A regular speaker at CCCC and other conferences, Herzberg has published articles on composition in the journals *MLN, College Composition and Communication*, and *Rhetoric Review*, and in the anthologies *The Politics of Writing Instruction* (1991) and *Contending with Words* (1991). Bizzell and Herzberg have collaborated on several successful books: *The*

Rhetorical Tradition (1990) was the winner of the Outstanding Book Award from the CCCC, *The Bedford Bibliography for Teachers of Writing* — now in its 4th edition and available on the World Wide Web at http://www.bedfordbooks.com, and *Negotiating Difference: Cultural Case Studies for Composition.*

Bizzell and Herzberg observe that instructors typically define research in two ways: as discovery or as recovery. Both definitions, they argue, are inadequate and contribute to ineffective assignments and teaching strategies. The authors ask instructors to recognize that research is a "social, collaborative act that draws on and contributes to the work of a community that cares about a given body of knowledge," and they suggest a range of activities to engage students as active participants in knowledge communities.

"Research" can be defined in several ways. First, it may mean discovery, as in the discovery of new information about the world by a researcher. We often call this work "original" research and think of the researcher as a solitary genius, alone in a study or, more likely, a laboratory. Second, "research" may mean the recovery from secondary sources of the information discovered by others. This is often the way we think of student research: students go to the library to extract information from books for a research paper. These two definitions call for some examination.

The first kind of research — discovery — seems more valuable than the second kind — recovery. Discovery adds to the world's knowledge, while recovery adds only to an individual's knowledge (some might add, "if we're lucky"). No matter how we protest that both kinds of research are valuable, there is a distinctly secondary quality to recovery. After all, recovery is dependent entirely upon discovery, original research, for its materials. Discovery actually creates new knowledge, while recovery merely reports on the results of the work of those solitary geniuses.

Common sense tells us that students, with rare exceptions, do not do original research until graduate school, if then. Students and teachers quite naturally share the feeling that research in school is, thus, mere recovery. Consequently, students and teachers often conclude that students are not likely to produce anything very good when they do this kind of research. Indeed, one cannot be doing anything very good while piling up the required number of facts discovered by others. Research-as-recovery seems to justify writing a paper by copying others' accounts of what they have discovered.

If we try, however, to remedy the defects of the research paper by calling for actual discovery, we run into more problems. Those who hope to do original research must know, before anything else, where gaps exist in current knowledge. And, of course, knowing where the holes are requires knowing where they are not. For most (perhaps all) students, this takes us back to research-as-recovery, that plodding effort to find out some of what others have already figured out.

Even research that evaluates sources of information, relates the accounts of information to one another, frames an argument that ties them together, and either reveals something important about the sources themselves or develops into a new contribution on the same topic requires, like discovery, a grasp of a field of knowledge that students cannot be expected to have.

The problem with both kinds of research, then, hinges on knowledge itself. The popular image of the solitary researcher in the lab or the library does not hint at the problem of knowledge — that these people are workers in knowledge who need knowledge as a prerequisite to their work. According to the popular image, they simply find facts. If that were all, presumably anyone could find them. But we know that is hardly the case.

What successful researchers possess that our students typically do not is knowledge, the shared body of knowledge that helps scholars define research projects and employ methods to pursue them. Invariably, researchers use the work of others in their field to develop such projects and consult others in the field to determine what projects will be of value. In short, all real research takes place and can only take place within a community of scholars. Research is a social act. Research is always collaborative, even if only one name appears on the final report.

This, then, is the third definition of research: a social, collaborative act that draws on and contributes to the work of a community that cares about a given body of knowledge. This definition is also a critique of the popular images that we have been examining. For, by the social definition of research, the solitary researcher is not at all solitary: the sense of what can and should be done is derived from the knowledge community. The researcher must be in constant, close communication with other researchers and will likely share preliminary results with colleagues and use their suggestions in further work. Her or his contributions will be extensions of work already done and will create new gaps that other researchers will try to close. Finally, his/her work of discovery is impossible without continuous recovery of the work of others in the community.

The social definition also allows us to revise the notion of research-as-recovery, for the recoverer in a community of knowledge is not merely rehashing old knowledge or informing himself/herself about a randomly chosen topic — he/she is interpreting and reinterpreting the community's knowledge in light of new needs and perspectives, and in so doing creating and disseminating new knowledge. The activity of interpretation reveals what the community values and where the gaps in knowledge reside. "Study knows that which yet it doth not know," as Shakespeare recognized long ago.

In many fields, the activities of synthesis and interpretation are primary forms of research. Think, for example, of the fields of history, philosophy, art and literary criticism, even sociology, economics, and psychology. But the important point is that no field of knowledge can do without such work. Clearly, the lab-science image of research is inaccurate, unrepresentative, and unhelpful. Research as a social act makes far more sense.

This new definition of research changes what it means for students to do research in school. In what ways do students participate in knowledge communities? One well-known and successful research assignment — the family history — suggests that in this very real community, student researchers find material to be interpreted, contradictions to be resolved, assertions to be supported, and gaps to be filled. They share the information and interpretations with the rest of the community, the family, who do not possess such a synthesis and are grateful to get it. But how do students fit into academic knowledge communities that are so much larger and colder than the family?

First, we must recognize that secondary and middle level students are novices, slowly learning the matter and method of school subjects. But they need not master the knowledge of the experts in order to participate in the sub-community of novices. They will need to know what other students know and do not know about a subject that they are all relatively uninformed about. In other words, they need to have a sense of what constitutes the shared body of knowledge of their community and a sense of the possible ways to increase that knowledge by useful increments. Imagine the classroom as a neighborhood in the larger academic community. Students contributing to the knowledge of the class are engaged in research in much the same way that expert researchers contribute to the larger community. They find out what is known — the first step in research — and identify what is unknown by sharing their knowledge amongst themselves. Then, by filling in the gaps and sharing what they find, they educate the whole community.

There are several practical implications for reimagining research in this way:

1. The whole class must work in the same area of inquiry — not the same topic, but different aspects of the same central issue. A well-defined historical period might do: by investigating work, play, social structure, literature, politics, clothing styles, food, and so on, students would become local experts contributing to a larger picture of the period. We will look at other examples later.

2. Students will need some common knowledge, a shared text or set of materials and, most of all, the opportunity to share with each other what they may already know about the subject. By collaborating on a questionnaire or interviewing each other, students learn valuable ways of doing primary research.

3. They will need to ask questions, critically examine the shared knowledge, and perhaps do some preliminary investigation to determine what the most tantalizing unknowns may be. Here again, some free exchange among class members will be helpful.

4. The exchange of ideas must continue through the process of discovery. Like expert researchers, students need to present papers or colloquia to the research community, distribute drafts and respond to feedback, and contribute to the work of others when they are able. Finally, their work must be disseminated, published in some way, and made available to the group. The early framework of the research community ought not to be reduced to a way to introduce the regular old term paper.

A perfectly good way to choose the general area of research for a class is simply to choose it yourself. Teachers represent the larger community and can be expected to know something about the topic at hand and provide guidance, so if the topic interests the teacher, all the better. Of course, the teacher can lean toward topics that may interest the class. Students may be asked to choose from among several possibilities suggested by the teacher, but it is likely to be needlessly daunting to the students to leave the whole selection process to them. Among the possibilities for class topics: utopia, Shakespeare's England, Franklin's America, the jazz age, the death of the dinosaurs, the year you were born, images of childhood, the idea of school, work and play, wealth and poverty, country and city, quests and heroes, creativity — it's easy to go on and on.

Central texts can be books, photocopied selections, a film, or videotapes. More's *Utopia* might work for some classes, but a utopian science fiction book might be better for others, and the description of the Garden of Eden, a well-known utopia, is only three pages long. Shakespeare plays are easy to come by, as is Franklin's *Autobiography* or selections from it. Not every topic will require such materials, of course. For some topics, the students' interviews or other initial responses might be compiled into the central text.

The shared knowledge of the group might be elicited through alternate writing and discussion sessions, the students answering questions like "what do you know about x?" or "what would you like to know about x?" Interviews and questionnaires also work, as noted. All of this preliminary reading, writing, and discussion will help to create a sense of community and give students a jump-start on writing for the group, rather than for the teacher. Needless to say, the teacher ought not to grade and need not even read such preliminary work, beyond requiring that it be done.

Identifying a gap in the group's knowledge and choosing a topic for individual research may still be difficult, and it helps to be armed with suggestions if the students run out of ideas or need to be focused. Have a list of questions about utopias, a list of attempted utopian communities, the names of prominent figures in the period under discussion, some key ideas or events or issues to pursue, and so on. Students may not see, in the central text, problems like class differences in opportunities for schooling, or assumptions about the place of women, or attitudes linked to local or historical circumstances. If discussion and preliminary research do not turn them up, the teacher can reasonably help out. We need not pretend that we are inventing a new field of inquiry, but we must beware of the temptation to fall back on assigned topics.

Having students share drafts and give interim reports takes time, but it is usually time well spent. Students can learn to provide useful feedback to other students on drafts of papers — teachers should not read every draft. Students acting as draft-readers can respond to set questions (what did you find most interesting? what do you want to learn more about?) or work as temporary collaborators in attacking problem areas or listen to drafts read aloud and give oral responses. Other kinds of sharing may be worthwhile. Annotated bibliographies might be compiled and posted so that resources can be shared. Groups might lead panel discussions to take the edge off formal presentations. Reading aloud and oral reporting are good ways, too, of setting milestones for writing, and public presentation is important for maintaining the sense of community. Oral reports, by the way, tend to be better as drafts than as final presentations — the feedback is useful then, and anxiety about the performance is muted. Publishing the final results is the last step — copies of the papers might be compiled with a table of contents in a ring binder and put on reserve in the school library, for example.

These activities do not eliminate problems of footnote form and plagiarism, but in the setting of a research community, the issues of footnoting and plagiarism can be seen in a fresh light. Students should be able to articulate for themselves the reasons why members of a community would want to enforce among themselves (and their novices) a common and consistent method of citation. When knowledge exists to be exchanged, footnotes facilitate exchange. So too with plagiarism: members of the community would love to see themselves quoted and footnoted, but not robbed.

An excellent way to teach citation and reinforce community cohesion is to ask students to cite each other. How do you cite another student's paper, especially in draft form? How do you cite an oral report? How do you thank someone for putting you onto an idea? These citation forms may be used rarely, but they are good ways to stir up interest in the need for and uses of footnotes.

If the students are discovering the process of drafting, peer-review, and interim reports for the first time, the problems of discussing work-in-progress may come up in that context. Many students have learned that it is "wrong" to look at someone else's paper and will just be learning about the way professionals share and help each other with their work. A good place to see how collaboration works is to look at the pages of acknowledgments in books. Students will find, in all of their textbooks, long lists of people who are acknowledged for help in the process of writing. Writing their own acknowledgments will allow students to talk about how their ideas were shaped by others, especially by those who cannot reasonably be footnoted.

If the social act of research is successful, students have the opportunity to learn that knowledge is not just found, but created out of existing knowledge. And if people create knowledge, it is reasonable to expect knowledge to change. What people regard as true may be something other than absolute fact. Indeed, it may be only a temporary formulation in the search for better understanding. We can hope that our students will develop ways to evaluate knowledge as a social phenomenon and progress toward a critical consciousness of all claims to knowledge.

BORROWING FROM THE SCIENCES:
A MODEL FOR THE FRESHMAN RESEARCH PAPER

Jeff Jeske

[*The Writing Instructor* 6 (1987): 62–67.]

An associate professor of English at Guilford College in Greensboro, North Carolina, Jeff Jeske directs the college's writing program, the writing across the curriculum initiative, and teaches classes in writing, American literature, and film. He has published in the *International Journal of Women's Studies,* the *Journal of the History of Ideas,* and *The Writing Instructor.* The article included here resulted from Jeske's work at the University of California – Los Angeles, where he developed courses designed to teach graduate students from a variety of disciplines how to write for publication.

Jeske recognizes that scientific models for writing offer English teachers an alternative to the more traditional approaches for teaching research in freshman writing classes. The format of the generic research paper, he claims, often encourages only the collection and assembly of information about a topic, and students view research as a teacher-sponsored exercise instead of seeing it as a process they can use to answer questions and solve problems. Jeske argues that teachers can use the format of the scientific paper to encourage students to consider actively the aims and methods of the process they use to research. His suggestions are particularly relevant for the increasing number of writing courses with cross-curricular emphasis.

An ongoing classified in the *Los Angeles Weekly* reads: "TERM PAPER ASSISTANCE: 15,728 papers to choose from, all subjects. Read first —

then buy. Custom research also available. Research Assistance, #####
Idaho Ave., West L.A., call ###-#### [numbers deleted]." This is one problem facing the instructor who assigns a research paper.

Another is the research paper itself, which has long had a not unde-
served reputation as a breakfast of troglodytes, a tedious enterprise best
described, like its grizzled great-uncle, the dissertation, as a transferring
of bones from one graveyard to another. Signaling its tired, formulaic nature,
one wag published a "Brief Guide to the Art of Marking Term Papers" in
the *Chronicle of Higher Education* a few years ago. It proposed that besides
the all-important counting of pages, all that was required of the grader was
to stick a "nice" somewhere in the first quarter of the paper, where the
thought might be original, and a "needs elaboration" toward the end, where
the writer likely ran out of steam; sprinkled between could be a few "What
is your source?'s" attached to random declarative sentences.

Although unhappy mutual tolerance has existed for generations, such is
no longer the case. Innocent freshmen are doubtless still willing to shoulder their cruel burden, but their mentors are not, for "the times they are
a' changing." As the gulf widens between old and new composition, all
weapons in the teacher's arsenal are being subjected to cold scrutiny. And
the research paper is not bearing up well. Clinton Burhans, Jr., for example, notes damagingly that a preoccupation with the research paper is
one of the hallmarks of the "traditional composition course," i.e., one that
is on the wrong side of "the knowledge gap."

Worse, Richard Larson asserts that the generic research paper is an
"artifice of the composition classroom" ("Richard L. Larson Responds").[1]
Because research differs from discipline to discipline, the only way an
English instructor can claim to teach research methodology is to teach a
field's specific forms — that is, blunder into foreign and thus dangerous
jungles of expertise. In other words, the freshman research paper not only
has no role in the new freshman English, but it cannot serve the Writing
across the Curriculum movement either. In short . . . death!

Professor Larson's proposed abolition of the research paper will not
likely occur, however: partly, doubtless, because of the conservatism of the
trade, and more importantly, because there are compelling reasons for
keeping the old steed saddled. For one thing, the research paper represents an informed immersion in activities which the student *will* use throughout her academic career. In response to Larson, James Doubleday identifies three of these as (1) learning the difference between summary and
paraphrase,[2] (2) gaining knowledge of reference sources, and (3) writing a
long paper. More abstractly, we know the research paper to be a microcosm of education itself, inasmuch as it requires first finding information
(and teaching oneself how to retrieve it in the process: the islander learning how to handle a pole rather than being doled out a fish) and then
evaluating, outside the classroom's *hortus conclusus,* what is relevant and
then what is valid, highly sophisticated cognitive activities.

The traditional research paper could use resuscitation, though, for the
objections which have been lodged all have partial validity: It definitely
needs retooling for its role in the new age of composition.

The following model has actually been around for a long while but at
higher strata in the academic atmosphere. I encountered it while working
with graduate and professional students and was immediately attracted by
the form's clear, crisp presentation of the research paradigm. Explained for
professional use by Robert A. Day in his *How to Write and Publish a
Scientific Paper,* the model is *de rigueur* in the medical sciences and used

with variations by the other hard sciences. I find it in the social sciences as well, and recognize it in the paradigms described in cross-curricular thesis and dissertation manuals. If there is an archetype for the research paper, this is it: the four-part format of Introduction, Materials and Methods, Results, and Discussion.

Besides providing experience with a form which many of my freshmen will later be expected to manipulate fluently, this model is particularly suited to students encountering professional research for the first time, for it can be used to encourage reflection on the research process itself. My interpretation of the model follows. The questions in each section suggest possible focal points for inquiry; I include them in the students' instructions.

I. Introduction
—What is your key question?
—Why is the problem significant?
—Why did you choose it?
—Was there a narrowing down process?
—Did you formulate a hypothesis?
—With what expectations did you begin your research?

The introduction of the standard experimental paper answers the question "What was the problem?" The professional researcher begins not with a topic, but with a specific, limited question; the purpose is to find answers, not to seek out an exercise in debate. Unlike the freshman's characteristic roaming through dark seas congested with towering icebergs of information, the researcher is thus sharply focused in her travel, and not as likely to return to port with an encyclopedia-style pastiche in tow. The energizing focus on question rather than static topic seems to encourage specificity as well as an active, questing spirit. Students in my Los Angeles theme course enthusiastically pursued such questions as Why did Marilyn Monroe commit suicide? Why are there no freeways in Beverly Hills? Why does Santa Monica have the nickname "The People's Republic of Santa Monica"? and Why is there a Venice in Southern California, complete with canals?

With its prompts to explain why the particular question was chosen, the form also encourages students to introduce a personal dimension to the paper and, given that more emphasis is placed on the question than on the answer, to be prepared to modify an initial hypothesis as the inquiry proceeds.

II. Materials and Methods
—What research strategy did you adopt?
—What were your primary sources of information, both inside and outside the library?
—How did you determine what these sources were?
—Which were the most useful? least useful?
—Did your focus shift? How did your attitude toward your topic evolve?
—How did you know when to stop?

The key question here is "How did you study the problem?" In professional research articles, this section is ordinarily the driest of the four, taken up with careful presentation of research design. In our use of the model, it can be the most personal and interesting, combining elements of the traditional literature search with a personal narrative of the student's investigation. I encourage students to be freewheeling and subjective in recounting their research experiences — the frustrations of library research, the blind alleys, the sudden insights, the twists and turns of their hypotheses, the creative extra-library techniques used to find the freshest, most pertinent information.

Teachers employing journals to elicit expressive writing can encourage students to use them here as records of research activity and hence as seed gardens for the Methods section. The goal, as in the Introduction, is for students to develop meta-awareness of themselves as researchers.

III. Results
—What did you find?
—Was it what you expected?
—How did you determine your sources' reliability?
—How did you resolve contradictory opinions?

Students present the material they found pertinent to their key question and also assess its quality. The assignment requires the students to present dispassionately what they've found and to organize it formally. (Because the key questions ordinarily begin with "Why?," we devote class time to discussing how to organize causal analysis.)

IV. Discussion
—What is your overall conclusion regarding the key question?
—What significance do your findings have?
—What boundaries or weak areas in your research should be pointed out to other researchers?
—Was this a difficult question to investigate?
—Are you satisfied with the thoroughness of your work?
—What did you learn about libraries and other sources of information?
—How would you evaluate your research guide (in our case, Melissa Walker's *Writing Research Papers: A Norton Guide*)?
—How could you make your research strategy more effective?

This section of the paradigm asks "What do your findings mean?" Unlike the professional researcher, though, we interpret "findings" to refer both to the topic and to the research process itself. Regarding the first, students are encouraged to meditate on the larger significance of what they've found; in class, we use a variant of Young, Becker, and Pike's particle-wave-field heuristic to see the topics in different contexts. Some students will have found that there is no answer to their key question; that is all right. Here they can assess the significance of there not being an answer. Or they may have found that their initial hypothesis was incorrect. That is all right, too; a key truth about research is that few hypotheses are not altered or modified in the course of one's investigation.

Just as importantly, we also use the Discussion to overview the research process itself. Students are encouraged to evaluate research strategy and their experience using it. What did they learn about doing research? What would they change? Successfully fusing this type of reflection with interpretation of the Results makes the Discussion section the most challenging to write — as it always is in the real world of research.

One of the model's advantages is its suppleness. In contrast to the traditional research paper, which Professor Larson describes as a "non-form of writing," this four-part model actually has many viable forms, depending on where the individual instructor decides to plot the assignment on such axes as expressive/transactional and topic-oriented/process-oriented. For example, he can emphasize a personal or an empirical tone — or he can encourage the student to follow the lead of the fine writers who synthesize the two.

Other benefits of the model:

- It encourages a free spirit of inquiry. The predetermined format enables the student to experiment with content.
- It provides a focus for discussing the writing of different fields.
- An instructor can bring in professional models to contrast from such sources as the *New England Journal of Medicine,* the *Journal of Social Welfare,* the *Journal of Paleontology* (and there are countless others).
- The four-part structure lends itself well to dividing the project into separate stages spread over time. Each section, with its distinct criteria for successful performance, can become a separate focus — or even a separate paper. The layout is also felicitous for the instructor who wishes to move from a personal to a more analytic mode of writing as the course progresses.

And of course there is one final benefit: This research paper is very difficult to plagiarize. It may finally offer a way to make the research paper vendors fold their tents and caravan into the great barren Beyond, where there will be much weeping and gnashing of teeth over bleached, though well-documented bones.

Notes

[1] See also Larson's "The 'Research Paper' in the Writing Course."

[2] William Irmscher makes the telling point that plagiarism often derives not from dishonesty but from ignorance: Students are often not taught how to read, absorb, quote, and paraphrase the works of others.

References

Burhans, Jr., Clinton S. "The Teaching of Writing and the Knowledge Gap." *College English* 45 (1983): 639–56.

Day, Robert A. *How to Write and Publish a Scientific Paper,* 2nd ed. Philadelphia: ISI Press, 1983, 26–39.

Doubleday, James F. "The 'Research Paper' in the Writing Course: A Comment," *College English* 46 (1984): 512–13.

Irmscher, William. *Teaching Expository Writing.* New York: Holt, Rinehart, and Winston, 1979, p. 61.

Larson, Richard L. "Richard L. Larson Responds." *College English* 46 (1984): 513–14.

———. "The 'Research Paper' in the Writing Course: A Non-Form of Writing." *College English* 44 (1982): 811–16.

Young, Richard, Alton L. Becker, and Kenneth L. Pike. *Rhetoric: Discovery and Change.* New York: Harcourt, Brace, and World, 1970, pp. 126–30.

HELPING STUDENTS USE TEXTUAL
SOURCES PERSUASIVELY

Margaret Kantz

[*College English* 52 (1990): 74–91.]

Margaret Kantz, assistant professor of English and director of freshman composition at Central Missouri State University, has written about composing processes in researched student papers. She contributed a chapter to *Reading to Write* (1990) by Linda Flower et al. and has published articles in *Poetics.*

The following article grew out of Kantz's own experiences as a student writer. In high school she wrote a term paper that received a lower grade than she thought it should and later discovered that the reason for the grade was the paper's lack of rhetorical concept. Since her discovery, Kantz has used her old paper as a teaching device, asking students to try to improve it.

Although the researched essay as a topic has been much written about, it has been little studied. In the introduction to their bibliography, Ford, Rees, and Ward point out that most of the over 200 articles about researched essays published in professional journals in the last half century describe classroom methods. "Few," they say, "are of a theoretical nature or based on research, and almost none cites even one other work on the subject" (2). Given Ford and Perry's finding that 84% of freshman composition programs and 40% of advanced composition programs included instruction in writing research papers, more theoretical work seems needed. We need a theory-based explanation, one grounded in the findings of the published research on the nature and reasons for our students' problems with writing persuasive researched papers. To understand how to teach students to write such papers, we also need a better understanding of the demands of synthesis tasks.

As an example for discussing this complex topic, I have used a typical college sophomore. This student is a composite derived from published research, from my own memories of being a student, and from students whom I have taught at an open admissions community college and at both public and private universities. I have also used a few examples taken from my own students, all of whom share many of Shirley's traits. Shirley, first of all, is intelligent and well-motivated. She is a native speaker of English. She has no extraordinary knowledge deficits or emotional problems. She comes from a home where education is valued, and her parents do reading and writing tasks at home and at their jobs. Shirley has certain skills. When she entered first grade, she knew how to listen to and tell stories, and she soon became proficient at reading stories and at writing narratives. During her academic life, Shirley has learned such studying skills as finding the main idea and remembering facts. In terms of the relevant research, Shirley can read and summarize source texts accurately (cf. Spivey; Winograd). She can select material that is relevant for her purpose in writing (Hayes, Waterman, and Robinson; Langer). She can make connections between the available information and her purpose for writing, including the needs of her readers when the audience is specified (Atlas). She can make original connections among ideas (Brown and Day; Langer). She can create an appropriate, audience-based structure for her paper (Spivey), take notes and use them effectively while composing her paper (Kennedy), and she can present information clearly and smoothly (Spivey), without relying on the phrasing of the original sources (Atlas; Winograd). Shirley is, in my experience, a typical college student with an average academic preparation.

Although Shirley seems to have everything going for her, she experiences difficulty with assignments that require her to write original papers based on textual sources. In particular, Shirley is having difficulty in her sophomore-level writing class. Shirley, who likes English history, decided to write about the Battle of Agincourt (this part of Shirley's story is biographical). She found half a dozen histories that described the circumstances of the battle in a few pages each. Although the topic was unfamiliar, the sources agreed on many of the facts. Shirley collated these facts into her own version, noting but not discussing discrepant details, borrowing what she assumed to be her sources' purpose of retelling the story, and modeling the narrative structure of her paper on that of her sources. Since the only comments Shirley could think of would be to agree or disagree with her sources, who had told her everything she knew about the Battle of Agincourt, she did not comment on the material; instead, she concentrated on telling the story clearly and more completely than her sources had done. She was surprised when her paper received a grade of C− . (Page 1 of Shirley's paper is given on page 391 as Appendix A.)

Although Shirley is a hypothetical student whose case is based on a real event, her difficulties are typical of undergraduates at both private and public colleges and universities. In a recent class of Intermediate Composition in which the students were instructed to create an argument using at least four textual sources that took differing points of view, one student, who analyzed the coverage of a recent championship football game, ranked her source articles in order from those whose approach she most approved to those she least approved. Another student analyzed various approaches taken by the media to the Kent State shootings in 1970, and was surprised and disappointed to find that all of the sources seemed slanted, either by the perspective of the reporter or by that of the people interviewed. Both students did not understand why their instructor said that their papers lacked a genuine argument.

The task of writing researched papers that express original arguments presents many difficulties. Besides the obvious problems of citation format and coordination of source materials with the emerging written product, writing a synthesis can vary in difficulty according to the number and length of the sources, the abstractness or familiarity of the topic, the uses that the writer must make of the material, the degree and quality of original thought required, and the extent to which the sources will supply the structure and purpose of the new paper. It is usually easier to write a paper that uses all of only one short source on a familiar topic than to write a paper that selects material from many long sources on a topic that one must learn as one reads and writes. It is easier to quote than to paraphrase, and it is easier to build the paraphrases, without comment or with random comments, into a description of what one found than it is to use them as evidence in an original argument. It is easier to use whatever one likes, or everything one finds, than to formally select, evaluate, and interpret material. It is easier to use the structure and purpose of a source as the basis for one's paper than it is to create a structure or an original purpose. A writing-from-sources task can be as simple as collating a body of facts from a few short texts on a familiar topic into a new text that reproduces the structure, tone, and purpose of the originals, but it can also involve applying abstract concepts from one area to an original problem in a different area, a task that involves learning the relationships among materials as a paper is created that may refer to its sources without resembling them.

Moreover, a given task can be interpreted as requiring an easy method, a difficult method, or any of a hundred intermediate methods. In this context, Flower has observed, "The different ways in which students [represent] a 'standard' reading-to-write task to themselves lead to markedly different goals and strategies as well as different organizing plans" ("Role" iii). To write a synthesis, Shirley may or may not need to quote, summarize, or select material from her sources; to evaluate the sources for bias, accuracy, or completeness; to develop original ideas; or to persuade a reader. How well she performs any of these tasks — and whether she thinks to perform these tasks — depends on how she reads the texts and on how she interprets the assignment. Shirley's representation of the task, which in this case was easier than her teacher had in mind, depends on the goals that she sets for herself. The goals that she sets depend on her awareness of the possibilities and her confidence in her writing skills.

Feeling unhappy about her grade, Shirley consulted her friend Alice. Alice, who is an expert, looked at the task in a completely different way and used strategies for thinking about it that were quite different from Shirley's.

"Who were your sources?" asked Alice. "Winston Churchill, right? A French couple and a few others. And they didn't agree about the details, such as the sizes of the armies. Didn't you wonder why?"

"No," said Shirley. "I thought the history books would know the truth. When they disagreed, I figured that they were wrong on those points. I didn't want to have anything in my paper that was wrong."

"But Shirley," said Alice, "you could have thought about why a book entitled *A History of France* might present a different view of the battle than a book subtitled *A History of British Progress.* You could have asked if the English and French writers wanted to make a point about the history of their countries and looked to see if the factual differences suggested anything. You could even have talked about Shakespeare's *Henry V,* which I know you've read — about how he presents the battle, or about how the King Henry in the play differs from the Henrys in your other books. You would have had an angle, a problem. Dr. Boyer would have loved it."

Alice's representation of the task would have required Shirley to formally select and evaluate her material and to use it as proof in an original argument. Alice was suggesting that Shirley invent an original problem and purpose for her paper and create an original structure for her argument. Alice's task is much more sophisticated than Shirley's. Shirley replied, "That would take me a year to do! Besides, Henry was a real person. I don't want to make up things about him."

"Well," said Alice, "You're dealing with facts, so there aren't too many choices. If you want to say something original you either have to talk about the sources or talk about the material. What could you say about the material? Your paper told about all the reasons King Henry wasn't expected to win the battle. Could you have argued that he should have lost because he took too many chances?"

"Gee," said Shirley, "That's awesome. I wish I'd thought of it."

This version of the task would allow Shirley to keep the narrative structure of her paper but would give her an original argument and purpose. To write the argument, Shirley would have only to rephrase the events of the story to take an opposite approach from that of her English sources, emphasizing what she perceived as Henry's mistakes and inserting comments to explain why his decisions were mistakes — an easy argument to write. She could also, if she wished, write a conclusion that criticized the cheerleading tone of her British sources.

As this anecdote makes clear, a given topic can be treated in more or less sophisticated ways — and sophisticated goals, such as inventing an original purpose and evaluating sources, can be achieved in relatively simple versions of a task. Students have many options as to how they can fulfill even a specific task (cf. Jeffery). Even children can decide whether to process a text deeply or not, and purpose in reading affects processing and monitoring of comprehension (Brown). Pichert has shown that reading purpose affects judgments about what is important or unimportant in a narrative text, and other research tells us that attitudes toward the author and content of a text affect comprehension (Asch; Hinze; Shedd; Goldman).

One implication of this story is that the instructor gave a weak assignment and an ineffective critique of the draft (her only comment referred to Shirley's footnoting technique; cf. Appendix A). The available research suggests that if Dr. Boyer had set Shirley a specific rhetorical problem such as having her report on her material to the class and then testing them on it, and if she had commented on the content of Shirley's paper during the drafts, Shirley might well have come up with a paper that did more than repeat its source material (Nelson and Hayes). My teaching experience supports this research finding. If Dr. Boyer had told Shirley from the outset that she was expected to say something original and that she should examine her sources as she read them for discrepant facts, conflicts, or other interesting material, Shirley might have tried to write an original argument (Kantz, "Originality"). And if Dr. Boyer had suggested that Shirley use her notes to comment on her sources and make plans for using the notes, Shirley might have written a better paper than she did (Kantz, "Relationship").

Even *if* given specific directions to create an original argument, Shirley might have had difficulty with the task. Her difficulty could come from any of three causes: 1) Many students like Shirley misunderstand sources because they read them as stories. 2) Many students expect their sources to tell the truth; hence, they equate persuasive writing in this context with making things up. 3) Many students do not understand that facts are a kind of claim and are often used persuasively in so-called objective writing to create an impression. Students need to read source texts as arguments and to think about the rhetorical contexts in which they were written rather than to read them merely as a set of facts to be learned. Writing an original persuasive argument based on sources requires students to apply material to a problem or to use it to answer a question, rather than simply to repeat it or evaluate it. These three problems deserve a separate discussion.

Because historical texts often have a chronological structure, students believe that historians tell stories and that renarrating the battle cast them as a historian. Because her sources emphasized the completeness of the victory/defeat and its decisive importance in the history of warfare, Shirley thought that making these same points in her paper completed her job. Her job as a reader was thus to learn the story, i.e., so that she could pass a test on it (cf. Vipond and Hunt's argument that generic expectations affect reading behavior. Vipond and Hunt would describe Shirley's reading as story-driven rather than point-driven). Students commonly misread texts as narratives. When students refer to a textbook as "the story," they are telling us that they read for plot and character, regardless of whether their texts are organized as narratives. One reason Shirley loves history is that when she reads it she can combine her story-reading strategies with her studying strategies. Students like Shirley may need to learn to apply basic organizing patterns, such as cause-effect and general-to-specific, to their texts. If, however, Dr. Boyer asks Shirley to respond to her sources in a way that is not compatible with Shirley's understanding of what such sources do, Shirley will have trouble doing the assignment. Professors may have to do some preparatory teaching about why certain kinds of tests have certain characteristics and what kinds of problems writers must solve as they design text for a particular audience. They may even have to teach a model for the kind of writing they expect.

The writing version of Shirley's problem, which Flower calls "writer-based prose," occurs when Shirley organizes what should be an expository analysis as a narrative, especially when she writes a narrative about how she did her research. Students frequently use time-based organizing patterns, regardless of the task, even when such patterns conflict with what they are trying to say and even when they know how to use more sophisticated strategies. Apparently such common narrative transitional devices such as "the first point" and "the next point" offer a reassuringly familiar pattern for organizing unfamiliar material. The common strategy of beginning paragraphs with such phrases as "my first source," meaning that it was the first source that the writer found in the library or the first one read, appears to combine a story-of-my-research structure with a knowledge-telling strategy (Bereiter and Scardamalia, *Psychology*). Even when students understand that the assignment asks for more than the fill-in-the-blanks, show-me-you've-read-the-material approach described by Schwegler and Shamoon, they cling to narrative structuring devices. A rank ordering of sources, as with Mary's analysis of the football game coverage with the sources listed in an order of ascending disapproval, represents a step away from storytelling and toward synthesizing because it embodies a persuasive evaluation.

In addition to reading texts as stories, students expect factual texts to tell them "the truth" because they have learned to see texts statically, as descriptions of truths, instead of as arguments. Shirley did not understand that nonfiction texts exist as arguments in rhetorical contexts. "After all," she reasoned, "how can one argue about the date of a battle or the sizes of armies?" Churchill, however, described the battle in much more detail than Shirley's other sources, apparently because he wished to persuade his readers to take pride in England's tradition of military achievement. Guizot and Guizot de Witt, on the other hand, said very little about the battle (beyond describing it as "a monotonous and lamentable repetition of the disasters of Crécy and Poitiers" [397]) because they saw the British invasion as a sneaky way to take advantage of a feud among the various branches of the French royal family. Shirley's story/study skills might not have allowed her to recognize such arguments, especially because Dr. Boyer did not teach her to look for them.

When I have asked students to choose a topic and find three or more sources on it that disagree, I am repeatedly asked, "How can sources disagree in different ways? After all, there's only pro and con." Students expect textbooks and other authoritative sources either to tell them the truth (i.e., facts) or to express an opinion with which they may agree or disagree. Mary's treatment of the football coverage reflects this belief, as does Charlie's surprise when he found that even his most comprehensive sources on the Kent State killings omitted certain facts, such as interviews with National Guardsmen. Students' desire for truth leads them to use a collating approach whenever possible, as Shirley did (cf. Appendix A), because students believe that the truth will include all of the facts and will reconcile all conflicts. (This belief may be another manifestation of the knowledge-telling strategy [Bereiter and Scardamalia, *Psychology*] in which students write down everything they can think of about a topic.) When conflicts cannot be reconciled and the topic does not admit a pro or con stance, students may not know what to say. They may omit the material altogether, include it without comment, as Shirley did, or jumble it together without any plan for building an argument.

The skills that Shirley has practiced for most of her academic career — finding the main idea and learning content — allow her to agree or disagree. She needs a technique for reading texts in ways that give her something more to say, a technique for constructing more complex representations of texts that allow room for more sophisticated writing goals. She also needs strategies for analyzing her reading that allow her to build original arguments.

One way to help students like Shirley is to teach the concept of rhetorical situation. A convenient tool for thinking about this concept is Kinneavy's triangular diagram of the rhetorical situation. Kinneavy, analyzing Aristotle's description of rhetoric, posits that every communicative situation has three parts: a speaker/writer (the Encoder), an audience (the Decoder), and a topic (Reality) (19). Although all discourse involves all three aspects of communication, a given type of discourse may pertain more to a particular point of the triangle than to the others, e.g., a diary entry may exist primarily to express the thoughts of the writer (the Encoder); an advertisement may exist primarily to persuade a reader (the Decoder). Following Kinneavy, I posit particular goals for each corner of the triangle. Thus, the primary goal of a writer doing writer-based discourse such as a diary might be originality and self-expression; primary goals for reader-based discourse such as advertising might be persuasion; primary goals for topic-based discourse such as a researched essay might be accuracy, completeness, and mastery of subject matter. Since all three aspects of the rhetorical situation are present and active in any communicative situation, a primarily referential text such as Churchill's *The Birth of Britain* may have a persuasive purpose and may depend for some of its credibility on readers' familiarity with the author. The term "rhetorical reading," then (cf. Haas and Flower), means teaching students to read a text as a message sent by someone to somebody for a reason. Shirley, Mary, and Charlie are probably practiced users of rhetorical persuasion in non-academic contexts. They may never have learned to apply this thinking in a conscious and deliberate way to academic tasks (cf. Kroll).

The concept of rhetorical situation offers insight into the nature of students' representations of a writing task. The operative goals in Shirley's and Alice's approaches to the term paper look quite different when mapped onto the points on the triangle. If we think of Shirley and Alice as Encoders, the topic as Reality, and Dr. Boyer as the Decoder, we can see that for Shirley, being an Encoder means trying to be credible; her relationship to the topic (Reality) involves a goal of using all of the subject matter; and her relationship to the Decoder involves an implied goal of telling a complete story to a reader whom Shirley thinks of as an examiner — to use the classic phrase from the famous book by Britton et al. — i.e., a reader who wants to know if Shirley can pass an exam on the subject of the Battle of Agincourt. For Alice, however, being an Encoder means having a goal of saying something new; the topic (Reality) is a resource to be used; and the Decoder is someone who must be persuaded that Alice's ideas have merit. Varying task representations do not change the dimensions of the rhetorical situation: the Encoder, Decoder, and Reality are always present. But the way a writer represents the task to herself does affect the ways that she thinks about those dimensions — and whether she thinks about them at all.

In the context of a research assignment, rhetorical skills can be used to read the sources as well as to design the paper. Although teachers have probably always known that expert readers use such strategies, the concept of rhetorical reading is new to the literature. Haas and Flower have shown that expert readers use rhetorical strategies "to account for author's purpose, context, and effect on the audience . . . to recreate or infer the rhetorical situation of the text" (176; cf. also Bazerman). These strategies, used in addition to formulating main points and paraphrasing content, helped the readers to understand a text more completely and more quickly than did readers who concentrated exclusively on content. As Haas and Flower point out, teaching students to read rhetorically is difficult. They suggest that appropriate pedagogy might include "direct instruction . . . modeling, and . . . encouraging students to become contributing and committed members of rhetorical communities" (182). One early step might be to teach students a set of heuristics based on the three aspects of the communicative triangle. Using such questions could help students set goals for their reading.

In this version of Kinneavy's triangle, the Encoder is the writer of the source text, the Decoder is the student reader, and Reality is the subject matter. Readers may consider only one point of the triangle at a time, asking such questions as "Who are you (i.e., the author/Encoder)?" or "What are the important features of this text?" They may consider two aspects of the rhetorical situation in a single question, e.g., "Am I in your intended (primary) audience?"; "What do I think about this topic?"; "What context affected your ideas and presentation?" Other questions would involve all three points of the triangle, e.g., "What are you saying to help me with the problem you assume I have?" or "What textual devices have you used to manipulate my response?" Asking such questions gives students a way of formulating goals relating to purpose as well as content.

If Shirley, for example, had asked a Decoder-to-Encoder question — such as "Am I in your intended audience?" — she might have realized that Churchill and the Guizots were writing for specific audiences. If she had asked a Decoder-to-Reality question — such as "What context affected your ideas and presentation?" — she might not have ignored Churchill's remark, "All these names [Amiens, Boves, Bethencourt] are well known to our generation" (403). As it was, she missed Churchill's signal that he was writing to survivors of the First World War, who had vainly hoped that it would be war to end all wars. If Shirley had used an Encoder-Decoder-Reality question — such as "What are you saying to help me with the problem you assume I have?" — she might have understood that the authors of her sources were writing to different readers for different reasons. This understanding might have given her something to say. When I gave Shirley's source texts to freshmen students, asked them to use the material in an original argument, and taught them this heuristic for rhetorical reading, I received, for example, papers that warned undergraduates about national pride as a source of authorial bias in history texts.

A factual topic such as the Battle of Agincourt presents special problems because of the seemingly intransigent nature of facts. Like many people, Shirley believes that you can either agree or disagree with issues and opinions, but you can only accept the so-called facts. She believes that facts are what you learn from textbooks, opinions are what you have about clothes, and arguments are what you have with your mother when you want to stay out late at night. Shirley is not in a position to disagree with the facts about the battle (e.g., "No, I think the French won"), and a rhetorical analysis may seem at first to offer minimal rewards (e.g., "According to the Arab, Jewish, and Chinese calendars the date was really . . .").

Alice, who thinks rhetorically, understands that both facts and opinions are essentially the same kind of statement: they are claims. Alice understands that the only essential difference between a fact and an opinion is how they are received by an audience. (This discussion is derived from Toulmin's model of an argument as consisting of claims proved with data and backed by ethical claims called warrants. According to Toulmin, any aspect of an argument may be questioned by the audience and must then be supported with further argument.) In a rhetorical argument, a fact is a claim that an audience will accept as being true without requiring proof, although they may ask for an explanation. An opinion is a claim that an audience will not accept as true without proof, and which, after the proof is given, the audience may well decide has only a limited truth, i.e., it's true in this case but not in other cases. An audience may also decide that even though a fact is unassailable, the interpretation or use of the fact is open to debate.

For example, Shirley's sources gave different numbers for the size of the British army at Agincourt; these numbers, which must have been estimates, were claims masquerading as facts. Shirley did not understand this. She thought that disagreement signified error, whereas it probably signified rhetorical purpose. The probable reason that the Guizots give a relatively large estimate for the English army and do not mention the size of the French army is so that their French readers would find the British victory easier to accept. Likewise, Churchill's relatively small estimate for the size of the English army and his high estimate for the French army magnify the brilliance of the English victory. Before Shirley could create an argument about the Battle of Agincourt, she needed to understand that, even in her history textbooks, the so-called facts are claims that may or may not be supported, claims made by writers who work in a certain political climate for a particular audience. She may, of course, never learn this truth unless Dr. Boyer teaches her rhetorical theory and uses the research paper as a chance for Shirley to practice rhetorical problem-solving.

For most of her academic life, Shirley has done school tasks that require her to find main ideas and important facts; success in these tasks usually hinges on agreeing with the teacher about what the text says. Such study skills form an essential basis for doing reading-to-write tasks. Obviously a student can only use sources to build an argument if she can first read the sources accurately (cf. Brown and Palincsar; Luftig; Short and Ryan). However, synthesizing tasks often require that readers not accept the authors' ideas. Baker and Brown have pointed out that people misread texts when they blindly accept an author's ideas instead of considering a divergent interpretation. Yet if we want students to learn to build original arguments from texts, we must teach them the skills needed to create divergent interpretations. We must teach them to think about facts and opinions as claims that are made by writers to particular readers for particular reasons in particular historical contexts.

Reading sources rhetorically gives students a powerful tool for creating a persuasive analysis. Although no research exists as yet to suggest that teaching students to read rhetorically will improve their writing, I have seen its effect in successive drafts of students' papers. As mentioned earlier, rhetorical reading allowed a student to move from simply summarizing and evaluating her sources on local coverage of the championship football game to constructing a rationale for articles that covered the fans rather than the game. Rhetorical analysis enabled another student to move from summarizing his sources to understanding why each report about the Kent State shootings necessarily expressed a bias of some kind.

As these examples suggest, however, rhetorical reading is not a magical technique for producing sophisticated arguments. Even when students read their sources rhetorically, they tend merely to report the results of this analysis in their essays. Such writing appears to be a college-level version of the knowledge-telling strategy described by Bereiter and Scardamalia (*Psychology*) and may be, as they suggest, the product of years of exposure to pedagogical practices that enshrine the acquisition and expression of information without a context or purpose.

To move students beyond merely reporting the content and rhetorical orientation of their source texts, I have taught them the concept of the rhetorical gap and some simple heuristic questions for thinking about gaps. Gaps were first described by Iser as unsaid material that a reader must supply to/infer from a text. McCormick expanded the concept to include gaps between the text and the reader; such gaps could involve discrepancies of values, social conventions, language, or any other matter that readers must consider. If we apply the concept of gaps to Kinneavy's triangle, we see that in reading, for example, a gap may occur between the Encoder-Decoder corners when the reader is not a member of the author's intended audience. Shirley fell into such a gap. Another gap can occur between the Decoder-Reality corners when a reader disagrees with or does not understand the text. A third gap can occur between the Encoder-Reality points of the triangle if the writer has misrepresented or misunderstood the material. The benefit of teaching this concept is that when a student thinks about a writer's rhetorical stance, she may ask "Why does he think that way?" When a student encounters a gap, she may ask, "What effect does it have on the success of this communication?" The answers to both questions give students original material for their papers.

Shirley, for example, did not know that Churchill began writing *The Birth of Britain* during the 1930s, when Hitler was rearming Germany and when the British government and most of Churchill's readers ardently favored disarmament. Had she understood the rhetorical orientation of the book, which was published eleven years after the end of World War II, she might have argued that Churchill's evocation of past military glories would have been inflammatory in the 1930s but was highly acceptable twenty years later. A gap between the reader and the text (Decoder-Reality) might stimulate a reader to investigate whether or not she is the only person having this problem; a gap between other readers and the sources may motivate an adaptation or explanation of the material to a particular audience. Shirley might have adapted the Guizots' perspective on the French civil war for American readers. A gap between the author and the material (Encoder-Reality) might motivate a refutation.

To discover gaps, students may need to learn heuristics for setting rhetorical writing goals. That is, they may need to learn to think of the paper, not as a rehash of the available material, but as an opportunity to teach someone, to solve someone's problem, or to answer someone's question. The most salient questions for reading source texts may be "Who are you (the original audience of Decoders)?"; "What is your question or problem with this topic?"; and "How have I (the Encoder) used these materials to answer your question or solve your problem?" More simply, these questions may be learned as "Why," "How," and "So what?" When Shirley learns to read sources as telling not the eternal truth but a truth to a particular audience and when she learns to think of texts as existing to solve problems, she will find it easier to think of things to say.

For example, a sophomore at a private university was struggling with an assignment that required her to analyze an issue and express an opinion on it, using two conflicting source texts, an interview, and personal material as sources. Using rhetorical reading strategies, this girl discovered a gap between Alfred Marbaise, a high school principal who advocates mandatory drug testing of all high school students, and students like those he would be testing:

> Marbaise, who was a lieutenant in the U.S. Marines over thirty years ago . . . makes it very obvious that he cannot and will not tolerate any form of drug abuse in his school. For example, in paragraph seven he claims, "When students become involved in illegal activity, whether they realize it or not, they are violating other students . . . then I become very, very concerned . . . and I will not tolerate that."
>
> Because Marbaise has not been in school for nearly forty years himself, he does not take into consideration the reasons why kids actually use drugs. Today the social environment is so drastically different that Marbaise cannot understand a kid's morality, and that is why he writes from such a fatherly but distant point of view.

The second paragraph answers the So what? question, i.e., "Why does it matter that Marbaise seems by his age and background to be fatherly and distant?" Unless the writer/reader thinks to ask this question, she will have difficulty writing a coherent evaluation of Marbaise's argument.

The relative success of some students in finding original things to say about their topics can help us to understand the perennial problem of plagiarism. Some plagiarism derives, I think, from a weak, non-rhetorical task representation. If students believe they are supposed to reproduce source material in their papers, or if they know they are supposed to say something original but have no rhetorical problem to solve and no knowledge of how to find problems that they can discuss in their sources, it becomes difficult for them to avoid plagiarizing. The common student decision to buy a paper when writing the assignment seems a meaningless fill-in-the-blanks activity (cf. Schwegler and Shamoon) becomes easily understandable. Because rhetorical reading leads to discoveries about the text, students who use it may take more interest in their research papers.

Let us now assume that Shirley understands the importance of creating an original argument, knows how to read analytically, and has found things to say about the Battle of Agincourt. Are her troubles over? Will she now create that A paper that she yearns to write? Probably not. Despite her best intentions, Shirley will probably write another narrative/paraphrase of her sources. Why? Because by now, the assignment asks her to do far more than she can handle in a single draft. Shirley's task representation is now so rich, her set of goals so many, that she may be unable to juggle them all simultaneously. Moreover, the rhetorical reading technique requires students to discover content worth writing about and a rhetorical purpose for writing; the uncertainty of managing such a discovery task when a grade is at stake may be too much for Shirley.

Difficult tasks may be difficult in either (or both of) two ways. First, they may require students to do a familiar subtask, such as reading sources, at a higher level of difficulty, e.g., longer sources, more sources, a more difficult topic. Second, they may require students to do new subtasks, such as building notes into an original argument. Such tasks may require task management skills, especially planning, that students have never developed and do not know how to attempt. The insecurity that results from trying a complex new task in a high-stakes situation is increased when students are asked to discover a problem worth writing about because such tasks send students out on a treasure hunt with no guarantee that the treasure exists, that they will recognize it when they find it, or that when they find it they will be able to build it into a coherent argument. The paper on Marbaise quoted above earned a grade of D because the writer could not use her rhetorical insights to build an argument presented in a logical order. Although she asked the logical question about the implications of Marbaise's persona, she did not follow through by evaluating the gaps in his perspective that might affect the probable success of his program.

A skillful student using the summarize-the-main-ideas approach can set her writing goals and even plan (i.e., outline) a paper before she reads the sources. The rhetorical reading strategy, by contrast, requires writers to discover what is worth writing about and to decide how to say it as or after they read their sources. The strategy requires writers to change their content goals and to adjust their writing plans as their understanding of the topic develops. It requires writers, in Flower's term, to "construct" their purposes for writing as well as the content for their paper (for a description of constructive planning, see Flower, Schriver, Carey, Haas, and Hayes). In Flower's words, writers who construct a purpose, as opposed to writers who bring a predetermined purpose to a task, "create a web of purposes . . . set goals, toss up possibilities . . . create a multidimensional network of information . . . a web of purpose . . . a bubbling stew of various mental representations" (531–32). The complex indeterminacy of such a task may pose an intimidating challenge to students who have spent their lives summarizing main ideas and reporting facts.

Shirley may respond to the challenge by concentrating her energies on a familiar subtask, e.g., repeating material about the Battle of Agincourt, at the expense of struggling with an unfamiliar subtask such as creating an original argument. She may even deliberately simplify the task by representing it to herself as calling only for something that she knows how to do, expecting that Dr. Boyer will accept the paper as close enough to the original instructions. My students do this frequently. When students decide to write a report of their reading, they can at least be certain that they will find material to write about.

Because of the limits of attentional memory, not to mention those caused by inexperience, writers can handle only so many task demands at a time. Thus, papers produced by seemingly inadequate task representations may well be essentially rough drafts. What looks like a bad paper may well be a preliminary step, a way of meeting certain task demands in order to create a basis for thinking about new ones. My students consistently report that they need to marshal all of their ideas and text knowledge and get that material down on the page (i.e., tell their knowledge) before they can think about developing an argument (i.e., transform their knowledge). If Shirley's problem is that she has shelved certain task demands in favor of others, Dr. Boyer needs only to point out what Shirley should do to bring the paper into conformity with the assignment and offer Shirley a chance to revise.

The problems of cognitive overload and inexperience in handling complex writing tasks can create a tremendous hurdle for students because so many of them believe that they should be able to write their paper in a single draft. Some students think that if they can't do the paper in one draft that means that something is wrong with them as writers, or with the assignment, or with us for giving the assignment. Often, such students will react to their drafts with anger and despair, throwing away perfectly usable rough drafts and then coming to us and saying that they can't do the assignment.

The student's first draft about drug testing told her knowledge about her sources' opinions on mandatory drug testing. Her second draft contained the rhetorical analysis quoted above, but presented the material in a scrambled order and did not build the analysis into an argument. Only in a third draft was this student able to make her point:

> Not once does Marbaise consider any of the psychological reasons why kids turn away from reality. He fails to realize that drug testing will not answer their questions, ease their frustrations, or respond to their cries for attention, but will merely further alienate himself and other authorities from helping kids deal with their real problems.

This comment represents Terri's answer to the heuristic "So what? Why does the source's position matter?" If we pace our assignments to allow for our students' thoughts to develop, we can do a great deal to build their confidence in their writing (Terri raised her D+ to an A). If we treat the researched essay as a sequence of assignments instead of as a one-shot paper with a single due date, we can teach our students to build on their drafts, to use what they can do easily as a bridge to what we want them to learn to do. In this way, we can improve our students' writing habits. More importantly, however, we can help our students to see themselves as capable writers and as active, able, problem-solvers. Most importantly, we can use the sequence of drafts to demand that our students demonstrate increasingly sophisticated kinds of analytic and rhetorical proficiency.

Rhetorical reading and writing heuristics can help students to represent tasks in rich and interesting ways. They can help students to set up complex goal structures (Bereiter and Scardamalia, "Conversation"). They offer students many ways to think about their reading and writing texts. These tools, in other words, encourage students to work creatively.

And after all, creativity is what research should be about. If Shirley writes a creative paper, she has found a constructive solution that is new to her and which other people can use, a solution to a problem that she and other people share. Creativity is an inherently rhetorical quality. If we think of it as thought leading to solutions to problems and of problems as embodied in questions that people ask about situations, the researched essay offers infinite possibilities. Viewed in this way, a creative idea answers a question that the audience or any single reader wants answered. The question could be, "Why did Henry V win the Battle of Agincourt?" or, "How can student readers protect themselves against nationalistic bias when they study history?" or any of a thousand other questions. If we teach our Shirleys to see themselves as scholars who work to find answers to problem questions, and if we teach them to set reading and writing goals for themselves that will allow them to think constructively, we will be doing the most exciting work that teachers can do, nurturing creativity.

Appendix A: Page 1 of Shirley's paper

The battle of Agincourt ranks as one of England's greatest military triumphs. It was the most brilliant victory of the Middle Ages, bar none. It was fought on October 25, 1414, against the French near the French village of Agincourt.

Henry V had claimed the crown of France and had invaded France with an army estimated at anywhere between 10,000[1] and 45,000 men[2]. During the siege of Marfleur dysentery had taken 1/3 of them[3], his food supplies had been depleted[4], and the fall rains had begun. In addition the French had assembled a huge army and were marching toward him. Henry decided to march to Calais, where his ships were to await him[5]. He intended to cross the River Somme at the ford of Blanchetaque[6], but, falsely informed that the ford was guarded[7], he was forced to follow the flooded Somme up toward its source. The French army was shadowing him on his right. Remembering the slaughters of Crécy and Poictiers, the French constable, Charles d'Albret, hesitated to fight[8], but when Henry forded the Somme just above Amiens[9] and was just

1. Carl Stephinson, Medieval History, p. 529.

2. Guizot, Monsieur and Guizot, Madame, The History of France, Volume II, p. 211.

3. Cyril E. Robinson, England: A History of British Progress, p. 145.

4. Ibid.

5. Winston Churchill, A History of the English-Speaking Peoples, Volume 1: The Birth of Britain, p. 403.

6. Ibid.

7. Ibid.

8. Robinson, p. 145.

9. Churchill, p. 403.

Works Cited

Asch, Solomon. *Social Psychology.* New York: Prentice, 1952.

Atlas, Marshall. *Expert-Novice Differences in the Writing Process.* Paper presented at the American Educational Research Association, 1979. ERIC ED 107 769.

Baker, Louise, and Ann L. Brown. "Metacognitive Skills and Reading." *Handbook of Reading Research.* Ed. P. David Person, Rebecca Barr, Michael L. Kamil, and Peter Mosenthal. New York: Longman, 1984.

Bazerman, Charles. "Physicists Reading Physics: Schema-Laden Purposes and Purpose-Laden Schema." *Written Communication* 2.1 (1985): 3–24.

Bereiter, Carl, and Marlene Scardamalia. "From Conversation to Composition: The Role of Instruction in a Developmental Process." *Advances in Instructional Psychology.* Ed. R. Glaser. Vol. 2. Hillsdale, NJ: Lawrence Erlbaum Associates, 1982. 1–64.

———. *The Psychology of Written Composition.* Hillsdale, NJ: Lawrence Erlbaum Associates, 1987.

Briscoe, Terri. "To Test or Not to Test." Unpublished essay. Texas Christian University, 1989.

Britton, James, Tony Burgess, Nancy Martin, Alex McLeod, and Harold Rosen. *The Development of Writing Abilities* (11–18). Houndmills Basingstoke Hampshire: Macmillan Education Ltd., 1975.

Brown, Ann L. "Theories of Memory and the Problem of Development: Activity, Growth, and Knowledge." *Levels of Processing in Memory.* Eds. Laird S. Cermak and Fergus I. M. Craik. Hillsdale, NJ: Laurence Erlbaum Associates, 1979. 225–58.

————, Joseph C. Campione, and L. R. Barclay. *Training Self-Checking Routines for Estimating Test Readiness: Generalizations from List Learning to Prose Recall.* Unpublished manuscript. Univesity of Illinois, 1978.

————, and Jeanne Day. "Macrorules for Summarizing Texts: The Development of Expertise." *Journal of Verbal Learning and Verbal Behavior* 22.1 (1983): 1–14.

————, and Annmarie S. Palincsar. *Reciprocal Teaching of Comprehension Strategies: A Natural History of One Program for Enhancing Learning.* Technical Report #334. Urbana, IL: Center for the Study of Reading, 1985.

Churchill, Winston S. *The Birth of Britain.* New York: Dodd, 1956. Vol. I of *A History of the English-Speaking Peoples.* 4 vols. 1956–58.

Flower, Linda. "The Construction of Purpose in Writing and Reading." *College English* 50 (1988): 528–50.

————. *The Role of Task Representation in Reading to Write.* Berkeley, CA: Center for the Study of Writing, U of California at Berkeley and Carnegie Mellon. Technical Report, 1987.

————. "Writer-Based Prose: A Cognitive Basis for Problems in Writing." *College English* 41 (1979): 1–37.

Flower, Linda, Karen Schriver, Linda Carey, Christina Haas, and John R. Hayes. *Planning in Writing: A Theory of the Cognitive Process.* Berkeley, CA: Center for the Study of Writing, U of California at Berkeley and Carnegie Mellon. Technical Report, 1988.

Ford, James E., and Dennis R. Perry. "Research Paper Instruction in the Undergraduate Writing Program." *College English* 44 (1982): 825–31.

Ford, James E., Sharla Rees, and David L. Ward. *Teaching the Research Paper: Comprehensive Bibliography of Periodical Sources,* 1980. ERIC ED 197 363.

Goldman, Susan R. "Knowledge Systems for Realistic Goals." *Discourse Processes* 5 (1982): 279–303.

Guizot and Guizot de Witt. *The History of France from the Earliest Times to the Year 1848.* Trans. R. Black. Vol. 2. Philadelphia: John Wanamaker (n.d.).

Haas, Christina, and Linda Flower. "Rhetorical Reading Strategies and the Construction of Meaning." *College Composition and Communication* 39 (1988): 167–84.

Hayes, John R., D. A. Waterman, and C. S. Robinson. "Identifying the Relevant Aspects of a Problem Text." *Cognitive Science* 1 (1977): 297–313.

Hinze, Helen K. "The Individual's Word Associations and His Interpretation of Prose Paragraphs." *Journal of General Psychology* 64 (1961): 193–203.

Iser, Wolfgang. *The Act of Reading: A Theory of Aesthetic Response.* Baltimore: The Johns Hopkins UP, 1978.

Jeffery, Christopher. "Teachers' and Students' Perceptions of the Writing Process." *Research in the Teaching of English* 15 (1981): 215–28.

Kantz, Margaret. *Originality and Completeness: What Do We Value in Papers Written from Sources?* Conference on College Composition and Communication. St. Louis, MO, 1988.

————. *The Relationship between Reading and Planning Strategies and Success in Synthesizing: It's What You Do with Them That Counts.* Technical report in preparation. Pittsburgh: Center for the Study of Writing, 1988.

Kennedy, Mary Louise. "The Composing Process of College Students Writing from Sources." *Written Communication* 2.4 (1985): 43–56.

Kinneavy, James L. *A Theory of Discourse.* New York: Norton, 1971.

Kroll, Barry M. "Audience Adaptation in Children's Persuasive Letters." *Written Communication* 1.4 (1984): 407–28.

Langer, Judith. "Where Problems Start: The Effects of Available Information on Responses to School Writing Tasks." *Contexts for Learning to Write: Studies of Secondary School Instruction.* Ed. Arthur Applebee. Norwood, NJ: ABLEX Publishing Corporation, 1984. 135–48.

Luhig, Richard L. "Abstractive Memory, the Central-Incidental Hypothesis, and the Use of Structural Importance in Text: Control Processes or Structural Features?" *Reading Research Quarterly* 14.1 (1983): 28–37.

Marbaise, Alfred. "Treating a Disease." *Current Issues and Enduring Questions.* Eds. Sylvan Barnet and Hugo Bedau. New York: St. Martin's, 1987. 126–27.

McCormick, Kathleen. "Theory in the Reader: Bleich, Holland, and Beyond." *College English* 47.8 (1985): 836–50.

McGarry, Daniel D. *Medieval History and Civilization.* New York: Macmillan, 1976.

Nelson, Jennie, and John R. Hayes. *The Effects of Classroom Contexts on Students' Responses to Writing from Sources: Regurgitating Information or Triggering Insights.* Berkeley, CA: Center for the Study of Writing, U of California at Berkeley and Carnegie Mellon. Technical Report, 1988.

Pichert, James W. "Sensitivity to Importance as a Predictor of Reading Comprehension." *Perspectives on Reading Research and Instruction.* Eds. Michael A. Kamil and Alden J. Moe. Washington, D,C.: National Reading Conference, 1980. 42–46.

Robinson, Cyril E. *England: A History of British Progress from the Early Ages to the Present Day.* New York: Thomas Y. Crowell Company, 1928.

Schwegler, Robert A., and Linda K. Shamoon. "The Aims and Process of the Research Paper." *College English* 44 (1982): 817–24.

Shedd, Patricia T. "The Relationship between Attitude of the Reader towards Women's Changing Role and Response to Literature Which Illuminates Women's Role." Diss. Syracuse U, 1975. ERIC ED 142 956.

Short, Elizabeth Jane, and Ellen Bouchard Ryan. "Metacognitive Differences between Skilled and Less Skilled Readers: Remediating Deficits through Story Grammar and Attribution Training." *Journal of Education Psychology* 76 (1984): 225–35.

Spivey, Nancy Nelson. *Discourse Synthesis: Constructing Texts in Reading and Writing.* Diss. U Texas, 1983. Newark, DE: International Reading Association, 1984.

Toulmin, Steven E. *The Uses of Argument.* Cambridge: Cambridge UP, 1969.

Vipond, Douglas, and Russell Hunt. "Point-Driven Understanding: Pragmatic and Cognitive Dimensions of Literary Reading." *Poetics* 13 (1984): 261–77.

Winograd, Peter. "Strategic Difficulties in Summarizing Texts." *Reading Research Quarterly* 19 (1984): 404–25.

RESPONDING TO PLAGIARISM

Alice Drum

[*College Composition and Communication* 37 (1986): 241–43.]

Vice president of the College and dean of Educational Services at Franklin and Marshall College in Lancaster, Pennsylvania, Alice Drum has published numerous articles in professional journals, including *World Literature Written in English* and *Magill's Literary Annual.* Currently, she is doing research on Jane Austen.

Drum wrote the following article as a response to a plagiarism case that was especially troubling to her. After the case was over she surveyed composition texts to see how they presented plagiarism. She concluded that many of the presentations were inadequate and that introductory writing courses needed to do more to prevent plagiarism. With its thorough coverage on pages 477–89, *The Bedford Handbook* answers Drum's call for more emphasis on teaching students how to avoid plagiarism.

Plagiarism is a disease that plagues college instructors everywhere. I believe that our reliance on the classic argument against plagiarism may be one of the reasons for its continued virulence. That argument reads something like this: Plagiarism is both legally and morally wrong because it involves the appropriation of words or ideas that belong to someone else and the misrepresentation of them as one's own. Unfortunately, we tend to place a great deal of emphasis on the first part of the process, the simple act of taking ideas, and very little on the second stage, the more complicated act of passing them off as one's own. In our conferences with students suspected of plagiarism, we carefully point out the legal and ethical implications of what they have done, but we neglect to mention the pedagogical implications of what they have not done — completed an assignment. As the continuing practice of plagiarism testifies, this emphasis on the legalistic rather than the pedagogical consequences of plagiarism has proved an ineffectual way of dealing with the problem. In its place, I would recommend a holistic approach, a recognition that plagiarism involves a student, an instructor, and the structure within which the two interact.

In the first place, we must admit that many students do not know how to avoid plagiarism, that most rhetoric textbooks are of little help in this respect, and that many college composition classes deal inadequately with the problem. The greatest weakness is with the textbooks. A random survey of thirty popular texts reveals that many provide no reference to plagiarism in the index, and that most contain at best a paragraph of explanation and definition. Most textbooks say, in effect, "Do not plagiarize," but they refuse to do much more than remonstrate against the practice. They seldom contain useful writing exercises on the paraphrase, the summary, and the precis, although such exercises would indicate to students that there are varied ways of avoiding plagiarism. Instead, the standard handbook emphasizes the mechanics of documentation — the presentation of footnotes and bibliography in the currently accepted form.

In the classroom, we take our cue from the handbooks and concentrate on rules rather than on the various ways of integrating source materials in a text. Avoiding plagiarism is not simply a matter of following accepted rules, however. If a student changes Harold Bloom's description of Milton, "the severe father of the sublime mode" (*Poetry and Repression*, p. 21), to "a severe father of sublimity," that student has not repeated more than three words in a row, thus adhering to one popular formula on how to avoid plagiarism. On the other hand, the student has not added anything that is original; clearly, the sentence needs a footnote. Occasionally, footnotes are omitted through oversight, but generally the need for documentation is clear to students, once they understand that avoiding plagiarism does not simply involve adhering to a formula but also involves dealing carefully with the style and the content of the original.

In my composition classes, to help students understand this principle, a research paper is due only after I have assigned and returned three or four preliminary assignments and after the students have participated in several research writing workshops. The preliminary assignments may include an abstract, a summary, a brief background paper. The writing workshops include sessions where the students analyze the style and the content of a selected passage and then attempt to put that passage in a different form. They may work on creating an effective paraphrase of a brief article; they may take a single sentence and rewrite it a number of times, making as many stylistic changes as possible without changing the content; they may rewrite a brief passage — an article from *Newsweek* — in the style of a well-known writer. The aim of these exercises is twofold: to help the students understand that writers do give an identity to their words, and to give students confidence in their own ability to create a style of their own in their writing.

These exercises are designed to correct unconscious plagiarism, but we all know that many acts of plagiarism are conscious ones. In regard to these cases, we must examine the myth that plagiarism has everything to do with some anonymous "other" — a critic, an expert — and nothing to do with the teacher of the class, who has, after all, made the assignment which the student has failed to complete. Because written assignments involve at least one, and probably all, of the steps of the cognitive process, they test the student's ability to collect evidence, make inferences, and render judgments. The professor's response in the form of a grade or a written commentary is a means of communicating his or her opinion of the student's intellectual maturity. When students fail to comply honestly with an assignment, the pedagogical process breaks down.

For this reason, the instructor — not deans, chairpersons, nor commissions — should handle initial cases of plagiarism. There are a number of benefits to be derived from this procedure. An important one is that we would not be perpetuating the myth that plagiarism has nothing to do with the instructor and the course. Another benefit is that students are more likely to be concerned about the response of a professor who represents a familiar face than they are about the response of a dean who represents anonymous authority. And professors, only too aware of the difficulties of dealing with bureaucracy, may be more inclined to confer with a student than to involve themselves in the time-consuming procedure of reporting plagiarism to someone else.

Instead, the penalty for plagiarism, at least for initial cases in introductory courses such as composition, should be meted out by the instructor. With initial cases, we can reasonably assume that either the students do not know how to avoid plagiarism or that they have been led to believe that it does not matter. We can assure them that the latter is not true, and we can provide instructions on how to avoid plagiarism in the future. Some persons may argue that the individual professor may not be harsh enough, that stringent punishments are needed to stop the widespread cheating on campuses today. But it can, also, be argued that legalistic punishments have not proved particularly effective, and that they necessitate extensive protections for the student and increasing complications for the professor who attempts to prove plagiarism. I am not arguing for permissiveness in regard to plagiarism, but rather for a recognition that it is at least as much a pedagogical offense as a legalistic one. Certainly, we must insist that we will not tolerate plagiarism, that students will receive significantly lowered grades when they plagiarize. But we should also admit that students may learn more from a second chance to complete an assignment than from an automatic failure in a course. With this alternative procedure, there should be added penalties and added work, but there would, also, be an opportunity for the student to learn how to deal with research material with integrity. And that, after all, is one of the reasons that we assign library papers.

PART TEN

SPECIAL TYPES OF WRITING: LITERATURE AND OTHER DISCIPLINES

One of the goals of first-year composition courses is to prepare students for the various kinds of writing they will be asked to do throughout their academic careers. Without question, students will have to write about literature or use those specific strategies to write about their reading in related courses. And, as more colleges and universities develop writing across the curriculum initiatives, students will be asked to write in a wider range of courses. In order to introduce students to the demands of writing in courses across the disciplines, instructors must be familiar with the theoretical principles informing the Writing Across the Curriculum (WAC) movement, which has various manifestations. At one end of the continuum are "writing to learn" approaches that are meant to increase students' engagement with and learning of a subject. At the other end of the continuum are "learning to write" approaches, in which students learn to write as members of specific disciplinary discourse communities. Students who practice writing for a variety of audiences and purposes will be prepared to engage more meaningfully in the various intellectual challenges they will face as they advance in their studies.

The following articles address several questions and issues that teachers face as they attempt to prepare a diverse student population to be effective writers and readers in courses across the curriculum:

- How can teachers interest students in approaching literature from different critical perspectives? Given the sophistication of current critical theory and the complexity of various interpretive approaches to literature, how can instructors teach writing about literature without introducing confusion and despair?
- What is WAC and where did it come from? How can teachers learn more about it?
- How can the principles of WAC help writing teachers prepare diverse students to become effective writers and readers in all of their academic work?
- How can teachers incorporate WAC principles in their writing courses?

WRITING ABOUT LITERATURE

A PASSAGE INTO CRITICAL THEORY

Steven Lynn

[*College English* 52 (1990): 258–71.]

Steven Lynn is professor of English and director of the Freshman Composition Program at the University of South Carolina, Columbia. He has published several articles on Samuel Johnson, including "Sexual Difference and Johnson's Brain," which appeared in *Fresh Reflections on Samuel Johnson* (1987), and an article in the 1990 edition of the annual *The Age of Johnson.* Extending the work he began in the article reprinted here, Lynn published *Texts and Contexts: Writing about Literature and Critical Theory* (1994).

In the introduction to "A Passage into Critical Theory," Lynn describes the situation that prompted the article: When he attempted to introduce instructors to contemporary literary criticism, they became confused and frustrated. This difficulty is analogous to the problems students have when their instructors try to teach the concept of differing critical perspectives. Lynn's overview demystifies various critical approaches and complements *The Bedford Handbook*'s discussion on being an active reader by offering teachers expanded options for helping student writers engage literary texts.

She might have deplored the sentiment, had it come from one of her students, "What we need," she was saying, trying hard not to whine, "is a short cut, a simple guide, a kind of recipe for each of these theories, telling us step by step how to make a particular reading." It was the second week of a three-week institute dedicated to the proposition that all teachers were created equal and that therefore all should share in the excitement and challenge of the ongoing transformation of literary criticism. But these teachers, it was clear, were just on the verge of saying, "Let's just pretend that nothing important has happened since, oh, 1967." I had whipped them into an evangelistic fever at the outset of the institute, ready to receive the spirit of critical theory; and they had read so much and worked so hard. But I nodded. She was right. They were mired in complexity and subtleties. I realized, of course, that no one whose loaf was fully sliced would seriously attempt an overview of recent critical theory in a few pages. But all they needed was to get their bearings, and then the confusion of ideas bouncing around in their heads would probably start falling into some comprehensible order. So I came up with the briefest of guides to some of the recent critical theory, an overview that would succeed when its users began to understand its limitations.

My strategy was to show how a single passage might be treated by a handful of different critical theories — certainly not every theory available, but enough to show how theory shapes practice and to help my students with those most puzzling them. Although multiple readings of the same work are easy to assemble and useful, my effort not only had the virtue of a calculated simplicity and brevity, it also displayed the same reader attempting to act as the extension of various different interpretive codes. The passage I chose, a wonderful excerpt from Brendan Gill's *Here at the New Yorker,* is itself brief, but also rich. In offering these notes I am assuming that my reader, like those teachers, knows enough about recent critical theory to be confused. Obviously, my theorizing will be alarmingly reductive, and the examples won't illustrate what any student at any level can produce, given a sketch of this or that theory. They illustrate only what I can do to provide in a very small space an example of a particular kind of critical behavior. But my teacher/students, as well as my student/students, have found these discussion/examples helpful, and so I'll proceed immediately to Gill's text and then mine, before anyone gets cut on any of these slashes.

Here's Gill's text:

> When I started at *The New Yorker,* I felt an unshakable confidence in my talent and intelligence. I revelled in them openly, like a dolphin diving skyward out of the sea. After almost forty years, my assurance is less than it was; the revellings, such as they are, take place in becoming seclusion. This steady progress downward in the amount of one's confidence is a commonplace at the magazine — one might almost call it a tradition. Again and again, some writer who has made a name for himself in the world will begin to write for us and will discover as if for the first time how difficult writing is. The machinery of benign skepticism that surrounds and besets him in the form of editors, copy editors, and checkers, to say nothing of fellow-writers, digs a yawning pit an inch or so beyond his desk. He hears it repeated as gospel that there are not three people in all America who can set down a simple declarative sentence correctly; what are the odds against his being one of this tiny elect?
>
> In some cases, the pressure of all those doubting eyes upon his copy is more than the writer can bear. When the galleys of a piece are placed in front of him, covered with scores, perhaps hundreds, of pencilled hen-tracks of inquiry, suggestion, and correction, he may sense not the glory of creation but the threat of being stung to death by an army of gnats. Upon which he may think of nothing better to do than lower his head onto his blotter and burst into tears. Thanks to the hen-tracks and their consequences, the piece will be much improved, but the author of it will be pitched into a state of graver self-doubt than ever. Poor devil, he will type out his name on a sheet of paper and stare at it long and long, with dumb uncertainty. It looks — oh, Christ — his name looks as if it could stand some working on.
>
> As I was writing the above, Gardner Botsford, the editor who, among other duties, handles copy for "Theatre," came into my office with the galleys of my latest play review in his hand. Wearing an expression of solemnity, he said, "I am obliged to inform you that Miss Gould has found a buried dangling modifier in one of your sentences." Miss Gould is our head copy editor and unquestionably knows as much about English grammar as anyone alive. Gerunds, predicate nominatives, and passive periphrastic conjugations are mother's milk to her, as they are not to me. Nevertheless, I boldly challenged her allegation. My prose was surely correct in every way. Botsford placed the galleys before me and indicated the offending sentence, which ran, "I am told that in her ninth decade this beautiful woman's only complaint in respect to her role is that she doesn't have enough work to do."
>
> I glared blankly at the galleys. Humiliating enough to have buried a dangling modifier unawares; still more humiliating not to be able to disinter it. Botsford came to my rescue. "Miss Gould points out that as the sentence is written, the meaning is that the complaint is in its ninth decade and has,

moreover, suddenly and unaccountably assumed the female gender." I said that in my opinion the sentence could only be made worse by being corrected — it was plain that "The only complaint of this beautiful woman in her ninth decade . . ." would hang on the page as heavy as a sash-weight. "Quite so," said Botsford. "There are times when to be right is wrong, and this is one of them. The sentence stands."

New Criticism

I'll start with New Criticism because modern literary study arguably begins with New Criticism, and because it is probably, even today, the most pervasive way of looking at literature. It emerged in the struggle to make literary criticism a respectable profession, which for many scholars meant making it more rigorous, more like the sciences — a goal embodied in Wellek and Warren's landmark *Theory of Literature* in 1949. Wellek's chapter on "The Mode of Existence of a Literary Work of Art" is crucial: "The work of art," Wellek asserts, is "an object of knowledge," "a system of norms of ideal concepts which are intersubjective" (p. 156). What Wellek means by this difficult formulation, at least in part, is that "a literary work of art is in exactly the same position as a system of language" (p. 152). Because the work has the same sort of stable and "objective" status as a language, existing in a "collective ideology," governed by enduring "norms," critical statements are not merely opinions of taste: "It will always be possible to determine which point of view grasps the subject most thoroughly and deeply," as "All relativism is ultimately defeated." This assumption is important, because although New Critics in practice have not always ignored authors, genres, or historical contexts, the purpose of their analysis of particular works, their "close reading," has been finally to reveal how the formal elements of the literary work, often thought of as a poem, create and resolve tension and irony. Great works control profound tensions, and therefore New Criticism's intrinsic analysis, dealing with the work in isolation, is implicitly evaluative.

Common sense might suggest that the function of criticism is to reveal the meaning of a work, but New Criticism attends to *how* a work means, not *what*, for a simple reason: As Cleanth Brooks puts it, the meaning of a work is "a controlled experience which has to be *experienced,* not a logical process" (p. 90). The meaning cannot, in other words, be summed up in a proposition, but the system of norms that constructs a reader's experience can be analyzed. So, the New Critic focuses on "the poem itself" (rather than the author, the reader, the historical context), asking, "What elements are in tension in this work?" and "What unity resolves this tension?"

In Gill's story, the most obvious tension might be seen as that between right and wrong (or editor versus writer, or the world versus *The New Yorker,* or grammar versus style, or confidence versus doubt, or something else). Whatever the basic tension is determined to be, it must somehow be resolved if the text succeeds, and New Criticism is inevitably teleological: Endings are crucial. Thus a New Critical reading of Gill's passage might well focus on the reconciliation at the end, when Botsford pronounces "right is wrong." The New Critic would then consider, "How does this idea fit into the system of the work's tensions, and how is the tension ordered and resolved?" The following paragraph briefly suggests the sort of discussion that might be produced in response:

> In Gill's story of the dangling modifier, Botsford solves the conflict between Miss Gould's rules and Gill's taste with a paradox that unifies the work: Sometimes "right is wrong." Miss Gould was right to spot the error, but Gill

was right to be wrong, to have written the sentence as he did. The irony of this solution is reinforced by various paradoxical images: For example, the dolphin is "diving skyward," an action that in its simultaneously downward ("diving") and upward ("skyward") implications embodies the same' logic as a wrong rightness. The "progress downward" of the writer, and even his "becoming seclusion" (appealing to others; unknown to others), convey the same image. In larger terms, the writer's "unshakable confidence" that quickly becomes a "dumb uncertainty" suggests the reversal that informs the story's truth. In such an upside-down world, we would expect to find the imagery of struggle and violence, and such is indicated by the "yawning pit" and the "army of gnats." Such tension is harmonized by Gill's brilliant conclusion: In writing, conducted properly, the demands of correctness and style are unified by the writer's poetic instincts, just as the story itself is resolved by the notion of a correct error.

Structuralism

At first glance, structuralism might appear to be simply the enlargement of New Criticism's project. But instead of focusing on the formal elements that create the experience of a particular work, structuralism aspired to deal, as Terry Eagleton says, "with structures, and more particularly with examining the general laws by which they work" (p. 94). In other words, the structuralist looks at a surface manifestation and theorizes about a deep structure, or s/he interprets surface phenomena in terms of this underlying structure.

In its most ambitious moments, structuralism may aspire to reveal anything from the structure of the human mind itself to the conventions of a literary form. Structuralists have tried, for instance, not only to isolate the conventions of certain kinds of narrative, such as the fantastic and science fiction, but also to determine what features allow us to identify a text as a story. Is Gill's passage a self-contained story, an entity in itself, or it is an excerpt, a fragment, a part of *Here at the New Yorker?* If we consider how we decide whether something is a story, we might well agree that a passage becomes a story when it fits our ideas of what a story is, when it satisfies certain general laws of discourse regarding a story. If we use a very simple and ancient notion of narrative structure, most readers would probably agree that Gill's text does have a beginning, a middle, and an end, moving from harmony, to complication and crisis, and finally to resolution. Readers might also agree it has a hero (the writer, who appears to be Gill), a helper (Botsford), and a villain (Miss Gould), features that Vladimir Propp finds, interestingly enough, in fairy tales. We can identify these elements, which we might argue are essential to a story, because we can relate this story to other ones and to a paradigm of stories. We can imagine (and perhaps even recall) other stories involving a confident neophyte who encounters destructive forces, descends into despair and near helplessness, and then finds an unexpected helper and vindication. Such structuralist analysis moves into the realm of archetypal criticism (as in Northrop Frye's work) when it seeks the universal patterns, the "archetypes" which are the foundation of the system of "literature," rather than isolating the structures and relationships within a particular system of discourse.

To produce a structuralist reading, then, exposing a text's conventions and operations, we must first identify the elements of the text — the genre, the agents, the episodes, the turning points, whatever. Structuralists are naturally attracted to charts and diagrams because these are helpful in reducing the complexity of a text to some understandable pattern, which can be compared to other patterns, or their transmutation, or absence. This concern with conventions rather than discrete works means that structuralism, unlike New Criticism, is not implicitly evaluative. *Gulliver's Travels* and *Gilligan's Island* are equally worthy of analysis, at least structurally: They may, in fact, illuminate one another, since textual conventions appear in the relationship of texts. If all the stories in our culture, regardless of characters or plot, end with a pack of multicolored dogs going off to hunt antelopes, as is indeed apparently the case in one African culture (Grimes, p. vii), then we recognize such an event as a discrete element: the ending element. In the case of Gill's text, one convention of a literary work that we surely recognize as missing is a beginning operation: a title. Does this lack alone disqualify this text as a literary story? If so, could we then add a title (what would it be?) and make the text into a story? If so, who would be the author of this story that didn't exist until we titled it? (We might also consider the status of this story before it was extricated from Gill's book.)

Because students' experience of literature may be limited, it's often helpful to supply comparable texts or to ask students to invent a comparable text, thus making the textual conventions easier to imagine. Here is my very limited attempt to think structurally about this excerpt, offering also another story to highlight the postulated form.

> The structure of Gill's text involves the repetition of an underlying sequence, in which a central figure encounters a contrary force that reverses his fortunes: x + y Æ anti-x. This sequence, which we see in the first two paragraphs, might be represented this way:
>
> 1. Unrealistic confidence ("unshakable confidence") + critical forces (editors, copy editors, and checkers) Æ unrealistic doubt ("dumb uncertainty").
>
> The same underlying structure appears in the last two paragraphs, except this time a particular example of the pattern is presented:
>
> 2. Specific instance: Unrealistic confidence ("boldly challenged her allegation") + critical force (Miss Gould) Æ unrealistic doubt ("Still more humiliating").
>
> In the final paragraph the pattern is inverted, as confidence becomes doubt, antagonistic forces become helpful, and doubt becomes confidence. This inversion, which is perhaps a common occurrence in the concluding element of a series, heightens by contrast the effect of the hero's success:
>
> 3. Unrealistic doubt (helpless to "disinter it") + a helpful force (Botsford) Æ realistic confidence (Gill's bold challenge, stoutly maintained, is upheld).
>
> The same underlying pattern can be seen in the following plot:
>
> 1. Dreaming of future glory as an artist, a student comes to study at the university and discovers that art professors systematically show students how incompetent they are.
> 2. The art student turns in a project, and one faculty member explains in public how the project is grossly wrong. The student did not realize that he had departed from the assignment.
> 3. The chairman of the department then responds to the faculty member's criticism, saying that the assignment was a foolish one, and the student has demonstrated admirable creativity in revising the professor's directions and producing a good project.

Deconstruction

New Criticism, like its sibling philosophy of writing instruction, Current-Traditional Rhetoric, is product-oriented. It is perhaps then not surprising that my New Critical reading of Gill's piece focuses on the centrality of error, one of C-T Rhetoric's fundamental concerns. At first glance, Gill's story may appear to deflate Error's terror, since being wrong turns out to be right. If we press this close reading, however, asking if the text might say something other than what it appears to say, we move into the realm of deconstruction. Composition students in particular might be sensitive to the way Botsford's paradox reverses itself, unravelling Gill's grammatical triumph and plunging "the writer" finally into an even dumber and darker uncertainty. It's bad enough for the writer at *The New Yorker,* not to mention the composer in Freshman English, if the rules of writing are so complex that not even three people in America "can set down a simple declarative sentence correctly," if an experienced and accomplished writer can commit a major blunder without knowing it and without being able to fix it when he does know it. But it's even worse if the rules obtain in one case and not in another, and the rules for determining such exceptions don't seem to exist but are rather invented and applied by whoever happens to be in charge. Basic writing students, mystified by the rules of Standard English, live in just such a nightmare, I suspect.

If we look again at Botsford's vindication, we see it is deceptive, for he does not actually say that sometimes right is wrong and wrong is right. He only says that sometimes "right is wrong." Certainly wrong is also occasionally wrong, and perhaps it is always wrong. But Botsford's apparent reversal of the dismantling of authors at *The New Yorker* is finally ambiguous, since we never know if the writer is ever correct, no matter what he does. "The sentence stands" indeed, but it stands with its error intact, a monument to Gill's inability and the inevitable error of writing — the way language masters us. The passage thus complements the deconstructive commonplace that reading is always misreading.

Although it has been asserted that poststructuralism is not an applicable method (see Tompkins), I am, I think, just applying some basic deconstructive moves to Gill's text, which seems especially receptive, given its overt oppositions and emphasis on language. And despite the reluctance of some theorists to risk the spectacle of defining deconstruction (an action that deconstruction, by definition, renders futile), useful and clear explanations are available. For example, Barbara Johnson says that deconstruction proceeds by "the careful teasing out of warring forces of signification within the text itself" (p. 5). Jonathan Culler says that "to deconstruct a discourse is to show how it undermines the philosophy it asserts, or the hierarchical oppositions on which it relies" (p. 86). This teasing out or undermining might be described as a three-step process: First, a deconstructive reading must note which member of an opposition in a text appears to be privileged or dominant (writers versus editors, error versus correctness, men versus women, etc.); second, the reading shows how this hierarchy can be reversed within the text, how the apparent hierarchy is arbitrary or illusory; finally, a deconstructive reading places both structures in question, making the text ultimately ambiguous. For students to deconstruct a text, they need to locate an opposition, determine which member is privileged, then reverse and undermine that hierarchy. Such activity often makes central what appears to be marginal, thereby exposing "hidden" contradictions. Deconstruction seems to me especially worthwhile because it encourages creativity (my students often enjoy the imaginative playfulness and punning of much poststructuralist criticism) and scrutiny (in order to deconstruct a work, one at least must read it carefully).

Thus, if structuralism shows how the conventions of a text work, then poststructuralism, in a sense, points out how they fail. In our time, the genres fiction and nonfiction have proved especially interesting. Gill's passage would appear to be nonfiction, since Gill really did work at *The New Yorker,* and his book obviously employs the operations of autobiography. But look at Miss Gould's uncannily apt name: She is a Miss Ghoul, having unearthed a "buried" dangling modifier, decomposing Gill's sentence; Botsford, perhaps played by Vincent Price, enters with "an expression of solemnity," carrying this mutilated modifier that the author finds himself unable to "disinter." Miss Gould may not drink human blood, but she does have some strange nutritional ideas: "gerunds, predicate nominatives, and passive paraphrastic conjugations are mother's milk to her." Fortunately, the editor, a gardener, or rather a Gardner, who has the final responsibility for nurturing, pruning, and harvesting the writer's sentences, knows how to deal with buried modifiers. A Botsford, he knows how to get over the unavoidable errors of prose, how to ford the botches of writing (ouch!). Thus, although we initially may place this piece into the nonfiction category, deconstruction calls such placement into question. People in nonfiction usually don't have symbolic numbers — do they? Of course, there was that White House spokesperson named Larry Speakes. And then my allergist in Tuscaloosa, whose name, prophetically enough, was Dr. Shotts. And a hundred other folks I've known with strangely meaningful names. Deconstruction typically leaves us in uncertainty, but with a richer understanding of the categories we have put in motion — thereby unavoidably functioning as a kind of cultural criticism, or at least a prelude to cultural criticism.

Although deconstructive critics may well deal with pervasive, basic issues, they may also choose some marginal element of the text and vigorously explore its oppositions, reversals, and ambiguities. In fact, for some critics, deconstruction is simply a name for "close reading" with a vengeance. The deconstructive critic, for example, might well decide to concentrate on the arguably marginal assertion that because of the editors' merciless correction, "the piece will be much improved." The New Critic, I think, would not be very likely to consider this assertion central, the key to the passage. Yet, proceeding from deconstructive assumptions, bringing the marginal to the center, here is what happened when I turned on this assertion:

> Gill's anecdote clearly sets the world's writers against the editors, and the latter control the game. The editors and their henchmen, the checkers and copy editors, get to say what is wrong. They get to dig the "yawning pit" in front of the helpless writer's desk; they determine the "tiny elect" who can write correctly; they make the scores and hundreds of "hen-tracks" on the writer's manuscript, which serve as testimony to the incompetence of writers, the near-impossibility of writing, and the arbitrary power of the editor. To be sure, it is acknowledged that these editorial assaults upon the writer serve their purpose, for "Thanks to the hen-tracks and their consequences, the piece will be much improved." But the cost is clearly terrible. Not only is the writer unable to write his own name with any confidence, he has become a "Poor devil," outside "the elect." In delivering his writing over to the editors, conceding their dominance, the writer inevitably places his own identity, perhaps even his own soul, in jeopardy, as the expostulation "oh Christ!" comes to be an invocation to the only power who can save the writer from the devil and the editor's destructive forces.

In fact, this story of the errors of writing actually reveals that the kingdom of editors is based upon a lie: It simply is not true, despite the beleaguered writer's admission under torture, that "the piece will be much improved" by editorial intervention. Miss Gould's enormous grammatical lore does not improve the piece at all; her effort nearly made it "worse." And Botsford's contribution involves simply leaving the piece as it was written — a strange method of improvement. This instance, in other words, suggests that the writer need not approach dissolution in order to compose his writing. At the same time, Gill can never become again like the gill-less dolphin of the first paragraph, confidently "diving skyward," for the dangling modifier remains, a part of the sea of language the author cannot leave. In the end, both writer and editor are defeated by their inability to control their language, as the status of the writer at *The New Yorker* becomes a paradigm for the alarming status of writing itself: deceptive, mute, and intractable, "The sentence stands," neither improved nor made worse.

Psychological Criticism

In its most commonsensical form, a psychological approach to a text simply involves focusing attention on the motivations and relationships involved in the text's production or consumption. The mental processes of author, character, and/or reader may be involved in such considerations. My students, who have seen their own writing covered by "pencilled hen-tracks of inquiry, suggestion, and correction," are easily interested in what Gill's passage implies about the emotional effects of criticism and why writers react so unconstructively and painfully to correction and advice. Whereas reader-response criticism would build a "reading" from such subjective reaction, psychological criticism would be more interested in analyzing (rather than expressing) the passage's effects. Obviously, terms like "ego," "anxiety," "unconscious," and "obsessive," would be handy in such an analysis, although an introduction to psychological concepts could quickly engulf a course in criticism. And one could easily spend several semesters exploring different psychological schools and the various ways they might influence our reading. My minimal (but still challenging) goal in an introduction to theory is to give my students an extremely basic understanding of some essential Freudian ideas and their application.

Many of my students think they already understand Freud: He's the guy who thought of everything in terms of sex. Freud did of course think that sexuality (in a large sense) pervades our lives, but it is also always in conflict with opposing forces. So that we can function in society, our drive toward pleasure is necessarily contained and suppressed, relegated in part to the unconscious, where it does not slumber peacefully away, but rather asserts itself indirectly, in dreams, jokes, slips of the tongue, creative writing. For instance, dreams of water, Freud tells us, harken back to "the embryo in the amniotic fluid in the mother's uterus"; dreams of diving into water may be expressing a desire to return to the womb (*Lectures*, p. 160). Repression of such desires becomes a problem when the unconscious enlarges its domain, creating hysterical, obsessional, or phobic neuroses that insistently express the desire while still disguising it. If the power of the unconscious begins to take over reality, creating delusion, then we have a psychosis.

This economy of desire is based on Freud's most outrageous (and undeniable) claim: That even infants are sexual beings. Freud's theory of the central sexual phenomenon of early childhood, admittedly based on the development of males, is laid out in a brief and accessible paper, "The Dissolution of the Oedipus Complex." Focusing first on the mother's breasts, the young boy invests his desire in his mother — he "develops an object-cathexis" for her, Freud says. As the boy's "sexual wishes in regard to his mother become more intense," his father is increasingly "perceived as an obstacle to them," thus originating what Freud calls "the simple positive Oedipus complex" (p. 640). The desire to supplant his father and join with his mother cannot be acted out, and it must be repressed, turned away from, put out of sight. This "primal repression" initiates the unconscious, engendering a "place" for repressed desires. If no more than a repression is achieved, however, the Oedipus complex "persists in an unconscious state in the id and will later manifest its pathogenic effect." This "pathogenic effect" can be avoided, Freud says, by "the destruction of the Oedipus complex," which "is brought about by the threat of castration" (p. 664). This threat is embodied in the father and perpetuated by the formation of the super-ego, which "retains the character of the father" (p. 642) and comes to stand for the restraints of "authority, religious teaching, schooling and reading." This constraining law in Lacan's reading of Freud is ultimately the system of language.

Even the most glimmering understanding of Freud, I would argue, can be useful: The idea of the unconscious, for instance, dispenses with the second-most-often-asked question in introductory courses — "Do you think the author really intended to mean any of that?" Further, my students generate thin and uninteresting readings more out of caution and a poverty of options than a plenitude of possibilities, and after an exposure to Freud, what interpretation can be immediately rejected as absurd? Even a basic understanding of "The Dissolution of the Oedipus Concept" opens up Gill's passage in ways my students have found liberating, comic, and revealing. For example, one of the most interesting problems in this passage is the apparent disparity between the emotional content and the actual events. We see a writer bursting into tears, hiding his head on his blotter; a writer who considers himself humiliated, who glares "blankly"; we even see a writer who is unsure of his very name. And what is the cause? A grammatical error? The scene makes so little logical sense that we may well wonder if it makes more psychological sense. The following reading tries to see what might happen when the Oedipal triangle, the unconscious, the super-ego, and the castration complex get Gill's passage on the couch:

> The dolphin diving skyward at the beginning of Gill's passage is an obvious Freudian image of birth, and an important clue to the psychic problems being addressed here. The writer moves from the buoyant amniotic ocean of pure pleasure and unthreatened ego, the world of "unshakable confidence," into the difficult reality of *The New Yorker*, the world of the anxious, neurotic writer. Gill's longing for an impossible return to the uncomplicated indulgence of an animal state, symbolized by the dolphin, conflicts with his unavoidable status in a parental society of traditions, gospels, grammatical rules, and "editors, copy editors, and checkers." The ambiguity of the image, "diving skyward," reflects this troubled position, suspended between the id's impossible nostalgia and the super-ego's stern correction. Gill's symbol for himself, the dolphin, is an interesting (and no doubt unconscious) play on his name: a "gill" is naturally associated with a fish, which becomes the dolphin; a dolphin, however, does not have a "gill," thus marking again the gulf between the burdened Gill and the free-floating dolphin.
>
> Does Freud's model of psychosexual development also help to explain how this loss of innocence leads to Gill's unexpectedly emotional reaction? Yes, startlingly well in fact, for analysis reveals how Gill's scene reenacts the traumatic dissolution of the Oedipus complex. To see how the Oedipal triangle shapes Gill's passage, how Gill's response bears the emotional

charge of reworking his way through this complex, we should first note the writer's special relationship to his editors: He owes his existence, as a writer anyway, to his editors. The union of Miss Gould and Gardner Botsford, in this case, allows "Brendan Gill" to appear. Miss Gould, the copy editor, the symbolic mother, stands for grammatical correctness. At *The New Yorker,* the writer's first desires must be for her "yes." But this identification with Miss Gould, or rather what she represents, is unavoidably frustrated. Like the child who desires union with his mother, the writer is ill-equipped to satisfy Miss Gould: not even one of the "tiny elect," the writer cannot possibly fill in the "yawning pit" of error.

But the writer, like the developing child, must also face the law of the father. Gardner Botsford, the symbolic father, the senior editor, must ultimately direct the writer's attention away from Miss Gould toward the proper object of his attention, outside *The New Yorker* family — the reader. We see that Gill does in fact reveal a turning away from Miss Gould, using in fact the same focus as the child who turns initially from the mother's breasts as an object of desire: Gill finds Miss Gould's "mother's milk," the predicate nominatives and such, distasteful. The way Gill chooses to present her name (not "Gloria Gould" but "Miss Gould") marks his recognition of her as a "Miss." As a by-the-book grammarian, she may also be a ghoul, bringing a deadly stiffness to what she handles. Gill's development as a writer thus requires him to reject her.

To see how this rejection is accomplished, again in terms of the Oedipus complex, we must observe how the writer's identification with his writing contributes to his extraordinary anxiety and its symptomatic distortions. Threats to his writing endanger his identity, his ego. Thus we see that although it is the writer's galleys that are covered with "inquiry, suggestion, and correction," Gill shifts these impressions to the writer, and further transforms them from "pencilled hen-tracks" into stings. It is not, as we might suppose, the particular work that may be attacked so much it dies, but instead the writer who may be "stung to death by an army of gnats." In reality, gnats do not, of course, have stingers; they bite, if anything. The dreamlike alteration here again substantiates the threat to his identity that the author has perceived: Being bitten to death by gnats is absurd, but being stung to death is a terrifying prospect.

At this point Freud's assertion that the dissolution of the Oedipus complex is accomplished by the threat of castration is especially helpful. Gardner Botsford, Gill's senior editor, his symbolic father, poses this threat. To see how Botsford plays this role, we must consider what he is threatening to remove. Botsford enters the scene with Gill's play review "in his hand," and we discover eventually that a part of this review has been illegitimately "buried," and may subsequently be removed, although Gill himself cannot see how to "disinter it." This threat to Gill's writing is charged by the fear of castration precisely because the writer identifies with his writing. It is no accident that the writer's "dumb uncertainty" becomes a paralyzed silence that threatens to erase the most public sign of his identity, as "his name looks as if it could stand some working on." His name, his signature, organizes the evidence of his potency, his ability (in a sense) to reproduce and promulgate himself. Thus, the writer may well "stare" at his name "long and long," once he realizes he may lose it if he cannot control the prose to which it is attached. Gill realizes that the editorial parents may correct and improve his "piece," but the cost may be terrible, as the piece may be separated from the writer, taken over by the authorities who control the emissions of his pen. Gill's image for what he has lost, the dolphin, thus becomes a rather blatant phallic symbol, reemerging as the pen (the grammatical penis) that the "dumb," unnamed writer loses. In other words, the writer must give up his "piece" to be published, to survive as a writer —

but then he is no longer the writer. He cannot get himself into print, so he submits to the authorities of culture, propriety, and correctness, having realized that the self may be cut off from the sign of its identity.

We now may see the fittingness of the error Miss Gould finds: A structure that is "dangling." The writer may see his own fate in the sentence that sticks out, for it suddenly has "assumed the female gender." We would have to agree that the writer who focuses his desire upon grammar and correctness will be impotent, emasculated. The writer, in order to thrive, must get beyond the desire to please the Miss Goulds of the world. We may also see now the fittingness of "Gardner" as the name for the symbolic father: So close to "gardener," Gardner is the one who has the power to prune, to root out, the writer who is stuck on the mother's milk of Miss Gould, grammar. Thus, Gill's story draws on his psychosexual development and an apparently unresolved Oedipus complex to rehearse in powerful terms the advantages of accepting the values of the father and shifting his desire to the reader. Gill evades symbolic castration. "The sentence stands," the father says, saving the writer's pen(is).

Feminist Criticism

I have only recently stopped being amazed at how easily and enthusiastically my students take to feminist criticism. Part of its appeal, I suppose, is its simplicity, at least on the surface: To practice feminist criticism, one need only read as a woman. Such a procedure quickly turns out to have a profound effect on the reader and the text — an effect that hardly can avoid being political. Whatever students' sexual politics might be, feminist criticism unavoidably involves them in significant, timely issues. I do not mean to say that feminist criticism is invariably easy: Reading as a woman, even if one is a woman, may be extremely difficult, requiring the reader to dismantle or discard years of learned behavior. And, of course, I am leaping over the difficult question of what "as a woman" actually means. Since we can't reasonably discuss, as Cheryl Torsney claims, "a single female sexuality" (p. 180), isn't it absurd to assume there is a distinctly feminine way of reading? How can a man even pretend to read "as a woman"?

But these questions need not be answered in order for students to attempt to undo their sexual assumptions, try out new ones, or simply sensitize themselves to the sexual issues present in a work. Feminist criticism thus involves students in reader-response and political criticism. Not all texts, of course, lend themselves easily to feminist criticism, but it is difficult to find one that completely resists a feminist stance. I have found that Gill's passage easily supports a familiar feminist observation, that language itself is phallocentric, as Hélène Cixous and Luce Irigaray have insistently argued. But the passage also repays a more aggressive and perhaps even outrageous (or outraged) approach. Both appear in the following analysis:

> We know not all the writers at *The New Yorker* were men, even some years ago during Brendan Gill's tenure. So, when Gill speaks of "some writer who has made a name for himself in the world," and about the editorial "machinery" that besets "him," Gill is of course referring to writers in the generic sense. One may still assert today, although less confidently than in 1975, that "himself" and "him" in this passage include "herself" and "her." Such a claim, that one sexual marker includes its opposite, is feeble — as if "white" included "black," or "totalitarian" included "democratic." But the motivations for such a claim are revealed even in this brief passage, for Gill's story not only contains this obvious pronominal bias, still accepted by some editors and writers; the story also conveys more subtle messages

about sexuality and sexual roles. It is, in fact, a not-so-subtle attack on the image of women.

Miss Gould functions as a familiar stereotype: the finicky spinster, a Miss Thistlebottom, who has devoted her life to English grammar and its enforcement. She is a copy editor, subservient to the male editor and writer, and her lack of imagination and taste testify to the wisdom of this power structure. This division of labor — male/creative, female/menial — is subtly reinforced by reference to the "hen-tracks" (not rooster tracks) that cover the writer's galley, thus further associating petty correction with the feminine, even though surely some copy editors could have been male. These "hen-tracks" are more than an aggravating correction, as they even come to threaten the writer's very identity. The effects of these hen-tracks, feminine marks of correction, allow Gill to assert the disabling consequences of the feminine upon the masculine: The writers become emotional, and even effeminately hysterical, crying on their blotters. Gill receives comfort and approval from the man, Botsford, but Miss Gould lacks the penetrating insight to deal properly with a problem as small as a grammatical error.

Gill's misogyny influences the passage in other ways. The metaphorical threat to the writer is distinctly gynecological, a "yawning pit." Miss Gould's shortcoming is that she fails maternally, providing indigestible "mother's milk." Even the error that Miss Gould locates is subtly connected to the feminine, for the problem with the sentence is that part of it has "assumed the female gender," which may be seen as the underlying problem for Gill: Something has assumed the female gender. That part of the sentence Miss Gould complains of, naturally, is a "complaint" — which, Gill and Botsford determine, should retain its feminine nature. The complaint itself seems strange: In the mode of feminine busybodies like Miss Gould, the nonagenarian laments not having "enough work to do." Miss Gould, similarly overzealous, has herself done more work than is reasonable, and Botsford's pronouncement that "The sentence stands" returns her to her place, negating her feminine fussiness, reasserting masculine mastery of the phallocentric world of writing.

Conclusion

One might want to point out, I suppose, that in offering this rehearsal of critical "approaches," I am assuming that plurality is better than unity, that the relative is better than the absolute (or even a quest for the absolute). And, given what I think we know about language and knowing, it seems silly to me to assume otherwise: As Jane Tompkins says, articulating a current commonplace, we are not "freestanding autonomous entities, but beings that are culturally constituted by interpretive frameworks or interpretive strategies that our culture makes available to us" (p. 734). In other words, the texts we read — when we look at books, at our world, at ourselves — are likewise constituted by these frameworks or strategies. Obviously, if this "reading" of meaning is correct, plurality offers us a richer universe, allowing us to take greater advantage of the strategies our culture makes available — strategies that do not approach a text, but rather make it what we perceive. Our students therefore should learn how to inhabit the theories mentioned here — and a good many others.

To be sure, such plurality is not always comfortable. Furthermore, if we should agree that the more strategies students can deploy (or be deployed by), the more power and insight they can potentially wield, then must we also agree there are no limits? Are all readings welcome, the more the merrier? My initial impulse is to say, "Yes, we can learn from any reading, from any set of interpretive assumptions. Come one, come all." We can see how readings that seem severely inattentive might offer useful insights:

Robert Crosman reveals, for example, how one student's reading completely missed the significance of the hair on the pillow at the end of "A Rose for Emily," and yet this reading, comparing Emily to the student's grandmother, profoundly enlarged Crosman's understanding of Faulkner's story. We can even imagine how ludicrous errors might stimulate our thinking: My student who thought *The Hamlet* was by Shakespeare did lead me to ask (mostly in an attempt to ease his embarrassment) about Shakespeare's influence on Faulkner — perhaps *The Hamlet* in some sense is by Shakespeare, or is shaped by *Hamlet*. But we must admit that most readings in violation of shared interpretive strategies will usually be seen as inferior, if not wrong, and that finding insight in such violations often seems an act of kindness, a salvage operation.

I can also imagine theoretical possibilities that would not be welcome in my critical home, should they ever appear: Nazi criticism, racist criticism, electroshock criticism, for example. In other words, if we are not freestanding autonomous entities, we are also not entirely helpless, simply the products of the interpretive operations we inherit, "a mere cultural precipitate," as Morse Peckham puts it (p. xviii). I would like to think we can resist; we can change; we can grow; we can, perhaps, in some sense, even get better. We can, that is, attempt to evaluate ways of making meaning, and their particular applications — and if we are very clever and very lucky, we may even modify interpretive frameworks, or possibly even invent new ones.

But only if we have some awareness that such frameworks exist.

References

Brooks, Cleanth. *The Well-Wrought Urn*. New York: Harcourt Brace, 1947.

Crosman, Robert. "How Readers Make Meaning." *College Literature* 9. (1982): 207–15.

Culler, Jonathan. *On Deconstruction: Theory and Criticism after Structuralism*. Ithaca, N.Y.: Cornell University Press, 1982.

Eagleton, Terry. *Literary Theory: An Introduction*. Minneapolis: University of Minnesota Press, 1982.

Freud, Sigmund. "The Dissolution of the Oedipus Complex." *The Freud Reader*. Ed. Peter Gay. New York: Norton, 1989, pp. 661–66.

———. *Introductory Lectures on Psychoanalysis*. Trans. and ed. James Strachey. New York: Norton, 1966.

Frye, Northrop. *Fables of Identity*. New York: Harcourt, 1951.

Gill, Brendan. *Here at the New Yorker*. New York: Random, 1975.

Grimes, Joseph. *The Thread of Discourse*. Paris: Mouton, 1975.

Johnson, Barbara. *The Critical Difference: Essays in the Contemporary Rhetoric of Reading*. Baltimore: Johns Hopkins University Press, 1980.

Peckham, Morse. *Explanation and Power: The Control of Human Behavior*. New York: Seabury, 1979.

Propp, Vladimir. *The Morphology of the Folktale*. Austin: University of Texas Press, 1968.

Tompkins, Jane. "A Short Course in Post-Structuralism." *College English* 50 (Nov. 1988): 733–47.

Torsney, Cheryl. "The Critical Quilt: Alternative Authority in Feminist Criticism." *Contemporary Literary Theory*. Ed. G. Douglas Atkins and Laura Morrow. Amherst: University of Massachusetts press, 1989, pp. 180–99.

Wellek, Rene, and Austin Warren. *Theory of Literature*. 1942. New York: Harcourt, 1977.

WRITING ACROSS THE CURRICULUM

WRITING ACROSS THE CURRICULUM: A BIBLIOGRAPHIC ESSAY

Patricia Bizzell and Bruce Herzberg

[From *The Territory of Language: Linguistics, Stylistics, and the Teaching of Composition.* Ed. Donald A. McQuade. Carbondale: Southern Illinois UP, 1986. 340–52.]

(For biographical information, see page 370.)

In this extensive bibliographical survey, Bizzell and Herzberg define writing across the curriculum (WAC), discuss its several manifestations, and offer an overview of WAC's origins and theoretical premises. They also examine problems associated with WAC initiatives and explore the future of the movement. They conclude their essay with a bibliography, current through 1985. Since Bizzell and Herzberg published their essay, the amount of published work on WAC has increased exponentially. Please see the Bibliography on page 415 for an extensive list of research on WAC.

"Writing across the curriculum" has come to mean three things to writing teachers in America. It denotes, first, a theory of the function of writing in learning; second, a pedagogy to encourage particular uses of writing in learning; and third, a program that applies the pedagogy in a particular school. American interest in the theoretical, pedagogical, and institutional aspects of writing across the curriculum has been growing rapidly in recent years, in part as a response to perceived declines in students' writing ability. Harvey Wiener, president of the Council of Writing Program Administrators, estimates that there are now about four hundred college-level writing-across-the-curriculum programs. Most American scholarship in the field is also recent, appearing after 1975.

The concept of writing across the curriculum was introduced in the 1960s by James Britton and his colleagues at the University of London Institute of Education. They studied language in secondary-level classrooms and found that most speaking, reading, and writing is used to convey information (Barnes et al.). In the London group's seminal work, *The Development of Writing Abilities* (11–18), Britton and his colleagues found that the overwhelming majority of student writing is "transactional," that is, writing used to convey information to a relatively distant and impersonal audience, usually the teacher in the role of examiner. Britton and his colleagues contrasted transactional writing with two other kinds, "poetic" and "expressive." Poetic writing allows the student to step back from the role of active participant in the world, to contemplate and speculate, and to share his or her thoughts with an intimate audience, for example, the teacher in the role of trusted adult. Expressive writing also allows students to explore ideas informally, but in expository modes such as the class journal rather than in fiction or poetry. (For summaries of the London group's work, see Applebee, "Writing"; Rosen; Shafer.)

The London group's studies in developmental psychology and the philosophy of language suggest that adolescents, like younger children, need to use language in personal, exploratory ways, with the support of a friendly audience, in order to learn (Britton). In other words, they need more opportunities for poetic and expressive writing. This need is particularly great for students whose social origins put them at a comparatively greater remove from school conventions of language use. Students need to be able to make connections in their own vernacular between school knowledge and their own interests and values before they can be expected to master transactional writing.

Out of this understanding of the function of the language in learning grew the London group's Writing across the Curriculum Project, headed by Nancy Martin. The Writing across the Curriculum Project published a series of pamphlets demonstrating, with many examples of expressive and poetic writing and talking, the academic benefits of allowing students to use language in the full range of ways. The pamphlets (*Information; Why Write?; Talking; Science; Options*) also suggest assignments for expressive and poetic writing in a variety of disciplines (see also Martin et al.).

A Language for Life, the report of the Bullock Commission, on which Britton served, advocates similar changes in language instruction across the curriculum (see Brunetti). This commission was appointed by then Secretary of State for Education and Science Margaret Thatcher to respond to Britain's version of the "back-to-basics" furor. Britton wrote the Bullock Report's chapters on early language development and collaborated on chapters dealing with writing instruction and language across the curriculum.

Britton and his colleagues were influenced by James Moffett's curriculum for *Teaching the Universe of Discourse* on the elementary and secondary levels, a curriculum recently detailed, with suggestions for college use, in Moffett's *Active Voice*. Moffett sorts language along a continuum from private, oral, concrete uses to public, written, abstract uses. Students will more easily master the full range of uses if they are encouraged to begin with those closest to their own speech. These beginning forms of language use are what Britton would call expressive — such as dialogues and letters — and poetic — such as plays and fictional autobiographies. Like Britton, Moffett does not aim to replace all transactional writing with expressive and poetic writing, but rather to help students feel comfortable with the full range of ways to use language to explore and communicate ideas.

Janet Emig was one of the first American theorists to make use of Britton's work. In *The Composing Processes of Twelfth Graders*, she revises Britton's classification of language uses. Her "reflexive" resembles his expressive, and her "extensive" resembles his transactional. Like Britton, she finds that when secondary-level students are given more opportunities to write reflexively, they engage in a more thoughtful writing process, write better and feel better about what they write, and learn more. Emig's argument for the importance of reflexive or expressive writing, however, differs from Britton's. In her seminal essay, "Writing as a Mode of Learning," Emig looks more to cognitive than to developmental psychology for evidence of the importance of all ways to use writing in learning. Whereas the London group emphasizes the continuity between speech and writing, Emig emphasizes the unique cognitive advantages conferred by writing. Writing requires imagining the audience and reinforces learning by involving hand, eye, and brain. The written text facilitates reflecting on and reformulating ideas. Writing thus becomes a central means to constitute and propagate knowledge.

Emig agrees with Britton that students must be given more opportunities to write reflexively (expressively) in all disciplines. Several studies have confirmed her finding that American students on the secondary and college levels do not have such opportunities now, because the great majority of the writing they do is transactional (Donlan; Tighe and Koziol; Eblen). The most comprehensive of these studies is Arthur N. Applebee's *Writing in the Secondary Schools: English and the Content Areas.* American interest in writing across the curriculum has been strengthened by the conjunction of findings that most student writing is transactional, and of widespread feelings that student writing ability is declining. Suspecting a causal relationship, many composition administrators have argued for a program to inform college faculty in all disciplines of the need for expressive and poetic writing, as well as the usual transactional assignments.

In addition to encouraging cross-disciplinary uses of expressive and poetic writing, some work on writing across the curriculum explores uses of language peculiar to the academy. The aim of this work is to reform freshman composition pedagogy as well as writing instruction in courses outside the English department. Elaine Maimon has argued that this new freshman composition pedagogy should teach academic discourse (*Instructor's Manual*). She explains that each academic discipline has its own way of making sense of experience, which is embodied in the discourse conventions of the discipline. Moreover, some discourse conventions are shared by all academic disciplines — that is, there is an academic discourse as well as disciplinary discourses. A. D. Van Nostrand argues that studying academic discourse teaches students how to find — or create — significant relationships between facts, rather than simply to report facts. The freshman composition course, where students learn what ways of relating facts are significant in the academy, is the place where they are initiated into academic discourse (Bizzell).

Writing program administrators have been eagerly exchanging ideas on how to implement the various aims of writing across the curriculum. A national network of writing-across-the-curriculum programs has been formed; several newsletters circulate. College-level writing-across-the-curriculum programs typically take one of two forms, Laurence Peters has found. One common kind of program is centered in an interdisciplinary freshman composition course. The other is centered in upper-level writing-intensive courses in various disciplines.

The most complete account of an interdisciplinary freshman composition course can be found in *Writing in the Arts and Sciences,* a textbook by Elaine Maimon and several of her colleagues from other departments at Beaver College. The book begins with the section "Writing to Learn," which discusses cross-disciplinary uses of expressive writing, heuristics, and informal academic writing, such as class notes and library work. The second major section, "Learning to Write," comprises chapters on discipline-specific discourse such as the humanities research paper, the social science case study, and the natural science laboratory report. A few other textbooks for writing across the curriculum have appeared, and more are likely to come out in the near future (Behrens; Bizzell and Herzberg). Another model for the interdisciplinary course has been developed by David Hamilton: students practice "serious parodies" of disciplinary discourse in order to grasp the underlying conceptual activities specific to each discipline (See also Rose, "Remedial Writing").

Writing-across-the-curriculum programs based in upper-level writing-intensive courses frequently stress the importance of expressive writing in all disciplines. Toby Fulwiler has shown how journals can be used both to explore academic content and to relate knowledge to one's own values ("Journals"). With Art Young, he has also edited a collection of essays on the teaching of poetic, expressive, and transactional writing in the Michigan Technological University writing-across-the-curriculum program. On the other hand, in collections such as those edited by C. William Griffin (*Teaching Writing*) and by Christopher Thaiss, the assumption is not necessarily that expressive writing needs to be increased. Rather, teachers in all disciplines should use writing for learning in ways particularly useful in their disciplines. (See also Odell.)

Faculty development has become an important aspect of writing across the curriculum. Professors who have not been trained to teach writing, whether they teach literature or other academic disciplines, often have too narrow a notion of "good" writing as grammatically correct writing. If they do not see themselves as writers, experiencing the complexities of the composing process, they often do not appreciate students' need for guidance through this process. They may be reluctant to take on the extra work of teaching writing, or fear that it will take time away from essential course content. They may be wary of the writing program administrator's expanded influence in college affairs.

This need for faculty development has prompted much work on how to start a writing-across-the-curriculum program and conduct writing workshops for faculty from all disciplines. Elaine Maimon has given practical advice on coping with intracampus politics ("Cinderella"; "Writing"). Some workshops, such as those conducted by Anne Herrington and Ann Raimes, seek to sensitize faculty to the ways they are teaching academic discourse and to make their assignment design and essay evaluation more effective through discussion of examples from their own courses (see also Rose, "Faculty Talk"; Walvoord). Another kind of workshop aims to develop faculty's view of themselves as writers by asking them to write expressively and to critique each other's work. Toby Fulwiler has been an influential proponent of such workshops ("Showing"). (See also Bergman, "Inclusive Literacy"; Freisinger.)

This American work on pedagogical and institutional concerns has relied for its theoretical underpinnings on the scholarship by Britton — by far the most frequently cited authority — Emig, and Moffett. Their work has helped us to understand the function of writing in the intellectual development of the individual student. But Britton, Emig, and Moffett have done most of their work on the elementary and secondary level. We are only now beginning to realize that new American theoretical work in writing across the curriculum is needed, work which addresses concerns particular to American, college-level writing instruction. This new theoretical work is beginning to take shape around the question of whether all students should be required to learn academic discourse. Mina Shaughnessy has diagnosed basic writers' fundamental problem as ignorance of academic discourse conventions.

In exploring this question, theorists are reexamining the importance of expressive writing in writing-across-the-curriculum programs. Expressive writing plays a part in most programs. It can be regarded as one important stage in a writing process which will issue eventually in finished pieces of academic writing. But C. H. Knoblauch and Lil Brannon have argued that keeping up a student-teacher dialogue through expressive writing should be the main goal of writing across the curriculum, because it is through such dialogue that inquiry methods are learned. They see the teaching of academic discourse as drill in "formal shells," leading to nothing more than "grammar across the curriculum." They fear that students whose home languages are at a relatively greater remove from academic discourse will be unduly penalized by a policy which requires all students to master academic discourse. These students will spend so much time on superficial aspects of academic discourse, such as Standard English usage, that they will have little time left for substantive learning.

Other theorists argue that learning and discourse conventions cannot be separated in the academy. Students must be able eventually to use academic discourse if they are to master the full complexities of academic thinking. The notion of dialogue or conversation as a mode of learning here is redefined to mean not a face-to-face encounter, but a sustained communal enterprise. Charles Bazerman has explained that learning how to enter this ongoing conversation means learning how the academic community talks and writes about what it does. As Elaine Maimon has argued, this is a matter of "Talking to Strangers" for students unfamiliar with the academic discourse community. But if students are not required to learn this discourse, they risk not participating fully in college intellectual life. To help them, we need more study of how this community develops and transmits its discourse conventions, a study in which scholars trained in literary criticism may be particularly well suited to engage (Maimon, "Maps and Genres").

Such study would help to return rhetoric to its eminent place in the curriculum. James Raymond has argued that rhetoric is the least reductive, most interdisciplinary methodology in the liberal arts. Taking a similar position, James Kinneavy has observed that increased attention to rhetoric helps faculty in all disciplines to communicate better with each other about the intellectual problems upon which they are working. They are thus better prepared to train their students not only to develop complex arguments within the disciplines but also to explain their areas of expertise cogently to a general audience. Kinneavy hopes that the spread of writing-across-the-curriculum programs will eventually revivify informed public discourse in our democracy, since citizens will be better able to sift evidence and evaluate debates on complex issues.

The study of "rhetoric across the curriculum," to coin a phrase, is becoming the study of how the academic community constitutes and legitimates its knowledge through its discourse. We are learning, as Kenneth Bruffee has shown, that knowledge is a "social entity," always collaboratively produced. From such study, too, we learn how other communities similarly constitute themselves in language. Because this is becoming the focus of rhetoric, literary critics have recently been studying it together with composition specialists. In one such fruitful exchange (Horner), eminent scholars agree that the establishment of English departments was justified by a false distinction between literary discourse and discourse that conveys information. This distinction leads to a separation between reading instruction, which focuses upon interpreting literary texts, and writing instruction, which focuses upon producing expository texts. Because this separation not only devalues composition studies but also impoverishes literary theory, it is now ending. A new kind of English department is emerging, united under a rhetorical paradigm, and well suited to study all kinds of discourse, not just fiction and poetry, and to foster rhetoric across the curriculum.

Bibliography

Applebee, Arthur N. "Writing across the Curriculum: The London Projects." *English Journal* 66 (1977): 81–85.

———. *Writing in the Secondary School: English and the Content Areas.* Urbana NCTE, 1981. Eighty-two percent of teachers surveyed agree that writing instruction is the responsibility of all faculty. But only 3 percent of lesson time is spent on writing of paragraph length or more. Very little attention is given to the writing process. Virtually all writing is informational (transactional), for an audience of teacher-as-examiner.

Barnes, Douglas, James Britton, and Harold Rosen. *Language, the Learner, and the School.* Harmondsworth: Penguin, 1969.

Bazerman, Charles. "A Relationship between Reading and Writing: The Conversation Model." *College English* 41 (1980): 656–61.

Behrens, Laurence. "Meditations, Reminiscences, Polemics: Composition Readers and the Service Course." *College English* 41 (1980): 561–70. Surveying composition readers, Behrens finds that almost all selections are meditations, reminiscences, or polemics. Most of the writing that students do in other courses, however, seeks to convey information, and students are better at conveying information than they are at writing meditations, reminiscences, and polemics. A new kind of reader is needed to "serve" students by teaching the kinds of writing they do in other courses.

Bergman, Charles A. "An Inclusive Literacy: U.S. Schools Are Teaching and Writing in All the Subject Disciplines." *AAHE Bulletin* (Dec 1982): 3–5. Bergman argues for writing across the curriculum as a way of demystifying the conventions of academic discourse, and describes the "conversation experience" of faculty at his university after a workshop with Kenneth Bruffee in which they learned to see themselves as writers.

———. "Writing across the Curriculum: An Annotated Bibliography." *AAHE Bulletin* (1983–84): 33–38. Bergman selects forty-one entries, citing some important theoretical works and a number of articles that describe writing-across-the-curriculum programs at specific schools.

Bizzell, Patricia. "College Composition: Initiation into the Academic Discourse Community." *Curriculum Inquiry* 12 (1982): 191–207. Bizzell argues that students' unequal distance from school discourse is a function of social class, that access to academic discourse is a prerequisite for social power, and that linguistically disenfranchised students can be helped by a writing-across-the-curriculum approach that seeks to demystify the conventions of academic discourse.

Bizzell, Patricia, and Bruce Herzberg. "Writing-across-the-Curriculum Textbooks: A Bibliographic Essay." *Rhetoric Review* 3 (Jan. 1985): 202–17.

Britton, James. *Language and Learning.* Harmondsworth: Penguin, 1970. Britton develops the theory that we construct our understanding of the world through language, an individual task shaped by social interaction.

Britton, James, et al. *The Development of Writing Abilities* (11–18). London: Macmillan Education, 1975; Urbana: NCTE, 1977.

Bruffee, Kenneth. "The Structure of Knowledge and the Future of Liberal Education." *Liberal Education* 67 (1981): 177–86. We have assumed that knowledge is determined by external reality and should be attained by individual effort in a hierarchical educational system. But the work of Einstein, Heisenberg, and Godel suggests that knowledge is created and promulgated through social activity. Hence education should be restructured for collaborative work, as in peer-tutoring workshops and writing-across-the-curriculum programs.

Brunetti, Gerald J. "The Bullock Report: Some Implications for American Teachers and Parents." *English Journal* 67 (1978): 58–64.

Bullock Commission. *A Language for Life.* London: HMSO, 1975.

Donlan, Dan. "Teaching Writing in the Content Areas: Eleven Hypotheses from a Teacher Survey." *Research in the Teaching of English* 8 (1974): 250–62.

Dunn, Robert F. "A Response to Two Views." *AAHE Bulletin* (Dec. 1982): 7–8.

Eblen, Charlene. "Writing-across-the-Curriculum: A Survey of a University Faculty's Views and Classroom Practices." *Research in the Teaching of English* 17 (1983): 343–48.

Emig, Janet. *The Composing Processes of Twelfth Graders.* Urbana: NCTE, 1971.

————. "Writing as a Mode of Learning." *College Composition and Communication* 28 (1977): 122–28. Rpt. in *The Writing Teacher's Sourcebook.* Ed. Gary Tate and E. P. J. Corbett. New York: Oxford UP, 1981. 69–78.

Freisinger, Randall R. "Cross-Disciplinary Writing Workshops: Theory and Practice." *College English* 42 (1980): 154+. Following Britton, Freisinger strongly defends the use of expressive writing in all disciplines, in spite of faculty resistance to this notion. He uses Piaget to argue that the absence of expressive writing retards cognitive development in college-age students.

Fulwiler, Toby. "Journals across the Disciplines." *English Journal* 69 (1980): 14–19. Fulwiler cites Britton and Emig on the need for expressive writing across the curriculum, and argues that journals have served this end well. He describes both the "academic journal," which focuses on course content, and the "personal journal," which focuses on ethical responses to course content.

————. "Showing, Not Telling, at a Writing Workshop." *College English* 43 (1981): 55–63. A good account of Fulwiler's methods in faculty workshops. He details five strategies and recommends conducting the workshop like a retreat.

Fulwiler, Toby, and Art Young, ed. *Language Connections: Writing and Reading across the Curriculum.* Urbana: NCTE, 1982. Twelve essays from the Michigan Tech writing-across-the-curriculum program, written by professors of literature, rhetoric, and reading. Essays address the interdisciplinary teaching of poetic, expressive, and transactional writing. The book includes three essays on reading, two on peer critiquing, and a selected bibliography.

Griffin, C. Williams, ed. *Teaching Writing in All Disciplines.* San Francisco: Jossey-Bass, 1982. Ten essays on writing-across-the-curriculum theory and practice, including John C. Bean, Dean Drenk, and F. D. Lee, "Microtheme Strategies for Developing Cognitive Skills"; Toby Fulwiler, "Writing: An Act of Cognition"; Elaine Maimon, "Writing across the Curriculum: Past, Present, and Future"; Chris Thaiss, "The Virginia Consortium of Faculty Writing Programs: A Variety of Practices"; Barbara Fassler Walvoord and Hoke L. Smith, "Coaching the Process of Writing."

Hamilton, David. "Interdisciplinary Writing." *College English* 41 (1980): 780+. Hamilton describes the Iowa Institute on Writing for writing program administrators, which developed an interdisciplinary freshman composition course using "serious parodies" of discourse modes of various disciplines, with the aim of teaching transferable processes of conceptualization. The article also analyzes the limitations of other interdisciplinary writing courses, such as those that ask students to write about their areas of expertise for a lay audience.

Herrington, Anne J. "Writing to Learn: Writing across the Disciplines." *College English* 43 (1981): 379–87. Following a defense of writing across the curriculum that draws on the work of Emig and Lee Odell, Herrington describes her workshops to help faculty design writing-intensive courses in their own disciplines. She describes good assignments in economics, sociology, and psychology.

Horner, Winifred, ed. *Composition and Literature: Bridging the Gap.* Chicago: U of Chicago P, 1983. Twelve essays by eminent literary critics and composition specialists, including Wayne Booth, E. P. J. Corbett, E. D. Hirsch, Jr., Richard Lanham, Elaine Maimon, and J. Hillis Miller.

Kinneavy, James L. "Writing across the Curriculum" *ADE Bulletin* 76 (1983): 14–21 Rpt. in *Profession* 83. Ed. Richard Brod and Phyllis Franklin. New York: MLA, 1983: 13–20.

Knoblauch, C. H., and Lil Brannon. "Writing as Learning through the Curriculum." *College English* 45 (1983): 465–74.

Maimon, Elaine. "Cinderella to Hercules: Demythologizing Writing across the Curriculum." *Journal of Basic Writing* 2 (1980): 3–11. Maimon describes and debunks several "myths" that obstruct writing-across-the-curriculum programs, such as the Myth of the Simple Rules, which leads misguided college deans to think that writing across the curriculum is simply a matter of enforcing a few grammar guidelines; the Myth of Cinderella, which casts writing teachers in a menial role; the Myth of Hercules, which envisions an effective program being launched by the writing program administrator alone; and more. This issue of *JBW* includes seven other essays on writing across the curriculum.

————."Maps and Genres" *Composition and Literature: Bridging the Gap.* Ed. Winifred Horner. Chicago: U of Chicago P, 1983: 110–25.

————."Talking to Strangers." *College Composition and Communication* 30 (1979): 364–69.

————."Writing in All the Arts and Sciences: Getting Started and Gaining Momentum." *Writing Program Administration* 4 (1981): 9–13. Maimon discusses administrative problems of launching writing-across-the-curriculum programs; how to deal with resistance within the English department; general curriculum guidelines. This issue of *WPA* also includes Toby Fulwiler, "Writing across the Curriculum at Michigan Tech," an account of his successful faculty seminars there; and a response to both Fulwiler and Maimon by Ann Raimes.

————. *Instructor's Manual: Writing in the Arts and Sciences.* Cambridge: Winthrop, 1981. Maimon, Elaine P., and Gerald L. Belcher, Gail W. Hearn, Barbara F. Nodine, and Finbarr W. O'Connor. *Writing in the Arts and Sciences.* Cambridge: Winthrop, 1981.

Martin, Nancy, et al. *Writing and Learning across the Curriculum 11–16.* London: Ward Lock, 1976.

Moffett, James. *Active Voice: A Writing Program across the Curriculum.* Upper Montclair: Boynton/Cook, 1981.

————. *Teaching the Universe of Discourse.* Boston: Houghton, 1969.

Odell, Lee "The Process of Writing and the Process of Learning." *College Composition and Communication* 31 (1980): 42–50. In faculty writing workshops, Odell discovered that writing in different disciplines requires a wide variety of conceptual activities; the inability to perform them is the chief cause of bad student writing. Workshops should not, therefore, seek to persuade faculty to teach any one heuristic method. Elements from a few powerful heuristics, however, can be combined to provide an invention method useful across the disciplines.

Peters, Laurence. "Writing across the Curriculum: Across the U.S." Writing to *Learn: Essays and Reflections by College Teachers across the Curriculum.* Ed. Christopher Thaiss. Fairfax: George Mason U Faculty Writing Program, 1982. 4–19.

Raimes, Ann. "Writing and Learning across the Curriculum: The Experience of a Faculty Seminar." *College English* 41 (1980): 797–801. To attend a seminar led by Raimes and Charles Persky, faculty in several disciplines received released time during the semester so that they could work on writing assignments and use student writing from current courses as the principal "text." Discussions focused on assignment design and essay evaluation.

Raymond, James C. "Rhetoric: The Methodology of the Humanities." *College English* 44 (1982): 778–83.

Rose, Mike. "Remedial Writing Courses: A Critique and a Proposal." *College English* 45 (1983): 109–28. Rose argues against the focus on personal writing common to many remedial composition programs, and for an interdisciplinary course that introduces developmental students immediately to college-level reading, writing, and thinking tasks.

————. "When Faculty Talk about Writing." *College English* 41 (1979) 272–79. A cross-disciplinary group of faculty, teaching assistants, and student counselors met to discuss their perceptions of student writing problems and agreed on some action — give professional recognition for composition teaching and research; teach academic discourse in freshman composition; and move university-wide standards for evaluating writing beyond a narrow focus on grammar.

Rosen, Lois. "An Interview with James Britton, Tony Burgess, and Harold Rosen. Closeup: The Teaching of Writing in Great Britain." *English Journal* 67 (1978): 50–58.

Shafer, Robert E. "A British Proposal for Improving Literacy." *Educational Forum* 46 (1981): 81–96 Shafer summarizes work of Britton and his colleagues, giving particular attention to theory. He discusses Britton's spectator/participant distinction; the work of Barnes and Rosen on the chasm between academic discourse and the students' own language; the influence of Sapir, Kelly, and Vygotsky; and the relation between speaking and writing.

Shaughnessy, Mina. "Some Needed Research on Writing." *College Composition and Communication* 28 (1977): 317–21. Shaughnessy argues that basic writers are those "unskilled in the rituals and ways of winning arguments in academe." To help them, we need a taxonomy of academic discourse conventions.

Thaiss, Christopher, ed. *Writing to Learn: Essays and Reflections by College Teachers across the Curriculum.* Fairfax: George Mason U Faculty Writing Program, 1982. Sixteen essays by professors of accounting, education, English, finance, mathematics, nursing, physical education, and psychology. They argue for the value of writing across the curriculum while describing classroom ideas that have worked well.

Tighe, M. A, and S. M. Koziol, Jr. "Practices in the Teaching of Writing by Teachers of English, Social Studies, and Science." *English Education* 4 (1982): 76–85.

Van Nostrand, A. D. "Writing and the Generation of Knowledge." *Social Education* 43 (1979): 178–80. This article heads a special section, "Writing to Learn in Social Studies," edited by Barry K. Beyer and Anita Brostoff, and aimed at secondary-level teachers.

Walvoord, Barbara E. Fassler. *Helping Students Write Well: A Guide for Teachers in All Disciplines.* New York: MLA, 1982. A good book for faculty who have not yet thought about how they teach writing. Walvoord concentrates on ways to respond effectively to student writing above the developmental level. Many specific examples of assignments and student papers.

Writing across the Curriculum Project. *From Information to Understanding: What Children Do with New Ideas.* London: Ward Lock, 1973; Upper Montclair: Boynton/Cook, 1983.

———. *Why Write?* London: Ward Lock, 1973; Upper Montclair Boynton/Cook, 1983. Children should be encouraged to write about knowledge important to them, rather than forced to learn particular essay forms.

———. *From Talking to Writing.* London: Ward Lock, 1973; Upper Montclair: Boynton/Cook, 1983. This pamphlet argues for expressive talk, but also argues that some kinds of thinking can only be accomplished in writing, because writing facilitates reflection and reformulation. Writing assignments should call on these unique powers rather than simply asking for a report on what has been learned.

———. *Writing in Science: Papers from a Seminar with Science Teachers.* London: Ward Lock, 1973.

———. *Keeping Options Open: Writing in the Humanities.* London: Ward Lock, 1973; Upper Montclair: Boynton/Cook, 1983.

STRANGERS IN ACADEMIA:
THE EXPERIENCES OF FACULTY AND
ESL STUDENTS ACROSS THE CURRICULUM

Vivian Zamel

[*College Composition and Communication* 46 (December 1995): 506–21.]

Professor of English Vivian Zamel directs the English as a Second Language Program at the University of Massachusetts–Boston.

She also teaches composition courses for ESL students and graduate courses in ESL theory and pedagogy. She has published widely on ESL writing and pedagogy in journals and collections, and has coauthored *The Discovery of Competence: Teaching and Learning with Diverse Student Writers* (1993).

In her work with faculty who are concerned about "underprepared" or "deficient" non-native language users, Zamel discovered that their discussions regularly led to "a consideration of the same kinds of pedagogical issues that are at the heart of writing across the curriculum initiatives." In an effort to understand more fully the experiences of faculty and ESL students across the curriculum, Zamel examines two opposing faculty views of ESL students and their use of language. Some faculty see ESL students in larger contexts and value their knowledge and abilities, in spite of their struggles with conventional academic language; other faculty continue to equate these struggles with abilities in language and cognitive/intellectual pursuits. Her survey of students confirms that the latter view is more prevalent among faculty, at least according to the courses and assignments that students encounter. Zamel proposes that faculty consider alternative ways to think about ESL students. Countering the inevitable argument from faculty that they would be compromising some sort of "standards," Zamel says that ESL students need "classroom exchanges and assignments that promote the acquisition of unfamiliar language, concepts, and approaches to inquiry."

When I go into a classroom these days, I look around and feel like I'm in a different country.

– Professor of Management

A few weeks ago a professor came by the reading, writing and study skills center where I tutor. He was with a young Asian woman, obviously one of his students. He "deposited" her in the center, claiming that she desperately needed help with her English. The woman stared into the distance with a frightened, nervous look on her face and tried to force a smile. She handed me a paper she had written on the labor union and asked if I could help her make corrections. After a short introductory discussion, we looked at the paper that we were about to revise — it was filled with red marks indicating spelling, punctuation, and grammar errors; the only written response was something along the lines of "You need serious help with your English. Please see a tutor."

– From a tutor's journal

Students in the lab speak to one another in their own language so that they make sure they know what they are doing. So they may look like they are not listening to the lab teacher. He feels so isolated from them. He feels he has no control, no power. So he may get angry.

– An ESL student

These comments show evidence of tensions and conflicts that are becoming prevalent in institutions of higher education as student populations become more diverse. One clear indication that faculty across the disciplines are concerned about the extent to which diverse student populations, particularly students whose native language is not English, constrain their work is the number of workshops and seminars that have been organized, and at which I have participated, in order to address what these faculty view as the "ESL Problem."[1] In the course of preparing to work with faculty, and in order to get a sense of their issues and concerns, I surveyed instructors about their experiences working with non-native speakers of English. As Patricia Laurence has pointed out, though we acknowledge and discuss the diversity of students, "we neglect the 'polyphony'" that represents faculty voices (24). While I did not receive many responses to my request for feedback, those responses that were returned did indeed reflect this polyphony.

Some faculty saw this invitation to provide feedback as an opportunity to discuss the strengths and resources these students brought with them, indicated that ESL students, because of their experience and motivation, were a positive presence in their classes, and noted the contributions ESL students made in discussions that invited cross-cultural perspectives. One professor took issue with the very idea of making generalizations about ESL students. But this pattern of response did not represent the attitudes and perspectives revealed by other faculty responses. One professor, for example, referred to both silent students, on the one hand, and "vocal but incomprehensible students" on the other. But, by far, the greatest concern had to do with students' writing and language, which faculty saw as deficient and inadequate for undertaking the work in their courses. I got the clear sense from these responses that language use was confounded with intellectual ability — that, as Victor Villanueva, recounting his own schooling experiences, puts it, "bad language" and "insufficient cognitive development" were being conflated (11).

In order to demonstrate the range of faculty commentary, I've selected two faculty responses, not because they are necessarily representative, but because they reveal such divergent views on language, language development, and the role that faculty see themselves as playing in this development. I've also chosen these responses because they may serve as mirrors for our own perspectives and belief systems, and thus help us examine more critically what we ourselves think and do, both within our own classrooms and with respect to the larger institutional contexts in which we teach. In other words, although these responses came from two different disciplines, it is critical for each of us to examine the extent to which we catch glimpses of our own practices and assumptions in these texts. The first response was written by an English Department instructor:

> One of my graduate school professors once told me that he knew within the first two weeks of the semester what his students' final grades would be. Recently I had a Burmese-born Chinese student who proved my professor wrong. After the first two essays, there was certainly no reason to be optimistic about this student's performance. The essays were very short, filled with second language errors, thesaurus words, and sweeping generalizations. In the first essay, it was obvious he had been taught to make outlines because that's all the paper was, really — a list. In the second essay, instead of dealing directly with the assigned text, the student directed most of his energy to form and structure. He had an introduction even though he had nothing to introduce. In his conclusion, he was making wild assertions (even though he had nothing to base them on) because he knew conclusions were supposed to make a point. By the fourth essay, he started to catch on to the fact that my comments were directed toward the content of his essays, not the form. Once he stopped worrying about thesis sentences, vocabulary, and the like, he became a different writer. His papers were long, thoughtful, and engaging. He was able to interpret and respond to texts and to make connections that I term "double face" as a way to comment on the ways in which different cultures define such terms

as "respect." Instead of 1 1/4 pages, this essay was seven pages, and it made several references to the text while synthesizing it with his experience as someone who is a product of three cultures. This change not only affected the content of his writing, but also his mechanics. Though there were still errors, there were far fewer of them, and he was writing well enough where I felt it was safe to raise questions about structure and correctness.

This response begins with the recognition that we need to be wary of self-fulfilling prophecies about the potential of students, and indeed this instructor's narrative demonstrates compellingly the dangers of such prophecies. This instructor goes on to cite problems with the student's performance, but he speculates that these problems may have to do with previous instruction, thus reflecting a stance that counteracts the tendency to blame students. Despite the student's ongoing difficulties, the instructor does not despair over the presence of second language errors, over the short essays, the "sweeping generalizations," the empty introduction, the "wild assertions." Instead, this instructor seems to persist in his attempts to focus the student on content issues, to respond to the student seriously, to push him to consider the connections between what he was saying and the assigned reading, to take greater risks, which he succeeds in doing "by the fourth essay." In this, I believe, we see the instructor's understanding that it takes multiple opportunities for students to trust that he is inviting them into serious engagement with the course material, that it takes time to acquire new approaches to written work. What seems to be revealed in this response is the instructor's belief in the student's potential, his appreciation for how language and learning are promoted, his refusal to draw conclusions about intellectual ability on the basis of surface features of language — all of which, in turn, helped the student become a "different writer," a change that affected the content of his writing, that had an impact on the very errors that filled his first papers, that even illuminated the instructor's reading of the assigned texts. This response suggests a rich and complicated notion of language, one that recognizes that language evolves in and responds to the context of saying something meaningful, that language and meaning are reciprocal and give rise to one another.

This response, especially the final section about surface level errors, foreshadows the other faculty response, which was written by an art history instructor and which reveals a very different set of assumptions and expectations:

> My experience with teaching ESL students is that they have often not received adequate English instruction to complete the required essay texts and papers in my classes. I have been particularly dismayed when I find that they have already completed 2 ESL courses and have no knowledge of the parts of speech or the terminology that is used in correcting English grammar on papers. I am certainly not in a position to teach English in my classes. (The problem has been particularly acute with Chinese/S. E. Asian students.) These students may have adequate intelligence to do well in the courses, but their language skills result in low grades. (I cannot give a good grade to a student who can only generate one or two broken sentences during a ten-minute slide comparison.)

The first assumption I see in this response is the belief that language and knowledge are separate entities, that language must be in place and fixed in order to do the work in the course. This static notion of language is further revealed by the instructor's assumption that language use is determined by a knowledge of parts of speech or grammatical terminology. Given this belief, it is understandable why she is dismayed by what she characterizes as students' lack of knowledge of grammar, a conclusion she has seemingly reached because her corrective feedback, presumably making use of grammatical terms, has not proven successful. This practice itself is not questioned, however; students or their inadequate English language instruction are held accountable instead. If students had been prepared appropriately, if the gatekeeping efforts had kept students out of her course until they were more like their native language counterparts, her commentary suggests, students would be able to do the required work. There is little sense of how the unfamiliar terms, concepts, and ways of seeing that are particular to this course can be acquired. Nor is there an appreciation for how this very unfamiliarity with the course content may be constraining students' linguistic processes. She does not see, focusing as she does on difference, how she can contribute to students' language and written development, how she can build on what they know. Despite indicating that students may have "adequate intelligence to do well in the course," she doesn't seem to be able to get past their language problems when it comes to evaluating their work, thus missing the irony of grading on the basis of that which she acknowledges she is not "in a position to teach." The final parenthetical statement reveals further expectations about student work, raising questions about the extent to which her very expectations, rather than linguistic difficulties alone, contribute to the "broken sentences" to which she refers.

What we see at work here is in marked contrast to the model of possibility revealed in the first response. What seems to inform this second response is a deficit model of language and learning whereby students' deficiencies are foregrounded. This response is shaped by an essentialist view of language in which language is understood to be a decontextualized skill that can be taught in isolation from the production of meaning and that must be in place in order to undertake intellectual work. What we see here is an illustration of "the myth of transience," a belief that permeates institutions of higher education and perpetuates the notion that these students' problems are temporary and can be remediated — so long as some isolated set of courses or program of instruction, but not the real courses in the academy, takes on the responsibility of doing so (see Rose, "Language"). Such a belief supports the illusion that permanent solutions are possible, which releases faculty from the ongoing struggle and questioning that the teaching-learning process inevitably involves.

In these two faculty responses, we see the ways in which different sets of expectations and attitudes get played out. In the one classroom, we get some sense of what can happen when opportunities for learning are created, when students are invited into a thoughtful process of engaging texts, when students' writing is read and responded to in meaningful and supportive ways. In the other classroom, although we have little information about the conditions for learning, we are told that one way that learning is measured is by technically correct writing done during a 10-minute slide presentation, and this, I believe, is telling. For students who are not adequately prepared to do this work, there is little, the instructor tells us, she can do. Given this deterministic stance, students are closed off from participating in intellectual work.

At the same time that I was soliciting faculty responses to get a sense of their perceptions and assumptions, I began to survey ESL students about what they wanted faculty to know about their experiences and needs in classrooms across the curriculum. I wanted, in other words, to capture the polyphony of students' voices as well. I felt that the work I was engaging in with faculty could not take place without an exploration of students' views, especially since, although faculty have little reservation discussing what they want and expect from students, informing us about their frustrations and disappointments, the students' perspective is one that faculty often hear little about. And since I have become convinced that our role in our institutions ought not to be defined solely by the service we perform for other faculty (either by making our students' English native-like or keeping the gates closed until this is accomplished) but in helping faculty understand the role they need to begin to play in working with all students, the students' perspective was critical.

Within the last two years, I have collected more than 325 responses from first and second year ESL students enrolled in courses across a range of disciplines.[2] I discovered from looking at these responses a number of predominant and recurring themes. Students spoke of patience, tolerance, and encouragement as key factors that affected their learning:

> Teachers need to be more sensitive to ESL students needs of education. Since ESL students are face with the demands of culture ajustment, especially in the classroom, teaches must be patients and give flexible consideration . . . .For example — if a teacher get a paper that isn't clear or didn't follow the assignment correctly, teacher must talk and communicate with the students.

Students articulated the kinds of assistance they needed, pointing, for example, to clearer and more explicitly detailed assignments and more accessible classroom talk:

> In the classes, most teachers go over material without explaining any words that seems hard to understand for us . . . .I want college teachers should describe more clearly on questions in the exams, so we can understand clearly. Also, I think the teachers should write any important information or announcement on the board rather than just speaking in front of class, because sometimes we understand in different way when we hear it than when we read it.

Students spoke with pride about how much they knew and how much they had accomplished through working, they felt, harder than their native English-speaking counterparts did, and they wanted faculty to credit and acknowledge them for this.

> I would like them to know that we are very responsible and we know why we come to college: to learn. We are learning English as well as the major of our choice. It is very hard sometimes and we don't need professors who claimed that they don't understand us. The effort is double. We are very intelligent people. We deserve better consideration . . . ESL students are very competent and deserve to be in college. We made the step to college. Please make the other step to meet us.

At the same time, an overwhelming number of students wanted faculty to know that they were well aware they were having language difficulties and appreciated responses that would help them. But they also expressed their wish that their work not be discounted and viewed as limited. They seemed to have a very strong sense that because of difficulties that were reflected in their attempts at classroom participation and in their written work, their struggles with learning were misperceived and underestimated:

> The academic skills of students who are not native speakers of English are not worse than academic skills of American students, in some areas it can be much better. Just because we have problems with language . . . that some professors hate because they don't want to spend a minute to listen a student, doesn't mean that we don't understand at all.

Students referred to professors who showed concern and seemed to appreciate students' contributions. But the majority of students' responses described classrooms that silenced them, that made them feel fearful and inadequate, that limited possibilities for engagement, involvement, inclusion.

While these students acknowledged that they continue to experience difficulties, they also voiced their concern that these struggles not be viewed as deficiencies, that their efforts be understood as serious attempts to grapple with these difficulties. While faculty may feel overwhelmed by and even resentful of working with such students, these students indicated that they expect and need their instructors to assist them in this undertaking, even making suggestions as to how this can be done. Indeed, the very kind of clarity, accessible language, careful explanation, and effort that faculty want students to demonstrate are the kinds of assistance students were asking of faculty. Without dismissing the concerns of the art instructor, these students nevertheless believed, as does the English instructor, that teaching ought to be responsive to their concerns.

Yet another source of information about students' classroom experiences comes from my ongoing case-study of two students who attended a composition course I taught two years ago and who have met with me regularly since that time to discuss the work they are assigned, their teachers' responses to and evaluation of their work, the classroom dynamics of their courses, the roles they and their teachers play, and the kinds of learning that are expected in their classes.

One of the students who has been participating in this longitudinal investigation is Motoko, a student from Japan who has taken a range of courses and is majoring in sociology. She described courses in which lively interaction was generated, in which students were expected to participate, to write frequent reaction papers and to undertake projects based on first-hand research, to challenge textbook material and to connect this material to their own lived experiences. But in most of her courses the picture was quite different. Lectures were pervasive, classes were so large that attendance wasn't even taken, and short answer tests were often the predominant means of evaluating student work. With respect to one class, for example, Motoko discussed the problematic nature of multiple-choice exams which, she believes, distort the information being tested and deliberately mislead students. In regard to another course, she described what she viewed as boring, even confusing lectures, but she perservered: "Because I don't like the professor, I work even harder. I don't want him to laugh at me. I don't want to be dehumanized. I came here to learn something, to gain something." In yet another course in which only the professor talked, she indicated that she was "drowning in his words." Even a class which assigned frequent written work, which Motoko completed successfully, disappointed her because she had such difficulty understanding the assignments and because her writing was not responded to in what she perceived as a thoughtful, respectful way. Motoko confided that despite her success in this course, she had lost interest in working on her papers.

The other student whose classroom experiences I've been following is Martha, a student from Colombia who, like Motoko, has taken a range of courses, and whose major is biology. Unlike Motoko, who had managed to negotiate "drowning words" and problematic assignments, Martha's sense of discouragement about the purposelessness of much of her work is far more pervasive. With respect to many of her courses, she complained about the absence of writing (which she views as essential for learning), the passive nature of class discussions, contrived assignments that "don't help her think about anything," and the lifeless comments she received. It was in her science courses, however, that she felt the greatest dissatisfaction and frustration. About one chemistry course, she spoke of "just trying to follow the lectures and get a grade in a huge class" that she characterized as a "disaster." She talked of the sense of superiority her professors project, of her inability to learn anything meaningful from assignments which require everyone "to come up with the same information." Her experiences have provoked her to write numerous pieces which reflect her growing sense of despair and which provide a rich commentary on her perspective and experiences. In one of these pieces she has labeled the way professors behave as "academic harassment." In yet another, she questions the purpose of schooling, assignments, and written work: "Each teacher should ask her or himself the next question: Why do I assign a writing paper on this class? Do you want to see creativity and reflection of students or do or want a reproduction of the same book concept?" She is frustrated by the "lack of connections with the material we listen on lectures," the "monotony of the teaching method," the "limited style of questions," the "stressful process of learning." She concludes:

> I have no new words in my lexicon. And how do I know that? From my writing. No fluency. Why? I don't write. I was moving forward and now I'm stagnant . . . .Frustration and lack of interest are the present feelings with my classes because there is not any planned "agenda" to encourage the students to improve ourselves by writing. There is no rich opportunity to break barriers and answer questions to others and also to myself. There is no REACTION and INTERACTION . . . It does not really matter how many courses the students take in order to improve skills of writing because what it counts is the responsibility encouraged by the teacher's method! the kind of responsibility developed around us is first with *ourselves!* It is an incentive for us to be listened and respected by our writing work! You get into it. Reading provides you grammar. Reading and writing are not separate in the process. It is a combined one. Doble team. Reacting and interacting.

This account, like others Martha has written, reveals her commitment to learning, her insightful understanding of how learning is both promoted and undermined, how writing in particular plays an essential role in this learning, how critical it is for teachers to contribute to and encourage learning. She, like Motoko and the other students surveyed, has much to tell us about the barriers that prevent learning and how these barriers can be broken. And lest we conclude that what these students perceive about their experiences is specific to ESL learners, recent studies of teaching and learning in higher education indicate that this is not the case. For example, Chiseri-Strater's ethnography of university classrooms reveals the authoritarian and limited ways that subject matter is often approached, the ways in which students, even those who are successful, are left silent and empty by the contrived and inconsequential work of many classrooms.

This ongoing exploration of the expectations, perceptions and experiences of both faculty and students has clarified much for me about the academic life of ESL students and what we ought to be doing both within our classrooms and beyond. Given the hierarchical arrangement of coursework within post-secondary schools, given the primacy accorded to traditional discipline-specific courses, it is not surprising that ESL and other writing-based courses have a marginalized position, that these courses are thought to have no authentic content, that the work that goes on in these courses is not considered to be the "real" work of the academy.

This view typically gets played out through coursework that is determined by what students are assumed to need in courses across the curriculum, coursework whose function it is to "guard the tower," to use Shaughnessy's term, and keep the gates closed in the case of students who are not deemed ready to enter ("Diving"). This often implies instruction that focuses on grammar, decontextualized language skills, and surface features of language. And we know from what faculty continue to say about these issues that this is precisely what is expected of English and ESL instruction — and, unfortunately, many of us have been all too ready to comply. Mike Rose speaks to the profoundly exclusionary nature of such a pedagogy and argues that a focus on mechanical skills and grammatical features reduces the complexity of language to simple and discrete problems, keeps teachers from exploring students' knowledge and potential, and contributes to the "second-class intellectual status" to which the teaching of writing has been assigned ("Language" 348). Furthermore, the problematic assumption that writing or ESL programs are in place to serve the academy, that their function is to benefit other academic studies, prevents us from questioning our situation within the larger institution. "Service course ideology," Tom Fox points out, "often leaves the curricular decisions in the hands of those who are not especially knowledgeable about writing instruction," which ultimately means that "political questions — in fact, *any* questions that challenge existing definitions of basic writing — become irrelevant to the bureaucratic task of reproducing the program" ("Basic" 67).

While skills-based and deficit models of instruction bring these kinds of pressures to bear on our work with students, our teaching has further been constrained by composition specialists who make claims about the need for students to adopt the language and discourse conventions of the academy if they are to succeed. David Bartholomae's article, "Inventing the University," is often cited and called upon to argue that students need to approximate and adopt the "specialized discourse of the university" (17). In the ESL literature, a reductive version of this position has been embraced by professionals who maintain that the role that ESL coursework ought to play is one of preparing students for the expectations and demands of discipline-specific communities across the curriculum. Such an approach, however, misrepresents and oversimplifies academic discourse and reduces it to some stable and autonomous phenomenon that does not reflect reality. Such instruction, like coursework shaped by limited conceptualizations of language, undermines *our* expertise and position. And because such instruction privileges and perpetuates the status quo, because it exaggerates the "distinctiveness of academic discourse [and] its separation from student literacy" (Fox, "Basic" 70), such a pedagogy has been characterized in terms of assimilation, colonization, domination, and deracination (Clark; Fox; Gay; Horner; Trimbur).

While there is growing debate about this instructional approach in the field of composition, there have been fewer attempts to problematize this model of teaching in ESL composition, where the norms and conventions of the English language and its discourses have particularly powerful political implications.[3] Hence the need to raise questions about such an instructional focus when it is applied to our work with non-native speakers of English. As I have argued elsewhere, we need to critique approaches that are reductive and formulaic, examine the notion that the language of the academy is a monolithic discourse that can be packaged and transmitted to students, and argue that this attempt to serve the institution in these ways contributes to our marginal status and that of our students.

Those of us who have tried to accommodate institutional demands have, no doubt, found this to be a troubling and tension-filled undertaking, since even when we focus on standards of language use or conventions of academic discourse, students, especially those who are still acquiring English, are not necessarily more successful in meeting the expectations of other faculty. There seems to be little carry-over from such instructional efforts to subsequent work since it is the very nature of such narrowly conceptualized instruction that undercuts genuine learning. As Fox argues, writing teachers who uphold a mythical and fixed set of institutional standards and skills are enacting a pedagogy that, however well-intentioned, is an "unqualifiable failure" ("Standards" 42). Those of us who have resisted and questioned such a pedagogy, embracing a richer and more complicated understanding of how language, discourse, and context are intertwined, may be able to trace the strides students make and to appreciate the intelligence their language and writing reveal, and yet find that this is not extended by other faculty who cannot imagine taking on this kind of responsibility.

We need to recognize that in the same way that faculty establish what Martha calls "barriers" between themselves and students, in the same way that faculty "exoticize" ESL students, we too, especially if our primary work is with ESL students, are perceived as "outsiders."[4] And as long as these boundaries continue to delineate and separate what we and other faculty do, as long as we are expected to "fix" students' problems, then misunderstandings, unfulfilled expectations, frustration, and even resentment will continue to mark our experiences. But this need not be the case. We are beginning to see changes in institutions in response to the growing recognition that faculty across the disciplines must take responsibility for working with all students. Studies, such as the ethnography undertaken by Walvoord and McCarthy, have documented the transformation of faculty from a range of disciplines who became more responsive to the needs of their students as they undertook their own classroom research and examined their own assumptions and expectations.

In my own work with faculty at a number of different institutions, including my own, what first begins as a concern about "underprepared" or "deficient" ESL students often leads to a consideration of the same kinds of pedagogical issues that are at the heart of writing across the curriculum initiatives. But these issues are reconsidered with specific reference to working with ESL students. Together, we have explored our instructional goals, the purposes for assigned work, the means for reading and evaluating this work, the roles that engagement, context, and classroom dynamics play in promoting learning. Through this collaboration faculty have begun to understand that it is unrealistic and ultimately counterproductive to expect writing and ESL programs to be responsible for providing students with the language, discourse, and multiple ways of seeing required across courses. They are recognizing that the process of acquisition is slow-paced and continues to evolve with exposure, immersion, and involvement, that learning is responsive to situations in which students are invited to participate in the construction of meaning and knowledge. They have come to realize that every discipline, indeed every classroom, may represent a distinct culture and thus needs to make it possible for those new to the context to practice and approximate its "ways with words." Along with acknowledging the implications of an essentialist view of language and of the myth of transience, we have considered the myth of coverage, the belief that covering course content necessarily means that it has been learned. Hull and Rose, in their study of the logic underlying a student's unconventional reading of a text, critique "the desire of efficiency and coverage" for the ways it "limit[s] rather than enhance[s] [students'] participation in intellectual work" (296), for the ways it undermines students' entry into the academy. With this in mind, we have raised questions about what we do in order to cover material, why we do what we do, what we expect from students, and how coverage is evaluated. And if the "cover-the-material" model doesn't seem to be working in the ways we expected, we ask, what alternatives are there?

We have also examined the ways in which deficit thinking, a focus on difference, blinds us to the logic, intelligence and richness of students' processes and knowledge. In *Lives on the Boundary,* Mike Rose cites numerous cases of learners (including himself) whose success was undercut because of the tendency to emphasize difference. Studies undertaken by Glynda Hull and her colleagues further attest to how such belief systems about students can lead to inaccurate judgments about learners' abilities, and how practices based on such beliefs perpetuate and "virtually assure failure" (325). The excerpt from the tutor's journal quoted at the beginning of this article, along with many of the faculty and student responses that I have elicited, are yet other indications of what happens when our reading of student work is derailed by a focus on what is presumed to be students' deficiencies. Thus we try to read students' texts to see what is there rather than what isn't, resisting generalizations about literacy and intelligence that are made on the basis of judgments about standards of correctness and form, and suspending our judgments about the alternative rhetorical approaches our students adopt.

In addition to working with faculty to shape the curriculum so that it is responsive to students' needs and to generate instructional approaches that build on students' competence, we address other institutional practices that affect our students. At the University of Massachusetts, for example, the Writing Proficiency Exam, which all students must pass by the time they are juniors, continues to evolve as faculty across the curriculum work together, implementing and modifying it over time. While the exam is impressive, immersing students in rich, thematically-integrated material to read, think about, and respond to, it nevertheless continues to be reconsidered and questioned as we study the ways in which the exam impinges on students' academic lives. And so, for instance, in order to address the finding that ESL students were failing the exam at higher rates than native speakers of English — a situation that is occurring at other institutions as well (see Ray) — we have tried to ensure that faculty understand how to look below the surface of student texts for evidence of proficiency, promoting a kind of reading that benefits not just ESL students but all students. The portfolio option, which requires students to submit papers written in courses as well as to write an essay in response to a set of readings, has proven a better alternative for ESL students to demonstrate writing proficiency. This is not surprising, given that the portfolio allows students to demonstrate what they are capable of when writing is imbedded within and an outgrowth of their courses.

Throughout this work, one of the most critical notions that I try to bring home is the idea that what faculty ought to be doing to enhance the learning of ESL students is *not* a concession, a capitulation, a giving up of standards — since the unrevised approaches that some faculty want to retain may never have been beneficial for *any* students. As John Mayher has pointed out, teaching and learning across college courses are by and large dysfunctional for all students, even those that succeed. What ESL students need — multiple opportunities to use language and write-to-learn, course work which draws on and values what students already know, classroom exchanges and assignments that promote the acquisition of unfamiliar language, concepts, and approaches to inquiry, evaluation that allows students to demonstrate genuine understanding — is good pedagogy for everyone. Learning how to better address the needs of ESL students, because it involves becoming more reflective about teaching, because it involves carefully thinking through the expectations, values, and assumptions underlying the work we assign, helps faculty teach everyone better. In other words, rather than seeing the implications of inclusion and diversity in opposition to excellence and academic standards (as they often are at meetings convened to discuss these issues), learning to teach ESL students, because this challenges us to reconceptualize teaching, contributes to and enhances learning, and for all students. As Gerald Graff has argued in response to those who voice their concerns about the presence of new student populations in their institutions and the negative consequences that this change brings,

> Conservatives who accuse affirmative action programs of lowering academic standards never mention the notorious standard for ignorance that was set by white male college students before women and minorities were permitted in large numbers on campus. It has been the steady pressure for reform from below that has raised academic standards. (88)

Needless to say, given the complexity of this enterprise, these efforts have not transformed classrooms on an institution-wide basis. As is obvious from the surveys and case studies I have undertaken, change is slow, much like the process of learning itself. Shaughnessy referred to the students who entered the CUNY system through open admissions as "strangers in academia" to give us a sense of the cultural and linguistic alienation they were experiencing (*Errors*). In listening to the comments of faculty (note, for example, the comment of the professor of management), it occurs to me that they too are feeling like strangers in academia, that they no longer understand the world in which they work. Janice Neulieb similarly points out that although it is common to view students as "other," as alienated from the academic community, our differing cultural perspectives result in our own confusion and alienation as well.

As we grapple with the kinds of issues and concerns raised by the clash of cultures in academia, we continue to make adjustments which, in turn, generate new questions about our practices. This ongoing dialogue is both necessary and beneficial. Like other prominent debates in higher education on reforming the canon and the implications of diversity, this attempt to explore and interrogate what we do is slowly reconfiguring the landscape and blurring the borders within what was once a fairly well-defined and stable academic community. According to Graff, this is all to the good because this kind of transformation can revitalize higher education and its isolated departments and fragmentary curricula. Within composition, the conflicts and struggles that inevitably mark the teaching of writing are viewed as instructive because they allow students and teachers to "reposition" themselves, raising questions about conventional thinking about instruction and challenging us to imagine alternative pedagogies (Lu; Horner). What Pratt calls the "contact zone," because it represents a site of contestation, is embraced because it enables us to redraw disciplinary boundaries, to reexamine composition instruction, and to revise our assumptions about language and difference.

When faculty see this kind of redefinition as a crisis, I invite them to reconsider their work in light of the way the word "crisis" is translated into Chinese. In Chinese, the word is symbolized by two ideographs — one meaning danger, the other meaning opportunity. Because the challenges that students bring with them may make us feel confused, uncertain, like strangers in our own community, there will be dissonance, jarring questions, ongoing dilemmas, unfulfilled expectations. We can see this reflected in the second faculty response, a response which insists that there are students who don't belong in the academy, that its doors be kept closed. But, as we saw in the first response, perplexities and tensions can also be generative, creating possibilities for new insights, alternative interpretations, and an appreciation for the ways in which these enrich our understanding. Seen from the fresh perspective that another language can provide, the Chinese translation of crisis captures the very nature of learning, a process involving both risk and opportunity, the very process that ideally students ought to engage in, but which we ourselves may resist when it comes to looking at our own practices. But as Giroux urges, teachers must "cross over borders that are culturally strange and alien to them" so that they can "analyze their own values and voices as viewed from different ideological and cultural spaces" (254–55). It is when we take risks of this sort, when we take this step into the unknown, by looking for evidence of students' intelligence, by rereading their attempts as coherent efforts, by valuing, not just evaluating, their work, and by reflecting on the critical relationship between our work and theirs, that opportunities are created not only for students but for teachers to learn in new ways.

Notes

[1] The acronym ESL (English as a Second Language) is used here because it is the commonly used term to refer to students whose native language is not English. Given the inherently political nature of working with ESL learners, it is important to note that at urban institutions, such as the University of Massachusetts at Boston, most of these students are residents of the United States. Furthermore, in the case of a number of these students, English may be a third or fourth language.

[2] This investigation of student responses was first initiated by Spack, whose findings were published in *Blair Resources for Teaching Writing: English as a Second Language.* My ongoing survey builds on her work.

[3] See, however, the work of Benesch, McKay, Raimes, and Zamel — all of whom have raised questions about the ideological assumptions underlying much ESL writing instruction.

[4] I am indebted here to Patricia Bizzell, whom I first heard use the term *exoticize* to characterize how faculty often react towards ESL students.

Works Cited

Bartholomae, David. "Inventing the University." *Journal of Basic Writing* 5 (Spring 1986): 4–23.

Benesch, Sarah. "ESL, Ideology, and the Politics of Pragmatism." *TESOL Quarterly* 27 (1993): 705–17.

Chiseri-Strater, Elizabeth. *Academic Literacies: The Public and Private Discourse of University Students.* Portsmouth: Boynton, 1991.

Clark, Gregory. "Rescuing the Discourse of Community." *CCC* 45 (1994): 61–74.

Fox, Tom. "Basic Writing as Cultural Conflict." *Journal of Education* 172 (1990): 65–83.

———. "Standards and Access." *Journal of Basic Writing* 12 (Spring 1993): 37–45.

Gay, Pamela. "Rereading Shaughnessy from a Postcolonial Perspective." *Journal of Basic Writing* 12 (Fall 1993): 29–40.

Giroux, Henry. "Postmodernism as Border Pedagogy: Redefining the Boundaries of Race and Ethnicity." *Postmodernism, Feminism, and Cultural Politics: Redrawing Educational Boundaries.* Ed. Henry Giroux. Albany: State U of New York P, 1991, 217–56.

Graff, Gerald. *Beyond the Culture Wars.* New York: Norton, 1992.

Horner, Bruce. "Mapping Errors and Expectations for Basic Writing: From 'Frontier Field' to 'Border Country.'" *English Education* 26 (1994): 29–51.

Hull, Glynda, and Mike Rose. "'This Wooden Shack Place': The Logic of an Unconventional Reading." *CCC* 41 (1990): 287–98.

Hull, Glynda, Mike Rose, Kay Losey Fraser, and Marisa Castellano. "Remediation as Social Construct: Perspectives from an Analysis of Classroom Discourse." *CCC* 42 (1991): 299–329.

Laurence, Patricia. "The Vanishing Site of Mina Shaughnessy's *Errors and Expectations.*" *Journal of Basic Writing* 12 (Fall 1993):18–28.

Lu, Min-Zhan. "Conflict and Struggle in Basic Writing." *College English* 54 (1992): 887–913.

Mayher, John S. "Uncommon Sense in the Writing Center." *Journal of Basic Writing* 11 (Spring 1992): 47–57.

McKay, Sandra Lee. "Examining L2 Composition Ideology: A Look at Literacy Education." *Journal of Second Language Writing* 2 (1993): 65–81.

Neuleib, Janice. "The Friendly Stranger: Twenty-Five Years as 'Other.'" *CCC* 43 (1992): 231–43.

Pratt, Mary Louise. "Arts of the Contact Zone." *Profession* 91 (1991): 33–40.

Raimes, Ann. "Out of the Woods: Emerging Traditions in the Teaching of Writing." *TESOL Quarterly* 25 (1991): 407–30.

Ray, Ruth. "Language and Literacy from the Student Perspective: What We Can Learn from the Long-term Case Study." *The Writing Teacher as Researcher.* Ed. Donald A. Daiker and Max Morenberg. Portsmouth: Boynton, 1990. 321–35.

Rose, Mike. *Lives on the Boundary: The Struggles and Achievements of America's Underprepared.* New York: Free P, 1989.

———. "The Language of Exclusion: Writing Instruction at the University." *College English* 47 (1985): 341–59.

Shaughnessy, Mina. "Diving In: An Introduction to Basic Writing." *CCC* 27 (1976): 234–39.

———. *Errors and Expectations.* New York: Oxford UP, 1977.

Spack, Ruth. *Blair Resources for Teaching Writing: English as a Second Language.* New York: Prentice, 1994.

Trimbur, John. "'Really Useful Knowledge' in the Writing Classroom." *Journal of Education* 172 (1990): 21–23.

Villanueva, Victor. *Bootstraps: From an American Academic of Color.* Urbana: NCTE, 1993.

Walvoord, Barbara E., and Lucille B. McCarthy. *Thinking and Writing in College: A Naturalistic Study of Students in Four Disciplines.* Urbana: NCTE, 1990.

Zamel, Vivian. "Questioning Academic Discourse." *College ESL* 3 (1993): 28–39.

EVOLVING PARADIGMS:
WAC AND THE RHETORIC OF INQUIRY

Judy Kirscht, Rhonda Levine, and John Reiff

[*College Composition and Communication* 45 (October 1994): 369–80.]

Judy Kirscht, Rhonda Levine, and John Reiff were all lecturers in the University of California, Santa Barbara Writing Program when they wrote this article. (John Reiff now teaches at Tusculum College in Tennessee.) Reiff and Kirscht helped develop the WAC program at the University of Michigan in the early 1980s; they have published in the *Journal of Advanced Composition*, the *Journal of Teaching Writing*, and the *English Teacher*. Levine has worked extensively at the University of California, Santa Barbara, on the relationships between social sciences research methods and discipline-specific writing, particularly in sociology.

As WAC has developed over the decades, it is often represented in terms of a "false dichotomy": teachers ask students to use "writing-to-learn" techniques, or they help students learn to write as members of discipline-specific discourse communities. In an attempt to resolve this conflict, the authors offer a different approach to WAC. Building on views of writing in academic disciplines that have developed from several decades of WAC initiatives, the authors describe a research assignment that integrates writing-to-learn strategies and helps students explore what it means to learn to write in a discipline. The authors discovered that this approach to research and writing helped to "push students toward more complex views" than they might have developed with a more traditional research assignment. The approach synthesizes the principles of writing-to-learn and writing-in-the-disciplines, offering teachers the opportunity to "collectively and consciously reshape our paradigms of writing."

In February, 1990, teams of faculty from ten university campuses gathered at the University of California, Santa Barbara, at a conference we organized to discuss the pedagogy and politics of "writing in the disciplines." Some teams were comprised of writing program lecturers at University of California campuses; teams from other universities consisted of tenure-track faculty in composition and other fields who were developing and teaching in WAC programs at their campuses. Discussion centered around the politics of WAC, institutional constraints, collegial networking, faculty development, and teaching models and objectives. Though participants welcomed such discussion, when group members began to name what they did and to define their goals, a level of conflict emerged that surprised us. Some participants spoke long and heatedly about the primacy of writing to learn, while others argued with equal heat for the power of discourse conventions in specific fields. A gap soon opened between the two groups that seemed almost unbridgeable.

Upon reflection, we realized that the conference was playing out in microcosm one of the major conflicts in our field — a conflict variously expressed as voice versus discourse, learning versus performance, process versus form. In this article we explore the theoretical and pedagogical implications of this conflict for writing across the curriculum. We argue that the conflict itself is based on a false dichotomy and that work in the social construction of knowledge — particularly the concept of "rhetoric of inquiry" — is capable of connecting both poles of that conflict in a powerful new synthesis with important implications for the field and for the classroom. John Nelson et al. use the term "rhetoric of inquiry" to point out that scholarly writing is argument on behalf of particular knowledge claims. While every scholar "relies on common devices of rhetoric," every field is also "defined by its own special devices and patterns of rhetoric" (4). Thus to study the rhetoric of inquiry is to connect "discussions of methodology to concrete inquiries in various contexts, and especially to the languages of their conduct" (5). Though this view of writing in the disciplines is not new, we will seek to demonstrate here its possibilities for opening up new and generative ways to explore the interaction of convention and growth in the classroom.

Writing-to-Learn vs. Writing-in-the-Disciplines

In the 1970s, faculty in many disciplines became increasingly aware of what they saw as deficiencies in their students' writing and looked to composition for help. The help they received, however, came from a field that was itself undergoing a major shift in both practice and theory. Practitioners such as Ken Macrorie, Peter Elbow, and Mina Shaughnessy were changing the face of composition instruction, while theorists such as James Britton, Donald Murray, James Moffett, and Janet Emig were linking these new practices to a new theory of writing development centered on process, a substantial change from the product focus of the current-traditional model. All of the faculty who responded to the call for help were informed by this shift to process; however, within this group two distinctly different orientations emerged. One group asked themselves: "What can composition contribute to teaching in other disciplines?" Their answer was, in brief, that it could offer the disciplines a sense of writing as an integral part of the learning process. The other group asked: "What kind of writing do you do in your discipline?" and proceeded to study the practice of the disciplines as discourse communities and the possibility of teaching these conventions in the composition class.

The hallmark of the first group, which we will call *writing-to-learn,* was its use of informal writing as a tool for learning. For instance, in "Journals Across the Disciplines," Toby Fulwiler offered perhaps a dozen different suggestions on integrating ungraded journals and in-class writing into courses throughout the curriculum. This group of WAC organizers assured other faculty that they had no interest in appointing biologists or sociologists as a new "grammar gestapo"; rather, their programs encouraged faculty to use writing flexibly as a tool for reaching their own course goals.

This process-based *writing-to-learn* model still characterizes much of the WAC movement. For example, a recent PBS video conference on WAC ("Issues and Conflicts in Writing Across the Curriculum," broadcast on February 27, 1991, from Robert Morris College) seemed designed to introduce this model to faculty and administrators unacquainted with WAC. In its opening segment, for instance, Bill Zinsser called writing "just thinking on paper" and Toby Fulwiler suggested that WAC be re-named "Language and Active Learning Across the Curriculum."

The hallmark of the second group, which we will call *learning-to-write-in-the-disciplines,* is teaching writing based on the understanding of the nature of discourse communities — that is, of their inquiry methods and conventions. The 1981 *Writing in the Arts and Sciences,* a textbook written by Elaine Maimon and her colleagues at Beaver College, exemplifies this approach. It creates writing assignments based on rhetorical situations in various disciplines. This group of WAC organizers created the context for faculty from other disciplines to help composition specialists understand the nature of academic writing in various disciplines and ways it could be taught.

The focus for this group of WAC organizers today is to see what is taking place in disciplinary writing, both for the individual and for the discipline . . . to be able to understand more deeply the dynamics of the texts with which our students work" (Bazerman, "Second Stage" 210). Even the video conference that we earlier characterized as an advertisement for *writing-to-learn* showed some recognition of this trend in WAC. In it, Anne Herrington said that WAC must give guidance in the methods of inquiry and its presentation associated with different fields — teaching students in anthropology, for instance, to first make observations and then inferences, or helping engineering students to first do evaluations that lead them to design recommendations. Art Young carried this point further when he distinguished between what he called WAC ("active learning in every discipline") and Writing in the Disciplines (which aims to make majors "proficient" in their fields — so that an engineering student, for example, will "read, write, and solve problems like an engineer").

The Effects of the Conflict

The distinction between *active-learning-in-every-discipline* and *writing-in-the-disciplines* is more than a difference in interest or approach to teaching; it represents a fundamental conflict in WAC, both as to its purpose and its understanding of writing. The differences between these approaches, evident for a long time in journal articles and papers at national conventions, became far clearer at the Santa Barbara conference, where small groups of both persuasions gathered for informal discussion. Under these circumstances it became clear that *writing-to-learn* and *learning-to-write-in-the-disciplines* had become more than theoretical constructs; they had become positions in a dichotomy and as such interfered with establishing a common language for dialogue. When we used the same terms, such as "writing as a process," "discourse conventions," or "writing as a means to or mode of learning," they functioned, in effect, as buzz words identifying ideological positions. In a sense these phrases were self-referential labels, and their function and power were based on the larger social network of values ascribed to them by the respective camps. It became clear that much of our discourse served more to mark our political locations in the field than to share what we knew, to learn from each other, or to describe our theory and practice.

On a more global level, we believe such polarization is going on across the field of composition and is, at best, reductive. It obscures the living interconnections between active learning and social communication; between individual experience and social act; and between the writer, in Faigley's words, as a "constituent of culture" (535) and, as we would add, a maker of that culture. When taken to an extreme, such prescriptive schema threaten to reduce writing to learn," on the one hand, to "Romantic expressivism" (Faigley 529–31) and the solipsistic acts of an individual "isolated from the social world" (Cooper 365); and, on the other hand, to reduce "learning to write in the disciplines" to passive, even mechanical, mimesis, a politically conservative mechanism for social control, and, finally, to a conventionalized commodity.

In a 1990 CCCC talk, Elaine Maimon called this opposition "a false dichotomy," and argued that the "search and destroy scholarship" which it engenders impedes our efforts to develop theory and to attain political status for the discipline of writing; such warfare, she argued, benefits only the "enemies of writing."

The Social Constructionist Resolution

We have found that the social constructionist view of cognitive psychologist Michael Basseches offers not only insight into why we adhere to such "killer dichotomies" (Berthoff 13), but also the possibility of resolving them as well. As Basseches explains,

> When adults systematize the world (1) using sets of fixed categories and (2) holding to static ontological and epistemological assumptions often associated with formal thought, their maintenance of cognitive equilibrium depends on their power to seal themselves off from anomalous data and discrepant viewpoints. (41)

In contrast, Basseches advocates a non-oppositional orientation which he calls "dialectical thinking." This view seeks to understand reality as an act of social construction by "describing fundamental processes of change and the dynamic relationships through which this change occurs" (30). From his perspective, then, false dichotomies are the byproducts of an undialectical way of looking at the world, fixing thinking within the closed boundaries of immutable systems and static antithetical terms. They allow for only one valid perspective and thus prevent those caught within this mode of thinking from using "multiple frames of reference," from adopting an integrative stance, and from achieving any resolution of the opposition at a higher level.

By refusing to venture beyond the boundaries of our assumptions, beliefs and the conceptual models that represent them, we maintain a sense of security about our purpose, value, and approach to writing. But this gain is offset by the limitations it imposes. When we think dialectically, in contrast, Basseches argues that we

> trade off a degree of intellectual security for a freedom from intellectually imposing limitations on oneself or other people. The open-mindedness thus gained is extremely important . . . because it facilitates the joining in collective meaning-making efforts with others whose reasoning is shaped by very different world-views or life contexts (34).

Such thinking promises more than an intellectual reconciliation based on political expediency, it offers a model that includes many perspectives on writing and, in fact, brings together ideas that have been developing in WAC for a long time.

Early on in WAC, we find theory and practice which attempt to forge a synthesis between *writing-to-learn* and *learning-to-write-in-the-disciplines.* For example, David Hamilton, in a 1980 *College English* article, advocated what he called "serious parodies" of science — assignments for composition students that immerse them in the kinds of thinking and problem-solving that scientists do. More recently, the work of social constructionists like Greg Meyers, Charles Bazerman, and Susan Peck MacDonald have shifted the discussion of writing in the disciplines from notions of fixed boundaries and prescriptive taxonomies to a view of disciplines as socially negotiated territory and conventions as representations of actions which emanate from a discipline's center of inquiry. In this framework, conventions work dialectically: as constraints, they help shape individual behavior, but they are also shaped and transformed by the contributions of those who work with and within them.

We believe these researchers are far from deserting the idea of writing as process; rather, they are, by extending it into its social context and into the inquiry process, opening the idea to its full complexity and to a view very similar to Basseches'. They are taking the "learning" in *writing-to-learn* beyond the assimilation of content into questions of how knowledge itself is constructed. If conventions are seen as rhetorical, as the way that questions are asked and answers sought in a given field, writing becomes a way not only to interact with declarative knowledge, but also to develop procedural knowledge concerning that field — to learn *how* knowledge has been constructed as well as *what* that knowledge is. WAC thus becomes a way into the inquiry practices of the fields.

Teaching the Rhetoric of Inquiry

Taught from this perspective, disciplinary-based writing becomes a highly imaginative activity, which opens up possibilities of new questions, new ways of seeing and organizing thought, new ways of talking about the world. This orientation shares with the *writing-to-learn* approach a goal of growth and with the *learning-to-write-in-the-disciplines* approach a concern with form, but these objectives are redefined by a recognition of their interdependence. Growth, here, is toward metacognition, the ability to take multiple perspectives, to integrate and synthesize, to exercise a self-conscious control over the forms of inquiry. Growth, in short, means movement toward dialectical thinking.

The disciplines are introduced as centers of inquiry rather than as banks of knowledge, and disciplinary conventions are presented as emerging from communally negotiated assumptions about what knowledge is and about the methods for shaping it. The forms and conventions of the disciplines become, in turn, tools used consciously to aid students in moving beyond the boundaries of previous belief systems and in exploring new perceptions. Using these forms means engaging in the inquiry process itself rather than teaching the conventions separate from the process — as has been done in composition classes based on the current traditional model. We recognize that this presents a problem for many composition teachers who do not feel competent to perform, much less teach, the methodologies that underlie the conventions of disciplines other than their own. Furthermore, many have been vehement, as we noted earlier, about staying within the bounds of their own disciplinary systems. But both Basseches' theory and our own classroom experiences suggest that the problem may lie more in writing teachers' reluctance to cross disciplinary boundaries than in their ability to understand new methodologies.

To illustrate the value of risking moves into such unfamiliar terrain, and the effect of this shift in perspective on the teaching of disciplinary conventions, we will describe the experience of developing and teaching an empirical study project as a part of an introductory composition course. The project was first developed by Judy Kirscht in consultation with an empirical psychologist, and such consultation is, of course, essential in the initial stages of course development. Once Kirscht was familiar with the psychologist's assumptions about knowledge, however, the inquiry process itself proved to be a variation on a familiar theme — an exploration of the critical thinking processes that also underlie composition and, we suspect, most other academic activities as well. The subject of study throughout the course, chosen for its familiarity and accessibility for both instructor and students, was contemporary social issues, an appropriate arena for exploring the social origins of knowledge.

"Empirical study report," here means the general format of "Introduction, Methods, Results, Discussion," a format which emerged in the natural sciences and is now used with variations in many fields. These conventions are introduced to students as a form which has evolved socially, as Bazerman has demonstrated in "Codifying the Social Scientific Style: The APA Publication Manual as a Behaviorist Rhetoric" (125). It is presented to students as a communally accepted way of looking at particular subject matter and of shaping and controlling what will count as knowledge in the field. Consequently, within any field, methods vary and evolve as the basic assumptions about what counts as knowledge change. Presented this way, the empirical method becomes a pair of glasses, consciously used, that enables the student and researcher alike to explore particular kinds of questions in particular ways and to see how belief is transformed by the methodology employed.

The difference between a positivist and a social constructionist view of the empirical study form — between "the way to think if you want to be a scientist and produce true knowledge," and "one way of thinking that produces a particular kind of knowledge" — is critical. In the latter view, the empirical study report becomes, as Frank D'Angelo has said of composition forms, "symbolic manifestations of underlying mental processes, not merely conventional static patterns" (56–57). Such forms are, as Richard Coe states, "generative because they are constraining" (17). Most importantly, the purpose in using empirical methodology in the composition classroom is not to prove, to close the system by arriving at certainty, but to raise new questions, to establish new theoretical grounds for plausible explanations and predictions.

Each section of the empirical study report reflects an aspect of the empirical inquiry process, and if taught this way, each section can also increase students' awareness of the social nature of that process. The "Introduction" presents a hypothesis — a claim which can be tested by the empirical method — and establishes the theoretical ground that produced that hypothesis. In this assignment, therefore, students must first decide what kinds of beliefs they can test using this method; if done in groups, the exercise emphasizes the social origins of hypotheses. When they examine claims such as "the [Gulf] war is just," "yellow ribbons express neutrality on [US involvement in] the war," "men and women express emotions differently," or "campus area merchants rip off students," they quickly discover that there are some things the empirical method cannot do. It cannot tell you, for instance, whether a war is just. And it cannot tell you anything about emotions, which are internal states.

Once students shape a belief, or hypothesis, in such a way that it can be referenced to verifiable physical evidence or agreed on definitions, they must discover the context from which that belief came. In science, as in any discipline, the context is the theoretical basis, what Basseches would call the system that both creates and constrains the questions (30); in the classroom, students must discover they, too, have such systems. Some beliefs, such as those about the Gulf War or other recent events, may seem fairly easy to source to their origins, but more often students have no idea how they came by their ideas; they first feel them simply as givens, much like the air that they breathe. Later they may discover that they share much the same processes of socialization and that their beliefs are the products of such processes. Even opinions whose sources are seemingly evident on a superficial level (such as beliefs about the Gulf War) turn out to have far deeper social roots.

Frequently, explorations into sources modify the beliefs, or hypotheses, themselves. For example, "the war is just" becomes "television shapes our views of the war." Under the rigors of definition, the hypothesis that "men and women express emotion differently" becomes "men and women express different emotions openly." Students find that hypotheses demand definitions, reasons, and arguments — and arguments bring the underlying social belief systems, or "theories," to light. One all-female group, for example, in exploring the sources of the hypothesis that women's fear of rape affects their behavior, discovered that the females had all received exactly the same warnings about behavior, and that those were the same warnings received by the female teacher a generation earlier. Later, during full-class discussion, a male student in the class pointed out that the "theory" they had unearthed assumed the rapist to be a stranger, and that none of the behavior modifications listed for study would protect women against rapes committed by males known to the victim. The study group, as Basseches would predict, initially resisted this "anomalous" information by insisting that date rape wasn't what they were studying. Eventually, however, the class persuaded them to include in their hypothesis the prediction that subjects would not take precautions against behavior they had not been socialized to expect, a prediction later supported by their results.

There is nothing, we think, very unfamiliar to composition teachers in this unearthing of assumptions and "theories" except that it takes place in a different inquiry community. The methodology of this particular community, however, demands a rigorous dissection of students' inference systems, and this is the process underlying the "Methods" section of empirical study reports. Of all the conclusions composition teachers have arrived at by examining texts without reference to the underlying inquiry process, the view of the "Methods" section as narrative is probably one of the most misleading. It is, of course, narrative in mode, but this statement misses the chief purpose of the section. To know what to do, the scientist needs to know the analytical strategies and procedures that are accepted in that research community and how to apply them to the project at hand. These are the norms that govern the critical analytical process of the discipline, that determine what will, at any given point in time, count as knowledge in the discipline. The purpose of communicating them here is social: to establish the researcher's authority as a member of the field and to allow others to assess the credibility of the results or replicate the work.

When students use a methodology instead of merely imitating a convention, they must struggle with both the demands and the constraints of that form. Specifically, they must decide whom they mean to include in their hypotheses (all people, or a limited sample?), how the hypothesis must be framed in order for it to be testable and what data they must observe in order to test it (what does "upset" look like?), what they must do to collect the data, and what sorts of reasoning they must use to get from that evidence to their claim. What generalizations will they have to make, and will they be able to make them? As they explore the possibilities for misinformation, misclassification, and misinterpretation at every step, their hypotheses undergo further limitation, revision, and clarification. Underlying the form of the "Methods" section of scientific reports, in short, is an extraordinary exercise in logic, an exploration into definition of terms, classification, causation, the dissection of inference, the discovery of assumption, the outlining of interpretive limits, all within the context of their own questions. This recursive exercise makes crystal clear that the heart of methodology is the examination of the researcher's own thinking process; sloppy logic here becomes confusion in the field — disagreements about what they are looking for, how to record it, what conclusions they can draw.

As students (in pairs) embark on the study itself it is wise to stress once again that their purpose is to gain new insight, not to prove that they are right, to open, not defend, their beliefs. The conviction that science produces certainty can lead to great consternation if their hypotheses fail — which they, of course, quite frequently do. It helps to tell them that points will be given not so much for being right as for discovering complexity. In one case, for example, people who were not wearing yellow ribbons thought, as the student/researcher did, that those who did wear them were ambivalent about the war; as it turned out, however, those who wore the ribbons were predominantly against the war, not ambivalent. Men and women did indeed express different emotions openly, but the interesting finding was that the men observed were easier to "read" than women. Usually, students are sufficiently intrigued by the new insights to compensate for the "failure" of the hypotheses, though not, again, without the ambivalence and confusion Basseches predicts when existing systems are challenged.

When students begin to write up their studies, the issue of subjectivity/ objectivity becomes central, masked by such questions as: "Can we express our own opinion?" and "Can we use '*I*'?" Such questions serve to highlight the place of the knower in empirical study. As Bazerman has demonstrated, the scientific community gradually eliminated the use of *I* from the empirical report as a reflection of the positivist's belief in an objective reality where hypotheses come from the data ("Codifying" 136–38). In the social constructionist composition class, however, the *I* reemerges as the originator of questions, the selector and interpreter of data, and the judge of significance. The purpose of the study report, however, is to share the investigator's explanations for phenomena in the outside world. It therefore follows that as the focus shifts from the researcher to the phenomenon to be explained, the grammar of the discourse shifts accordingly. When this logic is explained to students, some, as we would anticipate, feel deprived of the security given by the clear and simple subjective/objective distinction of the closed system. "Well, can we or can't we?" they ask.

These periods of confusion may be as significant as anything else that happens in such projects, for they suggest that students are moving into what Basseches refers to as "metapositions," temporary places beyond the boundaries of the old beliefs and conventions that mark motion toward greater inclusiveness (28, 41). Secondly, these periods of confusion suggest that in composition we may have socialized our students to ask questions that reinforce the separation of self and world, self and text, in nonproductive ways that give a skewed picture of what knowledge is and how it is constructed.

Once beyond this confusion, students find the writing task relatively simple, and their ease with it at this stage is evidence, we believe, that once the inquiry process is experienced self-consciously, the form becomes its logical expression. Each section of the report entails different cognitive activities, but activities they have already engaged in. Without knowing it, students have essentially written their "Introductions" when they constructed arguments for their hypotheses, and they've written their "Methods" sections when they designed their studies. Now they have to separate the data from the interpretation, the "what" from the "what it means," the "Results" from the "Discussion." Students who have gone through the process self-consciously have surprisingly little trouble with the distinction; nowhere is it clearer that demands of the form itself, from the introduction to the design to the collection of data, have guided the students' work. They return to the classroom with a very new sense of the problematic nature of data and the need to separate data from interpretation. Thus empirical methodology may itself move students a considerable distance toward a more transformational view of knowledge.

To reinforce this new and very fragile view, it is wise to make it very clear that credit will be given in the "Discussion" section of the report for their ability to draw implications from the specific data, for the thoroughness with which they critique their study — evaluating factors that might have influenced their data — and for the open and systematic way in which they explore other possible interpretations of those data. Despite this emphasis, the most common weakness of students' performance in this section is that they confine themselves to discussing only whether the main hypothesis was right or wrong, occasionally even ignoring their data to retain their previous position.

Despite this tendency to resist change, the empirical report form does seem to push students toward more complex views. When they finished the project and were asked to reflect on the experience, they responded not in terms of the restrictiveness of the form, but in terms of what happened to their hypotheses. Most often they expressed surprise: Things are more complicated than they thought. Though this response is unsophisticated, it is sufficient to convince us that if we do not separate form in our teaching from the processes that underlie it, it can work for students in generative and expansive ways.

Our experiences teaching discipline-based writing and our study of social construction and the rhetoric of inquiry have convinced us that the field has arrived at a transitional moment. To paraphrase Hairston, new "winds of change" are certainly blowing, carrying with them fresh ways of seeing, new sets of questions, and possibilities for shaping the field and the classroom. We in composition need to encourage this exploration in our research and teaching by letting go of false dichotomies, ideological labels, and embracing the questions and uncertainties of our own "anomalous data." Rather than calling for an "intellectual cease-fire," which maintains the status quo by locking the opposing camps into their respective positions, we need to recontextualize this debate as an open and fluid interaction between *writing-to-learn* and *writing-in-the-disciplines*, through which we collectively and consciously reshape our paradigms of writing.

Works Cited

Basseches, Michael. "Intellectual Development: the Development of Dialectical Thinking." *Thinking, Reasoning, and Writing*. Ed. Elaine Maimon, Barbara Nodine, and Finbarr O'Connor. White Plains, NY: Longman 1989. 23–45.

Bazerman, Charles. "Codifying the Social Scientific Style: The APA Publication Manual as a Behaviorist Rhetoric." *The Rhetoric of the Human Sciences: Language and Argument in Scholarship and Public Affairs*. Ed. John Nelson, Allan Megill, and Donald McCloskey. Madison: Wisconsin UP, 1987. 125–44.

———. "The Second Stage in Writing Across the Curriculum." *College English* 53 (1991): 209–12.

Berlin, James A. and Inkster, Robert P. "Current-Traditional Rhetoric: Paradigm and Practice." *Freshman English News* 8 (Winter 1980): 1–4, 13–14.

Berthoff, Ann E. "Killer Dichotomies: Reading In/Reading Out." *Farther Along: Transforming Dichotomies in Rhetoric and Composition*. Ed. Kate Ronald and Hephzibah Roskelly. Portsmouth: Boynton, 1990: 12–24.

Britton, James, Tony Burgess, Nancy Martin, Alex McLeod, and Harold Rosen. *The Development of Writing Abilities* (11–18). London: Macmillan, 1975.

Coe, Richard M. "An Apology for Form: or, Who Took the Form out of the Process?" *College English* 49 (1987): 13–28.

Cooper, Marilyn. "The Ecology of Writing." *College English* 48 (1986): 364–75.

D'Angelo, Frank. *A Conceptual Theory of Rhetoric*. Cambridge: Winthrop, 1975.

Elbow, Peter. *Writing Without Teachers*. Oxford UP, 1973.

Emig, Janet. "Writing as a Mode of Learning." *CCC* 28 (1977): 122–28.

Faigley, Lester. "Competing Theories of Process: A Critique and a Proposal." *College English* 48 (1986): 527–42.

Fulwiler, Toby. "Journals Across the Disciplines." *English Journal* 69.4 (1980): 14–19.

Hairston, Maxine. "The Winds of Change: Thomas Kuhn and the Revolution in the Teaching of Writing." *CCC* 33 (1982): 76–88.

Hamilton, David. "Interdisciplinary Writing." *College English* 41 (1980): 780–96.

Macrorie, Ken. *Telling Writing*. New Rochelle: Hayden, 1970.

Maimon, Elaine, Gerald Belcher, Gail Hearn, Barbara Nodine, and Finbarr O'Connor. *Writing in the Arts and Sciences*. Cambridge: Winthrop, 1981.

McDonald, Susan Peck. "Problem Definition in Academic Writing." *College English* 49 (1987): 315–31.

Moffett, James. *Teaching the Universe of Discourse.* Boston: Houghton, 1968.

Murray, Donald. "Teach Writing As Process, Not Product," *Rhetoric and Composition.* Ed. Richard L. Graves. New Rochelle: Hayden, 1976: 79–82.

Myer, Greg. "The Social Construction of Two Biologists' Proposals." *Written Communication* 2 (1985): 219–45.

Myer, Greg. "Writing Research and the Sociology of Scientific Knowledge: a Review of Three New Books." *College English* 48 (1986): 595–608.

Nelson, John S., Allan Megill, and Donald N. McCloskey, eds. *The Rhetoric of the Human Sciences: Language and Argument in Scholarship and Public Affairs.* Madison: Wisconsin UP, 1987.

Russell, David R. *Writing in the Academic Disciplines, 1870–1990: A Curricular History.* Carbondale: Southern Illinois UP, 1991.

Shaughnessy, Mina P. *Errors and Expectations.* Oxford UP, 1977.

PART ELEVEN

GRAMMAR BASICS

Though writing teachers no longer consider direct grammar instruction to be central to the teaching of writing, they recognize that students need understandable definitions of grammatical terms and concepts as they revise and edit. Part XI of *The Bedford Handbook* offers a straightforward explanation of the basics of grammar, providing students with an easy-to-use reference source.

The following article explores questions that teachers might confront as they consider how to encourage students to use the handbook's information on grammar:

- What are different definitions of *grammar*? How might these definitions help writing teachers? How can the different kinds of grammar contribute to the teaching of writing?
- How can teachers provide students with the information they need about grammar without hindering their development as writers?

GRAMMAR, GRAMMARS, AND THE TEACHING OF GRAMMAR

Patrick Hartwell

[*College English* 47 (1985): 105–27.]

Patrick Hartwell, professor of English at Indiana University of Pennsylvania, is interested in error analysis, basic writing, and literacy. His articles have appeared in *College English, Rhetoric Review*, and *Research in the Teaching of English*.

In the following article, Hartwell enters the ongoing debate about the role of grammar instruction in writing courses, observing that this is actually a debate about the sequence of instruction in composition classes: should teachers address word- and sentence-level concerns first, or should they use a "top-down" approach, attending first to issues of meaning and purpose? In his attempt to clarify the debate, Hartwell analyzes what we might mean by *grammar* and describes at least five meanings for the term. His discussion of those meanings can help new and experienced teachers be more specific in their use of grammar instruction and can help them understand more fully what they might or might not want to accomplish when presenting grammar to students.

For me the grammar issue was settled at least twenty years ago with the conclusion offered by Richard Braddock, Richard Lloyd-Jones, and Lowell Schoer in 1963.

> In view of the widespread agreement of research studies based upon many types of students and teachers, the conclusion can be stated in strong and unqualified terms: the teaching of formal grammar has a negligible or, because it usually displaces some instruction and practice in composition, even a harmful effect on improvement in writing.[1]

Indeed, I would agree with Janet Emig that the grammar issue is a prime example of "magical thinking": the assumption that students will learn only what we teach and only because we teach.[2]

But the grammar issue, as we will see, is a complicated one. And, perhaps surprisingly, it remains controversial, with the regular appearance of papers defending the teaching of formal grammar or attacking it.[3] Thus Janice Neuleib, writing on "The Relation of Formal Grammar to Composition" in *College Composition and Communication* (23 [1977], 247–50), is tempted "to sputter on paper" at reading the quotation above (p. 248), and Martha Kolln, writing in the same journal three years later ("Closing the Books on Alchemy," *CCC*, 32 [1981], 139–51), labels people like me "alchemists" for our perverse beliefs. Neuleib reviews five experimental studies, most of them concluding that formal grammar instruction has no effect on the quality of students' writing nor on their ability to avoid error. Yet she renders in effect a Scots verdict of "Not proven" and calls for more research on the issue. Similarly, Kolln reviews six experimental studies that arrive at similar conclusions, only one of them overlapping with the studies cited by Neuleib. She calls for more careful definition of the word *grammar* — her definition being "the internalized system that native speakers of a language share" (p. 140) — and she concludes with a stirring call to place grammar instruction at the center of the composition curriculum: "our goal should be to help students understand the system they know unconsciously as native speakers, to teach them the necessary categories and labels that will enable them to think about and talk about their language" (p. 150). Certainly our textbooks and our pedagogies — though they vary widely in what they see as "necessary categories and labels" — continue to emphasize mastery of formal grammar, and popular discussions of a presumed literacy crisis are almost unanimous in their call for a renewed emphasis on the teaching of formal grammar, seen as basic for success in writing.[4]

An Instructive Example

It is worth noting at the outset that both sides in this dispute — the grammarians and the anti-grammarians — articulate the issue in the same positivistic terms: what does experimental research tell us about the value of teaching formal grammar? But seventy-five years of experimental research has for all practical purposes told us nothing. The two sides are unable to agree on how to interpret such research. Studies are interpreted in terms of one's prior assumptions about the value of teaching grammar: their results seem not to change those assumptions. Thus the basis of the discussion, a basis shared by Kolln and Neuleib and by Braddock and his colleagues—"what does educational research tell us?" — seems designed to perpetuate, not to resolve, the issue. A single example will be instructive. In 1976 and then at greater length in 1979, W. B. Elley, I. H. Barham, H. Lamb, and M. Wyllie reported on a three-year experiment in New Zealand, comparing the relative effectiveness at the high school level of instruction in transformational grammar, instruction in traditional grammar, and no grammar instruction.[5] They concluded that the formal study of grammar, whether transformational or traditional, improved neither writing quality nor control over surface correctness.

After two years, no differences were detected in writing performance or language competence; after three years small differences appeared in some minor conventions favoring the TG [transformational grammar] group, but these were more than offset by the less positive attitudes they showed towards their English studies. (p. 18)

Anthony Petrosky, in a review of research ("Grammar Instruction: What We Know," *English Journal*, 66, No. 9 [1977], 86–88), agreed with this conclusion, finding the study to be carefully designed, "representative of the best kind of educational research" (p. 86), its validity "unquestionable" (p. 88). Yet Janice Neuleib in her essay found the same conclusions to be "startling" and questioned whether the findings could be generalized beyond the target population, New Zealand high school students. Martha Kolln, when her attention is drawn to the study ("Reply to Ron Shook," *CCC*, 32 [1981], 139–151), thinks the whole experiment "suspicious." And John Mellon has been willing to use the study to defend the teaching of grammar; the study of Elley and his colleagues, he has argued, shows that teaching grammar does no harm.[6]

It would seem unlikely, therefore, that further experimental research, in and of itself, will resolve the grammar issue. Any experimental design can be nitpicked, any experimental population can be criticized, and any experimental conclusion can be questioned or, more often, ignored. In fact, it may well be that the grammar question is not open to resolution by experimental research, that, as Noam Chomsky has argued in *Reflections on Language* (New York: Pantheon, 1975), criticizing the trivialization of human learning by behavioral psychologists, the issue is simply misdefined.

There will be "good experiments" only in domains that lie outside the organism's cognitive capacity. For example, there will be no "good experiments" in the study of human learning.

This discipline . . . will, of necessity, avoid those domains in which an organism is specially designed to acquire rich cognitive structures that enter into its life in an intimate fashion. The discipline will be of virtually no intellectual interest, it seems to me, since it is restricting itself in principle to those questions that are guaranteed to tell us little about the nature of organisms. (p. 36)

Asking the Right Questions

As a result, though I will look briefly at the tradition of experimental research, my primary goal in this essay is to articulate the grammar issue in different and, I would hope, more productive terms. Specifically, I want to ask four questions:

1. Why is the grammar issue so important? Why has it been the dominant focus of composition research for the last seventy-five years?
2. What definitions of the word *grammar* are needed to articulate the grammar issue intelligibly?
3. What do findings in cognate disciplines suggest about the value of formal grammar instruction?
4. What is our theory of language, and what does it predict about the value of formal grammar instruction? (This question — "what does our theory of language predict?" — seems a much more powerful question than "what does educational research tell us?")

In exploring these questions I will attempt to be fully explicit about issues, terms, and assumptions. I hope that both proponents and opponents of formal grammar instruction would agree that these are useful as shared points of reference: care in definition, full examination of the evidence, reference to relevant work in cognate disciplines, and explicit analysis of the theoretical bases of the issue.

But even with that gesture of harmony it will be difficult to articulate the issue in a balanced way, one that will be acceptable to both sides. After all, we are dealing with a professional dispute in which one side accuses the other of "magical thinking," and in turn that side responds by charging the other as "alchemists." Thus we might suspect that the grammar issue is itself embedded in larger models of the transmission of literacy, part of quite different assumptions about the teaching of composition.

Those of us who dismiss the teaching of formal grammar have a model of composition instruction that makes the grammar issue "uninteresting" in a scientific sense. Our model predicts a rich and complex interaction of learner and environment in mastering literacy, an interaction that has little to do with sequences of skills instruction as such. Those who defend the teaching of grammar tend to have a model of composition instruction that is rigidly skills-centered and rigidly sequential: the formal teaching of grammar, as the first step in that sequence, is the cornerstone or linchpin. Grammar teaching is thus supremely interesting, naturally a dominant focus for educational research. The controversy over the value of grammar instruction, then, is inseparable from two other issues: the issues of sequence in the teaching of composition and of the role of the composition teacher. Consider, for example, the force of these two issues in Janice Neuleib's conclusion: after calling for yet more experimental research on the value of teaching grammar, she ends with an absolute (and unsupported) claim about sequences and teacher roles in composition.

> We do know, however, that some things must be taught at different levels. Insistence on adherence to usage norms by composition teachers does improve usage. Students can learn to organize their papers if teachers do not accept papers that are disorganized. Perhaps composition teachers can teach those two abilities before they begin the more difficult tasks of developing syntactic sophistication and a winning style. ("The Relation of Formal Grammar to Composition," p. 250)

(One might want to ask, in passing, whether "usage norms" exist in the monolithic fashion the phrase suggests and whether refusing to accept disorganized papers is our best available pedagogy for teaching arrangement.)[7]

But I want to focus on the notion of sequence that makes the grammar issue so important: first grammar, then usage, then some absolute model of organization, all controlled by the teacher at the center of the learning process, with other matters, those of rhetorical weight — "syntactic sophistication and a winning style" — pushed off to the future. It is not surprising that we call each other names: those of us who question the value of teaching grammar are in fact shaking the whole elaborate edifice of traditional composition instruction.

The Five Meanings of "Grammar"

Given its centrality to a well-established way of teaching composition, I need to go about the business of defining grammar rather carefully, particularly in view of Kolln's criticism of the lack of care in earlier discussions. Therefore I will build upon a seminal discussion of the word *grammar* offered a generation ago, in 1954, by W. Nelson Francis, often excerpted as "The Three Meanings of Grammar."[8] It is worth reprinting at length, if only to re-establish it as a reference point for future discussions.

> The first thing we mean by "grammar" is "the set of formal patterns in which the words of a language are arranged in order to convey larger meanings." It is not necessary that we be able to discuss these patterns self-consciously in order to be able to use them. In fact, all speakers of a language above the age of five or six know how to use its complex forms of organization with considerable skill; in this sense of the word — call it "Grammar 1" — they are thoroughly familiar with its grammar.
>
> The second meaning of "grammar" — call it "Grammar 2" — is "the branch of linguistic science which is concerned with the description, analysis, and formulization of formal language patterns." Just as gravity was in full operation before Newton's apple fell, so grammar in the first sense was in full operation before anyone formulated the first rule that began the history of grammar as a study.
>
> The third sense in which people use the word "grammar" is "linguistic etiquette." This we may call "Grammar 3." The word in this sense is often coupled with a derogatory adjective: we say that the expression "he ain't here" is "bad grammar." . . .
>
> As has already been suggested, much confusion arises from mixing these meanings. One hears a good deal of criticism of teachers of English couched in such terms as "they don't teach grammar any more." Criticism of this sort is based on the wholly unproven assumption that teaching Grammar 2 will improve the student's proficiency in Grammar 1 or improve his manners in Grammar 3. Actually, the form of Grammar 2 which is usually taught is a very inaccurate and misleading analysis of the facts of Grammar 1; and it therefore is of highly questionable value in improving a person's ability to handle the structural patterns of his language. (pp. 300–301)

Francis' Grammar 3 is, of course, not grammar at all, but usage. One would like to assume that Joseph Williams' recent discussion of usage ("The Phenomenology of Error," *CCC*, 32 (1981), 152–168), along with his references, has placed those shibboleths in a proper perspective. But I doubt it, and I suspect that popular discussions of the grammar issue will be as flawed by the intrusion of usage issues as past discussions have been. At any rate I will make only passing reference to Grammar 3 — usage — naively assuming that this issue has been discussed elsewhere and that my readers are familiar with those discussions.

We need also to make further discriminations about Francis' Grammar 2, given that the purpose of his 1954 article was to substitute for one form of Grammar 2, that "inaccurate and misleading" form "which is usually taught," another form, that of American structuralist grammar. Here we can make use of a still earlier discussion, one going back to the days when *PMLA* was willing to publish articles on rhetoric and linguistics, to a 1927 article by Charles Carpenter Fries, "The Rules of the Common School Grammars" (42 [1927], 221–237). Fries there distinguished between the scientific tradition of language study (to which we will now delimit Francis' Grammar 2, scientific grammar) and the separate tradition of "the common school grammars," developed unscientifically, largely based on two inadequate principles — appeals to "logical principles," like "two negatives make a positive," and analogy to Latin grammar; thus, Charlton Laird's characterization, "the grammar of Latin, ingeniously warped to suggest English" (*Language in America* [New York: World, 1970], p. 294). There is, of course, a direct link between the "common school grammars" that Fries criticized in 1927 and the grammar-based texts of today, and thus it seems wise, as Karl W. Dykema suggests ("Where Our Grammar Came From," *CE*, 22 (1961), 455–465), to separate Grammar 2, "scientific grammar," from Grammar 4, "school grammar," the latter meaning, quite literally, "the grammars used in the schools."

Further, since Martha Kolln points to the adaptation of Christensen's sentence rhetoric in a recent sentence-combining text as an example of the proper emphasis on "grammar" ("Closing the Books on Alchemy," p. 140), it is worth separating out, as still another meaning of *grammar,* Grammar 5, "stylistic grammar," defined as "grammatical terms used in the interest of teaching prose style." And, since stylistic grammars abound, with widely variant terms and emphases, we might appropriately speak parenthetically of specific forms of Grammar 5 — Grammar 5 (Lanham); Grammar 5 (Strunk and White); Grammar 5 (Williams, *Style*); even Grammar 5 (Christensen, as adapted by Daiker, Kerek, and Morenberg).[9]

The Grammar in Our Heads

With these definitions in mind, let us return to Francis' Grammar 1, admirably defined by Kolln as "the internalized system of rules that speakers of a language share" ("Closing the Books on Alchemy," p. 140), or, to put it more simply, the grammar in our heads. Three features of Grammar 1 need to be stressed: first, its special status as an "internalized system of rules," as tacit and unconscious knowledge; second, the abstract, even counterintuitive, nature of these rules, insofar as we are able to approximate them indirectly as Grammar 2 statements; and third, the way in which the form of one's Grammar 1 seems profoundly affected by the acquisition of literacy. This sort of review is designed to firm up our theory of language, so that we can ask what it predicts about the value of teaching formal grammar.

A simple thought experiment will isolate the special status of Grammar 1 knowledge. I have asked members of a number of different groups — from sixth graders to college freshmen to high-school teachers — to give me the rule for ordering adjectives of nationality, age, and number in English. The response is always the same: "We don't know the rule." Yet when I ask these groups to perform an active language task, they show productive control over the rule they have denied knowing. I ask them to arrange the following words in a natural order:

> French   the   young   girls   four

I have never seen a native speaker of English who did not immediately produce the natural order, "the four young French girls." The rule is that in English the order of adjectives is first, number, second, age, and third, nationality. Native speakers can create analogous phrases using the rule — "the seventy-three aged Scandinavian lechers"; and the drive for meaning is so great that they will create contexts to make sense out of violations of the rule, as in foregrounding for emphasis: "I want to talk to the French four young girls." (I immediately envision a large room, perhaps a banquet hall, filled with tables at which are seated groups of four young girls, each group of a different nationality.) So Grammar 1 is eminently usable knowledge — the way we make our life through language — but it is not accessible knowledge; in a profound sense, we do not know that we have it. Thus neurolinguist Z. N. Pylyshyn speaks of Grammar 1 as "autonomous," separate from common-sense reasoning, and as "cognitively impenetrable," not available for direct examination.[10] In philosophy and linguistics, the distinction is made between formal, conscious, "knowing about" knowledge (like Grammar 2 knowledge) and tacit, unconscious, "knowing how" knowledge (like Grammar 1 knowledge). The importance of this distinction for the teaching of composition — it provides a powerful theoretical justification for mistrusting the ability of Grammar 2 (or Grammar 4) knowledge to affect Grammar 1 performance — was pointed out in this journal by Martin Steinmann, Jr., in 1966 ("Rhetorical Research," *CE,* 27 [1966], 278–285).

Further, the more we learn about Grammar 1 — and most linguists would agree that we know surprisingly little about it — the more abstract and implicit it seems. This abstractness can be illustrated with an experiment, devised by Lise Menn and reported by Morris Halle,[11] about our rule for forming plurals in speech. It is obvious that we do indeed have a "rule" for forming plurals, for we do not memorize the plural of each noun separately. You will demonstrate productive control over that rule by forming the spoken plurals of the nonsense words below:

thole   flitch   plast

Halle offers two ways of formalizing a Grammar 2 equivalent of this Grammar 1 ability. One form of the rule is the following, stated in terms of speech sounds:

a.   If the noun ends in /s z š ž č ǰ/, add /ɨz/;
b.   otherwise, if the noun ends in /p t k f Ø/, add /s/;
c.   otherwise, add /z/.

This rule comes close to what we literate adults consider to be an adequate rule for plurals in writing, like the rules, for example, taken from a recent "common school grammar," Eric Gould's *Reading into Writing: A Rhetoric, Reader, and Handbook* (Boston: Houghton Mifflin, 1983):

> *Plurals* can be tricky. If you are unsure of a plural, then check it in the dictionary.
> The general rules are:
> Add *s* to the singular: *girls, tables*
> Add *es* to nouns ending in *ch, sh, x* or *s; churches, boxes, wishes*
> Add *es* to nouns ending in *y* and preceded by a vowel once you have changed *y* to *i: monies, companies.* (p. 666)

(But note the persistent inadequacy of such Grammar 4 rules: here, as I read it, the rule is inadequate to explain the plurals of *ray* and *tray,* even to explain the collective noun *monies,* not a plural at all, formed from the mass noun *money* and offered as an example.) A second form of the rule would make use of much more abstract entities, sound features:

a. If the noun ends with a sound that is [coronal, strident], add /ɨz/;
b. otherwise, if the noun ends with a sound that is [non-voiced], add /s/;
c. otherwise, add /z/.

(The notion of "sound features" is itself rather abstract, perhaps new to readers not trained in linguistics. But such readers should be able to recognize that the spoken plurals of *lip* and *duck,* the sound [s], differ from the spoken plurals of *sea* and *gnu,* the sound [z], only in that the sounds of the latter are "voiced" — one's vocal cords vibrate — while the sounds of the former are "non-voiced.")

To test the psychologically operative rule, the Grammar 1 rule, native speakers of English were asked to form the plural of the last name of the composer Johann Sebastian *Bach,* a sound [x], unique in American (though not in Scottish) English. If speakers follow the first rule above, using word endings, they would reject a) and b), then apply c), producing the plural as /baxz/, with word-final /z/. (If writers were to follow the rule of the common school grammar, they would produce the written plural *Baches,* apparently, given the form of the rule, on analogy with *churches.)* If speakers follow the second rule, they would have to analyze the sound [x] as [non-labial, non-coronal, dorsal, non-voiced, and non-strident], producing the plural as /baxs/, with word-final /s/. Native speakers of American English overwhelmingly produce the plural as /baxs/. They use knowledge that Halle characterizes as "unlearned and untaught" (p. 140).

Now such a conclusion is counterintuitive — certainly it departs maximally from Grammar 4 rules for forming plurals. It seems that native speakers of English behave as if they have productive control, as Grammar 1 knowledge, of abstract sound features (± coronal, ± strident, and so on) which are available as conscious, Grammar 2 knowledge only to trained linguists — and, indeed, formally available only within the last hundred years or so. ("Behave as if," in that last sentence, is a necessary hedge, to underscore the difficulty of "knowing about" Grammar 1.)

Moreover, as the example of plural rules suggests, the form of the Grammar 1 in the heads of literate adults seems profoundly affected by the acquisition of literacy. Obviously, literate adults have access to different morphological codes: the abstract print -*s* underlying the predictable /s/ and /z/ plurals, the abstract print -*ed* underlying the spoken past tense markers /t/, as in "walked," /əd/, as in "surrounded," /d/, as in "scored," and the symbol /∅/ for no surface realization, as in the relaxed standard pronunciation of "I walked to the store." Literate adults also have access to distinctions preserved only in the code of print (for example, the distinction between "a good sailer" and "a good sailor" that Mark Aranoff points out in "An English Spelling Convention," *Linguistic Inquiry,* 9 [1978], 299–303). More significantly, Irene Moscowitz speculates that the ability of third graders to form abstract nouns on analogy with pairs like *divine: :divinity* and *serene: :serenity,* where the spoken vowel changes but the spelling preserves meaning, is a factor of knowing how to read. Carol Chomsky finds a three-stage developmental sequence in the grammatical performance of seven-year-olds, related to measures of kind and variety of reading; and Rita S. Brause finds a nine-stage developmental sequence in the ability to understand semantic ambiguity, extending from fourth graders to graduate students.[12] John Mills and Gordon Hemsley find that level of education, and presumably level of literacy, influence judgments of grammaticality, concluding that literacy changes the deep structure of one's internal grammar; Jean Whyte finds that oral language functions develop differently in readers and non-readers; José Morais, Jesús Alegria, and Paul Bertelson find that illiterate adults are unable to add or delete sounds at the beginning of nonsense words, suggesting that awareness of speech as a series of phones is provided by learning to read an alphabetic code. Two experiments — one conducted by Charles A. Ferguson, the other by Mary E. Hamilton and David Barton — find that adults' ability to recognize segmentation in speech is related to degree of literacy, not to amount of schooling or general ability.[13]

It is worth noting that none of these investigators would suggest that the developmental sequences they have uncovered be isolated and taught as discrete skills. They are natural concomitants of literacy, and they seem best characterized not as isolated rules but as developing schemata, broad strategies for approaching written language.

Grammar 2

We can, of course, attempt to approximate the rules or schemata of Grammar 1 by writing fully explicit descriptions that model the competence of a native speaker. Such rules, like the rules for pluralizing nouns or ordering adjectives discussed above, are the goal of the science of linguistics, that is, Grammar 2. There are a number of scientific grammars — an older structuralist model and several versions within a generative-transformational paradigm, not to mention isolated schools like tagmemic grammar, Montague grammar, and the like. In fact, we cannot think of Grammar 2 as a stable entity, for its form changes with each new issue of each linguistics journal, as new "rules of grammar" are proposed and debated. Thus Grammar 2, though of great theoretical interest to the composition teacher, is of little practical use in the classroom, as Constance Weaver has pointed out (*Grammar for Teachers* [Urbana, Ill.: NCTE, 1979], pp. 3–6). Indeed Grammar 2 is a scientific model of Grammar 1, not a description of it, so that questions of psychological reality, while important, are less important than other, more theoretical factors, such as the elegance of formulation or the global power of rules. We might, for example, wish to replace the rule for ordering adjectives of age, number, and nationality cited above with a more general rule — what linguists call a "fuzzy" rule — that adjectives in English are ordered by their abstract quality of "nouniness": adjectives that are very much like nouns, like *French* or *Scandinavian*, come physically closer to nouns than do adjectives that are less "nouny," like *four* or *aged.* But our motivation for accepting the broader rule would be its global power, not its psychological reality.[14]

I try to consider a hostile reader, one committed to the teaching of grammar, and I try to think of ways to hammer in the central point of this distinction, that the rules of Grammar 2 are simply unconnected to productive control over Grammar 1. I can argue from authority: Noam Chomsky has touched on this point whenever he has concerned himself with the implications of linguistics for language teaching, and years ago transformationalist Mark Lester stated unequivocally, "there simply appears to be no correlation between a writer's study of language and his ability to write."[15] I can cite analogies offered by others: Francis Christensen's analogy in an essay originally published in 1962 that formal grammar study would be "to invite a centipede to attend to the sequence of his legs in motion,"[16] or James Britton's analogy, offered informally after a conference presentation, that grammar study would be like forcing starving people to master the use of a knife and fork before allowing them to eat. I can offer analogies of my own, contemplating the wisdom of asking a pool player to master the physics of momentum before taking up a cue or of making a prospective driver get a degree in automotive engineering before engaging the clutch. I consider a hypothetical argument, that if Grammar 2 knowledge affected Grammar 1 performance, then linguists would be our best writers. (I can certify that they are, on the whole, not.) Such a position, after all, is only in accord with other domains of science: the formula for catching a fly ball in baseball ("Playing It by Ear," *Scientific American,* 248, No. 4 [1983], 76) is of such complexity that it is beyond my understanding — and, I would suspect, that of many workaday centerfielders. But perhaps I can best hammer in this claim — that Grammar 2 knowledge has no effect on Grammar 1 performance — by offering a demonstration.

The diagram on the next page is an attempt by Thomas N. Huckin and Leslie A. Olsen (*English for Science and Technology* [New York: McGraw-Hill, 1983]) to offer, for students of English as a second language, a fully explicit formulation of what is, for native speakers, a trivial rule of the language — the choice of definite article, indefinite article, or no definite article. There are obvious limits to such a formulation, for article choice in English is less a matter of rule than of idiom ("I went to college" versus "I went to a university" versus British "I went to university"), real-world knowledge (using indefinite "I went into a house" instantiates definite "I looked at the ceiling," and indefinite "I visited a university" instantiates definite "I talked with the professors"), and stylistic choice (the last sentence above might alternatively end with "the choice of the definite article, the indefinite article, or no article"). Huckin and Olsen invite non-native speakers to use the rule consciously to justify article choice in technical prose, such as the passage below from P. F. Brandwein (*Matter: An Earth*

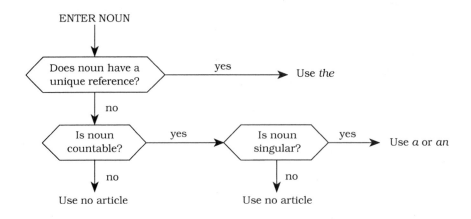

Science [New York: Harcourt Brace Jovanovich, 1975]). I invite you to spend a couple of minutes doing the same thing, with the understanding that this exercise is a test case: you are using a very explicit rule to justify a fairly straightforward issue of grammatical choice.

> Imagine a cannon on top of _____ highest mountain on earth. It is firing _____ cannonballs horizontally. _____ first cannonball fired follows its path. As cannonball moves, _____ gravity pulls it down, and it soon hits ground. Now _____ velocity with which each succeeding cannonball is _____ fired is increased. Thus, _____ cannonball goes farther each time. Cannonball 2 goes farther than _____ cannonball 1 although each is being pulled by _____ gravity toward the earth all _____ time. _____ last cannonball is fired with such tremendous velocity that it goes completely around _____ earth. It returns to _____ mountaintop and continues around the earth again and again. _____ cannonball's inertia causes it to continue in motion indefinitely in _____ orbit around earth. In such a situation, we could consider cannonball to be _____ artificial satellite, just like _____ weather satellites launched by _____ U.S. Weather Service. (p. 209)

Most native speakers of English who have attempted this exercise report a great deal of frustration, a curious sense of working against, rather than with, the rule. The rule, however valuable it may be for non-native speakers, is, for the most part, simply unusable for native speakers of the language.

Cognate Areas of Research

We can corroborate this demonstration by turning to research in two cognate areas, studies of the induction of rules of artificial languages and studies of the role of formal rules in second language acquisition. Psychologists have studied the ability of subjects to learn artificial languages, usually constructed of nonsense syllables or letter strings. Such languages can be described by phrase structure rules:

S ⇒ VX

X ⇒ MX

More clearly, they can be presented as flow diagrams, as below:

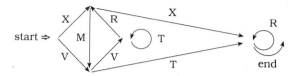

This diagram produces "sentences" like the following:

VVTRXRR.	XMVTTRX.	XXRR.
XMVRMT.	VVTTRMT.	XMTRRR.

The following "sentences" would be "ungrammatical" in this language:

*VMXTT.	*RTXVVT.	*TRVXXVVM.

Arthur S. Reber, in a classic 1967 experiment, demonstrated that mere exposure to grammatical sentences produced tacit learning: subjects who copied several grammatical sentences performed far above chance in judging the grammaticality of other letter strings. Further experiments have shown that providing subjects with formal rules — giving them the flow diagram above, for example — remarkably degrades performance: subjects given the "rules of the language" do much less well in acquiring the rules than do subjects not given the rules. Indeed, even telling subjects that they are to induce the rules of an artificial language degrades performance. Such laboratory experiments are admittedly contrived, but they confirm predictions that our theory of language would make about the value of formal rules in language learning.[17]

The thrust of recent research in second language learning similarly works to constrain the value of formal grammar rules. The most explicit statement of the value of formal rules is that of Stephen D. Krashen's monitor model.[18] Krashen divides second language mastery into *acquisition* — tacit, informal mastery, akin to first language acquisition — and formal learning—conscious application of Grammar 2 rules, which he calls "monitoring" output. In another essay Krashen uses his model to predict a highly individual use of the monitor and a highly constrained role for formal rules:

> Some adults (and very few children) are able to use conscious rules to increase the grammatical accuracy of their output, and even for these people, very strict conditions need to be met before the conscious grammar can be applied.[19]

In *Principles and Practice in Second Language Acquisition* (New York: Pergamon, 1982) Krashen outlines these conditions by means of a series of concentric circles, beginning with a large circle denoting the rules of English and a smaller circle denoting the subset of those rules described by formal linguists (adding that most linguists would protest that the size of this circle is much too large):

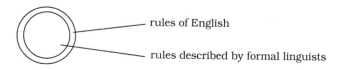

Krashen then adds smaller circles, as shown below — a subset of the rules described by formal linguists that would be known to applied linguists, a subset of those rules that would be available to the best teachers, and then a subset of those rules that teachers might choose to present to second language learners:

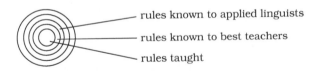

rules known to applied linguists

rules known to best teachers

rules taught

Of course, as Krashen notes, not all the rules taught will be learned, and not all those learned will be available, as what he calls "mental baggage" (p. 94), for conscious use.

An experiment by Ellen Bialystock, asking English speakers learning French to judge the grammaticality of taped sentences, complicates this issue, for reaction time data suggest that learners first make an intuitive judgment of grammaticality, using implicit or Grammar 1 knowledge, and only then search for formal explanations, using explicit or Grammar 2 knowledge.[20] This distinction would suggest that Grammar 2 knowledge is of use to second language learners only after the principle has already been mastered as tacit Grammar 1 knowledge. In the terms of Krashen's model, learning never becomes acquisition (*Principles*, p. 86).

An ingenious experiment by Herbert W. Seliger complicates the issue yet further ("On the Nature and Function of Language Rules in Language Learning," *TESOL Quarterly,* 13 [1979], 359–369). Seliger asked native and non-native speakers of English to orally identify pictures of objects (e.g., "an apple," "a pear," "a book," "an umbrella"), noting whether they used the correct form of the indefinite articles *a* and *an*. He then asked each speaker to state the rule for choosing between *a* and *an*. He found no correlation between the ability to state the rule and the ability to apply it correctly, either with native or non-native speakers. Indeed, three of four adult non-native speakers in his sample produced a correct form of the rule, but they did not apply it in speaking. A strong conclusion from this experiment would be that formal rules of grammar seem to have no value whatsoever. Seliger, however, suggests a more paradoxical interpretation. Rules are of no use, he agrees, but some people think they are, and for these people, assuming that they have internalized the rules, even inadequate rules are of heuristic value, for they allow them to access the internal rules they actually use.

The Incantations of the "Common School Grammars"

Such a paradox may explain the fascination we have as teachers with "rules of grammar" of the Grammar 4 variety, the "rules" of the "common school grammars." Again and again such rules are inadequate to the facts of written language; you will recall that we have known this since Francis' 1927 study. R. Scott Baldwin and James M. Coady, studying how readers respond to punctuation signals ("Psycholinguistic Approaches to a Theory of Punctuation," *Journal of Reading Behavior*, 10 [1978], 363–83), conclude that conventional rules of punctuation are "a complete sham" (p. 375). My own favorite is the Grammar 4 rule for showing possession, always expressed in terms of adding -'s or -s' to nouns, while our internal grammar, if you think about it, adds possession to noun phrases, albeit under severe stylistic constraints: "the horses of the Queen of England" are "the Queen of England's horses" and "the feathers of the duck over there" are "the duck over there's feathers." Suzette Haden Elgin refers to the "rules" of Grammar 4 as "incantations" (*Never Mind the Trees*, p. 9: see note 3).

It may simply be that as hyperliterate adults we are conscious of "using rules" when we are in fact doing something else, something far more complex, accessing tacit heuristics honed by print literacy itself. We can clarify this notion by reaching for an acronym coined by technical writers to explain the readability of complex prose — COIK: "clear only if known." The rules of Grammar 4 — no, we can at this point be more honest — the incantations of Grammar 4 are COIK. If you know how to signal possession in the code of print, then the advice to add -'s to nouns makes perfect sense, just as the collective noun *monies* is a fine example of changing *-y* to *-i* and adding *-es* to form the plural. But if you have not grasped, tacitly, the abstract representation of possession in print, such incantations can only be opaque.

Worse yet, the advice given in "the common school grammars" is unconnected with anything remotely resembling literate adult behavior. Consider, as an example, the rule for not writing a sentence fragment as the rule is described in the best-selling college grammar text, John C. Hodges and Mary S. Whitten's *Harbrace College Handbook*, 9th ed. (New York: Harcourt Brace Jovanovich, 1982). In order to get to the advice, "as a rule, do not write a sentence fragment" (p. 25), the student must master the following learning tasks:

Recognizing verbs.

Recognizing subjects and verbs.

Recognizing all parts of speech. (*Harbrace* lists eight.)

Recognizing phrases and subordinate clauses. (*Harbrace* lists six types of phrases, and it offers incomplete lists of eight relative pronouns and eighteen subordinating conjunctions.)

Recognizing main clauses and types of sentences.

These learning tasks completed, the student is given the rule above, offered a page of exceptions, and then given the following advice (or is it an incantation?):

> Before handing in a composition, ... proofread each word group written as a sentence. Test each one for completeness. First, be sure that it has at least one subject and one predicate. Next, be sure that the word group is not a dependent clause beginning with a subordinating conjunction or a relative clause. (p 27)

The school grammar approach defines a sentence fragment as a conceptual error — as not having conscious knowledge of the school grammar definition of *sentence*. It demands heavy emphasis on rote memory, and it asks students to behave in ways patently removed from the behaviors of mature writers. (I have never in my life tested a sentence for completeness, and I am a better writer — and probably a better person — as a consequence.) It may be, of course, that some developing writers, at some points in their development, may benefit from such advice — or, more to the point, may think that they benefit — but, as Thomas Friedman points out in "Teaching Error, Nurturing Confusion" (*CE*, 45 [1983], 390–399), our theory of language tells us that such advice is, at the best, COIK. As the Maine joke has it, about a tourist asking directions from a farmer, "you can't get there from here."

Redefining Error

In the specific case of sentence fragments, Mina P. Shaughnessy (*Errors and Expectations* [New York: Oxford University Press, 1977]) argues that such errors are not conceptual failures at all, but performance errors — mistakes in punctuation. Muriel Harris' error counts support this view ("Mending the Fragmented Free Modifier," *CCC*, 32 [1981], 175–182). Case studies show example after example of errors that occur *because* of instruction — one thinks, for example, of David Bartholomae's student explaining that he added an *-s to children* "because it's a plural" ("The Study of Error," *CCC*, 31 [1980], 262). Surveys, such as that by Muriel Harris ("Contradictory Perceptions of the Rules of Writing," *CCC*, 30 [1979], 218–220), and our own observations suggest that students consistently misunderstand such Grammar 4 explanations (COIK, you will recall). For example, from Patrick Hartwell and Robert H. Bentley and from Mike Rose, we have two separate anecdotal accounts of students, cited for punctuating a *because*-clause as a sentence, who have decided to avoid using *because*. More generally, Collette A. Daiute's analysis of errors made by college students shows that errors tend to appear at clause boundaries, suggesting short-term memory load and not conceptual deficiency as a cause of error.[21]

Thus, if we think seriously about error and its relationship to the worship of formal grammar study, we need to attempt some massive dislocation of our traditional thinking, to shuck off our hyperliterate perception of the value of formal rules, and to regain the confidence in the tacit power of unconscious knowledge that our theory of language gives us. Most students, reading their writing aloud, will correct in essence all errors of spelling, grammar, and, by intonation, punctuation, but usually without noticing that what they read departs from what they wrote.[22] And Richard H. Haswell ("Minimal Marking," *CE*, 45 [1983], 600–604) notes that his students correct 61.1 percent of their errors when they are identified with a simple mark in the margin rather than by error type. Such findings suggest that we need to redefine error, to see it not as a cognitive or linguistic problem, a problem of not knowing a "rule of grammar" (whatever that may mean), but rather, following the insight of Robert J. Bracewell ("Writing as a Cognitive Activity," *Visible Language*, 14 [1980], 400–422), as a problem of metacognition and metalinguistic awareness, a matter of accessing knowledges that, to be of any use, learners must have already internalized by means of exposure to the code. (Usage issues — Grammar 3 — probably represent a different order of problem. Both Joseph Emonds and Jeffrey Jochnowitz establish that the usage issues we worry most about are linguistically unnatural, departures from the grammar in our heads.)[23]

The notion of metalinguistic awareness seems crucial. The sentence below, created by Douglas R. Hofstadter ("Metamagical Themas," *Scientific American*, 235, No. 1 [1981], 22-32), is offered to clarify that notion; you are invited to examine it for a moment or two before continuing.

Their is four errors in this sentance. Can you find them?

Three errors announce themselves plainly enough, the misspellings of *there* and *sentence* and the use of *is* instead of *are*. (And, just to illustrate the perils of hyperliteracy, let it be noted that, through three years of drafts, I referred to the choice of *is* and *are* as a matter of "subject-verb agreement.") The fourth error resists detection, until one assesses the truth value of the sentence itself — the fourth error is that there are not four errors, only three. Such a sentence (Hofstadter calls it a "self-referencing sentence") asks you to look at it in two ways, simultaneously as statement and as linguistic artifact — in other words, to exercise metalinguistic awareness.

A broad range of cross-cultural studies suggest that metalinguistic awareness is a defining feature of print literacy. Thus Sylvia Scribner and Michael Cole, working with the triliterate Vai of Liberia (variously literate in English, through schooling; in Arabic, for religious purposes; and in an indigenous Vai script, used for personal affairs), find that metalinguistic awareness, broadly conceived, is the only cognitive skill underlying each of the three literacies. The one statistically significant skill shared by literate Vai was the recognition of word boundaries. Moreover, literate Vai tended to answer "yes" when asked (in Vai). "Can you call the sun the moon and the moon the sun?" while illiterate Vai tended to have grave doubts about such metalinguistic play. And in the United States Henry and Lila R. Gleitman report quite different responses by clerical workers and PhD candidates asked to interpret nonsense compounds like "house-bird glass": clerical workers focused on meaning and plausibility (for example, "a house-bird made of glass"), while PhD candidates focused on syntax (for example, "a very small drinking cup for canaries" or "a glass that protects house-birds").[24] More general research findings suggest a clear relationship between measures of metalinguistic awareness and measures of literacy level.[25] William Labov, speculating on literacy acquisition in inner-city ghettoes, contrasts "stimulus-bound" and "language-bound" individuals, suggesting that the latter seem to master literacy more easily.[26] The analysis here suggests that the causal relationship works the other way, that it is the mastery of written language that increases one's awareness of language as language.

This analysis has two implications. First, it makes the question of socially nonstandard dialects, always implicit in discussions of teaching formal grammar, into a non-issue.[27] Native speakers of English, regardless of dialect, show tacit mastery of the conventions of Standard English, and that mastery seems to transfer into abstract orthographic knowledge through interaction with print.[28] Developing writers show the same patterning of errors, regardless of dialect.[29] Studies of reading and of writing suggest that surface features of spoken dialect are simply irrelevant to mastering print literacy.[30] Print is a complex cultural code — or better yet, a system of code — and my bet is that, regardless of instruction, one masters those codes from the top down, from pragmatic questions of voice, tone, audience, register, and rhetorical strategy, not from the bottom up, from grammar to usage to fixed forms of organization.

Second, this analysis forces us to posit multiple literacies, used for multiple purposes, rather than a single static literacy, engraved in "rules of grammar." These multiple literacies are evident in cross-cultural studies.[31] They are equally evident when we inquire into the uses of literacy in American communities.[32] Further, given that students, at all levels, show widely variant interactions with print literacy, there would seem to be little to do with grammar — with Grammar 2 or with Grammar 4 — that we could isolate as a basis for formal instruction.[33]

Grammar 5: Stylistic Grammar

Similarly, when we turn to Grammar 5, "grammatical terms used in the interest of teaching prose style," so central to Martha Kolln's argument for teaching formal grammar, we find that the grammar issue is simply beside the point. There are two fully-articulated positions about "stylistic grammar," which I will label "romantic" and "classic," following Richard Lloyd-

Jones and Richard E. Young.[34] The romantic position is that stylistic grammars, though perhaps useful for teachers, have little place in the teaching of composition, for students must struggle with and through language toward meaning. This position rests on a theory of language ultimately philosophical rather than linguistic (witness, for example, the contempt for linguists in Ann Berthoff's *The Making of Meaning: Metaphors, Models, and Maxims for Writing Teachers* [Montclair, N.J.: Boynton/Cook, 1981]); it is articulated as a theory of style by Donald A. Murray and, on somewhat different grounds (that stylistic grammars encourage overuse of the monitor), by Ian Pringle. The classic position, on the other hand, is that we can find ways to offer developing writers helpful suggestions about prose style, suggestions such as Francis Christensen's emphasis on the cumulative sentence, developed by observing the practice of skilled writers, and Joseph Williams' advice about predication, developed by psycholinguistic studies of comprehension.[35] James A. Berlin's recent survey of composition theory (*CE*, 45 [1982], 765–777) probably understates the gulf between these two positions and the radically different conceptions of language that underlie them, but it does establish that they share an overriding assumption in common: that one learns to control the language of print by manipulating language in meaningful contexts, not by learning about language in isolation, as by the study of formal grammar. Thus even classic theorists, who choose to present a vocabulary of style to students, do so only as a vehicle for encouraging productive control of communicative structures.

We might put the matter in the following terms. Writers need to develop skills at two levels. One, broadly rhetorical, involves communication in meaningful contexts (the strategies, registers, and procedures of discourse across a range of modes, audiences, contexts, and purposes). The other, broadly metalinguistic rather than linguistic, involves active manipulation of language with conscious attention to surface form. This second level may be developed tacitly, as a natural adjunct to developing rhetorical competencies — I take this to be the position of romantic theorists. It may be developed formally, by manipulating language for stylistic effect, and such manipulation may involve, for pedagogical continuity, a vocabulary of style. But it is primarily developed by any kind of language activity that enhances the awareness of language as language.[36] David T. Hakes, summarizing the research on metalinguistic awareness, notes how far we are from understanding this process:

> the optimal conditions for becoming metalinguistically competent involve growing up in a literate environment with adult models who are themselves metalinguistically competent and who foster the growth of that competence in a variety of ways as yet little understood. ("The Development of Metalinguistic Abilities," p. 205: see note 25)

Such a model places language, at all levels, at the center of the curriculum, but not as "necessary categories and labels" (Kolln, "Closing the Books on Alchemy," p. 150), but as literal stuff, verbal clay, to be molded and probed, shaped and reshaped, and, above all, enjoyed.

The Tradition of Experimental Research

Thus, when we turn back to experimental research on the value of formal grammar instruction, we do so with firm predictions given us by our theory of language. Our theory would predict that formal grammar instruction, whether instruction in scientific grammar or instruction in "the common school grammar," would have little to do with control over surface correctness nor with quality of writing. It would predict that any form of active involvement with language would be preferable to instruction in rules or definitions (or incantations). In essence, this is what the research tells us. In 1893, the Committee of Ten (*Report of the Committee of Ten on Secondary School Studies* [Washington, D.C.: U.S. Government Printing Office, 1893]) put grammar at the center of the English curriculum, and its report established the rigidly sequential mode of instruction common for the last century. But the committee explicitly noted that grammar instruction did not aid correctness, arguing instead that it improved the ability to think logically (an argument developed from the role of the "grammarian" in the classical rhetorical tradition, essentially a teacher of literature — see, for example, the etymology of *grammar* in the *Oxford English Dictionary*).

But Franklin S. Hoyt, in a 1906 experiment, found no relationship between the study of grammar and the ability to think logically; his research led him to conclude what I am constrained to argue more than seventy-five years later, that there is no "relationship between a knowledge of technical grammar and the ability to use English and to interpret language" ("The Place of Grammar in the Elementary Curriculum," *Teachers College Record*, 7 [1906], 483-484). Later studies, through the 1920s, focused on the relationship of knowledge of grammar and ability to recognize error; experiments reported by James Boraas in 1917 and by William Asker in 1923 are typical of those that reported no correlation. In the 1930s, with the development of the functional grammar movement, it was common to compare the study of formal grammar with one form or another of active manipulation of language; experiments by I. O. Ash in 1935 and Ellen Frogner in 1939 are typical of studies showing the superiority of active involvement with language.[37] In a 1959 article, "Grammar in Language Teaching" (*Elementary English*, 36 [1959], 412-421), John J. DeBoer noted the consistency of these findings.

> The impressive fact is . . . that in all these studies, carried out in places and at times far removed from each other, often by highly experienced and disinterested investigators, the results have been consistently negative so far as the value of grammar in the improvement of language expression is concerned. (p. 417)

In 1960 Ingrid M. Strom, reviewing more than fifty experimental studies, came to a similarly strong and unqualified conclusion:

> direct methods of instruction, focusing on writing activities and the structuring of ideas, are more efficient in teaching sentence structure, usage, punctuation, and other related factors than are such methods as nomenclature drill, diagramming, and rote memorization of grammatical rules.[38]

In 1963 two research reviews appeared, one by Braddock, Lloyd-Jones, and Schorer, cited at the beginning of this paper, and one by Henry C. Meckel, whose conclusions, though more guarded, are in essential agreement.[39] In 1969 J. Stephen Sherwin devoted one-fourth of his *Four Problems in Teaching English: A Critique of Research* (Scranton, Penn.: International Textbook, 1969) to the grammar issue, concluding that "instruction in formal grammar is an ineffective way to help students achieve proficiency in writing" (p. 135). Some early experiments in sentence combining, such as those by Donald R. Bateman and Frank J. Zidonnis and by John C. Mellon, showed improvement in measures of syntactic complexity with instruction in transformational grammar keyed to sentence combining practice. But a later study by Frank O'Hare achieved the same gains with no grammar instruction, suggesting to Sandra L. Stotsky and to Richard Van de Veghe that active manipulation of language, not the grammar unit, explained the earlier results.[40] More recent summaries of research — by

Elizabeth I. Haynes, Hillary Taylor Holbrook, and Marcia Farr Whiteman — support similar conclusions. Indirect evidence for this position is provided by surveys reported by Betty Bamberg in 1978 and 1981, showing that time spent in grammar instruction in high school is the least important factor, of eight factors examined, in separating regular from remedial writers at the college level.[41]

More generally, Patrick Scott and Bruce Castner, in "Reference Sources for Composition Research: A Practical Survey" (*CE*, 45 [1983], 756–768), note that much current research is not informed by an awareness of the past. Put simply, we are constrained to reinvent the wheel. My concern here has been with a far more serious problem: that too often the wheel we reinvent is square.

It is, after all, a question of power. Janet Emig, developing a consensus from composition research, and Aaron S. Carton and Lawrence V. Castiglione, developing the implications of language theory for education, come to the same conclusion: that the thrust of current research and theory is to take power from the teacher and to give that power to the learner.[42] At no point in the English curriculum is the question of power more blatantly posed than in the issue of formal grammar instruction. It is time that we, as teachers, formulate theories of language and literacy and let those theories guide our teaching, and it is time that we, as researchers, move on to more interesting areas of inquiry.

Notes

[1] *Research in Written Composition* (Urbana, Ill.: National Council of Teachers of English, 1963), pp. 37–38.

[2] "Non-magical Thinking: Presenting Writing Developmentally in Schools," in *Writing Process, Development and Communication*, Vol. II of *Writing: The Nature, Development and Teaching of Written Communication*, ed. Charles H. Frederiksen and Joseph F. Dominic (Hillsdale, N.J.: Lawrence Erlbaum, 1980), pp. 21–30.

[3] For arguments in favor of formal grammar teaching, see Patrick F. Basset, "Grammar — Can We Afford Not to Teach It?" *NASSP Bulletin*, 64, No. 10 (1980), 55–63; Mary Epes et al., "The COMP-LAB Project: Assessing the Effectiveness of a Laboratory-Centered Basic Writing Course on the College Level" (Jamaica, N.Y.: York College, CUNY, 1979) ERIC 194 908; June B. Evans, "The Analogous Ounce: The Analgesic for Relief," *English Journal*, 70, No. 2 (1981), 38–39; Sydney Greenbaum, "What Is Grammar and Why Teach It?" (a paper presented at the meeting of the National Council of Teachers of English, Boston, Nov. 1982) ERIC 222 917; Marjorie Smelstor, *A Guide to the Role of Grammar in Teaching Writing* (Madison: University of Wisconsin School of Education, 1978) ERIC 176 323; and A. M. Tibbetts, *Working Papers: A Teacher's Observations on Composition* (Glenview, Ill.: Scott, Foresman, 1982).

For attacks on formal grammar teaching, see Harvey A. Daniels, *Famous Last Words: The American Language Crisis Reconsidered* (Carbondale: Southern Illinois University Press, 1983); Suzette Haden Elgin, *Never Mind the Trees: What the English Teacher Really Needs to Know about Linguistics* (Berkeley: University of California College of Education, Bay Area Writing Project Occasional Paper No. 2, 1980) ERIC 198 536; Mike Rose, "Remedial Writing Courses: A Critique and a Proposal," *College English*, 45 (1983), 109–128; and Ron Shook, Response to Martha Kolln, *College Composition and Communication*, 34 (1983), 491–495.

[4] See, for example, Clifton Fadiman and James Howard, *Empty Pages: A Search for Writing Competence in School and Society* (Belmont, Cal.: Fearon Pitman, 1979); Edwin Newman. *A Civil Tongue* (Indianapolis, Ind.: Bobbs-Merrill, 1976); and *Strictly Speaking* (New York: Warner Books, 1974); John Simons, *Paradigms Lost* (New York: Clarkson N. Potter, 1980); A. M. Tibbets and Charlene Tibbets, *What's Happening*

to American English? (New York: Scribner's, 1978); and "Why Johnny Can't Write," *Newsweek,* 8 Dec. 1975, pp. 58–63.

[5] "The Role of Grammar in a Secondary School English Curriculum." *Research in the Teaching of English,* 10 (1976), 5–21; *The Role of Grammar in a Secondary School Curriculum* (Wellington: New Zealand Council of Teachers of English, 1979).

[6] "A Taxonomy of Compositional Competencies," in *Perspectives on Literacy,* ed. Richard Beach and P. David Pearson (Minneapolis: University of Minnesota College of Education, 1979), pp. 247–272.

[7] On usage norms, see Edward Finegan, *Attitudes toward English Usage: The History of a War of Words* (New York: Teachers College Press, 1980), and Jim Quinn, *American Tongue in Cheek: A Populist Guide to Language* (New York: Pantheon, 1980); on arrangement, see Patrick Hartwell, "Teaching Arrangement: A Pedagogy," *CE,* 40 (1979), 548–554.

[8] "Revolution in Grammar," *Quarterly Journal of Speech,* 40 (1954), 299–312.

[9] Richard A. Lanham, *Revising Prose* (New York: Scribner's, 1979); William Strunk and E. B. White, *The Elements of Style,* 3rd ed. (New York: Macmillan, 1979); Joseph Williams, *Style: Ten Lessons in Clarity and Grace* (Glenview, Ill.: Scott, Foresman, 1981); Christensen, "A Generative Rhetoric of the Sentence," *CCC,* 14 (1963), 155–161; Donald A. Daiker, Andrew Kerek, and Max Morenberg, *The Writer's Options: Combining to Composing,* 2nd ed. (New York: Harper & Row, 1982).

[10] "A Psychological Approach," in *Psychobiology of Language,* ed. M. Studdert-Kennedy (Cambridge, Mass.: MIT Press, 1983), pp. 16–19. See also Noam Chomsky, "Language and Unconscious Knowledge," in *Psychoanalysis and Language: Psychiatry and the Humanities,* Vol. III, ed. Joseph H. Smith (New Haven, Conn.: Yale University Press, 1978), pp. 3–44.

[11] Morris Halle, "Knowledge Unlearned and Untaught: What Speakers Know about the Sounds of Their Language," in *Linguistic Theory and Psychological Reality,* ed. Halle, Joan Bresnan, and George A. Miller (Cambridge, Mass.: MIT Press, 1978), pp. 135–140.

[12] Moscowitz, "On the Status of Vowel Shift in English," in *Cognitive Development and the Acquisition of Language,* ed. T. E. Moore (New York: Academic Press, 1973), pp. 223–260; Chomsky, "Stages in Language Development and Reading Exposure," *Harvard Educational Review,* 42 (1972), 1–33; and Brause, "Developmental Aspects of the Ability to Understand Semantic Ambiguity, with Implications for Teachers," *RTE,* 11 (1977), 39–48.

[13] Mills and Hemsley, "The Effect of Levels of Education on Judgments of Grammatical Acceptability," *Language and Speech,* 19 (1976), 324–342; Whyte, "Levels of Language Competence and Reading Ability: An Exploratory Investigation," *Journal of Research in Reading,* 5 (1982), 123–132; Morais et al., "Does Awareness of Speech as a Series of Phones Arise Spontaneously?" *Cognition,* 7 (1979), 323–331; Ferguson, *Cognitive Effects of Literacy: Linguistic Awareness in Adult Non-readers* (Washington, D.C.: National Institute of Education Final Report, 1981) ERIC 222 857; Hamilton and Barton, "A Word Is a Word: Metalinguistic Skills in Adults of Varying Literacy Levels" (Stanford, Cal.: Stanford University Department of Linguistics, 1980) ERIC 222 859.

[14] On the question of the psychological reality of Grammar 2 descriptions, see Maria Black and Shulamith Chiat, "Psycholinguistics without 'Psychological Reality,'" *Linguistics,* 19 (1981), 37–61; Joan Bresnan, ed., *The Mental Representation of Grammatical Relations* (Cambridge, Mass.: MIT Press, 1982); and Michael H. Long, "Inside the 'Black Box': Methodological Issues in Classroom Research on Language Learning," *Language Learning,* 30 (1980), 1–42.

[15] Chomsky, "The Current Scene in Linguistics," *College English,* 27 (1966), 587–595; and "Linguistic Theory," in *Language Teaching: Broader Contexts,* ed. Robert C. Meade, Jr. (New York: Modern Language Association, 1966), pp. 43–49; Mark Lester, "The Value of Transformational Grammar in Teaching Composition," *CCC,* 16 (1967), 228.

[16] Christensen, "Between Two Worlds," in *Notes toward a New Rhetoric: Nine Essays for Teachers*, rev. ed., ed. Bonniejean Christensen (New York: Harper & Row, 1978), pp. 1–22.

[17] Reber, "Implicit Learning of Artificial Grammars," *Journal of Verbal Learning and Verbal Behavior*, 6 (1967), 855–863; "Implicit Learning of Synthetic Languages: The Role of Instructional Set," *Journal of Experimental Psychology: Human Learning and Memory*, 2 (1976), 889–94, and Reber, Saul M. Kassin, Selma Lewis, and Gary Cantor, "On the Relationship Between Implicit and Explicit Modes in the Learning of a Complex Rule Structure," *Journal of Experimental Psychology: Human Learning and Memory*, 6 (1980), 492–502.

[18] "Individual Variation in the Use of the Monitor," in *Principles of Second Language Learning*, ed. W. Richie (New York: Academic Press, 1978), pp. 175-185.

[19] "Applications of Psycholinguistic Research to the Classroom," in *Practical Applications of Research in Foreign Language Teaching*, ed. D. J. James (Lincolnwood, Ill.: National Textbook, 1983), p. 61.

[20] "Some Evidence for the Integrity and Interaction of Two Knowledge Sources," in *New Dimensions in Second Language Acquisition Research*, ed. Roger W. Andersen (Rowley, Mass.: Newbury House, 1981), pp. 62–74.

[21] Hartwell and Bentley, *Some Suggestions for Using Open to Language: A New College Rhetoric.* (New York: Oxford University Press, 1982), p. 73; Rose, *Writer's Block: The Cognitive Dimension* (Carbondale: Southern Illinois University Press, 1983), p. 99; Daiute, "Psycholinguistic Foundations of the Writing Process," *RTE*, 15 (1981), 5–22.

[22] See Bartholomae, "The Study of Error"; Patrick Hartwell, "The Writing Center and the Paradoxes of Written-Down Speech," in *Writing Centers: Theory and Administration*, ed. Gary Olson (Urbana, Ill.: NCTE, 1984), pp. 48–61; and Sondra Perl, "A Look at Basic Writers in the Process of Composing," in *Basic Writing: A Collection of Essays for Teachers, Researchers, and Administrators* (Urbana, Ill.: NCTE, 1980), pp. 13–32.

[23] Emonds, *Adjacency in Grammar: The Theory of Language-Particular Rules* (New York: Academic, 1983); and Jochnowitz, "Everybody Likes Pizza, Doesn't He or She?" *American Speech*, 57 (1982), 198–203.

[24] Scribner and Cole, *Psychology of Literacy* (Cambridge, Mass.: Harvard University Press 1981); Gleitman and Gleitman, "Language Use and Language Judgment," in *Individual Differences in Language Ability and Language Behavior*, ed. Charles J. Fillmore, Daniel Kemper, and William S.-Y. Wang (New York: Academic Press, 1979), pp. 103–126.

[25] There are several recent reviews of this developing body of research in psychology and child development: Irene Athey, "Language Development Factors Related to Reading Development," *Journal of Educational Research*, 76 (1983), 197–203; James Flood and Paula Menyuk "Metalinguistic Development and Reading/Writing Achievement," *Claremont Reading Conference Yearbook*, 46 (1982), 122–132; and the following four essays: David T. Hakes, "The Development of Metalinguistic Abilities: What Develops?," pp. 162–210; Stan A. Kuczaj, II, and Brooke Harbaugh "What Children Think about the Speaking Capabilities of Other Persons and Things," pp. 211–227, Karen Saywitz and Louise Cherry Wilkinson, "Age-Related Differences in Metalinguistic Awareness," pp. 229–250; and Harriet Salatas Waters and Virginia S. Tinsley, "The Development of Verbal Self-Regulation: Relationships between Language, Cognition, and Behavior." pp. 251–277; all in *Language, Thought, and Culture*, Vol. II of *Language Development*, ed. Stan Kuczaj, Jr. (Hillsdale, N.J.: Lawrence Erlbaum. 1982). See also Joanne R. Nurss. "Research in Review: Linguistic Awareness and Learning to Read," *Young Children*, 35, No. 3 (1980), 57–66.

[26] "Competing Value Systems in Inner City Schools," in *Children In and Out of School. Ethnography and Education*, ed. Perry Gilmore and Allan A. Glatthorn (Washington, D.C.: Center for Applied Linguistics, 1982), pp. 148–171; and "Locating the Frontier between Social and Psychological Factors in Linguistic Structure," in *Indi-*

vidual Differences in Language Ability and Language Behavior, ed. Fillmore, Kemper, and Wang, pp. 327–340.

[27] See, for example, Thomas Farrell, "IQ and Standard English," *CCC,* 34 (1983), 470–484, and the responses by Karen L. Greenberg and Patrick Hartwell, *CCC,* in press.

[28] Jane W. Torrey, "Teaching Standard English to Speakers of Other Dialects," in *Applications of Linguistics: Selected Papers of the Second International Conference of Applied Linguistics,* ed. C. E. Perren and J. L. M. Trim (Cambridge, Mass.: Cambridge University Press, 1971), pp. 423–428; James W. Beers and Edmund H. Henderson, "A Study of the Developing Orthographic Concepts among First Graders," *RTE,* 11 (1977), 133–148.

[29] See the error counts of Samuel A. Kirschner and C. Howard Poteet, "Non-Standard English Usage in the Writing of Black, White, and Hispanic Remedial English Students in an Urban Community College," *RTE,* 7 (1973), 351–355; and Marilyn Sternglass, "Close Similarities in Dialect Features of Black and White College Students in Remedial Composition Classes," *TESOL Quarterly,* 8 (1974), 271–283.

[30] For reading, see the massive study by Kenneth S. Goodman and Yetta M. Goodman, *Reading of American Children Whose Language Is a Stable Rural Dialect of English or a Language Other than English* (Washington, D.C.: National Institute of Education Final Report, 1978) ERIC 175 754; and the overview by Rudine Sims, "Dialect and Reading: Toward Redefining the Issues," in *Reader Meets Author/Bridging the Gap: A Psycholinguistic and Sociolinguistic Approach,* ed. Judith A. Langer and M. Tricia Smith-Burke (Newark, Del.: International Reading Association 1982), pp. 222–232. For writing, see Patrick Hartwell, "Dialect Interference in Writing: A Critical View," *RTE,* 14 (1980), 101–118; and the anthology edited by Barry M. Kroll and Roberta J. Vann, *Exploring Speaking-Writing Relationships: Connections and Contrasts* (Urbana, Ill.: NCTE, 1981).

[31] See, for example, Eric A. Havelock, *The Literary Revolution in Greece and its Cultural Consequences* (Princeton, N.J.: Princeton University Press, 1982); Lesley Milroy on literacy in Dublin, *Language and Social Networks* (Oxford: Basil Blackwell, 1980); Ron Scollon and Suzanne B. K. Scollon on literacy in central Alaska, *Interethnic Communication: An Athabascan Case* (Austin, Tex.: Southwest Educational Development Laboratory Working Papers in Sociolinguistics, No. 59, 1979) ERIC 175 276; and Scribner and Cole on literacy in Liberia, *Psychology of Literacy* (see note 24).

[32] See, for example, the anthology edited by Deborah Tannen, *Spoken and Written Language: Exploring Orality and Literacy* (Norwood, N.J.: Ablex, 1982); and Shirley Brice Heath's continuing work: "Protean Shapes in Literacy Events: Ever-Shifting Oral and Literate Traditions," in *Spoken and Written Language,* pp. 91–117; *Ways with Words: Language, Life and Work in Communities and Classrooms* (New York: Cambridge University Press, 1983); and "What No Bedtime Story Means," *Language in Society,* 11 (1982), 49–76.

[33] For studies at the elementary level, see Dell H. Hymes et al., eds., *Ethnographic Monitoring of Children's Acquisition of Reading/Language Arts Skills In and Out of the Classroom* (Washington, D.C.: National Institute of Education Final Report, 1981) ERIC 208 096. For studies at the secondary level, see James L. Collins and Michael M. Williamson, "Spoken Language and Semantic Abbreviation in Writing," *RTE,* 15 (1981), 23–36. And for studies at the college level, see Patrick Hartwell and Gene LoPresti, "Sentence Combining as Kid-Watching," in *Sentence Combining: Toward a Rhetorical Perspective,* ed. Donald A. Daiker, Andrew Kerek, and Max Morenberg (Carbondale: Southern Illinois University Press, in press).

[34] Lloyd-Jones, "Romantic Revels — I Am Not You," *CCC,* 23 (1972), 251–271; and Young, "Concepts of Art and the Teaching of Writing," in *The Rhetorical Tradition and Modern Writing,* ed. James J. Murphy (New York: Modern Language Association, 1982), pp. 130–141.

[35] For the romantic position, see Ann E. Berthoff, "Tolstoy, Vygotsky, and the Making of Meaning," *CCC*, 29 (1978), 249–255; Kenneth Dowst, "The Epistemic Approach," in *Eight Approaches to Teaching Composition*, ed. Timothy Donovan and Ben G. McClellan (Urbana, Ill.: NCTE, 1980), pp. 65–85; Peter Elbow, "The Challenge for Sentence Combining"; and Donald Murray, "Following Language toward Meaning," both in *Sentence Combining: Toward a Rhetorical Perspective* (in press; see note 33). and Ian Pringle, "Why Teach Style? A Review-Essay," *CCC*, 34 (1983), 91–98.

For the classic position, see Christensen's "A Generative Rhetoric of the Sentence" and Joseph Williams' "Defining Complexity," *CE*, 41 (1979), 595–609; and his *Style: Ten Lessons in Clarity and Grace* (see note 9).

[36] Courtney B. Cazden and David K. Dickinson, "Language and Education: Standardization versus Cultural Pluralism," in *Language in the USA*, ed. Charles A. Ferguson and Shirley Brice Heath (New York: Cambridge University Press, 1981), pp. 446–468; and Carol Chomsky, "Developing Facility with Language Structure," in *Discovering Language with Children*, ed. Gay Su Pinnell (Urbana, Ill.: NCTE, 1980), pp. 56–59.

[37] Boraas, "Formal English Grammar and the Practical Mastery of English." Diss. University of Illinois, 1917; Asker, "Does Knowledge of Grammar Function?" *School and Society*, 17 (27 January 1923), 109–111; Ash, "An Experimental Evaluation of the Stylistic Approach in Teaching Composition in the Junior High School," *Journal of Experimental Education*, 4 (1935), 54–62; and Frogner, "A Study of the Relative Efficacy of a Grammatical and a Thought Approach to the Improvement of Sentence Structure in Grades Nine and Eleven," *School Review*, 47 (1939), 663–675.

[38] "Research on Grammar and Usage and Its Implications for Teaching Writing," *Bulletin of the School of Education*, Indiana University, 36 (1960), pp. 13–14.

[39] Meckel, "Research on Teaching Composition and Literature," in *Handbook of Research on Teaching*, ed. N. L. Gage (Chicago: Rand McNally, 1963), pp. 966–1006.

[40] Bateman and Zidonis, *The Effect of a Study of Transformational Grammar on the Writing of Ninth and Tenth Graders* (Urbana, Ill.: NCTE, 1966); Mellon, *Transformational Sentence Combining: A Method for Enhancing the Development of Fluency in English Composition* (Urbana, Ill.: NCTE, 1969); O'Hare, *Sentence-Combining: Improving Student Writing without Formal Grammar Instruction* (Urbana, Ill.: NCTE, 1971); Stotsky, "Sentence-Combining as a Curricular Activity: Its Effect on Written Language Development," *RTE*, 9 (1975), 30–72; and Van de Veghe, "Research in Written Composition: Fifteen Years of Investigation," ERIC 157 095.

[41] Haynes, "Using Research in Preparing to Teach Writing," *English Journal*, 69, No. 1 (1978), 82–88; Holbrook, "ERIC/RCS Report: Whither (Wither) Grammar," *Language Arts*, 60 (1983), 259–263; Whiteman, "What We Can Learn from Writing Research," *Theory into Practice*, 19 (1980), 150–156; Bamberg, "Composition in the Secondary English Curriculum: Some Current Trends and Directions for the Eighties," *RTE*, 15 (1981), 257–266; and "Composition Instruction Does Make a Difference: A Comparison of the High School Preparation of College Freshmen in Regular and Remedial English Classes," *RTE*, 12 (1978), 47–59.

[42] Emig, "Inquiry Paradigms and Writing," *CCC*, 33 (1982), 64–75; Carton and Castiglione, "Educational Linguistics: Defining the Domain," in *Psycholinguistic Research: Implications and Applications*, ed. Doris Aaronson and Robert W. Rieber (Hillsdale, N.J.: Lawrence Erlbaum, 1979), pp. 497–520.

COMPUTERS AND WRITING

For more than a decade, the use of technology in writing classes has increased exponentially. Students come to college with advanced computer skills and extensive experience on the World Wide Web and Internet-based communications. Across the country, institutions invest substantial sums of money in computing facilities and electronic classrooms of various kinds. Technology is not only changing classroom practices, but it is also changing institutional structures and practices. The advent of "distance-learning" initiatives has resulted in "virtual classrooms" and "virtual universities." Writing teachers are often at the center of instructional technology initiatives, integrating technology in their own classes and participating in institutional decision-making processes to plan and implement the use of instructional technology across the campus.

The articles included in this appendix recognize that teachers are technologically literate, and they address several crucial issues that writing teachers face in their ongoing attempts to use technology effectively.

- How can we examine our uses of technology critically, carefully, and honestly? How can we resist the too-simple equation that more technology necessarily results in more effective learning or teaching?
- How is technology changing our understanding of "genre," of "publishing," of what it means "to write"?
- How does technology relate to literacy? How can teachers develop research agendas that will help them shape and control the use of instructional technologies rather than being shaped and controlled by technology?

THE RHETORIC OF TECHNOLOGY
AND THE ELECTRONIC WRITING CLASS

Gail E. Hawisher and Cynthia L. Selfe

[*College Composition and Communication* 42 (February 1991): 55–65.]

Gail E. Hawisher is associate professor of English and director of the Center for Writing Studies at the University of Illinois, Urbana. She has published widely in computers and composition studies. With Paul LeBlanc, she coedited *Re-imagining Computers and Composition: Teaching and Research in the Virtual Age*; with Cynthia Selfe, she coedited the *CCCC Bibliography of Composition and Rhetoric*, and they currently coedit *Computers and Composition*. Most recently she coauthored *Computers and the Teaching of Writing in American Higher Education, 1979–1994: A History*, with Cynthia Selfe, Charles Moran, and Paul LeBlanc. Cynthia Selfe, professor of composition and communications in the Department of Humanities at Michigan Technological University, has also published widely in computers and composition studies. She has coed-ited several books, including *Critical Perspectives on Computers and Composition Instruction and Evolving Perspectives on Computers and Composition Studies: Questions for the 1990s* with Gail Hawisher, *Computers and Writing: Theory, Research, Practice* with Deborah Holdstein, and *Literacy and Computers: The Complications of Teaching and Learning with Technology* with Susan Hilligoss.

In this article, Hawisher and Selfe look at the ways we use technology to teach writing and, more importantly, at the ways we represent our uses of technology. Although their 1991 article might seem dated, especially in a field where fundamentally innovative changes often occur more rapidly than in many other areas of educational practice, their cautions about the uses of technology continue to be valid. Although they recognize that technology en-ables teachers to reimagine composition instruction, the authors argue that teachers may be misrepresenting the value of technol-ogy, and that "it is not enough for teachers to talk about computer use in uncritical ways." Their article will help teachers view their electronic classes "as sites of paradox and promise, transformed by a new writing technology."

Since the mass production of the first fully-assembled microcomputer in 1977, technological change has influenced not only the ways in which we write but also, for many of us, the ways in which we teach writing.[1] In-creasing numbers of writing instructors now depend on computer-sup-ported classrooms and use online conferences that take place over com-puter networks as teaching environments. Writing instructors who hope to function effectively in these new electronic classrooms must assess ways in which the use of computer technology might shape, for better and worse, their strategies for working with students. Along with becoming acquainted with current composition theory, instructors, for example, must learn to recognize that the use of technology can exacerbate problems characteris-tic of American classrooms and must continue to seek ways of using tech-nology that equitably support all students in writing classes. All too fre-quently, however, writing instructors incorporate computers into their classes without the necessary scrutiny and careful planning that the use of any technology requires.

Such scrutiny will become increasingly important with computers, given the considerable corporate and community investment accompanying this technology as its use expands within our educational system. Unfortu-nately, as writing instructors, we have not always recognized the natural tendency when using such machines, as cultural artifacts embodying society's values, to perpetuate those values currently dominant within our culture and our educational system. This tendency has become evident as we continue to integrate computers into our efforts at writing instruction. In many English composition classes, computer use simply reinforces those traditional notions of education that permeate our culture at its most basic level: teachers talk, students listen; teachers' contributions are privileged; students respond in predictable, teacher-pleasing ways.

With the new technology, these tendencies are played out in classrooms where students labor at isolated workstations on drill-and-practice gram-mar software or in word-processing facilities where computers are arranged, rank and file, so that teachers can examine each computer screen at a moment's notice to check on what students are writing. What many in our profession have yet to realize is that electronic technology, unless it is considered carefully and used critically, can and will support any one of a number of negative pedagogical approaches that also grow out of our cultural values and our theories of writing.

As editors of *Computers and Composition,* a professional journal devoted to the exploration of computer use in English classes, we read primarily of the laudatory influence of computers in promoting a social construction of knowledge. Scant attention is paid, either in the manuscripts we receive or in the articles we read in other journals, to the harmful ways in which computers can be used even by well-meaning teachers who want to create community and social awareness within their classrooms. If electronic technology is to help us bring about positive changes in writing classes, we must identify and confront the potential problems that computers pose and redirect our efforts, if necessary, to make our classes centers of intellectual openness and exchange. We offer our critical perspectives as members of the composition community who strongly support the use of computers and electronic conferences for writing instruction. Our objections lie not in the use of computer technology and online conferences but rather in the uncritical enthusiasm that frequently characterizes the reports of those of us who advocate and support electronic writing classes.

In this paper, we examine the enthusiastic discourse that has accompanied the introduction of computers into writing classes and explore how this language may influence both change and the status quo in electronic classrooms. We do this by looking at published reports of computer use that appear in professional journals, by examining data about computer use collected through questionnaires completed by writing instructors at the 1988 Conference on Computers in Writing and Language Instruction (sponsored by the University of Minnesota at Duluth), and by comparing these analyses with a series of on-site classroom observations. After comparing these accounts of computer use, described through what we call the "rhetoric of technology," and our observations of electronic writing classes, we discuss how electronic technology can intensify those inequitable authority structures common to American education. Finally, we argue that computer technology offers us the chance to transform our writing classes into different kinds of centers of learning if we take a critical perspective and remain sensitive to the social and political dangers that the use of computers may pose.

All too often, those who use computers for composition instruction speak and write of "the effects of technology" in overly positive terms as if computers were good in and of themselves. As editors of a journal devoted to studies in computers and composition, we are most often sent glowing reports that fail to reconcile the differences between a visionary image of technology — what we want computers to do — and our own firsthand observations of how computers are being used in many classrooms around the country. Indeed, this distinctive "rhetoric" of technology seems to characterize more conference presentations, as well as many articles on computer use in other journals. This rhetoric — one of hope, vision, and persuasion — is the primary voice present in most of the work we see coming out of computers-and-composition studies,[2] and it is positive in the sense that it reflects the high expectations of instructors committed to positive educational reform in their writing classes. This same rhetoric, however, may also be dangerous if we want to think critically about technology and its uses.

The Rhetoric of Technology and Electronic Conferences

For an example of what we call the rhetoric of technology and of how it influences our perceptions and use of technology, we can turn to one specific computer application: electronic bulletin boards and conferences (i.e., conversing over networked computers). Among the claims made about using these electronic conference exchanges in writing classes are the following representative examples:

> Networks create an unusual opportunity to shift away from the traditional writing classroom because they create entirely new pedagogical dynamics. One of the most important is the creation of a written social context, an online discourse community, which presents totally new opportunities for effective instruction in writing. (Batson 32)

> Although I thought I might resent students intruding into my own time after school hours, I find instead that I enjoy our correspondences [over the network] — that I get to know students better and they know me better, too, a benefit that transfers to our classroom. (Kinkead 41)

> All the instructors in the pilot project [using an electronic conference for writing instruction] reported never having seen a group of first-year students, thrown randomly together by the registrar's computer, become as close as their students had. Students set up meetings in the library and in campus computer labs, came early to class and stayed late, made plans together for the next semester, and exchanged addresses. The computer, far from making the class more impersonal, fostered a strikingly close community in one of the nation's largest universities. (Shriner and Rice 476)

> Once people have electronic access, their status, power, and prestige are communicated neither contextually . . . nor dynamically. . . . Thus, charismatic and high status people may have less influence, and group members may participate more equally in computer communication. (Kiesler, Siegel, and McGuire 1125)

> On the network, students can work collaboratively to brainstorm, solve problems, experience writing as real communication with real people. . . . (Thompson 92)

> Those people with powerful ideas will have more influence than those with powerful personalities. . . . The democratization fostered by computer conferencing has other consequences as well. Just as nonverbal cues are missing in conferencing, so too are clues about an individual's status and position. (Spitzer 20)

The above comments represent a number of claims about writing instruction and how it can improve in carefully designed electronic settings: students experience different kinds of intellectual "spaces" in which they can learn differently and sometimes more effectively than in more traditional academic forums; instructors can become better acquainted with their students; many of the status cues marking face-to-face discourse are eliminated, thus allowing for more egalitarian discourse, with greater attention to the text at hand. Collaborative activities increase along with a greater sense of community in computer-supported classes.

Although these remarks reflect claims that we have also made and emphasize pedagogical goals that we too are committed to as specialists in computers and composition, they foreground positive benefits of using networked computers without acknowledging possible negative influences as well. The preceding comments suggest what the use of such networks should encourage, and in the best cases *is* encouraging, but they do not necessarily describe the less desirable outcomes that networks are also capable of supporting. More importantly, we have observed that this highly positive rhetoric directly influences the ways in which teachers perceive and talk about computer use in their classes. When we ask computer-using teachers about word processing in their writing classes (with and without networking) more often than not we again hear echoes of these same optimistic reports.

The Rhetoric of Technology and Computer-Supported Writing Classes

At the 1988 Conference on Computers in Writing and Language Instruction, we distributed lengthy open-ended questionnaires to writing instructors in an attempt to learn how the environment of a writing class — its social structures, discourse, and activities — might be shaped by the use of computers. Although we cannot claim that the answers regarding teaching and technology are representative of the profession as a whole, when considered with other commentary from publications and presentations we have seen, they seem typical of the rhetoric of computer-using instructors and are similar to the language that we ourselves use when talking of our electronic classrooms.[3]

Specifically, the instructors responding to our survey were asked the question, "Do you prefer teaching writing with traditional methods or with computers? Why?" As might be expected at a computers-and-writing gathering, all the respondents preferred teaching writing with computers and gave the following as their reasons, listed in order of their frequency:

1. Students spend a great deal of time writing.
2. Lots of peer teaching goes on.
3. Class becomes more student-centered than teacher-centered.
4. One-on-one conferences between instructor and students increase.
5. Opportunities for collaboration increase.
6. Students share more with other students and instructor.
7. Communication features provide more direct access to students, allowing teachers to "get to know" students better.

These comments are remarkably similar to the published claims about the use of online conferences that we have already examined. Note that these writing teachers, like their colleagues, also concluded that positive changes such as increased student participation and collaboration occurred in classes when they are computer-supported.

These comments illustrate the commitment of the teachers we surveyed to establishing a new kind of cooperative activity in their writing classes, one in which teaching and learning are shared by both instructors and students and through which traditional notions of teaching are altered. These instructors consider themselves not primarily as dispensers of knowledge but rather as collaborators within a group of learners supported by technology. In this sense, we considered the rhetoric of these instructors to be a reflection of their commitment to positive educational change; the survey respondents used the rhetoric of technology to describe a new cooperative electronic classroom shaped by a theory of teaching in which we understand knowledge as socially constructed by both teachers and students rather than as traditionally established. These teachers had come to see and talk about their classrooms in terms of groups of learners-in-progress working with instructors who are also learners (Lunsford and Glenn 186).

As we continued to analyze the open-ended responses to the question-naires, however, it became clear that when instructors foregrounded the beneficial influences of using computers, they often neglected to mention any negative effects of using the new technology. We recognized, as well, that this perspective was widespread and that the observations the survey teachers made were the same as those we had heard from writing instruc-tors at our own institutions. Moreover, at workshops we have conducted during the past two years, we continue to hear similar, positive reports that correspond to these earlier, more formal analyses.

Teaching Practices and the Computer-Supported Writing Class

Neither the published claims nor the survey responses, however, helped us to explain the less positive, more problematic uses of computers that we encountered during the past five years as we visited many other electronic writing classes around the country and made informal observations. Notes from a sampling of computer-supported classes we observed more formally in 1988 provided us with information about some of the more problematic social and pedagogical changes in electronic classes.[4] Both the formal and informal observations we made supported neither the teachers' responses in the questionnaires nor the published rhetoric of technology that had been our impetus for this study. In other words, we began to see that the language teachers used when they wrote about using computers some-times provided incomplete stories that omitted other possible interpreta-tions. Let us explain by using examples from those representative classes we formally observed in stand-alone computer classrooms.

First, however, it is important to note that our observations were limited and that we may well have missed day-to-day classroom dynamics. On other days, in some of the classes, the use of computers may indeed have fostered positive changes in the intellectual climate of the classroom. But we hope that by concentrating on some of the problematic aspects of these electronic classes, we can emphasize that computers do not automatically create ideal learning situations. This is not to say that electronic technol-ogy cannot encourage social interaction and cooperative undertakings but rather to stress, in Michel Foucault's words, that a technology cannot "guarantee" any behavior alone "simply by its nature" ("Space" 245); ac-cording to Foucault, the "architecture" of such electronic spaces is a highly political act in itself. Like the traditional classroom, the architecture of electronic spaces can put some students at a disadvantage, thwarting rather than encouraging learning.

In each of the ten classes we observed, with a few exceptions, there was a lot of writing going on. In fact, there was so much writing that we wondered sometimes why the time was set aside as class time, rather than as time that students could spend on their writing in a computer lab. We looked for exchanges and talk between instructor and student, and be-tween students — but what we commonly saw were not careful, two-way discussions of the writing problems students were encountering in their papers. Rather the instructors answered a series of one-time queries often having to do with mechanics or coming from the "does-this-sound-right" category. There were exceptions: sometimes an instructor moved from stu-dent to student and spent several minutes with each, talking about spe-cific writing problems highlighted on the computer screen. For the most part, though, instructors walked around the room, looking eager, we might add, for someone in the class to need them in some capacity. Although this observation seems to fit with one of the more frequent claims that teachers made for electronic writing classes — students do a lot of writing — the claim does not completely represent the classes we observed. The use of computers in these classes seemed to come between teachers and students, pre-empting valuable exchanges among members of the class, teachers and students alike.

Another kind of computer-supported class we observed reflected traditional practices of writing instruction in American classrooms. The instructor projected a student paper on an overhead projection system, and students critiqued various aspects of the paper. In each instance, classmates seemed to be searching for answers to the instructor's preset questions. And only three or four students were participating in these rather contrived discussions. This sort of class we saw as a variation on George Hillocks's presentational mode. Although the instructors were not lecturing, they had in mind answers that the students were to supply; hence, the discussion, in effect, became the instructor's "presentation." At these times we wondered about the advantage of having computers in the classroom. The use of technology in these classes, far from creating a new forum for learning, simply magnified the power differential between students and the instructor. Ostensibly computers were being used to "share" writing, but the effect of such sharing was to make the class more teacher-centered and teacher-controlled. Hence, describing technology as a mechanism for increasing the sharing of texts or bringing students and teachers together on a more equal basis again told only a part of the story.

Still another typical class we observed was one in which students were meeting in groups, often focusing on something written on the monitor or producing text on the screen. Yet the conversations we overheard only sometimes related to the task at hand — and often, once again, the effort put forth by students seemed to be one aimed at pleasing the instructor rather than one illustrative of active engagement with their classmates or the texts. This type of class seemed to fit with responses from the questionnaires that credited technology with encouraging "lots of peer teaching" or "more opportunities for collaboration." While such claims seemed outwardly to reflect the electronic writing class, they did not take into account the groups that we observed in which neither peer teaching nor collaboration among students occurred.

This realization, then, leads us to believe that it is not enough for teachers to talk about computer use in uncritical terms. We can no longer afford simply, and only, to dwell on the best parts, to tell stories about the best classroom moments, and to feature the more positive findings about computers. Rather, we must begin to identify the ways in which technology can fail us. We need to recognize the high costs of hardware and software, recognize that computers can, and often do, support instruction that is as repressive and lockstep as any that we have seen. We need to be aware of the fact that electronic classrooms can actually be used to dampen creativity, writing, intellectual exchanges, rather than to encourage them. We need to talk about the dangers of instructors who use computers to deliver drill-and-practice exercises to students or of instructors who promote the use of style analyzers to underscore student errors more effectively than they did five years ago with red pens.

How do we proceed then? We do not advocate abandoning the use of technology and relying primarily on script and print for our teaching without the aid of word processing and other computer applications such as communication software; nor do we suggest eliminating our descriptions of the positive learning environments that technology can help us to create. Instead, we must try to use our awareness of the discrepancies we have noted as a basis for constructing a more complete image of how technology can be used positively *and* negatively. We must plan carefully and develop the necessary critical perspectives to help us avoid using computers to advance or promote mediocrity in writing instruction. A balanced and increasingly critical perspective is a starting point: by viewing our classes as sites of both paradox and promise we can construct a mature view of how the use of electronic technology can abet our teaching.

Teaching Practices and Electronic Online Conferences

As a more specific example of how a critical perspective can help us to identify, and we hope avoid, the dangers that can accompany computer technology in writing classes, we turn again to the use of electronic conferences and bulletin boards. A critical re-examination of these online exchanges suggests that while conferences can help teachers create new and engaging forums for learning, they can also serve in ways that might inhibit open exchanges, reduce active learning, and limit the opportunities for honest intellectual engagement.

In the context of Foucault's description of disciplinary institutions as presented in *Discipline and Punish,* we can speculate as to how such conferences might work to the detriment of students and their learning. The electronic spaces created through networking, we learn by reading Foucault, might also be used as disciplinary technologies, serving to control students and their discourse. Of such technologies, Foucault writes:

> [They are] no longer built simply to be seen . . . , or to observe the external space . . . , but to permit an internal, articulated and detailed control — to render visible those who are inside it; in more general terms, an architecture that would operate to transform individuals: to act on those it shelters, to provide a hold on their conduct, to carry the effects of power right to them, to make it possible to know them, to alter them. (172)

This particular theoretical perspective, while it is highly incongruent with existing interpretations of conferences and what goes on in them, may at the same time enrich and problematize those interpretations.

A powerful metaphor to help us critically examine the uses of electronic forums is further elaborated in Foucault's discussion of Bentham's Panopticon, the perfect disciplinary mechanism for the exercise of power.[5] Originally designed as a circular prison building with a guard tower in the middle and the prisoners' cells arranged along the outside, the Panopticon, writes Foucault, is a "mechanism of power reduced to its ideal form" (*Discipline* 205), making it possible for wardens and guards to observe the behavior of inmates without they themselves being observed. Foucault argues that within such a space, because inmates do not know when they are being observed or ignored, prisoners are constantly and unrelentingly self-disciplining. Moreover, because surveillance is "unverifiable," it is all the more effective and oppressive. Although panoptic space differs from electronic bulletin boards and conferences in that students, unlike Bentham's inmates, can converse with one another over networks, those who have conversed over computers will recognize how eavesdropping and watching are made easy through the architecture of an electronic network.

Writing instructors can use networks and electronic bulletin boards as disciplinary mechanisms for observing students' intellectual contributions to written discussions. The institutional requirement of student evaluation contributes to this practice as instructors seek ways "to give students credit" for conference participation. Under certain conditions, without carefully thinking out the theoretical consequences, instructors enter conferences to read and monitor students' conversations without revealing themselves as readers and evaluators. We know after all that electronic conferences are, in some ways, spaces open to public scrutiny, places where individuals with the power of control over technology can observe conversations and participants without being seen and without contributing. When instructors take samples from network discussions into the classroom and use these as positive or negative examples, they are employing electronic conferences to discipline, to shape the conversations and academic discourse of their students.

Such a theoretical perspective reminds us that electronic spaces, like other spaces, are constructed within contextual and political frameworks of cultural values, a point that Shoshana Zuboff makes in her study of computer networking in the corporate environment. As in corporate settings, the architecture of computer networking may encourage "surveillance" of participants. Writing instructors praise online communication programs for helping them "get to know" students better, a phrase that survey instructors used in a positive sense but that Foucault includes to describe an architecture of control. Teachers who have easy access to students through a network can also "keep tabs" on student participation, blurring the thin line between "evaluating" contributions students make to electronic conferences and "inspecting" conversations that occur electronically.

Instructors inspecting electronic spaces and networked conversation have power that exceeds our expectations or those of students. In addition, many students who know a teacher is observing their conversation will self-discipline themselves and their prose in ways they consider socially and educationally appropriate. Constructing such spaces so that they can provide room for positive activities — for learning, for the resistant discourse characteristic of students thinking across the grain of convention, for marginalized students' voices — requires a sophisticated understanding of power and its reflection in architectural terms.

Conclusion

In this paper, we have suggested that the current professional conversation about computer use in writing classes, as evidenced in published accounts, is incomplete in at least one essential and important way. While containing valuable accounts of electronic classes, this conversation fails to provide us with a critical perspective on the problematic aspects of computer use and thus with a full understanding of how the use of technology can affect the social, political, and educational environments within which we teach. In making this point, we are not arguing against the use of computers in general or, more specifically, against the promising use of electronic conferences and bulletin boards. The central assumption underlying our argument is that writing instructors, by thinking critically and carefully about technology, can succeed in using it to improve the educational spaces we inhabit.

Our view of teaching and of how students learn invariably shapes our behavior in the classroom. The metaphors we build to house our professional knowledge exert powerful influence over us. Few of us, we would argue, construe our role as that of "controller," "gatekeeper," or "guard." We are more likely in the context of the writing class to think of ourselves as "teacher," "writer," and perhaps "expert." If we plan carefully and examine our integration of technology critically, computers have the potential for helping us shift traditional authority structures inherent in American education. We can, if we work at it, become learners within a community of other learners, our students. But the change will not happen automatically in the electronic classroom anymore than in a traditional classroom. We have to labor diligently to bring it about.

As teachers we are authority figures. Our culture has imbued us with considerable power within the confines of the classroom: we are the architects of the spaces in which our students learn. Although the use of computer technology may give us greater freedom to construct more effective learning environments, it may also lead us unknowingly to assume positions of power that contradict our notions of good teaching. Unless we remain aware of our electronic writing classes as sites of paradox and promise, transformed by a new writing technology, and unless we plan carefully for intended outcomes, we may unwittingly use computers to maintain rigid authority structures that contribute neither to good teaching nor to good learning.

Notes

[1] We gratefully acknowledge the insightful comments and excellent advice provided by Marilyn Cooper, Michigan Technological University, and Ron Fortune, Illinois State University.

[2] Exceptions to this optimistic discourse exist, of course, but these critical voices are less pervasive. For an interesting discussion of how an electronically networked writing class "mutinied" and lost "all sense of decorum about what [was] appropriate to say or write in an English class," see Marshall Kremers's article, "Adams Sherman Hill Meets *ENFI*."

[3] The open-ended questionnaires we analyzed were completed by 25 instructors from 10 different states, in addition to Washington, DC. Seventeen of the instructors taught in four-year colleges, four in community colleges, and four in high schools. First-year college writing classes were most frequently given as the course conducted on computers, but instructors also used computers to teach advanced composition, technical writing, business writing, pedagogy courses in composition instruction, and high-school writing courses. Although the majority of the 25 respondents taught in classrooms where stand-alone computers were the rule, several taught in networked environments in which students and instructors shared writing through electronic mail and bulletin boards.

[4] We observed ten first-year writing classes taught on computers during the summer and fall of 1988. All instructors had taught composition with computers for at least one year, and several had taught composition for five years or more. Some were teaching assistants, and some were full-time composition instructors.

[5] We are grateful to Vicki Byard, Purdue University, for bringing Foucault's treatment of Bentham's Panopticon to our attention at the 1989 CCCC in Seattle. In her insightful paper, "Power Play: The Use and Abuse of Power Relationships in Peer Critiquing," she suggested that even those approaches we use with the most liberating intentions may well prove disciplinary in nature.

Works Cited

Batson, Trent. "The ENFI Project: A Networked Classroom Approach to Writing Instruction." *Academic Computing* Feb.–Mar. 1988: 32–33.

Byard, Vicki. "Power Play: The Use and Abuse of Power Relationships in Peer Critiquing." Conference on College Composition and Communication Convention. Seattle, Mar. 1989.

Foucault, Michel. *Discipline and Punish: The Birth of the Prison.* Trans. Alan Sheridan. New York: Vintage, 1979.

———. "Space, Knowledge and Power." *The Foucault Reader.* Ed. Paul Rabinow. New York: Pantheon, 1984. 239–56.

Hillocks, George, Jr. *Research on Written Composition.* Urbana: NCTE, 1986.

Kiesler, Sara, Jane Siegel, and Timothy W. McGuire. "Social Psychological Aspects of Computer-Mediated Communication." *American Psychologist* 39 (Oct. 1984): 1123–34.

Kinkead, Joyce. "Wired: Computer Networks in the English Classroom." *English Journal* 77 (Nov. 1988): 39–41.

Kremers, Marshall. "Adams Sherman Hill Meets *ENFI*." *Computers and Composition* 5 (Aug. 1988): 69–77.

Lunsford, Andrea A., and Cheryl Glenn. "Rhetorical Theory and the Teaching of Writing." *On Literacy and Its Teaching: Issues in English Education.* Ed. Gail E. Hawisher and Anna O. Soter. Albany: State U of New York, 1990. 174–89.

Shriner, Delores K., and William C. Rice. "Computer Conferencing and Collaborative Learning: A Discourse Community at Work." *College Composition and Communication* 40 (Dec. 1989): 472–78.

Spitzer, Michael. "Writing Style in Computer Conferences." *IEEE Transactions on Professional Communications* 29 (Jan. 1986): 19–22.

Thompson, Diane P. "Teaching Writing on a Local Area Network." *T.H.E. Journal* 15 (Sept. 1987): 92–97.

Zuboff, Shoshana. *In the Age of the Smart Machine: The Future of Work and Power.* New York: Basic, 1988.

POSTINGS ON A GENRE OF E-MAIL

Michael Spooner and Kathleen Yancey

[*College Composition and Communication* 47 (May 1996): 252–78.]

Kathleen Yancey is associate professor of English at the University of North Carolina–Charlotte, and Michael Spooner is director of the Utah State University Press. These two collaborators have written other unconventional articles together, published either in print or electronically, addressing some of the same issues they raise in "Postings" — issues of textuality, technology, and collaboration. Their most recent article is published in *CCC*, Feb. 1998. Kathleen Yancey is best known for her work in writing assessment, including her most recent books (co-edited), *Situating Portfolios: Four Perspectives* (1997) and *Assessing Writing across the Curriculum: Diverse Approaches and Practices* (1997). Michael Spooner is best known as an editor and publisher of scholarly books, formerly at NCTE and now in Utah.

Except for the use of word-processing software, perhaps the most pervasive and visible way that technology is integrated into writing courses is through the use of e-mail. Students and teachers use e-mail for informal communications, to exchange responses about work in progress, to deliver written assignments, and for a variety of other activities. In this innovative and provocative article, Spooner and Yancey present a dialogic exploration of e-mail as an academic genre, broadly conceived. They present a wide-ranging discussion of the various potential uses of e-mail (and by extension, technology) for teaching and for scholarly work.

> Kathleen, How does this grab you for the opening? <mspooner>

I was talking with a novelist recently about various kinds of writing--nothing special, just happy-hour talk--and I found my earnest self assuring him that, oh yes, academic writing nowadays will tolerate a number of different styles and voices. (I should know, right? I'm in academic publishing.) He choked; he slapped my arm; he laughed out loud. I don't remember if he spit his drink back in the glass. Silly me, I was serious.

And, among other things, I was thinking about this essay/dialogue, in which we're turning discourse conventions of the net --often a rather casual medium--to some fairly stuffy academic purposes.

Interesting that you call it an essay/dialogue (nice slide, that one). But many readers will expect a "real" essay here--or, betterworse, an academic essay.

And we know what that means: a single voice, a single point (to which all the others are handmaidens), a coherence that's hierarchically anchored.

We couldn't say this in one voice. We--Griffin, Sabine, and Georgia notwithstanding--aren't one; we don't have identical points of view. This could have been an epistolary novel, were we novelists; it could have been a Platonic dialogue, except that most of Plato is single-minded essay in dialogic dress. This text takes the form of dialogue and is a dialogue.

Not just our own two voices here, either. Others interrupt us with commentary, obiter dicta, humor. All writers hear voices, but here we've made the convention/al choice to amplify those voices that inform us (or contradict us). It's different from essay, article, paper, dialogue, because this convention allows more juxtaposition with less predication. On the other hand, it's very like discourse on the net, but more coherent, more pre/ pared. This has been done before, even in the academic world. It reminds one of Winston Weathers's "Grammar B" discussions (1980), though we're not being as artistic as the authors he has in mind. But there is something about e-mail that brings this out, and I'm predicting it will be commonplace within a very short time.

It's too much to claim that it's Bakhtin uncovered, but that's its tenor. E-mail seems to make this aspect of language more obvious. The point is that reading this piece is in some way like e-mailing, feeling the staccato effect of jumbled messages, the sense of the incoherent ready to envelop you, the quick as well as the sustained. Voices always populate; the transmission of them on e-mail is just more obvious--flagrant, almost--celebratory.

To use the tropes and gestures of the net seemed an obvious decision in an article about the discourse of the net. Natural, too, because we've composed it entirely from e-mail exchanges. (In fact, I don't remember the last time I actually saw you: 1993?) Then there's the fact that we don't agree about the topic.

Our disagreement makes the blender-voice of many coauthored pieces virtually ;-) impossible for this one. Besides, the disagreement is part of the content. It's important to show that, while we do work toward each other, we finish feeling that there is still room for two separate soapboxes at the end. At least two.

I don't think we have an argument with each other so much, even though we do have more than a single point of view. But we write in different voices, and this is a problem if one insists on proper genres. Can't we just call it a text?

What is the difference between an article and an essay? A dialogue and a paper? Between hard copy and e-mail? Between what we are submitting and what certain readers expect? Those questions all center on genre--a central thread woven here. The essay genre becomes a place where genre itself is the topic of inquiry, even of dispute.

One thing we do agree about is that e-mail offers new ways of representing intellectual life. This is one way.

> :) This post has been smiley-captioned for the irony-impaired. :)   <skeevers>

The Digitized Word

E-mail is a floating signifier of the worst sort--whether it's called E-discourse, or VAX conferences, or whatever. So the first task is to narrow the focus. Let's look at these few dimensions.

• E-mail simple. Much like writing a letter, it is signalled by greetings, emoticons, closings, and other conventions; sometimes the author composes online, sometimes uploads a prepared text; author and topic are not unique, but audience is (as in letters). In its affective dimension, it feels like a hybrid form, combining elements one would expect in letters, on the phone, or in face-to-face conversation.

• E-mail on "lists"--electronic discussion groups. These groups have developed a new lexicon to cover unique rhetorical or technical functions online (e.g., flame wars, FTPs, lurkers, emoticons). Within the lists that I know, there is an evident territoriality (we who use the list, those who don't--benighted souls), but also an effort to democratize interaction. Some explicit conventions of interaction ("netiquettes") are established, others are in process, others implicit.

• E-mail in the classroom. Cooper and Selfe (1991) argue that democracy is closer in the computerized classroom. I wonder. I think a number of the features that seem to define lists do not obtain in the classroom--mostly authorial authority. But it does offer another kind of interaction, a chance to write differently, a different *opportunity* to learn.

• E-mail as resource. This is the networking function that Moran (1992) mentions--the thinking together that creates "a corporate, collaborative, collective 'self' that is more social and therefore more knowledgeable than the old."

• E-mail as mode of collaboration. As we write together/to(each)other, the author and audience elide; how does one represent that--in a single voice? in multiple voices? in CAPS? in multiple typefaces?

It's easier to see these as discrete categories in theory than in practice. For example, we've both taught students in at least the first four of these five dimensions, overlapping freely. In many classrooms, they use the fifth one, too.

It is also worth pointing out that merely *composing* on a computer does *not* make your list here. It is clearly electronic writing, but these days it has been absorbed into the normal. Not so long ago, using a computer at all to teach writing was considered so novel that many teachers bought books to help them do it (e.g., Rodrigues and Rodrigues, 1986). Now, many (I'd guess *most*) writing teachers and students compose with computers routinely. And, while electronic writing in the classroom offers some unique opportunities that progressive teachers are exploring, it hasn't *required* a shift in any single teacher's pedagogical values: while some classes are models of social constructivism, others are still cranking out those five-paragraph themes. That is, the machine will serve the most progressive and the most traditional practice with equal indifference.

On both counts, agreed. The second, first: the fact that a pedagogy seems innovative or uses new technology does not prevent it from simply reproducing the prior paradigm. Aviva Freedman and Peter Medway (1994) make this point when talking about journals, which they see, all claims notwithstanding, not as a new genre, but as another and unacknowledged kind of test--a replication of the same game:

> Although the writer's focus was now claimed to be solely on thinking about the topic, the rhetorical demands had not disappeared; they had simply taken a new form. Journals were, in our experience, still judged as *writing* and not just for the assistance they provided to the students' learning. The generic criteria were not made explicit, but, as Barnes and his colleagues found, clever students knew they were there. (18)

As to the first point about classroom e-mail practice *incorporating* many of the features articulated in the list above, again, agreed. But classroom e-mail is different in kind. Janet Eldred and Ron Fortune (1992) use classroom policy as the lens allowing us to see e-mail as its own type. Consider the case of the e-mail listserv group: subscribers presumably elect to subscribe, and there's no rule or convention or folkway that says they *must* participate. They may choose the Bartleby route, preferring not: they can lurk. But if an e-mail "discussion" group is a requirement of the course, lurking is not an option; it's forbidden.

The point? Classroom e-mail has a different set of conventions than other e-mails; precisely because it takes place in a different context, it inscribes a different ideology.

Vignette 1

They're mighty white, I think, as I wander into the IBM classroom. There are 18 of them, methods students and prospective teachers, and they're mighty female, too. On a second take, I see: they are all white, all women, and all anxious as they pose at keyboards, studiously avoiding them, carefully *not* touching them, collectively praying that our meeting in *this* classroom is a function of computer error. Computer error, after all, can be fixed.

Several tasks we have, I say. Write to Purdue's Online Writing Lab and secure some handouts that will help you. You are in groups, I say; here are the IDs. Read the Ednet discussions on grading, I tell them, as I hand out 13 pages of listserv discussions on grading.

Mimi says we shouldn't have to do this; we don't have any *real* students so we can't develop a grading philosophy *now*. Angie writes me an e-mail begging me to stop this exercise; it's too frustrating, and they already have too much to do.

They write, they cc to me. One group decides to number their posts to each other, in order to get a sense of chronology. They all greet each other as in a letter, and they all close: "See ya's!" and "Later's" predictably end the screen. They reassure each other that everyone is frustrated; they respond to each other's points, with varying detail. They share news. Kim writes, addressing me more as a friend than a teacher, remarking on the orange juice I might be drinking as I read her post. Through the opaque window of e-mail, she sees teacher as person. We begin to see each other a little differently, a little more fully. If the medium is the message, then affect is the medium.

Two weeks later a set of papers comes in. Sam's paper is among the best, and, to be honest, I'm a bit surprised at the quality of her work. Not that I thought she was incompetent, but she's the sort of student who's easy to overlook: compliant, not terribly vocal, older than the others--a "returning student." (And I admit: I'm troubled when she tells me, early on, that teaching will be *convenient,* easily slotted among motherhood, wifehood, the PTA, and Sunday school teaching.) More to the point perhaps, she's new to computers.

> Sitting at the computer the first day of class was more stress and agony than I had imagined. I had never used a computer before, and now I was expected to write with one. When our class did a SneakerNet as an opening exercise, I did not know how to scroll the screen and there wasn't time to ask for help . . . .

Sam chooses to take her midterm on computer, earns the highest A in the class. During our 14-day e-mail cycle, she posts among the highest number of messages (ten of them) in the class and writes on various topics--including appropriate uses for technology in the classroom. After the e-mail cycle is over, she continues to post. Always, she is aware of how the computer is changing her world, changing her.

> Hi, I saw something interesting in the Observer today. There was an article on computer-user language and do you know what "snail-mail" is? It refers to slower mail or any mail that is not e-mail! That meant something to me today but one week ago I wouldn't have understood that description.

Sam uses the occasion of composing her portfolio to look back-- "Putting together the portfolio was actually a review of the course" --and to anticipate what she will do next--take more coursework in computer technology, with specific application to teaching and to using writing with the computer.

At the end of the term, I attempt to distribute the collections I have maintained, in my closet of an office, to trashcans and bookshelves and file cabinets, as students drop by to collect their portfolios. Sam arrives; we talk. She regrets that her e-mail has been cancelled. Oh, yes, they do that fast, I say, once the term is over. I can co-sign for you if you'd like to have another account, I say. Well, maybe next fall, she says. See you soon, we say.

Thirty minutes later, she's back, asking me to co-sign. Welcome to the net. ;)

Virtually Yours

The emotional boundaries of our encounter seemed to have been much expanded by the e-mail that preceded it.

— John Seabrook

If you have been in love, if your lover could write, you know what I mean: it appears every day. It's transactive--not plain exposition, not pure narrative. It's a letter, but then, not the sort of letter you get from the bank or university. It's more like conversation. It's not conversation: it's one-way, and it's written. And it's written in the knowledge that days may pass between the writing and the reading--that in fact (though heaven forbid) it may be lost before it reaches you. As you read it, it speaks in the familiar voice of news, disappointments, and desires. It's affectionate--full of affect. Sometimes it's telegraphic, sometimes oblique, sometimes it includes a sort of lover's code: silly abbreviations <imho> <rotfl>, smiley faces :), Xs and Os.

> loved your smiley run over by a truck: ..-_   <lffunkhouser>

I want to argue that what e-mail writers are doing on the net does not in essence or in genre differ from what writers do off line. In some cases, it looks like a business letter. Sometimes it's a bulletin, sometimes a broadside, sometimes a joke, a memo, a grafitto, a book. In many one-to-one postings, e-mail shows all the features of the lovers' correspondence you used to read (or did you write it?) every day.

So e-mail is like a letter, a personal letter that allows both cognition and affect: is that it?

Often, yes. But often otherwise. I send and receive formal letters (a different genre, by most accounts) via e-mail, too. Also announcements, assignments, essays, one-liners, poems, and dirty jokes. Just like paper and ink, this technology allows a wide range of genres. *That's* the point.

So it's not a genre, you say. Well. There are several ways to look at this question: we could try older, more literary definitions of genre, grounded in form; we could include more recent rhetorically based definitions, more oriented to the social dimension; and we could speak from the vantage point of literary theory so dominated by interest in the ideological workings of genre.

Or we could simply listen in on the thing itself:

>I found myself writing to a friend last night . . . and thinking how there *is* a difference between writing and this spontaneous posting that we do.

>. . . our conversations seem much more like oral
conversation than like written correspondence.
<newmann>

>. . .there is an element of spontaneity. And the essen-
tials of conversation (as opposed to letter-writing)
are there: a topic focus, a variety of voices, and
statement-response structure. But unlike conversation, each of us can 1)edit and 2) speak without
interruption. <csjhs>

>. . . we all adopt a light, informal tone (and some real
wit too) that is too often missing from letters
typed on university letterhead. <harrism>

>If writing on the net is a hybrid, what shall we call it?
Well, it seems . . . to be kinda in between expressive
writing . . . and transactional. . . . Maybe we could
call it expractional? Or transpressive? Then, again, it
gets downright poetic at times. <ccrmitta>

These writers or speakers--or what shall we call them?
--seem to share common perceptions about e-mail, about its
friendliness, about its use for play as well as for thinking,
about its novelty, about its inability to be categorized
into any of the conventionalized
I don't seriously disagree with the schemes. I think this last point may
consensus expressed by these folks, but serve as a place to start.
there's something in it that troubles me:
I wonder if we've truly come far enough
in theorizing the electronic conference (whether one-on-one or
in a group) to decide what these folks are deciding.
The consensus is not limited to this group, of course; it's
repeated throughout the literature on computers and composi-
tion. And the consensus claims a great deal more than the
comments above reveal. For example, we're told that the net is
inherently non-hierarchical, "intrinsically communal," and that it
is challenging the "hegemony of the teacher" (respectively:
Zamierowski; Barker and Kemp; Cooper and Selfe). There's a
fervor about this body of opinion.

> The Internet's glorious egalitarianism is one of its chief
attractions for me. <csjhs>

But these community-enhancing qualities of the net seem more
assumed in the work on computers and composition than
demonstrated, and I'm not sure we have examined our as-
sumptions. Consider these few comments, selected from a single
discussion thread on a single list (Cybermind).

>. . . however much I may like these identity-erasing fa-
cilities of the Net, my actual feelings of community
are predicated on, and arise only with the revelation
of, identities. <malgosia>

>. . . my virtual communities are very dependent on gender and sexualities.   <lysana>

>Not everybody came here to form a community (maybe no one did; it wasn't on the agenda), and not everybody wants one.   <marius>

In Hawisher and LeBlanc's _Re-Imagining Computers and Composition: Teaching and Research in the Virtual Age_ (1992), Gail Hawisher acknowledges that ". . . as yet there are only a few studies of the electronic conference that have been conducted within composition studies" (84). She alludes to research in fields like distance education and information science, and she suggests that it supports the current heady consensus about computers in composition. In other publications, Hawisher has been careful not to overlook potential misuses of technology in pedagogy (e.g., 1991), and I don't necessarily doubt her here. There is surely research underway now specifically on issues in computers and composition, but in the meantime, should we rely on inference and extrapolation from other fields to give us the grounds for declaring utopia-at-hand in *writing*?

                                    But is this *writing*?

Isn't it?

In the same collection, Paul Taylor effectively summarizes the consensus when he says "computer conferencing is evolving into a new genre, a new form of communication that has not been possible before now" (145). Not to single out Taylor, but, when he (as momentary speaker for all this enthusiasm) applies Carolyn Miller's (1984) criteria for genre identification to computer conferencing, immediately he has to fudge.

> First, the associated texts must exhibit similarity in form. Although computer-based messages are not yet exceptionally uniform, they do display several common features. . . . Second, Miller states that the genre must be based on all the rhetorical elements in recurring situations. Do computer conferences arise from a genuine exigence relative to a specific audience? Only if we begin to narrow the terms somewhat--if we begin to see computer conferencing not as a single genre, but as a collection of related genres. (145)

A genre of genres? Wishful thinking. And I wish he'd bluffed --held out for a vision of one E- Genre. After all, if we equivocate on any of Miller's criteria, the whole case caves in. And he has to equivocate on two.

The facts are, on the one hand, that computer-based messages (whether in conference or not) come in a *very* wide variety of forms and, on the other hand, that they have common features with a zillion forms of *non*-computer-based writing: e.g., the memo, the report, the bulletin, the note, the list, the valentine. One could argue that the *only* distinctive feature of online writing is that it is transmitted via computer. And further, if we see computer conferencing "not as a single genre, but as a collection of genres," we're tripped again. Why gather them generically here? Why not let them individually stand where they were--with the memo, the report, the bulletin, and the others--where they have both formal and rhetorical *commonality? Just because we send them over the net? It seems to boil down to that.*

I can't see why the technology associated with a text is enough to warrant the claim of a distinctive genre. To my mind, we have to think of genres of writing as logically larger than the technologies through which we convey them.

I agree that today's technology shows much of the wonder and potential that these writers see in it. Perhaps the most careful, thorough exploration of this potential that I have read to date is in Richard Lanham's _The Electronic Word_ (1993) --a portion of which I actually received via e-mail from the publisher. This is the hopeful claim of the rhetorician that the computer is intrinsically a rhetorical device, and that through digitization it will inevitably democratize education in the liberal arts. Again, I don't much disagree about the computer's potential here--until we start using words like "intrinsic." Because it is quite clear that the same technology that stirs hopes like Lanham's for a postmodern avatar of the Rhetorical Paideia even now serves pedagogies of drill-and-skill, of Great Books, and other rigid traditional paradigms. The same technology.

My point is simply this: we are seeing a transition in the technology that delivers our written genres, not an innovation in genres themselves. And, in our enthusiasm for the (mere) technology, we are mistaking transition for innovation.

Vignette 2

These days <u>nothing stays buried</u>. . . .
Particularly not on a computer.
                                    – Gail Colins

"Do you mind if we take notes on the computer?" asks Tara (a pseudonym). "It's easier for us, but I know the clattering distracts some teachers."

These students are computer-literate--23 seniors in the Tech Writing program. They are also white, most of them are women, middle-class, and they're from predominantly religious, politically conservative, semi-rural communities in the West. All right: they're Mormon kids.

The computers are high-grade for the times (and for anywhere in the college of humanities): twenty workstations outfitted with network software and several industry-standard programs. There's e-mail with an uplink to Internet, and, oh yes, a couple of games. When I boot up, my machine plays a clip from Pink Floyd. "Hey! Teacher! Leave them kids alone!"

Like the others, Tara has never used the Internet, and she has only a general concept of a listserv or newsgroup. But she shrugs. It's just another network like the classroom LAN or the campus VMS. After minimal instruction from me, she attacks the subscribe routine through her workstation; she's an Internet list member within five minutes.

I ask the students to comment on the Internet discussions as well as other matters in their online journals. They are used to the idea--both writing such things and the process of saving their entries to a common area on the network. They know how to check back later for my replies. In one entry, Tara complains about how tedious the listserv of copyeditors can be.

I mean, it's interesting to see the comments on [whether to use] one space or two after a period, but is it really worth 25 postings?

In another, she reflects on the topic of obscenity on e-mail-- someone used the F-word in a realtime electronic conference in another class.

Since the letter was sent to the entire class as instructed, everyone got the message. Some people were offended, others were not. One general argument was that if you don't want to read that kind of thing, don't--delete it! The other argument was: even if you decide to immediately delete it, you have already been offended the instance [sic] the word hit your eyes.

In her journal, Tara didn't make any comments about the difference between online writing and writing to a printed page. Where she referred to online issues at all, she was concerned not with the writing, but with matters of propriety--the choices and judgment of individuals in relation to others--as in the two quotations above.

In other words, the technology was transparent to her. And, ironically, this is best illustrated by an amusing twist from the end of the quarter. Finals were over, students were gone, and I was clearing the journal directory. There I found a long letter from Tara to one of her classmates--evidently dropped into my space by mistake. Suddenly, I was a teacher picking up folded notes from the virtual classroom floor, somewhat stunned to see my best student write:

Well, I gotta go! Class is over! As you can see I find ways to entertain myself in class since I don't get anything out of the lectures!

Welcome to the net. ;)

A Virtual Genre

> If e-mail represents the renaissance of prose, why is so much of it so awful?
> – Philip Elmer-DeWitt

"Conceptual or substantive identity" and "procedural identity" are key terms that Larson (1982) used in arguing that the research paper as currently taught in freshman comp isn't a real paper. I liked the terms, and I thought they might help me think about genre--as having these kinds of identity.

Several articles composed via e-mail collaboration have been published by now; how did the authors know how to write them? How do we know what we're doing here? When I use e-mail in my class this term, I want the students to write *this way*--but what *is* this way? And what conventions should I point out to them as accepted? Students have enough trouble trying to navigate through "regular writing," yet if I want to extend the class and show them how we are working (e.g., in this paper), I have to help them do this. But *this* is still undefined.

>I just got a beep from you. Let me send this now,
and I'll read you, then finish.

<mspooner>

If you want to argue therefore that *this* is not a genre,
that's fine with me, but it doesn't absolve you of the need to
show students how to put such a piece together. There is still
a lot to be learned here about composing.

And the medium allows us to claim what is ours--as it
makes the audience real. The fictionalized audience itself
becomes a fiction, and the concept of author becomes more
collective. In other words, the rhe-
I'm in accord with you on the need torical situation is different--not theo-
for a social or purpose-oriented approach retically so much as really, practi-
to genre. I'll accept Swales's (1990) cally. According to a definition of
claim that "the principal criterial feature genre that is oriented to purpose or
that turns a collection of communicative to social action, this should make a
events into a genre is some shared set difference.
of communicative purposes" (51).
However, the mere fact that we can discover the several
different dimensions to electronic writing you described earlier
is evidence to me that we are not in the realm of a single
rhetorical situation. Among the five dimensions you listed are
family resemblances, but they do not represent a coherent set
of communicative purposes, let alone a coherent set of formal
conventions. By the logic of the social/purposive approach to
genre, electronic writing is no more one genre than writing on
clay tablets is one genre (cf. Swales on correspondence, p.
53). At best, we have a random clutch of communicative pur-
poses and an enthusiasm for tech novelty.

According to Swales, a genre is "a class of communicative events, the members of which share some set of communicative purposes" (58), and which can vary along three dimensions (at least): complexity of rhetorical purpose; degree
of advanced preparation or construction; and medium or mode
(62). Swales also talks about pre-genres and multi-genres: the
former too persuasive and fundamental to be generic, a place
of "life" from which other genres may emerge; and the latter,
the multi-genre, a larger category including several genres, as
in letters vs letters-of-condolence (58-61).

Could I get back to you by e-mail? I'm not comfortable
dealing with you in voice mode.   -- Anon.

Bakhtin seems to make the same distinction between
pre-generic and generic communications when he talks about
primary and secondary genres: secondary genres "absorb and
digest primary (simple) genres that have taken form in unme-
diated speech communication" (946). And as we might expect,
he describes secondary genres as arising "in more complex
and comparatively highly developed and organized cultural
communication (primarily written) that is artistic, scientific,
sociopolitical, and so on" (946). But what Bakhtin has done in
his formulation is to validate as genre what Swales calls pre-
genre, by classifying *all utterances* as participating in genre,

the distinction resting on the same features later identified by Swales, especially organized communication.

Others have made contributions to the definition that will help us. Lloyd Bitzer (1968) discusses rhetorical situations, like genres, and the role that recurrence plays: "The situations recur and, because we experience situations and the rhetorical responses to them, a form of discourse is not only established but comes to have a power of its own--the tradition itself tends to function as a constraint upon any new response in the form" (13). And, as Vincent Leitch (1991) says, the constraints--the conventions--helping to define genre act "as political instruments insuring order, effecting exclusions, and carrying out programs" (94). Genre is never innocent, he reminds us. Carolyn Miller (1984) makes the same point, but with greater attention to the role of social action in genre. Despite its ideological authority, however, genre is neither completely stable nor fixed. As Catherine Schryer (1993) observes, "Genres come from somewhere and are transforming into something else" (208).

> To be able to create discourse that will count as a certain kind of action, one has to be able to produce a text with the features that distinguish it as belonging to a certain genre. One has to know that form to be able to perform. (Fahnestock 1993)

The English novel as developing genre helps illustrate the concept. Its beginnings, most literary historians agree, took place during the seventeenth and eighteenth centuries. According to Walter Allen (1954), this was in part a function of literary history. Elizabethan drama, with both tragedy and comedy, with realistic characters and plots, with audiences of ordinary people, played an unwitting role in preparing for a new genre. History itself, the recorded variety, played another; written accounts of events and people and places, buttressed by diaries and autobiographies--the latter genre also evolving at this time--provided material and context for the novel, as well as a kind of preparation for the acceptance of the realistic as opposed to the fantastic/romantic.

But it was during the nineteenth century that the novel in England flourished. Why? History and the pre-generic "novels" no doubt played their parts, but a critical factor was simply the material conditions of the time, particularly as they affected a possible audience. Given the rise of the middle class in the nineteenth century, the celebration of a middle-class conception of family, the opportunity for leisure and some resources to fund it, the novel easily found a home within the lives of a large group of people. And of course the novel itself was delivered in various forms--through the penny papers and through single editions (which often became different versions of the novel), through the silent reading of an adult, through the performative reading of a mother to spouse and children.

> The episodic quality of the Victorian novel resulted, at least in part, from the penny paper distribution schedule. As important, the material conditions of the audience had everything to do with those

We would say now that this blurred Romantic conceptions of writer and reader. And didn't the audience influence both form and content, in effect pressing the author and publisher to reproduce middle-class ideologies?

As they are today, as well, or why are we writing this?

forms. The point here is that the genre "novel" took more than one form, and the form had everything to do with the means of delivery.

Yes, in fact, arguably, both author and audience were influenced by merchants, publishers, and schools, too.

So how is literary history relevant to our discussion? As a class of utterances, one could say, e-mail is "pre-genre"--i.e., in the process of becoming genre. We can see analogies between this process and the process that gave us the novel:

• The material conditions of the late 20th century have enabled a group of generally well-educated, relatively affluent people to communicate in a new medium.

• Many of these people believe that this form of communication is new, is different, and that it enacts new relationships between authors and readers. There is, in other words, an ideology already at work here, and it entails social action.

• E-mail seems currently, however, to function as a primary utterance. The conventions that its advocates cite as defining it seem closer to those "constraining" a phone conversation, which is itself not a genre. And a lack of consensus governing this "netiquette" suggests that it doesn't yet exert the conserving force characteristic of genre. Through recurrence, however, these conventions will become more stabilized, and will in turn define more clearly what is acceptable, what the boundaries will be.

• E-mail does also, however, seem to be challenging what we have taken to be both the role/authority of the author as well as the relationship between author and audience. As Jay David Bolter (1991) suggests,

> The electronic medium now threatens to reverse the attitudes fostered by the [printing] press, by breaking down the barrier between author and reader. . . . Anyone can become an author and send his merest thoughts over one of the networks to hundreds of unwilling readers. His act of "publication" is neither an economic nor a social event. (101)

If this observation is correct, then the rhetorical situation of e-mail is indeed different-- something beyond and apart from other genres. Moreover, as it becomes more stabilized, particularly with reference to rhetorical intent, we should see more clearly the features defining it.

All of which leads me to suggest that e-mail may be a genre-in-the-making.

I'm of two minds about this. In the first place, though Bolter's book, _Writing Space_ (1991), is stunning, sometimes I think he is plain wrong about one thing; the "publication" he mentions is indeed a social event, and it may be an economic one as well (as, obviously, in the case of the many merest advertisements online). I would suggest further that such phenomena as flaming and "cancelling" (censoring) are evidence that the "barrier between reader and author" is still intact, if it ever was. Besides, "Anyone" has always been an author (i.e., anyone with the means--just like today), and has always been considered important or not at the discretion of the reader.

There's yet one more factor. In a recent piece on writing-in-geography as genre, Bill Green and Allison Lee (1994) focus, if implicitly, on the identity a genre requires of its authors. They locate school writing and curriculum as special contexts with special rhetorical situations producing school genres.

> According to this formulation, curriculum work, as the provision of appropriate training in subject-disciplinary knowledge, has as part of its effect the projection and production of particular forms of student identity. This production is necessarily tied up with other major identity formations, such as gender, and connected to broader social power dynamics. For us, rhetoric is as much concerned with the formation of identities as the construction of texts. (210)

Another commentator on this scene, speaking of using e-mail in his own classes, also locates the identity issue as central. Russell Hunt (1994) sees e-mail as a device for forging and maintaining social relationships as well as for carrying on an intellectual discussion. The politics of e-mail, then, in the larger context are certainly those of the bourgeoisie, who--like other classes--seek to replicate their own ideology. Yes. But the politics are also those of the classroom, where identity formation is chief among its priorities.

I don't argue with the idea that rhetorical situations project and produce forms of identity--aside from my instinct that, for the sake of our postmodern anguish, we overstate this sort of thing. In any case, this doesn't establish that e-mail is a new rhetorical situation or genre; I believe Hunt could perceive the same identity effects by assigning a pen-pal unit. Exchange would be slower, but that has merely to do with the mechanics of the process. It's un-hip, I know, but I tend to believe that rhetorical situations are *not* defined by the mechanical process through which they travel, so much as by the social purposes of the rhetors. According to your sketch of the English novel, different media (penny papers, single editions) delivered a single genre. In that case, then (and I think in almost all cases), the genre is logically prior to the means of delivery. I don't doubt that new mechanics make new purposes possible (more about that in a minute), but I insist that we're overstating this effect. The purpose that an extant genre serves very rarely *disappears at the appearance of a new mechanical device. More likely, the new device is bent to the old rhetorical purpose.*

I think that's why most electronic communications are simply reproducing extant genres of writing instead of creating new ones. And for the same reason, I predict that we will see discourse communities online arrange themselves in terms of very familiar hierarchies and conventions. The page, the phone, the monitor is neither the utterance nor the context; it is merely the ground for them.

In fact, I see plenty of evidence on the net that this is true. The material conditions you mention fit here, I believe. One could argue that computer literacy lives within an even more elite socioeconomic hierarchy than does print literacy. But this is often quite forgotten by the users.

> >Distributed technology is the antithesis of the totalitarian apparatus, seems to me. Freedom of speech for anybody who owns a modem.
> <johnmc>

Leaving merely 90% of Americans disenfranchised. And how many Mexicans? How many Somalis and Burmese? In what may be a watershed article, even Selfe and Selfe, who have often led the optimism in the field of computers and composition, are now sounding a much-needed sobering note: "The rhetoric of technology obscures the fact that [computers] are not necessarily serving democratic ends" (1994).

We need to think of cyberspace as the commodity that it is, manufactured and marketed by today's captains of industry for the benefit of those who can afford it. So much of the "university view" of cyberspace seems naive on this point; we seem almost to believe in magic. As if this virtual reality we love were not constructed hammer-and-tongs by grunts in computer factories, packaged and sold by slick marketeers. As if Bill Gates got richer than God by magic. Perhaps this is because we in the university usually don't have to pay our way --access is our caste privilege. Perhaps it's because Bill Gates looks like us: he's a baby boomer, and very very smart. But the cold gray truth is that cyberspace and its equipment are created in the real world by the same socioeconomic structures that gave us the railroad, the automobile, and the petroleum industry. It is merely our place in the hierarchy that conceals the hierarchy from us. "Let them use modems," we say, in all earnest charity.

Even within the online world, true democracy is a polite fiction. Zamierowski (1994) argues that power on lists (electronic conferences) is not hierarchical; it gravitates merely toward wit and erudition, he says, as if those were the great equalizers. But aren't these plain old bourgeois values, revealing their source in our larger social structures? Besides, <imho> even this is a weak version of the truth. Perhaps *especially* on academic/professional lists, power gravitates toward prestige--prestige in written dialect and opinion at least (common surrogates for wit and erudition); and where user addresses include institutional identifiers, power gravitates toward prestige institutions. Some users even perceive a hierarchy among different lists and networks:

>Subscription requests are not automatic for this list. Your request has been forwarded to ykfok@ttacs.ttu.edu for approval.
<listproc>

>In my experience, most of the regular post-ers on *interesting* lists are not academics.   <artsxnet>

>Anti-AOL rantings routed to temp\trash\bigot\internet.
<lysana>

On less formal lists, power moves toward the most verbal and assertive users--whether they're witty and erudite or not. In other words, when people go online, they do not leave their biases behind. And, circling back, that's also why the "old" genres are being reproduced on the net instead of being replaced with new ones. If electronic communication is pre-generic, this is not because it's still young, but because it's indifferent: it is raw and mutable enough to handle the conflicted array of current genres just fine, thank you. And if you want to try a new one, that's fine, too.

When a new element such as e-mail enters the system that is our profession, it changes every element in that system. (Hawisher and Moran, 1993)

Among other things, postmodernism has concerned itself with the role of context in meaning. The strong position is that context *is* meaning, or that meaning is so context-bound that we cannot ascertain it apart from context. The literal sentence has become, quite literally, a dinosaur. We see the influence of this line of thinking on genre as well. Because genre occurs in context, it too derives meaning from the context, but--just as quickly--it shapes the context. (They are in dialogue.) As Freedman (1993) puts it: "genres themselves form part of the discursive context to which rhetors respond in their writing and, as such, shape and enable the writing; it is in this way that form is generative." (272). I think, then, that in order to declare something a genre, we'd have to describe the context in which it is likely to occur. How fixed is the context? How particularized? How quickly changing?

A Genre of Chaos

To most users of the Internet, unbridled freedom, even anarchy, are guiding principles.
— Peter Lewis

In my second mind, I'm beginning to think that, insofar as e-mail can be said to make new approaches possible, it might offer most advantage to the anarchic. In many ways, the TV with a remote controller is analogous. If we think of the remote controller as keyboard, and the TV hour as text to be created, then the channel-surfing teenager may be the most creative artist yet undiscovered.

Armed with a remote control, stocked with a cableful of channels, the home viewer creates montages of unspeakable originality, editing parallel transmissions into an individual blend. This art form is rhythmic, improvisational, and ironic. (Wittig 1994)

You get the idea. "Surrealism Triumphant," Wittig calls it (90), and it is founded in what is essentially a hermeneutic--or at least an aesthetic--of anarchy. Of course, it is worth noting that the TV artiste is improvising within a narrow range; he or she can only create from the very homogeneous values that TV offers. But at least the principle of random montage is evident.

When we recognize that the computer makes an analogous montaging potential available for the writer, we see some interesting new takes indeed on the scene of writing.

>Moments in MOOspace where multithread conversations become recombinant and seem to take on a life of their own. Part of one thread responding with amazing aptness to part of another. A kind of gift.   <swilbur>

Eventually--perhaps within a decade--electronic writing and publication will be boringly normal. Predictions about what will then be possible abound: multimedia and hypertext figure prominently; information transfer and storage beyond our wildest dreams. Our technology even now can accommodate not only combined media (e.g., the "publications" on CD-ROM), but combined voices, epistemologies, even intelligences, juxtaposed into densely populated canvasses of electronic text. We may be seeing, in other words, a collapse of written and visual and aural genres back into the collage of raw experience. Only this time, it would be a prepared rhetoric of chaos, a genre of chaos, perhaps, designed to exploit more of our native ability to process many channels of information simultaneously.

But even this doesn't represent a raw new frontier of human communication; it only brings our technology closer to a capacity for what we already do daily, unassisted, in spades. What dinner-table parent isn't all too familiar with multi-tasking? What child isn't alive to two worlds at once? (I return to my student Tara, who does fine work in my class while sending notes online to her girlfriend. The sneak.)

One issue, then, in this kind of discourse, is how to manage the multi-vocality and at the same time create enough coherence that a spectating conversationist can enter the fray, can discern what the fray is. *This* is what we need to teach our students.

*The period we are entering . . . will see the ascendance of a new aesthetic animated by the vision of the cultural world as composed of mobile, *interchangeable* fragments --common property--messages constantly in motion, ready to be linked into new constellations. . . . A perfume, a broken muffler, the texture of a boot, two bird calls, and an electronic message will be understood to form an inseparable and organic whole. (Wittig, 95)*

*Instead of hailing a brand-new genre, or speculating on pre-generic stases, perhaps we should reread your reference to Schryer: written forms have never been seamless wholes-- they come from and point to many directions *at once.* And maybe we should acknowledge that in the postmodern age, the* *reader, not the writer, is the real tyrant: multi-tasking, channel-surfing, capricious and fickle, free to interpret, misread, manipulate, and (horrors) apply. We're all guilty; we start at the end, in the middle, we don't finish, we joyously juxtapose bits of what we read with other readings, other experiences. But the point is that this is our most natural process. Both reader and writer are engaged constantly in making knowledge from a very random world.*

As our technology enables us to present multi-tasking in more and more tangible form, maybe we should be predicting not new genres, but the end of genre.

>Communities in cyberspace are "real"--but it's important to keep in mind that they are only rhetorical; they have no other dimension.   <baldwine>

Last winter someone told me that on e-mail, when we argue in words, we argue. (Decades ago, Scott Momaday said that we are constructed of words.) Words are, apparently, all we have. But we are production editors now, as well as writers, changing fonts and adding borders and lines, managing a rhetoric of the document to energize the text. Through the technology, we can more easily than ever make the multilayered "postmodern" dimension of writing evident.

Which brings us round to the beginning again. The technologies through which this dialogue/text (and I sense we are no closer to an answer, but do we need one?) is composed has made possible (or made convenient --for all but Joe perhaps) the performative stances we're taking in it. It allows us to use unfamiliar conventions in the familiar context of academic publishing, and in so doing it highlights the joints and seams in the process of making meaning through writing.

To call it the end of genre was flippant and extreme, of course (and very Net--they'd love this on Cybermind), and it doesn't address all kinds of cognitive theory about our need for schemata in processing information. Implicit in my argument all along has been that extant genres are functional mental frames, and the rise of e-mail doesn't eliminate the need for them. I see e-mail as merely a kind of tablet with courier attached. As such, it serves only to deliver extant genres more efficiently than we could deliver them before, and hence I think email itself doesn't destabilize current genres of writing.

But I still think e-mailing isn't writing--or not the discursive variety we're used to reading in academe. Our expectations will not the centre hold. This is the start of another kind of e-speech-that-is-writing: montage-like, quick, unpredictable in form and substance and tenor. That unpredictability, that flexibility, is its charm and thread. The linear and hierarchical, the neatly categorized, seen under erasure.

Well, yes. Where I wasn't being flip was in the sense that one can see e-mail as symbolic--I think you see it this way--as a harbinger, and multi-media as what it heralds. In that case, our tablet expands in many directions, and we see possibilities for combining text with graphics, with sound, with motion, in a wonderful stage-managed chaos of virtual communication. We become not only the production editors you mention, but the stars and directors of our own movies, or more likely (heaven help us) our own commercials.

Of course, montage and pastiche are increasingly chic now, partly as a function of a society that celebrates its difference by fragmentation. But it's also partly done in defense--to deconstruct before being deconstructed, partly to alleviate the anxiety of influence. In writing, electronic technology is the ideal medium for this. That is an important point, but it's one I think we don't fully comprehend yet. And it's one that is affecting us even as we write this, in ways we can't yet articulate. In other words, working on e-mail--constructing the messages within a pre-genre that is still being shaped itself--is constructing us, too.

We don't care. We have each other, on the Internet.   --Dave Barry

Works Cited

Allen, Walter. *The English Novel: A Short Critical History*. New York: Dutton, 1954.

<artsxnet>. "Hillbilly in Cyberspace." Cybermind Discussion List [online]. Available e-mail: CYBERMIND <LISTSERV@WORLD.STD.COM>. 6 July 1994.

Bakhtin, Mikhail. "The Problem of Speech Genres." *The Rhetorical Tradition*. Ed. Patricia Bizzell and Bruce Herzberg. Boston: Bedford, 1990. 944–64.

<baldwine>. "Define Cybermind." Cybermind Discussion List [online]. Available e-mail: CYBERMIND <LISTSERV@WORLD.STD.COM>. 6 July 1994.

Barker, Thomas, and Fred Kemp. "A Postmodern Pedagogy for the Writing Classroom." *Computers and Community*. Ed. Carolyn Handa. Portsmouth: Boynton, 1990. 1–27.

Barry, Dave. "Through Internet, Cybermuffin Shares Intimate Computer Secrets." Knight-Ridder Newspapers 6 Feb. 1994.

Bitzer, Lloyd. "The Rhetorical Situation." *Contemporary Rhetoric*. Ed. Douglas Ehninger. Glenview: Scott, 1972. 39–49.

Bolter, Jay David. *Writing Space*. Hillsdale: Erlbaum, 1991.

<ccrmitta>. "Email." Writing Center Discussion List [online]. Available e-mail: WCENTER <LISTPROC@UNICORN.ACS.TTU.EDU>. 1 Nov. 1993.

Colins, Gail. "The Freddy Krueger in Your Computer." *Working Woman* Apr. 1994: 62.

Cooper, Marilyn, and Cynthia Selfe. "Computer Conferences and Learning: Authority, Resistance, and Internally Persuasive Discourse." *College English* 52 (1991): 847–69.

<csjhs>. "Email." Writing Center Discussion List [online]. Available e-mail: WCENTER <LISTPROC@UNICORN.ACS.TTU.EDU>. 8 Nov. 1993.

———. "P\R." Writing Center Discussion List [online]. Available e-mail: WCENTER <LISTPROC@UNICORN.ACS.TTU.EDU>. 8 July 1994.

Eldred, Janet Cary, and Ron Fortune. "Exploring the Implications of Metaphors for Computer Networks and Hypermedia." Hawisher and LeBlanc 58–74.

Elmer-DeWitt, Philip. "Bards of the Internet." *Time* July 1994: 66–67.

Fahnestock, Jeanne. "Genre and Rhetorical Craft." *Research in the Teaching of English* 27 (1993): 265–71.

Freedman, Aviva. "Show and Tell? The Role of Explicit Teaching in the Learning of New Genres." *Research in the Teaching of English* 27 (1993): 222–52.

Freedman, Aviva, and Peter Medway, eds. *Learning and Teaching Genre*. Portsmouth: Boynton, 1994.

Green, Bill, and Allison Lee. "Writing Geography: Literacy, Identity, and Schooling." Freedman and Medway 207–24.

<harrism>. "Email." Writing Center Discussion List [online]. Available e-mail: WCENTER <LISTPROC@UNICORN.ACS.TTU.EDU>. 9 Nov. 1993.

Hawisher, Gail. "Electronic Meeting of the Minds: Research, Electronic Conferences, and Composition Studies." Hawisher and LeBlanc 81–101.

Hawisher, Gail, and Paul LeBlanc. *Re-Imagining Computers and Composition.* Portsmouth: Boynton, 1992.

Hawisher, Gail, and Charles Moran. "Electronic Mail and the Writing Instructor." *College English* 55 (1993): 627–43.

Hawisher, Gail, and Cynthia Selfe. "The Rhetoric of Technology and the Electronic Writing Class." *CCC* 42 (1991): 55–65.

Hunt, Russell. "Speech Genres, Writing Genres, School Genres, and Computer Genres." Freedman and Medway 243–62.

<johnmc>. "Elements of email Distribution." Megabyte University Discussion List [online]. Available e-mail: MBU-L <LISTPROC@UNICORN.ACS.TTU.EDU>. 5 July 1994.

Lanham, Richard. *The Electronic Word: Democracy, Technology, and the Arts.* Chicago: U of Chicago P, 1993.

Larson, Richard. "The 'Research Paper' in the Writing Course: A Non-Form of Writing." *College English* 44 (1982): 811–16.

Leitch, Vincent. "(De)Coding (Generic) Discourse." *Genre* 24 (Spring 91): 83–98.

Lewis, Peter H. "No More Anything Goes: Cyberspace Gets Censors." *New York Times* 29 June 1994: Business-Technology 3–4.

<lffunkhouser>. "Truck-Flattened Smiley." Copyediting Discussion List [online]. Available e-mail: COPYEDITING-L <LISTSERV@CORNELL.EDU>. 12 Feb. 1994.

<listproc>. "Subscribe CCCCC-L Michael S." Email to M. Spooner [online]. Available e-mail: <mspooner@cc.usu.edu>. 22 June 1994.

<lysana>. "Virtual Communities." Cybermind Discussion List [online]. Available e-mail: CYBERMIND<LISTSERV@WORLD.STD.COM>. 6 July 1994.

<malgosia>. "Virtual Communities." Cybermind Discussion List [online]. Available e-mail: CYBERMIND <LISTSERV@WORLD.STD.COM>. 4 July 1994.

<marius>. "Virtual Communities." Cybermind Discussion List [online]. Available e-mail: CYBERMIND <LISTSERV@WORLD.STD.COM>. 5 July 1994.

<mspooner>. "Early Final Thoughts." E-mail to K. Yancey [online]. Available e-mail: <mspooner@press.usu.edu>. 13 Dec. 1994.

Miller, Carolyn R. "Genre as a Social Action." *Quarterly Journal of Speech* 70 (1984): 151–67.

Moran, Charles. "Computers and English: What Do We Make of Each Other?" *College English* 54 (1992): 193–98.

<mullanne>. "Email." Writing Center Discussion List [online]. Available e-mail: WCENTER <LISTPROC@UNICORN.ACS.TTU.EDU>. 5 Nov. 1993.

<newmann>. "Email." Writing Center Discussion List [online]. Available e-mail: WCENTER <LISTPROC@UNICORN.ACS.TTU.EDU>. 29 Oct. 1993.

Rodrigues, Raymond, and Dawn Rodrigues. *Teaching Writing with a Word Processor.* Urbana: NCTE, 1986.

Schryer, Catherine. "Records as Genre." *Written Communication* 10 (1993): 200–34.

Seabrook, John. "E-mail from Bill." *The New Yorker* 10 Jan. 1994: 48–62.

——. "My First Flame." *The New Yorker* 6 June 1994: 70–79.

Selfe, Cynthia, and Richard J. Selfe, Jr. "The Politics of the Interface: Power and Its Exercise in the Electronic Contact Zone." *CCC* 45 (1994): 480–504.

<skeevers>. "Signature." Business Communication Discussion List [online]. Available e-mail: BIZCOM <LISTSERV@EBBS.ENGLISH.VT.EDU>. 6 June 1994.

Swales, John. *Genre Analysis: English in Academic and Research Discourse.* Cambridge: Cambridge UP, 1990.

<swilbur>. "Beauty in Cyberspace?" Cybermind Discussion List [online]. Available e-mail: CYBERMIND <LISTSERV@WORLD.STD.COM>. 5 July 1994.

Taylor, Paul. "Social Epistemic Rhetoric and Chaotic Discourse." Hawisher and LeBlanc 131–48.

Weathers, Winston. "Grammars of Style." *Rhetoric and Composition*. Ed. Richard L. Graves. Upper Montclair: Boynton, 1984. 133–47.

Wittig, Rob. *Invisible Rendezvous: Connection and Collaboration in the New Landscape of Electronic Writing*. Hanover: Wesleyan UP, 1994.

Zamierowski, Mark. "The Virtual Voice in Network Culture." *Voices on Voice: Perspectives, Definition, Inquiry*. Ed. Kathleen Yancey. Urbana: NCTE, 1994. 275–98.

WRITING THE TECHNOLOGY THAT WRITES US: RESEARCH ON LITERACY AND THE SHAPE OF TECHNOLOGY

Christina Haas and Christine M. Neuwirth

[From *Literacy and Computers: The Complications of Teaching and Learning with Technology*. Ed. Cynthia L. Selfe and Susan Hilligoss. New York: MLA, 1994. 319–35.]

Christina Haas is an assistant professor of English at Penn State University, University Park. In addition to her work in technology, her interests include technical discourse, reading and writing processes, and learning in the disciplines. Christine M. Neuwirth is an associate professor in the Department of English and the School of Computer Science at Carnegie Mellon University. She has published numerous articles and book chapters on computers and writing. And she has also designed and tested computer-based tools to support writing and collaborative writing.

As technology becomes a part of our classroom practices, we are challenged to justify its use and demonstrate how it enhances the learning experiences of our students. Research is one of the most commonly accepted ways we have to explain and justify our use of technology. Haas and Neuwirth argue for "a new, more complicated approach to research on computers and literacy," an approach that does not "assume that literacy 'technologies' are either straightforward or unproblematic." Instead of passively accepting technology as it is and as it becomes available to us, we must use our "knowledge of literacy, its myriad manifestations and its ramifications," and we "must become actively involved in shaping the complex technology that, in turn, shapes our literacy, our cultures, and ourselves." To that end, the authors outline a plan for initiating this kind of research agenda.

In "Literacy in Three Metaphors," Sylvia Scribner describes three ways of seeing literacy — as adaptation, as a state of grace, and as power. She argues that in fact all three views contribute — but each only partially — to understanding literacy, its nature and its implications. Scribner was one of the first scholars to bring to discussions of literacy an articulation of the many, often conflicting, definitions of the term and an awareness that the controversies in definition had, as she put it, "more than academic significance" (6). Cautioning against assumptions that literacy, or literacies, are straightforward and unproblematic, she instead demonstrates that differing views of literacy carry with them complex value systems and inherently competing agendas for action. And Scribner's cautions about oversimplifying literacy are ones those interested in computers and literacy might well take to heart. In this essay we put forth a caveat similar to Scribner's: researchers, teachers, and scholars in the field of English studies should not assume that literacy *technologies* are either straightforward or unproblematic. Views of computers, like views of literacy, are value-laden. Conceptions about what technology *is*, and how it comes to be, profoundly shape specific acts of computer-based reading and writing; they influence as well the construction of our individual and collective selves in *relation* to that technology.

The ultimate aim of this chapter is to argue for a new, more complicated approach to research on computers and literacy. The initial efforts at understanding and implementing computers in writing classrooms were full of enthusiasm, as English teachers and scholars began to recognize the new ways of writing and thinking that computers seemed to invite. This early work sought to document what many teachers and scholars felt intuitively: that writing with computers was more enjoyable, more efficient, yes, even "better." As Cynthia Selfe and Susan Hilligoss discuss in the introduction to this volume, however, these investigations were not simply guided by our enthusiasm; they were often derailed by it, as hastily and sometimes poorly designed studies yielded results that were difficult to interpret and less than conclusive.

A new, more mature research agenda will aid us in understanding how computer technologies, literacy, thinking, and culture are connected. Such research is crucial for informing the design of curricula for teaching writing and can guide the wise use of technology in writing. But an even more critical (and, to our minds, heretofore unacknowledged) justification for such research is that it can help authorize our voices not just in the proper *use* of computer technologies for literacy but in the very *shape* such technologies should take. A critical reason for conducting research, then, is to help us give shape to the technologies that, in turn, shape our literacy acts — to "write" the technology that "writes" us.

Prerequisite to this goal, however, is a need to adjust current thinking about technology. We begin this essay by critiquing three assumptions about computer technology that stand as serious personal, institutional, and cultural obstacles to research and, ultimately, to our free and critical authoring of technology for literacy. These assumptions place us in a subordinate position to technology and, in effect, silence us in the shaping of it. They take us out of the realm of technology development and critique and set us in positions to be merely receivers of technology.

The three assumptions are closely related: the first two assert that technology is either "transparent" or "all-powerful"; while seemingly disparate, these two assumptions actually share an "instrumental" view of technology. That is, they view technology as a means to produce reading and writing, which are somehow imagined to exist independently of and uninfluenced by that means. These two assumptions echo two of the metaphors Scribner discusses. Like literacy as adaptation, the "technology is transparent" assumption appeals to pragmatic values (e.g., increased efficiency) and has a certain commonsense appeal. Like literacy as a state of grace, the "technology is all-powerful" assumption grants certain privileges or virtues to technology and to those who possess or understand it.

These two assumptions are inherently bound to a third: an instrumental view of technology can lead us to forget that literacy is constituted by technology and to leave the work of technology to others. And a belief that "computers are not our job" means that the power (Scribner's third metaphor) to shape technology is by default left to others, to those unnamed "others" whose job it is to "do" computers. Together, these three assumptions negatively affect our understanding of the relation between technologies, individuals, and cultures; limit our power in the conduct of research; and, ultimately, impede our active authoring of technologies for literacy.

Technology Is Transparent

The assumption that technology is transparent is a belief that technologies for reading and writing are a distortionless window, through which we can see essential acts of thinking. In this view, "writing is writing is writing" (or "reading is reading is reading"), unchanged and unaffected by the mode of production and presentation. The essential processes of reading and writing are universal and unchanging: writers and readers simply exchange their pens and books for word processors, replace their face-to-face conversations with computer conferences, and continue to produce texts and construct meanings in the ways they always have.

The assumption that computers are transparent is evident in certain approaches to research and teaching and in most current theories of writing. The assumption is operating when teachers simply transfer "what works" in a traditional pen-and-book classroom to computer-based settings and assume that writing and learning will continue as usual. It is operating when researchers do not attend to the medium with which writers compose and ignore how processes and products may be influenced by various media. And it is operating when theorists attempt to explain composing and its myriad manifestations without examining, or at least acknowledging, the impact that technologies may have.[1]

A variant of the transparent technology assumption acknowledges that writing is *different* with computers — but limits the difference to an increase in efficiency. According to this aspect of the assumption, we can compose, revise, edit, and produce texts more quickly and with less effort with computers; therefore, using computers increases our efficiency as writers but makes no profound difference in *how* reading and writing get done. The belief that technology is a "win" because it increases our efficiency is open to critique: the very metaphor of "efficiency" equates literacy acts with production acts — a somewhat problematic equation (Olson).

Historical studies have documented the problems with the assumption that literacy technologies are transparent. For example, Elizabeth Eisenstein argues that the printing press was a revolutionary agent of change in medieval Europe — a chief contributor if not a prime cause of the rise of science, the growth of Protestantism, and the emergence of the middle class. While critiques of Eisenstein have also tended to act as a corrective on her sometimes overstated claims[2] (Grafton), the power of the printing press in shaping Western history is widely understood. Although the effects of new communication technologies on individuals and cultures are complex, multifaceted, and far from unitary, and while historians may argue about specific claims of degree or direction of such effects, the powerful shaping force of technologies on thinking and culture seems clear.

While it is too early for historical studies on the scale of Eisenstein's to examine the effects of computer technology on reading and writing, ample evidence shows that computer technology is not transparent; rather it can be a contributing agent to changes in both cognitive and social processes. In some of our own research, for instance, we found that writers may move away from note making and other planning activities more quickly when they use word processing (Haas, "Composing in Technological Contexts"). The writers we studied tended to begin production of sustained, connected discourse sooner than they did with pen and paper. The implications of this finding are troubling for teachers who wish to *delay* students' writing until exploration of the problem has been attempted, especially in the light of research results that show a link between initial planning and writing quality (Glynn et al.). And in a study of writing classrooms that use computer networks in addition to traditional modes of communication (face-to-face, paper, phone), we found a significant change in patterns of social interaction about writing, with teachers and students in the networked section interacting more than those in the traditional classroom, and teachers interacting more with less able students (Hartman et al.). These studies are important as a first step in understanding the dynamic relation between technologies and literacy. They also suggest that writing research that examines composing with traditional technologies may not be generalizable to those situations in which writers use computers. At the very least, we need to understand how writing and reading differ in different technological contexts, so that we can interpret research findings accordingly.

The most serious drawback to the transparent technology assumption, however, is that it invites a wholehearted acceptance of computer technology without any accompanying examination of its effects: the transparency myth (wrongly) precludes there *being* any interesting effects. Acceptance of this assumption leads to a belief that writers can *use* computer technology without being shaped by it; it discourages any examination of how computers shape discourse and, consequently, does not authorize us to take an active role in shaping technology. In adopting the transparent technology assumption, those of us in English studies put ourselves in a position to be influenced by technology but not to understand or control that influence.

Technology Is All-Powerful

The counterpart to the transparent technology myth is the assumption that computers are all-powerful. This assumption sees technology as an instrument that is self-determining. In this view, computer technologies will have far-reaching and profound — but essentially one-way — effects. The new technologies for literacy are such a powerful force that simply introducing them to writers or in writing classrooms will change writing and reading for the better, supplanting completely the old pen-and-book technologies. Although the "technology is transparent" and "technology is all-powerful" assumptions appear to be diametrically opposed — characterizing technology as either "all" or "nothing" — they both are based on an instrumental conception of technology, reducing and simplifying its nature and its effects.

An adherence to the "technology is all-powerful" assumption is evident when teachers assume that what they have known about language learning is now outmoded — the "rules" (i.e., our theories and our pedagogy) must be rewritten to accommodate computer technology, which is essentially a brand-new ball game. The assumption is also apparent when teachers expect benefits of technology to accrue similarly for all students and across contexts — as if the power of computers will overshadow or make irrelevant important differences between writers, tasks, contexts. In reality, a writer's particular background, skills, goals, and expectations will strongly determine the way the writer uses computers, as will the particular cultural, social, and educational setting within which he or she works. (Wahlstrom, ch. 8, and Moulthrop and Kaplan, ch. 9, discuss these issues in this volume.) Teachers should be aware of — and should help students become aware of — how individual, task, and situational differences help to determine the use, and usefulness, of various computer technologies.

Adherence to the "technology is all-powerful" stance is evident, too, when researchers and theorists assume that what we need to know about literacy will have to be rebuilt from the ground up — our old theories will be unable to account for literacy in the age of computers; they are not even useful starting points. Research influenced by the assumption looks for strong, unitary, one-way, and often only positive effects of technology. Under this assumption, research about computers and writing is not a way to determine how best to *use* technologies but simply a way to examine their effects. Studies become a justification *for* computers, rather than critical inquiry *about* computers.

One corrective to this assumption is to apply our current theories to think seriously about consequences of technology, both positive and negative. Davida Charney (ch. 10 of this volume) attempts such a corrective to this assumption, especially as it is manifested in much current thinking about hypertexts, when she examines the predictions that existing theories and research about reading would lead us to make concerning the impact of hypertexts. Another corrective is to realize that the effects of any technology are the result of certain cultural and cognitive ways of reasoning about and using that technology (Rubin and Bruce). That is, in a very real way, technologies are "made" through our thinking and talking about them. Consequently, technologies are continually evolving; they are not static but shaped subtly and constantly by the uses to which they are put and by the discourse that accompanies those uses. For example, any effect of computer networks on writing processes stems from a complex interaction between the technology itself and the teachers and students using the networks to achieve their goals (Neuwirth et al., "Why Write — Together").

The "technology is all-powerful" assumption also ignores the dynamic and complex relation between old and new technologies. Again, historical analyses of other literacy technologies provide illumination. Tony Lentz, in a recent study of orality and literacy in ancient Greece, shows compellingly how the "old" technology of orality and the "new" literacy actually existed side by side, in a symbiotic relation, each technology enriching the other. Another well-worn example is the computerized office that uses more paper than it did before the purchase of computers — to the chagrin of the office manager, who had justified the purchase of the machines by claiming that paper expenses would decrease.

In effect, this assumption errs by placing individual uses and motives, and cultural habits and beliefs, in a subordinate position to technology, which "determines" its own uses and effects. Like the "technology is transparent" stance, this one essentially remains non-critical and nonparticipatory; adherents believe (again incorrectly) that profound effects will accrue from technology but that we cannot control, predict, or even understand them. The assumption is detrimental to the conduct of literacy research because, while profound technology-based changes in literacy activity are expected to occur, researchers are not encouraged to ask questions or posit theories about how to account for these changes.

The belief that technology "determines" itself removes, in effect, the space where critique of technology takes place and silences us in the conversations that *do* determine the shape of technology.

Paradoxically, while human purposes and cultural contexts shape technologies, those same technologies exert a powerful influence on cultures and on individuals. The relation, then, between technologies, cultures, and individuals is a complex, multifaceted, and symbiotic one, with influence passing in all directions. Unless we recognize and are willing to explore this dynamic relation, we cannot be part of the dialogue that shapes technologies for literacies.

Computers Are "Not Our Job"

The final assumption may most directly and seriously stand in the way of our empowerment as shapers of technologies for literacy. The assertion that "computers are not our job" distances us from technology by invoking a division of labor: the study of English is our job; the study of computers is the work of others. The assumption has several manifestations, depending, in part, on the various, contested definitions of English studies. The narrowest traditional definition of the English profession is that the proper object of study in English is the preservation and interpretation of the best of our culture's literature, with "best" and "our culture" construed more or less broadly. The methods associated with this definition are primarily text-based analyses of written artifacts. This narrow definition, of course, affects far more than just studies of literacy and computers, since it excludes from sanctioned inquiry many objects having to do with literacy itself. Adherence to such a limited perspective results in the inadequate training of students to address objects beyond literary texts, including texts produced by students or in nonliterary settings, readers' responses to texts, the situations that give rise to texts and other utterances, and — of primary concern here — the media that shape those utterances.

Popularly associated with this narrow definition of the proper object of English studies is an anticomputer stance. Everyone (including those outside English studies) is familiar with the stereotypical image of the English professor as resistance fighter, a last bastion of humanism, refusing to have truck with the "tool of the devil" — that is, the latest innovation in computer technology, be it the word processing of a few years past or today's voice-annotated mail. To the extent that this antitechnological stance has any actuality, one of the forces that may be operating to produce it is the division of labor itself. As Richard Emerson notes, people often attempt to remain independent of what they do not control (e.g., computers), either by reducing investment in goals mediated by others (e.g., the production of manuscripts) or by maintaining alternatives for achieving those goals (e.g., pen and paper).

An anticomputer approach, however, is not a necessary concomitant of the narrow definition of English studies. A second, somewhat more sympathetic stance toward technology, but one that still holds to a traditional view of the proper province of English studies, is witnessed by professors of literature who have learned how to "message" on Humannet and by scholarly articles, such as Richard Lanham's "The Electronic Word: Literary Study and the Digital Revolution," that forecast a brave new world of electronic texts and counsel colleagues to embrace it or, at the least, brace for it. While the antitechnology stance tends to vilify technology and those who develop it, this second stance tends to revere it, even worship it: "The electronic word stands on our side in this endeavor [literary studies] and for that we should return thanks" (288).

But what unites these seemingly diametrically opposed stances is an instrumental view of technology, a view that technology is merely and simply a tool. This instrumental view is implied by the underlying shared assumption of the division of labor: we either choose (or are forced) to use computer technology, or we choose not to. But we do not contribute to its development. The social actors, the agents of development, are in some unspecified way the technology itself, evidenced in statements like "electronic 'texts' will redefine the writing, reading, and professing of literature" (Lanham, "Electronic Word" 265), a circumlocutory discourse that avoids facing the possibly painful thought that other people are redefining reading and writing, while humanists maintain the speculative high ground, remaining above the fray and remote from those actually involved in the process of shaping technology. In this view, technology may merit our attention because it is revolutionizing the study of books, but there is no suggestion that humanists should or even could participate in that revolution as social agents. Just as it is the job of creative writers to produce texts and the job of English scholars to critique them, according to the instrumental view of technology it is the technologists' job to create technology and the job of the cultural critic or teacher to interpret it and use it.

The division of labor and its attendant decisions about what to know and how knowledge of technology is to be formed limits the options available to members of a discipline who inherit it. The point is not that members are *forced* to conform but that the ways in which they are able to depart are restricted (Shumway). The restriction stems in part from members' education, which influences patterns of knowledge acquisition and discursive practices and, perhaps, in part from the ways in which specialization tends to produce, in those occupying a particular role, points of view and beliefs that are consistent with that role (Dearborn and Simon; Lieberman). Even those in English studies who see themselves as directly opposed to the traditional definition of English studies may in fact (perhaps because of background and training similar to their more traditional colleagues or because of the reward systems within traditional English departments) take the speculative high ground with regard to technology. These members of the discipline — whom we call composition scholars for ease of reference — operate from a somewhat broader definition of English studies, a definition that includes questions about the ways in which people interpret and produce texts as proper objects of study. These members often come from educational backgrounds appropriate to their less narrow definition of the field (with graduate work in rhetoric, education, or linguistics, for instance). Frequently these composition scholars run, or are closely tied to, writing programs; their research may center on the acquisition and use of discourse in varied settings; and, while their own departments may not widely share an interest in technology, groups such as the Fifth C (a special-interest group of the Conference on College Composition and Communication) and the spring Computers and Writing conference (held in 1991 in Biloxi, in 1992 in Indianapolis, and in 1993 in Ann Arbor) provide a community for scholars involved in teaching or using technology.

However, even these composition scholars may adhere to the "it's not our job" assumption, although it is often manifest in different ways. Because the assumption conditions attempts to understand technology in that members of this group may see themselves as users, but not as shapers, of technology, research in this community tends to pursue certain questions but not others. Researchers may ask, "Does computer technology improve writing quality?" and "How do computers affect the process of composing?" but too often avoid any inquiries concerning what shape computer-based literacy tools should take. These studies simply are not designed to produce knowledge about the shape of technology. For example, pretest-posttest designs with "the computer" as an undifferentiated treatment condition do not create knowledge that can shape technology, since they explain little about what characteristics of a particular technology are most salient or influential. Not surprisingly, implications are seldom drawn about specific features that are useful, or options that are needed for readers and writers.

Thus studies need not openly express the cultural dominant "computers are not our job" to support that dominant. Research that is concerned with literacy and computers but remains unconcerned with shaping that technology can have the same impact. Although few researchers doing investigations in literacy and computers would actively endorse the "computers are not our job" assumption, much of the work fails to provide grounds for opposition. Such opposition could come, for instance, from work that attend directly to the features of word processors that seem to be most valuable for various kinds of writing tasks or to ways in which groups of writers manage the conventions and procedures of computer mail in their collaborations.

This unwillingness, or inability, to address the issues surrounding technology's shape helps to explain recent exhortations to move beyond so-called basic questions concerning the relation of computers to writing processes and quality, to accept computer technology as a "given" and to go from there. Those exhortations depend on our belief that, because we have already chosen to use computers for writing and teaching and because "the computer" is given to us, complete and already formed, our inquiry should focus on how to use computers to meet such goals as "positive social and political change in our writing classrooms and our educational system" (Bridwell-Bowles 88). Such a stance implores teachers to "make a difference" in their classrooms — and, by implication, *only* in classrooms, since influence would not extend beyond that sphere. To hold to such a stance, one must ignore the critical role of technology in shaping response. In fact, the very shape of the technology used in the classroom, whether word processors, networks, or video displays, conditions the kinds of social and political change that can and will take place in classrooms.

The "computers are not our job" assumption is faulty for two major reasons. First, it ignores the fact that computer technologies — like other tools — are created by humans, usually with particular uses in mind. While tools are not always used as they were intended to be, those who fund, design, and build computer tools exert a powerful control over what kinds of activities those tools facilitate. As Richard Ohmann has pointed out, computers are developed "within particular social relations, and responsive to the needs of those with the power to direct [their] evolution" (680). A great deal of current scholarship acknowledges that theories of literacy shape literate practice. Similarly, computer scientists, actively working on the literacy tools of the future, are operating with their *own* theories of reading and writing, theories that may, in our estimation, be quite different from our own (see Charney, ch. 10 in this volume, for extended discussion of this issue). It is not the case that these developers will necessarily design and implement the same tools and features that researchers or teachers of literacy would. For instance, although writers may see a need for word processors that provide a margin in which collaborators can annotate texts, the technology itself simply does not have such a feature. Moreover, the feature is not going to be developed to be consistent with what researchers in English know about writing and reading processes without the hard work, planning, and execution by those with the technical skills (and resources) to make it happen (Neuwirth et al., "Issues in the Design"). It is, in fact, the skills, desires, and resources of those in a position to effect such decisions that has profound (if indirect) effects on literacy — not the technology itself.

Second, the "computers are not our job" assumption ignores the fact that decisions concerning technology are not infinitely retractable. It seldom suffices to criticize computers after the fact of their development. The QWERTY keyboard persists, although more effective keyboard layouts have been solidly demonstrated. Like the contents of Pandora's box, the QWERTY keyboard, once unleashed, cannot be recalled, despite known limitations. Thus interaction between those who know about literacy and those who know about computers, not after the artifact but during its shaping, is central to the development of the field of literacy and computers.

Research and the Future of Literacy Studies

At this point, it is tempting to see the division of labor as arbitrary and invidious, but such a view would be a mistake. Divisions of labor play important roles in our departments and in other cultural institutions as well. Divisions of labor, for instance, permit specialization by members of a discipline and allow for various economies of expertise. Further, such divisions can aid in overcoming the inherently limited knowledge and information-processing capacities of individual members of a group (J. D. Thompson).

It would be foolish, then, to do away entirely with divisions of labor and the rich range of perspectives and goal orientations they engender. But the failure to see task interdependencies between the goals we have and the goals of those in computer science and related fields has led to a territorialization and parochialism in research on literacy and computers that needs to be overcome. While it is not necessary for scholars of English studies to become computer scientists, cross-disciplinary inquiry on computers and literacy is necessary. It is not necessary to abandon our differences (in training, expertise, and goals), but it will be necessary to achieve more integration. To do so, we need to complicate our research to take into account a conception of computer technology that includes more than a simple instrumental view of technology — as either transparent or as allpowerful. Martin Heidegger, in *The Question Concerning Technology*, expressed it thus:

> The manufacture and utilization of equipment, tools, and machines, the manufactured and used things themselves, and the needs and ends that they serve, all belong to what technology is. The whole complex of these contrivances is technology. (288)

As we have argued, certain ways of thinking about technology and about our relation to it stand in the way of research that can authorize those in English studies to become active shapers of technologies for literacy. Discarding these assumptions means acknowledging that it *is* our job to reason about computer technology, to engage in the discourses that constitute that technology, and to bring our knowledge about literacy to bear on the design of tools for literacy. Further, it means acknowledging that individuals, cultures, and technologies exist in a complex and symbiotic relation, a relation that is still too little understood.

Those with a knowledge of literacy, its myriad manifestations and its ramifications, must become actively involved in shaping the complex of technology that, in turn, shapes our literacy, our cultures, and ourselves. We (and our students) are "written" by the technologies we use, or, more accurately, those with the knowledge, power, and desire shape the technologies that in turn shape us. We are advocating here that those in literacy studies take greater responsibility in "authoring" technology — that is, engaging in sustained and critical dialogue about technology, both its shape and its uses. (In this volume Hawisher, ch. 2, and Barton, ch. 3, take a first step in this direction in critiquing the habits of mind that underlie discussions of technology, both inside and outside English studies. However, neither author extends the argument to show how such critiques might usefully lead to our own involvement in critically authoring literacy technologies.)

Such authoring requires a change in numerous social and political values and institutional practices that work against the broadening of our authority. First, we need to alter our perceptions of ourselves and of one another: understanding computers and literacy is a task not for "individual" researchers but for research communities, whose members' often diverse ways of forming knowledge about computers and writing can, indeed must, be integrated. Members of the computers and literacy community certainly represent diverse methodologies, ask different kinds of questions, advocate differing solutions to common problems. However, we need to learn more about our colleagues' methods, questions, solutions, and problems. Common sense, if not humility, forces us to acknowledge that understanding the multifaceted relation between technologies, cultures, and individuals requires *all* of what we know — much more than any one of us can know.

Second, we need to support more contact across disciplinary boundaries. Certainly cross-disciplinary work will entail a great deal of effort and require a great deal of open-mindedness. Different groups may have different goals explicitly provided as a part of their task assignment. These goals may inherently conflict, as in the case of a computer scientist wanting to maximize functionality (i.e., by increasing the number of separate functions that a given computer feature might possess) and an English professor wanting to maximize learnability (by "keeping it simple"). Similarly, different groups have different areas of expertise: computer scientists know things about search and redisplay algorithms; English professors know things about reading and writing processes. Initiating and sustaining conversations in the face of such differences will be intimidating but crucial.

Finally, and perhaps most important in the long run, we must reduce the homogeneity of orientation and background of our students. We should introduce them to the varied ways of thinking and reasoning about technology (historical, cognitive, sociological), ways that may not always be our own. We must prepare them to traverse disciplinary and subdisciplinary boundaries. One way to accomplish this would be to recruit students who themselves have different disciplinary training and encourage them to work together on common problems. Another would be through the example of the discipline's rewards systems: policies should be established that credit publications about writing in journals of computer science, educational technology, and human factors, as well as in English journals, for hiring, promotion, and tenure.

Modifying our assumptions about technology and reconceiving the boundaries between our own work and those of our colleagues inside and outside our discipline is a first step. We must also embark on a research agenda that will authorize our voices in the dialogues that shape technology. Of course, these goals can and should be pursued concurrently. We cannot realistically expect to change institutional, educational, and cultural configurations and procedures before we begin our research. Indeed, our research ideally will contribute to such changes.

The general goals of such a research agenda would include increasing our knowledge of the relation between individuals and cultures, their literacies and their technologies for literacy. Discourse is inherently social but finds its voice through individuals within cultures. Research should tell us more about how literacy, and specifically literacy constituted by computer technology, mediates the relation between social and cultural groups and individual thinking. In general, then, research should ultimately contribute to a broader understanding of the complex interdependencies of literacy and technologies as they are manifested in cultures and in individuals.

A new research agenda would also have the more specific aim of increasing knowledge about computer features and configurations of uses that help or hinder literacy acts. As teachers, we want to contribute to an understanding of how computers can expand our students' use and knowledge of discourse. As researchers, we want to speak to the design and implementation, not merely the use, of computer technologies to support our pedagogical goals. Our aims, then, must include a consideration of how computer technologies should be implemented (the nuts and bolts of how computers get used in our classrooms) as well as how computer tools for literacy should be designed (software and hardware features that facilitate literacy acts). For instance, classroom-based questions might include the following: Which configuration of machines and software is best suited to particular writing tasks (individual or collaborative, short-term or long-term, routine or novel)? Which is best suited to specific pedagogical goals, such as extended development of ideas, coherent organization and fluid style, or the fruitful sharing of ideas by multiple writers? A question suggested by Betsy A. Bowen's essay in this volume (ch. 4) is, How might the *potential* for democratization inherent in computer networks be brought to fruition? What specific features should such technologies have? For example, Marlene Scardamalia et al. are working to shape a computer system in addition to examining its effects in classrooms. Such questions imply, of course, that researchers of technology and literacy must go beyond speculation and attend to actual classrooms, actual writers, and actual technology in use.

Classroom experiences are closely tied to a second goal: increasing our knowledge of specific hardware and software features that facilitate particular literacy acts. One way to pursue such a goal is to examine problem areas, mismatches between existing technology and writers' needs, goals, and prior experiences. For instance, our previous work on writers' reading from computer displays (Haas and Hayes) began, in a classroom, with complaints from freshman writing students about the lack of printing facilities available to them. This complaint, in turn, pointed to their continued use of hard copy throughout composing (see also Haas, "Seeing It on the Screen"). Systematic examination of their hard copy use eventually suggested the benefits of large-screen, high-resolution displays for complex literacy acts like composing and reading extended texts (Haas and Hayes; Haas, "Does the Medium Make a Difference?"; further corroboration is provided by Gould and Grischkowsky).

Such goals for research, of course, rest on theories of literacy — implicit or explicit. Consequently, clear articulation of theory must accompany any research agenda. Research should be driven by a theory of how literacy works, why and when people engage in literacy acts, how cultures and literacies constitute one another. For instance, the research on writers reading from computer displays described above rests on a particular theory of mind and human action suggesting that when writers have problems with computers — when they encounter mismatches between their practices of literacy and the available technologies — the writers are not simply "in error," do not merely need to be "weaned" to the new technology. Rather, they are demonstrating their cognizance of their own needs as literate agents, needs shaped by the literacy practice of their culture. An effective research agenda will include clear articulation of how specific theories of writing undergird research, justify questions, and help determine the interpretation of results. Further, results of research should explicitly feed back into theory — informing, testing, and enriching it. Research, then, becomes a way not simply to answer questions but also to open them up — a heuristic for inquiry.

A pluralistic variety of methods will be necessary to examine the symbiotic relation between technologies, cultures, and individuals. While no one study can address all aspects of this relation, collectively our methods should ultimately invite integration. And while no one researcher need be, or even can be, adept at all approaches, we should strive to understand the methodologies our colleagues use. The benefit of any one method is less important than rich and theory-driven questions, and rather than advocate techniques, we would advocate attention to the way specific questions call for particular methods. In general, we should apply methods that allow us to take both a "fine-grained" and a "wide-angle" view. Fine-grained research would examine individual writers and groups of writers, in detail and in situ, and might employ a range of observational methods (e.g., participant-observer research, interviews conducted over time) as well as more controlled studies of larger groups of writers and readers (Neuwirth and Kaufer, "Computers and Composition Studies"). New methods may also prove necessary and useful. A wide-angle view, drawing on clearly articulated theories and clearly specified research designs, would link disparate studies and examine issues that stretch across methods, across time, and across field of inquiry. Both approaches must be tied to research goals and should be theoretically grounded. A third view, one that might metaphorically be characterized as an "elapsed-time" view, would look at historical changes in literacy and technology and help ground all our research.

A final critical need is to expand the range of audiences to whom we speak. By looking within our own institution, we will undoubtedly find colleagues — in education, psychology, even in business and engineering — who are interested in decisions about the shape and implementation of technologies for literacy. Of course, in dialogues with these colleagues, we may find initial difficulties with terminology: where we would refer to "literacy acts," our colleagues may use different terms — "discourse production" and "comprehension" in psychology or education, for example; "information structuring" and "information management" in business. Such variations in terminology certainly imply some differences in theoretical perspectives and worldviews, but fruitful exchanges of ideas will still be possible and valuable. In addition, we should make our research accessible to designers involved in computer development, both hardware and software. Such cooperation may mean sitting on university task forces with our colleagues from computer science, publishing our results in journals read by computer scientists, attending conferences (like those sponsored by the Association for Computing Machinery) with developers and other computer professionals interested in education issues.

We can also expand our audience by making our research relevant and important to the work of our field generally. To do so, we might challenge our colleagues — who may themselves suffer from faulty assumptions like "computers are not my job" — to recognize what is at stake as literacies for technology evolve. As the new perspectives on literacy in this volume make clear, what is at stake is our active voice in the development of tools for literacy; indeed, what is at stake may be the very shape of literacy itself.[3]

Notes

[1] Hayes has recently proposed an adaptation of the 1981 Hayes and Flower process model of composing that recognizes the role technologies may play in writing, although his new model does not account for precisely *how* technology affects composing (Personal communication). Neuwirth and Kaufer offer one account of the role external representations can play in composing ("Role").

[2] Kaestle believes that this overstatement was deliberate — an attempt to disrupt the status quo assumptions about the presumably inconsequential effects of the rise of print.

[3] The authors would like to thank David Shumway, Nancy Kaplan, David Kaufer, Alan Kennedy, and Cheryl Geisler, who offered thoughtful comments on earlier drafts of this essay.

Works Cited

Bridwell-Bowles, Lillian. "Designing Research on Computer-Assisted Writing." *Computers and Composition* 7 (1988): 79–91.

Dearborn, Dewitt C., and Herbert A. Simon. "Selective Perception." *Sociometry* 21 (1958): 140–43.

Gould, John, and Nancy Grischkowsky. "Doing the Same Work with Hard Copy and with CRT Terminals." *Human Factors* 26 (1984): 323–37.

Haas, Christina, and John R. Hayes. "'What Did I Just Say?': Reading Problems in Writing with the Machine." *Research in the Teaching of English* 20.1 (1986): 22–35.

Heidegger, Martin. *The Question Concerning Technology and Other Essays*. New York: Harper, 1977.

Lanham, Richard A. "The Electronic Word: Literary Study and the Digital Revolution." *New Literary History* 20 (1989): 265–89.

Lentz, Tony M. *Orality and Literacy in Hellenic Greece*. Carbondale: Southern Illinois UP, 1989.

Lieberman, Seymour. "The Effects of Changes in Roles on the Attitudes of Role Occupants." *Human Relations* 9 (1956): 385–402.

Neuwirth, Christine M., and David S. Kaufer. "Computers and Composition Studies: Articulating a Pattern of Discovery." *Critical Perspectives on Computers and Composition Instruction*. Ed. Gail E. Hawisher and Paul LeBlanc. New York: Teachers Coll. P, 1989. 173–90.

Neuwirth, Christine M., David S. Kaufer, Ravinder Chandhok, and James H. Morris. "Issues in the Design of Computer Support for Coauthoring and Commenting." *Third Conference on Computer Supported Cooperative Work (CSCW '90)*. Baltimore: Assn. for Computing Machinery, 1990. 193–95

Neuwirth, Christine M., Michael Palmquist, Cynthia Cochran, Terilyn Gillespie, Karen Hartman, and Thomas Hajduk. "Why Write — Together — Concurrently on a Computer Network?" *Situated Evaluation of ENFI*. Ed. Bertram Bruce, Joy Peyton, and Trent Batson. Cambridge: Cambridge UP, in press.

Ohmann, Richard. "Literacy, Technology, and Monopoly Capital." *College English* 47 (1985): 675–89.

Rubin, Andee, and Bertram Bruce. *Alternate Realizations of Purpose in Computer-Supported Writing*. Tech. Rept. 492. Champaign: Center for the Study of Writing, 1990.

Scribner, Sylvia, and Michael Cole. *The Psychology of Literacy*. Cambridge: Harvard UP, 1981.

Shumway, David R. "Introduction." *Poetics Today* 9 (1988): 687–98.

Thompson, James D. *Organizations in Action*. New York: McGraw, 1969.

BIBLIOGRAPHY FOR FURTHER READING

This bibliography points out further books and articles related to the variety of topics discussed in *Background Readings*. For convenience, it follows the organization of *Background Readings*.

Part One: The Writing Process

Booth, Wayne C. "The Rhetorical Stance." *College Composition and Communication* 14 (1963): 139–45.

Coe, Richard M. "If Not to Narrow, Then How to Focus: Two Techniques for Focusing." *College Composition and Communication* 32 (1981): 272–77.

Cooper, Marilyn M. "The Ecology of Writing." *College English* 48 (1986): 364–75.

Ede, Lisa, and Andrea Lunsford. "Audience Addressed/Audience Invoked: The Role of Audience in Composition Theory and Pedagogy." *College Composition and Communication* 35 (1984): 155–71.

Elbow, Peter. "Closing My Eyes as I Speak: An Argument for Ignoring Audience." *College English* 49 (1987): 50–69.

Emig, Janet. *The Composing Processes of Twelfth Graders.* NCTE Research Rept. No. 13. Urbana: NCTE, 1971.

Flower, Linda. *The Construction of Negotiated Meaning: A Social Cognitive Theory of Writing.* Carbondale: Southern Illinois UP, 1994.

Flower, Linda, and John R. Hayes. "A Cognitive Process Theory of Writing." *College Composition and Communication* 32 (1981): 365–87.

Fulwiler, Toby, ed. *The Journal Book.* Portsmouth, NH: Boynton/Cook, 1987.

Harris, Joseph. *A Teaching Subject: Composition since 1966.* Englewood Cliffs: Prentice, 1997.

———. "Rethinking the Pedagogy of Problem-Solving." *Journal of Teaching Writing* 7 (1988): 157–65.

Hillocks, George, Jr. *Research on Written Composition.* Urbana: ERIC, 1986. 1–62.

———. *Teaching Writing as Reflective Practice.* New York: Teachers College P, 1995. 76–95.

Kinneavy, James L. *A Theory of Discourse.* New York: Norton, 1980. 17–40, 48–68.

Kroll, Barry. "Writing for Readers: Three Perspectives on Audience." *College Composition and Communication* 35 (1984): 172–85.

Marsella, Joy, and Thomas L. Hilgers. "Exploring the Potential of Freewriting." *Nothing Begins with N: New Investigations of Freewriting.* Ed. Pat Belanoff, Peter Elbow, and Sheryl I. Fontaine. Carbondale: Southern Illinois UP, 1991. 93–110.

Perl, Sondra. "Understanding Composing." *College Composition and Communication* 31 (1980): 363–69.

Perl, Sondra, ed. *Landmark Essays on Writing Process.* Davis, CA: Hermagoras, 1994.

Porter, James E. *Audience and Rhetoric.* Englewood Cliffs: Prentice, 1992.

Pratt, Mary Louise. "Arts of the Contact Zone." *Profession* 91 (1991): 33–40.

Rafoth, Bennett A. "Discourse Community: Where Writers, Readers, and Texts Come Together." *The Social Construction of Written Communication.* Ed. Bennett A. Rafoth and Donald L. Rubin. Norwood, NJ: Ablex, 1988. 131–46.

Roth, Robert G. "The Evolving Audience: Alternatives to Audience Accomodation." *College Composition and Communication* 38 (1987): 47–55.

Selzer, Jack. "Exploring Options in Composing." *College Composition and Communication* 35 (1984): 276–84.

Tobin, Lad, and Thomas Newkirk, eds. *Taking Stock: The Writing Process Movement in the '90s*. Portsmouth, NH: Boynton/Cook, 1994.

Williams, James D. *Preparing to Teach Writing*. Belmont: Wadsworth, 1989. 3–14, 27–49.

Young, Richard, and Yameng Liu, eds. *Landmark Essays on Rhetorical Invention in Writing*. Davis, CA: Hermagoras, 1994.

Planning, Drafting, and Revising

Bruffee, Kenneth A. "Writing and Collaboration." *Collaborative Learning: Higher Education, Interdependence, and the Authority of Knowledge*. Baltimore: Johns Hopkins UP, 1993. 52–62.

Corbett, Edward P. J. *Classical Rhetoric for the Modern Student*. 3rd ed. New York: Oxford UP, 1990.

Elbow, Peter. *Writing with Power: Techniques for Mastering the Writing Process*. New York: Oxford UP, 1981.

Faigley, Lester, and Stephen Witte. "Analyzing Revision." *College Composition and Communication* 32 (1981): 440–14.

Flower, Linda, et al. "Detection, Diagnosis, and the Strategies of Revision." *College Composition and Communication* 37 (1986): 16–55.

Harris, Muriel. "Collaboration Is Not Collaboration Is Not Collaboration: Writing Center Tutorials vs. Peer-Response Groups." *College Composition and Communication* 43 (1992): 369–83.

Hilbert, Betsy S. "It Was a Dark and Nasty Night It Was a Dark and You Would not Believe How Dark It Was a Hard Beginning." *College Composition and Communication* 43 (1992): 75–80.

Lanham, Richard. *Revising Prose*. New York: Scribner's, 1979.

Lindemann, Erika. *A Rhetoric for Writing Teachers*. 3rd ed. New York: Oxford UP, 1995. 21–34, 105–25, 216–45.

Murray, Donald. *The Craft of Revision*. 2nd ed. Orlando: Harbrace, 1995.

Nelson, Victoria. *Writer's Block and How to Use It*. Cincinnati: Writer's Digest Books, 1985.

Podis, JoAnne M., and Leonard A. Podis. "Identifying and Teaching Rhetorical Plans for Arrangement." *College Composition and Communication* 41 (1990): 430–42.

Raymond, Richard C. "Teaching Students to Revise: Theories and Practice." *Teaching English in the Two-Year College* 16 (1989): 49–58.

Young, Richard. "Recent Developments in Rhetorical Invention." *Teaching Composition: 12 Bibliographic Essays*. Ed. Gary Tate. Fort Worth: Texas Christian UP, 1987. 1–38.

Wall, Susan V. "The Languages of the Text: What Even Good Students Need to Know about Re-Writing." *Journal of Advanced Composition* 7 (1987): 31–40.

Willis, Meredith Sue. *Deep Revision: A Guide for Teachers, Students, and Other Writers*. New York: Teachers and Writers Collaborative, 1993.

Responding to Student Writing

Belanoff, Pat, and Marcia Dickson, eds. *Portfolios: Process and Product*. Portsmouth, NH: Boynton/Cook, 1991.

Cooper, Charles R., and Lee Odell, eds. *Evaluating Writing: Describing, Measuring, Judging*. Urbana: NCTE, 1977.

Garrison, Roger. "One-to-One: Tutorial Instruction in Freshman Composition." *New Directions for Community Colleges* 2 (Spring 1974): 55–84.

Harris, Muriel. *Teaching One-to-One*. Urbana: NCTE, 1986.

Murray, Donald M. "Teaching the Other Self: The Writer's First Reader." *College Composition and Communication* 33 (1982): 140–47.

Robertson, Michael. "Is Anybody Listening?" *College Composition and Communication* 37 (1986): 87–91.

Straub, Richard. "The Concept of Control in Teacher Response: Defining the Varieties of 'Directive' and 'Facilitative' Commentary." *College Composition and Communication* 47 (1996): 223–51.

Straub, Richard, and Ronald F. Lunsford. *Twelve Readers Reading: Responding to College Student Writing.* Cresskill, NJ: Hampton, 1995.

White, Edward M. *Assigning, Responding, Evaluating: A Writing Teacher's Guide.* 3rd ed. New York: St. Martin's, 1995.

Williams, James D. *Preparing to Teach Writing.* Mahwah, NJ: Erlbaum, 1996. 255–99.

Paragraphs

Bamberg, Betty. "What Makes a Text Coherent?" *College Composition and Communication* 34 (1983): 417–29.

Braddock, Richard. "The Frequency and Placement of Topic Sentences in Expository Prose." *Research in Teaching Writing* 8 (1974): 287–304.

Brostoff, Anita. "Coherence: 'Next to' Is Not 'Connected to.'" *College Composition and Communication* 32 (1981): 278–94.

Christensen, Francis. "A Generative Rhetoric of the Paragraph." *Notes toward a New Rhetoric: Six Essays for Teachers.* New York: Harper, 1967. 52–81.

D'Angelo, Frank. "The Topic Sentence Revisited." *College Composition and Communication* 37 (1986): 431–41.

Haswell, Richard H. "Textual Research and Coherence: Findings, Intuition, Application." *College English* 51 (1989): 305–19.

Laib, Nevin. "Conciseness and Amplification." *College Composition and Communication* 41 (1990): 443–59.

Lindemann, Erika. *A Rhetoric for Writing Teachers.* 3rd ed. New York: Oxford UP, 1995. 141–57.

Popken, Randell L. "A Study of Topic Sentence Use in Academic Writing." *Written Communication* 4 (1987): 209–28.

Witte, Stephen P., and Lester Faigley. "Coherence, Cohesion, and Writing Quality." *College Composition and Communication* 32 (1981): 189–204.

Choosing Formats and Document Design

Anderson, W. Steve. "The Rhetoric of the Résumé." Annual Meeting of the Coll. English Assn. Clearwater Beach, FL. 12–14 Apr. 1984. *ERIC.* CD-ROM. SilverPlatter, 1995.

Hall, Dean G., and Bonnie A. Nelson. "Initiating Students into Professionalism: Teaching the Letter of Inquiry." *Technical Writing Teacher* 14 (1987): 86–89.

Hawisher, Gail E., and Charles Moran. "Electronic Mail and the Writing Instructor." *College English* 55 (1993): 627–43.

Humphries, Donald S. "Making Your Hypertext Interface Usable." *Technical Communication* 40 (1993): 754–61.

Kostelnick, Charles. "The Rhetoric of Text Design in Professional Communication." *Technical Writing Teacher* 17 (1990): 189–202.

———. "Visual Rhetoric: A Reader-Oriented Approach to Graphics and Designs." *Technical Writing Teacher* 16 (1989): 77–88.

Lanham, Richard A. *Revising Business Prose.* 3rd ed. New York: Prentice, 1991.

Lay, Mary M. "Nonrhetorical Elements of Layout and Design." *Technical Writing: Theory and Practice.* Ed. Bertie E. Fearing and W. Keats Sparrow. New York: MLA, 1989. 72–85.

Mansfield, Margaret A. "Real World Writing and the English Curriculum." *College Composition and Communication* 44 (1993): 69–83.

Matalene, Carolyn B., ed. *Worlds of Writing: Teaching and Learning in Discourse Communities of Work.* New York: McGraw, 1989.

Mendelson, Michael. "Business Prose and the Nature of the Plain Style." *Journal of Business Communication* 24 (Spring 1987): 3–18.

Norman, Rose. "Resumex: A Computer Exercise for Teaching Résumé Writing." *Technical Writing Teacher* 15 (Spring 1988): 162–66.

Odell, Lee, and Dixie Goswami, eds. *Writing in Nonacademic Settings*. New York: Guilford, 1986.

Parker, Roger C. *Looking Good in Print: A Guide to Basic Design for Desktop Publishing*. 2nd ed. Chapel Hill: Ventana, 1990.

Pickett, Nell Ann. "Achieving Readability through Layout." *Teaching English in the Two-Year College* 10 (1984): 154–56.

Redish, Janice C., Robbin M. Battison, and Edward S. Gold. "Making Information Accessible to Readers." *Writing in Nonacademic Settings*. New York: Guilford, 1986. 129–54.

Shenk, Robert. "Ghost-Writing in Professional Communications." *Journal of Technical Writing and Communication* 18 (1988): 377–87.

Special Issue: Visual Communication. *Journal of the Society for Technical Communication* 40 (1993).

Part Two: Critical Thinking and Argument

Bator, Paul. "Aristotelian and Rogerian Rhetoric." *College Composition and Communication* 31 (1980): 427–32.

Bean, John C. *Engaging Ideas: The Professor's Guide to Integrating Writing, Critical Thinking, and Active Learning in the Classroom*. San Francisco: Jossey-Bass, 1996.

Bizzell, Patricia. "The 4th of July and the 22nd of December: The Function of Cultural Archives in Persuasion, as Shown by Frederick Douglass and William Apess." *College Composition and Communication* 48 (1997): 44–60.

Browne, M. Neil, and Stuart M. Keeley. *Asking the Right Questions: A Guide to Critical Thinking*. 4th ed. Englewood Cliffs: Prentice, 1994.

Carella, Michael J. "Philosophy as Literacy: Teaching College Students to Read Critically and Write Cogently." *College Composition and Communication* 34 (1983): 57–61.

Clark, John H., and Arthur W. Biddle, eds. *Teaching Critical Thinking: Reports from across the Curriculum*. Englewood Cliffs: Prentice, 1993.

Dyrud, Marilyn A. "Teaching Logic." Oregon Council of Teachers of English Spring Conf. Bend, OR. 6–7 Apr. 1984. *ERIC*. CD-ROM. SilverPlatter, 1995.

Fahnestock, Jeanne, and Marie Secor. "Teaching Argument: A Theory of Types." *College Composition and Communication* 34 (1983): 20–30.

Fishman, Stephen M., and Lucille Parkinson McCarthy. "Teaching for Student Change: A Deweyan Alternative to Radical Pedagogy." *College Composition and Communication* 47 (1996): 342–66.

Fulkerson, Richard. "Technical Logic, Comp-Logic, and the Teaching of Writing." *College Composition and Communication* 39 (1988): 436–52.

Kaufer, David S., and Christine M. Neuwirth. "Integrating Formal Logic and the New Rhetoric: A Four Stage Heuristic." *College English* 45 (1983): 380–89.

Lamb, Catherine E. "Beyond Argument in Feminist Composition." *College Composition and Communication* 42 (1991): 11–24.

Lazere, Donald. "Teaching the Political Conflicts: A Rhetorical Schema." *College Composition and Communication* 43 (1992): 194–213.

McCleary, William J. "A Case Approach for Teaching Academic Writing." *College Composition and Communication* 36 (1985): 203–12.

Rapkin, Angela A. "The Uses of Logic in the College Freshman English Classroom." *Activities to Promote Critical Thinking: Classroom Practices in Teaching English*. Urbana: NCTE, 1986. 130–35. *ERIC*. CD-ROM. SilverPlatter, 1995.

Secor, Marie J. "Recent Research in Argumentation Theory." *Technical Writing Teacher* 14 (1987): 337–54.

Trail, George Y. "Teaching Argument and the Rhetoric of Orwell's 'Politics of the English Language.'" *College English* 57 (1995): 570–83.

Zeller, Robert. "Developing the Inferential Reasoning of Basic Writers." *College Composition and Communication* 38 (1987): 343–45.

Parts Three and Four: Clear Sentences and Word Choice

Effective Sentences

Carkeet, David. "Understanding Syntactic Errors in Remedial Writing." *College English* 38 (1977): 682–86, 695.

Christensen, Francis. "A Generative Rhetoric of the Sentence." *Notes toward a New Rhetoric: Six Essays for Teachers.* New York: Harper, 1967. 1–22.

Corbett, Edward P. J. "Approaches to the Study of Style." *Teaching Composition: 12 Bibliographical Essays.* Ed Gary Tate. Fort Worth: Texas Christian UP, 1987. 83–130.

Corbett, Edward P. J. *Classical Rhetoric for the Modern Student.* 3rd ed. New York: Oxford UP, 1990. 398–403, 404–23.

Crowhurst, Marion. "Sentence Combining: Maintaining Realistic Expectations." *College Composition and Communication* 34 (1983): 62–72.

Elbow, Peter. "The Challenge for Sentence Combining." *Sentence Combining: A Rhetorical Perspective.* Ed. Don Daiker, Andrew Kerek, and Max Morenberg. Carbondale: Southern Illinois UP, 1985. 232–45.

Faigley, Lester. "Names in Search of a Concept: Maturity, Fluency, Complexity, and Growth in Written Syntax." *College Composition and Communication* 31 (1980): 291–300.

Freeman, Donald C. "Linguistics and Error Analysis: On Agency." *The Territory of Language.* Ed. Donald McQuade. Carbondale: Southern Illinois UP, 1986. 165–73.

Graves, Richard L. "Symmetrical Form and the Rhetoric of the Sentence." *Rhetoric and Composition: A Sourcebook for Teachers and Writers.* Ed. Richard L. Graves. Portsmouth, NH: Boynton/Cook, 1984, 119–27.

Kolln, Martha. *Understanding English Grammar.* 4th ed. New York: Macmillan, 1994. 349–90.

Laib, Nevin. "Conciseness and Amplification." *College Composition and Communication* 41 (1990): 443–59.

Lanham, Richard. *Style: An Anti–Textbook.* New Haven: Yale UP, 1978.

Lindemann, Erika. *A Rhetoric for Writing Teachers.* 3rd ed. New York: Oxford UP, 1995. 158–69.

Noguchi, Rei R. *Grammar and the Teaching of Writing: Limits and Possibilities.* Urbana: NCTE, 1991. 38–58.

Pixton, William H. "The Dangling Gerund: A Working Definition." *College Composition and Communication* 24 (1973): 193–99.

Shaughnessy, Mina P. *Errors and Expectations: A Guide for the Teacher of Basic Writing.* New York: Oxford UP, 1979. 44–89.

Walker, Robert L. "The Common Writer: A Case for Parallel Structure." *College Composition and Communication* 21 (1970): 373–79.

Walpole, Jane R. "The Vigorous Pursuit of Grace and Style." *Writing Instructor* 1 (1982): 163–69.

Weaver, Constance. *Teaching Grammar in Context.* Portsmouth, NH: Boynton/Cook, 1996. 102–47.

Williams, James D. *Preparing to Teach Writing.* Mahwah, NJ: Erlbaum, 1996. 301–02, 306.

Williams, Joseph M. *Style: Ten Lessons in Clarity and Grace.* 5th ed. New York: Longman, 1997. 140–44.

Word Choice

Balester, Valerie M. *Cultural Divide: A Study of African-American College-Level Writers.* Portsmouth, NH: Boynton/Cook, 1993. 77–151.

Corbett, Edward P. J. *Classical Rhetoric for the Modern Student.* 3rd ed. New York: Oxford UP, 1990. 438–47.

Devet, Bonnie. "Bringing Back More Figures of Speech into Composition." *Journal of Teaching Writing* 6 (1987): 293–304.

Frank, Francine Wattman, and Paula A. Treichler, et al. *Language, Gender, and Professional Writing: Theoretical Approaches and Guidelines for Nonsexist Usage.* New York: MLA, 1989.

Giannasi, Jenefer M. "Language Varieties and Composition." *Teaching Composition.* Ed. Gary Tate. Rev. ed. Fort Worth: Texas Christian UP, 1987.

Labov, William. *Language in the Inner City: Studies in the Black English Vernacular.* Philadelphia, U of Pennsylvania P, 1972.

Lanham, Richard. *Revising Prose.* New York: Prentice, 1991.

Lutz, William. *Quarterly Review of Doublespeak.* Urbana: NCTE.

Lutz, William. *The New Doublespeak: Why No One Knows What Anyone's Saying Anymore.* New York: Harper, 1996.

Miller, Casey, and Kate Swift. *The Handbook of Non-Sexist Writing.* 2nd ed. New York, Harper, 1992.

Williams, James D. "Nonstandard English." *Preparing to Teach Writing.* Mahwah, NJ: Erlbaum, 1996. 160–76.

Williams, Joseph M. *Style: Ten Lessons in Clarity and Grace.* 5th ed. New York: Longman, 1997. 159–84.

Part Five: Grammatical Sentences

Bamberg, Betty. "Periods Are Basic: A Strategy for Eliminating Comma Faults and Run–on Sentences." *Teaching the Basics — Really!* Ed. Ouida Clapp. Urbana: NCTE, 1977. 97–99.

Byrony, Shannon. "Pronouns: Male, Female, and Undesignated." *ETC.: A Review of General Semantics* 45 (1988): 334–36.

Caroll, Joyce Armstrong, and Edward E. Wilson. *Acts of Teaching: How to Teach Writing.* Englewood, CO: Teacher Ideas, 1993. 223–39.

Epes, Mary. "Tracing Errors to the Sources: A Study of the Encoding Processes of Adult Basic Writers." *Journal of Basic Writing* 41 (1985): 4–33.

Harris, Joseph. *A Teaching Subject: Composition since 1966.* Upper Saddle River, NJ: Prentice, 1997. 76–90.

Harris, Muriel. "Mending the Fragmented Free Modifier." *College Composition and Communication* 32 (1981): 175–82.

Hull, Glynda. "Constructing Taxonomies for Error." *A Sourcebook for Basic Writing Teachers.* Ed. Theresa Enos. New York: McGraw, 1987. 231–44.

Kagan, Dona M. "Run–on and Fragment Sentences: An Error Analysis." *Research in the Teaching of English* 14 (1980): 127–38.

Kolln, Martha. "Everyone's Right to Their Own Language." *College Composition and Communication* 37 (1986): 100–02.

Kroll, Barry, M. and John C. Schafer. "Error Analysis and the Teaching of Composition." *College Composition and Communication* 29 (1978): 242–48.

Mathews, Alison, and Martin S. Chodorow. "Pronoun Resolution in Two–Clause Sentences: Effects of Ambiguity, Antecedent Location, and Depth of Imbedding." *Journal of Memory and Language* 27 (1988): 245–60.

Moskovit, Leonard. "When Is Broad Reference Clear?" *College Composition and Communication* 34 (1983): 454–69.

Noguchi, Rei R. *Grammar and the Teaching of Writing: Limits and Possibilities.* Urbana: NCTE, 1991.

Shaughnessy, Mina P. *Errors and Expectations: A Guide for the Teacher of Basic Writing.* New York: Oxford UP, 1979. 16–43, 135.

Sklar, Elizabeth S. "The Tribunal of Use: Agreement in Indefinite Constructions." *College Composition and Communication* 39 (1988): 410–22.

Williams, Joseph M. "The Phenomenology of Error." *College Composition and Communication* 32 (1981): 152–68.

Wolfram, Walt, and Ralph W. Fasold. *The Study of Social Dialects in American English.* Upper Saddle River: Prentice, 1974.

Part Six: English as a Second Language

Bizzell, Patricia, and Bruce Herzberg. "Teaching English as a Second Language." *The Bedford Bibliography for Teachers of Writing.* Boston: Bedford, 1996. 117–22.

Celce-Murcia, Marianne, Diane Larsen-Freeman, and Stephen Thewlis. *The Grammar Book: An ESL/EFL Teacher's Course.* Boston: Heinle, 1983.

Chappel, Virginia A., and Judith Rodby. "Verb Tense and ESL Composition: A Discourse Level Approach." Annual Convention of Teachers of English to Speakers of Other Languages. Honolulu. 1–6 May 1982. *ERIC.* CD-ROM. SilverPlatter, 1995.

Cook, Lenora, and Helen C. Lodge, eds. "Voices in English Classrooms: Honoring Diversity and Change." *Classroom Practices in Teaching English* 28. Urbana: NCTE, 1996.

Dean, Terry. "Multicultural Classrooms, Monocultural Teachers." *College Composition and Communication* 40 (1989): 23–37.

Fox, Helen. *Listening to the World: Cultural Issues in Academic Writing.* Urbana: NCTE, 1994.

Harris, Muriel, and Tony Silva. "Tutoring ESL Students: Issues and Options." *College Composition and Communication* 44 (1995): 525–37.

Leki, Ilona. "Coaching from the Margins: Issues in Written Response." *Second Language Writing: Research Insights for the Classroom.* Ed. Barbara Kroll. Cambridge: Cambridge UP, 1990. 57–68.

Master, Peter. "Teaching the English Articles as a Binary System." *TESOL Quarterly* 24 (1990): 461–78.

Nelson, Gayle L., and John M. Murphy. "Peer Response Groups: Do L2 Writers Use Peer Comments in Revising Their Drafts?" *TESOL Quarterly* 27 (1993): 135–41.

Rinnert, Carol, and Mark Hansen. "Teaching the English Article System." Japan Association of Language Teachers' International Conference on Language Teaching and Learning. Seiri Gakuen, Hamamatsu, Japan. 22–24 Nov. 1986. *ERIC.* CD-ROM. SilverPlatter, 1995.

Parts Seven and Eight: Punctuation and Mechanics

Bruthiaux, Paul. "Knowing When to Stop: Investigating the Nature of Punctuation." *Language and Communication* 13 (1993): 27–43.

———. "The Rise and Fall of the Semicolon: English Punctuation Theory and English Teaching Practice." *Applied Linguistics* 16 (1995): 1–14.

Connors, Robert J., and Andrea A. Lunsford. "Exorcising Demonolatry: Spelling Patterns and Pedagogies in College Writing." *Written Communication* 9.3 (1992): 404–28.

Cruttenden, Alan. "Intonation and the Comma." *Visible Language* 25.1 (1991): 54–73.

Dawkins, John. "Teaching Punctuation as a Rhetorical Tool." *College Composition and Communication* 46 (1995): 533–48.

Dobie, Ann R. "Orthographical Theory and Practice, or How to Teach Spelling." *Journal of Basic Writing* 5 (Fall 1986): 41–48.

Hassett, Michael. "Toward a Broader Understanding of the Rhetoric of Punctuation." *College Composition and Communication* 47 (1996): 419–21.

Martin, Charles L., and Dorothy E. Ranson. "Spelling Skills of Business Students: An Empirical Investigation." *Journal of Business Communication* 27.4 (1990): 377–400.

Meyer, Charles F. *A Linguistic Study of American Punctuation.* New York: Lang, 1987.

Meyer, Charles F. "Teaching Punctuation to Advanced Writers." *Journal of Advanced Composition* 6 (1985–1986): 117–29.

Meyer, Emily, and Louise Z. Smith. *The Practical Tutor.* New York: Oxford UP, 1987. 177–201, 286–96.

Shaughnessy, Mina. *Errors and Expectations: A Guide for the Teacher of Basic Writing.* New York: Oxford UP, 1979. 14–33, 36–38, 160–86.

Vasallo, Phillip "'How's the Weather': Ice-Breaking and Fog-Lifting in Your Written Messages." *ETC: A Review of General Semantics* 50 (1993–94): 484–91.

"Vygotsky and the Bad Speller's Nightmare." *English Journal* 80.8 (1991): 65–70.

Part Nine: Researched Writing

Bean, John C. "Encouraging Engagement and Inquiry in Research Papers." *Engaging Ideas: The Professor's Guide to Integrating Writing, Critical Thinking, and Active Learning in the Classroom.* San Francisco: Jossey, 1996. 197–214.

Brent, Doug. *Reading as Rhetorical Invention: Knowledge, Persuasion, and the Teaching of Research-Based Writing.* Urbana: NCTE, 1992.

Coon, Anne C. "Using Ethical Questions to Develop Autonomy in Student Researchers." *College Composition and Communication* 40 (1989): 85–89.

Daemmrich, Ingrid. "A Bridge to Academic Discourse: Social Science Research Strategies in the Freshman Composition Course." *College Composition and Communication* 40 (1989): 343–48.

Dellinger, Dixie G. "Alternatives to Clip and Stitch: Real Research and Writing in the Classroom." *English Journal* 78 (1989): 31–38.

Dixon, Deborah. *Writing Your Heritage: A Sequence of Thinking, Reading, and Writing Assignments.* Berkeley: National Writing Project, 1993.

Fulkerson, Richard. "Oh, What a Cite! A Teaching Tip to Help Students Document Researched Papers Accurately." *Writing Instructor* 7 (1988): 167–72.

Gibson, Craig. "Research Skills across the Curriculum: Connections with Writing-across-the-Curriculum." *Writing across the Curriculum and the Academic Library: A Guide for Librarians, Instructors, and Writing Program Directors.* Ed. Jean Sheridan. Westport: Greenwood, 1995. 55–70.

Holland, Robert M., Jr. "Discovering Forms of Academic Discourse." *Audits of Meaning: A Festschrift in Honor of Anne E. Berthoff.* Ed. Louise Z. Smith. Portsmouth, NH: Boynton/Cook, 1988. 71–79.

Johnson, Jean. *The Bedford Guide to the Research Process.* 3rd ed. Boston: Bedford, 1997.

Kennedy, Mary Lynch. "The Composing Process of College Students Writing from Sources." *Written Communication* 2 (1985): 434–56.

Kleine, Michael. "What Is It We Do When We Write Papers like This One — And How Can We Get Students to Join Us?" *Writing Instructor* 6 (1987): 151–61.

Kroll, Barry M. "How College Freshmen View Plagiarism." *Written Communication* 5 (1988): 203–21.

Lazere, Donald. "Teaching the Political Conflicts: A Rhetorical Schema." *College Composition and Communication* 43 (1992): 194–213.

Lutzker, Marilyn. *Research Projects for College Students: What to Write across the Curriculum.* Westport: Greenwood, 1988.

Macrorie, Ken. *The I-Search Paper.* Rev. ed. of *Searching Writing.* Portsmouth, NH: Boynton/Cook, 1988.

Marino, Sarah R., and Elin K. Jacob. "Questions and Answers: The Dialogue between Composition Teachers and Reference Librarians." *The Reference Librarian* 37 (1992): 129–42.

Neverow-Turk, Vara. "Researching the Minimum Wage: A Moral Economy for the Classroom." *College Composition and Communication* 42 (1991): 477–83.

Page, Miriam Dempsey. "'Thick Description' and a Rhetoric of Inquiry: Freshmen and the Major Fields." *Writing Instructor* 6 (1987): 141–50.

Penrose, Ann M., and Cheryl Geisler. "Reading and Writing without Authority." *College Composition and Communication* 45 (1994): 505–20.

St. Onge, Keith R. *The Melancholy Anatomy of Plagiarism.* Lanham, MD: UP of America, 1988.

Schmersahl, Carmen B. "Teaching Library Research: Process, Not Product." *Journal of Teaching Writing* 6 (1987): 231–38.

Sherrard, Carol. "Summary Writing: A Topographical Study." *Written Communication* 3 (1986): 324–43.

Strickland, James. "The Research Sequence: What to Do before the Term Paper." *College Composition and Communication* 37 (1986): 233–36.

Tyryzna, Thomas N. "Research outside the Library: Learning a Field." *College Composition and Communication* 37 (1986): 217–23.

Williams, Nancy. "Research as a Process: A Transactional Approach." *Journal of Teaching Writing* 7 (1988): 193–204.

Zebroski, James Thomas. "Using Ethnographic Writing to Construct Classroom Knowledge." *Thinking through Theory*. Portsmouth: Boynton/Cook, 1994. 31–43.

Zemelman, Steven, and Harvey Daniels. "Collaborative Research and Term Papers." *A Community of Writers*. Portsmouth, NH: Boynton/Cook, 1988. 256–67.

Part Ten: Special Types of Writing

Writing about Literature

Beach, Richard. *A Teacher's Introduction to Reader-Response Theories*. Urbana: NCTE, 1993.

Biddle, Arthur W., and Toby Fulwiler, eds. *Reading, Writing, and the Study of Literature*. New York: McGraw, 1989.

Chamberlain, Lori. "Bombs and Other Exciting Devices, or the Problem of Teaching Irony." *College English* 51 (1989): 29–40.

Commeyras, Michelle. "Using Literature to Teach Critical Thinking." *Journal of Reading* 32 (1989): 703–07.

Dragga, Sam. "Collaborative Interpretation." *Activities to Promote Critical Thinking: Classroom Practices in Teaching English*. Urbana: NCTE, 1986. 84–87. ERIC. CD-ROM. SilverPlatter, 1995.

Gould, Christopher. "Literature in the Basic Writing Course: A Bibliographic Survey." *College English* 49 (1987): 558–74.

Herrington, Anne J. "Teaching, Writing, and Learning: A Naturalistic Study of Writing in an Undergraduate Class." *Writing in Academic Disciplines*. Ed. David Jolliffe. Norwood, NJ: Ablex, 1988. 133–66.

Holman, C. Hugh, and William Harmon. *A Handbook to Literature*. 7th ed. New York: Macmillan, 1996.

Hull, Glynda, and Mike Rose. "'This Wooden Shack Place': The Logic of an Unconventional Reading." *College Composition and Communication* 41 (1990): 287–98.

Lentriccia, Frank, and Thomas McLaughlin, eds. *Critical Terms for Literary Study*. 2nd ed. Chicago: U of Chicago P, 1995.

Lindemann, Erika. "Freshman Composition: No Place for Literature." *College English* 55 (1993): 311–16.

MacDonald, Susan Peck, and Charles R. Cooper. "Contributions of Academic and Dialogic Journals to Writing about Literature." *Writing, Teaching, and Learning in the Disciplines*. Ed. Ann Herrington and Charles Moran. New York: MLA, 1992.

Moran, Charles, and Elizabeth F. Penfield. *Conversations: Contemporary Critical Theory and the Teaching of Literature*. Urbana: NCTE, 1990.

Meyer, Emily, and Louise Z. Smith. "Reading and Writing about Literature." *The Practical Tutor*. New York: Oxford UP, 1987. 256–85.

Oster, Judith. "Seeing with Different Eyes: Another View of Literature in the ESL Class." *TESOL Quarterly* 23 (1989): 85–102.

Reilly, Jill M., et al. "The Effects of Prewriting on Literary Interpretation." Annual Meeting of the Amer. Educ. Research Association. San Francisco. Apr. 16–20, 1986. ERIC CD-ROM. SilverPlatter, 1995.

Roskelly, Hephzibah. "Writing to Read: The Stage of Interpretation." 1988: ERIC. CD-ROM. SilverPlatter, 1995.

Steinberg, Erwin R., Michael Gamer, Erika Lindemann, Gary Tate, and Jane Peterson. "Symposium: Literature in the Composition Classroom." *College English* 57 (1995): 265–318.

Swope, John W., and Edgar H. Thompson. "Three R's for Critical Thinking about Literature: Reading, 'Riting, and Responding." *Activities to Promote Critical Thinking: Classroom Practices in Teaching English.* Urbana: NCTE, 1986. 75–79. ERIC. CD-ROM. SilverPlatter, 1995.

Tate, Gary. "A Place for Literature in Freshman Composition." *College English* 55 (1993): 317–21.

Wentworth, Michael. "Writing in the Literature Class." *Journal of Teaching Writing* 6 (1987): 155–62.

Young, Art, and Toby Fulwiler, eds. *When Writing Teachers Teach Literature: Bringing Writing to Reading.* Portsmouth, NH: Boynton/Cook, 1995.

Writing across the Curriculum

See Bizzell and Herzberg, "Writing across the Curriculum: A bibliographic Essay" on p. 411.

Part Eleven: Grammar Basics

Baron, Dennis. *Grammar and Good Taste: Reforming the American Language.* New Haven: Yale UP, 1982.

Connors, Robert J. "Grammar in American College Composition: An Historical Overview." *The Territory of Language: Linguistics, Stylistics, and the Teaching of Composition.* Ed. Donald A. McQuade. Carbondale: Southern Illinois UP, 1986. 3–22.

Crowley, Sharon. "Linguistics and Composition Instruction: 1950–1980." *Written Communication* 6 (1989): 480–505.

Harris, Muriel, and Katherine E. Rowan. "Explaining Grammatical Concepts." *Journal of Basic Writing* 8.2 (1989): 21–41.

Lindemann, Erika. *A Rhetoric for Writing Teachers.* 3rd ed. New York: Oxford UP, 1995. 68–86.

Noguchi, Rei R. *Grammar and the Teaching of Writing: Limits and Possibilities.* Urbana: NCTE, 1991.

Parker, Frank, and Kim Sydow Campbell. "Linguistics and Writing: A Reassessment." *College Composition and Communication* 44 (1993): 295–314.

Quirk, Randolph, and Sidney Greenbaum. *A Concise Grammar of Contemporary English.* New York: Harcourt, 1975.

Sedgwick, Ellery. "Alternatives to Teaching Formal, Analytical Grammar." *Journal of Developmental Education* 12 (Jan. 1989): 8+.

Weaver, Constance. *Teaching Grammar in Context.* Portsmouth, NH: Boynton/Cook, 1996.

Appendix: Computers and Writing

Curtis, Marcia S. "Windows on Composing: Teaching Revision on Word Processors." *College Composition and Communication* 39 (1988): 337–44.

Crew, Louie. "The Style-Checker as Tonic, Not Tranquilizer." *Journal of Advanced Composition* 8 (1988): 66–70.

Holdstein, Deborah H., and Cynthia L. Selfe, eds. *Computers and Writing: Theory, Research, Practice.* New York: MLA, 1990.

Sudol, Ronald A. "The Accumulative Rhetoric of Word Processing." *College English* 53 (1991): 920–33.

Tuman, Myron C., ed. *Literacy Online: The Promise (and Peril) of Reading and Writing with Computers.* Pittsburgh: U of Pittsburgh P, 1992.

———. *Word Perfect: Literacy in the Computer Age.* Pittsburgh: U of Pittsburgh P, 1992.

Ilona Leki, "Classroom Expectations and Behaviors," from *Understanding ESL Writers: A Guide for Teachers*, reprinted by permission of Ilona Leki: *Understanding ESL Writers: A Guide for Teachers* (Boynton/Cook Publishers, A Subsidiary of Greenwood Publishing Group, Portsmouth, NH, 1992).

Erika Lindemann, "Prewriting Techniques," from *A Rhetoric for Writing Teachers* by Lindemann, Erika. (Oxford University Press, New York, NY, 1995); reprinted with permission. "Responding to Student Writing," from *A Rhetoric for Writing Teachers* by Lindemann, Erika (Oxford University Press, New York, NY, 1995); reprinted with permission. "Teaching about Sentences" from *A Rhetoric for Writing Teachers* by Lindemann, Erika (Oxford University Press, New York, NY, 1995); reprinted with permission

Min-Zhan Lu, "Conflict and Struggle: The Enemies or Preconditions of Basic Writing?," *College English*, December 1992. Copyright © 1992 by the National Council of Teachers of English. Reprinted with permission.

Dennis A. Lynch, Diana George, and Marilyn Cooper, "Moments of Argument: Agonistic Inquiry and Confrontational Cooperation," from *College Composition and Communication*, February 1997. Copyright © 1997 by the National Council of Teachers of English. Reprinted with permission.

Steven Lynn, "A Passage into Critical Theory," *College English*, March 1990. Copyright © 1990 by the National Council of Teachers of English. Reprinted with permission.

Casey Miller and Kate Swift, "Introduction: Change and Resistance to Change," from *The Handbook of Nonsexist Writing*, Second Edition by Casey Miller and Kate Swift. Copyright © 1980, 1988 by Casey Miller and Kate Swift. Reprinted by permission of HarperCollins Publishers, Inc.

Ruth Mirtz, "A Conversation about Small Groups." From *Small Groups in Writing Workshops: Invitations to a Writer's Life*, edited by Brooke, Mirtz, and Evans. Copyright © 1994 by the National Council of Teachers of English. Reprinted with permission.

Douglas Park, "Analyzing Audiences," *College Composition and Communication*, December 1986. Copyright © 1986 by the National Council of Teachers of English. Reprinted with permission.

Mike Rose, "Rigid Rules, Inflexible Plans, and the Stifling of Language: A Cognitivist Analysis of Writer's Block," *College Composition and Communication*, December 1980. Copyright © 1980 by the National Council of Teachers of English. Reprinted with permission.

Mariolina Salvatori, "Conversations with Texts: Reading in the Teaching of Composition," *College English*, April 1996. Copyright © 1996 by the National Council of Teachers of English. Reprinted with permission.

Ann L. Schlumberger and Diane Clymer, "Tailoring Composition Classes to ESL Students' Needs," *Teaching English in the Two-Year College*, May 1989. Copyright © 1989 by the National Council of Teachers of English. Reprinted with permission.

Nancy Sommers, "Responding to Student Writing," *College Composition and Communication*, May 1982. Copyright © 1982 by the National Council of Teachers of English. "Revision Strategies of Student Writers and Experienced Adult Writers," *College Composition and Communication*, December, 1980. Copyright © 1980 by the National Council of Teachers of English. Reprinted with permission.

Michael Spooner and Kathleen Blake Yancey, "Postings on a Genre of E-mail," *College Composition and Communication*, May 1996. Copyright © 1996 by the National Council of Teachers of English. Reprinted with permission.

Elizabeth Tebeaux, "The Trouble with Employees' Writing May be Freshman Composition," *Teaching English in the Two-Year College*, February 1988. Copyright © 1988 by the National Council of Teachers of English. Reprinted with permission.